The European Economy in an American Mirror

T0326160

In this book an important array of international contributors take the temperature of the American and European economies and draw comparisons between them. The volume is organised into two broad parts – one dealing with competitiveness, the other exploring the relationship between institutions and markets.

Europe's economy is under strain due to lagging productivity growth, population ageing, the difficulties of adjustment in an enlarged European Union, and the challenges of globalization. In comparison with America, rates of growth of GDP per capita and labour productivity growth are anaemic, raising questions about the viability of a distinct European model. From observations like these, observers draw the conclusion that Europe will feel irresistible pressure to allow its policies and institutions to converge toward those of the United States. But how far and how fast are uncertain. Understanding how the US and European economies will evolve requires understanding the influence of history and balancing the roles of institutional inheritance and global competition. This volume brings together specialists from both sides of the Atlantic to analyse the current state of both economies and their responses to the changing global environment.

This book will be of particular relevance to postgraduate and postdoctoral students undertaking research in all areas of European Integration and International Political Economy, while also being appropriate for a professional audience.

Barry Eichengreen is George C. Pardee and Helen N. Pardee Professor of Economics and Political Science at the University of California, Berkeley, Research Associate of the National Bureau of Economic Research, and Research Fellow of the Centre for Economic Policy Research. **Michael Landesmann** is Scientific Director of the Vienna Institute for International Economic Studies (wiiw) and Professor of Economics and Head of Department at Johannes Kepler University, Linz, Austria. **Dieter Stiefel** is Professor at the Department for Social and Economic History and at the Department of Economics at Vienna University.

Routledge studies in the modern world economy

The European Economy
in an American Mirror

**Edited by Barry Eichengreen,
Michael Landesmann and
Dieter Stiefel**

Routledge
Taylor & Francis Group

LONDON AND NEW YORK

First published 2008
by Routledge
2 Park Square, Milton Park, Abingdon, Oxon OX14 4RN

Simultaneously published in the USA and Canada
by Routledge
711 Third Avenue, New York, NY 10017

Routledge is an imprint of the Taylor & Francis Group, an informa business

First issued in paperback 2011

Typeset in Times by Wearset Ltd, Boldon, Tyne and Wear

British Library Cataloguing in Publication Data
A catalogue record for this book is available from the British Library

Library of Congress Cataloging in Publication Data
A catalog record for this book has been requested

ISBN13: 978-0-415-77172-6 (hbk)
ISBN13: 978-0-203-94571-1 (ebk)
ISBN13: 978-0-415-51277-0 (pbk)

Contents

Contributors

Karl Aiginger
Austrian Institute of Economic Research

Bart van Ark
University of Groningen

Alan J. Auerbach
University of California, Berkeley

Tito Boeri
Bocconi University and Fondazione Rodolfo Debenedetti

Marco Buti
European Commission

Élie Cohen
CNRS-Sciences Po and Conseil d'analyse économique, Paris

Barry Eichengreen
University of California, Berkeley

Richard B. Freeman
Harvard University

Michael Gehler
University of Hildesheim

Robert J. Gordon
Northwestern University, NBER, and CEPR

Michael Landesmann
Vienna Institute for International Economic Studies (wiiw) and Johannes Kepler University Linz

Jonah D. Levy
University of California, Berkeley

Peter H. Lindert
University of California, Davis

Dennis C. Mueller
University of Vienna

Rainer Münz
Hamburg Institute of International Economics and Erste Bank

Giovanni Peri
University of California, Davis

Karl Pichelmann
European Commission and Institut d'Etudes Européennes, Université Libre de
   Bruxelles

Jean Pisani-Ferry
Bruegel, Brussels and Université Paris-Dauphine

Andreas Resch
University of Economics and Business Administration, Vienna

Werner Roeger
European Commission

Gérard Roland
University of California, Berkeley

André Sapir
Université Libre de Bruxelles, Bruegel and Centre for Economic Policy
   Research (CEPR)

Jan Pieter Smits
University of Groningen

Dieter Stiefel
University of Vienna

Agnes Streissler
Austrian Chamber of Labour

Acknowledgements

The editors gratefully acknowledge the financial support of the Austrian Marshall Plan Foundation under its Austrian-Berkeley Program and of the Institute for European Studies, University of California, Berkeley, for hosting two conferences at which the papers collected in this volume were presented and discussed.

Introduction

Barry Eichengreen and Michael Landesmann

Commentators are fond of emphasizing the differences between the US and European economies. America is characterized by high levels of income inequality but also by high social mobility that allows individuals to move between less- and better-paying jobs. While Europe suffers from less inequality, it also enjoys less social mobility. Europe displays higher rates of unemployment, but Europeans typically enjoy shorter work weeks and take more weeks of holiday. It is more difficult in Europe to start a new company, terminate redundant workers, and reorganize production with the goal of cutting labour costs. The European economy is more heavily unionized, and industry-wide wage agreements leave less scope for wage differentials between more- and less-productive firms and regions. European finance remains bank based, in contrast to the United States where stock and bond markets are better capitalized. America outstrips Europe as the home of the leading research universities and the residence of Nobel Prize winners; its economy benefits from closer university–industry collaboration.

All this would seem to give the United States a leg up in exploiting the latest information and communications technologies. And yet the most advanced European economies continue to surpass the United States in terms of output per hour worked, what many economists would regard the best summary measure of overall productivity. As faithful BMW owners will attest, Europe's capacity for quality production, grounded in its ability to train skilled technicians and tailor technology to local needs, remains unsurpassed.

Admittedly, all this is a bit of a caricature. Both the American and European economies are well managed. Both allow considerable play for the operation of market forces. Both enjoy strong rule of law, independent judiciaries, and reliable contract enforcement. Both have vigorous competition policies and reasonably effective institutions of corporate governance (recent corporate scandals notwithstanding to the contrary). Both economies are continental in scope and trade extensively with the rest of the world. Both apply minimal restrictions on inward and outward foreign investment. Both enjoy low and stable inflation. Both have legions of skilled workers and creative entrepreneurs. From the perspective of the rest of the world, the US and European economies resemble one another more than they differ.

Moreover, the two economies feel the same external pressures. Both are experiencing growing competition from lower-wage emerging markets, above all China. Both feel pressure to outsource service sector employment to India. Both worry that major corporations are contemplating new investments not at home but in lower-cost economies in other parts of the world. Both have mixed feelings about immigration from significantly poorer countries.

Thus the development of radical new technologies, the emergence of emerging markets, the advent of more intense international competition, and other changes in the world economy pose similar challenges for the US and Europe. They pose the question of how their respective economic and social systems will adapt. Will they respond differently, reflecting the two economies' different economic and institutional inheritances? And, if so, which response will be more effective? Or will external pressures force their economic systems to converge? For example, now that controls on international capital movements have been lifted and the disciplines of the World Trade Organization require members to admit qualified foreign financial institutions, will their financial systems converge? And if Continental Europe acquires an Anglo-American-style financial system, will impatient financial markets force firms to pressure workers to the point where it acquires Anglo-Saxon-style labour markets as well? Will the institutional differences between the US and European economies ultimately disappear?

To be sure, there are no simple answers to these questions. Since history casts a long shadow, convergence is likely to remain partial. The historical inheritance being deeply entrenched, convergence will have significant institutional obstacles to overcome. At the same time, the pressure for convergence is undeniable. This is most evident in finance, where the tyranny of distance and influence of geography have been all but completely erased. But similar pressures are far from absent in other sectors.

Understanding how the US and European economies will evolve thus requires understanding the influence of history and balancing the roles of institutional inheritance and global competition. Making a start on this is our goal in the present volume. It brings together specialists from both sides of the Atlantic to analyse the current state of the US and European economies and their responses to the changing global environment. A number of the chapters are historical, reflecting our conviction that historical experience and socioeconomic inheritance continue to shape both the current performance of the European and American economies and their future responses. Others are institutional, reflecting the importance of institutional constellations as carriers of history. Where some chapters examine specific institutions and markets, others are macroeconomic in focus, indicative of our belief that an adequate analysis must consider both macro and micro factors. Finally, some chapters consider political aspects of the comparison, such as US and European foreign policies, on the grounds that politics and foreign policies importantly influence the lay of the economic land.

The collection is organized into two parts, one on competitiveness and employment and the other on markets and institutions, and encompasses seven topics: growth and productivity, labour markets, fiscal policy, institutions, the Welfare State, governance, and trans-Atlantic relations. Although the chapters that follow analyse both economies, they are mainly concerned with Europe's prospects and thus use US performance as a way of helping to identify and answer the key questions. In effect, we seek to view the European economy in an American mirror.

Growth and productivity performance

Growth performance relative to the United States has been of concern to European policy-makers for several decades. Western Europe stopped converging toward US income per capita in the 1970s. While catch-up in productivity levels (measured either by GDP per hour worked or total factor productivity) continued for longer, albeit at slower rates, the Europe–US productivity gap began widening again in the 1990s. The failure of Europe to converge to US levels of income and to match its recent rates of productivity growth provided the motivation for the Single Market Program, economic and monetary unification (EMU), and the Lisbon Agenda to make Europe the world's most productive economy by 2010.

Robert Gordon decomposes the income-per-capita gap between the US and Europe into differences in labour input and productivity. He shows that the EU-15 (the 15 members of the European Union prior to the most recent enlargement) had reached almost 90 per cent of US productivity levels by 2004 (measured by output per hour worked), whereas incomes per capita were still only 69 per cent of US levels. By definition, the difference in the two ratios is attributable to the difference in hours worked per capita. This last difference can in turn be decomposed into differences in hours worked per employed person, differences in the share of the labour force in employment, and differences in the share of the population of working age that is counted as part of the employed or unemployed labour force (the participation rate).

Gordon criticizes the interpretation of authors like Blanchard (2004) that Europeans work fewer hours because they have a stronger taste for leisure – because they prefer longer vacations, a shorter work week etc. He shows that the Europe–US gap is due less to differences in hours worked per person than to differences in the participation rate, something that is not obviously related to the taste for extended summer holidays and short work weeks. This difference in participation rates is concentrated among the relatively young (those aged 15 to 24) and relatively old (those aged 55 to 64) which is less plausibly a function of society-wide differences in the taste for leisure than it is of public policies to limit the competition for scarce jobs felt by prime-age workers. Moreover, the difference in hours worked is of relatively recent vintage: where hours worked per capita in Europe were still 20 per cent higher than in the US in 1960 and 2 per cent higher even in 1970, by 2004 they were 23 lower. This shift is more easily explained by changes in policies and incentives than by a sudden, inexplicable shift in tastes. Since 1995, furthermore, there was a significant improvement in employment and participation rates in Europe, a break that seems to have resulted from labour market and pension reforms (and from special efforts to reduce youth unemployment), not from some mysterious shift in individual preferences.

To be sure, incomes are only one dimension of living standards. Gordon adjusts them for the greater use of energy per unit of GDP in the US, the value of more leisure and early retirement in Europe, and the effects of a large prison population in the US. Adjusting for these factors, the difference in living standards falls from 31 to 20 per cent. As Gordon observes, still other dimensions of the welfare comparison could be explored: access to medical care and education, ease of assimilating immigrants, and economic and social discrimination.

Bart van Ark and Jan Pieter Smits then analyse the relative facility of the United States and Europe in adopting new information and communication technologies (ICT) and examine lessons from the diffusion of earlier general-purpose technologies (GPTs) like electricity. The comparison leads the authors to predict significant additional productivity enhancement, ICT still being less pervasive than electricity. They find that adoption in the service sector has been less rapid in Europe, where limits on shopping hours, transport and land-use regulations, restrictive hiring and firing rules, and regulatory barriers slow diffusion. Research has shown that the recent productivity growth differential between the US and Europe is concentrated in service industries, and in retail trading and business services in particular, where the obstacles to adoption are particularly formidable.

Karl Aiginger and Michael Landesmann put Europe's growth and productivity performance in a wider context. The "Wider Europe" to which they refer encompasses not only current and prospective EU members but also other regions, such as the successor states to the former Soviet Union, parts of the Middle East and North Africa, linked to the European Union. The authors emphasize the extent of heterogeneity within the EU (which has increased with recent waves of enlargement) and in addition the growing diversity in incomes, productivity growth rates, and institutional arrangements in this wider European space.

Aiginger and Landesmannn first document heterogeneity within "Old Europe" (the EU-15), contrasting growth and productivity in Scandinavia and the large continental European economies. They then consider the impact of eastward enlargement on Europe's growth and competitiveness. While incorporation into the European Union encourages catching-up, such processes can take a long time. Given the diversity of developmental starting points, Wider Europe comprises a region with a very wide range of *Standortfaktoren* (wage and productivity levels, skill endowments, quality of institutions, etc.), which poses political problems. From a more narrowly economic standpoint, it opens up an unprecedented range of location options for firms and facilitates their efforts to develop cross-European production networks as a way of enhancing productivity and profitability.

Labour markets

Differences in labour markets have been a major focus of research and policy debate in the literature on the US and European economies, not to say that many firm conclusions have emerged. One reason for this, according to Richard Freeman, is excessive reliance on aggregate cross-country data. Aggregate data limited to easily standardized dimensions of labour market structure, he argues, are incapable of capturing much of the relevant institutional detail. As a result, many results obtained by earlier authors are not robust to changes in specification, measurement, and sample. The most promising direction for research is that concerned with the interaction of institutions, economic shocks and behavioural responses, yet even here international comparisons of aggregate time series data do not yield convincing results. Freeman suggests using micro-data and laboratory experiments to shed more light on the posited interactions.

Tito Boeri argues that Europe has in fact undertaken significant labour market reforms in the past 20 years, notably by scaling back traditional employment protections. But there has been less progress in product markets. This asymmetry is rooted partly in political economy and partly in differences in market structures. Changes in labour market regulation can be applied to new labour-force entrants without scaling back the protections extended to existing workers. But this approach is not feasible in product markets, since differentiated treatment that favours some firms over others would be corrosive of competition. Hence product–market reforms must be applied across the board rather than being phased in incrementally. This means that they will be more strongly resisted by entrenched interests.

Karl Pichelmann and Werner Roeger ask whether reforms that raise employment and participation rates could have a negative impact upon productivity growth. A priori the answer is unclear. More workers would raise the labour/capital ratio and thus depress productivity in the short run, something that may have been working to slow European productivity growth in recent years. Moreover, those who move out of unemployment or inactivity may be less skilled and experienced than those already in employment. However, in their empirical analysis, Pichelmann and Roeger find that there is no genuine trade-off between policies that raise the employment rate and policies that foster productivity growth (the so-called "twin pillars" of the Lisbon Agenda).

The US and European labour markets are also increasingly affected by immigration. In his analysis of this phenomenon, Rainer Münz insists on comparable definitions of immigrants as "foreign born", where most European statistics use citizenship rather than place of birth to define immigrants, rendering trans-Atlantic comparisons problematic. Münz shows that most EU-15 countries are now net recipients of immigrants. As of 2004, the immigrant stock in the EU-25 was some 35 million out of a population of 456 million, or roughly 8 per cent of Europe's population. If one considers only immigrants from non-EU countries, the ratio falls to 5 per cent. The US, meanwhile, had a stock of 33 million immigrants in a population of 290 million, or 12.5 per cent of its population. So there is some truth in the conventional wisdom that the US is more open to immigration.

Data on employment growth point in the same direction. Thus, third country nationals accounted for 13 per cent of employment growth in Europe in the period 1997–2002. Including foreign-born naturalized citizens, immigrants accounted for perhaps 20 per cent of employment growth. Again this is less than in the US, where foreign-born accounted for nearly half of the net increase in the labour force. Once more the conclusion is that the US is more open to immigrants.

Giovanni Peri focuses on differences in the attractiveness of Europe and the US as destinations for highly-educated immigrants. In fact, net flows of highly-educated individuals are slightly negative in Europe, in contrast to the situation in the US and the other immigration countries. Although it is well known that immigrants are more strongly represented amongst the least and most educated groups, Peri shows that the complementarity between immigrants and natives in terms of differences in skill levels is stronger in the United States. The implication is that America's native population is more positively affected, which may in turn explain the somewhat more favourable public perception of immigration in that country.

Fiscal policy

The public sector has played a critical role in the development of employment and competitiveness on both sides of the Atlantic. The two concluding chapters of Part I examine its influence in detail. Focusing on Europe, Marco Buti and André Sapir distinguish two perspectives on fiscal policy: the Musgrave public-finance view that sees the state as correcting market failures and the Buchanan public-choice view that sees it as operating in the interest of specific groups. They identify three corresponding phases in the development of European fiscal policy. First was the postwar "golden age", when high growth and low unemployment supported complementary state–economy relations. This was followed by a period in which the compatibility of growth, stability and social cohesion dissolved, with adverse consequences for the public finances. Slower GDP growth and lower employment rates meant rising public expenditure. In turn rising public expenditure meant higher social insurance contributions and taxes, with negative incentive effects on investment. Buti and Sapir speak here of a shift from the benign view of the role of public finance associated with Musgrave to a more sceptical view emphasizing an inbuilt bias towards an increased role of state. The way out of this dilemma, according to authors like Buchanan and Tullock, is to restore fiscal discipline by limiting policy-makers' discretion. Thus the third phase in the development of European fiscal policies involved attempting to counteract deficit bias through the rules associated with the Maastricht Treaty and the Stability and Growth Pact. Buti and Sapir discuss in detail the rationale for this rules-based approach, why it unravelled, and its uncertain future.

In contrast to its rise in Europe, federal government spending in the US has held steady, as a share of GDP, since the 1960s, as Alan Auerbach shows. Outlays have fluctuated in a narrow range between 16 and 20 per cent despite a steady decline in military spending after the Vietnam period and an increase in entitlement programmes (which have more than doubled as a share of GDP). There is remarkably little to distinguish recent spending levels from this longer term trend. What sets this recent period apart, rather, is the sharp drop in federal revenues as a share of GDP, reflecting the discretionary tax cuts adopted at the beginning of the decade – something that has no counterpart in Europe. The result has been a sharp shift from budget surpluses to deficits, raising questions about the sustainability of US spending patterns.

Institutions

In opening Part II, Elie Cohen and Jean Pisani-Ferry return to the question of whether different varieties of capitalism can persist in an era of globalization – whether we should expect to see the persistence of a distinctively European social market economy or convergence to the US model of unbridled market capitalism. The authors emphasize the pressures for convergence, which they illustrate through a discussion of the retreat of industrial policy in the face of globalization and European integration, and the impact of these forces on the conduct of monetary and fiscal policy, which is subject to quasi-constitutional constraints and locked in by the liberal economic philosophy of the late 1980s and early 1990s. At the same time they highlight the importance of institutions and ideology as sources of inertia, taking as examples the European Central Bank's statutory price stability objective and the excessive deficit procedure of the Maastricht Treaty. On balance their picture is one of pressure for convergence but also of sources of resistance.

Jonah Levy describes Europe's economic reforms under the label "progressive liberalism", which he defines as the effort to fuse a liberal concern for efficiency with a Rawlesian commitment to support the disadvantaged. Levy offers a number of examples of how European governments have implemented liberalizing reforms while minimizing increases in inequality: deficit reduction in Italy and Sweden; tax relief in France, the Netherlands and Britain; and efforts to boost labour market participation in the Netherlands and Sweden. He suggests that there is scope for further steps in these directions. He then gives examples of how inefficient social spending can be curtailed through stronger targeting and by setting up more effective administrative procedures, such as curtailment of excesses of disability pay, early retirement, and protections for well-situated self-employed or public sector workers.

The Welfare State

The size and structure of the Welfare State is a key difference between the US and European models. In Europe, comprehensive social protection is a fundamental right, as Agnes Streissler describes, while the US, after moving closer to the European model during the New Deal and the Great Society era, diverged from this European conception in the 1980s and 1990s. The outcome is that social protections are targeted more narrowly in the United States. The results show up in higher overall poverty rates, low health provisions, lower life expectancy, and high crime rates amongst particular groups of society in the United States.

Peter Lindert asks whether a large welfare state has a negative impact on the sustainable rate of economic growth and, more generally, whether provision of a generous social safety net has a cost in terms of output and economic growth. While there is some evidence of negative effects of unemployment compensation on labour utilization and hence on GDP per capita, these are more than offset by the pro-growth effects of other social transfers. Among pro-growth policies Lindert counts those that invest in career continuity and skill accumulation (such as parental leave provisions and public day care) as well as public health expenditure. Comparing the tax mixes of high-budget welfare states with the tax mixes of low-budget states such as the United States, he concludes, contrary to much conventional wisdom, that the former may in fact be more pro-growth on balance.

Governance

Two chapters address frameworks for corporate behaviour. In his chapter on insolvency procedures, Dieter Stiefel shows that the American system is more debtor friendly. US procedures encourage restructuring insolvent enterprises, a process in which sitting management plays a major role. In Europe, in contrast, management quickly loses its power to court-appointed administrators. European procedures more frequently result in the closure of enterprises, although in France there is involvement by the state to safeguard jobs. The UK is the most extreme case of a creditor-oriented system, while Germany became less creditor-oriented as a result of the experience of reunification.

Andreas Resch similarly analyses the evolution of European competition and US anti-trust laws and their prospects for convergence. He distinguishes four phases of European competition policy: the period prior to the First World War, the interwar period, the era of competition policy under American influence after the Second World War, and recent developments including the development of EU-level competition policy. Resch shows how this history gave Europe's capital markets, corporate governance and competition policy their distinctive characteristics. Among these was a rather positive attitude towards cartels as a vehicle for advancing the interests of powerful national business groups and buttressing market stability. In contrast, reservations about the operation of cartels, grounded in considerations of competitive efficiency, received less attention. With the US occupation of Germany after the Second World War, American anti-trust attitudes encouraged a less friendly attitude toward cartels. But, notwithstanding this American influence, Europe's financial and corporate structures proved remarkably robust. Corporate control by blockholders, inter-locking directorates and supervisory boards, strong positions of banks as share-holders and financiers, close state–economy relations, barriers to the entry or growth of new firms, and closed job markets for managers all remained in place throughout the 1960s. At this point these arrangements began to change in response to the pressures of international competition. Resch points to the role of European integration, from the establishment of the European Coal and Steel Community onwards, in developing a transnational competition policy in con-junction with trade liberalization and the creation of the Common Market. While it took some time for an effective competition policy to develop at the European level, from the 1960s onwards EU policies have played an increasingly promi-nent role, particularly in encouraging a new emphasis on promoting market integration and reducing barriers to entry.

Although there has been significant convergence of capital markets and corporate governance between Europe and the United States, important differ-ences remain. US anti-trust law has developed out of the common law tradition in which rulings are governed by efficiency considerations. In Europe, in con-trast, the competition authorities have adopted a less permissive position on ver-tical restraints and mergers. Given the path dependence of Europe's economic structures, Resch cautions against the dangers of attempting to prematurely har-monize Europe's rules and regulations with those of the United States.

The other aspect of governance considered in this volume is political gover-nance at the level of the European Union. Dennis Mueller asks whether the EU would be better organized federally or confederally. As the EU grows larger, collective decision making, like that presupposed by the advocates of federal-ism, will become more difficult. In addition, insofar as heterogeneity increases with EU enlargement, there is a growing danger that the centralized provision of public goods will become less well attuned to the preferences of a majority of residents. At the same time, the higher levels of residential mobility implied by federation – mobility between different communities providing different bundles of public goods – may permit citizens to sort themselves into communities char-acterized by more homogeneous preferences. Of course, how much scope exists for this in a Europe where individuals have preferences not just for different bundles of public goods but also for a particular geographic location is an open question.

These observations underscore the complexity of the political and economic choices confronting the European Union. Gérard Roland addresses the debate over the European constitution in this light. He observes that French and Dutch voters, while both rejecting the draft EU constitution in referenda in 2005, did so for quite different reasons: dissatisfaction with the economy and the political situ-ation in France, fear of loss of sovereignty in the Netherlands. Roland suggests that the failure of their referenda had less to do with the constitution's provisions per se than with the document's role as a flash point for other concerns. Judged on its merits, he argues, the constitution would have created fewer problems than it solved. In particular, it would have enhanced the flexibility in provision of public goods on which Dennis Mueller places such weight. Thus, the constitution envisaged procedures that would have considerably reduced transaction costs associated with any future moves in European integration while at the same time respecting national sovereignty. Its flexibility would also have allowed for enhanced cooperation among sub-groups of members.

While defending the broad outlines of the constitution, Roland also acknowledges that revision will be necessary before it can be resubmitted to the voters. Doing otherwise would tarnish the EU's democratic credentials. Of course, this approach heightens uncertainty, since it is not obvious what will emerge from the Pandora's Box of substantial revision. In addition, Roland suggests that better economic performance will help to put voters in a more ratification-friendly state of mind.

Transatlantic relations

In the final chapter Michael Gehler offers an account of the evolution of post-Second World War US–European relations. These were characterized by both supportive and critical phases in the US government's attitude toward European integration, depending on the foreign policy context (the Cold War, the Iran crisis) or whether there was competition between the US and Europe in international relations. Gehler discusses Europe's difficulties in overcoming the polyphony of middle sized powers pursuing diverse foreign policy traditions and shows how this continues to shape US–European relations. Nonetheless, tension between the US and Europe over the war in Iraq, different conceptions of how to move forward in the Middle East, a widening gap in military-technological capabilities between Europe and the US, different conceptions of national sovereignty and the rule of law in global affairs, and a yearning for peaceful resolution of global conflicts have led to more assertiveness on the part of Europe. Combined with new challenges (security issues related to migration, relations with Russia, conflict in the Balkans, Caucasus and Middle East), this should lead to a strengthening of Europe's formulation of a common foreign and security policy.

Convergence or continued differentiation and rivalry?

The European model is under strain due to lagging productivity growth, population ageing, the difficulties of adjustment in an enlarged European Union, and the challenges of globalization. Be that as it may, the presence of deeply-embedded structures inherited from the past will continue to slow convergence with the US model – which itself is a moving target.

Moreover, the image of a single European model is itself a simplification. Europe always has been and likely always will be home to a number of different economic models, each of which continues to undergo its own distinct evolution. To be sure, pressure for convergence is evident here as well: policy learning, harmonization through EU mandates, and market forces all play a role in what some authors refer to as the "bounded convergence" of institutional arrangements. But it is important to bear in mind that heterogeneity within Europe has increased as a result of EU enlargement and formation of a wider European space. In labour market institutions, tax and spending structures, social insurance, pensions, and the provision of public services in education and health care, the diversity of organizational forms remains pronounced. The EU, for its part, has virtually no mandate to pursue harmonization in these areas.

At the same time, there is pressure to strengthen the supply side of the European economy in order to close the efficiency and innovation gap relative to the United States. Key issues here include higher education reform, the strengthening of university–business links, and reducing start-up and growth barriers for small and medium-sized enterprises (including the provision of venture capital finance and the cutting of red-tape, etc.). There are some signs that European innovation systems are seeking to emulate successful features of the Anglo-Saxon model in all these areas, albeit slowly. That there remain deficiencies in exploiting productivity potential and initial institutional efficiency gaps is precisely why convergence toward US levels of income and productivity is still possible. The result need not be unbridled US-style capitalism; rather, it can be an updated European model. But real reform at both the national and EU levels will be needed to make this vision a reality.

Part I

Competitiveness and employment

1 Comparing welfare in Europe and the United States*

Robert J. Gordon

1 Introduction

Starting immediately after the Second World War with a level of labour productivity barely half that of the United States, by the mid-1990s Europe had caught up to near parity and some nations had exceeded the American level of productivity.[1] Yet over the same period Europe's relative per-capita income did not exhibit a similar catching-up process. The ratio of European to US income per capita since 1970 has stagnated at between 70 and 75 per cent. How could Europe be so productive and yet so poor?

The data on both labour productivity (Y/H) and real GDP per capita (Y/N) come from the invaluable Groningen data bank, which provides inter-country comparisons with two base years and weighting schemes.[2] Averaging these two data sources, we find that Europe's (EU-15) productivity level by 1995 had reached 97.5 per cent of the US and then by 2004 fell back to 89.7 per cent. Three European countries had exceeded the US level – France was at 117.3 per cent in 1995 and 113.2 per cent in 2004; Belgium was at 113.2 per cent in 1995 and 106.5 per cent in 2004; the Netherlands was at 116.4 per cent in 1995 and fell back to 98.9 per cent in 2004.

But none of these countries had come close to catching up with the level of US real GDP per capita. In the 1995–2004 period, averaging the same two data sources, France achieved no better than 77.5 per cent of the US level in 1995 and this ratio had fallen back to 73.4 per cent by 2004. Thus the Y/N ratio for France was fully 40 points below its Y/H ratio in 1995 and a similar 40 points in 2004. By definition, this discrepancy is due to a precipitous decline in hours per capita in France relative to the US over the past four decades. For the EU-15 the same discrepancy in 2004 was 20 percentage points, with a productivity ratio to the US of 89 per cent and an income-per-capita ratio of 69 per cent.

How are these large differences to be interpreted? At one extreme, if the decline in European hours per capita consisted entirely of voluntarily-chosen long vacations that could be valued at the after-tax market wage, then the entire discrepancy would represent an undercounting of European welfare compared to the United States. This position is taken by Blanchard (2004: 4), who writes that 'The main difference is that Europe has used some of the increase in productivity to increase leisure rather than income, while the United States has done the opposite.' An alternative interpretation is that the rise in the Europe:US productivity ratio was artificial, as Europe made labour expensive and forced firms to slide northwest up their labour demand curves, cutting low-productivity jobs and retaining high-productivity workers while forcing the low-productivity workers into unemployment or out of the labour force entirely. Under this interpretation the decline in hours per capita is largely involuntary and does not represent unmeasured welfare.

This chapter investigates two aspects of welfare comparisons between Europe and the United States. First, we provide a breakdown of the sources of the decline in European hours per capita into falling hours per employee, lower labour-force participation, and a higher unemployment rate, and we examine the pattern of these differences by age group. Our interpretation combines elements of the emphasis by Alesina, Glaeser, and Sacerdote (2006) on the political process rather than voluntary choice, the much-discussed Prescott (2004) interpretation that traces *all* of the decline in hours per capita to high labour taxes in Europe, and the more recent Ljungqvist–Sargent interpretation that places more emphasis on European social benefits than on labour taxes. On the European side there is controversy regarding the interpretation of reduced hours per capita. How much of reduced hours reflects voluntary choices of, say, longer vacations, and how much represents structural elements and political choices that have reduced working hours per week, reduced labour-force participation through exclusion of youth from the marketplace and through early retirement, and raised the unemployment rate?

The second aspect of the welfare comparison concerns not the interpretation of hours in Europe but rather output, the numerator of both the Y/N and Y/H ratios. Is the translation of output to welfare different in the United States than in Europe? This part of the chapter involves comparisons that are less frequently discussed. The claim that US GDP is overstated for welfare comparisons begins with its harsh climate that requires higher expenditures on energy to achieve a given level of interior comfort. Another portion of US GDP goes to maintaining an enormous prison system that currently incarcerates two million Americans, mostly for minor drug offences. A more controversial claim is that longstanding US policies have encouraged the inefficient low densities of metropolitan areas, adding to traffic congestion, commuting times, and air pollution.

Plan of the chapter

The chapter begins by comparing productivity and per-capita income in Europe and the United States. The difference between the Europe:US productivity and per-capita-income ratios is by definition the ratio of hours per capita, and this is then decomposed into its three main components: hours per employee, the employment rate, and the labour force participation rate (LFPR). The chapter then reviews explanations of differences between Europe and the United States in these three components, starting with an examination of patterns of the employment rate and LFPR across age groups, highlighting the stark differences between Europe and the US for youth and senior citizens in contrast to the relative similarity for prime-age adults. We use the age distribution of differences between Europe and the US to assess the plausibility of the alternative explanations introduced above, namely voluntarily-chosen leisure, political mechanisms, high labour taxes, and high social benefits.

The last part then turns to the translation between GDP and welfare. We examine a wide range of issues including energy use, prison incarceration, urban density, public transit, and the role of immigration. To what extent does a comparison of American and European welfare depend on subjective tastes on each side of the Atlantic for the various attributes of high or low urban density?

2 The evidence: productivity converges but per-capita income does not

In this section we examine the basic data on output per capita and output per hour and then subsequently turn to the explanations.[3] To allow for the initial stage of rapid postwar reconstruction in Europe, each of our graphs begins in 1960 rather than 1950. Figure 1.1 displays real GDP per capita for the EU-15 as compared to the United States, and the log scale shows how remarkably constant has been the gap between the two series since about 1970, after a period of European catch-up prior to 1970. Somewhat remarkably, despite the widespread impression that Europe continued to catch up after 1970, the annual growth rate for the US from 1970–2004 was 2.05 per cent, slightly ahead of the European growth rate of 1.97 per cent. Consequently, the ratio of European to US per-capita output retreated slightly from 71.2 per cent in 1970 to 69.2 per cent.

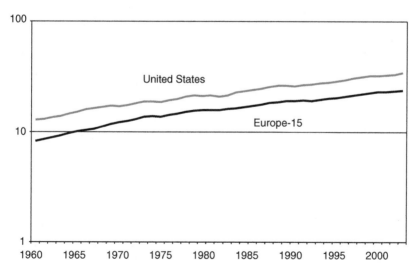

Figure 1.1 Real GDP per capita, Europe-15 and United States, 1960–2004, in thousands of averaged 1990 G-K and 2002 E-K-S US dollars.

Figure 1.2 provides the dramatically different comparison of real GDP per hour in Europe as compared to the United States. Continuing its rapid productivity growth of 1960–70, Europe continued to catch up until 1995, reaching a ratio of 97.4 per cent. The growth rate of labour productivity in Europe from 1970–95 was a robust 2.77 per cent per year, almost double the United States rate of 1.43 per cent per year. This relationship was completely reversed after 1995, with the European rate falling to 1.53 per cent per year, almost a full percentage point behind the US rate of 2.46 per cent per year.

Shifting from the raw data to the percentage per-capita income (Y/N) and productivity (Y/H) ratios of Europe to the US, the dramatic contrast in the timing and magnitude of changes of these ratios is displayed in Figure 1.3. The productivity ratio rises steeply until 1995, holds at a plateau near 100 per cent until 2000, and then enters into a decline during 2001–04. In contrast the per-capita income ratio first reaches 70 per cent in 1970 and then fluctuates in a narrow range between 71 and 76 per cent until 2004, when it falls back below 70 per cent. The 1982 peak in this ratio is artificial, as it reflects the US recession of that year rather than progress for Europe.

Decomposition of the decline in Europe:US hours per capita

By definition, real output *(Y)*, population *(N)*, hours of work *(H)*, and employment *(E)*, are related as:

$$Y/N = Y/H * H/E * E/N \qquad (1)$$

which states that output per capita equals labour productivity times annual hours

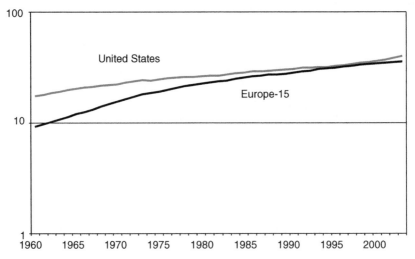

Figure 1.2 Real GDP per hour, Europe-15 and United States, 1960–2004, in thousands of averaged 1990 G-K and 2002 E-K-S US dollars.

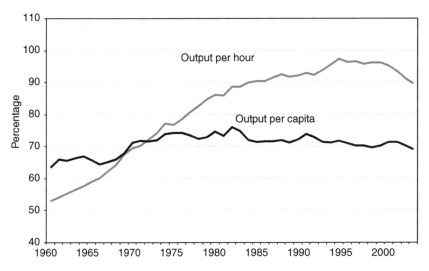

Figure 1.3 Ratio of Europe-15 to the United States, output per capita and output per hour, 1960–2004.

per employee, times employment per capita. Subsequently we will further subdivide changes in the *E/N* ratio into its two components, the employment rate *(E/L)* and the labour force participation rate *(L/N)*.

$$E/N = E/L * L/N = (1 - U/L) * L/N \tag{2}$$

where *U/L* is the unemployment rate.

In Figure 1.4 the dashed grey line is the ratio of the two lines in Figure 1.3, namely the Europe:US ratio of output per capita divided by the Europe:US ratio of output per hour. By definition, the dashed grey line equals hours per capita and is labelled as such in Figure 1.4. This shows a decline from 120 per cent in 1960 to 102 per cent in 1970 to 74 per cent in 1995 and then a slight recovery to 77 per cent in 2004.

By definition any changes in hours per capita (H/N) must be explained by changes in the same direction in the product of the hours:employee and employment:population ratios, as shown in Figure 1.4 by the solid grey and solid black lines, respectively. An important finding is that the decline in the hours per capita ratio has been explained more by the decline in the employee to population ratio than by the hours to employee ratio. Thus we can reject Blanchard's (2004) overly facile explanation, as quoted above, that the differential behaviour of European productivity to European per-capita income is simply a matter of the voluntary choice of shorter hours. Also, we note two interesting aspects of timing that may help to distinguish alternative hypotheses. First, much of the decline in the employee:population ratio had already occurred by 1970, whereas the decline in the ratio for hours per employee was more gradual. Second, there

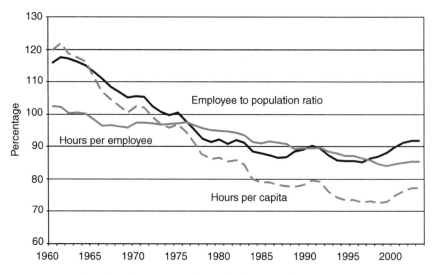

Figure 1.4 Ratio of Europe-15 to the United States, hours per capita, hours per employee, and employees per capita, 1960–2004.

was a distinct turnaround in the employee:population ratio after 1995 but not in the hours:employee ratio.

The time-series plots of the three ratios in Figure 1.4 are summarized in Table 1.1, which displays both levels and growth rates for 1960, 1970, 1995, and 2004. Starting in the first column with hours per capita, we find a steady decrease at an annual rate of −1.6 per cent for 1960–70 and −1.3 per cent for 1970–95, followed by a turnaround to a positive growth rate of 0.5 per cent for 1995–2004. Hours per employee also declined relatively steadily from 1960–95, with respective 1960–70 and 1970–95 growth rates of −0.5 and −0.4 per cent, and this decline continued after 1995 at an annual growth rate of −0.2 per cent. The 'residual,' employment per capita, declined steadily in 1960–70 and

Table 1.1 Levels and growth rates of three ratios of Europe to the United States, 1960–2004, per cent

	Hours per capita	*Hours per employee*	*Employees per capita*
1960	119.8	102.4	115.9
1970	102.4	97.4	105.6
1995	73.6	87.1	85.7
2004	77.2	85.4	91.7
Annual growth rates			
1960–70	−1.6	−0.5	−0.9
1970–95	−1.3	−0.4	−0.8
1995–2004	0.5	−0.2	0.8

1970–95 at respective growth rates of −0.9 and −0.8 per cent, followed by a sharp turnaround after 1995 to +0.8 per cent. This turnaround in the behaviour of employment per capita may be helpful in assessing alternative hypotheses to explain Europe's low hours per capita.

The time series of hours per employee and the employment:population ratio

Having examined the Europe:US ratios corresponding to equation (1) above, we now return to the raw numbers for Europe and the US separately. As shown in Figure 1.5, hours per employee in 1960 were higher in Europe, 2,082 hours per year compared to 2,033 hours in the United States. From 1960 to 1975 hours in Europe declined slightly faster than in the US, in 1975 reaching 1,827 for Europe and 1,878 for the US. After 1975 there was a sharp divergence, so that by 2004 hours in the US had barely declined, from 1,878 to 1,817, whereas the decline in Europe was much more significant, from 1,827 to 1,552. Those like Prescott (2004) who attribute the entire decline in hours to high European labour taxes need to show that these taxes increased in Europe relative to the US steadily throughout the post-1960 period and particularly between 1975 and 1990.

Perhaps the most interesting of our comparison charts is Figure 1.6, which shows the employment:population ratio in Europe and the US separately. In the United States, we take for granted the increase in this ratio that occurred between 1965 and 1985 due to the entry of females into the labour force. Over the period plotted in Figure 1.6 the US ratio increased from 35.8 per cent in 1963 to 47.5 per cent in 1990 and then flattened out to an identical 47.5 per cent

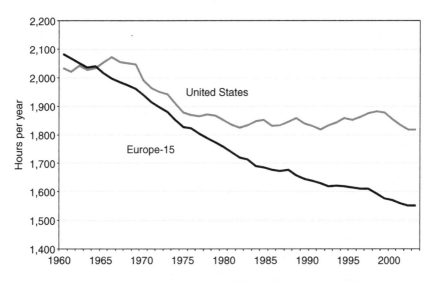

Figure 1.5 Hours per employee, Europe-15 and United States, 1960–2004.

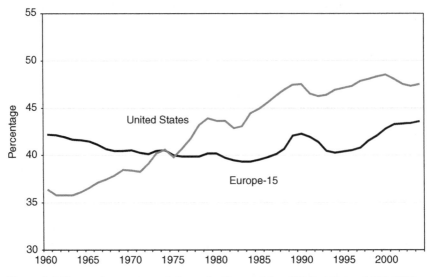

Figure 1.6 The employment:population ratio, Europe-15 and United States, 1960–2004.

in 2004. In contrast, the European ratio actually fell from 42.2 per cent in 1960 to 39.3 per cent in 1983, followed by a small recovery to 40.3 per cent in 1994 and then a substantial revival to 43.6 per cent in 2004.

Why did the entry of females into the labour force in Europe not generate the same rise in the employment:population ratio in Europe as in the US in the 1965–85 period? This puzzle is partly explained by the sharp increase in European unemployment that occurred over the same time interval; an increase in the unemployment rate reduces the ratio of employment to the labour force, apparently by enough to offset the role of females who would have been expected to increase the labour force participation rate. Another possibility is that a trend to earlier retirement ages pushed down the labour force participation rate by enough to offset the increase in the female labour force participation rate. It is worth noting that fertility rates in the United States are substantially higher than in Europe, implying that more European women have time free from raising children and would thus be expected to have a higher labour force participation rate than in the United States.

3 Interpreting changes in hours per capita

Until now we have examined time-series changes in the key components of hours per capita in Europe vs. the United States. The pattern of changes over time may be more consistent with some types of explanations than others, helping us to discriminate among them. Age is another dimension that may help us with this discrimination, for instance, an explanation for falling hours per capita in Europe based on higher labour taxes would tend to have an impact upon workers of all ages up to retirement age rather than have a disproportionate effect on one age group or another.

The age distribution of unemployment and labour force participation

Unemployment rates by five-year age groups are shown for the EU-15 and United States in Figure 1.7. The unemployment rate is uniformly higher across all age groups.[4] These differences can be assessed using absolute or relative differences. For teenagers the European rate is 22.0 per cent vs. 13.9 for the US, an absolute gap of 8.1 points and a relative gap that is 59 per cent of the US rate. The lowest absolute gap is for age group 45–49, where the European rate is 6.0 and the US rate is 2.8, for an absolute gap of 3.2 points and a relative gap of 114 per cent. Because the absolute and relative differences occur for all age groups, this evidence would seem to endorse a single explanation such as high labour taxes.

However, as shown in Figure 1.8, the behaviour of the labour force participation rate is quite different. For the prime-age groups from 30 to 44 the rates in Europe are identical to the United States. The big differences are for the young and particularly for the older age groups. The absolute shortfall for Europe is 11.7 points for age 15–19, 10.7 points for age 20–24, 12.1 points for age 55–59, and a huge 22.8 points for age 60–64. These differences do not seem consistent with Prescott's (2004) labour tax explanation and may be more compatible with the Alesina *et al.* (2006) emphasis on the political process which may have included pressure for pension schemes that encourage early retirement. The low

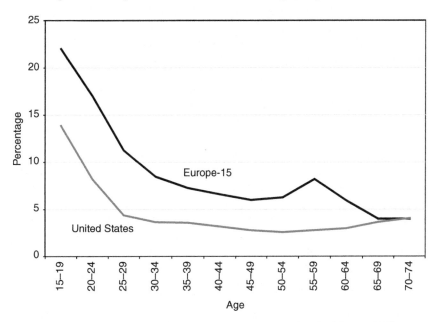

Figure 1.7 Unemployment rates by age group, Europe-15 and United States, 2002.

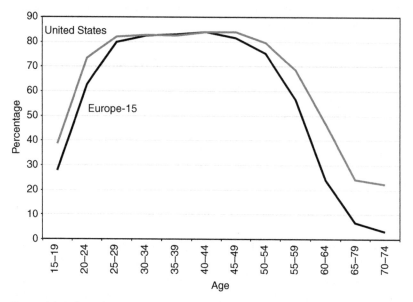

Figure 1.8 Labour force participation rates by age group, Europe-15 and United States, 2002.

participation for the older groups in Europe may also be compatible with the Ljungqvist–Sargent (2006) preference for an explanation based on European social welfare policies rather than labour tax rates.

By definition, the employment rate *(E/L)* times the LFPR *(L/N)* equals the employment:population ratio *(E/N)*, for which we have already examined time-series changes in Figure 1.4 and Table 1.1. Figure 1.9 shows the employment:population ratio by age group, and this combines the age pattern of unemployment in Figure 1.7 and of the LFPR in Figure 1.8. Because unemployment is higher at every age group in Europe, the prime-age groups that in Figure 1.8 have the same LFPR as in the US have lower *E/N* ratios in Figure 1.9. But the overall pattern is the same, with larger absolute and relative differences for the youngest and oldest age groups.

The aggregation of the group-specific unemployment rate and the LFPR depend on the relative size of each group. As shown in Figure 1.10, Europe's population structure is more heavily weighted to the older age groups, as would be expected with lower fertility, higher life expectancy, and a smaller flow of immigration. All the European age groups starting with age 50–54 have a higher weight than in the US, and all younger age groups have a higher weight in the US except for age groups 25–34.

Summary of findings on changes in hours per capita

Changes in hours per capita in Europe compared to the US can be divided into two categories – changes in hours per employee *(H/E)* and in employment per

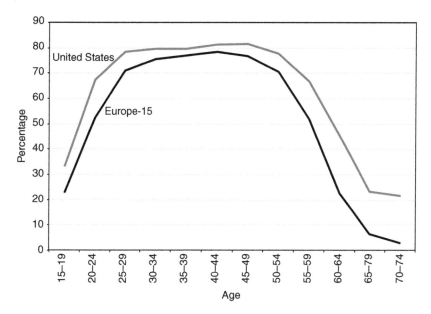

Figure 1.9 Employment/population ratios by age group, Europe-15 and United States, 2002.

capita *(E/N)*, and the latter can be further subdivided into changes in the employment rate *(E/L)* and changes in the labour force participation rate *(L/N)*. We have learned from Figure 1.4 and Table 1.1 that the post-1960 period can be divided into two distinct phases split at 1995. Between 1960 and 1995, fully two-thirds of the decline in hours per capita was accounted for by the employment ratio *(E/N)* and only one-third by hours per employee *(H/E)*. This provides a useful dose of scepticism for Blanchard's previously cited view that Europeans used their high productivity to purchase more leisure; leisure in the form of shorter hours per employee were only one-third of the story through 1995.

Fully two-thirds was a very different story of high unemployment and low labour force participation, hardly an outcome of voluntary choice. But an additional dimension of evidence in Table 1.1 is that the Europe:US ratio for employment per capita *(E/N)* turned around after 1995 while the hours per employee ratio, while declining more slowly, did not turn around. All this suggests that a different set of factors may have been driving changes in the hours ratio from the employment per capita ratio.

While we do not have graphs on the time-series behaviour of the split of the employment ratio between the unemployment rate and the labour force participation rate, we can calculate the importance of each of these components for a single year, 2002. Using US population weights as in Figure 1.10 to aggregate across age groups, with EU unemployment and LFPRs the Europe:US employment ratio *(E/N)* would have been 86.2 per cent. Continuing with US population

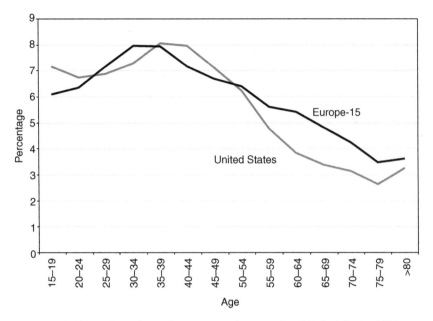

Figure 1.10 Share of population by age group, Europe-15 and United States, 2002.

weights, with US age-specific unemployment rates that *E/N* ratio would have risen to 90.8 per cent, and obviously to 100.0 per cent with US age-specific unemployment rates and labour force participation rates. Thus we conclude that in 2002, of the gap of 13.8 per cent between the European and US *E/N* ratio, less than one-third (4.4/13.8) is explained by higher European age-specific unemployment rates and more than two-thirds (9.2/13.8) by lower European age-specific labour force participation rates.

4 Distinguishing among alternative hypotheses

In recent journal and conference discussions most of the attention has focused on single-cause explanations of the secular decline in hours per capita in Europe, such as Prescott's labour taxes or Alesina's politically powerful unions. However, our examination of the data suggests that a multi-cause nuanced set of explanations might better fit the facts, including the post-1995 turnaround in the Europe:US employment per capita *(E/N)* ratio and the sharp differences in the Europe:US ratios of labour force participation by age group.

As we discuss and criticize the alternative hypotheses, we should focus on welfare implications of the extra hours of the year spent by Europeans in non-market work instead of market work. Conventional economic analysis values leisure at the marginal after-tax wage. If a single cause like higher labour taxes causes a substitution from work to leisure, the value of the extra leisure consumed would be measured by the area under the labour supply curve. Since discussions of labour taxes assume that there is no income effect, because tax revenues are rebated to the population through government expenditures and transfers, the effect of taxes is to create a pure substitution effect. If we imagine an upward sloping labour supply curve extending between the 2004 European *H/E* annual total of 1,550 hours and the US ratio of 1,811 hours, then presumably the average value of the extra leisure in Europe is halfway between the marginal after-tax wage that Europeans receive today and the higher marginal after-tax wage that Europeans would receive in a hypothetical world in which taxes are levied at American rates. A basic question, however, is whether this valuation of leisure should be applied to the entire reduction in hours per capita that includes the effects of higher unemployment and lower labour force participation rates, or only to the one-third of the drop in European hours per capita consisting of lower hours per employee, i.e. vacations and shorter working weeks.

Prescott on labour taxes

The Prescott (2004) explanation claims that the entire difference between Europe and the US not just for hours per employee but for hours per capita can be explained by higher tax rates on labour. The key to this demonstration, as explained by Alesina *et al.* (2006: 13), is that Prescott chooses a functional form that delivers a very high elasticity of labour supply, that is, a response of around -0.8 in logs to $1/(1-t)$, where t is the tax rate on labour income. Alesina and co-authors show that the data require an even higher elasticity of -0.92, which is the ratio of the -29.7 per cent log difference between European and American hours, divided by the 32.4 per cent log difference in the marginal tax rate expressed as $1/(1-t)$. They reject the Prescott assumptions after reviewing the micro labour supply literature that shows uncompensated labour supply elasticities for men that are close to zero, that labour supply elasticities for married women are high enough so that European tax rates could explain the entire Europe:US difference, and finally that taking all the evidence together tax rate differences can explain at best one-half of the hours per capita difference.

A further weakness in the Prescott argument comes from the time series evidence. Most of the increase in tax rates occurred between the 1960s and mid-1980s, whereas the decline in hours continued at least through 1995. As we have noted, after 1995 the decline in hours per employee continued at a slower rate whereas the decline in employees per capita turned around into an increase. A final problem is that high tax rates may be standing as a proxy for a whole range of variables that differ between Europe and the US but are not included explicitly in the simplistic cross-country correlations between tax rates and hours per capita, namely 'generous welfare systems, workplace regulations, unemployment compensation programmes, powerful unions, generous social security systems, etc.' (Alesina *et al.*, 2006).

The Welfare State

Some critics, particularly Ljungqvist and Sargent (2006), criticize Prescott's assumption that labour taxes are entirely redistributed to households as lump-sum transfers that are valued as if they were privately purchased goods and services. It is this device that allows Prescott to ignore income effects, and in turn to overstate the portion of changing work hours attributable to changing tax rates. These authors also criticize Prescott for ignoring the fact that in the early 1970s tax rates in France and Germany were already 10 points higher than in the US, but hours per capita were basically the same, as shown above in Figure 1.4.

Ljungqvist and Sargent (2006: 43–44) emphasize the different welfare implications of the 'national family perspective' implicit for Prescott, in which the entire population is viewed as a set of representative agents. When higher taxes reduce labour force participation, there are voluntary transfers between working and non-working members of the 'national family.' In reality, however, most non-employed heads of households in Europe are not supported by voluntary intra-family transfers but rather by welfare systems that not only support reduced hours per capita but also 'strain social insurance systems and government finances.'

These authors argue that reforming European welfare systems would raise hours per capita more than cutting labour tax rates. They support their view in part by pointing to the fact that Europeans worked as much as Americans in the early 1970s despite higher labour tax rates, because Prescott's hypothetical costless lump-sum redistribution within the national family was not in fact available. 'Tax revenues were funnelled to public goods and government expenditures that were poor substitutes for private consumption. The negative income effect of taxation worked in favour of sustaining high employment in the European welfare states' (Ljungqvist and Sargent, 2006: 45).

An additional consequence of generous welfare benefits is to encourage workers to remain unemployed for long periods of time after negative demand or productivity shocks. With heterogeneous workers who have previously accumulated skills, there will be a loss of those skills over prolonged spells of unemployment. The skill set of workers will no longer be high enough to warrant their high reservation wage, and they 'become discouraged and are likely to fall into long-term unemployment or end up in other government programmes, such as disability insurance and early retirement' (Ljungqvist, 2006: 75).

Unionization and regulation

Alesina and co-authors make much of the higher penetration of unions in Europe than in the United States. As is well known, unions in the United States had a negligible role prior to the 1930s, were legitimized by New Deal legislation, reached their peak of influence in the 1940s and 1950s and began to decline in importance from the late 1960s. Some authors, including Goldin and Margo (1992) have stressed the role of unions in helping achieve the 'great compression' of income equality during their strong period and more recently Dew-Becker and Gordon (2005), among others, have attributed part of the decline in real incomes of the bottom half of the income distribution relative to the top 10 per cent to the decline of US union penetration.

In contrast, 'union strength reached a peak in most European countries in the late 1970s and early 1990s' (Alesina *et al.*, 2006: 29). These authors trace two channels between high unionization and lower hours. First, unions keep wages artificially high and thus restrict employment, and in this sense their effect on labour demand is just like a labour tax. Second, unions may pursue a political agenda to reduce work hours in order to force firms to hire more unionized workers to achieve the tasks that need to be done. They derive several propositions from a simple model, (1) that regulations limiting work hours will decrease productivity per worker but will raise productivity per hour, (2) that total hours worked under unionization will be lower and productivity per hour will be higher, and (3) that unions impede the reallocation of labour in response to sectoral shocks and can cause a decrease in overall hours worked, in comparison to an increase in hours worked in response to sectoral shocks in a competitive economy.

The authors support their emphasis on unions by displaying a negative correlation between union coverage and hours of work that they claim is at least as high as that between marginal tax rates and hours of work.[5] However, this kind of cross-section evidence is fragile, both because of the large size of the outliers, and also because there is no attempt to model the time-series properties of unionization vs. the pattern of European hours per capita. Neither the Alesina *et al.* (2006) paper nor its discussants recognize the sharp turnaround in the Europe:US employment:population ratio, and without recognizing this important phenomenon they provide no explanation for it related to taxes, unions, or anything else.

These authors go beyond a simplistic reliance on union density to provide numerous examples in individual European countries in which unions promoted policies like 'work less, work all' which reflected the belief that an enforcement of regulations that reduced work hours would create more jobs. Since this political pressure required that wages per job remain fixed, it forced upwards the wage per hour and ensured that hours per capita would decline. Examples are given for France, Germany, and Italy of union political involvement not only in shortening work hours without pay reductions, but also in 'promoting and defending the Welfare State in general and public pension systems in particular' (Alesina and Glaeser, 2004). They cite not only the push for early retirement but also the role of unions in negotiating early retirement schemes for older workers in cases where the closing of a large plant might otherwise cause unemployment. They attribute the concern of unions with early retirement to the political power of older workers within the union hierarchy itself.

We have already seen that perhaps the most important single source in Europe's reduction in hours per capita relative to the US is early retirement, as shown by the age-specific labour force participation rates in Figure 1.8. Thus, a key difference between the leading authors is that Blanchard implicitly assumes that early retirement has been voluntary, Prescott assumes that early retirement is an endogenous response to high labour taxes, and Alesina *et al.* regard early retirement as the outcome of a political process led by unions who were involved in a political philosophy of work sharing regardless of whether workers actually want to stop working and live off pension income. Below we provide an example of the enormous cost to any society of early retirement.

Evaluation

Why does it matter whether the decline in the Europe:US ratio of hours per capita is mainly caused by higher labour taxes, by the Welfare State, or political pressure engineered by unions? The simple Prescott tax story allows us to interpret the entire decline in European hours per capita as voluntarily-chosen leisure, while the Welfare State and political stories imply that European households are not receiving leisure that they value as highly as in the standard economics textbook story.

One line of criticism of the Alesina emphasis on unions is that the timing is wrong. As shown by Rogerson (2006: 83), union density averaged over 19 European countries rose through the late 1970s and fell until 1995, reaching a level that was little different from the starting value of 1960. If unions became strong and then became weak, why was their political influence still strong enough to explain low European hours per capita in 2004? Rogerson supports his scepticism by showing that union density and a measure of employment protection have very little explanatory power for changes in European hours per capita. This criticism falls into the trap of simple correlation and ignores inertia in the political process. It is possible that Europe could still be suffering from legislation that unions successfully pushed when they were strong in the 1980s but which opposing political forces have thus far been unable to overturn. The demonstrations in Paris in April, 2006, against modest reforms in labour market regulations suggest the power of such political inertia.

None of the explanations reviewed from the recent literature has any explanation of the post-1995 reversal in the ratio of the Europe:US employment: population *(E/N)* ratio. Most observers are startled to find that employment has grown faster relative to population in Europe than in the US, where hours of work in 2005:Q4 were still 3.0 per cent below their peak levels in 2001:Q1. There is a chicken and egg aspect to this phenomenon of growing work hours in Europe and shrinking work hours in the US over the past half-decade. Is the phenomenon to be explained as an autonomous shift in the incentives for work hours in Europe vs. the US, as is implicitly assumed by most of the literature reviewed above, or is the behaviour of work hours a by-product of differences in productivity growth in Europe compared to the US that emerge from a totally different set of factors? For instance, the productivity literature shows that half of the difference in US compared to European productivity growth since 1995 occurred in retail trade, and this is in turn attributed to land use and other regulations which have made it much easier in the US to develop 'big box' retailing by firms such as Wal-Mart, Target, Home Depot, Best Buy, and others. Simple single-cause explanations of falling hours in Europe, such as 'higher taxes,' 'welfare state,' and 'unions' appear to have missed completely the post-1995 turnaround and the related chicken–egg question.

The literature reviewed here revolves around much more complex issues than Blanchard's (2004) sanguine view, quoted above, that Europeans have voluntarily chosen more leisure and so their relative well-being is better represented by the Europe:US productivity ratio in Figure 1.3 than by the Europe:US ratio of output per capita. Any suggestion that Europeans have a different 'taste for leisure' than Americans ignores the fact that Europeans worked longer hours than Americans during the 1945–73 era of postwar reconstruction, so their passion for long vacations and short weekly hours of work is a recently-acquired taste.

The Alesina approach questions whether Europeans really have chosen such long vacations voluntarily; could this outcome be the result of union or parliamentary politics? American workers seem happy to be bribed to work long hours for premium overtime pay; as the quip goes, 'Compulsory overtime is an unmitigated evil that every one of my workers wants his fair share of.'[6]

Early retirement and the idle European youth

Perhaps the most convincing aspects of the Alesina approach is the interplay between the political process and early retirement in Europe. If individual households in a welfare state are given the option of a defined benefit government-funded pension plan that allows them to retire at nearly full pay at age 58, they would be crazy to turn down the option of receiving the same income for not working as they would receive for working. The costs of early retirement to society can be illustrated by a simple example.

Consider an economy that initially has people work from ages 20 to 65 and then retire from ages 65 to 84. There is no private saving. A 30 per cent tax finances pay-as-you-go pensions with a balanced government budget. This tax finances a level of consumption during the 20 years of retirement equal to consumption during the 45 years of work. Now let the politicians reduce the retirement age from 65 to 55. Instead of 45 years of work financing 20 years of retirement, now 35 years of work finances 30 years of retirement. The tax rate must increase to 45.6 per cent. Even ignoring the Prescott-like withdrawal of work hours that reduces market GDP, there is a 25.1 per cent decline in consumption during both work years and retirement years.

With a few additional assumptions, we can translate this decline in market consumption into a welfare measure. Let us assume that hours that are normally spent by current workers in leisure-time activities, i.e. on weekday evenings and on weekends, are valued at 4/3 of the after-tax market wage, but that hours switched from work to weekday leisure as a result of early retirement are valued at 2/3 of the after-tax market wage. Total welfare is market consumption plus the total value of leisure. The early retirees continue to enjoy high-valued weekday evening and weekend leisure but switch from market consumption to low-valued weekday daytime leisure. A simple simulation shows that as a result of the decline in market consumption of 25.1 per cent determined above, total welfare declines by 22.6 per cent and the value of extra leisure as a result of early retirement offsets only 10 per cent of the loss of market consumption that results from early retirement.

The time-study research by Freeman and Schettkat (2005) provides another qualification regarding the value of leisure time gained by those who are not working. They contrast the United States with Germany and find that part of the difference in hours per capita does not represent more leisure in Germany but more household production. German mothers cook more at home, American mothers more frequently go out to eat as they spend their higher market income on market consumption. Higher labour force participation in the US brings not only the benefits of higher market incomes which allow the substitution of restaurants and hired help for household drudgery, but also provides for greater socialization as people remain in an organized social context during the workday in contrast to loneliness at home.

We learned from Figures 1.6 and 1.7 that a major contributor to lower labour force participation in Europe compared to the US is not only early retirement but also lower participation and higher unemployment among youths aged 15 to 29. The French riots of the *banlieue* in 2005 remind us that many European youths are marginalized from contact with the market economy. Are unmarried Italian 30-year-old males sitting at home, insisting that their mothers cook for them and do their laundry, because they have a special taste for leisure or because the economy and society do not provide sufficiently rewarding jobs for them?[7]

Differences in the economic environment of American and European youth are pervasive. Because of the flexibility of American labour markets, American youths easily find after-school jobs in fast-food restaurants and other service outlets. Instead of receiving government-funded tuition block grants for college, American youths are expected both by their parents and by colleges to work part-time during the school year and full-time during the summer. They are early to adopt a culture of work rather than idleness, and this continues after graduation from college. In contrast, judging from the low employment:population ratios for Europeans aged 15 to 29, much of the time in this European age group is wasted, especially when we recognize the share of American youths compared to European youths going to college and hence removed from the employment:population ratio.

5 By how much does American GDP overstate welfare?

Until this point, the chapter has been about welfare interpretations of the decline in European hours per capita relative to the US that by definition explain why Europe performs so much better in comparison with American productivity than in comparison with American output per capita. This final section addresses several issues that concern the numerator of the productivity and output per capita ratios, namely real GDP itself. How much does measured real GDP with typical PPP exchange rate translations exaggerate or understate welfare in Europe vs. the United States?

A considerable part of the US advantage in cross-country comparisons of living standards must stem from the much larger size of average American dwelling units, both their internal dimensions and the amount of surrounding land. Fully three-quarters of the American housing stock consists of single-family detached and attached units. The median living area in the detached units is 1,720 square feet, with an average acreage for all single-family units of 0.35 (equivalent to a lot size of 100 by 150 feet). Another figure that must seem unbelievable to Europeans is that 25 per cent of American single-family units rest on lots of one acre or more. Available data, although patchy for Europe, suggest that the average American dwelling unit is at least 50 to 75 per cent larger than the average European unit.[8] Since construction of new units and imputed rent on old units are included in GDP comparisons across countries, our Europe:US ratio of per capita output in Figure 1.3 already incorporates the superiority of the US housing stock (as long as the cross-country PPP-based price indexes make adequate allowance for housing quality).

Yet a European might retort that, while the gap between US and European standards already includes the housing difference, it also includes activities that are not welfare-enhancing. A significant fraction of GDP in the US does not improve welfare but rather involves fighting the environment whether created by nature or man-made decisions. The climate is more extreme in America than in Europe (excluding the ex-USSR), and this means that some GDP is spent on larger air-conditioning and heating bills than in Europe to attain any given indoor temperature. Some of the US GDP is spent on extra highways and extra energy to support the dispersion of the American population into huge metropolitan areas spreading over hundreds or even thousands of square miles, in many cases with few transport options other than the car. European real GDP is held down by the correctly measured high price of petrol, but sufficient credit is not given for convenience benefits from frequent bus, subway, and train (including TGV) public transit.

While an economist's first reaction is that the dispersion of US metropolitan areas must be optimal, since people have chosen to buy houses in the outer suburbs, a more careful reaction would be to view the American dispersion as related to public policy in addition to private choice, especially subsidies to interstate highways in vast amounts relative to public transport, local zoning measures in some suburbs that prohibit residential land allocations below a fixed size, e.g. two acres, and the infamous and politically-untouchable deduction of mortgage interest payments from income tax. Europeans enjoy shopping from small individually-owned shops on lively central city main streets and pedestrian arcades, and recoil with distaste from the ubiquitous and cheerless American strip malls and big-box retailers – although Carrefour, Ikea and others provide American-like options in some European cities. To counter the effects of

American land use regulations that create overly-dispersed metropolitan areas, Europeans counter with their own brand of land use rules that preserve greenbelts and inhibit growth of suburban and exurban retailing and have indirectly prevented Europeans from enjoying either the low prices or high productivity growth of American 'big box' retailers.

Tastes are, in part, the result of circumstances and habit, and to the European critique many Americans would deliver a counter-retort. An American mother of two small children wants nothing to do with schlepping those kids through endless tunnels while making connections on the London or Paris subways, or with waiting in the rain for the next bus, or with shopping for groceries more often than once per week. The three-quarters of American households living in single-family units treasure their backyards, decks, and barbeques and do not want to be forced to go to a public park for outdoor recreation – whose barbeque grill would they use?

Even if part of American energy use is not welfare-enhancing, either because it offsets the harsh climate or politically-motivated 'excess dispersion' of American metropolitan areas, how much could this possibly be worth? Figure 1.11 displays the time path of energy consumption per dollar of GDP in the US and Europe since 1980. Despite the continuation of low gasoline taxes in the US, the gap between American and European energy use has narrowed and now amounts to no more than 2 per cent of GDP. If we take half of that gap as welfare-enhancing (the value of heating large interior spaces and driving larger cars and trucks), and the other half as non-welfare-enhancing (offsetting the harsh climate and unnecessary driving caused by excess dispersion and the lack of public transit), the energy story emerges with an overstatement of US welfare by only 1 per cent of GDP. Other US expenditures, including keeping two million people in prison, might add another 1 per cent of GDP in non-welfare-enhancing activities.

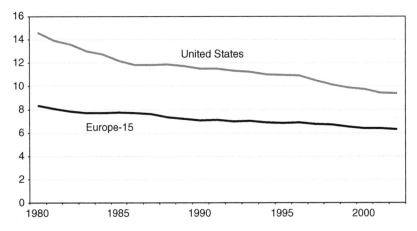

Figure 1.11 BTUs of energy consumption per dollar of GDP, Europe-15 vs. United States, 1980–2002.

6 Conclusion

This chapter examines two classes of arguments implying that standard PPP-based ratios of European output per capita relative to that of the United States understate true European welfare. The first set of debates which takes up most of the chapter concerns the interpretation of the puzzle, 'why is Europe so productive yet so poor?' What explains the fact that in the mid-1990s Europe almost caught up to the US level of productivity but remains far behind with a ratio of its per-capita income that has languished at between 70 and 75 per cent since 1970? Arithmetic isolates a decline in the Europe:US ratio of hours per capita as the sole cause of this puzzle, but then the questions begin.

This chapter provides a detailed review of debates involving four leading interpretations of the relative decline in European hours per capita. These are that most or all of the difference represents a different taste for leisure in Europe, that all of the difference reflects high taxes on labour in Europe, that much of the difference represents the effects not of high taxes but of an overly-generous Welfare State, and finally that hours per capita have been driven down not by voluntary choices but by political pressure initiated by unions that have promoted legislation ratifying a shorter working week, long vacations, and early retirement.

In sorting through the debate about these explanations, we examine data that allows us to make three distinctions that rarely appear in the literature. First, the time-series evidence shows that only one-third of the relative decline in European hours per capita was due to a decline in hours per employee, i.e. the famous European long vacations and short working week. The remaining two-thirds was divided into roughly two-thirds due to falling labour force participation and the remaining one-third to rising unemployment, both corrected for differences between the US and Europe in the composition of the working-age population by age group.

Second, the time-series data show a distinct turnaround after 1995. While hours per employee continued to fall in Europe relative to the US, albeit at a slower rate, there was a complete turnaround in the behaviour of employment per capita, from 35 years of steady decline to nine years since 1995 of steady increase. None of the literature on European hours calls attention to this turnaround nor provides any explanation of this phenomenon.

Third, our examination of European vs. US unemployment rates and labour force participation rates by age group shows another little-discussed contrast. The unemployment rate is higher across the board in every European age group, and in several age groups the unemployment rate in 2002 was double that in the same US age group. But for labour force participation the pattern is completely different. Among prime-age workers (aged 30–44) European participation rates are identical to those in the US, whereas participation rates are much lower in the 15–29 and 50–65+ age groups. These patterns make it unlikely that a single explanation of lower European hours per capita can suffice. For instance, if high labour taxes are the dominant cause of falling European hours per capita, why did this not affect the labour force participation rate of prime-age Europeans at all?

We emerge convinced that markets work, and that there is some role for higher taxes and more generous welfare benefits in reducing hours per capita. But the tax-and-benefits story cannot explain all of the differences by age group and cannot explain the post-1995 turnaround in the employment:population ratio. The Alesina explanation of political pressure from unions provides at least one plausible explanation of early retirement ages in Europe, which are entirely a political phenomenon built into the legislation that sets retirement ages in government-funded pension schemes. In a back-of-the-envelope calculation, we conclude that early retirement is perhaps the most significant cause of Europe's low standard of living. In our example, a reduction of the retirement age from 65 to 55 with a balanced-budget government-funded pension scheme and no private saving would reduce market consumption by 25 per cent and reduce welfare by 22 per cent, leaving only a 3 per cent offset from the value of the leisure of early retirees.

Regarding the post-1995 turnaround, we enter the world of conjecture. In earlier work (Gordon, 1997), I suggested that there was a tradeoff between unemployment and productivity, using the standard textbook labour supply and demand diagram. Anything that made labour more expensive in Europe, including a high minimum wage and high taxes, would push firms northwest up the labour demand curve, would cut low marginal-productivity jobs, would reduce hours and employment, and would raise average productivity. In contrast, the United States with its flexible labour markets, lower taxes, and lower minimum wage would emerge with lower average productivity and higher hours and employment. This point was illustrated with four examples of low skilled employment in the US that barely exist in Europe, namely grocery baggers, bus boys, parking lot attendants, and valet parking (although the *Voiturier* has recently emerged in central Paris).

My conjecture is that since 1995 Europe has become less unlike the United States, helping to explain the turnaround in the employment:population ratio. While differing across European countries, there has been the introduction of flexible employment contracts, a weakening of employment protection enforcement, and a reduction in the real minimum wage. In contrast, in the US the relative decline in hours per capita has a different source, an explosion of productivity growth that has enabled firms to cut costs, particularly labour costs.

The last part of the chapter is about possible dimensions in which measured PPP GDP overstates welfare in the United States compared to Europe. The easiest case to make is that the US has a harsher climate and so some of the extra energy consumption in the US (measured relative to GDP) is not welfare-enhancing. A more debatable position is that the US has long instituted policies that have created overly-dispersed metropolitan areas with few public transit options, also leading to excess energy use. However, the extra use of energy in the US compared to Europe is currently worth only around 2 per cent of GDP, so that any allowance for 'excess' energy use could at most account for only

1 per cent of GDP. Our discussion of GDP overstatement also makes an allowance of 1 per cent of GDP for excessive incarceration in prisons.

Table 1.2 summarizes the results of the chapter. In the top line we start with a Europe:US ratio of 68.8 per cent for real GDP per capita and in the next-to-bottom line we contrast that with a ratio of 89.2 per cent for productivity, i.e. real GDP per hour. How much can we add to the initial ratio of 68.8 per cent? By far the largest addition is 7.9 points to reflect the value of leisure reflected in declining European hours per employee, much of which involves longer vacations and shorter working weeks, which are doubtless of considerable value. These extra hours of leisure in Europe are valued at two-thirds of the market wage. However, for the reduction in the employment:population ratio, we view this as largely involuntary and, using our example of early retirement, providing a relatively small value of additional leisure. This adds another 0.9 per cent. The two adjustments to real GDP add 2.0 points for excess US energy use and wasted resources created by excess incarceration and the creation of a gigantic prison population of two million people, who in their future life are deprived of educational and job opportunities as a result of their prison records.

Adding together these supplements to the European standard of living raises the ratio from the initial 68.8 per cent at the top of Table 1.2 to a more robust 79.6 per cent, and this explains slightly more than half of the initial 20 point gap between the Europe:US ratio of output per capita to output per hour.

There are many other dimensions of these welfare comparisons that should be explored in future research. There is increasing distress in the US about our dysfunctional medical care system that makes medical care insurance a benefit of employment instead of a right of citizenship. Day-to-day employment decisions of American workers and bankruptcy or relocation decisions by American firms are distorted by the failure of the US to adopt a citizenship-based medical care system. Numerous other examples could be provided of welfare issues that favour one side of the Atlantic or another, e.g. the inferiority of US math and science education at the secondary level, the superiority of US higher education and its worldwide attraction to graduate students, and the greater ability of the US compared to countries like France in assimilating immigrants. This chapter begins the process not just of debating the causes of relatively low hours per capita in Europe but also of rethinking the translation of real GDP into welfare comparisons across countries and regions.

Table 1.2 Summary of adjustments to the Europe-to-US ratio of per-capita income, 2004

	Europe-to-US ratio of real GDP per capita	Adjustment to leisure component of hours	Adjustment to GDP
Market PPP ratio of Y per capita	68.8		
Add: 2/3 of difference in hours per employee (11.8)		7.9	
Add: 1/10 of difference in employment per capita (8.6)		0.9	
Add: half of energy use difference			1.0
Add: prisons and other			1.0
Sum of market PPP ratio and above additions	79.6		
Market PPP ratio of Y per hour	89.2		
Percentage of difference explained	52.9		

Notes

* The author is grateful for comments on earlier versions by Lou Cain, Paul David, Jean-Paul Fitoussi, Robert M. Solow, and seminar participants at Northwestern, M.I.T., the Economic History Association, OFCE in Paris, the University of Oviedo, and the DEMPATEM conference in Seville.

Ian Dew-Becker was the peerless research assistant who created the aggregated European data for the charts and tables; Chris Taylor and Rob McMenamin helped in the final stages of preparing this chapter.

1 All references to 'Europe' in this chapter refer to the 15 members of the European Union prior to May 1, 2004, the so-called 'EU-15.'
2 These are the 'G-K' (Geary-Khamis) weights calculated in 1990 dollars and the 'E-K-S' (Eltetö, Köves, and Szulc) weights calculated in 2002 dollars. For a year like 1980, the average of the G-K and E-K-S data show that the Europe:US ratio of per-capita income is 74.4 per cent, almost identical to Neary's (2004) preferred 'QUAIDS' index number method that yields 74.3 per cent. All data on productivity, income per capita, and hours per capita come from the Groningen economy-wide data base at www.ggdc.net/index-dseries.html.
3 As indicated before, all data on GDP, population, and hours come from the Groningen economy-wide data base, which has assembled data for many countries going back to 1950.
4 Our OECD data source does not provide rates for European age groups above 65. In Figure 1.7 these are assumed to be the same as in the United States, leading to the artificial impression that unemployment rates converge in the older age groups.
5 This comparison is not appropriate, because the measure of hours in the tax correlation is H/N but is H/E in the union correlation.
6 I owe the quip to Robert M. Solow, a discussant of an earlier version of this chapter.
7 Roughly 52 per cent of Italians between the ages of 20 and 34 live at home with their parents (Rhoads, 2002).
8 Average estimated useful floor space of dwellings in 1997 or 1998 was 2,058 square feet for the United States and 995 for the average of Austria, Denmark, Finland, and Switzerland (none of the large European countries are listed). For newly-constructed dwellings, 'average living floor space' for Germany and Italy was 969. See United Nations, *Annual Bulletin of Housing and Building Statistics for Europe and North America 2000*, pp. 21 and 24, obtained from www.unece.org/env/hs/bulletin/00pdf/h10.pdf. An alternative measure for the United States in 1997 is a median square footage of all existing single detached and mobile homes (68 per cent of all housing units) equal to 1,720. For all newly-constructed privately-owned single-family houses in 1999 the median was 2,030 and the average was 2,225. See *Statistical Abstract of the United States: 2000*, Tables 1211 and 1197, respectively. The former table is the source of the average lot size data given in the text. All available data for the US seem to refer only to single-family units and omit apartments in multi-family units, which presumably are smaller in size.

References

Alesina, A. and Glaeser, E. (2004) *Fighting Poverty in the U.S. and Europe: A World of Difference.* Oxford, UK: Oxford University Press.

Alesina, A., Glaeser, E. and Sacerdote, B. (2006) 'Work and Leisure in the United States and Europe: Why So Different?' *NBER Macroeconomics Annual 2005* 20: 1–64.

Blanchard, O. (2004) 'The Economic Future of Europe,' *Journal of Economic Perspectives* 18(4), Fall: 3–26.

Dew-Becker, I. and Gordon, R.J. (2005) 'Where Did the Productivity Growth Go?

Inflation Dynamics and the Distribution of Income,' *Brookings Papers on Economic Activity* 36(2): 67–127.

Freeman, R. and Schettkat, R. (2005) 'Jobs and Home Work: Time Use Evidence,' *Economic Policy* 41: 6–50.

Goldin, C. and Margo, R.A. (1992) 'The Great Compression: The Wage Structure in the United States at Mid-Century,' *Quarterly Journal of Economics* 107 (February): 1–34.

Gordon, R.J. (1997) 'Is There a Tradeoff between Unemployment and Productivity Growth?' in D. Snower and G. de la Dehesa (eds) *Unemployment Policy: Government Options for the Labour Market.* Cambridge, UK: Cambridge University Press, pp. 433–463.

Ljungqvist, L. (2006) 'Comment' in Alesina, A., Glaeser, E. and Sacerdote, B. (2006) 'Work and Leisure in the United States and Europe: Why So Different?' *NBER Macroeconomics Annual 2005* 20: 65–77.

Ljungqvist, L. and Sargent, T.J. (2006) 'Indivisible Labor, Human Capital, Lotteries, and Personal Savings: Do Taxes Explain European Employment?' presented at NBER Macroannual conference, April 7–8.

Neary, J.P. (2004) 'Rationalizing the Penn World Table: True Multilateral Indices for International Comparisons of Real Income,' *American Economic Review* 94(5): 1411–1428.

Prescott, E.C. (2004) 'Why Do Americans Work So Much More than Europeans?' *Federal Reserve Bank of Minneapolis Quarterly Review* 28(1): 2–13.

Rhoads, C. (2002) 'Short Work Hours Undercut Europe in Economic Drive,' *Wall Street Journal*, August 8, p. A1.

Rogerson, R. (2006) 'Comment' in Alesina, A., Glaeser, E. and Sacerdote, B. (2006) 'Work and Leisure in the United States and Europe: Why So Different?' *NBER Macroeconomics Annual 2005* 20: 79–95.

2 Technology regimes and productivity growth in Europe and the United States

A comparative and historical perspective

Bart van Ark and Jan Pieter Smits[1]

1 Introduction

Explosive growth of investment in information and communication technology (ICT) was at the centre of the unrealistic expectations that surrounded the 'new economy' hype of the late 1990s. The slowdown in investment in ICT since 2000 has somewhat tempered the enthusiasm, but the question remains how much ICT contributes to productivity growth in the longer run. As ICT can typically be characterized as a General Purpose Technology (GPT), one would expect longlasting effects beyond the investment cycle.

Strikingly with the boom in ICT investment during the 1990s, labour productivity growth in the US accelerated from 1.1 per cent in 1987–95 to 2.5 per cent in 1995–2004. In contrast, average annual growth rate of labour productivity, measured as value added per hour worked, in the European Union fell from 2.3 per cent to 1.4 per cent over the same period.[2]

The acceleration in productivity growth in the US has spurred a burst of academic research on both sides of the Atlantic. Most of the macroeconomic research concluded that ICT accounted for much of the acceleration in productivity growth in the US.[3] In Europe, attention focused on how much of the slower productivity growth could be tied to differences in ICT diffusion relative to the US. Various studies at the economy-wide level suggested that slower growth rates of ICT investment were an important factor in explaining the poorer European productivity performance.[4]

The macroeconomic studies only provided indirect evidence on the differential productivity effects of the *production* versus the *use* of ICT. The production effects of ICT mainly relate to the comparative advantage of the US in ICT-producing industries, in particular the production of semiconductors and computer hardware. Only a limited number of small European countries, notably Finland and Ireland, have similar comparative advantages in the production of telecommunication equipment and computer hardware respectively. Despite very rapid technological change (and related TFP growth) in these industries, these effects are not very large at the aggregate level due to the small share of these industries in total GDP in Europe.

More important for the aggregate productivity effect is the differential impact of ICT on the productivity growth in some typical ICT-using industries. Several industry level studies have pointed at the US advantages from the use of ICT on productivity in service industries. Three major service industries account for most of the US growth advantage, namely wholesale and retail trade and the financial securities industry.[5]

Hence, not unlike the electric motor – and any other general purpose technology – the economic impact of ICT partly derives from its production but also, and foremost, from its applications to business processes, and the production of new products and services.[6] The combination of the *macro-based evidence* that countries in Europe have somewhat lower investment in ICT with the *industry-level evidence* that intensive ICT users have shown slower productivity growth in Europe, suggests that one of the principal factors in explaining the slower European productivity growth is the failure to exploit the productivity effects from ICT.

In this chapter our aim is to draw on historical parallels between the ICT era on productivity and earlier episodes of rapid technological change, namely the introduction of steam during the nineteenth century and that of electricity during the early twentieth century. Most of the historical literature on the impact of GPTs on growth derives from experiences in the United Kingdom and the United States, largely because of the ample availability of historical data for these countries. But these two countries were typically at the frontier of the new technological paradigms in steam (UK) and electricity (US). The experience of follower countries may be different and more strictly based on the diffusion of the GPT rather than invention itself. In a companion paper we have documented the evidence on the diffusion and productivity of steam, electricity and ICT in great detail for the Netherlands (van Ark and Smits, 2005). With additional access to (admittedly more limited) data at macro and industry level for Finland, Sweden, the United Kingdom and the United States, we can test whether our main conclusions from the Dutch case also hold for other countries.

The chapter proceeds as follows. In section 2 we review the long-term evidence on the contribution of earlier GPTs to productivity growth from macroeconomic studies. Hence we look at adoption rates for steam and technology and discuss the possible relationship to productivity growth. In section 3 we adopt an industry perspective to look at the extent to which differences in productivity growth may be related to the technology diffusion. In section 4 we return to the recent evidence of the contribution of ICT to productivity growth, and discuss the parallels with the earlier GPT episodes to assess the implications for the future effects of ICT on productivity growth. In the concluding section (5) we discuss the role of non-technological factors interacting with the relationship between technology and productivity.

2 A macro perspective on technology and productivity in historical perspective

Research into the interrelatedness of technological breakthroughs and subsequent phases of economic growth goes back to the work of Kondratieff and has been revived by, among others, Landes (1969), Rosenberg (1982) and Freeman and Soete (1997). The latter two state that there are 'systematic interdependencies of myriad technical and organizational innovations. Like Hamlet's troubles, they come not single but in battalions. Process innovations, product innovations, organizational innovations and material innovations are all interdependent in mechanization, electrification or computerization' (Freeman and Soete, 1997: 31). If we accept the notion that radical new technologies arise in clusters which create new potential for growth, it is possible that long-term changes in economic growth performance are somehow linked to changes in technological systems.

The first explicit and quantitative comparison of different phases of technological change originates from Paul David (1989, 1990), who drew an analogy between the introduction of electricity around the turn of the nineteenth century and the introduction of ICT during the 1970s and 1980s. David emphasizes the time lag between invention and productivity advances, as both the United Kingdom and the United States experienced a vigorous expansion of technology during the period 1900–13, but a relatively slow growth of productivity. Only after 1913 could a significant acceleration in productivity be observed for both countries.

Steam diffusion

Recent research into the impact of steam on productivity growth reveals that even in the United Kingdom, the technology leader in the era of steam, the diffusion of this technology was rather slow and had a limited effect on productivity growth (Crafts, 2004a, b). Watt's improved steam engine was patented in 1769, but it was only in 1830 that use of steam was at the same level as that of water power. The relatively low level of diffusion is reflected in the low share of steam engines in the capital stock. Around 1830 this share amounted to a mere 1.5 per cent of the total capital stock in Britain (Crafts, 2004a: 341).

It was only during the 1850s, due to the development of high pressure steam power, that savings in coal consumption per hour resulted in a decline in the costs of steam power. Yet, even during the second half of the nineteenth century, large parts of the British economy (such as agriculture and non-transport services) remained virtually untouched by steam.[7] It is therefore not surprising that the impact of steam technology on productivity growth has been quite modest. On the basis of growth accounting techniques, Crafts (2004a, b) shows that TFP growth in Britain only showed a modest acceleration from 0 to 0.3 per year on average between 1760–80 and 1780–1831, and that productivity growth was steady but unspectacular at 0.75 for the remainder of the nineteenth century.

More or less the same trends can be discerned in countries on the European continent, which mainly depended on the import of steam technology from the UK. Although evidence on the diffusion of steam is lacking for most European continental countries, research into the diffusion of steam in the Netherlands reveals that traditional techniques based on wind and water energy prevailed because they proved to be cheaper for a considerable length of time (Smits, 1995; Smits et al., 2001). It was only after scale constraints were being removed that the use of steam became viable in the 1850s and 1860s. For example, the share of machines that are steam driven shows an increase from 13 per cent of the total number of machines in 1860 to 39 per cent in 1880 and then a rapid acceleration to 61 per cent of total machinery in 1890. However, as adoption of steam has been faster for bigger machines than for smaller machines, an upper bound estimate suggests that steam power accounted for as much as 81 per cent of total power by 1890 (van Ark and Smits, 2005). It should be noted, however, that the evidence of steam power which came relatively late to the Netherlands may not only be contrasted to the United Kingdom but also to other continental European countries. Due to the large share of agriculture, trade and personal services in GDP, relatively large segments of the Dutch economy were not affected by this new technology (van Ark and Smits, 2005).

Electricity diffusion

The next technological paradigm produced much faster rates of adoption and higher rates of growth, especially in the United States. However, as pointed out by David (1989), there was still as much as 40 years between the major technological innovations in the field of electricity and the upsurge of labour productivity in the manufacturing sector, although the time-lag was much shorter than for steam (about 80 years). The first experiments with electricity were conducted by Galvani in the 1790s. In 1819 the phenomenon of electromagnetic induction was discovered which was the basis for the development of the dynamo in 1831. It was only after 40 years that, due to a large series of incremental innovations, electricity could be used for commercial purposes. Moreover, in the early years the diffusion of electricity may also have been hampered by the fact that parts of the economy were 'locked' into steam technology. Only when electricity became a cheap alternative to other forms of motive power, electrical motors diffused rapidly through the economy.

Even in the United States (which was the productivity leader from the late nineteenth century onwards) electrical power still made a low contribution to total power in industry around 1900 (4 per cent). This share grew almost exponentially in the following decades. Around 1910 the share of electricity accounted for 25 per cent of total power, for 50 per cent in 1919, 75 per cent in 1929 and 87 per cent in 1938 (Edquist and Henrekson, 2004).

Continental European countries showed approximately the same pace in adopting this new technology. In Germany, the Netherlands, Sweden and Finland the rate of electrification almost reached the US level on the eve of the First World War. The rate of electrification amounted to 22 per cent in Germany

1906–07, 25 per cent in the Netherlands in 1912 and even 32 per cent in Finland in 1913.[8] During the 1920s and 1930s the share of electricity in total industrial power supply converged to a level of more than 85 per cent in all countries. Only in the United Kingdom electrification proceeded at a lower speed (10 per cent of industrial motive power supplied by electrical motors around 1906–07), preventing British entrepreneurs from investing rapidly in new technologies.

Not only did electricity diffuse at more or less the same speed on both sides of the Atlantic, changes in the rate of labour productivity growth bear some similarities as well. Especially in the case of the productivity leader (the United States) the productivity improvement proved to be exceptionally fast. David and Wright (1999) show that US labour productivity growth increased from 4.5 per cent a year in the period 1909–19 to 5.6 per cent in 1919–29. Using a growth accounting methodology with refined calculations of the contributions of factor inputs and total factor productivity, Gordon (1999, 2000) confirms the rapid acceleration in US productivity after 1913. TFP increased at 1.6 per cent per year on average during the whole period 1913–72, compared to 0.6 per cent from 1870–1913. However, with further adjustments for the composition of labour and capital and some adjustments for changes in retirement age of the capital stock, the acceleration is somewhat more modest, from 0.5 per cent from 1870–1913 to 1.0 per cent from 1913–72.

In most other countries industrial labour productivity growth accelerated after 1913, and in particular during the 1910s and 1920s, which was the period in which the larger part of the manufacturing sector started to use electricity as its main source of power. Table 2.1 presents evidence regarding the labour productivity performance from 1870 to 1938. The growth figures for the period 1913–38 indicate that productivity growth in most European countries was close to the growth rates in the US, with the exception of Belgium and the United Kingdom. It is remarkable that productivity growth was rather low in precisely those two countries which performed relatively strongly in the steam era. This can probably be explained by 'lock in' effects in old technologies.

Table 2.1 Average annual growth of labour productivity (GDP per hour worked), 1870–1938 (in %)

	1870–1913	1913–38	of which	
			1913–29	1929–38
United States	1.9	2.1	2.4	1.5
Belgium	1.2	1.5	1.8	1.0
Finland	1.8	2.1	2.2	2.0
Netherlands	1.3	1.8	2.8	−0.1
Sweden	1.7	2.0	1.5	2.9
United Kingdom	1.2	1.2	1.4	0.8

Source: Maddison (1995).

In conclusion, it is very likely that in the United States as well as in Europe, labour productivity growth was somehow related to the rapid diffusion of electricity in the industrial sector, and this is confirmed elsewhere in the literature. For example, for Finland, Myllyntaus (1991) has pointed out how electrification promoted the modernization of production processes. De Jong (2003) draws the same conclusion for the Netherlands.

But can the diffusion of electricity be solely responsible for the acceleration in growth? There are strong indications that the relationship is more complex than is often assumed for at least two reasons. First, although the rate of electrification had reached more or less the same levels on both sides of the Atlantic in the 1930s, productivity increases in the US remained above that of most European countries until the 1950s, after which the European post-war 'catching up' effect began to kick in. Second, already before the age of electrification, productivity growth in the US was higher than in most (continental) European countries. Indeed David (1989) shows that only 25 per cent of the differences in the growth rates of industrial labour productivity can be ascribed to the diffusion of electrical motors. This conclusion is in line with recent work by Gordon (2003), who argues that not only technology, but also political and historical factors explain the US miracle during the 'One Big Wave' of the period 1913–72. From this perspective, the focus shifts from purely technological factors to the institutional context in which diffusion occurs. We return to this issue in the concluding section of the chapter.

3 An industry perspective

In order to further clarify the effects of technology diffusion on productivity differentials, it is useful to also focus on the industry level. There are strong indications that not all key technologies are easily applicable in large segments of the economy. It is therefore useful to make a distinction between technologies which have been diffused in a limited number of industries and those which have been used economy-wide in most industries.

Diffusion of steam and electricity at industry level

Research into the diffusion of steam shows that, even in the case of Britain, only a limited number of branches were affected during the late eighteenth and early nineteenth centuries. Apart from shipping and railway transport, only textiles, mining and metals strongly benefited from the diffusion of steam. The diffusion may have been even less in countries with a low share of textiles, mining and metals in total industrial value added. For example, in the Netherlands the low levels of investment in steam technology are mainly due to the nature of economic specialization. From the late middle ages onwards the Dutch had been specializing in agriculture and trade, activities in which steam was not easily applicable. A comparison between Belgium (a classic example of a successful follower of Britain during the first industrial revolution) and the Netherlands (known for its late and slow diffusion) shows that the differences in amount of horse power per inhabitant between the two countries is, for 82 per cent, explained by differences in the output structure. In Belgium, the key sectors of the first industrial revolution contributed much more to GDP than in the Netherlands. But even in the Netherlands, steam power was used in manufacturing industries to different degrees. For example, in metal products and engineering the share of steam-driven machines was close or even at 100 per cent by 1890, whereas it was no more than 40 per cent in other manufacturing industries such as food manufacturing, chemicals and woodworking (Lintsen *et al.*, 1992).

Compared to steam, electricity is clearly much more of a general purpose technology as it was applicable in more sectors of the economy (see also section 2). Even though it was originally confined to lighting and railways and tramways during the very early phase, it quickly spread throughout manufacturing and beyond to services.

The productivity effects from electricity

In section 2 it has already been discussed that the impact of steam on productivity growth in the UK was limited to a few industries (Crafts, 2004a, b). The productivity impact of steam may have been even lower in the case of most other countries. For example, in the Netherlands, only six out of 26 industries scored labour productivity growth rates of more than 3 per cent on average per year between 1860 and 1890. These industries, which accounted for only 16 per cent of the total labour force, were all manufacturing industries including printing (7 per cent per year), metals (4.2 per cent), paper (4.2 per cent), woodworking (4.2 per cent), textiles (3.7 per cent) and clothing and cleaning (3.1 per cent). It should be stressed that these are labour productivity growth rates, which therefore include the effects from capital deepening.

In the United States, the diffusion of the electrical motor boosted productivity growth in large parts of the manufacturing sector. Growth rates of labour productivity were much higher during the period 1919–29 than in the previous period (1909–19) (David and Wright, 1999). This strong growth occurred in a wide range of sectors from the food-processing industries and the chemical industries (petrochemicals in particular) to the iron and steel industry. The first two industries especially had witnessed rather low growth rates in earlier periods due to the fact that steam technology could not be applied on a large scale in these branches. It is interesting to note that the productivity increases in the electrical machinery industry in the US remained relatively modest. This result confirms the importance of technology use to exploit the productivity effects.

Table 2.2 compares the productivity performance in the US and three continental European countries. The European 'followers' also enjoyed widespread productivity benefits from electrification, showing patterns of development which closely resembled those of the United States. Large parts of the industrial sector in the Netherlands, Finland and Sweden enjoyed productivity benefits from this new technology. Since 1919 productivity growth in Sweden occurred

Table 2.2 Labour productivity growth (GDP per person employed) in manufacturing industries, beginning of twentieth century

	United States		Sweden			Finland		Netherlands			
	1909–19	1919–29	1913–19	1919–29	1929–39	1901–20	1920–38	1900–13	1913–21	1921–29	1900–38
Food	1.3	2.9	0.0	2.8	2.1	0.3	3.3	−1.0	−2.7	6.9	2.7
Textiles	0.2	4.1	−0.6	1.6	1.0	0.3	1.1	2.7	1.6	0.2	−1.0
Wood products	−1.8	2.1	0.0	0.3	1.1	0.2	2.7	11.3	−0.2	−25.6	6.3
Paper			−2.1	4.5	3.0						
paper	1.3	5.7				3.0	7.9	2.6	−7.9	12.1	12.1
printing	1.2	1.5				−1.2	4.0	2.8	2.7	6.7	9.4
Chemicals			−5.7	11.5	4.6	3.2	5.0	0.6	9.8	1.4	10.0
chemical	0.2	4.0									
petroleum	2.7	5.9									
Rubber and leather			−2.5	0.1	1.0						
rubber	6.2	6.7				−0.9	3.7	0.7	5.7	−5.2	6.5
leather	−1.1	3.3				−0.7	4.2	−0.8	1.3	4.2	0.4
Metal			−2.2	4.3	2.8						
iron and steel	2.8	4.4									
non-ferrous metals	2.1	2.7									

Sources: United States: David and Wright (1999); Sweden: Edquist and Henrekson, (2004); Finland: Hjerppe, (1990); Netherlands: Smits *et al.* (2000).

throughout the industrial sector. Productivity growth increased most rapidly in food products, paper, chemicals and metal products. In Finland, productivity growth was strong across manufacturing with the exception of textiles. The Dutch economy showed larger differences between industries but in most cases productivity growth has accelerated since 1913. On the whole, these data suggest that productivity growth became a much more general phenomenon since 1920, as is indicated by the declining standard deviations of industry growth rates.

It should be stressed, however, that authors have generally not found a clear significant statistical relationship between technological diffusion and productivity growth at the industry level (Edquist and Henrekson, 2004), hence some caution is required in directly relating technology diffusion to productivity growth at industry level.

Another way to look at the impact of technology diffusion originates from Harberger (1998), who suggests looking at the distribution of industry contributions to aggregate productivity growth. In the case that only a few industries account for most of the aggregate productivity growth, Harberger speaks of a 'mushroom' type of growth. When industries contribute more equally to productivity growth, this may be referred to as a 'yeast' type of growth.

The results from David and Wright on total factor productivity growth in the aggregate manufacturing sector, reported above from 1919–29, clearly suggest a 'yeast' type of growth. In contrast, Harberger (1998) himself, who focussed on the US experience during the post-Second World War II period, found more of a mushroom-type growth process. In his view mushroom growth resulted from real cost reductions (which is one possible interpretation of TFP) which stemmed 'from 1001 different causes' (Harberger, 1998: 4–5). Comparing the two studies might indicate that the strong early impact of electricity across the economy relates to a surge in productivity, which was followed by a more ad-hoc process of different inventions and innovations during the mature period of technology use.[9] The growth experience during the latter period may also represent the petering-out of the economy-wide diffusion process with some industries realizing growth effects through a continuous stream of new innovations, whereas in many other industries the new technology only created a once-for-all level effect.

Table 2.3 shows summary measures of the distribution of industry contributions to aggregate labour productivity growth in the Netherlands from 1860 to 2003, using historical national accounts for the period 1800–1921 in combination with historical data and current national accounts data from Statistics Netherlands (Smits *et al.*, 2001; van Ark and De Jong, 1996). The first measure in the table shows the aggregate productivity growth rate, which is the sum of all industry contributions. The second measure shows the cumulative labour share of industries with a positive contribution to productivity growth. The latter may be interpreted as a measure of the pervasiveness of growth.

The third measure indicates the distribution of the productivity gains between industries. This distribution measure is closer to 0 when the pattern is more 'yeast-like' and closer to 1 when it is more 'mushroom-like'.[10]

Table 2.3 Summary characteristics of distribution of industry contributions to aggregate labour productivity growth, Netherlands, 1860–2003

Technology regime	Period	Aggregate annual labour productivity growth rate	Cumulative labour share of industries with positive contributions to productivity	Distribution of productivity gains between industries (0 = equal; 1 = unequal) *
Steam era	1860–90	0.8[a]	42	0.50
Initial electricity era	1900–38	4.4[a]	85	0.28
Mature electricity era	1950–73	3.3[a]	>80	na
Initial ICT era	1977–95	2.0[b]	89	0.35
Maturing ICT era	1995–2003	1.0[b]	71	0.49

Note
* calculated as the ratio of the space between the curve representing the cumulative contribution of industries to aggregate productivity growth and the diagonal and the total area between the curve and the horizontal axis.
a per person employed
b per hour worked

In line with the observations above, Table 2.3 shows that the growth pattern was clearly more 'mushroom-like' during the steam era and more 'yeast-like' during the electricity era. In particular during the first few decades of the twentieth century, productivity growth was more pervasive compared to the late nineteenth century. Moreover, productivity growth rates during this period were substantially higher than during the period 1860–90. Electricity has probably been an important factor contributing to the improved productivity performance during the 'big wave' of the twentieth century. Its application was widespread and went well beyond the manufacturing sector. The distribution of industry contributions during the 'mature' electricity era also looks somewhat more unequal than during the 'early' electricity period. At the same time aggregate productivity growth is considerably lower in the second subperiod compared to the first.

Summary of the evidence for the pre-ICT era

The most important conclusions from the study of the two previous technology regimes are threefold. First, the diffusion of electricity appears to have been faster and more widespread across industries than for steam. The differences in adoption rates between countries are limited, and appear mainly due to differences in industrial structure. Second, the effect of electricity on productivity appears faster and more pervasive than for steam in both the 'leading' country (the US) as well as in the following countries. Still, aggregate productivity growth rates have been higher in the US than in Europe for the first half of the twentieth century. Third, although technology diffusion appears to be related to productivity growth, other factors such as the performance of the technology innovation system, other sources of comparative advantage, the functioning of markets and organizational changes probably also interact with productivity growth (see section 5).

4 Implications from the historical evidence for the ICT era

The experiences with the most recent technology regime, related to information and communication technology (ICT), can now be put in historical perspective. To do so, we first look at the recent evidence on ICT diffusion and productivity at macro level, followed by a comparison of industry productivity performance with the earlier periods.

The diffusion of ICT

Recent data on ICT investment from the Groningen Growth and Development Centre show a clear upward trend in investment in ICT as a percentage of total investment in non-residential equipment.[11] This is a useful measure of the diffusion of the new technology. Table 2.4 shows that the ICT investment share in the EU-15 has been about half of that in the US. It increased rapidly in both

Table 2.4 ICT investment as percentage of total non-residential investment (current prices), 1976–2004

	1976	1995	2000	2004
Finland	5.8	25.8	26.3	27.6
Sweden	9.1	23.5	30.5	22.9
Belgium	7.7	18.0	24.2	20.1
Denmark	7.7	19.1	19.5	19.6
United Kingdom	4.8	21.7	25.0	18.4
Netherlands	6.3	13.1	17.7	17.1
Germany	8.1	13.3	17.4	16.1
Italy	7.6	14.8	16.1	15.5
Austria	6.9	12.4	13.7	13.1
Portugal	9.2	12.2	12.4	12.9
France	5.1	9.0	12.8	11.4
Greece	4.1	10.0	12.8	10.9
Spain	5.5	9.7	11.9	10.4
Ireland	3.3	9.6	14.2	8.8
European Union	6.8	14.3	17.6	15.2
United States	12.4	24.8	30.3	29.5

Source: Groningen Growth and Development Centre (www.ggdc.net/dseries/growth-accounting. shtml).

Note
Countries ranked in descending order of shares in 2004.

regions, but the gap between the two regions has not narrowed much during the past three decades. In some countries, however, ICT investment intensity is almost as high as in the United States, notably in some of the Scandinavian countries such as Sweden and Finland.

Strikingly, the ICT investment shares have fallen somewhat since 2000. It is important to examine which parts of the economy are responsible for this possible slowdown in technology diffusion. One possibility is that the collapse of the 'new economy' hype, referred to in the introduction, has mainly affected ICT-producing industries in the hardware, software and telecommunication sectors. Another, more serious, problem would be that the diffusion of ICT to its main users, notably market services such as trade, transport and financial services, has slowed down.

For a limited number of countries (France, Germany, the Netherlands, United Kingdom and the United States) we also have information on ICT investment shares for individual industries, as obtained from the Groningen Growth and Development Centre. Table 2.5 shows that the ICT investment shares are generally highest in ICT production industries. Their behaviour is rather volatile and there may be large differences in the composition of production of ICT goods.

With the exception of France, the investment shares in market services are generally about half of those in ICT production. However, as market services account for a much bigger share of the economy's output, their contribution to

Table 2.5 ICT investment as percentage of total non-residential investment by major industry group (current prices), 1987–2003

	1987	*1995*	*2000*	*2003*
France				
Market economy	10.2	11.5	16.0	14.5
ICT production	14.7	15.5	18.3	17.3
Market services*	14.1	14.6	19.6	18.2
Production industries**	4.4	5.6	8.9	8.3
Germany				
Market economy	13.8	14.0	17.7	16.5
ICT production	30.7	38.6	33.3	34.4
Market services*	13.0	12.9	17.8	17.1
Production industries**	9.6	10.1	13.3	11.5
Netherlands				
Market economy	13.9	15.8	21.1	22.7
ICT production	34.8	37.9	28.3	38.7
Market services*	16.2	17.9	23.9	25.3
Production industries**	7.4	8.3	11.6	11.6
United Kingdom				
Market economy	10.7	18.5	22.1	20.0
ICT production	20.8	47.1	50.8	36.5
Market services*	10.5	18.8	20.0	20.6
Production industries**	8.4	9.7	9.7	10.5
United States				
Market economy	21.5	26.1	34.0	34.3
ICT production	47.9	50.5	62.1	62.3
Market services*	24.1	29.1	35.9	38.0
Production industries**	11.3	13.8	16.3	16.7

Source: Groningen Growth and Development Centre (www.ggdc.net/dseries/iga.shtml).

Notes
* excluding ICT services: telecommunication services (ISIC 64).
** excluding ICT manufacturing: electrical and optical equipment (ISIC 30–33).

aggregate growth is likely to be much bigger than for ICT production. The US ICT investment share in market services is much higher than in any of the European countries, and has shown a continuous increase since 1987, whereas the shares in European countries have increased more slowly or stalled. Indeed, there is considerable evidence that US service industries have applied ICT more intensively to improve delivery processes and create new services.[12]

The productivity effects of ICT use

Using a growth accounting decomposition technique, the impact from ICT on productivity for the EU and the US can be compared (Timmer and van Ark,

2005; van Ark and Inklaar, 2005). In the light of the previous discussion it is most sensible to focus on the effect of ICT use in market services. This can only be done for the same countries as those mentioned above (namely France, Germany, the Netherlands, the UK and the US) for which ICT investment data at industry level are available. Table 2.6 shows the percentage point contribution of market services to labour productivity growth in the aggregate market economy, as well as the percentage point contribution of the underlying sources of growth in market services, i.e. ICT capital, non-ICT capital, labour quality and total factor productivity.

Table 2.6 shows that the year 1995 is an important breakpoint in the comparative performance of the EU versus the US. Whereas US productivity growth accelerated significantly, it slowed down in all European countries, and in particular in France and Germany. The US growth resurgence since 1995 was to a large extent (almost 75 per cent) due to a faster productivity growth in market services. This was considerably more than in the European countries, in particular in France and Germany where the contribution of market services even declined.

Faster labour productivity growth in US market services appears to be due partly to a faster growth in ICT capital deepening in the US, but due mostly to an improvement in TFP growth. Since 1995, TFP has contributed as much to labour productivity growth as ICT capital deepening. ICT capital contributes much less to productivity growth in market services in all European countries, and TFP growth is even negative (with the exception of the UK).

The superior performance of the US market services sector is mainly due to three major service industries, namely wholesale and retail trade and the financial securities industry. Since 2000, the contribution of business services to aggregate productivity growth has also improved in the US. In contrast, in European countries these service industries mostly show a productivity slowdown – or at best stability – since 2000.

Finally, as for the earlier GPT eras, it is interesting to look at the degree of 'yeastiness' or 'mushroomness' of productivity during the ICT era. Using the Harberger method, Table 2.7 shows the summary statistics for France, Germany, the Netherlands, the UK and the US for aggregate total factor productivity growth rates in the market sector of the economy, the cumulative value added share of industries with a positive contribution to TFP growth, and the distribution of the productivity gains between industries (which is closer to 0 when the pattern is more 'yeast-like' and closer to 1 when it is more 'mushroom-like'). In contrast to the measures shown in Table 2.3, the figures here refer to Total Factor Productivity (and not to labour productivity) and the industry shares are obtained on the basis of value added instead of labour.[13]

Table 2.7 shows that despite the decline in TFP growth in the continental European countries and the TFP acceleration in the US, the share of industries with positive TFP contributions has remained in between half and two-thirds of value added in all cases. The continental European countries show a striking tendency towards greater 'mushroom-type' growth since 1995 as the distribution factor has increased well above 0.5, and even to 0.76 in the Netherlands. In

Table 2.6 Contributions of market services and underlying sources to market economy labour productivity growth, 1987–2003

	France	Germany	Netherlands	United Kingdom	United States
1987–95					
Market economy labour productivity growth	2.4	2.6	1.7	3.0	1.4
Contribution of market services	0.5	0.9	0.5	1.0	0.5
of which:					
ICT capital deepening	0.2	0.3	0.3	0.3	0.4
Non-ICT capital deepening	0.2	0.3	0.2	0.5	0.1
Labour quality growth	0.1	0.1	0.1	0.4	0.2
Total factor productivity growth	0.0	0.2	−0.2	−0.2	−0.1
1995–2003					
Market economy labour productivity growth	1.8	2.1	1.4	2.6	3.5
Contribution of market services	0.1	0.3	0.6	1.3	2.0
of which:					
ICT capital deepening	0.3	0.4	0.6	0.5	0.8
Non-ICT capital deepening	0.0	0.1	0.3	0.4	0.3
Labour quality growth	0.1	0.0	0.1	0.1	0.1
Total factor productivity growth	−0.4	−0.2	−0.3	0.2	0.8

Source: van Ark and Inklaar (2005).

contrast, the distribution factor in the UK and the US has declined to around 0.5, which suggests a greater 'yeastiness' of growth compared to the pre-1995 period for the latter two countries.

How do the results for the ICT era compare to the earlier GPT phases? Table 2.3 in section 3, which shows Harberger summary statistics for labour productivity growth in the Netherlands, suggests a somewhat more 'mushroom' type process for the ICT era compared to the electricity age. For TFP, there is less information for historical comparisons except for the US. But even the US TFP rates for the most recent period cannot be directly compared with those for the early electricity phase, as no estimates are available beyond manufacturing. But if the diffusion of electricity in manufacturing during the early electricity phase can be compared with the diffusion of ICT in the service sector recently, the diffusion process was again clearly more 'yeasty' in the first period. However, for the mature electricity phase during the post-Second World War period, Harberger (1998) suggests a more 'mushroom' type of growth pattern for the US private economy.

Strikingly, when comparing the US estimates for the period 1987–95 with those for 1995–2003, the trend for ICT appears to be opposite to that for electricity. Instead of moving from yeasty to mushroom growth, Table 2.7 suggests a trend from mushroom growth to a more 'yeasty' pattern of productivity growth. The distribution factor in the third column of Table 2.7 clearly suggests a more equal distribution of productivity growth during the latter period. However, a more 'yeasty' process of growth cannot yet be observed for the European countries with the possible exception of the United Kingdom.

There may be various reasons for explaining the difference in distribution of productivity gains between the electricity era and the ICT age. First, the technical impact of electricity may have been more widespread in first instance, followed by a broad range of innovations during the maturity phase, affecting sectors very differently. ICT application may have been more 'mushroom'-like right from the beginning. The technical features of electricity and ICT deserve more research to better understand these differences. Second, the trend towards greater 'yeastiness' in the US vis-à-vis greater 'mushroom' type growth in Europe during the ICT era may be related to non-technological factors that support or inhibit entrepreneurs exploiting the productivity advantages of the exploitation of ICT. The latter issue will be addressed in more detail in the concluding section of this chapter.

5 Concluding remarks

Although the diffusion of ICT across industries seems somewhat slower in Europe than in the United States, ICT is widely applied across industries in the economy, in particular across a wide range of market service industries. The biggest difference between the EU and the US, however, seems to arise from the much smaller productivity effects from ICT. The fundamental question that arises is: is this difference simply due to a time-lag effect, as was also observed

Table 2.7 Summary characteristics of distribution of industry contributions to aggregate total factor productivity growth in the market sector during the ICT-era, 1987–2003

Country	Period	Aggregate total factor productivity growth rate in market economy	Cumulative value added share of industries with positive contributions to TFP growth	Distribution of TFP gains between industries (0 = equal; 1 = unequal)*
France	1987–95	1.4	65	0.45
	1995–2003	1.1	60	0.54
Germany	1987–95	1.2	63	0.51
	1995–2003	0.7	67	0.67
Netherlands	1987–95	0.6	52	0.61
	1995–2003	0.3	56	0.76
United Kingdom	1987–95	1.1	65	0.56
	1995–2003	1.2	60	0.50
United States	1987–95	0.6	57	0.65
	1995–2003	1.3	64	0.52

Source: Inklaar and Timmer (2007), Table 3

Note

* calculated as the ratio of the space between the curve representing the cumulative contribution of industries to aggregate TFP growth and the horizontal axis and the space between the diagonal and the horizontal axis.

earlier for electricity and steam, meaning that Europe will catch up with the US soon? Or is the EU–US differential due to other (non-technological) factors related to differences in knowledge infrastructure, general comparative advantages, the functioning of markets and organizational changes? The latter might mean that the US advantage in ICT use over Europe will remain in the longer term.

Although non-technological factors also played a role in determining the productivity effect from electricity, technological factors such as the shift from shafts to wires in the production system may have dominated the diffusion process in those industries (Devine, 1983). In contrast, various authors have indicated the importance of non-technological factors in determining the productivity effect from ICT. For example, McGuckin and van Ark (2001) and McGuckin *et al.* (2005) argue that structural impediments in product and labour markets hamper the successful implementation of ICT across service industries in Europe. Limits on shopping hours and transport regulations and restrictive hiring and firing rules as well as other restrictive labour regulations make it hard for producers to control their organizations reaping the full benefits from ICT. Furthermore, barriers to entry also limit competitive pressure. Eichengreen (2004) reports evidence on the payoff from IT capital formation, which appears greatest in countries where telecom infrastructure is most extensive, where financial markets are best developed, and where regulatory burdens are lightest. Gordon (2004), who focuses in part on the large contribution of retailing to productivity growth in the US, calls attention to regulatory barriers and land-use regulations in Europe that inhibit the development of large scale retail formats.

However, one must be careful not to embrace a simple story that is based only on excessive European regulation. For example, the more rapid take-off of wireless technology in Europe suggests that some regulation, for example setting standards, can be productivity enhancing as well. Gordon (2004) points at the different public and social choices in Europe concerning the dispersion of metropolitan areas, the promotion of public transport, the taxing of home ownership, etc. These factors may determine different effects from ICT diffusion on productivity growth. Still, the question of why most European economies have so far been unable to use ICT more productively on smaller-scale operations remains an important issue for the research agenda.

Historical parallels offer some lessons and should temper exaggerated expectations. But the present evidence on steam and electricity, representing very different technologies with different applications and potential, cannot be imposed directly on the present experience. Also, time will need to tell part of the story of the effects of ICT on productivity.

In sum, the most important finding in this chapter is that technology diffusion and the productivity effects do not always follow the same pattern across industries, over time or across countries. The reasons for these differences are related to factors which often go beyond the application of the technology itself. A better understanding of these non-technological factors and a study of their impact in an historical perspective requires the further development of technology diffusion indicators at industry level, computations of related capital concepts and TFP, and quantitative analysis of institutional and policy variables in relation to TFP.

Notes

1 We acknowledge Robert Inklaar for assistance in preparing the 'Harberger summary statistics' for this chapter.
2 See McGuckin and van Ark (2005) and www.ggdc.net/dseries/totecon.shtml.
3 See Jorgenson (2001), Gordon (2003), Jorgenson *et al.* (2003) and Oliner and Sichel (2000, 2002).
4 See Daveri (2002) and Timmer and van Ark (2005).
5 For the US, see Bosworth and Triplett (2007). For Europe, see van Ark *et al.* (2003) and Inklaar *et al.* (2005).
6 Bresnahan and Trajtenberg (1995).
7 See also Nuvolari (2004). In the US the diffusion of steam also went at slow speed and left large parts of the economy unaffected. In the late 1830s only 5 per cent of total power supply in industry was provided by steam. Even in key sectors of the first industrial revolution such as textiles, metals and machinery, the share of steam in the total supply of power amounted to only 25 per cent in 1870 and 33 per cent in 1910 (Edquist and Henrekson, 2004).
8 Data on the rate of electrification are derived from Byatt (1979) for the United States and Germany, de Jong (2003) for the Netherlands and Jalava (2003) for Finland.
9 The comparison between the David and Wright (1999) and Harberger (1998) studies is affected by the fact that former focusses on the manufacturing sector only.
10 See van Ark and Smits (2005) for a more detailed description of our application of the Harberger model to the Dutch data. See Inklaar and Timmer (2007) for a more detailed discussion of the type of summary measures presented in Table 2.3.
11 See www.ggdc.net/dseries/growth-accounting.shtml and Timmer and van Ark (2005).
12 See, for example, OECD (2004). McGuckin *et al.* (2005) present substantial evidence of rapid ICT diffusion in US retail trade services compared to European countries.
13 This is more in line with the original Harberger (1998) method. See Inklaar and Timmer (2007) for a more detailed discussion of these summary measures.

References

Ark, B. van and de Jong, H.J. (1996) 'Accounting for Economic Growth in the Netherlands since 1913', *The Economic and Social History in the Netherlands* 7: 199–242.

Ark, B. van and Inklaar, R. (2005) 'Catching Up or Getting Stuck? Europe's Troubles to Exploit ICT's Productivity Potential', Research Memorandum GD-79, Groningen Growth and Development Centre, September (available online: www.ggdc.net/pub/gd79.pdf).

Ark, B. van and Smits, J.P. (2005) 'Technology Regimes and Growth in the Netherlands, An Empirical Record of Two Centuries', Groningen Growth and Development Centre, mimeographed (www.rug.nl/economie/_shared/pdf/medewerkers/arkHhVan/tech_nology_phases.pdf).

Ark, B. van, Inklaar, R. and McGuckin, R.H. (2003) ' "Changing Gear" Productivity, ICT and Service Industries: Europe and the United States', in J.F. Christensen and P. Maskell (eds) *The Industrial Dynamics of the New Digital Economy*. Cheltenham: Edward Elgar Publishing, pp. 56–99.

Bosworth, B. and Triplett, J. (2007) 'Services Productivity in the United States: Griliches' Services Volume Revisited', in E.R. Berndt and C.M. Hulten (eds) *Hard-to-Measure Goods and Services: Essays in Honor of Zvi Griliches*, NBER, Chicago University Press (www.nber.org/books/CRIW03-BH/bosworth-triplett3-24-05.pdf).

Bresnahan, T.F. and Trajtenberg, M. (1995) 'General purpose technologies: "Engines of growth"?', *Journal of Econometrics* 65(1): 83–108, January.

Byatt, I.C.R. (1979) *The British Electrical Industry 1875–1914: The Economic Returns to a New Technology*. Oxford: Clarendon Press.

Crafts, N.F.R. (2004a) 'Steam as a General Purpose Technology: A Growth Accounting Perspecitive', *The Economic Journal* 114(493): 338–351.

Crafts, N.F.R. (2004b) 'Productivity Growth in the Industrial Revolution: A New Growth Accounting Perspective', *Journal of Economic History* 64(2): 521–535.

Daveri, F. (2002) 'The New Economy in Europe, 1992–2001', *Oxford Review of Economic Policy* 18, 345–362.

David, P.A. (1989) 'Computer and Dynamo. The Modern Productivity Paradox in a Not-too-Distant Mirror', in OECD, *Technology and Productivity*, Paris, pp. 315–347.

David, P.A. (1990) 'The Dynamo and the Computers: A Historical Perspective on the Modern Productivity Paradox', *American Economic Review, AEA Papers and Proceedings 1990*, 80(2): 355–361.

David, P.A. and Wright, G. (1999) 'Early Twentieth Century Productivity Growth Dynamics: An Inquiry into the Economic History of Our Ignorance', University of Oxford, Papers in Economic History, No. 33.

Devine, W. (1983) 'From Shaft to Wires: Historical Perspective on Electrification', *Journal of Economic History* 43(2): 347–372.

Edquist, H. and Henrekson, M. (2004) 'Technological Breakthroughs and Productivity Growth', SSE/EFI Working Paper Series in Economics and Finance, No. 562, Stockholm School of Economics.

Eichengreen, B.J. (2004) 'Productivity Growth, the New Economy, and Catching Up', *Review of International Economics* 12(2): 243–245.

Freeman, C. and Soete, L. (eds) (1997) *The Economics of Industrial Innovation*, 3rd edition. London/Washington: Pinter.

Gordon, R.J. (1999) 'Interpreting the "One Big Wave" in U.S. Long-term Productivity Growth', in B. van Ark, S.K. Kuipers and G. Kuper (eds) *Productivity, Technology, and Economic Growth*. Kluwer Publishers, pp. 19–65.

Gordon, R.J. (2000) 'Does the "New Economy" Measure up to the Great Inventions of the Past?', *Journal of Economic Perspectives* 14(4): 49–77.

Gordon, R.J. (2003) 'Exploding Productivity Growth: Context, Causes, and Implications', *Brookings Papers on Economic Activity* 34(2): 207–298.

Gordon, R.J. (2004) 'Why was Europe Left at the Station When America's Productivity Locomotive Departed?', NBER Working Paper No. 10661, Cambridge, Mass.

Harberger, A.C. (1998) 'A Vision of the Growth Process', *American Economic Review* 88(1): 1–32.

Hjerppe, R. (1996) *Finland's Historical National Accounts 1860–1994*, University of Jyväskylä, Jyväskylä.

Inklaar, R.C. and Timmer, M.P. (2007) 'On Yeast and Mushrooms: Patterns of Industry-Level Productivity Growth', *German Economic Review* 8(2): 174–187.

Inklaar, R.C., O'Mahony, M. and Timmer, M.P. (2005) 'ICT and Europe's Productivity Performance; Industry-level Growth Account Comparisons with the United States', *Review of Income and Wealth* 51(4): 505–536.

Jalava, J. (2003) 'Electrifying and Digitalizing the Finnish Manufacturing Industry: Historical Notes of Diffusion and Productivity', Discussion Papers no. 870, ETLA, Helsinki.

Jong, H.J. de (2003) *Catching up Twice: The Nature of Dutch Industrial Growth during the Twentieth Century in a Comparative Perspective*. Berlin: Akademie Verlag.

Jorgenson, D.W. (2001) 'Information Technology and the US Economy', *American Economic Review* 91(1): 1–32.

Jorgenson, D.W., Ho, M.S. and Stiroh, K.J. (2003) 'Lessons for Europe from the US Growth Resurgence', *CESifo Economic Studies* 49: 27–48.

Landes, D. (1969) *The Unbound Prometheus*. Cambridge: Cambridge University Press.

Lintsen, H.W., Bakker, M.S.C., Homburg, E., van Lente, D., Schot, J.W. and Verbong, G.P.J. (1992) *Geschiedenis van de techniek in Nederland. De wording van een moderne samenleving, 1800–1990*. Zutphen, Stichting Historie der Techniek-Walburg Pers.

Maddison, A. (1995) *Monitoring the World Economy, 1820–1920*. Paris: OECD.

McGuckin, R.H. and van Ark, B. (2001) 'Making the Most of the Information Age: Productivity and Structural Reform in the New Economy', *Perspectives on a Global Economy*, Report 1301–01-RR, October.

McGuckin, R.H. and van Ark, B. (2005) *Performance 2005: Productivity, Employment and Income in the World's Economies*, Research Report R-1364–05-RR. New York: The Conference Board.

McGuckin, R.H., Spiegelman, M. and van Ark, B. (2005) *The Retail Revolution. Can Europe Match US Productivity Performance?*, Research Report R-1358–05-RR. New York: The Conference Board.

Myllyntaus, T. (1991) *Electrifying Finland: The transfer of a new technology into a late industrialising country*. London: Macmillan and ETLA.

Nuvolari, A. (2004) *The Making of Steam Technology. A Study of Technical Change during the British Industrial Revolution*, ECIS, Eindhoven University of Technology.

OECD (2004) *The Economic Impact of ICT. Measurement, Evidence and Implications*, Paris.

Oliner, S.D. and Sichel, D.E. (2000) 'The Resurgence of Growth in the Late 1990s: Is Information Technology the Story?' *Journal of Economic Perspectives* 14(4): 3–22.

Oliner, S.D. and Sichel, D.E. (2002) 'Information Technology and Productivity: Where Are We Now and Where Are We Going?' *Federal Reserve Bank of Atlanta Economic Review*, 3rd Quarter 2002, 87(3): 15–44.

Rosenberg, N. (1982) *Inside the Black Box: Technology and Economics*. Cambridge: Cambridge University Press.

Smits, J.P. (1995) *Economic Growth and Structural Change in the Dutch Service Sector 1850–1913*, PhD Thesis, Free University Amsterdam.

Smits, J.P., Horlings, E. and van Zanden, J.L. (2001) *Dutch GNP and its Components, 1800–1913*, Groningen Growth and Development Centre.

Timmer, M.P. and van Ark, B. (2005) 'IT in the European Union: A driver of productivity divergence?', *Oxford Economic Papers* 57(4): 693–716.

3 Longer-term competitiveness of the Wider Europe

Karl Aiginger and Michael Landesmann

1 Introduction

This chapter covers a wide range of issues at the cost of a relatively discursive style: We first review some findings concerning growth and productivity developments US–EU over the most recent decades (sections 2 and 3); we shall qualify these findings by taking a broader view of the notion of 'competitiveness' (section 4) and point to the heterogeneity of performance within Europe, particularly with regard to the relative success stories of the Northern economies (Denmark, Finland, Sweden) which are often cited as a 'model' option for the rest of Europe (section 5). We then turn our attention to the recent process of EU Enlargement and discuss its impact upon the EU's growth perspectives (section 6) and then to the Wider European region and its neighbourhood (section 7). We make some comparisons of the position of the Wider Europe in the global economy in relation to other regionalist entities (US and East Asia) in section 8. We end with some remarks concerning the outlook for Europe's competitiveness (section 9) and a discussion of some implications of the analysis for US–European transatlantic relationships and Europe's global role (section 10).

2 Evolution of US–Europe competitiveness 1970–2005

In this section we shall review the principal features of US–European competitiveness.

1   Europe[1] was on a catching-up path as regards real income developments relative to the United States in the post-war period until the early 1980s (see Figure 3.1). After that, the catching-up process in GDP per capita came to a halt and Europe first held its relative position vis-à-vis the US and, from 1995 onwards, lost ground. Productivity catching-up continued at rates which differed depending upon which measure of productivity is used (total factor productivity, GDP per employee or GDP per hour worked) until 1995, after which Western Europe fell behind. The measured 'gap' in productivity levels and real income vis-à-vis the US is smallest when measured as GDP per hour worked and largest when the standard real income measure is used (GDP per capita).

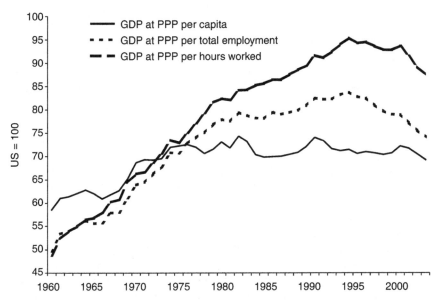

Figure 3.1a European catching-up in GDP per capita, productivity per worker and per hour, 1960–2004 (US = 100).

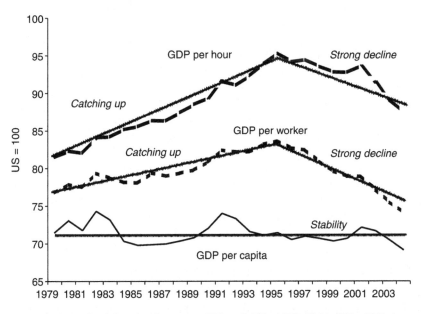

Figure 3.1b Productivity developments, US and EU, 1979–2004 (US = 100) (source: Own calculations using data from the Groningen Growth and Development Centre and The Conference Board, Total Economy Database, January 2005, www/ggdc.net).

2   Using the terminology of growth theory, we can speak of 'conditional convergence' between the US and Europe, in that productivity and real income catching-up has taken place but come to a halt before the gap has been fully closed. Growth analysts in this case search for 'conditioning factors', i.e. structural and institutional factors which can account for the inability of economies to fully close the gap vis-à-vis more advanced economies. A 'falling behind', as witnessed after 1995, would require further explanation.

3   The main factor accounting for the discrepancy between the productivity gap (amounting currently to about 10 per cent, if measured by GDP per hour worked) and the real income gap (amounting to about 30 per cent) lies in the lower levels of utilization of the labour force in Europe as compared to the US.[2] Three factors in turn account for this: (i) generally lower participation rates (this refers to the share of the population of working age who are looking for jobs; this is especially true for females in general and then, across genders, amongst the older (55–64) age group and the youngest (15–24) age group); (ii) lower employment rates (the share of people who find jobs out of those who are counted as part of the labour force[3]) or, inversely, higher unemployment rates; and (iii) lower numbers of hours worked per person employed (shorter working week, more part-time jobs, more holiday entitlements).

4   As regards the measurement of productivity, there are problems in comparing productivity levels between the US and Europe: specifically problematic are different methods used to account for quality improvements; the major problem of measurement of productivity in the services sector; difficulties of measuring the significance of the 'informal sector' and of 'outsourced homework' (for the latter, see Freeman and Schettkat, 2005). Recent studies emphasize particularly the difference in productivity levels which have opened up over the period 1995–2003 in the ICT-using services industries (retail and wholesale trade, finance/insurance) (see McGuckin and van Ark, 2005; O'Mahony and van Ark, 2003; Gordon, 2004).

Thus, never having fully caught up with the US in levels, GDP, real income and productivity growth all moved onto a lower growth path in Europe compared to the US from the mid-1990s onward. This is a cause for soul-searching in Europe as regards the factors responsible and policy options available to counter this.

3 Factors accounting for lower growth in Europe

The period since 1995 (when the strong take-off in growth took place in the US and the growth performance in Europe lagged behind) is still too short to allow us to dissect in a convincing manner the reasons for Europe's relatively disappointing growth performance. However, we shall try to summarize some of the research findings on this:

Differences in the conduct of monetary and fiscal policy

There is general acknowledgement that the conduct of monetary and fiscal policy has been quite different over the period 1995–2005. Europe was pre-occupied in the latter half of the 1990s with preparing the ground for European Monetary Integration; in this context, the Maastricht criteria imposed relatively strict conditions on those economies which were still far from the fiscal and monetary targets set by these criteria. Overall one can say that the restrictive macroeconomic policy scenario in Europe differed from the accommodating conduct of monetary policy by the Fed in the US (Greenspan was guided by the idea that the 'potential growth path' of the US economy had shifted; and so far he has been proven right). After the collapse of the stock-market boom and the aftermath of September 11, both monetary and fiscal policy were again more responsive and expansionary in the US than in Europe, leading to a deteriora-tion in fiscal and external balances in the US while Europe continued on its relatively low growth path, which by itself generated a crisis in the fulfillment of the fiscal targets implied by the Growth and Stability Pact (GSP). More recently, the turnaround of the US in interest rate policy was again more dra-matic than in the Euro-zone.

Strengths and weaknesses in the US and European 'innovation systems'

Innovation indicators (patents, citations, Nobel prizes) reveal a strong and sus-tained gap between the US and Europe. Studies have pointed out the much higher proportion of private business R&D spending in the US compared to Europe (while public spending ratios in GDP are similar); the much better developed interface of university–business links; the existence of the world's best research universities (which are much more open to international talent than European universities and research institutes) and – similarly – the world's best business schools; the better developed venture capital markets providing the backbone to the setting-up and continued growth of research-intensive SMEs. Europe has made some small steps in closing these gaps and, so far, too little to fulfil the ambitious goals of the Lisbon Agenda. The relative weakness of these features of the European innovation system show up in a lag in the introduction and diffusion of the most recent crops of new innovations, particularly informa-tion technology in the 1990s and bio-technology currently (see also Figure 3.2 and Appendix Table 3A.1 on 'growth drivers'). Estimates of the productivity growth gap in the 1990s attributes about a 0.5 per cent annual difference in pro-ductivity growth between the US and the EU to slower introduction and dif-fusion of information technology (see e.g. O'Mahony and van Ark, 2003; Denis *et al.*, 2004).

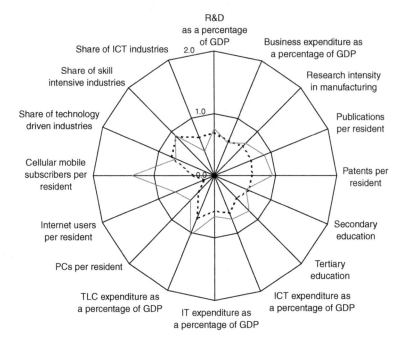

Figure 3.2 Growth drivers: Europe vs. USA (source: Aiginger and Landesmann (2002); see Appendix Table 3A.1 for more detailed descriptions of individual headings).

Note
Each indicator outside the unit circle shows a superior performance of Europe vs. the USA; black (interrupted) line: early 1990s; light (continuous) line: late 1990s.

Ageing problem and differences in migration policy

Europe has a more serious ageing problem. Between 1960 and 2000, the average dependency ratio (defined as the number of persons aged above 60 years per 100 persons aged 15–59 years) for the EU-15 rose from 26 to 35. Meanwhile the dependency ratio for the US remained almost constant at around 25. In the EU-15, by the mid-1970s the fertility rate had already dropped below 2.1 per woman, the natural replacement rate, and declined steadily thereafter, while it remained at that level in the US at the beginning of the twenty-first century. Forecasts of the dependency ratio in the EU-15 are 47 in 2020 and 70 in 2050. The European Commission estimates that the pure demographic effect of ageing would be an increase in public expenditure (related to pensions and health care) of eight points of GDP between 2000 and 2050 (see Sapir *et al.*, 2004: 118). The implication of an ageing population for skill acquisition, skill development, organizational flexibility, openness to innovation and entrepreneurship, labour mobility, etc. have not been systematically explored but should not be ignored. The same can be said for differences in migration flows and the differences between the US and Europe in the ease of integration of new migrants into the host population's culture and labour market opportunities; we shall return to this below.

The negative spiral of ageing, declining productivity, increasing social security costs, and implications for employment

Support for the European welfare system was generous in the period of relatively high productivity growth and relatively healthy demographic structures after the Second World War. With the decline of productivity growth and the ageing process, together with rising labour market problems which manifested themselves in low employment rates and sustained unemployment, the burden for maintaining social services expressed itself in high and rising social insurance contributions in the wage bill. This in turn increased labour costs, which provided incentives to save labour in production – particularly in highly labour-intensive activities (see the sharply rising capital/labour ratios in Europe in comparison with the US over the 1980s and 1990s; Appendix Figure 3A.1). This contributed to the employment problem, particularly affecting the low-wage (and low skill) segment where the sensitivity to labour costs is particularly high. This further reduces employment rates (waves of early retirements and problems with low-qualified youths) and increases in turn the burden on those in jobs to provide the funds to maintain welfare services.

The unfulfilled integration pay-offs of the Single Market

The Single Market Program in 1992, which was designed to remove barriers across all markets within the European Union, went along with high expectations as regards both static and dynamic efficiency gains (see Emerson *et al.*, 1988). Ex post research indicates that the liberalization, particularly in services, utilities and banking, proceeded much more slowly than envisaged. The gains from market integration were consequently lower. As economic growth is affected by other factors (such as the framework for short-run macroeconomic policies) it is nearly impossible to isolate the specific effects of market integration; however, some evidence suggests that higher degree of market regulation and barriers to entry and exit affect Europe's relative growth performance (see, for example, the evidence presented in Nicoletti and Scarpetta, 2003).[4]

The European 'success stories'

It should not be overlooked that Europe can also claim a number of success stories in which innovation systems were very successful and welfare systems were revamped (see, for example, Aiginger, 2004b). Some of the Scandinavian countries (Sweden, Finland, Denmark) developed a highly trained work-force, increased their R&D spending ratios above the US levels and successfully emphasized active labour market policies so that unemployment rates could be kept low (or fell strongly after the impact of shocks). R&D intensive industries in these countries dominate industrial production and exports. They are in the very top league as regards the production and diffusion of IT technologies and their fiscal situation is very satisfactory (see Figure 3.4 below as well as Figure 3A.2 on growth drivers vis-à-vis the US). Another example is Ireland, which had a successful growth phase in the 1990s based on a sustained effort to improve the quality of its labour force. It consolidated macroeconomically and undertook successful industrial policies which attracted a large amount of FDI which, in turn, contributed strongly to upgrading its industrial structure. Having been in the group of least developed economies in the EU until the 1980s, Ireland now belongs to the richest group of countries and shows clear signs of labour shortages.

4 Beyond growth dynamics

The competitiveness of nations is intensively discussed (see Aiginger and Landesmann, 2002). An assessment of competitiveness has to include market results as well as the conditions of the social, fiscal and environmental conditions under which the results are achieved. This section therefore compares the performance of Europe and the US, including broad indicators on economic welfare.

Growth of output and productivity

As discussed in section 2, economic growth as measured by real GDP grew faster in Europe until the early 1970s. The catching-up process then stagnated and, particularly since 1990, the US has been outperforming Europe: it was less affected by the crisis of 1993, achieved higher growth during the second half of the decade and was more resistant to the downturn of 2001/03. For the period 1990–2004, this difference in GDP growth amounted to 1.14 per cent per annum and 22 per cent cumulatively. The difference in productivity per hour worked was 18 per cent (lower in Europe than in the US) in 1980; this difference declined to 5 per cent in 1995. The difference has then widened to about 13 percentage points in 2004 (see Table 3.1b). The relative improvement on the employment side in Europe since 1995 – one of the factors accounting for lower relative labour productivity performance – has been heralded as good news reflecting labour market and pension reforms (Tables 3.1a and 3.2).[5]

Other components of welfare

Broader comparisons of welfare include: (1) employment and unemployment; (2) distribution of incomes; (3) comprehensiveness of the coverage of social and health risks; and (4) preservation of environment and prudent use of resources. These considerations imply that a more broadly defined economic concept of

Table 3.1a Europe's growth performance relative to the US

	Growth of real GDP		Productivity growth per worker		Employment growth	
	EU	USA	EU	USA	EU	USA
1961–70	4.80	4.22	4.51	2.14	0.28	2.04
1971–80	2.97	3.25	2.59	1.11	0.37	2.11
1981–90	2.41	3.17	1.71	1.32	0.69	1.83
1991–95	1.52	2.48	1.94	1.41	−0.41	1.05
1996–2000	2.70	4.14	1.28	2.10	1.41	1.99
2001–05	1.57	2.75	0.93	2.38	0.63	0.36
1996–2005	2.13	3.44	1.10	2.24	1.02	1.17
1961–2000	4.11	4.67	3.48	2.11	0.61	2.51

welfare embraces employment, income distribution, the comprehensiveness of the social net and ecological conservation.

Concepts of welfare could also be extended to life expectancy, security, cultural goals, the rule of law, and other aspects of human development (see Figure 3.3). The broader the set of goals to be evaluated, the more difficult it is to measure these goals, and the more difficult it is to determine the relative weights of the individual objectives and make a general assessment.

We have already discussed differences with respect to employment and unemployment. The employment rate is currently about 13 percentage points higher in the US, namely 76 per cent versus 67 per cent (see Table 3.3). Until the mid-1970s, the share of employment for the working-age population was higher in Europe than in the US (the employment rate was 70 per cent in Europe, as compared to 66 per cent in the US in 1960). Why the curves crossed is beyond the scope of this chapter (see the discussion by Gordon, 2006, in this volume). One relationship to be explored is the causality between population growth, GDP growth and employment rate in rich economies, especially when population growth is fed through migration flows (on this see e.g. Borjas, 2001). Second, at the lower end of the wage spectrum, US labour became comparatively cheap, increasing the labour intensity of US growth. The US created 78 million new jobs between 1960 and 2000, Europe 42 million. Employment creation in recent years has accelerated in Europe: between 1996 and 2004, the EU-15 created 15.4 million jobs (the US 14 million). Even during three years of slow growth (2001–03) employment has, in contrast to experiences during other periods of sluggish growth, been increasing (while it fell in the US), although many jobs are part-time. Unemployment in 2005 was 5.1 per cent in the US and 8 per cent in Europe (2004).

The social net is more generous in Europe. Net public spending on welfare is about 16 per cent in the US and 24 per cent in Europe. Most Europeans have government funded or commanded health insurance, pensions are higher, retirement can be started earlier and the contribution provided through public schemes is higher. Unemployment payments are higher in relation to income

Table 3.1b Differences in income per capita, per worker and per hour, EU-15/US

	GDP per capita			GDP per worker			GDP per hour		
	EU-15 1,000 euro	USA	EU-15/US	EU-15 1,000 euro	USA	EU-15/US	EU-15 euro	USA	EU-15/US
1980	16.30	22.31	0.73	39.84	51.16	0.78	23.00	27.93	0.82
1990	20.08	27.88	0.72	47.43	58.66	0.81	28.82	32.25	0.89
1995	21.30	29.81	0.71	52.52	62.79	0.84	32.53	34.13	0.95
2000	23.93	33.85	0.71	55.81	70.69	0.79	34.90	37.63	0.93
2002	24.43	34.08	0.72	56.26	72.94	0.77	35.52	38.83	0.91
2004	24.92	36.02	0.69	57.12	77.08	0.74	36.24	41.44	0.87

Source: Own calculations using data from the Groningen Growth and Development Centre and The Conference Board, Total Economy Database, January 2005, www.ggdc.net.

Table 3.2 Employment and unemployment

	Employment rate			Working hours per year and per person			Unemployment rate		
	EU	USA	USA/EU	EU	USA	USA/EU	EU	USA	USA/EU
1980	64.34	71.01	1.10	1,769	1,853	1.05	5.6	7.1	1.26
1985	60.81	72.63	1.19	1,700	1,853	1.09	9.6	7.2	0.75
1990	64.34	77.83	1.21	1,676	1,840	1.10	7.5	5.5	0.73
1995	62.10	77.26	1.24	1,644	1,859	1.13	10.0	5.6	0.56
2000	65.81	79.65	1.21	1,598	1,878	1.18	7.6	4.0	0.53
2005	66.74	76.06	1.14	1,577	1,817	1.15	8.0	5.2	0.65

Source: Own calculations using Eurostat (AMECO).

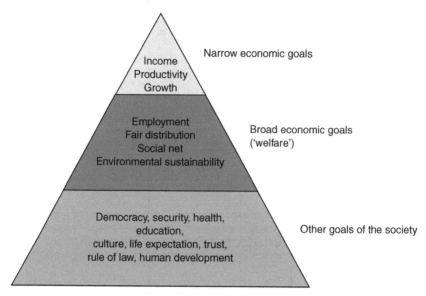

Figure 3.3 Hierarchy of economic and social goals.

(replacement rate), they are paid for a longer period of time, and fall back payments (social assistance) are relatively high and essentially unlimited in time.

Income is distributed less evenly in the US. The top 20 per cent earns 45 per cent of total income, while the bottom 20 per cent earns 4.8 per cent, which results in an inequality ratio of 9.4. In Europe, the corresponding numbers are 38.5 per cent for the top 20 per cent and 8.3 per cent for the bottom 20 per cent, resulting in a ratio of 4.7. The lowest ratio in Europe is 3.2 for Austria, followed by the Scandinavian countries and Belgium; Portugal is the only country where inequality nears US levels. The uneven distribution of income is increasing in many countries, but it is greatest in the US. Contrary to common expectation, the poverty rate is not rising in the US in the long run: it dropped from 22 per cent in 1960 to a historic low of 11.1 per cent in 1973. It later increased to 15.2 per cent in 1983, following the shift in economic policy by the Reagan Administration and the increase in unemployment. It declined in the 1990s to 11.3 per cent and has been increasing slightly since the most recent recession. The reason for the relatively low level of poverty despite increasing income inequality is the relatively high employment rate (amongst men and women).

Other indicators underline the greater downside risk of American society. The number of homeless, illiteracy rates, the share of population in prison, homicides, the relative prevalence of drugs and guns, racial discrimination, and the discrepancies between living standards in slums and suburbs illustrate the point. On the other hand, data on mobility reveal that expected upward mobility is greater, although the difference between the US and Europe in actual mobility is less than commonly believed (Alesina *et al.*, 2001). Immigration flows are

Table 3.3 Broad indicators of economic welfare

	EU-15	USA	Top 3[7] European countries	Big 3[7] European countries
Employment rate 2004	66.5	75.9	72.9	64.8
Employment generation in millions 1996/2004	15.4	14.0	0.6	5.6
Unemployment rate 2005	8.0	5.1	7.1	9.0
Net social expenditures (public and private)[1]	24.9	23.4	26.4	21.2
Net social expenditures (public)[1]	24.0	16.4	24.3	18.7
Income distribution[2]				
Share of top 20%	38.5	45.2	34.9	38.7
Share of low 20%	8.3	4.8	9.7	7.9
Relation of top 20%/low 20%	4.7	9.4	3.6	4.9
Energy consumption in Mtoe/GDP[3]	0.15	0.26	0.16	0.14
Carbon dioxide in t/GDP[3]	0.31	0.57	0.27	0.29
Self assessment of happiness[4]	7.05[5]	7.60	7.87	6.87
Self assessment of life satisfaction[4]	6.81[5]	7.46	7.75	6.68
Health adjusted life expectancy (at birth)[6]	70.14	67.60	70.67	70.83
Persons sentenced to prison per 100,000	65	469		

Notes
1 Adema (2001) OECD, Society at a Glance, 2003.
2 IMD, Competitive Yearbook, 1999.
3 Total Primary Energy Supply, OECD, International Energy Agency.
4 Veenhoven (1997).
5 Four largest EU countries only (Germany, France, Italy, United Kingdom).
6 OECD, Society at a Glance, 2003.
7 See section 5, Table 3.4.

larger in the US than in the EU. There is also evidence of a difference in the skill mix of migrants between the US and Europe, particularly in the relative attractiveness of the US research institutions and labour markets to highly talented and skilled migrants (on this, see chapters by Peri and Münz in this volume).

Europe is definitely leading the US in ecological performance. Energy consumption per GDP is 73 per cent higher in the US than in Europe (US 0.26 Mtoe/GDP, Europe 0.15 Mtoe/GDP); carbon dioxide is 84 per cent higher relative to GDP. With respect to the dynamics of emissions, Europe is at least trying to fulfil the Kyoto targets of reducing greenhouse gases, while the US is not.

Europeans have more leisure time; this is the other side of the employment picture: as mentioned earlier the share of population in work is smaller by 13 percentage points, and there are 16 per cent fewer working hours per year (more vacations, fewer weekly hours). It is difficult to assess the extent to which these differences are voluntary and to what extent they are by-products of the economic environment – such as the lack of full-time jobs or jobs for workers of particularly vulnerable age groups, those who have problems entering the job market in the first place, and those who have lost their jobs and have little chance of regaining employment. Gordon (2002: 10) ventures the 'wild guess that about one third of the difference represents voluntary chosen leisure and the remaining two thirds represent a lack of employment opportunities'.

How can these factors be weighted? One way of attaining an overall assessment by means of socio-economic research is to formulate two internationally comparable questions, namely whether a person is happy and whether (s)he is satisfied with her/his life. Results indicate that people are influenced by income, but the rankings ascribed to income and self assessments of life satisfaction are not redundant. For both subjective indicators, Americans rank higher in terms of satisfaction, namely 7.6 for 'happiness' on a scale of ten versus 7.1 for the four largest European countries (Germany, France, the United Kingdom, Italy). For 'life satisfaction', the US rating is 7.5, while the corresponding value for the four largest European countries is 6.8. Interestingly, intra-country differences within the US are smaller than in France and the United Kingdom (see Veenhoven, 1997, and Deutsche Bank Research, 2006).

5   Performance differences across European countries and their relation to the welfare system and welfare reforms

Differences across European countries in dynamics have become larger in the 1990s. We will use this cross-country difference to qualify the standard judgements made regarding the determinants of growth differentials between the US and Europe. Specifically, if the high welfare costs were at the heart of the European problem of low dynamics, the countries with comprehensive welfare and high taxes should be the worst performing countries.

Sweden, Finland and Denmark are the three countries outperforming the European average, if we combine growth of output, productivity and employment to measure 'overall economic performance'. These three countries are welfare states of the Nordic type; they are characterized by high re-distributive policies and a high degree of government involvement. We follow Aiginger (2004b) using indicators on growth of output, productivity and employment, but the same conclusions are reached by assessments of the competitiveness of European countries by IMD, the World Economic Forum and in studies on country growth differences by the OECD.[6]

These successful countries can be seen as following a 'three tiers' strategy (see Aiginger, 2004b). First, they contained private and public costs in order to regain profitability and fiscal balance. Second, they fine-tuned their welfare systems and liberalized part-time work as well as product markets in order to improve incentives. Third, investment in growth was increased significantly, surpassing that of the large European economies in research input and output, in education expenditures and quality, and in information technology. In contrast, the large continental economies (Germany, France and Italy) under-performed in terms of investments in such growth drivers.

The structures and policies of the most successful European countries are very different from the US as far as welfare and government involvement are concerned, as well as in their commitment to training and redistribution as goals of labour market policy. Their labour market policy offers a rather high degree of flexibility for firms (easy dismissals, low corporate taxes), but also provides security to individuals in helping them to find new jobs and to upgrade qualifications. The system has been coined 'flexicurity' and builds on the importance of 'active labour market policies' in these economies. These countries give high priority to new technologies, the efficiency of production, and the competitiveness of firms. They rely on a proactive industrial policy with government-supported strategies for information technology and agencies promoting research, regional policies, and clusters. They suffered a severe crisis (mostly in the early 1990s) in which many of the problems suspected to dampen growth in a highly developed Welfare State occurred (costs increasing faster than productivity, problems with fiscal sustainability). But they changed course without abandoning the goals of the Welfare State and without giving up ecological goals. The specific reform agenda has prompted discussion of the feasibility of a reformed European Model which combines welfare and sustainability on the one hand with efficiency and economic incentives on the other hand.[7]

To summarize the basic differences between the New and the Old Welfare State, here are some of the main points (see also Table 3.5):

- The social system remains inclusive and tight, but the social benefits depend on the individual's inputs, they may be conditional on certain obligations; replacement rates are lower than they used to be to provide better incentives to work.
- Taxes are relatively high, but in line with expenditures, even in the demanding sense of aiming at positive balances to take care of future pensions or to repay current debt.
- Wages are high, but the individual's position is not guaranteed. Assistance

Table 3.4 Performance of top 3 and big 3 European countries relative to the EU and the US

	Top 3 European countries	Big 3 European countries	EU-15	USA
Real growth of GDP 1996–2005	2.8	1.6	2.1	3.4
Macro productivity growth 1996–2005	1.9	0.9	1.2	2.2
Employment rate; average 1996–2005	71.4	62.8	64.4	77.4
Unemployment rate; average 1996–2005	8.2	9.5	8.8	5.3
Inflation rate; average 1996–2005	1.6	2.1	2.1	2.5
Public debt in % of GDP 2005	44.6	79.6	64.3	63.5
Budget deficit in % of GDP 2005 (deficit −)	1.4	−3.3	−2.5	−4.0
Taxes in % of GDP 2005	55.4	46.6	45.3	29.5
GDP per capita at PPP 2005	27.4	24.7	25.1	36.1

Source: Own calculations using Eurostat (AMECO).

Note
Top 3 countries: Denmark, Finland, Sweden. Big 3 countries: Germany, France, Italy.

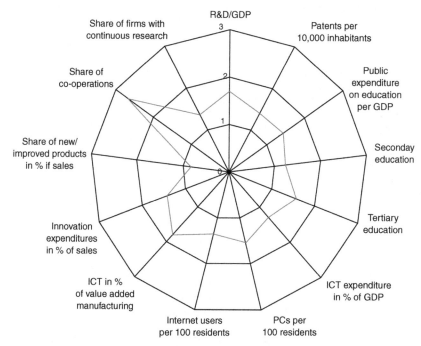

Figure 3.4 Investment in future growth; top 3 European countries vs. big 3 European countries.

Note

Values outside the unit circle indicate greater investment by the top three countries (in the last year that the indicator was available; usually 1999 or 2000).

and training opportunities that are personalized, less bureaucratic and centralized are offered to people losing their jobs.

• Welfare-to-work elements have been introduced, usually on a decentralized, sometimes even private basis; conditions vary according to problem size and problem class, the background philosophy being one of providing assistance while keeping work search incentives intact.

• Part-time work and adaptation of work to life cycle is encouraged, and social benefits are pro rata extended to part-time work, which becomes an individual right and a measure voluntarily taken to enforce, rather than prevent, gender equality.

• Technology policy and adoption of new technologies, rather than subsidizing old industries, are a precondition for the survival of the Welfare State.

• Even where welfare costs are streamlined and incentives are improved, the welfare system offers comprehensive insurances against economic and social risks and a broad coverage of health risks.

• Environmental and social goals as well as equity of income distribution and prevention of poverty are high on the political agenda.

• Government and public institutions play a proactive role in promoting

Table 3.5 Old Model versus New European Model of a Reformed Welfare State

Old model of European Welfare	*The new model of leading three countries*
Welfare pillar	
Security in existing jobs	Assistance in finding a new job
High replacement ratios	Incentives to accept new jobs (return to
Structural change in existing firms (often	labour force)
large firms)	Job creation in new firms, in services, in
Comprehensive health coverage, pensions,	self-employment
education	Coverage dependent on personal
Regulation of labour and product markets	obligations
Focus on stable, full-time jobs	Flexibility as a strategy for firms and as a
Early retirements	right for employees
	Part-time work as individual choice
	(softened by some rules)
	Encouraging employment for elderly
	workforce
Policy pillar	
Focus on price stability	Focus on growth and new technologies
Asymmetric fiscal policy (deficits)	Fiscal prudence (but flexible in crisis)
Incentives for physical investment	Incentives for research, education, and
Subsidies for ailing firms (public ownership)	new technologies
Industrial policy for large firms	Industrial areas, business–university nexus
Local champions, permissive competition	Start-ups, venture capital, services
policy	Enforce current strengths (cluster and
	regional policy) and competition

innovation, efficiency, and structural change, in upgrading qualifications, and in life-long learning. Public institutions also provide the largest part of education and health care.

*   Social partners (institutions comprising representatives of firms and employees) determine many elements of wage formation and play a decisive role in shaping labour laws, in certain institutional developments, and in the formulation of economic policy in general.
*   Government is large and taxes are high, even if mechanisms are put in place to limit increases in spending and for achieving a sound fiscal policy in periods of increasing demand.

6 The impact of enlargement on Europe's growth prospects

With the fall of the Iron Curtain and the ensuing rapid process of East–West European economic integration, culminating – so far – in the accession of 12 new countries to the European Union in 2004 and 2006, the diversity of living standards and the differentiation of structural and systemic (institutional and behavioural) features within the European Union has vastly increased.

Figures 3.5a and 3.5b show the dispersion of GDP per capita across the

European continent, first in relation to the shares which the different countries represent in Europe's population (Figure 3.5a) and then in relation to their shares in Europe's GDP (measured in PPP) (Figure 3.5b). We see that the dispersion of income (between the richest and poorest of the EU-25 economy) has dramatically increased through the recent wave of enlargement, and that further prospective waves bringing in the candidate countries and potential future applicants (the countries in the ACS and SEE groups[8]) would lead to further dispersion.

We shall shortly review developments in Central and Eastern Europe from the early 1990s and then refer to current developments and the impact of enlargement upon the EU economy and governance issues.

Transition in Central and Eastern Europe and (re)integration into the European economy

The starting point of the transformation processes in 1989 in Eastern Europe meant an enormous change in economic structure, trade arrangements, adjustments in the policy tools used and, of course, fundamental institutional and behavioural changes. After a difficult transitional period in which the 'newly emerging market economies' (NEMs) of Eastern Europe experienced a dramatic recession (mostly induced by a radical shift from one system of allocation (planning) towards another (markets) as well as the sudden regime switch towards very far-reaching trade, exchange rate and price liberalization), the more successful of the Central and Eastern European economies (Poland, the Czech and Slovak Republics, Hungary, Slovenia and the Baltics) gradually regained stability and, from the mid- to late 1990s, started to grow at rates which were double those of the EU-15. Together with systemic and macroeconomic changes came important structural transformations: there was an influx of foreign direct investment and upgrading of industrial production structures, technologies, and product quality. All this took place at a relatively rapid pace (see Landesmann, 2000; Landesmann and Stehrer, 2002; Landesmann, 2003). The current trade and production integration between the new members and the 'old EU' (the EU-15) is strong, particularly with the neighbouring countries, Austria, Germany, Italy and Greece. There have been significant developments in terms of cross-border production networks and the development of an industrial production belt (in cars, machinery, electrical goods, etc.) in the border regions of the new members with the old EU. A 'new division of labour' has developed, with medium-tech industrial production stages shifting towards the new members. The EU-15 countries, on the other hand, benefit from a high demand in the new members for financial and business services. In these areas they have substantial trade surpluses, while the new members have increasingly become important locations for industrial production (see Figure 3A.3).

The impact upon the EU economy and the EU policy framework

Much more differentiation and coping with heterogeneity

The new European Union is characterized by a much wider range of real income levels, productivity and wage levels than the EU-15 (the range of real income differences – at the national level – between the richest and poorest EU member in the 'old EU' was of the order of 40 per cent; in the new EU this range has expanded to about 70 per cent; see Figure 3.5). Sectoral structures still differ

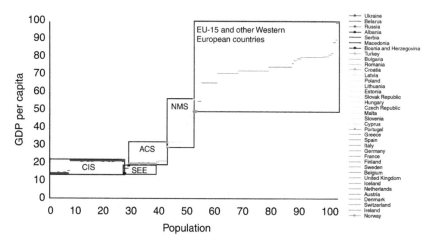

Figure 3.5a Income levels in the Wider Europe region: GDP per capita (PPP) vs. share of population, 2004.

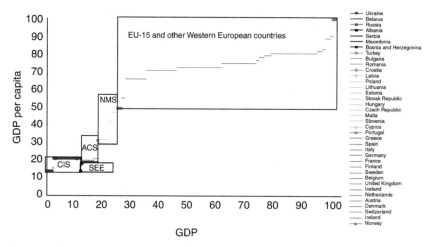

Figure 3.5b Income levels in the Wider Europe region: GDP per capita (PPP) vs. share of GDP, 2004.

substantially between the NMS and the OMS (see the shares of agriculture and services in GDP, but more importantly in employment; Table 3.6) and even more so in the candidate countries. This indicates still substantial forthcoming processes of sectoral structural adjustment. The regional dimension (below country level) shows a further increase in regional disparities (e.g. a large share of the poorest regions of the EU-25 is in the new member countries; see Landesmann and Roemisch, 2005). There are opportunities and challenges in this increase in heterogeneity: the opportunities lie in the possibilities of complementarities in comparative advantage structures and the increased scope for production location decisions and the setting-up of production networks by EU and international companies across the enlarged European Union. The challenges lie in cohesion policies on the one hand, which will have to be applied at both national and European levels and difficult adjustment processes in the old EU members which face the difficult task of adapting economic structures that result from the new division of labour in Europe and globally (see, e.g., Sinn, 2005).

Challenges for decision-making structures and the conduct of macroeconomic policies

Decision-making in the EU has become a major problem with 27 members (and will become more so as more countries enter): the changes that were to be introduced with the new Constitution would have eased these problems, but, at the same time, would have generated a new dynamic of coalition-building which is untested in its potential efficiency or inefficiency. The conduct of macroeconomic policy is in a state of disarray, with monetary policy having been centralized (for the Euro-zone) and a clear – and unlikely to be changed – constitutional role being given to the ECB to conduct monetary policy in line with the former Bundesbank model. On the other hand, fiscal policy coordination and the framework for the Growth and Stability Pact (GSP) are in a state of flux and a major factor in a feeling of disenchantment with the overall macroeconomic policy framework. Reform of the GSP reflects efforts at rational reform of the fiscal policy framework in the direction of an orientation towards 'longer-run fiscal sustainability' and a complex web of particular countries' interests given their economic positions (France, Germany; new members). There are definitely new challenges created by the increased heterogeneity which get reflected in differences in trend growth paths, different inflation scenarios reflecting catching-up processes, and different demographic situations which would allow different longer-run fiscal and debt arrangements; it has been acknowledged that such increased heterogeneity should be reflected in a reformed GSP. However, the unclear division of powers between the Commission, the councils of ministers and the 'Euro-group' to initiate and carry through reforms have made it difficult to go beyond a marginal reform package and find a longer-term solution.

Table 3.6 Central and East European new EU member states (NMS-8): an overview of economic fundamentals, 2004

	NMS-4[1]	NMS-8[2]	EU-15	AC-3[3]	Turkey	Ukraine
Population – thousands, average	27,693.3	72,962.9	385,059.0	33,894.5	72,003	47,281
GDP in EUR at exchange rates, EUR bn	226.03	459.08	9,793.85	105.97	243.04	52.17
GDP in EUR at ER, per capita	8,162	6,292	25,435	3,127	3,375	1,103
GDP in EUR at PPP, EUR bn	394.84	868.97	9,383.48	250.92	486.07	280.85
GDP in EUR at PPP, per capita	14,258	11,908	24,369	7,403	6,750	5,920
GDP at constant prices, 1990 = 100	121.4	132.2	131.6	103.8	162.1	61.0
GDP at constant prices, 1995 = 100	132.3	140.0	121.6	122.0	138.4	127.6
GDP at constant prices, 2000 = 100	114.6	114.7	106.1	123.9	114.1	141.1
GDP, p.a. growth (per cent, 1990–2004)	1.4	2.0	2.0	0.3	3.5	−3.5
GDP, p.a. growth (per cent, 1995–2004)	3.2	3.8	2.2	2.2	3.7	2.7
GDP, p.a. growth (per cent, 2000–04)	3.5	3.5	1.5	5.5	3.3	9.0
Gross value added, in % of GDP[4]						
Agriculture, forestry, fishing	2.9	2.9	1.8	10.3	11.7	10.8
Industry total	30.7	28.2	24.3	30.6	28.2	32.6
Services	56.8	59.2	66.5	47.7	62.3	47.3
Employed persons in, LFS in % of total[5,6]						
Agriculture, forestry, fishing	5.2	12.3	3.9	25.9	34.0	23.1
Industry total	36.8	32.1	24.3	30.5	23.0	25.6
Services	57.9	55.5	71.9	43.5	43.0	51.3
Public sector expenditures, EU-def., in % of GDP[7]	47.1	46.8	48.0	36.1	32.6	29.4
General government deficit, in % of GDP av. 2000–04	−5.4	−4.2	−1.5	−2.7	−11.3	−0.5

Sources: wiiw, EUROSTAT, AMECO, ILO.

Notes

1 NMS-4: Czech Republic, Hungary, Slovak Republic, Slovenia.
2 NMS-8: Czech Republic, Estonia, Hungary, Latvia, Lithuania, Poland, Slovak Republic, Slovenia.
3 AC-3: Bulgaria, Croatia, Romania.
4 Data 2003 for Romania, Turkey, NMS-4 and NMS-10 (NMS-8 plus Malta and Cyprus).
5 Bulgaria, Croatia employment by registration.
6 Ukraine employment by registration, data 2003.
7 EU-15 and NMS according to EU definition (excessive deficit procedure); Bulgaria, Romania, Turkey and Ukraine national definition; Croatia IMF-definition and data 2003.

The future of EU policy programmes

The year 2005 saw conflicts emerge over the next Financial Framework as expenditure plans for EU programmes had to be finalized for the period 2007–13. The major spending components in the EU budget are the Common Agricultural Policy (CAP) and the Structural and Cohesion Funds. The plan submitted by the European Commission (see Figure 3.6) envisaged a decline in the share of spending on the CAP (currently amounting to about 45 per cent of overall spending), constancy in the finance provided for Structural and Cohesion Funds (currently amounting to about 35 per cent), and an increase in spending on the Lisbon Agenda, particularly for research, and on international development and common foreign policy programmes. The Commission's proposal wanted to keep the commitment of member states to the EU budget at current levels (1.27 per cent of EU GNI) but was countered by the position taken by the group of 'net payers' which wants to reduce the commitment ceiling to 1 per cent. A compromise was struck, reducing the commitment to 1.06 per cent of GNI. Furthermore a conflict erupted between the UK and France, when the UK (which held the EU presidency in the second half of 2005) sought to reopen negotiations with respect to reforming the CAP before finalizing the 2007–13 Financial Framework. Allocations to the CAP budget for this period had been fixed by the acceptance in 2002 of a limited reform package pushed through by Commissioner Fischler. In any case, the current situation seems to indicate continued conflicts over the three major EU expenditure items, the CAP, Structural/Regional policies and innovation-support measures which should go some way towards achieving the Lisbon Agenda objectives. There is currently no willingness to increase the overall EU budget and thus shift expenditure structures between the EU and national levels.

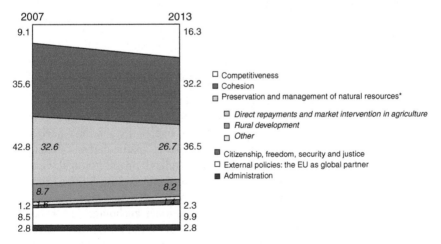

Figure 3.6 The composition of expenditures of the European Union's budget in 2007 and 2013 according to the European Commission's proposal (in %) (source: Richter (2005)).

Note
The internal distribution of 'Preservation, etc.' is indicated by the figures in italic.

Hence the EU will remain a midget in budgetary terms, which constitutes a major difference with respect to the federal structure in the US.

The impact upon 'model competition' within the enlarged European Union

Over the past few years it has become clear that the new members have embarked upon a path which will enhance 'model competition' within the enlarged European Union. While earlier in the transition there were indications that the NMS would follow the social-democratic, corporatist approach of their immediate neighbours (Germany and Austria), more recent developments indicate a turn towards a more liberal economic orientation. There have been moves towards flat tax or near flat tax regimes in a succession of NMS, there have been developments towards a stronger mix of private–public segments in the health and education systems, and the overall fiscal constraints (given the pressures to fulfil GSP criteria and ambitions to join EMU) point towards a reduced role of the (inherited large) state in economic life. Pension reforms, privatization of utilities, and the presence of foreign investors have moved in many of the new member countries beyond the levels achieved in many of the 'old' member states. In most of the NMS there is – after the dismantling of the Communist trade union organizations – also relatively low union membership and hence little basis for developing strong social partnership arrangements. The presence of a group of fast growing economies, attractive to FDI (which mostly comes from the EU-15), with low wages and a tendency towards very low corporate tax rates, and more liberal corporate regulations (in shop opening hours, shift work, standards of safety regulations), introduces new momentum into the already diverse picture of 'model competition' in the European Union previously characterized by Anglo-Saxon, Scandinavian, corporatist continental, Southern cohesion country models, and the Irish catching-up model (which many of the NMS want – in part – to emulate[9]).

7 The concept of the 'Wider Europe' and its neighbourhood

'Enlargement' and 'Association' have been buzzwords in the European integration process for 25 years and will continue to be so at least for the coming decade. The track record shows, first, that – over a longer time horizon – integration with the European Union benefits particularly catching-up economies, previously the cohesion countries (Ireland, Spain, Portugal, Greece) and most recently the new members from Central and Eastern Europe. Second, the benefits of enlargement accrue in part in advance of actual membership. In a phase of catching-up or 'transition' the institutional anchorage (or 'lock-in') with the more mature institutional and legal frameworks of Western Europe is an important factor in tipping developments towards institutional and economic upgrading. The same can be said for the economic integration process through trade liberalization, FDI flows, the entry of foreign banks, fiscal and monetary policy coordination with more advanced, high income economies. These provide a major spur for upgrading economic structures and in the conduct of economic policy. Hence Association and prospects for EU membership provide a major pull for economies which are (1) less developed than the EU and (2) in the EU's neighbourhood so that substantive economic integration provides a realistic scenario.

In the following we shall discuss the various 'layers' of the Wider Europe and the impact that tighter economic and political integration in the Wider Europe will have for Europe's competitiveness and position in the global economy.

Layers of the Wider Europe

The EU-25

The EU-25 is characterized by increased economic heterogeneity and unresolved governance structures as regards its own functioning. These two issues are core issues in the political debate in Europe and will absorb many of the resources of the political establishment devoted to EU integration over the current decade. The reform backlog and the growth weaknesses of the larger continental European economies (Germany, France, Italy) indicate that there will be a phase in which national political processes will be the determining factor in tackling economic reforms, while the resources and instruments available at the EU level are too weak to play a decisive role in this respect over the coming years.

In spite of the setback over the acceptance of the European Constitution, there seems to be nonetheless a continuous push and – in the final analysis – inescapable dynamic towards further enlargement (in Southeast Europe) and increased ties with neighbouring countries and regions.

The follow-up round of enlargement (Romania, Bulgaria, Croatia)

This further enlargement will take place in 2007–09. Negotiations with Croatia were delayed as it was dragging its feet to comply with the Hague Tribunal to extradite accused war criminals, but they are now on course. The issues with this further round of enlargement are no different from those of the previous round: there will again be transitory arrangements with respect to full participation in EU programmes and the opening up to full mobility of labour which should ease adaptation from the EU-25 side. Given that the countries join after the principal decisions regarding the 2007–13 Financial Framework have been taken, they have very limited influence on the budget over the first period of their EU membership. The increase in membership numbers from this wave of enlargement will not make a significant difference with respect to the already problematic state of decision-making processes in the EU of (then) 28 members.

The 'rest of the Balkans' (Macedonia, Serbia, Montenegro, Bosnia-Herzegovina, Albania, potentially Kosovo) and Turkey

This is a 'weightier' enlargement in terms of numbers (5–7 new members) and also in economic terms, because of the big weight of Turkey and some very poor countries and regions (in the Balkans and Eastern Anatolia). The adjustment processes required from the then EU 33–35 would therefore be far more difficult and put new strain on cohesion policies and decision-making structures. From today's perspective it looks as if a 'special partnership' arrangement with Turkey is the most likely outcome, although there is no way to foresee developments over the coming decade (both within the EU and in Turkey). The rest of Southeast Europe (Western Balkans) is likely to gain full membership because of its small economic weight, and the incentive to support political and economic stabilization in the region and to provide contiguity for the EU geographic entity. One reason that the 'special partnership' option with Turkey might be the more probable outcome is that it might also provide a precedent on how to deal with other weighty aspirants such as Ukraine or Belarus. The likely time horizon for the West Balkan enlargement is 2013–17.

Ukraine, Russia, CIS

Russia is already strongly linked through trade with the EU, and the other CIS countries remain strongly linked to Russia but also increasingly to the EU (see Astrov and Havlik, 2004). Links with the EU, furthermore, provide more scope and incentive for upgrading production and expenditure structures and, most importantly, institutions. This provides the 'pull' to Association and, for some countries (Ukraine, Moldova, Georgia), full membership of the EU, although the possibility of an EU of 35–37 by 2020 has become much less likely after the Constitution debacle. That this region might form part of an economic entity with considerable market integration and policy coordination is more likely.

MENA region

Many authors have written about an EU 'soft-power' effect on the Middle East, the Eastern Mediterranean, Iran, and Northern Africa. Developmental prospects of this region are strongly linked to tighter economic relationships with the EU. The question is whether a more forceful EU 'neighbourhood policy' can influence socio-economic and political blockages to economic development. One of the most important issues with potentially far-reaching social and economic consequences lies in the strong demographic complementarity of this region with the enlarged EU, but difficult issues of migration policy will have to be resolved.[10]

Complementarities and growth impetus from a 'Wider Europe' – a 'regionalist' arrangement

There are good reasons why 'Wider Europe' can – and already does – provide significant growth stimulus for the enlarged European Union. Figure 3.7 presents the differences of growth rates of the EU-15, the EU-25, the EU-28+Balkans and Turkey, and finally the EU-28+Balkans+Turkey+Ukraine over the years 2002–04 and then a projection for the period 2005–20.[11] The Wider Europe (defined here as the last group, i.e. excluding Russia and any other CIS country except Ukraine) displays a significant growth differential compared to the EU-15 (this differential amounted to 0.6 per cent in 2002, 0.7 per cent in 2003, and 0.8 per cent in 2004). With assumptions about differential growth rates also for the future for the EU-15, the NMS, the Balkans, Turkey and Ukraine, we see that while the EU-15 is assumed to grow at the rate of 2.3 per cent per annum, the Wider Europe region would grow at 3.1 per cent per annum. Due to the differential growth performances of the non-EU-15 members of the Wider Europe region, the weights in the overall GDP of the Wider Europe region would shift as well: using purchasing power estimates, the weight of the EU-15 in the Wider Europe region was 83.7 per cent in 2000; it would fall to 73.2 per cent in 2020; that of the NMS-10 was 7.6 per cent in 2000 and is projected to rise to 10.7 per cent in 2020; the Balkan region plus Turkey amounted to 6.8 per cent in 2000 but would account for 11.7 per cent of Wider Europe GDP in 2020; and Ukraine moves from 1.9 per cent to 4.5 per cent. Hence the non EU-15 countries would together account for about 27 per cent of Wider Europe GDP in 2020 as compared to 16.3 per cent in 2000.

More important are the structural aspects of the integration processes which are likely to deepen further within Wider Europe and in relation to the neighbouring region (particularly MENA-20 and Russia). We have already pointed out that the much increased heterogeneity in wage and productivity levels in the Wider Europe region provides a scope to gain from an increased division of labour built upon exploiting comparative advantages, and from the increased scope for vertical differentiation, fragmentation and integration of production stages across the wider European economic space. This can enhance the internationalization of a wide range of European businesses (not only the very large enterprises). Additionally, the presence of fast-growing economies exerts strong pressure for productivity and quality upgrading in the advanced Western European countries, as maintaining their high income positions depends upon continuous and successful attempts to upgrade their skill and production structures and improve framework conditions. These pressures are already evident in the Western European economies, where they have been met with varying success (see Germany and France vs. Scandinavian economies discussed earlier).

The crucial issue is that painful structural adjustment processes are needed to reap the gains from regional and global integration and the emerging new division of labour. Particularly negatively affected are low- and medium-qualified jobs in advanced economies, not just in industry but also in some services (tourism, distribution, post and telecommunications, health and welfare services). The pressure on these jobs in so-called 'tradable' sectors has been apparent for a long time; more recently 'outsourcing' and fragmentation possibilities have expanded strongly in what used to be 'non-tradable' sectors due to improved logistics, communications and transportation technologies. There is also increased competitive jobs pressure within countries through increased migration flows. The nature of these pressures depends upon the skill structures of migrants, labour market institutions (such as minimum wage legislation, controls on illegal migrants, etc.) and migration policies designed to affect the supply structure of migrants and the dynamics of their positions on host countries' labour markets. The above processes of direct and indirect labour market integration within the Wider Europe's regionalist and global context will shape labour market developments in Western Europe to an increasing degree. An important question in this respect is whether the New European (Scandinavian) social model – discussed in section 5 – will remain viable and become more or less likely as an option also for the larger continental European economies.

8 The Wider Europe in its global context

Both the US and the EU have increasingly come under competitive pressure from a widening group of successful Asian economies. The emergence of China and India as major exporting nations has added to the impact of globalization upon the 'older' advanced economies (US, EU, Japan). There is a shift in world market shares towards the group of catching-up economies, first of all in goods trade (see Figure 3.8), but there is also the potential for an increased position of some of these economies in the services trade.[12]

Globalization has both a truly global and a 'regionalist' dimension. If one looks at trade flows, one can perceive a distinct orientation of a group of catching-up economies towards the advanced economies of their respective region: thus there is an overwhelming trade orientation of the Central and Eastern European countries

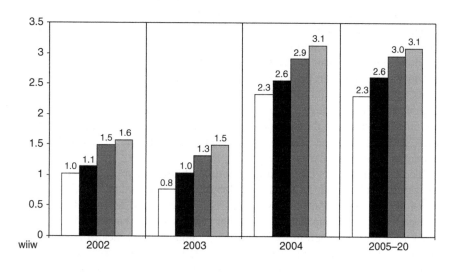

□ EU-15   ■ EU-25   ■ EU-25 + 4 CC + SEE-4   ▨ EU-25 + 4 CC + SEE-4 + UA

Figure 3.7 Growth of gross domestic product: EU-15, EU-25 and Wider Europe % annual change, 2005 and 2005–20 forecasts.

Note
Own calculations (wiiw and Ameco databases) and projections.

(and, previously, of the Southern cohesion countries) towards the EU-15, while they trade very little with, for example, the US. Mexico is singularly dependent upon trade with the US, and Japan has strong trade links with the economies of Southeast Asia and very little trade with the catching-up economies in the other regionalist blocs (on this see Figure 3.9). Hence there is a strong regional dependence between the set of catching-up economies and the large neighbouring 'Northern' economies. One relative exception is the Asian economies, which have made strong inroads into all the three Northern economies' markets (i.e. into the US, EU, and Japanese markets).

In this context, Wider Europe is somewhat special, as compared to North America (NAFTA) and South-Southeast Asia. Wider Europe shows a much stronger continuum of differentiation in behavioural and institutional developmental levels, and in productivity and wage levels, than does NAFTA, in that the gaps between the US and Canada, on the one hand, and Mexico, on the other hand, are vast. The other distinct, but related feature of the Wider Europe is that it occupies a mid-position between the US, which is a well-established federal state, and the Asian region, which is made up of a collection of nation states each following its own national development agenda. Europe is undergoing the (protracted) birth pangs of an evolving agenda of delegating and redistributing powers between the supra-national, national and regional levels. This can mean a considerable transitory disadvantage, as these developments mean that the allocation of powers to the different levels is in a state of flux. This can result in a major gap in the efficiency of governance structures for a considerable period of time relative to the maturely functioning structures of a large federal state such as the US. On the other hand, we cannot exclude the possibility that the types of supra-national and national state structures which might evolve from this phase of European economic and political integration might equip Europe with more appropriate (and effective) institutional structures for the twenty-first century.

As to Asia, it has developed successful structures for the (mostly) mercantilist strategy pursued at the national state level, but so far lacks institutions for conflict resolution and for proper regional economic integration. Institution-building at the supra-national level is so far practically non-existent.

9 Outlook on Europe's competitiveness

Priorities in Europe's development policies

Demographic factor and migration policy

Adjustments to the 'demographic traverse' (the strong jump in expected old age dependency ratios) is now a high priority in attempts to reform pension systems. But equally important would be to support labour market adjustments to increase employment rates of the older cohorts; to focus training and retraining institutions on this task; to adjust employment contracts, etc. Furthermore, there

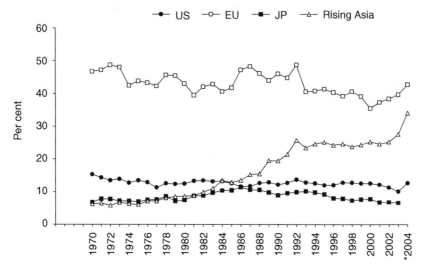

Figure 3.8a Shares in world merchandise exports (including Intra-EU).

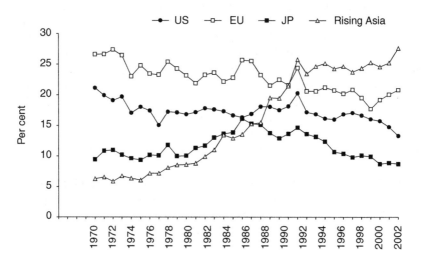

Figure 3.8b Shares in world merchandise exports (excluding Intra-EU) (source: UN Comtrade).

Note
Rising Asia comprises China, India, Hong Kong, Singapore, Taiwan, Korea, Philippines, Thailand, Malaysia, Indonesia.

has to be a major move on migration policy, both as regards selectivity at entry and with continued integration into the host societies. Migration can play a major role in improving mobility features of the European labour markets (see also Borjas, 2001) and in contributing to skill availability and entrepreneurship in a service and knowledge-based economy.

Further moves on market integration

The potential for market integration is still far from being fully exploited (see the earlier discussion in section 3). There are many residual entry barriers, especially in services, labour markets and financial markets. The issues have become more sensitive with the increase in the dispersion of developmental levels across the enlarged EU – as the recent crisis around the Commission's Services Directive has shown. This will require a parallel strategy of speeding up convergence processes, gradual harmonization, and further market integration in these sensitive areas.

European innovation system

This refers to efforts to increase corporate R&D spending, improve spill-over effects of public spending efforts on private R&D activity, develop complementarities of R&D policies at European, national and regional levels, encourage the further development of university–business links, develop research institutions and research networks of global excellence, develop venture capital finance and improve corporate legal governance frameworks, and openness to highly trained non-EU nationals. In all these areas there are substantial reforms across EU member states and gradual improvement in the EU's standing relative to the US. At the same time, new competitive pressures are emerging from the strong emphasis in many Asian economies on developing innovation capacities and a strong skills base.

Gradualist transformation of European social policies

These should become more targeted towards the most vulnerable groups; see also Levy (2006). However, a high degree of heterogeneity will likely be preserved reflecting country preferences (and levels of economic and social development). This heterogeneity also provides the basis for continued 'model competition' and the spread of better practice policies across Europe (see also Boeri, 2002). Distributive, employment and growth (and competitiveness) goals have to be looked at interdependently in reforming social policy frameworks.

Labour market (specifically educational and training) policies

This refers to policies targeted at low- and high-skill segments, and at different age segments and genders. The aim is to continue to increase participation rates with emphasis on those groups where these rates continue to remain very low by international comparison. Avoidance of a low-wage (working poor) segment through intensified efforts in educational and training upgrading is another desirable goal. This should specifically extend to immigrant groups to avoid sedimentation.

In addition, there is a host of other policies undergoing reform at the EU and national levels in the light of the debates over the Lisbon Agenda. These include regional policies, cross-European infrastructural policies, and remnants of industrial policy (see Sapir *et al.*, 2004).

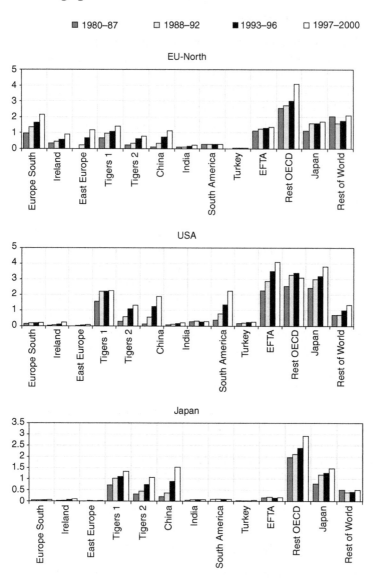

Figure 3.9 Import penetration ratios in total manufacturing.

Two possible scenarios

One can envisage both optimistic and pessimistic scenarios in Europe's development.

Continued slow growth scenario

Gaps in innovation systems persist; demographic developments take their toll, and migration and other policies are not courageously developed; asymmetry between centralized monetary policy and badly coordinated and badly designed (rule-based) fiscal policy persists; growth stimulus for the wider economic space does not materialize as economic and political crises intervene in the Balkans, the CIS and Turkey.

Catching-up scenario

Benefit from diffusion of latest generalized process technologies (GPTs) allows Europe to follow the improved productivity performance of the US; significant improvements of European innovation systems (at European, national and local levels), including university–business links, cross-European networks of excellence and development of top universities, venture capital institutions and changes in corporate governance structures – all of which should contribute to Europe positioning itself closer to the global technology and innovation frontier. This would also involve improvement and harmonization of EU immigration and intra-EU migration policies; reforms and targeting a new 'European social and labour market model' (see Aiginger, 2004a and b, and section 5 in this chapter).

The authors give a 50-50 chance to either of the two scenarios materializing.

10 Europe's limited global role

The EU will remain Europe-oriented in both the above outlined scenarios. The basic pre-occupation with deepening and widening will continue to occupy a large part of the European political agenda and available resources. In foreign relations, the EU's relations with its immediate neighbourhood (see section 8 above) will dominate; there will also be an interest in building a wider 'regionalist perspective' including the Middle East, North Africa and CIS.

There will continue to be an interest in maintaining an independent stance towards the US. There will be no complete convergence of US–European 'models'; this provides grounds for 'model competition' and also potentially an alternative option in countries/regions that develop an antagonistic or critical stance towards the US (and the 'US model').

Europe has to be seen as a regional entity (East/Southeast Asia is also increasingly developing into one) with distinct interests. It will want (or be pushed) to play an enhanced role on the global stage which will increasingly be shaped by the complex relationships among such regional entities (US and NAFTA; EU and Wider Europe; Russia and CIS; China, Japan and East Asia).

The main 'pull' of the European Union as a 'model' is the role it plays in countries that are politically and socially unstable and for which targeting an association with or accession to the European Union provides an anchor in institutional and political development (given the conditionality the EU imposes on association and accession). Such an anchor has been shown to have been of crucial importance in those transition economies which have now become members of the EU; it has already played this role (and will, hopefully, continue to play) in the Balkans, some CIS countries (Ukraine, Georgia), and Turkey. It is possible that the EU can play a similar role in the future in other CIS countries (Caucasus, Belarus, Moldavia, possibly Russia), the Middle East and North Africa. However, the resources the EU can devote to encourage such processes are negatively affected by the recent 'Enlargement fatigue', the limits of its budget, and concern about the EU's capacity to adjust its decision-making procedures to further widening without strengthening its internal functioning. Nonetheless, the EU's efforts in these neighbouring regions can constitute a significant complementarity to US foreign policy.

Given the current state of Europe's integration process, it seems clear that Europe and the US will play different roles on wider globalization issues: Europe will have a regional political and strategic agenda (i.e. within its 'neighbourhood') while limiting itself to looking at wider global issues (e.g. the rise of China) predominantly in economic relations terms. The US, on the other hand, is not handicapped by basic structural transformations in its decision-making mechanism. Hence it will act as a well-defined strategic actor on geo-political issues. Take the example of China's exchange rate policy: both the EU and the US are interested in appreciation of the Chinese currency, but the US has to consider a much wider range of geo-strategic and economic issues when pressuring China into an appreciation (the future of the Asian political and economic alignments, the impact upon the general long-run relationship between the various regional powers, the impact upon the international financial architecture, etc.), which is not much of an issue for the EU which does not intend to play a significant role in Asian political and strategic relations. The same applies to developments in sub-Saharan Africa and the rise of India.

11 Conclusions

This chapter has presented some of the problems related to the issue of Europe's longer-term competitiveness. It has discussed problems of its internal functioning, the picture of heterogeneity it presents, and the difficulties of its governance problems in its current historical juncture as a collection of highly interdependent nation states on a clear path towards harmonization and coordination of most of their policies but without strong (or efficient) institutional and budgetary features at the European level.

Europe will remain pre-occupied with deepening and widening issues for a long time to come. Enlargement – which will be an ongoing process over the next two decades – will exert overall a growth boost to the European Union, although cohesion and governance problems get compounded by it.

The 'regionalist perspective' of the Wider Europe construct will be of crucial importance for transatlantic relationships, insofar as the Wider Europe and its neighbourhood is also of crucial strategic interest to the US. Apart from this, the competition of a 'reformed European model' with the 'US–Anglo-Saxon model' will provide for continued – hopefully creative – tension.

Appendix

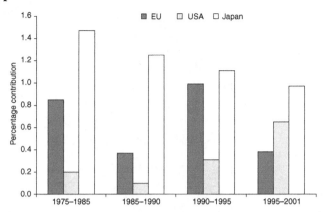

Figure 3A.1 Capital deepening (source: European Competitiveness Report 2001, Commission staff working document). Figures indicate the contribution of the growth of capital stock per employee to overall labour productivity growth.

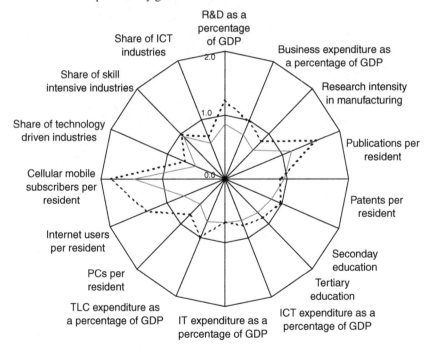

Figure 3A.2 Growth drivers Sweden, Finland and Denmark vs. USA (source: Aiginger and Landesmann (2002); see Appendix Table 3A.2 for more detailed descriptions and individual headings).

Note
Top 3: Sweden, Finland, Denmark. Each indicator outside the unit circle shows a superior performance of the top 3 European countries vs. the USA. Interrupted line: early 1990s; continuous line: late 1900s.

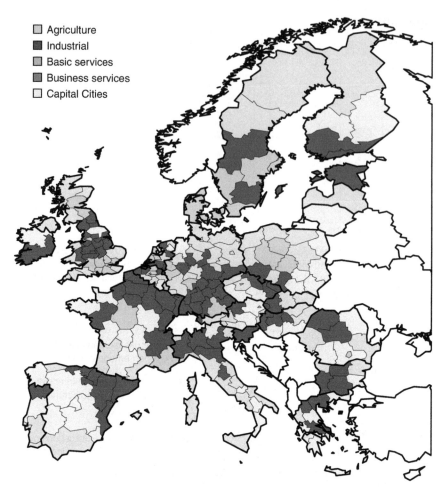

Figure 3A.3 Specialization of regions (NUTS 2 level) in the enlarged EU.

Note
Specialization of a region has been defined in terms of the largest deviation of the sectoral share of employment of a region relative to the national employment structure.

Legend:
- ☐ Agriculture
- ■ Industrial
- ▨ Basic services
- ▨ Business services
- ☐ Capital Cities

Table 3A.1 Differences in determinants of long-term growth (growth drivers): EU-15 vs. USA

	Position of EU to USA		
	EU/USA First year	EU/USA Last year	Absolute change
Indicators an R&D: input and output			
Total expenditure on R&D in % of GDP 1992/2001	0.693	0.733	0.040
Business Enterprise expenditure on R&D (BERD) in % of GDP 1992/98	0.606	0.564	−0.042
Research intensity in manufacturing 1990/98	0.652	0.623	−0.029
Publications per inhabitant 1992/99	0.646	0.878	0.232
Patents per resident 1990/97	0.617	0.554	−0.064
Indicators on education system: input and output			
Percentage of the population that has attained at least upper secondary education, by age group (1998)	0.609	0.795	0.186
Percentage of the population that has attained at least tertiary education, by age group (1998)	0.514	0.694	0.181
Indicators an ICT production and use			
ICT expenditure in % of GDP 1992/2000	0.654	0.731	0.077
Information technology (IT) expenditure in % of GDP 1992/2000	0.568	0.493	−0.075
Telecommunication (TLC) expenditure in % of GDP 1992/2000	0.749	1.135	0.385
PCs per inhabitant 1992/99	0.369	0.481	0.112
Internet users per inhabitant 1992/99	0.178	0.584	0.406
Cellular Mobile Subscribers per 100 capita 1992/99	0.356	1.271	0.914
Indicators on share of 'progressive' industries (see Section 5)			
Share of technology driven industries in nominal value added 1990/98	0.826	0.757	−0.069
Share of skill-intensive industries in nominal value added 1990/98	0.920	0.895	−0.025
Share of ICT industries in nominal value added 1990/98	0.723	0.475	−0.248

Notes

First (last) year means that year in the 1990s for which earliest (or latest) data are available (both are indicated after the name of the variable). For percentage with secondary and tertiary education the older (45–54) and the younger (25–34) age groups are compared.

Table 3.4.2 Large countries persistently behind, while top performers catch up with the USA

	Position of large countries EU to USA			Position of leading 3 EU to USA		
	First year	Last year	Absolute change	First year	Last year	Absolute change
Indicators on R&D: input and output						
Total expenditure on R&D in % of GDP 1992/2001	0.838	0.714	−0.124	0.861	1.231	0.370
Business Enterprise Expenditure on R&D (BERD) in % of GDP 1992/98	0.766	0.672	−0.094	0.753	0.967	0.215
Research intensity in manufacturing 1990/98	0.766	0.690	−0.075	0.636	0.834	0.198
Publications per inhabitant 1992/99	0.767	0.990	0.223	1.158	1.589	0.430
Patents per resident 1990/97	0.961	0.803	−0.159	0.953	0.888	−0.086
Indicators on education system: input and output						
Percentage of the population that has attained at least upper secondary education, by age group (1998)	0.759	0.856	0.097	0.816	0.970	0.154
Percentage of the population that has attained at least tertiary education, by age group (1998)	0.595	0.722	0.128	0.748	0.870	0.123
Indicators on ICT: production and use						
ICT expenditure in % of GDP 1992/2000	0.740	0.736	−0.004	0.703	0.796	0.093
Information technology (IT) expenditure in % of GDP 1992/2000	0.692	0.596	−0.097	0.681	0.680	−0.001
Telecommunication (TLC) expenditure in % of GDP 1992/2000	0.794	0.974	0.180	0.730	0.993	0.262
PCs per inhabitant 1992/99	0.445	0.529	0.084	0.556	0.790	0.234
Internet users per inhabitant 1992/99	0.169	0.585	0.416	0.712	1.363	0.651
Cellular Mobile Subscribers per 100 capita 1992/99	0.359	1.116	0.757	1.461	1.841	0.380
Indicators on share of 'progressive' industries (see Section 5)						
Share of technology driven industries in nominal value added 1990/98	0.945	0.859	−0.086	0.561	0.696	0.135
Share of skill-intensive industries in nominal value added 1990/98	0.978	0.933	−0.045	0.980	0.976	−0.003
Share of ICT industries in nominal value added 1990/98	0.819	0.535	−0.284	0.628	0.715	0.087

Notes

First (last) year means that year in the 1990s for which earliest (or latest) data are available (both are indicated after the name of the variable). For percentage with secondary and tertiary education the older (45–54) and the younger (25–34) age groups are compared. Large European countries: Germany, France, United Kingdom. Leading European countries: Sweden, Finland, Denmark.

Notes

1 Unless otherwise stated we shall refer to 'Europe' as Western Europe including the European Union members prior to May 2004 (i.e. the EU-15) as well as the other countries of Western Europe such as Switzerland, Norway, Iceland and Liechtenstein. The 'Wider Europe' includes the previous group plus the countries which joined the EU after May 2004 as well as current and future candidate countries of the EU. The concept of Wider Europe will be discussed in the later sections of this chapter.

2 If we take the year 2003, the EU per capita income level was 71 per cent of the US level. Productivity (in terms of output per hour worked) accounted for just 8 percentage points of this 29 percentage point difference. Of the remaining 21 percentage point gap, roughly 75 per cent was associated with fewer working hours (per person employed). The other 25 per cent came from lower participation rates, i.e. lower employment relative to the total population, and involved differences in such things as retirement ages (earlier in Europe) and unemployment rates (higher in Europe). It is interesting to see the changes in the components which make up the gap in per capita income between the EU and the US: in 1990 the gap in income per capita between the EU and the US amounted to 27 percentage points: lower productivity accounted for 10 points, fewer hours worked for 8 points and lower participation rates for 9 points. In 2003 the gap amounted to 29 percentage points: of these 8 points were accounted for by productivity, 15 points by hours worked and 7 points by the difference in participation rates. (The information in this note is extracted from R.H. McGuckin and B. van Ark: *Performance 2004: Productivity, Employment and Income in the World's Economies*, The Conference Board, New York, 2004).

3 Thus the difference in employment rates in 2002 between the US and the EU for men in the age group 15–64 was 5.1 percentage points, for women 10.7 points; for men in the age group 25–54 there was no difference between the US and the EU (for women 5.0), while for the age groups 15–24 the difference was 13.4 for men and 17.1 for women and for the age group 55–64, 15.8 points for men and 22.2 for women. Source: OECD, Employment Outlook, 2003, Tables B, C, D; see also Freeman and Schettkat (2005).

4 A contributory factor to the slow accrual of a growth dividend from the Single Market programme is the resistance put up by large incumbent (and state-backed) firms especially in some of the large continental European economies (France, Italy, Germany) to implement fully the non-discrimination obligations of the Single Market. Such companies were used to a strong domestic market position and preferential treatment by national and local governments and thus had much to lose from a full implementation of the Single Market programme. The defensive strategies often pursued by these companies (e.g. Italian and French car manufacturers) prevented a forward-looking restructuring strategy to exploit the potential of a liberalized EU-wide market. This might explain the difference to the more successful adjustment of large companies in smaller EU economies (such as in Sweden, Finland, Denmark, the Netherlands) which were – given the relatively smaller size of the domestic market – already highly export-market oriented even before the implementation of the Single Market rules. Nonetheless, the scenario for the privileged companies of the large continental economies seems to be changing (see Pisani-Ferry, 2006).

5 See also Pichelmann and Roeger (2006).

6 Ranking the countries according to the indicators in Table 3.4 reveals Ireland as the top-performing country, followed by Sweden, Denmark and Finland. While Ireland is a remarkable story of catching up and finally forging ahead (in a subset of indicators, not in income per head or wages per worker), we consider the other three as important examples of how mature and rich countries can continue to grow and call them 'top 3 European countries'.

7 For earlier suggestions along this line see Aiginger (2002), Aiginger and Landesmann (2002) and Aiginger (2004a); see also Levy (2006) and in this volume. The basic

unresolved issue here is whether the large continental European countries (France, Germany, Italy) can be reformed along the experiences of the Scandinavian countries or whether the experiences cannot be easily replicated in larger, more heterogeneous states. Furthermore there is a question of whether the 'Northern model' is itself sustainable in the context of further pressures of globalization (see, for example, the recent widespread discussion on out-sourcing).

8 ACS refers to accession and candidate countries including Bulgaria and Romania which have joined the European Union in 2007 and Croatia and Turkey which have the status of candidate countries. SEE refers to the other countries of Southeast Europe (Albania, Serbia, Montenegro, Bosnia-Herzegovina, Macedonia).

9 While some of the policies which made Ireland very attractive to foreign investors are emulated, such as low corporate tax rates, other elements – such as a very strong public effort towards training and the development of excellent educational institutions as well as elements of an active industrial policy – are less noticed and, given the fiscal constraints in the NMS, feature less in their policy strategies.

10 The following are some figures on the demographics of the Wider Europe and its neighbours: Western and Central Europe's (i.e. EU-25 plus EEA plus Switzerland) total population size will remain roughly stable over the next 20 years (2003: 467 million; 2025: 466 million). In the Rest of Eastern Europe plus Turkey and Central Asia the population will also remain stable over the next 25 years (2000: 405 million; 2025: 407 million); there is a mix here with positive population growth in Azerbaijan, Turkey and most parts of Central Asia and considerable demographic decline in Russia, most Balkan countries and Ukraine. In Europe's southern and southeastern neighbours (the Middle East, North Africa, and the Gulf states, i.e. MENA-20) the population will grow steadily from 316 million in 2000 to 492 million in 2025 (i.e. a 56 per cent rise) and to 638 million by 2050 (+73 per cent). Together with these differences in overall population growth there are major differences in the shares of people of working age and those older than 65 in the various regions, e.g. in the absence of massive recruitment of economically active migrants, the number of people between 15 and 64 will decrease in the Western and Central European region from 312 million in 2000 to 295 million in 2025 (−5.5 per cent) to 251 million in 2050 (−20 per cent), while the number of people older than 65 will increase from 73 million in 2000 to 104 million by 2025 (+42.5 per cent) and then to 125 million in 2050 (+71 per cent). In contrast, the number of people between the ages of 15 and 64 in the MENA-20 region will increase from 187 million in 2000 to 323 million in 2025 (+73 per cent) and to 417 million by 2050 (+123 per cent). The demographic complementarity between the Western and Central European region and the MENA-20 region should be obvious from this. All the above information is extracted from Holzmann and Muenz (2004), pp. 15–16.

11 Detailed assumptions behind these projections can be obtained from the authors.

12 One reason for a catching-up of some economies in business services is the pressure which Chinese dominance in manufacturing production imposes upon other Asian economies and which makes a specialization on business and financial services attractive to these economies within the context of increasing intra-Asian trade flows. This comes on top of the opportunities which global outsourcing of services represents for countries like India.

References

Adema, W. (2001) 'Net Social Expenditure, 2nd Edition', Labour Market and Social Affairs Occasional Paper, No. 52, OECD, Paris.

Aiginger, K. (2002) 'Growth Difference between Europe and the US in the Nineties: Causes and Likelihood of Persistence', European Forum Working Paper 1/2002, Stanford University, 15 November.

Aiginger, K. (2004a) 'Economic Agenda of the 21st Century', *Review of International Economics* 12(2): 187–206.

Aiginger, K. (2004b) 'The three tier strategy followed by successful European countries in the 1990s', *International Review of Applied Economics* 18(4): 399–422.

Aiginger, K. and Landesmann, M. (2002) 'Competitive Economic Performance: USA vs EU', Research Report 291. Vienna: The Vienna Institute for International Economic Studies (wiiw).

Alesina, A., Glaeser, E. and Sacerdote, B. (2001) 'Why Doesn't the US Have a European-Style Welfare State?', NBER Working Paper, No. 8524.

Astrov, W. and Havlik, P. (2004) 'European Union, Russia and Ukraine: Creating New Neighbourhoods', Research Report 305. Vienna: The Vienna Institute for International Economic Studies (wiiw).

Bassanini, A., Scarpetta, S. and Hemmings, P. (2001) 'Economic Growth: The Role of Policies and Institutions. Panel Data Evidence from OECD Countries', Economics Department Working Paper, No. 283, OECD, Paris.

Bassanini, A., Scarpetta, St. and Visco, I. (2000) 'Knowledge, Technology and Economic Growth: Recent Evidence from OECD Countries', Economics Department Working Papers, No. 259, OECD, Paris.

Boeri, T. (2002) *Social Policy: One for all?*, Bocconi University and Fondazione Rodolfo Debenedetti.

Boeri, T. (2007) 'Convergence via Two-Tier Reforms and Growthless Job Creation in Europe' (Chapter 5, this volume).

Borjas, G. (2001) 'Does Immigration Grease the Wheels of the Labor Market?', *Brookings Papers on Economic Activity* 2001(1): 69–133.

Denis, C., McMorrow, K. and Roeger, W. (2004) 'An Analysis of EU and US Productivity Developments (a Total Economy and Industry Level Perspective)', European Commission, DG Economic and Financial Affairs; Economic Papers 208; Brussels.

Deutsche Bank Research (2006) 'Measures of Well-being', *Current Issues*, September, Frankfurt.

Emerson, M., Aujean, M., Catinat, M., Goybet, Ph. and Jacquemin, A. (1988) *The Economics of 1992*. Oxford: Oxford University Press.

European Commission (1998, 1999, 2000) *The Competitiveness of European Manufacturing*, Brussels: EU Commission.

European Commission (2000) 'Innovation in a Knowledge Driven Economy', Annex, European Innovation Scoreboard, Brussels.

Freeman, R.B. and Schettkat, R. (2005) 'Marketization of Household Production and the EU-US gap in work', *Economic Policy*, January, pp. 7–50.

Gordon, R.J. (2002) 'Two Centuries of Economic Growth: Europe Chasing the American Frontier', Paper prepared for the Economic History Workshop, Northwestern University, October 2002.

Gordon, R.J. (2004) 'Why was Europe Left at the Station when America's Productivity Locomotive Departed?', National Bureau of Economic Research, No. 10661; Cambridge, Mass.

Gordon, R.J. (2007) 'Comparing Welfare in Europe and the United States' (Chapter 1, this volume).

Holzmann, R. and Muenz, R. (2004) *Challenges and Opportunities of International Migration for the EU, Its Member States, Neighboring Countries and Regions: A Policy Note*, Institute for Futures Studies, Stockholm.

Jorgenson, D.W. and Stiroh, K.J. (2000a) 'Raising the Speed Limit: US Economic

Growth in the Information Age', Economics Department Working Papers No. 261, OECD, Paris (ECO/WKP 2000–2034).

Jorgenson, D.W. and Stiroh, K.J. (2000b) 'US Economic Growth in the Information Age, Brooking Papers on Economic Activity', 1, pp. 125–211.

Landesmann, M. (2000) 'Structural Change in the Transition Economies, 1989–1999', in: *United Nations – Economic Commission for Europe: Economic Survey of Europe*, 2000, No. 2/3, pp. 95–117, Geneva.

Landesmann, M. (2003) *wiiw Structural Report – 2003*, The Vienna Institute for International Economic Studies (wiiw), Vienna.

Landesmann, M. and Roemisch, R. (2005) 'Regional developments in the New Members and Candidate Countries of the European Union', in J. Eriksson, B.O. Karlsson and D. Tarschys (eds) *Adapting EU Cohesion Policy to the Needs of New Member States*, SIEPS Report, Stockholm.

Landesmann, M. and Stehrer, R. (2002) 'Evolving Competitiveness of CEECs in an Enlarged Europe', *Rivista di Politica Economia*, 2002, 92/1, pp. 23–87.

Levy, J. (2007) 'Between Neo-Liberalism and No Liberalism: Progressive Approaches to Economic Liberalization in Western Europe' (Chapter 12, this volume).

McGuckin, R.H. and van Ark, B. (2005) *Performance 2005: Productivity, Employment and Income in the World's Economies*, The Conference Board, May 2005.

McMorrow, K. and Roeger, W. (2001) 'Potential Output: Measurement Methods, "New" Economy Influences and Scenarios for 2001–2010, A Comparison of the EU15 and the US', European Commission, Economic Papers No. 150.

Münz, R. (2007) 'Migration, Labour Markets, and Integration of Migrants: An Overview for Europe with a Comparison to the US' (Chapter 7, this volume).

Nicoletti, G. and Scarpetta, S. (2003) 'Regulation, Productivity and Growth: OECD Evidence', OECD Working Paper 2003/1, Paris.

Nordhaus, W.D. (2001) 'Productivity Growth and the New Economy', Working Paper W8096, NBER, Cambridge, Mass.

OECD (2001a) *The Impact of Information and Communication Technologies on Output Growth: Issues and Preliminary Findings*, Paris.

OECD (2001b) *The New Economy: Beyond the Hype, Final Report on the OECD Growth Project*, Paris.

Oliner, S.D. and Sichel, D.E. (2000) 'The Resurgence of Growth in the Late 1990s: Is Information Technology the Story?', *Journal of Economic Perspectives*, 14(4), pp. 3–22.

O'Mahony, M. and van Ark, B. (2003) *EU productivity and competitiveness: an industry perspective*, European Commission, Enterprise publications, Brussels.

Peri, G. (2007) 'International Migrations: Some Comparisons and Lessons for the European Union' (Chapter 8, this volume).

Pichelmann, K. and Roeger, W. (2007) 'Employment and Labour Productivity in the EU: Reconsidering a Potential Trade-off in the Lisbon Strategy' (Chapter 6, this volume).

Pisani-Ferry, J. (2006) 'Financial Integration and European Priorities', Third Conference of the Monetary Stability Foundation, Frankfurt am Main, 6–7 July.

Richter, S. (2005) 'Scenarios for the Financial Redistribution across Member States in the European Union in 2007–2013', *wiiw Research Reports*, No. 317, The Vienna Institute for International Economic Studies (wiiw), Vienna, April.

Sapir, A. and Pisani-Ferry, J. (2006) *Last Exit to Lisbon*, Breughel Policy Brief, March, Brussels.

Sapir, A., Aghion, Ph. and Bertola, G. (2004) *An Agenda for a Growing Europe – The Sapir Report*. Oxford: Oxford University Press.

Sinn, H.W. (2005) 'Basar-Oekonomie Deutschland; Exportweltmeister oder Schlus-slicht?', *IFO Schnelldienst* 58(6), pp. 3–42.

Veenhoven, R. (1997) 'Advances in Understanding Happiness', *Revue Quebecoise de Psychologie*, 18, pp. 29–74.

Wykoff, A. (2000) *Differences in Economic Growth across the OECD in the 1999s: The Role of Innovation and Information Technologies*, DSTI/STP/ICCP.

Wyplosz, C. (2006) 'European Monetary Union: the dark sides of a major success', *Economic Policy*, 46, April, pp. 207–261.

4   How well do the clothes fit?

Priors and evidence in the debate over
flexibility and labour market
performance

Richard B. Freeman

All the people standing by and at the windows cheered and cried, 'Oh, how
splendid are the Emperor's new clothes. What a magnificent train! **How well the
clothes fit!**'.... But among the crowds a little child suddenly gasped out, 'But he
hasn't got anything on'.

(Hans Christian Andersen, *The Emperor's New Clothes*[1])

1 Introduction

Many economists and policy-makers believe that institutions and policies
designed to protect workers have distorted labour markets in ways that impede
full employment. International agencies, such as the OECD in its 1994 Jobs
Study and the IMF in its 2003 analysis, proclaim that the road to full employment in advanced Europe requires reforms of those institutions and policies. But
there is considerable disagreement over the evidentiary base on which this recommendation rests. Baker *et al.* (2004) and Baccaro and Rei (2005) have found
that models which purportedly show that institutions adversely affect unemployment are non-robust to specification, measurement, and additional years of data.
Blanchard and Wolfers (2000) and Ljungquist and Sargent (2004) argue that the
only way to explain the increased rate of unemployment in Europe compared to
the US is through the interaction of institutions and economic shocks. For its
part, the OECD recognizes that the evidence is more equivocal than it first
claimed.[2] At the same time, Bassanini and Duval (2006; also chapter 7 of
OECD, 2006) estimate that changes in tax and labour policies explain about half
of the 1982–2003 changes in unemployment among countries along lines of
earlier OECD pronouncements.

Why have economists failed to reach consensus on the effects of labour institutions on labour outcomes? What research programme might best illuminate the
issues in the debate over institutions and outcomes?

This chapter seeks to explain the disagreement in terms of the weak cross-
country aggregate data on which analysts focus and the lack of any clear alternative to the distortionist view of institutions/policies. The weak data allows

analysts with strong priors that institutions cause labour market problems to maintain their beliefs and analysts who believe the opposite to maintain their views. In addition, the lack of a clear alternative to the orthodox view produces a one horse race instead of robust competition between hypotheses. Models in which institutions, policies, and economic shocks interact make even greater demands on the data, which risks propagating disagreements endlessly.

I argue that researchers need information from sources beyond cross-country time series data to escape this cul-de-sac: micro studies of individual responses to policies and institutional arrangements, experimental investigations of posited interactions, and simulations of institutions operating in different environments; and that a Coase theorem/efficient bargaining hypothesis that labour institutions and policies affect the distribution of employment and earnings more than they affect aggregate outcomes provides an alternative interpretation of empirical findings.

2 The debate: 'Resolved, labour policies/institutions are the prime cause of unemployment'

The 1994 Jobs Study of the OECD (OECD, 1994a, 1994b) brought the claim that labour institutions were the primary cause of unemployment in advanced countries to the centre of policy debate. The Jobs Study listed ten recommendations to reduce unemployment and improve economic performance. Five were boilerplate platitudes: good macro-economic policy; enhanced technological knowledge; elimination of impediments to creation of enterprises; improved education and training; enhanced product market competition. Four recommendations called for labour market deregulation: increased flexibility of working time; making wage and labour costs more flexible by removing restrictions; reforming employment security provisions; and reforming unemployment and related benefit systems. The last recommendation endorsed active labour market policies – training programmes, job-finding assistance to workers, subsidies to employers to hire long-term unemployed or disabled workers, and special programmes for youths leaving school.[3] Most analysts and policy-makers interpreted the Jobs Study as blaming the economic problems of advanced Europe on inflexible regulated labour markets.

The OECD Jobs Study was accompanied by two volumes of supporting research and followed by numerous studies and reviews of studies, many given in the OECD's annual Employment Outlook. Layard *et al.* (1994) and Nickell (1997) with various co-authors and diverse other economists have also estimated the effect of institutions on outcomes. In the January 2005 *Economic Journal*, Nickell *et al.* summarized this work with the claim that 'the broad movements in unemployment in the OECD can be explained by shifts in labour market institutions' (p. 1).

As OECD economists have examined the evidence more carefully, however, the OECD has moderated its initially strong claims. The 2004 OECD Employment Outlook admitted that 'the evidence of the role played by EPL (employment protection legislation) on aggregate employment and unemployment rates remains mixed' (p. 81); and expressed concern that the temporary contracts that replaced permanent jobs in some countries (such as Spain) produced labour market duality between those with permanent contracts and those with temporary contracts and job insecurity that were themselves a problem. The Outlook argued for 'the *plausibility* (my italics) of the Jobs Strategy diagnosis that excessively high aggregate wages and/or wage compression have been impediments' to jobs, while admitting that 'this evidence is somewhat fragile'. With respect to unionism, it accepted that the effect of collective bargaining 'appears to be contingent upon other institutional and policy factors that need to be clarified to provide robust policy advice' (p. 165). Chapter 6 of the 2006 Outlook stressed that the institutions of low unemployment European countries differ greatly from those in the US and UK (Table 6.3). This is a significant admission because once one allows that there is no single way to attain full employment, it is difficult to argue for a 'peak' form of capitalism to which each country should strive[4] by adopting the same policies and institutions.

Still, many economists hold to the claim that institutions/policies are the reason for European unemployment. In 2003, the IMF published an article in its World Economic Outlook that predicted that unemployment in Europe would fall massively below US levels if European countries deregulated their labour market and product markets:

> labour reforms could produce output gains of about 5 per cent and a fall in the unemployment rate of about 3 percentage points ... those benefits could be **doubled** by simultaneous efforts to increase competition in the product market.[5]
>
> [...]
>
> high unemployment is largely structural in nature – and thereby potentially affected by institutions – rather than cyclical (and therefore determined by the business cycle and macroeconomic policies). (Enact the reforms and) ... **unemployment could fall by about 6.5** percentage points.[6]

Using the newest OECD measures of institutions/policies and testing carefully for the robustness of results, Bassanini and Duval (2006), have found that 'changes in policies and institutions between 1982 and 2000 are estimated to explain 47 per cent of the cross country variance of observed unemployment changes' (p. 13). Consistent with many other studies, they reject the once prevalent claim that employment protection laws affect aggregate unemployment and find that changes in tax wedges – the gap between what employers pay to workers and take-home pay – are important in changing unemployment, while the generosity of unemployment benefits also contributes to the observed pattern. Mirroring some earlier studies, they also find that some forms of centralized or coordinated bargaining and active labour market programmes reduce unemployment.

3 The rebuttal: labour policies/institutions are a minor element in joblessness

Critics of the claim that pro-worker institutions and policies have caused Europe's unemployment problems argue that: (1) the cross-country data do not support the claims; (2) micro-economic data show responses to unemployment benefits and related programmes that suggest only modest effects of institutions/policies on aggregate unemployment; (3) the programmes have income insurance and distributional benefits that outweigh their effects on joblessness.

Most critical analyses focus on the cross-country time series data on which OECD analyses are based. One line of criticism is that the measures of dependent and independent variables in these studies are flawed. The key variable, unemployment, has been measured differently across counties and over time. Blanchflower and Freeman (1993) documented the many changes in definition of unemployment in the UK over time, which meant that unemployment was lower towards the end of the Thatcher period than at the outset simply because the government changed definitions. Swedish economists note that the low unemployment rate in Sweden understates true joblessness because so many jobless persons are on labour market programmes and long-term sickness leave. With respect to the explanatory variables, Atkinson and Micklewright (1991) have criticized the measures of unemployment benefits, which categorized countries with drastically different benefits systems similarly. Martin (1996) noted some of the problems in measuring the replacement rates in an international comparison. Howell *et al.* (2006) document some of the issues in measuring policy variables and the way OECD has worked to improve the variables, from crude estimates of employment protection legislation every few years to annual estimates that pinpoint changes in the laws, and from gross replacement measures of the incentives facing workers to remain on unemployment benefits as opposed to finding work quickly. In 2006 the OECD will have a long time series of net replacement rates that Howell *et al.* (2006) believe will weaken the estimated effects of unemployment benefits on unemployment.

Another line of criticism has focused on the tendency for analysts to stress evidence favourable to the view that institutions cause joblessness while downplaying evidence that runs counter to the hypothesis. Blanchflower (2001) notes 'only a weak positive relation in the OECD between unemployment and benefits' (p. 390) and '*no* support (from a 1999 OECD report) ... for the belief that unions, benefits, the tax wedge, ALMP spending or earnings dispersion influence unemployment ... contrary to the claims made in Layard et al., which appear to be based on mis-specified cross-country unemployment regressions' (p. 392). Taking a sharper line, Blanchard and Wolfers (2000) suggest that one reason is a form of regression-mongering, in which the models used to make the case against institutions 'are in part the result of economic Darwinism ... measures ... constructed ex post facto by researchers who were not unaware of unemployment developments' (p. 18). As an example of this form of analysis,

Blanchflower notes that some models include country dummy variables that effectively remove observations that fail to fit the orthodox model.

The third and arguably most important line of criticism is that the time series models that find that the institutions adversely affect aggregate outcomes are not robust. In a volume devoted to debunking the Jobs Study claims, Baker *et al.* (2005) document this point in great detail. They show that estimated coefficients on labour institutions disappear or become statistically insignificant when researchers make modest changes in the measures of institutions, countries covered, and time period. Models that cover more years, countries, and measures than earlier studies 'provide little support for those who advocate comprehensive deregulation of OECD labour markets' (p. 106). They conclude that there is a 'yawning gap between the confidence with which the case for labour market deregulation has been asserted and the evidence that the regulating institutions are the culprits' (p. 198). In a similar vein, Baccaro and Rei (2005) found that 'changes in real interest rates and in an index of central bank independence are positively associated with changes in unemployment. All other institutional variables are instead generally insignificant or negatively signed, except the unionization rate.' They concluded that there seems to be no generalized unemployment-increasing effect of institutions in OECD countries in the period under consideration (1960–98). Restrictive macroeconomic policies appear to play a more important role (p. 1).

Critics of the labour institution/policy hypothesis also note that microeconomic studies of government programmes rarely obtain the large responses required for the programmes to have a major impact on joblessness. Studies that relate exit rates from unemployment to the characteristics of unemployment insurance programmes usually find that job-finding rates rise sharply when the unemployed exhaust benefits. But the coefficients on duration are rarely large enough to explain the huge cross-country differences in unemployment. It is possible that the larger effects found in some cross-section time series studies are the 'true' ones, but Holmlund has pointed out that the estimates from the time series suffer from a major flaw that is likely to bias upward their estimates of the impact of unemployment benefits on unemployment. The studies do not take account of the endogeneity of unemployment benefits on the level of unemployment. In the US, benefits typically last 26 weeks but additional weeks of benefits are often available during times of high unemployment. Analyses of the US that regressed unemployment on increased duration of benefits would get the causal relation wrong: the rate of unemployment induces the change in policy, not the reverse. In other countries the policy responses may be different – Sweden reduced its replacement rate when the fiscal expense of high unemployment created a budget crisis – and at this writing intends to reduce the rate in a period of low unemployment. But the criticism remains. We do not know if positive associations between unemployment insurance (UI) and unemployment reflect 'the rise in unemployment driven by more generous UI system? … or (if) the rise in unemployment increased the political pressure to make UI more generous?' (p. 128).

The third objection to the claim that weakening labour institutions/policies will resolve joblessness problems is that those policies provide desirable benefits to recipients that outweigh any adverse effects on their job-finding behaviour. The purpose of unemployment benefit programmes, after all, is not to elongate spells of joblessness – that is an unintended and undesirable side effect – but to provide income support (insurance) to workers who lose their job. Moreover, evidence that more generous UI benefits increase the time the unemployed are on the dole does not give good insight into what happens to people when they exit the benefit system. In the UK, tightening the unemployment benefit system reduced numbers on the dole, many of whom disappeared from official records rather than necessarily finding jobs in the legitimate economy.

Similarly, institutional wage determination that raises pay at the bottom of the earnings distribution is designed to raise earnings, not reduce employment. Whether the benefits of these programmes in fact exceed their costs requires analyses of both sides of the equation. Neither those favourable to these interventions nor those opposed have provided the benefit calculations needed for rational policy decisions (Blank and Freeman, 1994).

4 Interactions and configurations

The basic fact about unemployment rates among OECD countries is that unemployment rose in Europe from below to above US rates, while the institutional differences between US and European styles of capitalism remained largely intact. To attribute changes in unemployment between the two systems to institutions requires that some other factors change as well – the economic environment/shocks. This line of thinking has led to analyses of the interaction between the environment/shocks and institutions/policies and directed attention at potential interactions among institutions or policies themselves.

While appealing, analyses of interactions make great demands on limited data and risk creating the social science equivalent of epicycles to account for observed patterns across countries. The problem is that there is a large number of possible *configurations* of institutions and economic shocks relative to the number of cross-country observations on which to assess their impact on outcomes.[7] By configurations I mean combinations of institutional arrangements, such as collective bargaining coverage, centralization of wage setting, employment protection laws, government regulation of wages, affirmative action policies, etc. Consider the problem of analysing four institutions, all coded as 0/1 so that a country has or does not have a given institution, and with institutions measured so that having one implies less reliance on decentralized markets. An experimental design to assess the impact of institutions would require analysis of 32 ($= 2^4$) logically possible configurations.[8]

The social world does not provide the evidence needed to assess these possibilities. Invariably there are no observations for some configurations, either because they are impossible to fit together or because of historical circumstance. There will also be some combinations for which the observation is a single country, which makes it indistinguishable from anything else unique about that country. With only 30 or so advanced countries, highly correlated outcomes, and infrequent changes in institutions, the number of configurations can easily exceed the number of independent data points.

To deal with the problem of excessive configurations, analysts of labour institutions have aggregated arrangements into simpler categories: 'neo-corporatist' economies vs. 'liberal' economies, and so on. But there is no uniform agreement about these groupings. For example, Japan combines company level unionism and profits-related bonuses with a strong employer federation, the Shunto offensive, and a sense of national unity. Is this neo-corporatist or liberal, or does Japan merit its own categorization? As long as countries have many institutions that differ in many ways, researchers risk forming classifications or groupings that support their priors rather than test those views.

Another difficulty in analysing how institutions affect outcomes is that institutions change over time as their members and leaders learn from experience. Unions, government regulators, and employer federations do not respond in the same way to the same stimuli regardless of past events any more than does any other economic agent. As cases in point, consider the way the British and German unions behaved in the 1970s compared to the way they acted in the 1990s. In the 1970s, the British unions were troglodytes, opposed to seemingly rational economic thought and responsibility towards the UK economy. German unions were widely praised as responsible economic agents. In the 1990s the British unions were the modernizers, with the TUC endorsing 'value added' unionism on the notion that only if unions could add value to the performance of firms would they be able to improve the well-being of workers. By contrast, the German unions seemed incapable of adjusting to the economic realities of post-unification Germany and globalization. Recognizing that unions learn from the past, one would not want to assume that unions would respond to some future inflationary shock as they did to the 1970s inflation.

Since interactions among institutions and between institutions and the economic environment are almost certainly part of economic reality, it is important to deal with these issues up front in the debate over labour institutions. But the time series cross-country data can provide only limited insight into them.

5 The debate continues: the effect of priors

The IMF's 2003 study provides the best example of how priors have affected analysis. This study produced extreme claims about the virtues of favoured policies and apparent blindness to evidence against the claims.[9] As noted earlier, the IMF concluded that labour market 'reforms' would reduce EU unemployment from 8.0 per cent to 5.0 per cent and raise GDP by 5 per cent, and that labour and product market reforms together would reduce EU unemployment by 6.5 points to 1.5 per cent! These are extraordinary claims. In 2003 many advanced European countries had unemployment rates below 6.5 per cent – Austria, Denmark, Eire, Netherlands, Luxembourg, Portugal, Sweden, Norway, and the United Kingdom, so the 6.5 point drop would put them into negative unemployment terrain. Since this cannot occur, rates would have to fall by more than 6.5 points in other countries. Moreover, the nominally flexible US did not have anything close to the predicted 1.5 per cent rate of unemployment. In 2003 the US unemployment rate was 6.0 per cent. That the EU would have one-fourth the unemployment rate that the US had if the EU had flexible US institutions seemed prima facie nonsense. If the US couldn't attain 1.5 per cent unemployment with these institutions or even the 5.0 per cent unemployment rate predicted for European countries if they adopted US style labour practices, why should European countries do so well?

The excessive claim does not come from erroneous empirical work. The analysis in the article shows nothing like these effects. This analysis estimates a vector of 'Institution-Adjusted Unemployment Rates' for OECD countries – unemployment rates minus the estimated impact of institutions on unemployment – which closely track actual changes in unemployment rates. The article informs the reader that this means that *'Institutions ... hardly account for the growing trend observed in most European countries and the dramatic fall in U.S. unemployment in the 1990s'* (my italics).[10] As a case in point, Germany had broadly unchanged institutions while unemployment rose by about 6 percentage points. No change in institutions and higher unemployment – just the sort of conclusion one might have expected from one of the critics of the IMF position. But, despite this finding, the article concluded that weakening institutions would reduce unemployment to 1.5 per cent. It reached this conclusion by focusing on cross section regressions that showed that institutions '... alone explain a good deal of the cross-country differences in unemployment rates'. In the context of US–EU differences, this is a nearly circular argument: the US has different institutions and lower unemployment than Europe, so those institutions must explain the difference in unemployment.

Bassanini and Duval (2006) offer more compelling evidence on the potential adverse impact of institutions and policies on unemployment and employment. They relate *changes* in outcomes to *changes* in institutions and policies among OECD countries and undertake robustness checks on findings and examine the effects of variables not only on unemployment rates but also on the employment of specific groups. This allows for more subtle analyses of particular policies. For instance, since unemployment insurance programmes rarely cover youths, measures of the generosity of UI should have no effect on youth employment/unemployment. If regressions show such an effect, it is likely that something is wrong with the model. Similarly, other policies/institutions – such as early retirement systems, childcare facilities – that affect some groups and not others also provide internal tests of causal relations: if spending on childcare affects behaviour of people without children, it is likely that the variable is standing in for something else. Differencing variables between groups likely to be affected by a policy/institution and those unlikely to be affected provides a stronger test of the impact of policies/institutions than standard time series cross-country analyses.

In fact, Bassanini and Duval find that the benefit replacements rate reduces youth employment by more than it reduces the employment of prime age males! (table 2.3 baseline equation vs. table 2.1 baseline equation.) They note that this is 'rather surprising' (p. 47) but then argue that it could reflect indirect effects. The most plausible indirect effect, however, is that it reduces the job search of prime age workers, which should increase the probability that youths find jobs, deepening the puzzle. Similarly, they find that 'minimum wage hikes significantly increase youth employment rates' (p. 47), which is hard to believe, and spend some effort in undermining the plausibility of this result so that no one draws a strong policy conclusion from this. But they put no such effort into searching for factors that might undermine results favourable to the hypothesis that institutions/policies have caused unemployment. My guess is that endogeneity of minimum wage policy explains their positive result – as governments raise the minimum in good times. This raises the question of whether many of the other statistical findings also reflect simultaneous determination of outcomes and policies. Critics of the hypothesis that institutions and policies cause unemployment have sought weaknesses in the Bassanini and Duval analysis (Howell *et al.*, 2006).

6 Where is the alternative hypothesis?

A strong claim and rebuttal suffice for debate tournaments and court trials, not for analyses of the impact of labour institutions and aggregate economic outcomes. If labour institutions and policies are not the root cause of Europe's poor employment performance, what is? If labour institutions/policies have minimal impact on aggregate outcomes, what do they do that generates controversy about them?

On the issue of causes, there are three competing hypotheses. One is that it is the change in the economic environment/shocks and interaction of institutions and economic shocks described earlier. Another hypothesis is that it reflects differing macro-economic policies. Every study finds a strong link between measures of macro-economic performance and unemployment or employment. Baccaro and Rei trace this to interest rate and the independence of central banks. A third hypothesis is that variation in product market rules and regulations accounts for different unemployment outcomes. May the hypotheses battle in the squared circle and the best one win.

On what labour institutions actually do, the evidence is compelling that they reduce inequality of pay compared to pay in competitive markets.[11] In countries like the US in which decentralized labour markets set pay, dispersion of earnings is lower in unionized workplaces than in nonunionized workplaces; falls for the same workers when they move from nonunion to union settings, and increases when they move in the opposite direction. Across countries, dispersion of pay tends to be lower in countries with high rates of collective bargaining coverage than in countries with low rates of collective bargaining. Over time, moreover, dispersion decreases in countries when institutions play a greater role in pay setting and increases when institutional pay setting gets weaker. For example, when Italy used the Scala Mobile to set pay, inequality fell rapidly whereas when it scrapped that form of national pay bargaining, inequality began to rise.[12]

The key question is whether shifts in the distribution of income and capital from the high paid to the lower paid persons affect aggregate outcomes. The part of economic analysis associated with the Coase theorem and efficient bargaining suggests that these redistributions would have little or no effect on aggregate outcomes. Consistent with this, research on employment protection laws has largely concluded that these laws redistribute joblessness from the prime age generally male workers to other groups without noticeably affecting overall unemployment.[13] Also, minimum wage studies that find little impact on employment could also be interpreted in this vein (Card and Krueger, 1997). But some other policies – tax wedges and unemployment benefits – do not seem to fit into an efficient bargaining world.

7 Conclusion: doing better

As the OECD generates increasingly better measures of the key variables, as time generates additional observations, and as countries alter their policies, the debate over the impact of labour institutions and policies will continue. Hopefully, careful dissections of studies with seemingly contradictory findings – Bassanini and Duval vs. Baccaro and Rei – will uncover which assumptions or data choices explain the results. If I am right and the data are weaker than the priors of researchers, there will be no closure until we bring additional evidence and insight to the debate. There is need for additional micro evidence, not only of government programmes but also of firms, whose organization is sufficiently complicated to provide insight into interactions of institutions at a higher level. There are lots of firms and lots of changes in labour practices among them, so there is no lack of data. There is also need for more sophisticated priors in analysis of data. Economics has theories that deal with non-competitive markets – monopsony theory for instance (Manning, 2005) – but most economists hold the prior that markets operate according to the competitive model unless proven otherwise. Analyses of financial markets have forced economists to go beyond the first approximation 'efficient market model' into behavioural finance, which has led to very different priors about behaviour from the traditional rational actor. If it is necessary to develop more realistic priors about behaviour in finance, where all that matters is money, then surely it is necessary to do so in labour, where market participants are concerned with much more than monetary considerations.

One way to develop more realistic priors about how people and institutions operate in aggregate economies is to make greater use of laboratory experiments. Experimental economics (see Kagel and Roth, 1995) has generated findings about behaviour in diverse situations – the ultimatum game, the dictator game, the prisoners dilemma game, and public goods games, that have implications for labour institutions; about the conditions under which supply and demand do or do not clear markets. While the jump from laboratory experiments to actual institutions is a large one, knowledge of what experimental economics has found should help us form better priors about what to expect from labour institutions.

We can also make greater use of artificial agent modelling. This form of modelling can help us develop priors about the interaction among decision units. The Sante Fe stock market model (Le Baron, 2002), for example, shows how competing strategies adopted by agents with bounded rationality can interact to produce swings in stock market values that more resemble the actual swings than the random fluctuations in any efficient market model. Models of labour economic institutions have focused on issues relating to the matching of firms and workers (Neugart, 2004; Pingle and Tesfatsion, 2003) but they could not also examine other institutions or issues – for instance the high dispersion of wages in labour markets. Al Roth (2002) and Roth and Peranson (1999) have shown the value of combining modelling with the design of new institutional forms for specific labour markets. These models provide powerful priors for what to expect from actual institutions or changes in institutions.

Because the problem of determining the effect of institutions and policies on outcomes is difficult, we need all of the weapons at our disposal to attack it. If there is a single lesson to draw from the debate based on cross-country time series data, it is that continued regression mongering of these data is not enough.

Notes

1 www.mindfully.org/Reform/Emperors_New_Clothes.htm.
2 The evolving views of the OECD can be seen in various *Employment Outlooks* (1995, 1996, 1997, 1999).
3 Martin (1998).
4 Freeman (2000).
5 IMF (2003), chapter 4, p. 129.
6 IMF (2003), chapter 4, p. 131.
7 Charles Ragin (1987) has done the most to analyse the problem of inferring relations from configurations.
8 If we used a high/medium/low categorization, we would have 81 ($=3^4$) possible configurations.
9 Freeman (2005) provides a more detailed analysis of this study.
10 IMF (April 2003), figure 4.4, p. 134.
11 The situation is more ambiguous in developing countries since unions do not represent workers in the informal sector and rarely represent rural workers, who are paid less than those in the modern sector.
12 Erickson and Ichino (1995); Manacorda (2004).
13 Patterns in strikes run counter to a Coase theorem interpretation. If management and workers lose from strikes, they should come to an agreement without strikes or lockouts.

References

Atkinson, A. and Micklewright, J. (1991) 'Unemployment Compensation and Labor Transitions: A Critical Review', *Journal of Economic Literature* 29, 1679–1727.

Baccaro, L. and Rei, D. (2005) 'Institutional Determinants of Unemployment in OECD Countries: a time series cross-section analysis (1960–98)', International Institute for Labor Studies Discussion Paper DP/160/2005, International Institute for Labor Studies, Geneva.

Baker, D., Glyn, A., Howell, D. and Schmitt, J. (2004) 'Labor Market Institutions and Unemployment: A Critical Assessment of the Cross-Country Evidence', in D. Howell (ed.) *Fighting Unemployment: The Limits of Free Market Orthodoxy*. Oxford: Oxford University Press.

Bassanini, A. and Duval, R. (2006) 'Employment Patterns in OECD Countries: Reassessing the Role Policies and Institutions', OECD Economic Department Working Paper 486, June.

Blanchard, O. and Wolfers, J. (2000) 'Shocks and Institutions and the Rise of European Unemployment: The Aggregate Evidence', *Economic Journal* 110(1): 1–33.

Blanchflower, D.G. (2001) 'Unemployment, Well-Being, and Wage Curves in Eastern and Central Europe', *Journal of the Japanese and International Economies* 15: 364–402.

Blanchflower, D.G. and Freeman, R. (1993) 'Did the Thatcher Reforms Change British Labour Performance?', NBER Working Paper No. W4384, June.

Blank, R.M. and Freeman, R.B. (1994) 'Evaluating the Connection between Social Protection and Economic Flexibility', in Rebecca M. Blank (ed.) *Social Protection vs. Economic Flexibility: Is There a Tradeoff?*, National Bureau of Economic Research – Comparative Labor Markets Series, University of Chicago.

Card, D. and Krueger, A.B. (1997) *Myth and Measurement*. Princeton, NJ: Princeton University Press.

Erickson C. and Ichino, A. (1995) 'Wage Differentials in Italy: Market Forces, Institutions and Inflation', in R. Freeman and L. Katz (eds) *Differences and Changes in Wage Structure*. University of Chicago Press.

Freeman, R.B. (1995) 'The Limits of Wage Flexibility to Curing Unemployment', *Oxford Review of Economic Policy* 11(1) (Spring): 214–222.

Freeman, R.B. (2000) 'Single peaked vs. diversified capitalism: The relation between economic institutions and outcomes', Working Paper 7556 (February), National Bureau of Economic Research.

Freeman, R.B. (2005) 'Labour Market Institutions Without Blinders: The Debate over Flexibility and Labour Market Performance', NBER Working Paper 11246.

Holmlund, B. (1998) 'Unemployment Insurance in Theory and Practice', *Scandinavian Journal of Economics* 100(1): 143–145.

Howell, D., Baker, D., Glyn, A. and Schmitt, J. (2006) 'Are Protective Labor Market Institutions Really at the Root of Unemployment? A Critical Perspective on the Statistical Evidence', CEPTR, 14 July 2006.

International Monetary Fund (IMF) (1999) 'Chronic Unemployment in the Euro Area: Causes and Cures', Chapter 4 in *World Economic Outlook* (May). Washington, DC: IMF.

IMF (2003) 'Unemployment and Labor Market Institutions: Why Reforms Pay Off', Chapter 4 in *World Economic Outlook* (April). Washington, DC: IMF.

Kagel, J.H. and Roth, A.E. (eds) (1995) *The Handbook of Experimental Economics*. Princeton, NJ: Princeton University Press.

Layard, R., Nickell, S. and Jackman, R. (1994) *The Unemployment Crisis*. Oxford: Oxford University Press.

LeBaron, B. (2002) 'Building the Santa Fe Artificial Stock Market', Working Paper, Brandeis University, June.

Ljungqvist, L. and Sargent, T.J. (1998) 'The European Unemployment Dilemma', *Journal of Political Economy* 106(3): 514–550.

Ljungqvist, L. and Sargent, T.J. (2004) 'European Unemployment and Turbulence Revisited in a Matching Model', *Journal of the European Economic Association.* 2(2–3) (April/May): 456–468.

Manacorda, M. (2004) 'Can the Scala Mobile Explain the Fall and Rise of Earnings Inequality in Italy? A Semiparametric Analysis, 1977–1993', *Journal of Labor Economics* 22(3): 585–613.

Manning, A. (2005) *Monopsony in Motion: Imperfect Competition in Labor Markets.* Princeton, NJ: Princeton University Press.

Martin, J. (1996) 'Measures of Replacement Rates for the Purpose of International Comparisons, A Note', *OECD Economic Studies*, No. 26, 1996/1: 100–115.

Martin, J. (1998) 'What Works Among Active Labor Market Policies: Evidence from OECD Countries' Experiences', www.rba.gov.au/PublicationsAndResearch/Conferences/1998/Martin.pdf.

Neugart, M. (2004) 'Endogenous matching functions: an agent-based computational approach', *Advances in Complex Systems* 7(2): 187–202.

Nickell, S. (1997) 'Unemployment and Labor Market Rigidities: Europe versus North America', *Journal of Economic Perspectives* 11(3) (Summer): 55–74.

Nickell, S.J. and Bell, B. (1996) 'Changes in the Distribution of Wages and Unemployment in the OECD Countries', *American Economic Review, Papers and Proceedings*, 86(5): 302–308.

Nickell, S., Nunziata, L. and Ochel, W. (2005) 'Unemployment in the OECD since the 1960s: What Do We Know?', *Economic Journal* 115 (January): 1–27.

Organization for Economic Cooperation and Development (OECD) (1994a) *OECD Jobs Study, Evidence and Explanations, Part I: Labor Market Trends and Underlying Forces of Change.* Paris: OECD.

OECD (1994b) *OECD Jobs Study, Evidence and Explanations, Part II: The Adjustment Potential of the Labor Market.* Paris: OECD.

OECD (1995) *OECD Jobs Study, Taxation, Employment, and Unemployment.* Paris: OECD.

OECD (1996) *OECD Employment Outlook.* Paris: OECD.

OECD (1997) 'Economic Performance and the Structure of Collective Bargaining', OECD Employment Outlook (July). Paris: OECD.

OECD (1999) *Implementing the Jobs Study.* Paris: OECD.

OECD (2002) *OECD Employment Outlook.* Paris: OECD.

OECD (2004) *OECD Employment Outlook.* Paris: OECD.

OECD (2006) *OECD Employment Outlook.* Paris: OECD.

Pingle, M. and Tesfatsion, L. (2003) 'Evolution of Worker-Employer Networks and Behaviors Under Alternative Non-Employment Benefits: An Agent-Based Computational Study', *Computing in Economics and Finance* 7, Society for Computational Economics, pp. 1–33.

Ragin, C. (1987) *The Comparative Method*, University of California Press.

Roth, A.E. (2002) 'The Economist as Engineer: Game Theory, Experimentation, and Computation as Tools for Design Economics', Fisher-Schultz Lecture, *Econometrica* 70(4) (July): 1341–1378.

Roth, A.E. and Peranson, E. (1999) 'The Redesign of the Matching Market for American Physicians: Some Engineering Aspects of Economic Design', *American Economic Review* 89(4) (September): 748–780.

5 Convergence via two-tier reforms and growthless job creation in Europe

Tito Boeri

1 Introduction

The Lisbon liberalization agenda has been a major failure. Broadly speaking, too many targets were set and too many messages were lost in the translation from Brussels to the EU capitals.

But failures of the Lisbon process were less evident in labour than in product markets. There were more reforms in labour markets, albeit less coherent than the few that occurred in product markets. And more progress was made in labour also in terms of outcomes, as the growth of employment rates in several countries exceeded the Lisbon employment targets.

Why were there more reforms in labour than in product markets? I argue in this chapter that asymmetries in the speed of reforms in product and labour markets can be explained by the nature of political obstacles. Labour market reforms can be applied only to new entrants in the market without affecting the regulations applied to existing workers. These two-tier strategies are feasible in product markets, since incumbent firms can easily drive away new entrants.

Will labour market reforms continue to pay off in terms of employment growth? Economic theory suggests that we should expect significant *net* job creation effects from these type of reforms. Yet, two-tier labour market reforms have a transitional 'honeymoon' job creating effect, which has been so far ignored by the literature. Clearly, the honeymoon cannot go on forever and there are already indications that the job generation potential of these asymmetric reforms is fading away. There is also some risk that dual reforms, rather than creating a consensus for further reforms, end up increasing opposition to further reforms in both labour and product markets. Reforms of social policies adapting them to the new contractual arrangements and, more broadly, dual labour market regimes may reduce this risk.

The chapter is organized as follows. First, we review structural reforms in labour and product markets and their interaction in industrial countries, drawing on a detailed inventory of reforms assembled at Fondazione Rodolfo Debenedetti. Unlike other studies, we focus on changes over time rather than on cross-sectional differences in reforms.

Second, we evaluate the political obstacles to reforms in labour and product markets, trying to understand the reasons of the observed asymmetries in the pace of reforms in the two areas. Third, we dwell on the effects of these asymmetric reforms, arguing that they may well be responsible for the rather positive employment performance of Europe in recent years.

The final remarks discuss possible improvements of the Lisbon process enabling it to further reforms of labour markets and strengthen the pace of reforms in product markets.

2 Taking stock of reforms

My main source of information on labour market reforms in this section is the 'Social Policy Reform Inventory' assembled by the Fondazione Rodolfo Debenedetti. It draws on a variety of sources (including country economic reviews carried out by OECD, Income Data Source studies, EC-MISSOC reports, etc.) and it takes stock of reforms carried out in Europe in the field of non-employment benefits (encompassing not only unemployment benefits, but also the various cash transfers provided to individuals in working age), provisions for retirement (relevant in determining participation among older workers) as well as employment protection. It complements the information provided by the OECD indicators in that it offers more insights on qualitative features of institutions and on political opposition to reforms. We may observe significant reform activity even at times in which the regulatory indicator exhibits small changes or no variation at all. This may point to unsuccessful attempts of Governments to bypass political resistance to reforms.

Details on the inventory of social policy reforms and on each single regulatory change are offered in the webpage of Fondazione Rodolfo Debenedetti (www.frdb.org). Hence, we can confine ourselves herein just to providing information on the criteria followed in the classification of the reforms.

The frdb inventory of reforms is organized along two main dimensions. On the one hand, reforms are classified on the basis of their broad orientation, that is, whether they tend to reduce or increase the generosity of public pensions and non-employment benefits and make employment protection more or less stringent. It should be stressed that increasing rewards from labour market participation does not necessarily mean simply phasing out existing cash transfers mechanisms to non-employed individuals. It may also involve the introduction of wage subsidies, employment-conditional incentives or activation policies (including sanctions) for beneficiaries of existing schemes.

Table 5.1 documents an acceleration of reforms increasing labour market flexibility and rewards from labour market participation in the last six-year period (roughly corresponding to a Parliamentary term) covered by the data.

Unfortunately, there is not an inventory of reforms in the product market area to draw upon. We were forced in this case to define and measure reforms as changes in the values of the regulatory indicators devised by OECD. This rules

Table 5.1 Average number of reforms per year and country

	1985–90	1991–96	1997–2002
Employment protection legislation	0.05	0.14	0.31
Non-employment benefits	0.09	0.33	0.82

out the possibility of reforms moving in opposite directions within the same year, a rather frequent event in the case of labour market reforms. Thus, we are likely to underestimate the total number of reforms that occurred in the product market area.

In order to obtain our proxy-reforms, we focused on regulatory indicators for which there was a time-series at yearly frequencies. These cover a few service sectors (airlines, telecoms, electricity, gas, postal services, railways and road freight) and a range of regulatory areas (barriers to entry, public ownership, constraints to business operation and, wherever applicable, price controls). As we are particularly interested in evaluating changes that occurred in the structure of markets, notably the evolution in the degree of competition in the different industries, we carried out this exercise only limited to the regulations on barriers to entry.

The results of this exercise are displayed in Table 5.2. Once more, we group reforms six-year time-period, and we classify them by orientation (increasing or decreasing competition) and scope (radical if they involve a step change of the indicator corresponding to at least one-third of its potential range, marginal otherwise).

In the case of product markets, the acceleration of reforms took place mainly in the first half of the 1990s. There has been much less reform activity in product than in labour markets. In particular, in the 2002–03 period, the OECD counted nine reforms in the labour market area (and another six being proposed by governments but not yet implemented) and five in the product market area (with another three being proposed).

These indices also do not point to a convergence across countries in the degree of liberalization of product markets. The countries with more regulated product markets to start with are not necessarily those doing most in liberalizing them. In the case of labour markets, we instead observe a significant and positive correlation between the number of reforms reducing the strictness of employment protection and the initial value of the EPL index, which suggests that countries that are most 'rigid' are indeed more active in liberalizing labour markets (Figure 5.1).

Overall, wide differences persist between the US and Europe and within the EU itself in terms of labour and product market regulations. However, some convergence has been observed in the last decade in the strictness of employment protection legislation thanks to a series of small reforms in the countries which had the strictest provisions to start with.

Table 5.2 'Reforms' of product market regulations (1985–98, European Union)

	Increasing competition			Decreasing competition			Total per row	Of which decreasing (%)
	1985–90	1991–96	1997–98	1985–90	1991–96	1997–98		
Airlines								
Marginal	0	5	13	0	0	0	**18**	100
Radical	3	9	0	0	0	0	**12**	100
Telecom								
Marginal	4	45	9	0	0	0	**58**	100
Radical	0	4	8	0	0	0	**12**	100
Electricity								
Marginal	1	4	3	0	0	1	**9**	88.89
Radical	1	3	2	0	0	0	**6**	100
Gas								
Marginal	0	8	0	0	0	1	**9**	88.89
Radical	1	1	0	0	0	1	**3**	66.67
Post								
Marginal	6	5	2	1	0	0	**14**	92.86
Radical	3	3	0	0	0	0	**6**	100
Railways								
Marginal	0	0	0	0	0	0	**0**	–
Radical	0	5	0	0	0	0	**5**	100
Road								
Marginal	11	0	1	0	0	0	**12**	100
Radical	4	1	1	0	0	0	**6**	100
Total per column	**34**	**93**	**39**	**1**	**0**	**3**	**170**	**97.65**
Average per year	5.07	16.03	19.05	0.02	0	1.05	12.14	

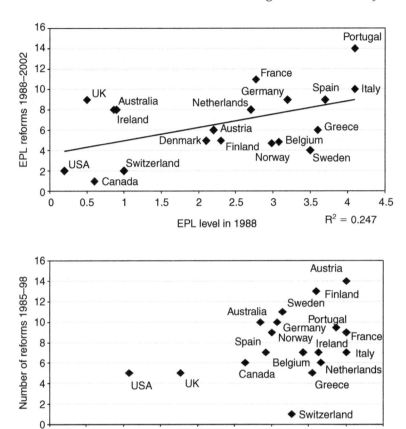

Figure 5.1 Convergence and divergence in reform efforts.

3 Why these asymmetries?

As shown above, an intensification of reform efforts in the labour market area in recent years has not been paralleled by major variations in the values of the OECD aggregate indicators of labour market regulation. There are many reforms, but not much change in the aggregate indicators of the strictness of employment protection or in the generosity of unemployment benefit systems.

These reforms are asymmetric in that they change regulations only for a subset of the population. Reforms of EPL, in particular, involved often only specific segments of the workforce. Unbundling reforms is therefore a viable strategy for implementing politically difficult reforms. In addition to employment protection legislation, this approach has been followed in designing pension reforms, where preferences over reform options are deeply shaped by individuals' characteristics.

Political support for reforms of EPL from different socio-economic groups can be well characterized on the basis of a survey carried out by Fondazione Rodolfo Debenedetti in April 2002 on a representative sample of Italians (1,000 individuals aged 16 to 80). All respondents were asked whether they preferred a flexible 'labour market regime in which it is relatively easy to find a job, but it is likewise easy to lose a job' or a rigid labour market in which jobs are difficult to find but last longer. In particular, being aged more than 55 yields a 20 per cent higher probability (than the baseline) of voting in favour of employment protection. Low educational attainment also plays in favour of stronger employment protection (+12 per cent) and even more so when interacted with the fact of having lost a job (+40 per cent). Finally, residence in depressed labour markets (e.g. in the Mezzogiorno) also increases support to employment protection. Thus, reforms of EPL are more likely to win support if concentrated on some socio-economic groups, such as high-skill types, youth, and those living in relatively dynamic labour markets.

Political support for pension reforms likewise interacts meaningfully with personal characteristics. This can be better appreciated once again with the help of survey data. Surveys suggest that individual features such as age, income and education play an important role in shaping the evaluation of these reform options. In particular, younger, more educated, richer males tend to approve reforms shrinking the size of pay-as-you-go systems, while the fact of being a member of a trade union, living in poor regions or having a left-wing ideology plays in the opposite direction.

Clearly not all of these heterogeneities in preferences can be exploited in devising feasible reform trajectories. For instance, there are constitutional rules or ethical considerations preventing the enforcement of reforms which create long-lasting asymmetries across workers with different educational attainment. Other asymmetries can instead be exploited: many pension reforms in Europe (e.g. the Italian 1995 reform, the Swedish 1998 reform) involved only the youngest workers, leaving the rules unaltered for the older workers. The reason for creating these two-tier systems is essentially political: younger workers are more favourable to pension reforms reducing the state monopoly in retirement provision and expanding the scope of supplementary, private pensions.

A similar approach underlines the introduction of flexible contractual arrangements limited to new hires or school-leavers (as in the case of the contracts combining fixed-term durations and a training component). In principle, these reforms eventually change the rules for everybody. As young workers age, all pensions will be paid according to the new rules; insofar as labour turnover changes the stock of jobs, only the new contracts are enforced. The crucial issue is the length of the transition from one system to another: a too-long transition exposes a country to the risk of getting caught in an equilibrium with a two-tier regime (Saint-Paul, 2000). In this respect the Swedish pension reform was better designed than the Italian one. The former exempted only 10 per cent of the workers from the new (less generous) rules, while in Italy the new DC rules were introduced on a flow, pro-rata basis for no more than 60 per cent of the eligible population. Only in 2065 will the transition to the new system be complete.

Summarizing, reforms done at the margin and the unbundling of reforms offer powerful ways of implementing politically difficult reforms. The trick is to devise them in such a way as to gradually extend the new rules to everybody. There are indeed potential distortions associated with the long-term maintenance of a two-tier system: the speed of the transition from the old to the new ones is therefore crucial in this strategy.

Unfortunately, this reform strategy does not seem to be viable in the case of product markets. A marginal reform (similar to those applied in the labour market) limited to a specific sector (e.g. in the provision of a public utility) would result in a market with different rules applied to different firms. On the one hand, incumbent firms would operate under the traditional set of protection, and rents (i.e. government subsidies). On the other hand, new entrants would be forced to operate without these rents. This cannot work as the incumbent firm (a former monopolist) would easily drive the new competitive fringe out of business.

The above suggests a fundamental difference between product market and labour market reforms. In the case of the latter, marginal reforms are politically feasible. In the case of the former, reforms need necessarily to be more fundamental and must completely change the rules governing the competitive structure. Thus, the result in section 3 should not come as a surprise: in the product market we observe more radical reforms than in the labour market. Only *radical* reforms are likely to have a long-lasting impact on the functioning of the product market. Marginal reforms in the product market are just not sustainable.

Lacking the possibility of engineering marginal reforms, radical reforms in a specific industry turn out to be politically difficult. First, the lobbying power of incumbents is strong. Aware of the risk of radical reforms, existing monopolists are likely to oppose by all means any radical reform proposal. The second reason is more subtle and has to do with the marginal propensity to push and resist reform by the active population. Arguably, the mass of voters within the population would certainly have the *aggregate* political power to enforce a radical reform in a specific goods sector. The issue is whether such political power is exploited in equilibrium. Each individual tends to see his/her position in the economic system more as worker rather than consumer. While individuals are willing to demonstrate and oppose structural reforms in the labour market, the same political energy seems to be absent when lobbying for radical reforms in the product market. Within Europe in the last ten years, there are plenty of examples of long-lasting strikes aimed at preventing structural reforms of the European welfare states (e.g. Italy, 1994 and 2002; France, 1995). Conversely, the same people have not engaged in long strikes aimed at implementing market reform for specific industries.

The above helps to explain why there is stronger status quo bias in product markets. In product markets reforms unavoidably hit the incumbents, while in labour markets it is possible to concentrate regulatory changes on new entrants.

Marginal reforms are a powerful force for the convergence of institutions as they are more successful in the countries which need more deregulation of labour markets: temporary contracts were adopted just in the countries where the rules for incumbents were most restrictive.

4 Two-tier reforms and the honeymoon

In recent years several European countries, and notably most Mediterranean countries coming from strict EPL regimes, experienced protracted employment growth despite moderate output growth. This performance stands in contrast with the 'jobless growth' of the 1980s and mid-1990s. As discussed in Boeri and Garibaldi (2005), the asymmetric labour market reforms in the area of employment protection legislation (EPL), which have been documented in Section 2, may contribute to explain this 'honeymoon effect' on job creation.

The traditional analysis on the effects of EPL – pioneered by Nickell (1986), Bentolila and Bertola (1990) and Bertola (1990) – suggests that one should not expect any sizeable permanent employment effect associated with EPL reforms. The reduction in EPL is bound to increase employment volatility over the business cycle but should not have any obvious effect on average labour demand. This is because EPL affects both the creation and destruction margins (incentives to hire and to dismiss workers) and there is no reason to believe a priori that one effect could dominate the other. While these studies focus mainly on the steady state effects of reforms, little research has been carried out on the transitional dynamics of EPL reform.

However, when temporary contracts are introduced, firms exploit hiring flexibility in good business conditions but do not exploit downward flexibility in bad times, since they are constrained by the stock of insider workers. As a result, the lower the employment attrition, the larger the employment increase during the transition, as suggested in Figure 5.2. A honeymoon effect in employment emerges. Eventually, the employment gains are dissipated by the decline of insider workers. As the firm expands in good periods, its employment pool expands along a downward sloping labour demand, with additional workers who are less productive at the margin. In such a setting, average productivity should fall eventually, as the firm also gains downward flexibility, inducing a fall in average productivity.

Table 5.3 points out another common denominator of these country experiences, namely the strong contribution offered by temporary contracts (including fixed-term contracts, according to the definition provided by Eurostat) to job creation: in Spain the increase of the stock of 'temporary workers' was 2.5 times larger than the increase in the overall stock of jobs, pointing to strong substitution of permanent with fixed-term contracts. In the other countries liberalizing less than Spain the use of these contractual types, the contribution of temporary contracts to job creation is of the order of 35 to 60 per cent. Notice further that the Netherlands is the only country where employment growth did not accelerate after the reforms (growth rates reported in parentheses). This is because this

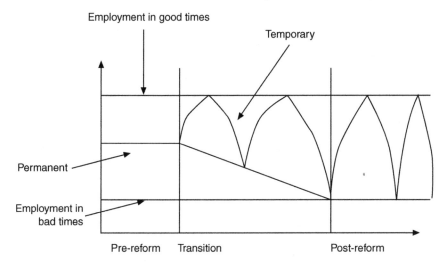

Figure 5.2 The honeymoon effect.

country had already embarked on a large scale substitution of full-time with part-time jobs in the decade before reforming EPL. Notice that employment growth was not concentrated in low educated positions. With the exception of Portugal, Eurostat (2005) records a decline in the total number of employed persons with primary or lower educational attainments. This is relevant in discussing the labour productivity developments in the various countries.

5 Final remarks

There is currently a disconnect between the rhetoric of the intergovernmental meetings and public debate in individual countries. At Council meetings, the Heads of Governments make ambitious commitments, but, as soon as they are back home, they adjust their language under pressure from national lobbies. Four years ago in Barcelona, European leaders officially committed to increase the effective retirement age by five years before 2010. Back home, they forgot to inform their compatriots of this historic (but perhaps not very popular) decision.

The entire Lisbon process somewhere got 'lost in translation'. In order to revitalize it, a common language should be adopted.

First, there ought to be fewer targets. Lisbon-1 had 117 indicators. Lisbon-2 (the Action plan subsequently delivered by the Commission) still has too many. In order to select the relevant indicators, the Commission may choose only those targets which (1) refer to variables under the control of Governments (otherwise one may end up rewarding lucky Governments), and (2) are consistent with the allocation of tasks envisaged in the Constitution signed in Rome. It is easy to check that most 'Lisbon indicators' fail either (1) or (2). For

Table 5.3 Job creation in the honeymoon

	Pre-reform		Post-reform	
Belgium	1987–96		1997–2004	
ΔE^1	318,000	(0.92)	301,000	(0.98)
$\Delta ETEMP^1$	27,000	(1.72)	108,000	(0.37)
$\Delta ETEMP/\Delta E$ (%)	8.49		35.88	
$\Delta LOWEDU/\Delta E$ (%)^2	–		−25.25	
Spain	1981–86		1987–95	
ΔE	−586,000	(−0.70)	852,000	(0.68)
$\Delta ETEMP$	1,226,000	–	2,033,000	(15.69)
$\Delta ETEMP/\Delta E$ (%)	–		238.62	
$\Delta LOWEDU/\Delta E$ (%)	–		28.01	
Italy	1986–96		1997–2004	
ΔE	−563,000	(−0.25)	2,107,500	(1.30)
$\Delta ETEMP$	387,000	(5.31)	728,420	(7.71)
$\Delta ETEMP/\Delta E$ (%)	–		34.56	
$\Delta LOWEDU/\Delta E$ (%)	–		−40.19	
Netherlands	1987–98		1999–2004	
ΔE	1,557,000	(2.22)	500,750	(1.10)
$\Delta ETEMP$	352,000	(6.12)	241,000	(4.99)
$\Delta ETEMP/\Delta E$ (%)	–		48.13	
$\Delta LOWEDU/\Delta E$ (%)	–		−37.84	
Portugal	1989–95		1996–2004	
ΔE	−124,000	(−0.39)	683,080	(1.71)
$\Delta ETEMP$	−272,000	(−6.62)	403,830	(12.94)
$\Delta ETEMP/\Delta E$ (%)	–		59.12	
$\Delta LOWEDU/\Delta E$ (%)	–		58.42	
Sweden	1995–96		1997–2004	
ΔE	−63,000	(−0.78)	373,000	(1.19)

Source: European Labour Force Survey.

Notes
1 Average yearly rate in parentheses.
2 Data on employment by education available only since 1992.

instance, EU-wide targets in terms of employment rates (overall and by gender or age groups) do not satisfy either of the two criteria. After all, it makes little sense to ask Sweden (currently having an employment-to-population ratio higher than the US) to increase the employment rate even further when there are other countries having almost 50 per cent of the population in working age out of work. An indicator passing (1) and (2) is instead a targeted yearly inflow of legal migrants relative to the European population. This would prevent lack of coordination in migration policies from creating a 'race to the top' in migration restrictions as happened in the case of the Eastern enlargement. Another example of a Lisbon target is an EU-wide R&D spending threshold, possibly associated with enforceable sanctions for countries systematically deviating from the target. Clearly, only by having fewer targets one can combine carrots and sticks.

Second, there ought to be one national Lisbon plan (rather than a number of parallel plans, from stability and convergence to competition, from poverty to employment) encompassing all the various dimensions of economic policy, as these are interconnected (not lastly because of the overall fiscal constraint). This unique plan should be approved not only by Governments but also by national Parliaments, which should receive in time the commentaries of the Commission to the plans produced by national Governments. This would put supra-national authorities in a position to talk directly to European citizens, highlighting the advantages of competition and other public goods provided at the European level. Clearly, supra-national authorities will have to show themselves to be up to this task. They should be precise in documenting the costs for families and firms of delays in, say, regulating highway tolls and allowing for more competition in the banking sector. The Commission is in the position to do this as it can compare the performance of countries that have reformed these policies with those of countries that have not.

References

Bentolila, S. and Bertola, G. (1990) 'Firing Costs and Labour Demand: How Bad is Eurosclerosis?', *Review of Economic Studies* 57: 381–402.

Bertola, G. (1990) 'Job Security, Employment, and Wages', *European Economic Review* 57(4), 851–879.

Boeri, T. and Garibaldi, P. (2007) 'Two Tier Reforms of Employment Protection: a Honeymoon Effect?', *Economic Journal*, forthcoming.

Cohen, E. and Pisani-Ferry, J. (2005) 'Economic Institutions and Policies in the US and the EU: Convergence or Divergence?', paper presented at the second annual Berkeley-Vienna Conference, Berkeley, 12–13 September 2005.

Freeman, R. (2005) 'Improving Labor Market Performance without Throwing in the Social Welfare Towel', paper presented at the second annual Berkeley-Vienna Conference, Berkeley, 12–13 September 2005.

Nickell, S. (1986) 'Dynamic Models of Labor Demand', in O. Ashenfelter and R. Layard (eds) *Handbook of Labor Economics*. Amsterdam: North-Holland.

Roland, G. (2005) 'Europe's Constitutional Imbroglio', paper presented at the second annual Berkeley-Vienna Conference, Berkeley, 12–13 September 2005.

Saint-Paul, G. (2000) *The Political Economy of Labour Market Institutions*, Oxford: Oxford University Press.

6 Employment and labour productivity in the EU

Reconsidering a potential trade-off in the Lisbon strategy

Karl Pichelmann and Werner Roeger

1 Introduction

At their summit meeting in Lisbon in 2000, EU leaders set the ambitious goal for the EU of becoming the world's most competitive economy by 2010 and agreed on a comprehensive structural reform agenda to boost employment and liberalize markets, now known as the 'Lisbon strategy'. The overarching objective of this strategy is to enhance the capacity of the EU economy to generate high rates of non-inflationary growth over a prolonged period. This requires pressing ahead with deep, comprehensive reforms of product, capital and labour markets, backed up by a sound macroeconomic policy-mix aiming at sustained rates of growth close to potential within an environment of price stability.

Motivated by the observation of a persistent income gap with the US and a widespread perception of falling even further behind, the Lisbon strategy involves efforts on several fronts both to improve labour market performance and to raise productivity growth in the EU. This twin aspiration is neatly encapsulated in the phrase 'more and better jobs', which implies higher employment rates but also more productive, higher-quality employment.

The strategy sets explicit targets for 'more jobs': an employment rate of as close as possible to 70 per cent and a female employment rate of over 60 per cent by 2010. The Stockholm summit a year later added a further target of an employment rate of 50 per cent for older working-age people. Given the rate of employment growth required to meet these targets, the Lisbon conclusions also established an implicit target for productivity growth with the statement that – if the recommended measures were implemented against a sound macroeconomic background – it should be possible to achieve 3 per cent GDP growth.

These targets have met with criticism in some quarters. Some regarded them as over-ambitious, particularly since the European Council (as opposed to individual Member States) lacks full control of the necessary instruments to meet its objectives. There were doubts about whether a credible strategy had been set out, or even whether EU leaders realized the extent of the reforms that would be required. Others pointed to the risk of policy distortions – there are many ways to raise employment rates, for example, but not all of them are fully consistent with raising economic welfare. On the other hand, the Lisbon targets appeared to score an initial public relations success, being widely interpreted as a signal that the EU was taking economic reform seriously. (Even then, however, it was noted that this might damage the credibility of similar exercises were the targets to be missed by a wide margin.)

Two clear advantages of the Lisbon strategy, and especially the employment rate targets, are often overlooked in these discussions. First, the commitment to raising employment rates (i.e. raising labour force participation as well as reducing unemployment) represents clear rejection of an idea that has been one of the great weaknesses of European employment policy in recent decades, namely that high unemployment can be cured by discouraging labour supply. If this seems obvious today, it is not so long ago in some countries that married women were discouraged from working, while older workers were actively encouraged to quit the labour market through early retirement schemes, partly in response to high unemployment. Even more recently, governments in some EU Member States were entertaining a similar notion – that employment of persons might be boosted by means of regulatory restrictions on hours worked.

Second, the Lisbon strategy embodies the idea that structural improvements in the functioning of markets are required for a sustained increase in employment rates and higher productivity growth. Clearly, at any given moment, output and (un-)employment are determined by real demand in the economy. However, over the longer term, real demand will generally tend towards a level consistent with stable inflation, this level being determined by overall supply conditions in the economy. By focusing on the functioning of labour, product and capital markets, as well as investments in R&D and human capital, the Lisbon strategy seeks to raise employment and growth potential in a sustainable manner.

In addition, while one may ask whether the employment rate is the ideal variable to target, there is no doubt that low employment rates in several EU Member States are a symptom of poor labour market performance, and that improving labour market performance would lead to both higher employment rates and greater economic welfare. The benefits of higher employment rates for the sustainability of the public finances (at least in the short-to-medium term) were also noted.

Against this background, this chapter focuses on a crucial question for the strategy of 'more and better jobs': whether and in what sense there are trade-offs between employment growth and productivity growth. Concern has been raised in some quarters that raising the employment rate in the EU will result in lower productivity growth. Indeed, there is a grain of truth in this: a rising employment rate implies that productivity growth will be temporarily below full potential, simply because the number of workers per unit of capital is increasing. In addition, those who move from unemployment or inactivity into employment are likely, on average, to have a relatively low level of productivity, at least at first.

However, as will be argued in the chapter, there are three reasons why this is not a cause for concern. First, the temporary negative effect on productivity growth is estimated to be rather small. Second, even if growth in productivity –

GDP per employed person – is negatively affected, a higher employment rate unambiguously raises growth in GDP per capita in the short term. Newly employed people clearly contribute more to GDP than they used to, even if their productivity is below average. Third, there are few reasons to think that a higher employment rate has any negative implications for longer-term productivity growth, which is what really matters for the competitiveness and dynamism of the EU economy. These points – important ones for the Lisbon strategy – are supported by two separate pieces of analysis: an econometric analysis of the dynamic response of productivity to structural employment shocks, and a simulation based on the Commission's macroeconomic model. Thus, we conclude that there is no genuine trade-off between policies to raise the employment rate and policies to foster productivity growth.

2 More and better jobs – an example of goal inconsistency?

Background considerations

At the moment, EU GDP per capita in purchasing power parities is around 70 per cent of the US level, with one-third of the gap due to productivity differentials and two-thirds due to a lower labour input (i.e. a lower employment rate and hours worked compared with the US). Consequently, improving the EU's productivity performance and raising employment is fundamental to increasing the long-term growth potential of the EU economy.[1] However, several observers have argued that the twin goals of raising both employment rates and productivity growth may be difficult, or even impossible to pursue simultaneously, given a perceived negative trade-off between employment and productivity.

The basic argument for the existence of a negative relationship between employment and productivity is derived from straightforward comparative–static reasoning. For any standard production function, average factor productivity will decrease with rising output as the expansion of production will require the introduction of less and less productive factors into operation – less fertile soil, older and less efficient equipment and machinery, workers with lower abilities and skills, etc. Then, obviously, higher employment will inevitably be associated with lower output per worker and vice versa. Thus, in such a comparative–static setting it is easy to construe a situation where, for example, regulations and restrictions excluding low productivity workers from employment result in a higher level of actual labour productivity, but this will come at the price of lower employment; similarly, reform efforts to price back low productivity workers into employment will mean more jobs, but this will be associated with lower overall productivity.

In comparing labour productivity levels across countries, such considerations of a comparative–static nature can be useful. There appears to be widespread agreement that measured labour productivity in Europe relative to the US may be upwardly biased as a result of the exclusion of more low productivity workers. Indeed, the EU employment rate falls short of US levels by almost

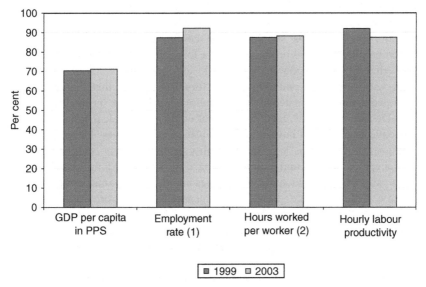

(1) Employment rate = 100 * (GDP per capita / Labour productivity per person employed)

(2) Hours worked per worker = 100 * (Labour productivity per person employed / Hourly labour productivity)

Figure 6.1 Decomposing the GDP gap (US = 100).

10 per cent, with lower participation rates and higher unemployment rates disproportionately affecting low skill workers. In a similar vein, the capital/labour ratio is typically higher in the EU than in the US, driving up measured labour productivity in Europe. Thus, both economic theory and quick inspection of a few figures suggest that one should control for these effects in productivity comparisons. Obviously, in consequence, a Europe at full employment may well see a significantly larger labour productivity gap vis-à-vis the US than current actual figures suggest.

By how much could the productivity gap rise? A simple calculation can be performed focusing on comparisons of total factor productivity levels, using the following relationship:

(1) $Y/L = (K/L)^{1-\alpha} \cdot \text{TFP}$

where Y/L denotes measured labour productivity, TFP is total factor productivity, K/L is the capital intensity of production and $1-\alpha$ is the capital elasticity of output in the constant-returns Cobb-Douglas case. For the calculation, GDP and the capital stock in PPP are taken from the AMECO data base. Employment is civilian employment (LFS). Hours worked come from the GGDC (Groningen Growth and Development Centre). The results suggest that the productivity gap between the euro area and the US, shown in Figure 6.2, may be some 6 percentage points

wider than the actual figures indicate. However, the notion of a negative relationship between employment and productivity levels emerging in comparative–static considerations should not be confused with a genuine trade-off
between employment and productivity in a long run dynamic sense. One of the
'big' stylized facts in economics is that in the long run, technical progress is
neutral with respect to employment. History has told us that the process of
capital accumulation and technological innovation has not meant the 'end of
work'. Despite notions of 'factories without workers', it is clear from an overall
perspective that workers have not been replaced by machines. In standard economic growth theory this long run neutrality proposition has been captured by
the concept of labour-augmenting technical progress.[2] Along this balanced
growth path, labour productivity, real wages and the capital intensity of production grow at the same rate, driven by (exogenous) technical progress. Technical
progress is called total factor productivity growth, indicating that this concept
should not be seen in a narrow engineering sense. Given that TFP determines
standards of living in the long run, clearly policy-makers want it to grow faster
than in recent years.

Actual labour productivity growth can of course deviate from the balanced
labour productivity growth rate over the short-to-medium term due to capital-
labour substitution; faster than 'balanced' productivity growth indicates labour
shedding, and a shortfall of actual relative to 'balanced' productivity growth is
a characteristic of what is loosely called labour-intensive growth. Obviously,
then, employment neutrality will not hold over the short-to-medium term.[3] In
consequence, pressing ahead with labour market reforms may entail a temporary reduction in measured productivity growth below potential, but this should
not be regarded as a trade-off in any sense. A higher employment rate implies

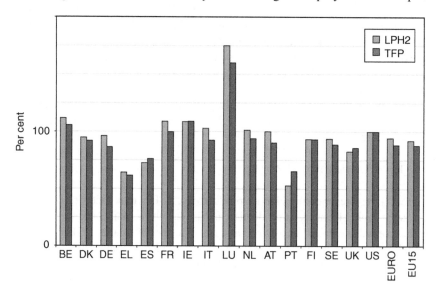

Figure 6.2 TFP and labour productivity gap (source: Commission services).

an unambiguous increase in GDP per capita with no negative implications for the long-run productivity growth of the existing workforce. Thus, there is no inherent problem with acting on both fronts simultaneously, raising the 'balanced' rate of productivity growth using all the available instruments to stimulate TFP growth, whilst at the same time encouraging the labour-intensive growth in the medium term that is needed to move towards full employment.[4]

The dynamic employment-productivity relationship in recent years

EU employment and productivity growth patterns have diverged sharply in recent years. Compared with the first half of the 1990s, the period since then has witnessed a significant increase in the contribution of labour to EU GDP growth, but unfortunately this has been accompanied by a reduction in the contribution from labour productivity, with labour productivity growth having come down by about one percentage point.

Figure 6.3, as a starting point for the analysis, decomposes labour productivity growth into its two components, with the US and the Rest of World included for comparison purposes. The productivity growth slowdown is evident, with the EU's long established superiority in terms of labour productivity growth having disappeared over recent years.

From a purely growth accounting perspective,[5] the 1 percentage point decline in EU labour productivity emanates from two sources. First, 50 per cent can be attributed to a reduction in the contribution from capital deepening, i.e. lower investment. Second, the remaining 50 per cent appears to emanate from deterioration in total factor productivity, i.e. a decline in the overall efficiency of the production process. On top of this, cyclical conditions are estimated to have depressed annual labour productivity growth by around 0.5 percentage points in recent years.

By comparison, over the same timeframe, the US has been able to combine a strong employment performance with an acceleration in labour productivity

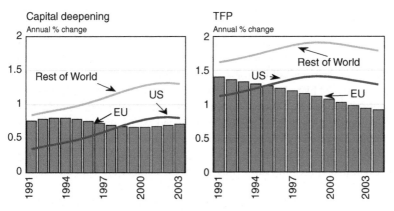

Figure 6.3 Decomposition of labour productivity trends (source: Commission services).

growth. Against this background, this section investigates to what extent the recent slowdown in labour productivity growth may merely reflect a response to a series of positive shocks to labour supply and jobs emanating from structural reforms and employment-friendly wage developments.

The benign interpretation of observed productivity growth trends sees the recent deterioration in performance mainly as the mirror image of structural labour market improvements. In this view the EU may now simply be in a transition phase whereby wage moderation and positive labour supply shocks may have initially created a negative trade-off between employment and productivity growth, basically via a temporary decline in capital-labour substitution. However, the dynamic adjustment path towards a new equilibrium with higher employment and lower structural unemployment will also involve capital accumulation that should eliminate the trade-off over the medium-term.

The more pessimistic view, on the other hand, is that the labour productivity growth slowdown reflects a genuine negative shock, either in the form of a decline in total factor productivity growth or additional pressures on capital productivity; clearly, in such a scenario, prospects for a recovery of labour productivity growth are bleaker.

Obviously, both interpretations contain an element of truth, posing the analytical challenge of inferring the relative magnitude of the employment and productivity shocks and their respective consequences for overall productivity and employment developments. The picture is complicated by a third possible factor, namely aggregate demand. Both fiscal consolidation and precautionary household savings could have contributed to a decline in growth and, in particular, of productivity growth.

We have employed both a structural VAR analysis and a simulation using the Commission's QUEST model to study these three shocks: shocks to employment, shocks to productivity and shocks to aggregate demand; and to measure their relative importance for productivity and employment. What is of interest in the context of this chapter is the dynamic response of productivity to structural employment shocks. In technical terms, we use a structural VAR (SVAR) methodology, based on Stock and Watson (1988) and Blanchard and Quah (1989), for the identification of structural shocks. The intuition for identification in Blanchard and Quah is based on the idea that demand shocks only have temporary effects while supply shocks have permanent effects. Stock and Watson extend this approach and allow for separate supply contributions from labour and productivity (TFP). In order to identify different supply contributions, namely those coming from employment and those coming from productivity, additional identification criteria must be introduced. Stock and Watson use long run restrictions implied by the neoclassical growth model for that task. The neoclassical growth model appears to be suitable, since there are at least three important features in the long run trends which are compatible with this model:

- A close trend correlation between the growth of labour productivity and capital intensity.

- Capital intensity and productivity grow at a similar rate in the long run.
- If one looks over long periods of time and across the EU and the US, the employment rate appears to be unrelated to productivity growth.

Using the neoclassical growth model this leads to the imposition of the following long run restrictions:

- The labour market shock can have short and long run effects on employment, productivity and inflation.
- The productivity shock can have long run effects on productivity and inflation but only short and medium run effects on employment. This constraint arises from the assumption that real wages are indexed to productivity in the long run.
- The demand shock can have a long run effect on inflation but not on employment and productivity. No long run constraint is imposed on inflation.

These three types of restrictions imply a triangular long run structure between the growth rate of employment (Δh), productivity ($\Delta(y - h)$) and inflation (π) on the one hand, and the corresponding shocks to employment (v), productivity (e) and demand (d) on the other. If one defines the vector $\Delta x_t = [\Delta h_t, \Delta(y_t - h_t), \Delta \pi_t]$ and the vector $\xi_t = [v_t, e_t, d_t]$, then the moving average representation of this model is given by:

$$\Delta x_t = A(L)\xi_t \text{ with } A(1) = \begin{bmatrix} a_{11} & 0 & 0 \\ a_{21} & a_{22} & 0 \\ a_{31} & a_{32} & a_{33} \end{bmatrix}$$

where the matrix $A(1)$ shows the long run restrictions. This particular structure is particularly suited to test for the short, medium and long run effects of an employment shock. Allowing for a non-zero long run productivity effect of an employment shock allows one to test for labour quality effects associated with a permanent change in the employment rate. A similar analysis of the employment effects of productivity shocks has been conducted by Galí (1999).

The empirical results are presented in two steps. In step one, the impulse responses from the estimated VAR are presented. These responses give the impact on employment and productivity of a unit shock to employment, productivity and demand. Recall that the identifying restrictions imply that temporary unit shocks to employment can have permanent effects on employment and productivity, while a unit shock to demand (inflation) can only have temporary effects.

In order to evaluate the quantitative magnitudes of these shocks, they are compared to similar shocks simulated with the Euro area QUEST model. This comparison shows whether orders of magnitude from these shocks are similar when two very distinct empirical tools are used, with the VAR model imposing very little economic structure (apart from the long run constraints), while

QUEST consists of explicitly estimated structural equations and estimated adjustment lags.

Employment shock: A positive employment shock initially leads to an increase in productivity; however, this short run positive effect in the VAR model is partly spurious. In the medium and long run the effect on productivity is negative, i.e. an increase in employment is associated with a decrease in labour quality. Note, though, that this negative long run effect is estimated to be small: a shock which leads to a permanent increase in the level of employment of about 1 per cent is associated with a long run productivity level effect of about −0.1 per cent.[6] Analysis based on QUEST model simulations yields fairly similar results to the VAR approach, but the negative impact upon the productivity level is stronger (−0.3 instead of −0.1) over the medium term; moreover, the QUEST model analysis does not reveal any short run increase in productivity.

Productivity shock: A positive productivity shock is associated, in the short run, with a small negative employment effect. The order of magnitude of the employment effect is only about one-tenth of the size of the productivity shock. By implication, this analysis suggests that a structural slowdown in labour productivity growth will, by itself, not be associated with an expansion of employment. Again, in the QUEST model analysis a qualitatively similar pattern to the VAR emerges, but the short run negative employment response appears to be somewhat stronger.

Demand shock: The demand shock is initially associated with a positive employment and productivity effect. This result appears quite plausible, since a demand shock is likely to lead to better capacity utilization in the short run. As the demand effect fades away and employment is slow to adjust, the productivity effect turns negative and dies out within a year.

In the second step of the empirical analysis, the shocks are cumulated over the period 1995q1 to 2003q4[7] in order to derive an estimate of the structural component in employment growth and its likely impact on productivity and vice versa. The results of this exercise are depicted in Figure 6.6. The cumulated size of the employment shock over the period 1995–2003 is estimated at about 5 per cent. Thus, roughly one half of the overall observed employment expansion over that period is attributed to structural trend improvements. According to the VAR approach the cumulated productivity cost of this structural employment expansion may have amounted to three-quarters of a per cent; the QUEST model simulations would put the productivity cost somewhat higher at 1.5 per cent. Translated into year-on-year figures using a mid-point between the VAR and QUEST estimates, this implies a reduction in annual productivity growth of around two-tenths of a percentage point, equivalent to some 20 per cent of the observed total productivity growth slowdown, which could be attributed to positive structural shocks in the labour market.

A further result of the VAR model relates to the question of the structural

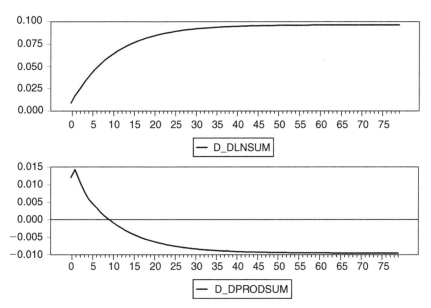

Figure 6.4a Employment shock.

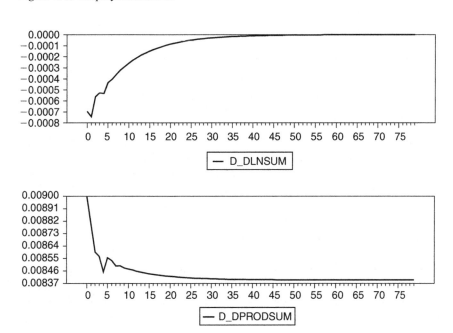

Figure 6.4b Productivity shock.

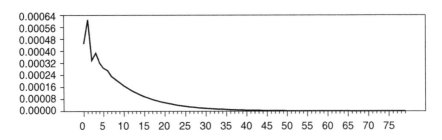

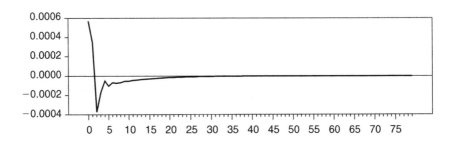

Figure 6.4c Demand shock (source: Commission Services).

Note
Upper panel: employment response; lower panel: productivity response.

versus temporary nature of the productivity growth slowdown. Based on the underlying assumptions on the short, medium and long-term impact of the various shocks, the VAR model attributes most of the decline in productivity to a structural trend decline in productivity growth. As can be seen from Figure 6.7, the autonomous shock to productivity explains a decline in the level of productivity of almost 5 per cent, which would translate into an annual average productivity growth rate effect of the order of -0.6 percentage points. This is fully consistent with the growth accounting result given earlier of a decline in TFP of the order of half of a percentage point, with TFP considered to be a reflection of the structural component of the productivity trend.

Figure 6.7 also indicates that the autonomous productivity shock is unable to explain the increase in employment. Therefore, it is necessary to look separately at both shocks in order to give a complete picture of both the employment and productivity developments. However, the overall conclusion from the analysis suggests that the decline in productivity growth is to a large extent structural in nature, i.e. not induced by the positive employment shock.

The empirical results presented above are broadly in line with other available evidence on structural labour market improvements as indicated by a trend increase in participation and a reduction in structural unemployment. Moreover, relating the productivity effect to real wage moderation also suggests that the

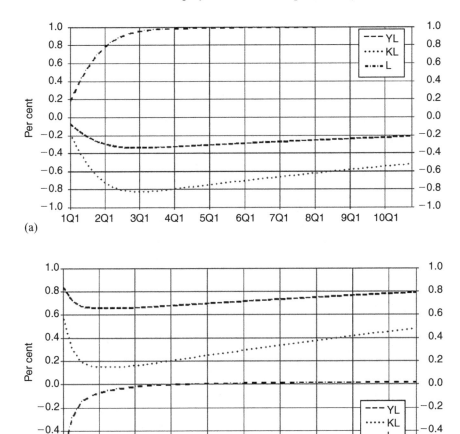

Figure 6.5 Employment shock (a), Productivity shock (b) (source: Commission services).

estimated impact on short run productivity developments is of a reasonable order of magnitude. A stylized number for real wage moderation in the past ten years or so would put the average annual reduction in real efficiency wages at slightly less than half a per cent. Thus, back-of-the-envelope calculations would suggest that real wage moderation could, on average, have reduced annual actual labour productivity growth relative to its balanced steady-state rate by about two-tenths of a percentage point, which is well within the range derived from the VAR and QUEST model approaches. Further corroborating evidence stems from growth regressions suggesting that about 25 per cent of the productivity decline is due to the increase in employment.[8]

In summary, and recalling that the overall slowdown in average annual productivity growth has amounted to about one percentage point, it emerges as a

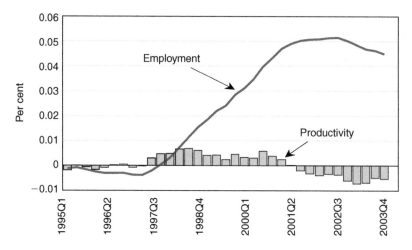

Figure 6.6 Cumulated euro area employment shock.

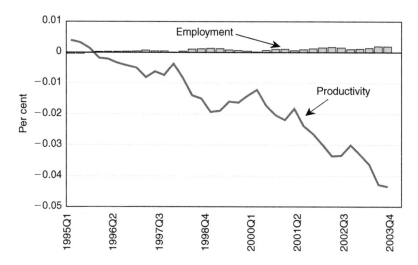

Figure 6.7 Cumulated euro area productivity shock.

fairly robust result that only some 20 per cent of this reduction can be attributed to the dynamic response of productivity to positive structural shocks in the labour market.

3 Conclusions

The analysis in this chapter challenges the notion of a genuine trade-off between employment and productivity growth. Obviously, misguided policies to exploit such a trade-off have to be avoided. However, there are no reasons to think that structural labour market reforms boosting employment will entail negative implications for longer-term productivity growth. In particular, this chapter reaches the following conclusions:

- The negative relationship between productivity and employment in comparative–static analyses should not be interpreted as a genuine trade-off.
- However, all else equal, a move towards full employment is likely to see a widening of the labour productivity gap between Europe and the US.
- The dynamic response of productivity to positive labour supply and wage shocks may entail a temporary reduction in productivity growth rates, which, in principle, could be considered as benign; in any case, the size of a negative effect of this type is estimated to be small.
- The increase in employment in the EU-15 since the mid-1990s has been to a significant extent the result of such positive labour market shocks, with about one half of the additional jobs attributed to structural improvements.
- Positive employment shocks can only account for a very small fraction of the observed productivity slowdown; consequently, the decline of labour productivity growth must be considered as predominantly caused by other factors and probably not just a temporary phenomenon. Indeed, a cyclical pick-up in labour productivity growth after the recent period of weak output growth should not divert attention from the 'deeper' structural problem of a slowdown in trend productivity growth.

The implications of the above findings for the Lisbon strategy are straight-forward. 'The more jobs the better' may serve as a simple catch-phrase characterizing the principal goal of labour market reform efforts since there is no genuine trade-off – in the sense of a difficult decision to be made – between policies to raise the employment rate and policies to foster productivity growth. Of course, misguided policies attempting to exploit such a trade-off have to be avoided – if, for example, policy-makers promoted sectors with low productivity *growth* prospects, if they introduced unnecessary regulations leading to 'over manning', if they discouraged young people from pursuing further education, or if they used funds for public training programmes in an unproductive manner, then employment might be raised at the expense of longer-term productivity potential. However, none of these policies is advocated in the EU's economic and employment policy framework and, in consequence, the employment strategy should not be blamed for the dismal productivity performance in recent years.

Notes

1 See Pichelmann and Roeger (2004) for an analysis of potential growth in the EU.
2 Labour augmenting technical progress is equal to Harrod-neutral technical progress when the capital stock grows at the same rate as output, thus leaving the capital/output ratio constant. For a Cobb-Douglas production function this 'balanced' labour productivity growth rate is defined as TFP growth divided by the labour share.
3 Gordon (1995) provides a neat theoretical and empirical investigation as to how a productivity-unemployment trade-off might emerge and how it will subsequently be eliminated through a dynamic path of capital adjustment.
4 Obviously, misguided policies attempting to exploit a perceived trade-off have to be avoided, for example unnecessary regulations leading to 'over manning'.
5 See Denis *et al.* (2004) for a detailed interpretation of recent productivity trends in Europe.
6 In fact, the hypothesis of a zero long run productivity effect cannot be rejected at standard significance levels.
7 It should be noted that this provides an estimate of the overall magnitude of the shocks, but not of the impact these shocks have had on the macroeconomic aggregates.
8 See EU Economy Review 2003, Table A3.

References

Blanchard, O. and Quah, D. (1989) 'The Dynamic Effects of Aggregate Demand and Supply Disturbances', *American Economic Review* 79(4): 655–673.

Denis, C., McMorrow, K. and Roeger, W. (2004) 'An analysis of EU and US productivity developments (a total economy and industry level perspective)', Economic papers No. 208, EU Commission, Directorate-General for Economic and Financial Affairs.

Elmeskov, J., Martin, J.P. and Scarpetta, S. (1998) 'Key lessons for Labour Market Reforms: Evidence from OECD Experiences', *Swedish Economic Policy Review*, 5: 205–252.

European Commission (2003) EU Economy 2003 Review, European Economy, No. 6, Luxembourg: Office for Official Publications of the EU.

Galí, J. (1999) 'Technology, Employment, and the Business Cycle: Do Technology Shocks Explain Aggregate Fluctuations?', *American Economic Review* 89: 249–271.

Gordon, R.J. (1995) 'Is There a Trade-off between Unemployment and Productivity Growth?', *CEPR Discussion Paper* No. 1159.

Pichelmann, K. and Roeger, W. (2004) 'The EU Growth Strategy and the Impact of Ageing', *Review of International Economics*, Special Issue: The Economic Agenda of the 21st Century.

Stock, J.H. and Watson, M.W. (1988) 'Testing for Common Trends', *Journal of the American Statistical Association* 83: 1097–1107.

7 Migration, labour markets, and integration of migrants

An overview for Europe with a comparison to the US

Rainer Münz[1]

1 Introduction

Between 1750 and 1976 Europe was the prime source region of world migration sending some 70 million people – the equivalent of one-third of its population growth – overseas. During the last 50 years, however, all countries of Western Europe[2] gradually became destinations for international migrants (Table 7.1). Several of the new EU member states in Central Europe and the Mediterranean also follow that pattern (Table 7.2).[3] It is likely that, sooner or later, this will be the case in other new EU member states and accession countries[4] as well. Many Europeans, however, still do not see their homelands as immigration countries – in particular not as destinations for permanent immigrants. This counter-factual perception of demographic realities has become an obstacle to the development and implementation of proactive migration regimes and comprehensive integration programmes. As a consequence it might be more difficult for the EU and its member states to attract the mix and kind of migrants this world region will need to recruit in the future for demographic and economic reasons.

2 Migration and population

In early 2006, the total population of Western and Central Europe, the Balkans and Turkey was 594 million. The European Union (EU-27) had 491 million inhabitants: of these, 389 million were either citizens or foreign residents of the 15 pre-enlargement Member States (EU-15). The other 102 million were citizens or foreign residents of the 12 new EU Member States (EU-12; of them: 101 million in Central Europe, the Baltic States and Southeastern Europe). Seventy-nine million people were living in EU candidate countries[5] (of them: 72 million in Turkey), another 12 million people in the rest of Western Europe,[6] and 17 million in other Western Balkan countries.[7]

In absolute terms, Germany has by far the largest foreign-born population (10.1 million), followed by France (6.4 million), the UK (5.4 million), Spain (4.8 million) and Italy (2.5 million). Relative to population size, two of Europe's smallest countries – Luxembourg (37.4 per cent) and Liechtenstein (33.9 per cent) –

Table 7.1 Cumulative net migration flows in Europe, 1950–2005

| | Cumulative net flows (+inflow, -outflow) | | | | | | | | | |
| | 1950–60 | | 1961–70 | | 1971–80 | | 1981–90 | | 1991–2000 | |
	In thousands	Annual rate in ‰	In thousands	Annual rate in ‰	In thousands	Annual rate in ‰	In thousands	Annual rate in ‰	In thousands	Annual rate in ‰
Total EU-25	**-2,284**	**-0.6**	**148**	**0.0**	**3,078**	**0.7**	**2,926**	**0.7**	**7,343**	**1.7**
Austria	-129	-1.8	67	0.9	79	1.0	138	1.8	238	3.0
Belgium	86	0.9	114	1.2	111	1.1	28	0.3	142	1.4
Cyprus[1]	n.a.	n.a.	-31	-5.3	-147	-29.9	21	3.9	68	10.5
Czech Republic	37	0.4	-99	-1.0	-18	-0.2	-39	-0.4	87	0.8
Denmark	-59	-1.3	34	0.7	22	0.4	45	0.9	133	2.6
Estonia	58	4.8	90	7.0	63	4.4	32	2.1	-147	-10.2
Finland	-85	-1.9	-178	-3.9	4	0.1	44	0.9	60	1.2
France	973	2.1	2,033	4.2	605	1.2	494	0.9	227	0.4
Germany[2]	1,011	1.4	1,488	2.0	1,505	1.9	2,022	2.6	3,347	4.1
Greece	-201	-2.4	-397	-4.7	258	2.9	220	2.2	718	6.8
Hungary	-190	-1.9	6	0.1	-19	-0.2	-167	-1.6	177	-1.7
Ireland	-392	-13.8	-140	-4.9	105	3.3	-204	-5.8	112	3.1
Italy	-1,014	-2.0	-972	-1.9	-84	-0.2	-132	-0.2	410	0.7
Latvia	62	3.0	133	5.9	98	4.0	74	2.9	-172	-6.9
Lithuania	-112	-4.1	43	1.5	52	1.6	86	2.4	-217	-6.0
Luxembourg	7	2.2	16	4.9	27	7.6	16	4.4	39	9.6
Malta	n.a.	n.a.	-54	-16.8	-3	-1.0	4	1.2	16	4.3
Netherlands	-164	-1.4	113	0.9	330	2.4	206	1.4	370	2.4
Poland	-308	-1.0	-300	-1.0	-307	-0.9	315	0.9	-543	-1.4
Portugal	-637	-7.2	-1,306	-14.5	383	4.3	-209	-2.1	199	2.0
Slovakia	73	1.8	-92	-2.1	-41	-0.9	-36	-0.7	-48	0.9
Slovenia	-50	-3.2	14	0.9	62	3.5	25	1.3	-9	0.5

Spain	−796	−2.6	−608	−1.9	144	0.4	−227	−0.6	1,302	3.3
Sweden	85	1.1	223	2.9	84	1.0	172	2.1	200	2.3
United Kingdom	−539	−1.0	−49	−0.1	−235	−0.4	−2	0.0	634	1.2
EU Member States of 2007										
Bulgaria	−165	−2.0	−20	−0.2	−134	−1.5	−351	−3.9	−370	−4.4
Romania	−179	−0.9	−116	−0.6	−109	−0.5	263	1.2	−533	−2.3
EU–27	**−2,628**	**−0.7**	**12**	**0.0**	**2,835**	**0.6**	**2,838**	**0.6**	**6,440**	**1.4**
EU candidate countries										
Croatia	−140	−3.3	−1	0.0	−28	−0.6	−6	−0.1	−201	−4.2
Macedonia	10	0.7	−37	−2.5	1	0.1	−253	−12.6	−10	−0.5
Turkey[3]	25	0.1	−488	−1.6	−488	−1.2	−488	−1.0	−513	−0.8
Other EEA and Switzerland										
Iceland	0	0.0	−5	−2.6	−5	−2.3	0	0.0	2	0.8
Liechtenstein	0	4.9	2	10.5	2	8.4	2	7.5	2	6.5
Norway	−23	−0.6	1	0.0	40	1.0	58	1.4	102	2.4
Switzerland	307	5.8	326	5.6	−89	−1.4	255	4.0	251	3.6
Other Southeastern Europe										
Albania[4]	7	0.4	7	0.4	−6	−0.3	−43	−1.5	−311	−9.6
Bosnia[5]	−182	−5.7	−224	−6.3	−133	−3.4	−20	−0.5	−350	−8.8
Moldova	n.a.	n.a.	n.a.	n.a.	n.a.	n.a.	n.a.	n.a.	n.a.	n.a.
Serbia, Montenegro[6]	−111	−1.4	−29	−0.3	−29	−0.3	174	1.7	−1	0.0

Source: Brücker (2002); Laczko and Münz (2003); UN Population Division Migration Data Base (2006), author's calculations.

Notes
1 1971–2005: Since 1971, Greek part of Cyprus only.
2 1951–90: Migration between East (GDR) and West Germany (FDR) not included.
3 1961–90: Estimates for Turkey based on an average for 1961–90.
4 1971–80: Data for 1978 missing.
5 2001–05: Provisional data.
6 1961–80: Estimates for Serbia based on an average for 1961–80.

Table 7.2 Demographic indicators 2005 in Europe

	Pop. January 2005 in 1,000	Births	Deaths	Nat. pop. change	Net migration	Total pop. change	Pop. January 2006 in 1,000
		per 1,000 population					
EU 27	**488,910**	**10.5**	**9.9**	**0.6**	**3.7**	**3.9**	**490,816**
Germany	82,501	8.4	10.1	-1.7	1.2	-0.5	82,456
France	60,561	12.6	8.8	3.7	1.7	5.4	60,892
UK	60,035	11.9	9.9	2.0	3.3	5.3	60,354
Italy	58,462	9.9	10.4	-0.5	5.8	5.3	58,772
Spain	43,038	10.9	8.8	2.1	15.0	17.1	43,781
Poland	38,174	9.4	9.7	-0.3	-0.3	-0.7	38,148
Bulgaria	7,761	9.0	14.6	-5.6	-1.8	-7.4	7,704
Netherlands	16,306	11.6	8.4	3.1	-1.2	2.0	16,338
Greece	11,076	9.4	9.2	0.2	3.1	3.3	11,112
Portugal	10,529	10.5	9.7	0.8	3.9	4.7	10,579
Belgium	10,446	11.4	10.0	1.4	3.2	4.6	10,494
Czech Republic	10,221	10.0	10.5	-0.5	3.5	2.9	10,251
Hungary	10,098	9.6	13.5	-3.9	1.8	-2.1	10,076
Sweden	9,011	10.4	9.9	0.5	2.7	3.2	9,040
Austria	8,207	9.4	9.0	0.4	7.4	7.8	8,270
Romania	21,659	10.2	12.3	-2.1	-0.5	-2.5	21,604
Denmark	5,411	11.8	10.3	1.6	1.4	3.0	5,428
Slovakia	5,385	10.0	9.8	0.2	0.8	0.9	5,390
Finland	5,237	11.0	9.2	1.8	1.7	3.5	5,255
Ireland	4,109	15.3	6.5	8.8	11.4	20.2	4,193
Lithuania	3,425	8.9	12.9	-4.0	-3.0	-7.0	3,401
Latvia	2,306	9.3	14.2	-4.9	-0.5	-5.4	2,294
Slovenia	1,998	8.8	9.2	-0.5	3.6	3.1	2,004

Estonia	1,347	10.6	13.1	−2.5	−0.3	−2.8	1,343
Cyprus[i]	749	10.9	6.7	4.1	27.2	31.3	773
Luxembourg	455	11.5	7.6	3.9	3.4	7.3	458
Malta	403	9.9	7.2	2.7	5.0	7.8	406
Other EEA							
Iceland	294	14.2	6.2	7.9	2.0	10.0	297
Liechtenstein	35	10.8	6.4	4.5	3.8	8.3	35
Norway	4,606	12.4	8.8	3.7	4.7	8.4	4,645
EEA	**464,423**	**10.5**	**9.7**	**0.7**	**3.7**	**4.4**	**466,484**
Switzerland	7,415	9.6	8.3	1.3	4.7	6.0	7,460
Accession countries	**105,472**	**16.0**	**8.3**	**7.6**	**−4.1**	**3.5**	**106,276**
Croatia	4,444	9.4	11.1	−1.7	2.6	0.9	4,448
Bulgaria	7,761	9.0	14.6	−5.6	−1.8	−7.4	7,704
Romania	21,659	10.2	12.3	−2.1	−0.5	−2.5	21,604
Turkey[ii]	71,609	18.9	6.2	12.6	−5.9	6.7	72,520

Source: EUROSTAT, Cronos Database.

Notes
i Greek part of Cyprus only.
ii Data for Turkey on net migration are from 2003.

Table 7.3 Foreign-national and foreign-born population in EU-27, 2005

	Foreign nationals[1]		Foreign born	
	(in thousands)	*%*	*(in thousands)*	*%*
EU-27	**23,895**	**4.7**	**40,501**	**8.3**
Austria	523	6.4	1,234	15.1
Belgium	272	2.6	1,186	11.4
Bulgaria	26	0.3	104	1.3
Cyprus[2]	65	9.4	116	13.9
Czech Republic	254	2.5	453	4.4
Denmark	268	4.9	389	7.2
Estonia	244	18.1	202	15.2
Finland	108	2.1	156	3.0
France	3,263	5.6	6,471	10.7
Germany	6,739	8.9	10,144	12.3
Greece	762	7.0	974	8.8
Hungary	142	1.4	316	3.1
Ireland	223	5.5	585	14.1
Italy	2,402	4.1	2,519	4.3
Latvia	103	3.9	449	19.5
Lithuania	21	0.6	165	4.8
Luxembourg	177	39.0	174	37.4
Malta	13	3.2	11	2.7
Netherlands	699	4.3	1,736	10.6
Poland	49	0.1	703	1.8
Portugal	449	4.3	764	7.3
Romania	26	0.1	103	0.6
Slovakia	22	0.4	124	2.3
Slovenia	37	1.9	167	8.5
Spain	2,984	6.9	4,790	11.1
Sweden	463	5.1	1,117	12.4
United Kingdom	2,856	4.8	5,408	9.1

Source: Foreign-born population: OECD Data Base (2006), UN (2006); foreign-national population: Community Labour Force Survey, Eurostat; various national sources; author's calculations, see Münz *et al.* (2007).

Notes
1 EU citizens from other Member States and third country nationals.
2 Greek part of Cyprus only.

have the largest stock of immigrants, followed by non-EU/EAA country Switzerland (22.9 per cent) and two Baltic States (Latvia 19.5 per cent and Estonia 15.4 per cent), Austria (15.1 per cent), Ireland (14.1 per cent), Cyprus (13.9 per cent), Sweden (12.4 per cent) and Germany (12.3 per cent). In the majority of West European countries, the foreign-born population accounts for 7–15 per cent of total population. In the majority of new EU Member States in Central and Southeastern Europe (excluding the Baltic States, Cyprus and Slovenia), the share of foreign-born is still below 5 per cent (see Table 7.3).

In 2005, Europe still experienced a population increase. In the 30 EU/EAA countries and Switzerland, total population growth was two million. But 11 of

Table 7.4 Immigrant population (15+ years) of known origin by education level and country of birth, EU-15, 2002[1] (percentages)

Education level[2] completed (in per cent)	Immigrant population by known country of birth									EU-15 total population
	EU West[2]	EU South[3]	EU-8 + CEE[4]	Turkey	Africa, Middle East	USA, Canada, Australia	Latin America, Caribbean	Asia	Total immigrants	
Low[5]	30.9	76.8	40.8	69.2	58.6	11.6	33.9	41.0	51.8	43.4
Medium[6]	37.8	15.6	39.5	22.5	24.5	34.7	33.0	31.5	28.2	39.4
High[7]	31.3	7.6	19.7	8.4	17.0	53.8	33.0	27.5	20.0	17.2
Total (per cent)	100.0	100.0	100.0	100.0	100.0	100.0	100.0	100.0	100.0	100.0
Total (in 1,000s)	2,774	2,801	1,628	766	3,084	346	224	966	12,589	312,639

Notes
1 LFS 2002, Data for Germany and Italy not available;
2 EU-15 residents born in another EU-15 country (except Italy, Greece, Portugal, or Spain) or born in Iceland, Liechtenstein, Norway, or Switzerland;
3 EU-15 residents born in Italy, Greece, Portugal, or Spain but living in another EU-15 country;
4 EU-15 residents born in new EU member states (EU-10), EU candidate countries (except Turkey), other countries in Central/Eastern Europe and the Balkans, Russia, Belarus, Ukraine, Caucasus, Central Asia;
5 Completed primary education only;
6 Completed lower or upper secondary education only;
7 Completed at least tertiary education.

the 30 EEA countries (as well as EU candidate country, Croatia[8]) had an excess of deaths over births. In the coming years, the number of countries with declining domestic population will increase. The other 20 countries still experienced some natural population growth. Net migration was positive in 25 of the 30 EU/EAA countries (plus Switzerland, Table 7.2).

Recent flows

In 2005, today's 30 EU and EEA countries plus Switzerland had an overall positive net migration rate of 3.4 per 1,000 inhabitants and a net migration gain of 1.8 million people. Migration accounted for almost 85 per cent of Western and Central Europe's total population growth of two million people in 2005. In absolute numbers for 2005, net migration was largest in Spain (+652,000) and Italy (+338,000), followed by the UK (+196,000), France (+103,000), Germany (+99,000), Portugal (+64,000), Austria (+61,000) and Ireland (+47,000).[9] Among the new EU Member States (EU-10) the Czech Republic experienced the largest net migration gain (+36,000). In addition, Cyprus, Hungary, Malta, Slovakia, Slovenia and Croatia also had a positive migration balance.

Several countries, in particular the Czech Republic, Italy, Greece, Slovenia and Slovakia, only showed a population growth because of immigration. In other countries, for example Germany and Hungary, recent population decline would have been much larger without a positive migration balance.

Relative to population size, Cyprus[10] had the largest positive migration balance (+27.2 per 1,000 inhabitants), followed by Spain (15.0 per 1,000), Ireland (+11.4), Austria (+7.4), Italy (+5.8), Malta (+5.0), Switzerland (+4.7), Norway (4.7) and Portugal (+3.8). On the other hand, Lithuania (-3.0 per 1,000 inhabitants), Bulgaria (-1.8), the Netherlands (-1.8), Latvia (-0.5), Romania (-1.5), Poland (-0.3), and Estonia (-0.3) had a negative migration balance.

Comparisons with the US suffer from the lack of population registers in North America. But estimates that include both legal and irregular migrants put the US foreign-born population at 36 million people. In fiscal year 2004 the US admitted 1.3 million legal permanent immigrants (3.9 per 1,000 inhabitants) and some 1.5 million temporary migrants.[11] Net migration only accounted for over one-third of US population growth.

3 Gates of entry, relevance of labour migration

EU and EEA citizens are more or less free to move within Western and Central Europe, to take residence and to join the workforce in any other EU/EEA member states (and Switzerland). Restrictions only apply to citizens of new EU member states in Central Europe (EU-10) seeking employment in another EU country.[12] The transitional regime limiting the free movement of workers from new member states (except Cyprus and Malta) following enlargement of the European Union on 1 May 2004 and January 2007 allows other EU countries to decide to postpone the opening of their national labour markets up to a maximum period of seven years. Initially only three countries, the UK, Ireland and Sweden had opened their labour markets to newly arriving EU citizens from Central Europe and the Baltics. As a result Ireland (2004–06: +160,000) and the UK (2004–06: +427,000) experienced unprecedented gross inflows from new EU member states, mainly from Poland, Lithuania and Slovakia (Tamas and Münz, 2006). In 2006–07 Finland, Greece, Italy, the Netherlands, Portugal and Spain followed their example. Since 2007 a similar transitional regime limits the free movement of Bulgarian and Romanian workers. So far only a few EU countries (including the Czech Republic, Estonia, Finland, Poland, Slovakia and partly France) have opened their labour markets for workers from Bulgaria and Romania.

The key gates of entry for third-country nationals entering the EU as permanent migrants are employment, family reunion[13] and family formation, the inflow of asylum seekers (some 300,000 applications in EU-27 annually),[14] and the inflow of co-ethnic 'return' migrants and their dependent family members.[15] In 2001 some 40 per cent of the residence permits were granted in EU-15 for employment and another 30 per cent for family reunifications.[16] However, on the one hand these numbers do not account for seasonal and temporary labour migration, which is quite common in countries like Austria, Germany, France, Italy and Spain. On the other, they do not include irregular immigration.[17]

For a select number of EU member states, the relative importance of employment, family reunion, asylum and other reasons for immigrants to enter the Union is known. Entry visa or residence permits granted for work purposes accounted for over 40 per cent of all permits in Denmark, Portugal and Switzerland (2004). In the UK, Finland, Austria, Italy and the Netherlands their share was 30–35 per cent. In Austria, France, Germany, Italy, Sweden and Switerland over 50 per cent of residence permits were granted for purposes of family formation/reunion (2004). In Italy, Norway and the UK, asylum and the admission of quota refugees played a quantitatively significant role (2004: over 20 per cent of all permits).[18] In the UK, employment was the reason for entry in only 27 per cent of the cases, as was family reunion (also 27 per cent).[19]

For the EU overall, nearly 40 per cent of all residence permits were granted for the purpose of employment whereas 30 per cent were granted for the purpose of family reunion. These figures, however, do not give the full picture. For example, in several EU countries economic migration takes place to a larger extent in the form of seasonal and temporary labour migration (some 600,000–800,000 persons admitted annually in the EU and other countries of Western Europe)[20] as well as in the form of irregular labour migration of at least the same magnitude. The latter only becomes statistically visible on the occasion of so-called amnesties and regularization programmes. During the period 1995–2005 some 3.7 million migrants were formally regularized in EU-15.[21] An unknown number of EU-12 citizens living in EU-15 acquired legal resident status when their countries of origin became EU member states in 2004 and 2007.[22]

Table 7.5 Foreign-born labour force and foreign-nationals labour force in selected countries of Western and Central Europe in 2004

Country	Foreign-born labour force[1] total (in thousands)	Foreign-born labour force as % of total labour force	Foreign-national labour force[2] total (in thousands)	Foreign-national labour force as % of total labour force
Austria	585	15.3	320	8.4
Belgium	512	11.5	357	8.0
Czech Republic	109	1.2	36	0.7
Denmark	161	5.9	107	3.9
Finland	70	2.6	41	1.5
France	2,990	11.3	1,444	5.4
Germany	4,800	12.2	3,539	9.0
Greece[3]	402	8.5	303	6.4
Hungary[4]	85	2.1	30	0.7
Ireland	188	10.0	112	5.9
Italy[4]	1,350	5.6	759	32
Luxembourg	88	45.0	88	45.0
Netherlands	929	11.1	299	3.6
Norway	167	7.1	88	3.8
Portugal[4]	379	7.3	150	2.9
Spain[4]	2,241	11.2	1,852	9.3
Sweden	606	13.3	204	4.5
Switzerland	1,022	25.3	889	22.0
United Kingdom	2,759	9.6	1,557	5.5
Total	19,443	8.6	12,175	5.4

Source: OECD (2006), World Bank, World Development Indicators database.

Notes

1 Intra-EU migrants from other EU Member States and migrants born in third countries.
2 EU citizens from other EU Member States and third country nationals.
3 Data based on third country nationals entering Greece for legal employment.
4 Substantial irregular foreign workforce not included in country results.

Education levels

The skills profile of the foreign-born population is markedly different from that of the total EU-15 population (Table 7.4). Both people with low formal education[23] (immigrants: 52 per cent; EU-15 average: 43 per cent) and with high formal education[24] (immigrants: 20 per cent; EU-15 average: 17 per cent) are overrepresented among immigrants. People with medium formal education[25] are underrepresented (immigrants: 28 per cent; EU-15 average: 39 per cent). This is mainly a result of labour markets primarily creating demand for high- and low-skilled migrants.

Immigrants from Southern Europe living in another EU country as well as immigrant populations from Turkey, North Africa/Middle East and sub-

Table 7.6 Immigrant population of working age (15–64 years) and known origin by labour force status, gender, and region of birth, EU-15, 2002[1] (percentages)

Labour force status		Immigrant population by known region of birth				EU-15 total population
		EU-15[2]	*EU-10[3]*	*Rest of the world*	*Total immigrants*	
Total	Employed	67.3	62.0	57.0	61.3	64.2
	Unemployed	4.5	5.2	8.2	6.6	5.4
	Inactive	28.2	32.8	34.8	32.1	30.4
	Total (per cent)	100.0	100.0	100.0	100.0	100.0
	Active (per cent)	71.8	67.2	65.2	67.8	69.6
	Unemployment rate (per cent)	6.2	7.7	12.6	9.7	7.8
	Total (in 1,000s)	4,559	461	6,546	11,566	250,433
Male	Employed	75.3	69.8	68.5	71.2	72.9
	Unemployed	4.7	4.8	9.2	7.3	5.4
	Inactive	20.1	25.4	22.3	21.5	21.7
	Total (per cent)	100.0	100.0	100.0	100.0	100.0
	Active (per cent)	79.9	74.6	77.7	78.5	78.3
	Unemployment rate (per cent)	5.9	6.4	11.9	9.3	6.9
	Total (in 1,000s)	2,239	189	3,284	5,714	125,441
Female	Employed	59.6	56.6	45.3	51.5	55.5
	Unemployed	4.3	5.5	7.1	5.9	5.3
	Inactive	36.1	37.9	47.5	42.5	39.2
	Total (per cent)	100.0	100.0	100.0	100.0	100.0
	Active (per cent)	63.9	62.1	52.5	57.5	60.8
	Unemployment rate (per cent)	6.7	8.9	13.6	10.3	8.7
	Total (in 1,000s)	2,319	272	3,262	5,853	124,993

Notes
1 LFS 2002, Data for Germany and Italy not available;
2 EU-15 residents born in another EU-15 country or born in Iceland, Liechtenstein, Norway, or Switzerland;
3 EU-15 residents born in the new EU member states (EU-10).

Saharan Africa have relatively high proportions of people with low skills (Southern EU: 78.6; TY: 69.2; MENA: 58.6). In contrast, immigrant groups from North-western Europe living in another EU country and, in particular, immigrants from other industrialized world regions (North America, Australia/ New Zealand: 58.3; Latin America: 33.0) have higher proportions of highly-skilled people.

Work force

In 2005 there were some 317 million working age (15–64) people living in Western and Central Europe (EU-25, EEA and Switzerland). Of them, 209 million were actually employed, resulting in an overall employment rate of 65 per cent. Another 19.5 million were seeking a job, for an overall unemployment rate of 8.6 per cent. Twelve million foreign nationals (other EU citizens and third country nationals) are part of Western Europe's workforce. But the number of immigrants (born in another EU country or in a third country) in the labour market amounts to 19 million (Table 7.5).

Between 1997 and 2002 the number of people gainfully employed[26] in the EU-15 increased by about 12 million, out of which 9.5 million were EU nationals and more than 2.5 million third-country nationals. While the share of third-country nationals in total EU employment was just 3.6 per cent in 2002, they contributed to employment growth by 13 per cent during the period 1997–2002 (Table 7.6).[27] If we account for foreign-born third-country nationals and natural-ized EU citizens the contribution of immigrants to employment growth was of the order of 20 per cent (Table 7.6).[28]

In 1997, the employment rates of EU nationals had already reached 79 per cent for the medium-skilled and 88 per cent for the high-skilled. In 2002 they had risen further to 82 per cent and 89 per cent respectively. A similar develop-ment is true for legal foreign residents in EU-15.

The number of medium skilled third-country nationals increased by 50 per cent and that of high-skilled third-country nationals doubled, amounting to more than 60 per cent of the total increase in employment.[29] This reflected cyclical growth in employment and the migrants' over-proportional contribution to the increase during 1997–2002, a period of economic and employment growth (Table 7.7). The situation for the low-skilled is less favourable, with more modest employment increase, but was nonetheless stronger for third-country than EU-nationals.[30]

4 Employment and unemployment rates

The employment rate of working age adults (15–64 years) varies with place of origin (Table 7.8). EU working age adults had an overall employment rate of 64.2 per cent and an unemployment rate of 5.4 per cent in 2002. Immigrants from Western and Southern Europe living in another EU country and from other industrialized countries have higher employment rates (Western and Southern

Table 7.7 Distribution of employment growth by country of origin or nationality and gender of worker, EU-15,[1] 1997–2003: citizenship and country of birth compared (percentages)

Nationality or country of birth	Citizenship or nationality of persons in the additional workforce					
	Male		Female		Total	
	Foreign nationals and citizens	Foreign born and native born	Foreign nationals and citizens	Foreign born and native born	Foreign nationals and citizens	Foreign born and native born
Other EU-15	1.3[2]	2.2[3]	1.8[2]	3.2[3]	1.8[2]	2.6[3]
EU-10+CEE[6]	3.9	2.7	5.6	4.1	3.3	4.8
Other Europe	0.1	0.1	1.4	0.6	0.1	1.0
North Africa	0.3	0.4	0.6	1.2	0.3	0.9
North America, Australia	0.4	0.2	0.3	−0.2	0.3	0.0
Other	7.3	5.5	13.4	10.1	6.3	11.6
Nationals/natives	85.9[4]	88.4[5]	78.1[4]	81.8[5]	87.3[4]	80.1[5]
Unknown	0.7	0.5	−1.2	−0.7	0.6	−1.0
Total	100.0	100.0	100.0	100.0	100.0	100.0

Source: Labour Force Survey 2003.

Notes
1 Data for Germany and Italy not available;
2 EU-15 legal residents with citizenship of another EU-15 member state;
3 EU-15 residents born in another EU-15 member state;
4 EU-15 nationals residing in their country of citizenship;
5 EU-15 natives residing in their country of birth;
6 New EU member states (EU-10), EU candidate countries (except Turkey), other countries of Central/Eastern Europe and the Balkans, Russia, Belarus, Ukraine, Caucasus, Central Asia.

Table 7.8 Immigrant population of working age (15–64 years) and known origin by labour force status, gender, and country of birth, EU-15, 2002[1] (percentages)

Labour force status		Immigrant population by known country of birth								Total immigrants	EU-15 total population
		EU-West[2]	EU-South[3]	EU-10 + CEE[4]	Turkey	Africa, Middle East	USA, Canada, Australia	Latin America, Caribbean	Asia		
Total	Employed	67.1	67.3	63.2	50.0	51.4	76.3	62.7	58.6	61.3	64.2
	Unemployed	4.7	4.2	7.8	9.2	9.8	3.5	8.3	5.2	6.6	5.4
	Inactive	28.1	28.4	29.0	40.8	38.7	20.2	29.0	36.2	32.1	30.4
	Total (per cent)	100.0	100.0	100.0	100.0	100.0	100.0	100.0	100.0	100.0	100.0
	Active (per cent)	71.8	71.5	71.0	59.2	61.2	79.8	71.0	63.8	67.9	69.6
	Unemployment rate (per cent)	6.5	5.9	11.0	15.5	16.0	4.4	11.7	8.2	9.7	7.8
	Total (in 1,000s)	2,587	2,145	1,516	772	2,706	456	217	1,166	11,565	250,433
Male	Employed	75.0	75.3	72.7	65.1	62.6	86.0	73.9	73.2	71.2	72.9
	Unemployed	5.2	4.1	7.6	11.6	11.4	3.2	5.4	6.0	7.3	5.4
	Inactive	19.9	20.5	19.7	23.4	25.9	10.9	20.7	20.8	21.5	21.7
	Total (per cent)	100.0	100.0	100.0	100.0	100.0	100.0	100.0	100.0	100.0	100.0
	Active (per cent)	80.2	79.4	80.3	76.7	74.0	89.2	79.3	79.2	78.5	78.3
	Unemployment rate (per cent)	6.5	5.2	9.5	15.1	15.4	3.6	6.8	7.6	9.3	6.9
	Total (in 1,000s)	1,182	1,135	696	398	1,442	221	92	548	5,714	125,441
Female	Employed	60.5	58.3	55.1	33.9	38.7	67.5	54.0	45.6	51.5	55.5
	Unemployed	4.3	4.4	7.9	6.9	8.0	3.4	11.1	4.7	5.9	5.3
	Inactive	35.2	37.3	37.0	59.2	53.3	29.1	34.9	49.8	42.5	39.2
	Total (per cent)	100.0	100.0	100.0	100.0	100.0	100.0	100.0	100.0	100.0	100.0
	Active (per cent)	64.8	62.7	63.0	40.8	46.7	70.9	65.1	50.3	57.4	60.8
	Unemployment rate (per cent)	6.6	7.0	12.5	16.9	17.1	4.8	17.1	9.3	10.3	8.7
	Total (in 1,000s)	1,405	1,010	820	375	1,264	234	126	619	5,853	124,993

Notes
1 LFS 2002, Data for Germany and Italy not available;
2 EU-15 residents born in another EU-15 country (except Italy, Greece, Portugal, or Spain) or born in Iceland, Liechtenstein, Norway, or Switzerland;
3 EU-15 residents born in Italy, Greece, Portugal, or Spain but living in another EU-15 country;
4 EU-15 residents born in new EU member states (EU-10), EU candidate countries (except Turkey), other countries in Central/Eastern Europe and the Balkans, Russia, Belarus, Ukraine, Caucasus, Central Asia.

Table 7.9 Legal foreign resident population of working age (15–64) by labour force status, gender and region of nationality, EU-15, 2002[1] (percentages)

Labour force status		Legal foreign resident population by nationality				EU-15 total population
		EU-15[2]	EU-10[3]	Rest of the world	Total LFRs	
Total	Employed	67.2	60.4	52.5	58.6	64.2
	Unemployed	5.1	6.7	9.7	7.7	5.4
	Inactive	27.7	33.0	37.8	33.6	30.4
	Total (per cent)	100.0	100.0	100.0	100.0	100.0
	Active (per cent)	72.3	67.0	62.2	66.4	69.6
	Unemployment rate (per cent)	7.0	10.0	15.5	11.7	7.8
	Total (in 1,000s)	4,206	449	6,059	10,714	250,433
Male	Employed	74.6	73.9	64.6	68.9	72.9
	Unemployed	5.7	6.8	11.7	9.1	5.4
	Inactive	19.7	19.3	23.7	22.0	21.7
	Total (per cent)	100.0	100.0	100.0	100.0	100.0
	Active (per cent)	80.3	80.7	76.3	78.0	78.3
	Unemployment rate (per cent)	7.1	8.5	15.3	11.7	6.9
	Total (in 1,000s)	2,208	176	3,087	5,471	125,441
Female	Employed	59.1	51.6	40.1	47.9	55.5
	Unemployed	4.4	6.6	7.6	6.3	5.3
	Inactive	36.6	41.8	52.4	45.8	39.2
	Total (per cent)	100.0	100.0	100.0	100.0	100.0
	Active (per cent)	63.4	58.2	47.6	54.2	60.8
	Unemployment rate (per cent)	6.9	11.3	15.9	11.6	8.7
	Total (in 1,000s)	1,997	273	2,972	5,242	124,993

Notes
1 LFS 2002, Data for Italy not available;
2 EU-15 nationals+nationals of Iceland, Liechtenstein, Norway and Switzerland living in (another) EU-15 country;
3 Nationals of EU-10 (new member) states living in an EU-15 country.

EU: 67 per cent; North America, Australia: 76 per cent) and lower unemployment rates (Western EU: 4.7 per cent, Southern EU: 4.2 per cent, North America/Australia: 3.5 per cent) than those of the total EU-15. The opposite is true for immigrants from other parts of the world. Employment rate is particularly low and unemployment correspondingly high among immigrants from Turkey (50 per cent and 9.2 per cent), Middle East/Africa (51 per cent and 9.8 per cent), and Asia (59 per cent and 5.2 per cent). Immigrants from the new EU member states, the Balkans and Eastern Europe (collectively the Central and Eastern Europe Countries=EU-10+CEE) and from Latin America have almost the same employment rate (63 per cent) as the EU-15 average, but higher unemployment (Balkans, Eastern Europe: 7.8 per cent, Latin America: 8.3 per cent).

Foreign-born men only have a slightly lower employment rate (71 per cent) and higher unemployment (7.3 per cent) than the total EU-15 male population (73 per cent and 5.4 per cent respectively). Employment is high among male immigrants from other EU member states, the Americas and Australia, Latin America, and the Caribbean (75 per cent, 86 per cent, and 74 per cent respectively). Only male immigrants from Turkey and also Africa and the Middle East have significantly lower employment rates (65 per cent and 63 per cent respectively) and much higher unemployment (11.6 per cent and 11.4 per cent respectively).

Differences are larger among women. Female immigrants from Turkey and from Africa and the Middle East have particularly low employment rates (34 per cent and 39 per cent respectively) and high unemployment rates (6.9 per cent and 8.0 per cent respectively) relative to all EU-15 women (55 per cent and 5.3 per cent respectively). The opposite is true for women from Western EU countries (61 per cent and 4.3 per cent) and from N. America and Australia (68 per cent and 3.4 per cent). Women from Asia have particularly low employment and unemployment rates (46 per cent and 4.7 per cent respectively). Women from Latin America have particularly high unemployment (11.1 per cent).

When comparing legal foreign residents with the EU-15 average, the differences are much larger (Table 7.9). The overall employment rate of other EU citizens residing in the EU-15 but outside their country of citizenship, and of third-country nationals, is only 59 per cent as compared with an average of 64 per cent for the EU-15 as a whole. The unemployment rate of foreign residents is 7.7 per cent as compared with an average of 5.4 per cent for the EU-15 as a whole. Among foreign men the employment rate is 69 per cent and the unemployment rate is 9.1 per cent, as compared with EU-15 averages of 73 per cent and 5.4 per cent respectively. Among foreign women, the employment rate is 48 per cent and the unemployment rate 6.3 per cent, compared with averages of 56 per cent and 5.3 per cent respectively for all EU-15 women.

A comparison of rates of employment computed for the foreign-born and those computed for the legal foreign resident population (Table 7.10) shows clear discrepancies, especially regarding persons associated with the new EU member states, the Balkans and Eastern Europe, Turkey, Africa and the Middle

Table 7.10 Employment rates of working age legal foreign resident population and immigrant population with country of birth known, by national- ity or country of birth, and gender, EU-15, 2002

Nationality or country of birth	Employment rate					
	Male		Female		Total	
	Foreign national[1]	Foreign born[2]	Foreign national[1]	Foreign born[2]	Foreign national[1]	Foreign born[2]
EU-15[3]	74.6	75.3	59.1	59.6	67.2	67.3
Non EU-15 Europe	64.6	68.5	40.1	45.3	52.5	57.0
North Africa	55.3	62.6	24.8	38.7	41.5	51.4
North America	85.9	86.0	67.5	67.5	76.8	76.3
Turkey	61.3	65.1	31.6	33.9	47.5	50.0
Total[4]	68.9	71.2	47.9	51.5	58.6	61.3
EU-15 average	**72.9**	**72.9**	**55.5**	**55.5**	**64.2**	**64.2**

Notes
1 LFS 2002, data on foreign nationals for Italy not available;
2 LFS 2002, data on foreign born for Germany and Italy not available;
3 EU-15 nationals/people born in EU-15 and currently living in EU-15, but outside their country of citizenship or birth;
4 All foreign nationals/all migrants.

Table 7.11 Legal foreign resident population of working age (15–64) by labour force status, gender, and country of nationality, EU-15, 2002[1] (percentages)

Labour force status		Legal foreign resident population by nationality									EU-15 total population
		EU-West[2]	EU-South[3]	EU-10 + CEE[4]	Turkey	Africa, Middle East	USA, Canada, Australia	Latin America, Caribbean	Asia	Total LFRs	
Total	Employed	67.5	66.9	60.7	47.5	41.5	76.8	62.6	56.6	58.6	64.2
	Unemployed	4.0	5.9	8.9	10.1	12.8	3.1	9.6	5.9	7.7	5.4
	Inactive	28.5	27.1	30.4	42.4	45.7	20.1	27.8	37.5	33.6	30.4
	Total (per cent)	100.0	100.0	100.0	100.0	100.0	100.0	100.0	100.0	100.0	100.0
	Active (per cent)	71.5	72.8	69.6	57.6	54.3	79.9	72.2	62.5	66.3	69.6
	Unemployment rate (per cent)	5.6	8.1	12.8	17.5	23.6	3.9	13.3	9.4	11.6	7.8
	Total (in 1,000s)	2,027	2,310	1,861	2,121	1,373	383	115	525	10,715	250,433
Male	Employed	75.5	73.9	70.3	61.3	55.3	85.9	77.1	74.1	68.9	72.9
	Unemployed	4.6	6.4	9.4	13.0	15.6	3.6	4.2	7.5	9.1	5.4
	Inactive	19.9	19.7	20.3	25.7	29.0	10.4	18.8	18.4	22.0	21.7
	Total (per cent)	100.0	100.0	100.0	100.0	100.0	100.0	100.0	100.0	100.0	100.0
	Active (per cent)	80.1	80.3	79.7	74.3	70.9	89.5	81.3	81.6	78.0	78.3
	Unemployment rate (per cent)	5.7	8.0	11.8	17.5	22.0	4.0	5.2	9.2	11.7	6.9
	Total (in 1,000s)	975	1,293	842	1,131	748	192	48	239	5,468	125,441
Female	Employed	60.1	58.1	52.8	31.6	24.8	67.5	52.2	42.0	47.9	55.5
	Unemployed	3.5	5.3	8.4	6.9	9.5	2.6	13.4	4.5	6.3	5.3
	Inactive	36.4	36.6	38.7	61.5	65.7	29.8	34.3	53.5	45.8	39.2
	Total (per cent)	100.0	100.0	100.0	100.0	100.0	100.0	100.0	100.0	100.0	100.0
	Active (per cent)	63.6	63.4	61.2	38.5	34.3	70.1	65.6	46.5	54.2	60.8
	Unemployment rate (per cent)	5.5	8.4	13.7	17.9	27.7	3.7	20.4	9.7	11.6	8.7
	Total (in 1,000s)	1,052	1,016	1,018	989	624	191	67	286	5,243	124,993

Notes
1 LFS 2002, Data for Italy not available;
2 EU-15 nationals (except Italy, Greece, Portugal, Spain) + nationals of Iceland, Liechtenstein, Norway, or Switzerland living in (another) EU-15 country;
3 Nationals of Italy, Greece, Portugal, or Spain living in another EU-15 country;
4 Nationals of new EU member states (EU-10), EU candidate countries (except Turkey), other countries in Central/Eastern Europe and the Balkans, Russia, Belarus, Ukraine, Caucasus, or Central Asia living in an EU-15 country.

Table 7.12 Employment rate of working age (15–64 years) population born in or nationals of Maghreb and Turkey and resident in selected EU countries, 2002[1]: two concepts compared

	Immigrants from Maghreb countries[2]	Nationals of Maghreb countries	Immigrants from Turkey	Nationals of Turkey
Belgium	34.5	21.6	31.9	26.2
Denmark	43.5	36.4	46.7	30.8
Germany	n/a	47.1	n/a	48.5
Greece	63.2	75.0	57.1	57.1
Spain	56.3	57.0	n/a	37.9
France	50.8	39.1	42.2	50.6
Netherlands	53.2	41.9	55.9	57.0
Austria	55.6	42.9	59.8	33.3
Sweden	44.3	34.5	50.0	44.4
UK	65.3	60.4	55.9	26.2

Notes
1 LFS 2002;
2 Algeria, Morocco, Tunisia.

East (Table 7.11). Such discrepancies, however, vary by country of residence. This is exemplified in a cross-country comparison of immigrants from and nationals of the Maghreb[31] and Turkey (Table 7.12). In most EU-15 countries, which in the past received immigrants from the Southern and/or Eastern Mediterranean, the immigrants born in Turkey and the Maghreb have higher employment rates than Algerian, Moroccan, Tunisian and Turkish citizens living in these countries. For Turks this is true in Belgium, Denmark, Austria, Sweden, and the UK. For Maghreb citizens the differences are visible in France, Belgium, the Netherlands, and Denmark. This can be interpreted as a result of particularly exclusionary mechanisms in labour markets of these countries affecting foreign nationals more adversely than naturalized citizens. But such discrepancies are almost nonexistent when comparing immigrants from other EU member states, North America and Australia as well as Latin America with nationals of the same regions living in EU-15 (Table 7.10).

In the US, the foreign-born population is also extremely heterogeneous with respect to labour market performance as measured by labour force participation and unemployment rates. Among persons between the ages of 15 and 64, the US-born population as well as North/West European, Canadian, and African immigrants to the US have labour force participation rates of over 72 per cent. In contrast, Mexican, Caribbean, West Asian, Caribbean and Central American immigrants have considerably lower rates of labour force participation (between 62 and 66 per cent).[32]

Likewise, in the US there is strong variation in unemployment rates between groups. North/West European and Canadian immigrants have the lowest unemployment rate (3.1 per cent); moreover, the rate for several other immigrant

Table 7.13 Immigrant workforce of known origin by ISCO[1] skill level and country of birth, EU-15, 2002[2] (percentages)

ISCO skill level	Immigrant workforce by known country of birth								Total immigrant workforce	EU-15 total workforce
	EU West[2]	EU South[3]	EU-10 + CEE[4]	Turkey	Africa, Middle East	USA, Canada, Australia	Latin America, Caribbean	Asia		
Highly-skilled non-manual	49.9	20.9	20.1	21.4	35.8	64.7	36.5	38.8	34.9	36.8
Medium-skilled non-manual	11.7	6.9	5.4	6.6	11.1	12.6	12.4	9.4	9.3	12.9
Low-skilled non-manual	13.0	13.1	16.0	14.2	12.5	7.5	20.4	17.5	13.7	14.0
Skilled manual	10.4	32.0	22.1	22.6	15.7	5.8	11.7	6.5	17.7	17.7
Non-skilled manual	14.5	27.0	36.4	34.7	24.2	7.5	19.0	27.6	24.0	17.9
Armed Forces	0.5	0.1	–	0.5	0.7	2.0	–	0.1	0.4	0.7
Total (per cent)	100.0	100.0	100.0	100.0	100.0	100.0	100.0	100.0	100.0	100.0
Total (in 1,000s)	1,758	1,527	959	380	1,391	348	137	691	7,191	161,906

Notes

1 International Standard Classification of Occupations;
2 LFS 2002, Data for Germany and Italy not available;
3 EU-15 residents born in another EU-15 country (except Italy, Greece, Portugal, Spain) or born in Iceland, Liechtenstein, Norway, or Switzerland;
4 EU-15 residents born in Italy, Greece, Portugal, or Spain but living in another EU-15 country;
5 EU-15 residents born in the new EU member states (EU-10), EU candidate countries (except Turkey), other countries in Central/Eastern Europe and the Balkans, Russia, Belarus, Ukraine, Caucasus, Central Asia.

Table 7.14 Legal foreign resident workforce by ISCO[1] skill level and nationality, EU-15, 2002[2] (percentages)

ISCO skill level	Legal foreign resident workforce by nationality									EU-15 total workforce
	EU West[3]	EU South[4]	EU-10 + CEE[5]	Turkey	Africa, Middle East	USA, Canada, Australia	Latin America, Caribbean	Asia	Total LFR workforce	
Highly-skilled non-manual	53.7	21.1	17.9	12.1	19.9	68.0	27.4	32.7	29.0	36.8
Medium-skilled non-manual	11.5	6.8	5.3	6.1	7.8	11.9	12.3	5.4	7.8	12.9
Low-skilled non-manual	12.6	16.0	16.1	12.3	13.8	6.5	23.3	25.3	14.5	14.0
Skilled manual	9.6	24.6	24.7	27.7	24.2	4.4	15.1	7.7	19.9	17.7
Non-skilled manual	12.5	31.5	36.0	41.7	34.2	7.5	21.9	29.0	28.6	17.9
Armed Forces	0.1	–	–	0.1	0.2	1.7	–	–	0.1	0.7
Total (per cent)	100.0	100.0	100.0	100.0	100.0	100.0	100.0	100.0	100.0	100.0
Total (in 1,000s)	1,378	1,541	1,122	995	567	294	73	297	6,267	161,906

Notes
1 International Standard Classification of Occupations;
2 LFS 2002, Data for Italy not available;
3 EU-15 nationals (except Italy, Greece, Portugal, or Spain) + nationals of Iceland, Liechtenstein, Norway, or Switzerland living in (another) EU-15 country;
4 Nationals of Italy, Greece, Portugal, or Spain living in another EU-15 country;
5 Nationals of new EU member states (EU-10), EU candidate countries (except Turkey), other countries in Central/Eastern Europe and the Balkans, Russia, Belarus, Ukraine, Caucasus, Central Asia who are living in an EU-15 country.

groups is less than that for the US-born population (5.6 per cent). Other groups have unemployment rates that are almost double that of the American-born population: rates for Mexican (9.4 per cent), Caribbean (9.3 per cent) and Central American (8.4 per cent) immigrants are particularly high.[33]

5 Occupational structure and industry structure

On the whole the occupational structure of foreign-born workers in Europe (as identified in the LFS) is different from the EU-15 average (Table 7.13). Immigrant workers are underrepresented in medium-skilled non-manual positions (immigrants: 9 per cent; EU-15 average: 13 per cent) and over-represented in non-skilled manual positions (immigrants: 24 per cent; EU-15 average: 18 per cent). Immigrants from Northwestern Europe living elsewhere in the EU, as well as immigrants from other industrialized countries (North America, Australia/ New Zealand), predominantly occupy highly skilled non-manual positions (Western EU immigrants: 50 per cent, North American immigrants: 65 per cent, EU-15 average: 37 per cent). Immigrants from Southern Europe living elsewhere in the EU (skilled manual: 32 per cent, unskilled manual: 27 per cent), as well as immigrants from the Balkans, Central and Eastern Europe (skilled manual: 22 per cent, unskilled manual: 36 per cent) and from Turkey (skilled manual: 23 per cent, unskilled manual: 35 per cent), are disproportionately active in skilled and unskilled manual positions (EU-15 average skilled manual: 18 per cent, unskilled manual: 18 per cent). Immigrants from North Africa/ Middle East and sub-Saharan Africa as well as from Asia have an average representation in highly skilled non-manual positions[34] but are disproportionately active in unskilled manual positions (Africa: 24 per cent, Asia: 28 per cent).

In comparison with the overall EU population (Table 7.14), legal foreign residents on average are less concentrated in highly skilled non-manual positions (29 per cent, EU-15 average: 37 per cent), but they are over-represented in skilled manual (20 per cent, EU-15: 18 per cent) and particularly in unskilled manual positions (29 per cent, EU-15: 18 per cent). These differences between the foreign-born and foreign nationals are significant for the following regions of origin and groups of foreign nationality: Turkey, North Africa/Middle East and sub-Saharan Africa, Latin America and the Caribbean. Such differences are less pronounced but still visible for migrants from/nationals of Southern Europe and Asia. And there are only very small differences for migrants from or nationals of Northwestern Europe and North America, Australia/New Zealand.

Differences between the industrial distribution of immigrant and overall EU-15 workforce are accentuated when comparing the latter with the legal foreign resident workforce. Foreign nationals are more frequently employed in manufacturing, construction, hotels and restaurants, and research and development than the EU-15 average (Table 7.15). At the same time they are less likely to work in the public sector, in particular public administration and education (Table 7.16). Such differences point to the fact that many foreign residents take

Table 7.15 Immigrant workforce of known origin by sector/industry (NACE) and country of birth, EU-15, 2002¹ (percentages)

NACE sector or industry	Immigrant workforce by country of birth									EU-15 total workforce
	EU West²	EU South³	EU-10 + CEE⁴	Turkey	Africa, Middle East	USA, Canada, Australia	Latin America, Caribbean	Asia	Total immigrant workforce	
Agric., fishing, mining	0.4	0.4	0.3	0.3	0.2	0.9	–	0.2	0.3	0.3
Manufacturing	16.4	18.2	19.4	25.3	15.6	11.2	14.9	18.1	17.4	20.9
Construction	6.4	18.8	15.7	12.3	8.8	3.3	7.5	2.2	10.4	8.2
Wholesale, retail trade	13.5	13.0	11.8	16.6	14.7	9.1	11.9	16.2	13.6	15.2
Hotels, restaurants	5.9	7.8	10.1	10.4	5.9	3.6	15.7	13.5	7.9	4.4
Trans., storage, communication	6.2	5.1	5.0	5.7	7.1	3.9	6.0	9.4	6.2	6.5
Financial intermediation	4.3	1.7	1.1	1.4	2.3	7.3	2.2	3.1	2.8	3.5
Real estate, renting, research	14.4	9.8	12.1	10.4	13.2	22.7	14.2	10.9	12.8	9.7
Public administ., defence	4.8	4.1	1.6	2.7	8.1	5.7	3.0	3.7	4.7	7.9
Education	8.9	4.3	3.9	4.9	7.8	11.8	5.2	5.6	6.6	7.2
Health, social work	12.8	6.5	9.2	6.0	10.7	10.6	8.2	12.7	10.1	10.2
Personal services	5.6	3.7	4.0	3.5	4.2	9.7	8.2	3.5	4.6	5.0
Private households	0.5	6.6	5.9	0.5	1.7	0.3	3.0	1.0	2.8	1.1
Total (per cent)	100.0	100.0	100.0	100.0	100.0	100.0	100.0	100.0	100.0	100.0
Total (in 1,000s)	1,706	1,365	933	367	1,351	331	134	680	6,867	155,470

Notes
1 LFS 2002, Data for Germany and Italy not available;
2 EU-15 residents born in another EU-15 country (except Italy, Greece, Portugal, or Spain) or born in Iceland, Liechtenstein, Norway, or Switzerland;
3 EU-15 residents born in Italy, Greece, Portugal, or Spain but living in another EU-15 country;
4 EU-15 residents born in new EU member states (EU-10), EU candidate countries (except Turkey), other countries in Central/Eastern Europe and the Balkans, Russia, Belarus, Ukraine, Caucasus, Central Asia.

Table 7.16 Legal foreign resident workforce by sector/industry (NACE) and nationality, EU-15, 2002[1] (percentages)

NACE sector or industry	Legal foreign resident workforce by nationality									EU-15 total workforce
	EU West[2]	EU South[3]	EU-10 + CEE[4]	Turkey	Africa, Middle East	USA, Canada, Australia	Latin America, Caribbean	Asia	Total LFR workforce	
Agriculture, fishing, mining	0.4	0.2	0.4	1.4	0.2	0.7	–	–	0.5	0.3
Manufacturing	17.5	25.6	22.9	38.4	19.4	11.8	12.7	18.8	23.8	20.9
Construction	5.9	13.5	15.8	10.0	16.1	2.5	8.5	2.4	10.8	8.2
Wholesale, retail trade	12.8	11.5	12.6	13.9	14.8	8.2	14.1	16.1	12.8	15.2
Hotels, restaurants	7.1	12.6	10.5	7.2	7.9	3.9	19.7	21.9	9.9	4.4
Trans., storage, communications	6.4	5.0	4.5	5.9	7.0	4.3	5.6	6.2	5.6	6.5
Financial intermediation	4.7	1.8	1.3	0.9	1.5	7.2	1.4	2.4	2.4	3.5
Real estate, renting, research	15.3	10.6	10.8	9.4	12.8	23.7	12.7	10.3	12.2	9.7
Public administ., defence	3.2	2.1	1.1	1.8	3.0	3.6		1.4	2.2	7.9
Education	8.5	3.0	2.6	1.8	4.3	12.2	4.2	4.1	4.5	7.2
Health, social work	11.2	5.5	8.2	4.3	7.2	10.4	5.6	11.3	7.7	10.2
Personal services	6.6	4.3	4.1	4.5	3.3	11.5	12.7	3.8	5.1	5.0
Private households	0.5	4.3	5.3	0.4	2.6		2.8	1.4	2.5	1.1
Total (per cent)	100.0	100.0	100.0	100.0	100.0	100.0	100.0	100.0	100.0	100.0
Total (in 1,000s)	1,343	1,518	1,103	994	541	279	71	292	6,141	155,470

Notes
1 LFS 2002, Data for Italy not available;
2 EU-15 nationals (except Italy, Greece, Portugal, Spain) + nationals of Iceland, Liechtenstein, Norway, or Switzerland living in (another) EU-15 country;
3 Nationals of Italy, Greece, Portugal, or Spain living in another EU-15 country;
4 Nationals of new EU member states (EU-10), EU candidate countries (except Turkey), other countries in Central/Eastern Europe and the Balkans, Russia, Belarus, Ukraine, Caucasus, Central Asia.

up less stable jobs in manufacturing, construction and tourism. And they clearly reflect the exclusion of third-country nationals from important parts of the public sector while naturalized immigrants have access to this segment of the labour market.

In the US, Mexican and Central American immigrants are heavily concentrated in manufacturing, construction, and accommodation and food services industries, both relative to the US-born population and other immigrant groups. In contrast, African and Caribbean immigrants are strongly represented in education, health, care and social services, and, like Mexicans and Central Americans, in accommodation and food services. Other immigrant groups, namely those from Northern/Western Europe and Canada and Eastern Europe are more strongly represented than the US-born population in some high-skill industries: professional, science, management and administration, finance, insurance and real estate, and information technology.[35]

6 Economic inclusion and exclusion of migrants

In Europe over the last decade, third-country nationals' unemployment has remained higher than EU nationals' unemployment (Table 7.9). Third-country nationals (designated 'Rest of the World') have much lower employment rates than EU-nationals (12 percentage points lower in 2002), in particular, in the prime-age group (20 percentage points lower) and for the high-skilled. The gap is, on average, wider for women than for men, within all working age groups.[36]

In more than half of the EU-15 this gap has been shrinking over the last decade. From 1994 to 2002, the employment rates of non-EU nationals improved significantly in Portugal (+28 percentage points), Spain, (+22 percentage points), Denmark (+18 percentage points), the Netherlands (+16 percentage points), Ireland (+13 percentage points) and Finland (+12 percentage points).[37] In Portugal and Denmark the employment rate of non-EU nationals increased by more than 10 percentage points. Smaller increases were recorded in the United Kingdom, Sweden and Greece. The employment rates for non-EU nationals remained below average in France and Belgium, and there was a decline in the employment rates of non-EU nationals in Austria (−3.5 percentage points),[38] Luxembourg (−3.1 percentage points) and Germany (−2.0 percentage points).[39]

Migrant workers and employees originating from non-Western and non-EU countries are not only concentrated in a few sectors, but within them, in the lower skilled segments. A growing number of them are employed in the health and care sector as well as in education. Domestic services also play an important role, though this is not always visible in available statistics due to the high proportion of irregular migrants working in this sector. By contrast, young people of foreign origin tend to be increasingly working in jobs closer to the native profile.[40]

Whether these changes mean a better starting point for migrants' longer-term integration into the labour market is questionable, as they still tend to remain concentrated in low quality service jobs offering little room in terms of adaptability and mobility.

Table 7.17 Employment rates of working age legal foreign residents and immigrants of known origin by nationality or country of birth, gender, and educational attainment, EU-15, 2002

Nationality	Foreign nationals (LFRs)[1]					
	Male			Female		
	Low education[2]	Medium education[3]	High education[4]	Low education[2]	Medium education[3]	High education[4]
Turkey	55.5	73.3	–	27.9	49.7	–
North Africa	49.3	65.0	67.5	18.9	32.7	49.1
North America	–	79.6	87.3	–	60.6	76.9
EU-10+CEE	61.3	76.1	77.8	45.7	60.2	53.3
EU-West[5]	59.5	78.5	87.8	35.0	61.3	78.0
EU-South[5]	66.9	80.3	84.3	52.3	67.8	69.8
EU-15 average	**60.9**	**76.3**	**85.8**	**36.9**	**63.3**	**78.6**

Country of birth	Foreign born (immigrants)[6]					
	Male			Female		
	Low education[2]	Medium education[3]	High education[4]	Low education[2]	Medium education[3]	High education[4]
Turkey	58.4	75.3	–	25.5	49.3	76.9
North Africa	51.6	68.4	79.9	25.1	48.5	66.0
North America	–	82.3	87.6	–	58.9	78.5
EU-10+CEE	64.5	77.1	80.5	46.5	59.9	63.1
EU-West[7]	59.7	74.4	86.1	41.7	61.6	76.8
EU-South[7]	71.6	76.2	85.6	53.4	62.4	77.4
EU-15 average	**60.9**	**76.3**	**85.8**	**36.9**	**63.3**	**78.6**

Notes
1 LFS 2002, data on foreign nationals for Italy not available;
2 Primary education only;
3 Lower or upper secondary education completed;
4 Tertiary education completed;
5 EU-15 nationals living in EU-15 but outside their country of citizenship;
6 LFS 2002, data on foreign born for Germany and Italy not available;
7 People born in EU-15 but living in EU-15 outside their country of birth.

The distinction, however, tends to be less marked if one compares native-born with foreign-born workers and employees (Table 7.16). This is to be expected as naturalized citizens tend to be better integrated than legal foreign residents. However discrepancies exist between immigrants from non-industrialized countries and Europe's majority populations.

Those third-country nationals who entered the EU in recent years tend, on average, to have a higher skill level than those established in the EU for a decade or longer. Yet their activity rates are lower and their unemployment rates higher than for longer established immigrants. In 2002, the employment rate of migrants originating from non-EU countries who arrived in 2001 (45 per cent) was nearly 20 points below that of those who arrived ten years earlier.[41]

Differences in employment, economic performances and integration of third-country nationals are strongly correlated with the country of origin. The employment rate of legal foreign residents from North Africa and Turkey is systematically lower than for EU nationals at any skill level (Table 7.17). This gap is more marked for women. Again the differences are somewhat less pronounced if native-born vs. foreign-born populations are compared (instead of citizens vs. foreign residents).[42] In contrast, citizens of Balkan countries have employment rates that are equal to or exceed EU nationals' levels both for men and women. The same is true for North Americans and Australians residing in Europe as well as for citizens of Northwestern Europe residing in another EU member state.

In order to get a more accurate and complete picture of the economic position and performance of migrants in Europe, the focus has to shift beyond the foreign resident/foreign national population. Naturalization in many EU-15 countries has drastically increased during the 1990s and the beginning of the twenty-first century, leaving foreign nationals less and less representative of the migrant population. As a result, the economic position of the foreign-born population in EU-15 differs less on average from that of the total European population than does the economic position of the foreign resident population. The latter are in a less favourable economic position.

If one only looks at foreign nationals, i.e. disregarding persons who have naturalized in the receiving country, one could derive an overly negative picture. One might even get the impression that the economic position of migrants is deteriorating, particularly in EU countries with a longer tradition of immigration and higher naturalization rates.[43] But European Labour Force Survey data show that immigrants in Europe are apparently more successful than is suggested by the surveys and data that focus on foreign nationals. Thus, differences between traditional countries of immigration – such as Australia, Canada and the US[44] – and European countries are probably smaller than assumed.[45] Nevertheless for certain immigrant groups – in particular those coming from middle- and low-income countries – considerable employment gaps remain. The LFS data also make clear that immigrants who do not naturalize within the first 10–15 years are especially likely to remain in low-skill and low-paid employment. This sectoral concentration of foreign residents can partly be explained by labour shortages and lower requirements in terms of specific skills. Such circumstances may provide immigrants and their children with an opportunity to enter the EU labour market. However, relatively large numbers of non-EU nationals in some sectors with limited rights or scope for labour market mobility will not be in a strong position regarding wages and job-quality.[46]

Therefore integration of third-country nationals newly arriving and residing in Europe remains an important issue for the EU, its member states and

European civil society.[47] In recent years a growing number of EU member states have introduced integration programmes, ranging from language training courses to civic education.[48]

In contrast to many EU member states, economic integration of newcomers in the US is primarily based on the power of labour market absorption. In the rapidly expanding economy of the 1990s, this seemed to be justified as immigrants found employment in a wide range of occupations and industrial sectors, and many groups had both high rates of labour force participation and low to modest unemployment levels. It is also clear that some groups fared far better than others, and that many individuals, even after many years of residence in the United States, remain in low-skill and low-paid employment.[49] The absence of integration policies and programmes in the US seemingly had few immediate negative consequences in the context of an expanding and, by European standards, much less regulated labour market open to regular and irregular immigrants. But it has also been argued that the lack of attention to utilizing and/or developing the human capital of newcomers so that they might effectively participate in a knowledge-based economy may simply create a more daunting set of long-term problems for immigrants and their children.[50]

The analysis for Europe clearly shows the importance of citizenship for the process of integration. There is, however, no simple causality. On the one hand naturalization may help to gain access to certain segments of the labour market and to reduce discrimination. On the other hand it is evident that successful integration of immigrants makes it more likely that they become citizens of the receiving country.[51] In any case the results clearly show that sustained efforts for the economic and civic integration of immigrants and their native-born children (i.e. the so-called second generation) are necessary.[52] This goes along with efforts of the EU to implement anti-discrimination and equal opportunities legislation in all its member states.[53]

7 Demographic imbalances

As outlined above, Europe's demographic situation is characterized by low fertility, increasing life expectancy, and the prospect of shrinking domestic populations in the decades to come. The data for 2000–05 show that the number of countries with a shrinking domestic population is growing; the number of countries with a negative migration balance is now very small. This contrasts with the situation in neighbouring regions to the South and Southeast, where fertility is much higher, albeit declining, life expectancy is also increasing, and overall population is projected to continue to grow at a high pace.

Low fertility and increasing life expectancy in Europe both reverse the age pyramid, leading to a shrinking number of younger people, an ageing work force, and an increasing number and share of older people. According to Eurostat data and projections by the United Nations, Western and Central Europe's[54] total population size will slightly increase during the next 20 years (2005: 472

million, 2025: 479 million) and start to decrease only during the following decades (to 462 million by 2050). However, the number of people between ages 15 and 64 would decrease from 317 million in 2005 to 302 million (or −5 per cent) until 2025 and to 261 million (−18 per cent) by 2050.[55]

In the same period, in Western and Central Europe the number of people over 65 years of age will increase from 79 million in 2005 to 107 million by 2025 (+35 per cent) and to 133 million in 2050 (+68 per cent). As a result, the old age dependency ratio (population 65+ divided by population 15–65) is likely to increase from 26 per cent in 2005 to 35 per cent until 2025 and 51 per cent by 2050.

The situation in the Balkans and in the European CIS countries[56] is similar to the one in the EU-27. Sustained endogenous population growth, however, is expected for Albania, Azerbaijan, Kosovo, Macedonia, Turkey, and most parts of Central Asia,[57] but many Balkan countries, Russia, and Ukraine face considerable demographic decline.[58]

In contrast, the situation in Europe's Southern and Southeastern neighbour regions, i.e. in the Middle East and North Africa (MENA-14[59] and the Gulf States) is characterized by higher – but declining – fertility, rising life expectancy, and sustained demographic growth. Total population in MENA-14 will grow steadily from 313 million in 2005 to 438 million by 2025 (+40 per cent) and to 557 million by 2050 (+78 per cent). During this period, in MENA-14 the number of people between ages 15 and 64 will almost double: from 195 million in 2000 to 289 million by 2025 (+48 per cent) and to 365 million by 2050 (+78 per cent). At the same time, this region also faces an ageing problem as its population over age 65 will grow almost five-fold over the next 45 years.

The change in the economically-active population, however, will be smaller than the projected changes for the age group 15–64, because only 60–80 per cent of this age group are currently employed or self-employed. Today, Western and Central Europe's labour force is 227 million. After 2010, this region (EEA and Switzerland) can expect a decrease in the active population. By 2025 the decrease will reach −16 million (compared to 2005). During the same period (2005–25), the active or job-seeking population will still rise by seven million people in the EECA-20 and by 66 million in MENA-14. In EECA-20, this increase will mainly take place in Turkey and Central Asia. In countries such as Bulgaria, Moldova, Romania, Serbia and Montenegro,[60] the active or job-seeking population is already shrinking.[61]

Throughout the twenty-first century, Western and Central Europe will be confronted with a rapidly decreasing native workforce (−44 million until 2050) while the potentially active population will continue to grow in Europe's Southern and Southeastern neighbour regions (+118 million until 2050 for MENA-14) and in Turkey (+16 million until 2050).

For Europe, the main challenge is the changing ratio between economically-active and retired persons, i.e. the old age support ratio. With a projected employment rate of 70 per cent, the number of employed persons per person aged 65 and over will decline from 2.7 in 2010 to some 2.2 in 2020 and to only

1.5 in 2040. If, after reaching the so-called Lisbon target, the employment rate were to rise further to 75 per cent between 2010 and 2020, the decline in this ratio would be attenuated, reaching 2.4 in 2020 and 1.8 in 2040.[62]

In North Africa and the Middle East, the main challenge is to absorb those currently unemployed and those entering the labour market in the next two decades. In order to fully cope with this challenge, the MENA-14 countries would have to create 45 million new jobs until 2010 and more than 100 million until 2025, while Europe is confronted with choices concerning higher retirement age, higher labour force participation of women, and the recruitment of immigrants. The current labour market conditions in many MENA countries raise doubts whether these economies will be able to absorb the significant expansion of the labour force. As a consequence of persistent, large-scale unemployment in most MENA-14 countries, migration pressures on the contracting labour markets in Europe will increase.

8 Outlook

Europe's demographic situation is characterized by longevity and low fertility. This leads to ageing and eventually shrinking domestic populations and workforces. Given the high levels of employment already reached by skilled EU-nationals, recruitment of migrants from third countries is increasingly appearing as the main way of responding to the growing demand for medium and high-skilled labour. At the same time, Europe has a continuing need for low-skilled labour.[63] For these reasons, during the twenty-first century, all present EU+EEA member states and EU candidate countries will either remain or become immigration countries.

After 2010, many countries will have to develop pro-active migration policies to meet burgeoning demographic and economic needs. For a relatively short period of time, European East–West migration will continue to play a role.[64] But in the medium and long term, potential migrants will inevitably be recruited from other regions. In this context, Europe will have to compete with traditional countries of immigration – in particular Australia, Canada, and the USA – for qualified migrants to fill labour gaps. The main challenge will be to put Europe in a position that allows the EU and its member states to attract and recruit migrants matching EU labour market needs, as well as to sustain economic growth and provide support for the public pension system. In this context a pro-active approach to immigration can play a crucial role in tackling shortages of labour and skills, provided the qualifications of immigrants are appropriate.[65]

There are, however, significant impediments to deriving accurate projections to help with the middle- and long-term planning of policies to meet labour supply requirements. This is partly linked to problems with predicting phenomena that are influenced by complex, often volatile economic factors, and that may also be significantly affected by unforeseeable policy developments in years to come. Accurate projections are also difficult to disaggregate, especially regarding occupations and skills requirements. In any case, while demographic projections give a clear picture for the next 40 years, projections of emerging skills gaps cannot realistically cover more than a 15-year time frame at most. More accurate or disaggregated projections may not even be possible for such a time span.[66]

The migrants most likely to help match shortages of labour and skills and with the best chances to integrate are probably those able to adapt to changing conditions, by virtue of their qualifications, experience and personal abilities. Future selection mechanisms of a pro-active migration policy must be put in order to assess both qualifications and adaptability of potential immigrants.[67] Given international competition for talent and skills, European countries and the EU as a whole will not only have to establish selection and admission mechanisms, but will also have to offer the migrants sufficiently attractive conditions.

At the same time, given the political sensitivity of immigration, it is likely that governments will find it difficult to justify introducing programmes in the absence of already existing acute labour shortages. Even if projections predict quantitative and qualitative shortages with a sufficient degree of certainty, governments may require more tangible 'proof' in order to convince their electorates of the need for additional foreign labour. This implies that while projections may provide a basis for policy planning in the areas of education, labour market, welfare or social reforms, because of the special political sensitivity linked to immigration, it is likely that migration policy will remain subject to more short-term, ad hoc planning.[68] In this context the EU is well placed to develop medium- and long-term migration policies able to cope with the demographic and economic challenges for Europe described in this chapter.

Today, both Europe and North America are home or host to about one-fifth of the world's migrant population each. Along with the US and Canada, Western Europe has become one of the two most important destinations on the world map of international migration. And, given foreseeable demographic and economic imbalances, it is not only likely but also necessary that Europe remains on that map and continues to manage economically-motivated migration for its own benefit. In this context, future labour market needs will lead to increased competition among EU member states and between OECD countries as they will try to recruit attractive potential immigrants. Such a competition calls for policy coordination and for sustained efforts in the area of integration to ensure equal opportunities for the actors involved. When putting this in historical perspective, we might conclude that for Europe, in contrast to the US, net gains from migration and the possibility of moving towards pro-active migration policy are relatively new phenomena.

Appendix: definitions of terms

Geographic entities

EU-27: The current European Union, consisting of the EU-15 plus the EU-12 (see below).

EU-15: The 15 states that comprised the European Union prior to May 1, 2004, including: Austria, Belgium, Denmark, Finland, France, Germany, Greece, Ireland, Italy, Luxembourg, the Netherlands, Portugal, Spain, Sweden and the United Kingdom.

EU-12: The 12 EU member states admitted on May 1, 2004 and on January 1, 2007, including Bulgaria, Cyprus, Czech Republic, Estonia, Hungary, Latvia, Lithuania, Malta, Poland, Romania, Slovakia and Slovenia.

EU-10: The Central European EU member states admitted on May 1, 2004 and on January 1, 2007, including Bulgaria, Czech Republic, Estonia, Hungary, Latvia, Lithuania, Poland, Romania, Slovakia and Slovenia.

EU candidate countries: Countries scheduled for admission to the EU, currently including Croatia (not before 2010), Macedonia and **Turkey**.

European Economic Area (EEA): With the 1995 enlargement of the European Union, the EEA remained in existence to enable its three non-EU members (Norway, Iceland, and Liechtenstein) to participate in the Common Market. Switzerland decided not to join the EEA, but is associated with the EU by bilateral treaties.

Western Europe: EU-15, Iceland, Norway and Switzerland.

EU West: EU-15 (except Italy, Greece, Portugal, and Spain) plus Iceland, Liechtenstein, Norway and Switzerland.

EU South: Italy, Greece, Portugal and Spain.

CEE: Central and Eastern Europe: the countries of Eastern Europe, the Balkans, Turkey and Central Asia, including: Albania, Armenia, Azerbaijan, Belarus, Bosnia and Herzegovina, Bulgaria, Croatia, Georgia, Kazakhstan, Kyrgyzstan, Moldova, Montenegro, Romania, Russian Federation, Serbia (including Kosovo), Tajikistan, Turkmenistan, Ukraine, and Uzbekistan.

EECA-20: CEE countries plus Turkey.

MENA-14: Countries of the Middle East (without the Gulf States) and North Africa including Algeria, Djibouti, Egypt, Iran, Iraq, Israel, Jordan, Lebanon, Libya, Morocco, Syria, Tunisia, West Bank and Gaza, and Yemen.

Immigration and labour terms

International migrant: A person living for 12 months or more outside of his/her country of birth or citizenship (UN definition).

Foreign-born: A person born in a country other than the one in which he/she resides (regardless of his/her citizenship).

Migrant: Persons moving (or having moved) from one country to another.

Immigrant: Term synonymous to 'foreign-born' with the prospect of long-term or permanent residence. (In the US this term is reserved for persons who are granted lawful permanent residence in the United States.)

Foreign National: Defined as a person who is a citizen of a country other than the one in which he/she resides.

Legal Foreign Resident: Defined as 'foreign national' who is lawfully residing in a country other than the one in which he/she is a citizen. This includes not only foreign-born individuals but also many persons who were born in their current country of residence but at birth acquired only the foreign citizenship held by their parents.

Irregular Migrant: Persons resident in a country without legal permission to be there; also referred to as 'undocumented,' 'unauthorized,' 'unlawful' or 'illegal' migrants.

Regularization: A government programme granting a large number of irregular migrants authorization to remain in their country of residence. In some countries such programmes are also called 'legalization' or 'amnesties.'

Worker: In the EU sometimes also used as an equivalent to 'blue-collar' worker.

Employee: In the EU sometimes also used as an equivalent to 'white collar' workers; the term does not include the self-employed or contract workers.

Gainful employment: Defined as workers/employees with salary plus self employed persons in the working age population. This term usually excludes people working as dependent family members without pay or for benefits in kind in a family owned farm or business.

Notes

1 This chapter profited from discussions between the author and services of the European Commission as well as from discussions with a number of scholars and senior civil servants active in the fields of migration and integration. European Labour Force Survey data were provided by Eurostat and additional analysis by Heinz Fassmann (University of Vienna) and Florin Vadean (HWWI).
2 Western Europe is defined as the EU-15, Iceland, Liechtenstein, Norway and Switzerland, with 393 million inhabitants.
3 In 2006, Cyprus (Greek part only), the Czech Republic, Hungary, Slovakia, and Slovenia already have a positive migration balance.
4 Candidate countries with possible EU membership are Croatia and Macedonia. Turkey will not be admitted to the EU before 2015–2020.
5 Croatia, Macedonia and Turkey.
6 Iceland, Liechtenstein, Norway and Switzerland.
7 Albania, Bosnia-Herzegovina, Macedonia, Montenegro, Serbia (including Kosovo).
8 Excess of deaths over births in: Bulgaria, Croatia, Romania.
9 Net flow of migrants (regardless of citizenship; without seasonal workers) according to Eurostat (Cronos data base).
10 Greek part of Cyprus only.
11 Non-immigrant visas for foreign migrants arriving for business, pleasure, work, educational and other purposes. Many of these non-immigrant legal foreign residents later manage to adjust their status in the US and become permanent immigrants (Gozdziak and Martin, 2004). Some are even able to adjust their status after irregular entry (Massey and Malone, 2002). Statistically they only become visible as 'immigrants' in the year that this adjustment takes place.
12 According to the transitional arrangements (2+3+2 regulation) the EU-15 can apply national rules on access to their labour markets for the first two years after enlargement. After two years (new EU Member States of 2004: already in 2006; new EU Member States of 2007: in 2009) the European Commission reviews the transitional arrangements. Member States that wish to continue national measures for up to another three years. At the end of this period (new EU Member States of 2004: in

2009; new EU Member States of 2007: in 2011) all Member States will be invited to open their labour market entirely. Only if countries can show serious disturbances in the labour market or a threat of such disturbances, will they be allowed to resort to a safeguard clause for a maximum period of two years. From 2011/2013 all Member States will have to comply with the Community rules regulating the free movement of labour.

13 The European Union sees 'the right to family reunification (...) as an indispensable instrument for integration.' The European Directive on Family Unification adopted by the Council in September 2003 therefore 'recognises the right to family reunification for third-country nationals holding a residence permit of one year or more who have reasonable prospects of obtaining permanent residence. Member States will be entitled to require for the exercise of this right that third-country nationals comply with integration measures in accordance with national law. An essential provision for the integration of family members is that they be entitled, in the same way as the applicant, to access to employment, education and vocational training' (Commission of the European Communities, 2003a).

14 EU-25+EEA+Switzerland, among them 382,000 in the EU-15 and 30,000 in the ten new EU member states (then still accession countries). The US, in FY 2001, admitted 97,000 refugees and 11,000 asylum seekers. The European directive on 'minimum standards for the qualification and status of third-country nationals and stateless persons as refugees or as persons who otherwise need international protection contains a specific chapter regulating the content of international protection and specifying the rights to be enjoyed by a refugee or person granted subsidiary protection. These require Member States to provide programmes tailored to the needs of refugees to facilitate their integration into society' (Commission of the European Communities, 2003a).

15 These two related inflows are of particular relevance for countries like Germany (ethnic German Aussiedler), Greece (Pontian Greeks) and Hungary (ethnic Hungarians).

16 Source: European Commission (2003b).

17 Münz (2004).

18 OECD (2006).

19 In January 2005 The European Commission published a 'Green Paper' on economic migration following a 'proposal for a directive on the conditions of entry and residence of third-country nationals for the purpose of paid employment and self-employed economic activities' which failed to get sufficient support in the Council. The idea behind the proposal for the directive and the Green Paper 'is both to provide a pathway for third-country workers which could lead to a more permanent status for those who remain in work, while at the same time giving a secure legal status while in the EU to those who return to their countries of origin when their permit expires' (Commission of the European Communities, 2005a).

20 Admitted by France, Germany, Italy, Sweden and Switzerland (see OECD/Sopemi, 2004).

21 The US on the basis of the 1986 Immigration Reform and Control Act legalized 2.8 million irregular foreign residents. For regularization in Europe and the US see Papademetriou and Jachimowicz, 2004. In 2005 Spain offered regularization to some 800,000 irregular migrants.

22 Tamas and Münz (2006).

23 Only primary education completed.

24 Tertiary education completed.

25 Lower or higher secondary education completed.

26 Defined as the number of people gainfully employed (i.e. workers/employees with salary plus self employed persons) in the working age population (15–64) in the European Labour Force Survey (LFS). This figure excludes people working as dependent family members without pay or for benefits in kind in a family-owned farm or business.

27 Commission of the European Communities (2004c).
28 For comparison, between 1996 and 2000, foreign-born workers accounted for nearly half of the net increase in the US labour force; see Mosisa (2002).
29 Commission of the European Communities (2004b).
30 Commission of the European Communities (2004b).
31 Algeria, Morocco, Tunisia.
32 US Census results of 2000; see Ray (2004). For a critical review of these findings see Lowell (2004).
33 US Census results of 2000; see Ray (2004), Lowell (2004).
34 This could well be influenced by an over representation of skilled migrants in the LFS.
35 US Census results of 2000; see Ray (2004).
36 Commission of the European Communities (2003b).
37 Finland since entering EU in 1995.
38 Austria since entering EU in 1995.
39 See Commission of the European Communities (2003b), Ray (2004).
40 See OECD/Sopemi (2003, 2004).
41 Calculations kindly provided by European Commission services.
42 See Münz and Fassmann (2004).
43 In the decade 1992–2001 some 5,855,000 people were naturalized in the EU-15 (OECD/Sopemi, 2003).
44 See Lowell (2004), Papdemetriou and O'Neill (2004).
45 See Münz and Fassmann (2004).
46 See Commission of the European Communities (2003a).
47 See Commission of the European Communities (2000, 2003).
48 For a summary of such integration programmes see Bade, Bommes and Münz (2004), Ray (2004), Tijdelijke Commissie onderzoek Integratiebeleid (2004), Heckmann and Schnapper (2003).
49 The US-born population also experienced varying degrees of socio-economic mobility during the 1990s.
50 See Ray (2004).
51 This can be demonstrated for Canada (see DeVorez and Pivnenko, 2004) and for Sweden (see Bevelander, 2000).
52 'Since the launch of the European Employment Strategy (EES) in 1997, the integration of disadvantaged groups, including migrant workers and ethnic minorities, as well as combating discrimination, have been key features of the employment guidelines. In its Communication of 17 July 2002, the Commission reviewed the experience of five years of the EES and identified major issues for the debate on its future. These include reducing the employment gap between EU nationals and non-EU nationals, promoting full participation and employment for 2nd generation migrants, addressing the specific needs of immigrant women, fighting illegal immigration and transforming undeclared work into regular employment' (Commission of the European Communities, 2003a).
53 'The EU has also put in place a legal framework to combat discrimination – which can seriously impede the integration process – and in particular common minimum standards to promote equal treatment and to combat discrimination on grounds of racial or ethnic origin, religion or belief, age, disability and sexual orientation. Directives approved at EU level in 2000 will give important new rights both to arriving migrants and to established ethnic minorities in the EU. The scope of Community legislation banning racial discrimination is wide and covers employment, education, social security, health care, access to goods and services and to housing. Although the directives do not cover discrimination on grounds of nationality, and are without prejudice to the conditions relating to the entry and residence of third country nationals and to any treatment, which arises from their legal status, they do apply to all persons

resident in the Member States, including third country nationals. In addition, several activities aiming at exchange of experiences and good practice are carried out under the accompanying programme to combat discrimination. The Commission also supports the work of the European Monitoring Centre on Racism' (Commission of the European Communities, 2003a) see also EUMC (2003).

54 The 30 EEA countries and Switzerland.
55 Holzmann and Münz (2005).
56 EECA-20 countries in Europe are Albania, Armenia, Azerbaijan, Belarus, Bosnia-Herzegovina, Bulgaria, Croatia, Georgia, Macedonia, Moldova, Montenegro, Romania, Russian Fed., Serbia, Turkey, Ukraine.
57 EECA-20 countries in Asia are Kazakhstan, Kyrgyz Rep., Tajikistan, Turkmenistan, Uzbekistan.
58 Holzmann and Münz (2005).
59 MENA-16 countries are Algeria, Djibouti, Egypt, Iran, Iraq, Israel, Jordan, Lebanon, Libya, Morocco, Syria, Tunisia, West Bank and Gaza, and Yemen.
60 Without Kosovo.
61 Holzmann and Münz (2005).
62 Holzmann and Münz (2005).
63 See Commission of the European Communities (2004).
64 See Fassmann and Münz (2002), Krieger (2004).
65 See Commission of the European Communities (2003), Holzmann and Münz (2004).
66 See Boswell *et al.* (2004).
67 See Holzmann and Münz (2004); for the experiences of traditional countries of immigration see Papademetriou and O'Neil (2004).
68 See Boswell *et al.* (2004).

Bibliography

Apap, J., de Bruycker, Ph. and Schmitter, C. (2000) 'Regularisation of Illegal Aliens in the European Union. Summary Report of a Comparative Study', *European Journal of Migration and Law* 2: 3–4.

Bade, K., Bommes, M. and Münz, R. (eds) (2004) *Migrationsreport 2004*. Frankfurt/M. New York: Campus.

Bevelander, P. (2000) *Immigrant Employment Integration and Structural Change in Sweden: 1970–1995*. Lund Studies in Economic History 15. Lund: University Press.

Boswell, Ch., Stiller, S. and Straubhaar, T. (2004) *Forecasting Labour and Skills Shortages: How Can Projections Better Inform Labour Migration Policies?* Paper prepared for the European Commission, DG Employment and Social Affairs. Brussels: European Commission; Hamburg: HWWA.

Brücker, H. (2002) 'Can International Migration Solve the Problems of European Labor Markets?' *UNECE Economic Survey of Europe* 2, pp. 109–142.

Commission of the European Communities (2000) *Communication from the Commission to the Council and the European Parliament. On a Community Integration Policy*, COM (2000) 757 final. Brussels.

Commission of the European Communities/Eurostat (2002a) *The Social Situation in the European Union 2002*. Luxembourg: EC.

Commission of the European Communities (2002b) *Communication from the Commission to the Council and the European Parliament. Integrating Migration Issues in the European Union's Relations with Third Countries*, COM (2002) 703 final. Brussels.

Commission of the European Communities (2003a) *Communication from the Commis-*

sion to the Council and the European Parliament on Immigration, Integration and Employment, COM (2003) 336 final. Brussels.

Commission of the European Communities (2003b) *Employment in Europe 2003*. Luxembourg: EC.

Commission of the European Communities (2004a) *Communication from the Commission to the Council, the European Parliament, the European Economic and Social Committee and the Committee of the Regions. First Annual Report on Migration and Asylum*, COM (2004) 332 final. Brussels.

Commission of the European Communities (2004b) Third Report on Economic and Social Cohesion. Brussels.

Commission of the European Communities (2004c) *Employment in Europe 2004*. Luxembourg: EC.

Commission of the European Communities (2005a) *Green Paper on an EU Approach to Managing Economic Migration*, COM (2005) 36 final. Brussels.

Commission of the European Communities (2005b) *Report on the Functioning of the Transitional Arrangements set out in the 2003 Accession Treaty (period 1 May 2004–30 April 2006)*, COM (2006). Brussels.

Commission of the European Communities (2005c) *Policy Plan on Legal Migration*, COM (2005) 669 final. Brussels.

Commission of the European Communities (2005d) *Priority actions for responding to the challenges of migration: First follow-up to Hampton Court*, COM (2005) 621 final. Brussels.

Commission of the European Communities (2005e) *A Common Agenda for Integration: Framework for the Integration of Third-Country Nationals in the European Union*, COM (2005) 389 final. Brussels.

Commission of the European Communities (2005f) *Common Actions for Growth and Employment: The Community Lisbon Programme*, COM (2005) 330 final. Brussels.

Commission of the European Communities (2005g) *Integrated Guidelines for Growth and Jobs*, COM (2005) 141 final. Brussels.

Constant, A. and Zimmermann, K.F. (2005) *Immigrant Performance and Selective Immigration Policy: A European Perspective*, National Institute Economic Review 194: 94–105.

Coppel, J., Dumont, J. and Visco, I. (2001) *Trends in Immigration and Economic Consequences*, OECD Economic Department Working Paper 284, Paris: OECD.

DeVoretz, D.J. (2006) *Immigration Policy: Methods of Economic Assessment*, International Migration Review 40(2): 390–418.

DeVorez, D. and Pivnenko, S. (2004) *The Economics of Canadian Citizenship*. Paper presented at the Workshop 'Immigrant Ascension to Citizenship, Recent Policies and Economic and Social Consequences', Malmø University, Malmø: IMER.

Einaudi, L. (2004) *Historical Approaches to Legal and Illegal Migration for Employment in Italy and France*. Paper presented at the 2nd Stockholm Workshop on Global Mobility Regimes. Stockholm: IFS.

European Monitoring Centre on Racism and Xenophobia (EUMC) (2002) *Anti-discrimination Legislation in EU Member States*. Vienna: European Monitoring Centre on Racism and Xenophobia.

European Monitoring Centre on Racism and Xenophobia (EUMC) (ed.) (2003) *Migrants, Minorities and Employment: Exclusion, Discrimination and Anti-Discrimination in 15 Member states of the European Union*. Report prepared by the International Centre for Migration Policy Development (ICMPD). Luxembourg: EC.

Fassmann, H. and Münz, R. (2002) 'EU Enlargement and Future East-West Migration,' in F. Laczko, I. Stacher and A. Klekowski von Koppenfels (eds) *New Challenges for Migration Policy in Central and Eastern Europe.* Geneva: TMC Asser Press, pp. 59–86.

Gozdziak, E. and Martin, S. (2004) *The Economic Integration of Immigrants in the United States: A Review of the Literature.* Paper prepared for the 'U.S.-EU Seminar on Integrating Immigrants into the Workforce', Washington, DC, June 28–29, 2004.

Heckmann, F. and Schnapper, D. (eds) (2003) *The Integration of Immigrants in European Societies: National Differences and Trends of Convergence.* Stuttgart: Lucius and Lucius.

Holzmann, R. and Münz, R. (2004) *Challenges and Opportunities of International Migration for the EU, Its Member States, Neighboring Countries and Regions: A Policy Note.* Washington, DC: World Bank; Stockholm: Institute for Futures Studies.

Holzmann, R. and Münz, R. (2005) *Europe, North Africa and the Middle East: Diverging Trends, Overlapping Interests, Possible Arbitrage through Migration.* Paper presented at the joint workshop on 'The Future of Demography, Labour Markets, and the Formation of Skills in Europe, and its Mediterranean Neighbourhood'. Brussels, 4–5 July 2005.

Independent High-Level Study Group (2003) *An Agenda for a Growing Europe. Making the EU Economic System Deliver.* Report of an Independent High-Level Study Group initiated by the President of the European Commission. Brussels.

Krieger, H. (2004) *Migration Trends in an Enlarged Europe.* Dublin: European Foundation for the Improvement of Living and Working Conditions.

Laczko, F. and Münz, R. (2003) 'International Labour Migration and Demographic Change in Europe,' in: *International Organization for Migration* (ed.) World Migration 2003. Geneva: IOM, pp. 239–258.

Lowell, L.B. (2004) *Immigrant Labor Market Assimilation in the United States: A critique of Census data and Longitudinal Outcomes.* Paper prepared for the 'U.S.-EU Seminar on Integrating Immigrants into the Workforce', Washington, DC, 28–29 June 2004.

Massey, D.S. and Malone, N. (2002) 'Pathways to Legal Immigration', *Population Research and Policy Review* 21(6).

Mosisa, A.T. (2002) 'The role of foreign-born workers in the US economy', *Monthly Labor Review,* May 2002, pp. 3–14.

Münz, R. and Fassmann, H. (2004) *Migrants in Europe and their Economic Position: Evidence from the European Labour Force Survey and from Other Sources.* Paper prepared for the European Commission, DG Employment and Social Affairs. Brussels: European Commission; Hamburg: HWWA.

Münz, R. and Ulrich, R. (2003) 'The ethnic and demographic structure of foreigner and immigrants in Germany,' in R. Alba, P. Schmidt and M. Wasmer (eds) *Germans or Foreigners?* New York, Basingstoke: Palgrave-Macmillan, pp. 19–44.

Münz, R., Straubhaar, T., Vadean, F. and Vadean, N. (2007) 'What are the Migrants' Contributions to Employment and Growth? A European Approach,' Hamburg HWWI, Paris: OECD.

Neuckens, D. (2001) *Regularization Campaigns in Europe.* Brussels: Platform for International Cooperation on Undocumented Migrants (PICUM).

Niessen, J. and Schibel, Y. (2003) *EU and US Approaches to the Management of Immigration: Comparative Perspectives.* Brussels: Migration Policy Group.

Organization for Economic Co-operation and Development (ed.) (2003) *Trends in International Migration: Sopemi 2002.* Paris: OECD.

Organization for Economic Co-operation and Development (ed.) (2004) *Trends in International Migration: Sopemi 2003*. Paris: OECD.

Organization for Economic Co-operation and Development (2006) *International Migration Outlook: Sopemi 2006*. Paris: OECD.

Papademetriou, D. and O'Neil, K. (2004) *Efficient Practices for the Selection of Economic Migrants*. Paper prepared for the European Commission, DG Employment and Social Affairs. Brussels: European Commission; Hamburg: HWWA.

Papademetriou, D., O'Neil, K. and Jachimowicz, M. (2004) *Observations on Regularization and the Labor Market Performance of Unauthorized and Regularized Immigrants*. Paper prepared for the European Commission, DG Employment and Social Affairs. Brussels: European Commission; Hamburg: HWWA.

Passel, J. (2002) New Estimates of the Undocumented Population in the United States. *Migration Information Source*. Washington, DC: Migration Policy Institute, www.migrationinformation.org/ feature/display.cfm?ID=19.

Portes, A. and Rumbaut, R.G. (1990) *Immigrant America: A Portrait*. Berkeley: University of California Press.

Ray, B. (2004) *Practices to Promote the Integration of Migrants into Labour Markets*. Paper prepared for the European Commission, DG Employment and Social Affairs. Brussels: European Commission; Hamburg: HWWA.

Tamas, K. and Münz, R. (2006) *Labour Migrants Unbound? EU Enlargement, Transitional Measures and Labour Market Effects*. Stockholm: Institute for Future Studies.

Tijdelijke Commissie onderzoek Integratiebeleid (2004) *Onderzoek integratiebeleid, Rapport Bruggen bouwen*. Eindrapport, 28689, nr. 9, Kammerstuck 2003–2004, Amsterdam: Tweede Kamer.

United Nations (2005) *World Population Prospects. The 2004 Revision*. Population Division, Department of Economics and Social Affairs, New York: UN.

United Nations High Commissioner for Refugees (2004) *Asylum Applications Lodged in Industrialized Countries: Levels and Trends, 2000–2003*. Geneva: UNHCR.

United Nations Population Division (2002) *International Migration Report 2002*. New York: UN.

United Nations Population Division (2003) *World Population Prospects – The 2002 Revision*. New York: UN.

US Department of Labor (2002) *Developments in International Migration to the United States: 2002*. Washington, DC.

World Bank (2005) *Global Economic Prospects 2006: Economic Implications of Remittances and Migration*. Washington, DC: The World Bank.

8 International migrations

Some comparisons and lessons for the European Union

Giovanni Peri[1]

1 Introduction

During the 1990s, the world experienced an increase in the flows of goods, capital and people across countries, making 'globalization' a buzzword in the media and political discourse. While economists generally consider this trend beneficial, a heated debate concerning the 'discontented' or the 'losers' has held centre-stage in the theatres of politics, economics and the media.[2] The increased trade in manufacturing products and the outsourcing of traditionally skilled services to developing countries have compelled some trade economists to think more carefully about some of the particulars of extant trade theories.[3] Certainly no aspect of globalization is regarded with more anxiety (or bound to produce more pronounced changes to society) than the large migratory flows of workers who seize economic opportunities by moving across countries. The United States, always a powerful attractor of migrants, has recently regained the position it held at the beginning of the twentieth century as the quintessential immigration country. Similarly Canada and Australia have experienced very large and growing inflows of immigrants in recent decades. On the other hand, the European Union, a frequent point of departure for immigrants in the past (headed mainly to North America, and Australia) is now becoming the destination of choice for a growing number of Turks, North Africans and Eastern Europeans.[4]

This collection of internationally mobile workers, with varying skills, educational attainments and abilities, represents an extraordinary potential resource for both the US and the EU. From a political and economic point of view, however, native citizens more often than not perceive immigration as a threat. Immigrants are often seen as harbingers of job loss and wage reductions for home-born workers, or the unwitting disseminators of traditions and values that 'corrupt' the authenticity of native institutions. In extreme cases, they are seen as a threat to national security. As social scientists, therefore, we are compelled to analyse more carefully the determinants and consequences of these migration flows in order to separate incorrect perceptions from reality. In the wake of the escalation of fear and intolerance for foreigners emerging in the EU, along with mounting uneasiness in foreign-born communities (for example, in the urban peripheries of

France) it is particularly important to focus on immigration and internal mobility in the European Union, looking into both its causes and consequences. One critical aspect of immigration (little inquired in the international literature due to the lack of systematic cross-country data) is the education and skills of migrants vis-à-vis those of natives. Attracting highly skilled engineers or scientists is likely to depend on different factors, and has different consequences, from attracting low skilled manual workers. Some countries (such as Canada and Australia) have immigration systems that aim at selecting immigrants based on their skills (schooling, abilities). Others, like the US, keep only general quotas for immigrants and favour family reunifications, but also maintain special channels to allow highly trained professionals into the country (like the H1B visa programmes). The EU is currently debating which system to adopt and thus needs a clear understanding of the determinants and consequences of immigration on which to base such a decision.

Recent studies have made important progress in analysing both the determinants of international migration[5] and the effects[6] of such migration on natives. While several issues are still debated, this chapter follows a standard approach in analysing the determinants of international migration by means of a gravity equation that includes geographic and economic determinants. We then build on previous work (mainly Borjas, 2003 and Ottaviano and Peri, 2005) in order to evaluate the impact of immigration on the wages of natives.

This chapter uses data made available only recently (March 2005) on the stock of international migrants in OECD countries, as measured by censuses held in each country in the year 2000. Individuals over 15 years of age residing in each of 28 OECD countries are classified according to their country of birth and their schooling level, as recorded by the census of the country of residence. This allows one to contruct a cross-sectional picture of the stock of foreign-born workers in each couhtry by education group. We use these data together with country-level data on education, population and wages to establish facts and to highlight some correlations, with particular attention to the European Union (EU15) in comparison with the main immigration economies (the US, Canada, Australia and Switzerland). Studying the mobility of highly educated individuals (i.e. people with tertiary education) serves as a central focus of this chapter and reveals interesting and important facts. In particular we find that four general features clearly characterize the current state of the EU vis-à-vis the US and other important immigration economies:

1   The European Union exhibits surprisingly low levels of long-run cross-country mobility of its labour force. While migration flows between EU countries are known to be lower than migration flows between US states, we are surprised to find that this gap remains even after controlling for economic and geographic determinants. This is true even for the most educated workers. Far from being an integrated labour market like the US, the union of European countries seems to have no particular effect in facilitating the long-run mobility of residents.

2   The European Union lags far behind the US and other immigration coun-
     tries (Canada, Australia, Switzerland) in its ability to attract immigrants,
     including highly educated ones. While part of the difference in attracting
     highly educated workers can be explained by lower returns to education in
     continental Europe relative to the US, a large and significant difference per-
     sists even after controlling for this.

3   Interestingly, we find that the educational distributions of foreign born in
     immigration countries like the US, Canada and Australia and Switzerland
     are 'complementary' to the distribution of skills of native born. Specifically,
     the educational group comprising the largest share in the native population
     has the smallest share among foreign-born individuals. This fact, emerging
     from our calculations of the wage effects of immigrants, implies that these
     countries receive an influx of immigrants with skills that are relatively
     scarce in the home country, hence driving up home wages. In contrast, the
     EU attracts immigrants in largest proportion among less educated workers
     (with primary education degrees) who constitute the largest educational
     groups for natives as well. The educational distribution of immigrants to the
     EU therefore replicates (rather than complements) the education of its
     native population and hence may be more harmful to their wages.

4   Finally, Great Britain appears to be most similar to the immigration
     economies (USA, Canada, Australia) in terms of its ability to attract skilled
     immigrants and in the schooling distribution of these immigrants. Its fea-
     tures should perhaps serve as helpful guidelines for other EU countries. On
     the other hand, Germany and France appear to attract mainly unskilled
     workers, and share an apparent inability to consistently attract highly edu-
     cated migrants.

These four features characterizing the migration behaviour of workers with different levels of education, particularly 2 to 4, are the outcomes of differences not
only in immigration policies but also in labour markets, higher education policies and economic performances. The labour market and education opportunities often serve as the main pull factors that attract educated immigrants, while
immigration policies themselves simply act as a device for regulating the flows.
Attracting immigrants from the pool of highly educated people will probably
require the EU to reform its labour and goods markets to facilitate higher
competition and to redefine its tertiary education strategies, on top of reforming
its immigration laws.

The rest of the chapter is organized as follows. Section 2 describes the data
and presents some statistics on international migration flows across OECD
countries and their composition by education. We devote particular attention to
describing the EU as a whole and its main economies as the countries of
destination for international migrants. Section 3 analyses the determinants of
bilateral migration using a gravity model, and section 4 focuses on migratory
flows of highly educated workers. Section 5 describes the skill composition of
natives and immigrants in both the EU and main immigration countries, and

section 6 calculates the impact of immigration on the wages of natives. Some interesting implications for the political economy of immigration emerge from this section. Section 7 concludes the chapter.

2 Description of the data and summary statistics on migration

Several sources collect data on yearly migratory flows across countries (for example, the International Migration Statistics for OECD countries and the Continuous Reporting System on Migration, SOPEMI). However there is little information on the level of schooling or on other measure of the skills of these migrants. In order to have accurate information on these variables one has to rely on population censuses held by each country to record the stock of foreign born and their schooling. Recently, the OECD has gathered comparable data on the presence of foreign born grouped by levels of education and country of birth from censuses of all the developed countries (OECD, 2005). Three education groups can be consistently tracked across countries: people with primary education (some education or the full primary degree), people with secondary education (some education or the full secondary degree) and people with tertiary education. We will refer to these three groups as 'low,' 'intermediate' and 'high' levels of education, respectively. These educational categories are consistent with those of the Barro and Lee (2000) data set on education across countries based on the International Standard Classification of Education (ISCED).[7] These data allow us to construct the stock of migrants for a matrix of all OECD countries (country of origin by country of destination). These stocks measure the long-run outcomes of migratory processes and are less subject to yearly fluctuations. They constitute a measure of long-run migratory behaviour across countries and skills. The data on country population, GDP and area are from the Penn World Tables release 7.0. The data on wages for each schooling group are calculated using average wages (from average GDP per capita) and the estimated returns to schooling specific to each country, reported by Bils and Klenow (2001). Finally, all the bilateral geographical data (distance, border dummies and language dummies) are taken from Glick and Rose (2002).

The EU relative to other OECD economies

First consider the overall size of the stocks of immigrants and emigrants for the countries of the European Union, together with the same stocks for the other OECD economies. Table 8.1 reports some shares that provide an idea of the ability of each OECD economy to attract foreign born as well as the propensity of its natives to migrate abroad. Column 2 reports the share of foreign born in the resident population, while column 3 reports people who were born in the country and reside abroad as a share of the total born in the country. These values thus provide information on the stocks of immigrants (column 2) and emigrants (column 3) for each OECD country in year 2000. Column 1 reports the difference between immigrants and emigrants (with a positive sign indicating net immigration and a negative sign indicating net emigration) as share of the total population born in the country. While most of the current issues in the European Union and the US concern the presence of foreign-born immigrants as a share of total residents (column 2) it is also interesting to analyse the magnitude of the stock of emigrants and the balance of the two. In Table 8.1 countries are ranked in decreasing order of the percentages reported in column 1, i.e. from the largest net 'attractors' of immigrants to the largest net 'suppliers' of emigrants (as percentage of their population). Excluding the extremely small country of Luxembourg we call 'immigration' countries the four countries at the top of the list (all outside the EU). They are, in decreasing order, Australia, Switzerland, Canada and the United States. These countries exhibit extremely high net immigration rates, equal, respectively, to 27 per cent, 23 per cent, 19 per cent and 13.5 per cent of their native populations.

While Australia and the US are purely countries of immigration (as their stock of emigrants is less than 2 per cent of their native-born populations), around 5 per cent of the native populations of Switzerland and Canada have emigrated abroad (mainly to the EU and the US, respectively). They attract, however, a far larger number of immigrants, resulting in large net migrations. Compared to these economies, the EU15,[8] considered as a whole, maintains a substantially smaller share of foreign-born residents (i.e. those born outside the EU). This percentage is equal to 7.2. On the other hand, 3 per cent of EU natives reside outside the EU, so the net immigration rate is a scant 4.7 per cent, less that a third of the US's rate and less than a fifth of Australian's rate.

Looking at countries within the EU, some such as Sweden, Austria and Belgium can be characterized as relatively 'open' economies from a migratory point of view, with large percentages of both immigrants and emigrants. Others such as France and Germany are mainly immigration economies, while a few such as Ireland and Portugal remain net emigration economies. The percentages in Table 8.1 however do not distinguish between whether immigrants and emigrants are going from/to other countries within the EU or outside of it. As our focus is on the EU as a whole, we make the distinction between mobility inside and outside of the EU in Figure 8.1. Note also two other typologies among the migratory patterns of OECD economies. First, some of the major countries of emigration into the EU and the US, such as Turkey, Poland, Hungary and Mexico, are within the group of OECD countries analysed in this study. Mexico in particular is a pure emigration economy, with 9 per cent of its native people living abroad, mostly in the US. Second, some OECD countries essentially close off labour flows altogether. Most notably, Japan has a stock of immigrants and emigrants smaller than 1 per cent of its population. While we hardly think that this is applicable to the EU, the case of Japan shows that it is possible to run a developed economy geographically closed to less developed ones and to resist immigration pressures almost entirely.

Figure 8.1 shows the foreign-born population as a percentage of the total residents in each of the EU15 countries (with the exception of Italy, due to lack

Table 8.1 Stock of immigrants and emigrants in OECD countries. Census 2000, population aged 15 years and older

Country	1 Net immigrant stock as share of total natives	2 Stock of foreign born as share of residents	3 Stock of residents abroad as share of total born
Luxembourg	0.358	0.326	0.112
Australia	**0.275**	**0.230**	**0.024**
Switzerland	**0.230**	**0.224**	**0.055**
Canada	**0.191**	**0.193**	**0.046**
USA	**0.135**	**0.123**	**0.005**
Sweden	0.107	0.120	0.029
Austria	0.091	0.125	0.049
France	**0.090**	**0.100**	**0.021**
Germany	**0.087**	**0.121**	**0.048**
New Zealand	0.081	0.195	0.138
Belgium	0.080	0.107	0.038
The Netherlands	0.067	0.101	0.043
EU15[a]	**0.047**	**0.072**	**0.030**
Norway	0.045	0.073	0.033
Greece	0.039	0.103	0.071
Spain	0.036	0.053	0.020
Denmark	0.034	0.068	0.037
UK	**0.027**	**0.083**	**0.060**
Japan	0.005	0.010	0.005
Hungary	−0.004	0.029	0.032
South Korea	−0.005	0.003	0.008
Turkey	−0.013	0.019	0.031
Poland	−0.015	0.021	0.034
Finland	−0.032	0.025	0.055
Portugal	−0.069	0.063	0.119
Mexico	−0.094	0.005	0.090
Ireland	−0.121	0.104	0.191

Source: Author's calculations on OECD (2005) data set.

Note

a Excluding Italy for which data on country of birth of residents are not available.

of data). The countries are arrayed from left to right in decreasing order of total percentage of foreign born. The share of the bar that is coloured in a darker shade represents immigrants from other EU countries, the portion coloured in the lighter shade measures the share of immigrants born outside the EU. Aside from the very small and highly 'international' country of Luxembourg, Germany and Austria exhibit the greatest ability to attract 'extra-communitarian' immigrants (interestingly, Greece is the next highest for share of foreign born, mostly coming from Turkey and Cyprus). The Netherlands, France and the UK also attract non-trivial percentages of extra-communitarians.

Surprisingly, for all countries except Ireland and Luxembourg, the share of immigrants from outside the EU is larger than the share from inside the EU.

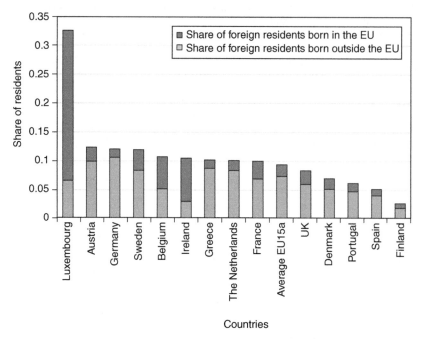

Figure 8.1 Stock of immigrants in the EU countries, Census 2000, population 15 years and older (source: Author's calculations on OECD (2005) data).

Note

a Excluding Italy for which data on country of birth of residents are not available.

Considering the complete elimination of political barriers to the movement of labour since 1992, the strong cultural and linguistic commonalities within the EU, and the geographic proximity of these countries, one marvels at the trivial degree of mobility of EU citizens. On average only 2.2 per cent of the residents of an EU country are born in a different EU country. Section 3 below will inquire more formally about the low cross-country mobility of Europeans. Here it is enough to mention that taking the US as a model of an integrated labour market, and considering cross-state mobility as a measure of internal mobility, the percentage of US residents born in one state and living (working) in a different state was, on average in year 2000, around 30 per cent. This is 15 times larger than the cross-country analogue for Europeans.

In short, while the EU15 is still far from attracting the percentages of extra-communitarian immigrants comparable to those found in Australia, Canada and the US, some of its countries maintain shares of extra-communitarians close to 10 per cent of their populations. Overall though, the long-run mobility of EU citizens across EU countries is extremely low.

Education of immigrants

This chapter focuses on the skill composition of immigrants. Our goal is to characterize the different determinants and consequences of the international mobility of people with different levels of human capital (education). Human capital is a fundamental determinant of productivity (Hall and Jones, 1999), innovation and growth (Jones, 2002) across countries. Moreover, workers with different educational attainments embody different amounts of human capital and are imperfect substitutes in production (Katz and Murphy, 1992; Ciccone and Peri, 2005). Therefore it is important to analyse the international migration of workers with a particular focus on their educational levels. Considering the EU15 as one economy, Table 8.2 (divided into three parts, a, b and c) reports the net immigration rate (immigrants minus emigrants) as a percentage of the total resident population for each of the three schooling groups, for both the four main immigration countries and the EU15. Table 8.2a, column 1 shows the immigration rates of individuals with tertiary education for each economy. The absolute number of net immigrants with tertiary education is reported in column 2 and the total number of residents with tertiary education in column 3. Tables b and c do the same for individuals with secondary and primary education. The classification of education levels into the three groups follows the International Standard Classification of Education (ISCED). In particular the group of 'primary school educated' includes the categories ISCED 0, 1 and 2. The group of secondary school educated includes ISCED 3 and 4 and the group of tertiary educated includes ISCED 5 and 6. Each table ranks the four immigration countries and the EU in decreasing order of immigration rate for each group. A very important fact is established in Table 8.3, substantiating the fears of Europeans that many of their best brains are leaving the EU to the US and other advanced economies. While Australia, Canada, Switzerland and the US attract a large number of highly educated foreigners (these include professionals, engineers, scientists, and managers with crucial roles in promoting the productivity and growth of the host country) the EU15 experiences a net loss of highly educated individuals.

Between 15 and 36 per cent of the population with tertiary education in the US, Canada, Australia and Switzerland are foreign born. In contrast, the EU cannot even attract enough foreign born to make up for its brain drain. While the net drain is small, the gross numbers reveal that 2.5 million college-educated Europeans live abroad and only 2.44 million foreign college-educated workers operate in Europe. This is perhaps the most alarming figure of the whole chapter.[9]

In relative terms the ability of Australia to attract highly-educated foreign born is the most extraordinary: a third of the resident population with tertiary education is foreign born. In terms of sheer quantities the United States attracts the largest share of internationally mobile highly educated workers with an impressive 7.5 million tertiary-educated foreign born. This is like adding to the US the highly educated population of a country as large as Canada. Talents from all over the world are attracted in very large numbers to jobs in the US.

Table 8.2 Net stock of immigrants by education level Census 2000, age 15 and older

a: Net immigrant stock, tertiary education

Country	Net immigrant stock as share of total resident	Net immigrant stock	Total residents
Australia	0.264	1,345,326	5,076,425
Canada	0.204	1,610,587	7,867,545
Switzerland	0.184	184,061	1,000,155
USA	0.132	7,803,770	59,187,830
EU15	−0.001	−62,617	43,980,128

b: Net immigrant stock, secondary education

Country	Net immigrant stock as share of total resident	Net immigrant stock	Total residents
Australia	0.350	739,139	2,110,946
Canada	0.178	1,519,130	8,556,870
Switzerland	0.132	351,938	2,657,729
USA	0.110	11,819,336	107,889,714
EU15	0.006	551,853	86,310,119

c: Net immigrant stock, primary education

Country	Net immigrant stock as share of total resident	Net immigrant stock	Total residents
Switzerland	0.385	419,608	1,090,638
USA	0.300	12,474,002	41,597,025
Australia	0.293	1,268,208	4,324,802
Canada	0.234	1,419,656	6,057,084
EU15	0.034	3,574,683	104,822,511

Source: Author's calculations based on OECD (2005) data.

The ability to attract immigrants into the EU exceeds its stock of emigrants exclusively in the category of less educated workers, where the net stock of immigrants is 3 per cent of the resident population. Notice also that relative to Australia and Canada (countries that disproportionately attract highly educated workers), Switzerland and the US disproportionately attract the group of less educated workers. An impressive 30 per cent of less educated workers in the US were foreign born in the year 2000. Notice, however, that both in relative and absolute terms the number of natives with only primary education is much smaller in the US than in the EU. While the group of US-born residents with a college degree (see column 3 of Table 8.2a) is 40 per cent larger than the corresponding group for the EU15, US natives with primary education are less than

Table 8.3 Geographic determinants of bilateral migration

Dependent variable: Ln (stock migrants)	I: All groups	II: Tertiary education only (16 yrs +)	III: Secondary education only (12–16 yrs)	IV: Primary education only (0–11 yrs)
Ln (distance)	−1.29** (0.09)	−1.21** (0.15)	−1.39** (0.16)	−1.27** (0.17)
Common border	0.74** (0.21)	0.41 (0.34)	0.59 (0.36)	1.21** (0.39)
Common language	0.45** (0.15)	0.47* (0.22)	0.45 (0.27)	0.42 (0.29)
Trade agreement	0.20* (0.11)	0.17 (0.17)	0.18 (0.19)	0.28 (0.21)
Within EU	−0.02 (0.10)	0.13 (0.12)	−0.10 (0.24)	−0.20 (0.26)
Country of origin effect	Yes	Yes	Yes	Yes
Country of destination effect	Yes	Yes	Yes	Yes
Tertiary education dummy	0.43** (0.08)	n.a.	n.a.	n.a.
Secondary education dummy	0.42** (0.08)	n.a.	n.a.	n.a.
Observations	2,268	756	756	756
R²	0.71	0.76	0.74	0.72

Notes

Dependent variable: natural logarithm of the total stock of emigrants in each schooling group in year 2000. The zero values (only 2% of the total) have been substituted with ones.

Number of countries is 28. Each one has 27 observations on gross emigrants. Education groups are 3.

Specification I: People 15 years of age and older, all schooling groups pooled.

Specification II: Only people 15 years and older with some tertiary education.

Specification III: Only people 15 years and older with some secondary education.

Specification IV: Only people 15 years and older with some tertiary education.

Standard errors are clustered by country couple

* = significant at 5%, ** = significant at 10%.

half of EU15 natives with primary education. We can then say that the US economy is progressively substituting natives with foreign born in the low education groups. We will come back on this point later.

All in all, the EU exhibits a much lower capability of attracting immigrants within any skill group, and perhaps most alarmingly, this inability is particularly apparent for the group of the most highly educated workers.

3   Determinants of emigration and the EU effect

The simple statistics presented above are suggestive of two important characteristics of migration in the EU: a low degree of internal mobility and a low ability to attract foreign immigrants, including the highly educated. We need a more structured econometric analysis, however, in order to better understand the causes of these two phenomena. Low internal mobility, for instance, may be due to the equalization of wages across EU countries, which would weaken incentives to migrate. Alternatively, genuine barriers to mobility may exist. Similarly, inability to attract highly skilled foreigners may be a consequence of low wage compensation, or of unattractive post-tertiary education systems, or of hostile immigration policies and other institutional features that penalize immigrants in this group. To shed light on these issues we use the data on the bilateral stocks of emigrants across all OECD countries (by origin and destination) and perform an econometric analysis using a gravity equation that includes the economic and geographic characteristics of countries (of origin and destination) in order to explain these flows. Moreover we differentiate migrants across the three education groups to determine whether they respond differently to economic and geographic incentives and, in general, whether some groups are more mobile than others.

A gravity approach

The basic gravity regression, used to analyse gross trade flows between countries, assumes that (the natural logarithm of) those flows depends on the size of each of the two trading countries (measured as their GDPs) and on factors that can influence bilateral trade costs (distance, contiguity, trade agreements, common culture, access to the sea and so on).[10]

The gravity equation has also been used in the international migration literature. Early work by Helliwell (1998) uses it to analyse migration between US states and Canadian provinces, and more recently Karemera *et al.* (2000) use this framework to analyse immigration in North America, while Mayda (2005) adapts it to a panel of international migration flows. In its most basic form the gravity equation for migratory flows explains total emigration from a country of origin to a country of destination using the economic characteristics of the two countries (population and GDP per person) along with bilateral geographic characteristics (distance, common border, access to sea, common language and trade agreements). Occasionally, if the data allow it, more characteristics of both the country of origin and country of destination are included in order to account for immigration policies and other relevant characteristics. Our empirical strategy follows the general guidelines described above with a novel feature. We include as dependent variables different education groups separately and, correspondingly, we enter as explanatory variables the economic characteristics relevant to each education group (their wage, their population) in the country of origin and of destination. We run some specifications pooling the education groups together and others separating the three groups.

Geographic determinants

In order to analyse the effects of bilateral characteristics (such as distance, sharing a border or speaking a common language) on the emigration flows of each skill group, we first run a generalized gravity equation in which we control for all possible characteristics (economic and non-economic) of the countries of origin and destination by including origin and destination dummies. The data set includes 756^{11} observations on gross emigration rates between 28 OECD countries for each of three schooling groups. We use these observations to estimate the effects of geographic (and other bilateral) variables after controlling for 28 country of origin effects and 28 country of destination effects. The basic regression, whose estimated coefficients are reported in Table 8.3, is as follows:

$$\ln(E_{k,i,j}) = \alpha_i + \beta_j + \gamma_k + b_1 \ln(dist_{i,j}) + b_2 (bord_{i,j}) + b_3 (lang_{i,j}) + b_4 (tradeag_{i,j}) + \varepsilon_{i,j} \tag{1}$$

$E_{k,i,j}$ is the total number of emigrants in education group k, born in country i (called the country of origin) and residing in country j (called the country of destination). α_i is a set of 28 country of origin fixed effects, while β_j are 28 country of destination fixed effects. γ_i are education-specific effects and capture the higher or lower propensity of a skill group to migrate. The other variables are relative to each couple (i and j). They capture, respectively, the distance between the two countries $(dist_{i,j})$ and the presence of a common border $(bord_{i,j})$, a common language $(lang_{i,j})$ or a trade agreement between the countries $(tradeag_{i,j})$. Each of these variables affects the costs of migration and therefore may affect migratory flows. ε_{ijk} is a zero-mean random error. As there may exist correlation in the shocks to gross migration for different skills between a particular pair of countries, we cluster the standard errors by country-pair. Specification I of Table 8.3 reports the estimated coefficients of regression (1) while the other three specifications (II, III and IV) report the coefficients for the same regression run separately for each skill group, i.e. allowing for different effects of each explanatory variable on the emigration flows of each group. Finally in each regression we include a dummy (labelled 'within EU') that takes a value of one if the two countries (origin and destination) are both within the EU15 and zero otherwise. A positive and significant value of this variable implies that migration within EU countries is more intense than between two average OECD countries, once we control for the bilateral characteristics that affect migration.

Specification I of Table 8.3 shows that all the bilateral variables have the expected signs and enter significantly in the regression. As the dependent variable is measured in natural logs (we add one to the very few cells with 0 emigrants) the coefficients are elasticities. Reducing distance by half (50 per cent) increases emigration flows by 65 per cent. Sharing a border increases overall migration between two countries by 74 per cent, while speaking a common language increases migration by 45 per cent, and belonging to the same trade agreement increases it by 20 per cent. Moreover, for a given set of bilateral characteristics, the group of individuals with intermediate or high education exhibits a tendency to migrate 43 per cent more than the group with low education (the omitted dummy). Finally, confirming the statistics on low mobility within the EU, the regression shows no significant effect of belonging to the EU on cross-country migration. This is surprising as there are usually very restrictive immigration policies across countries, while there are no formal restrictions on labour mobility across EU countries.

Considering the mobility of each education group (column II to IV), a few interesting indications emerge. First, highly educated workers appear to be less sensitive to distance and common borders. Highly educated people are likely to be better informed and better equipped to seize good job opportunities in distant countries. However, linguistic commonality plays a bigger role for highly educated, whose jobs no doubt involve professional skills in which mastering a language is crucial. On the other hand, the importance of a common border for migration of low educated people is substantial. The existence of informal networks and word-of-mouth information, particularly strong in the presence of geographic contiguity, may be the main channel to foster the migration of less educated workers. The effect of sharing a border is large and statistically significant only for the group of less educated individuals. Finally the 'within EU' effect is not significant for any skill group. Its point estimate is positive for the highly educated and negative for the other two groups, but highly insignificant for all. The EU thus far has not promoted cross-country integration of labour markets at any level of skill.

Economic determinants

Specification (1) absorbs all the idiosyncratic characteristics of the countries of origin and destination into dummies. This is convenient because it solves the problem of country-specific omitted variables; however it does not provide any understanding of what economic characteristics of the country of origin and destination affect the magnitude of emigration flows. In this section we more closely follow the traditional gravity specification by including, as potential determinants of emigration, the sizes of the country of origin and destination (measured by the population born in each of the two) and the average wage of the education group in both countries. Since we maintain the three education groups as the primary unit of analysis, we need to identify both the size and the wage of each group within each country (origin and destination). Specifically we run the following regression:

$$\ln(E_{k,i,j}) = \alpha_1 \ln(pop_{k,i}) + \alpha_2 \ln(pop_{k,j}) + \beta_1 \ln(w_{k,i}) + \beta_2 \ln(w_{k,j}) + b_1 \ln(dist_{i,j})$$
$$+ b_2(bord_{i,j}) + b_3(lang_{i,j}) + b_4(tradeag_{i,j}) + \varepsilon_{i,j} \quad\quad (2)$$

The variable $pop_{k,i}$ measures the total population with schooling level k born in country i, and $w_{k,i}$ is the average wage of workers in education group k in country i. In order to measure these variables we need additional data and assumptions. We calculate the population size of each skill group using population data from the Penn-World Tables (release 7.0) and the share of population in each schooling group using the Barro and Lee (2000) data set, which is currently updated to the year 1999. The wage for each skill group is harder to find for a large set of countries. As such we calculate them as follows. We assume that the average wage in a country is proportional to the average GDP per capita and is earned by workers with the average schooling level of the country. Then we construct the wage for each education group in each country using the estimated returns to schooling specific to the country, taken from Bils and Klenow (2001) and we use the median years of schooling for each skill group (taken from the Barro and Lee (2000) data set and relative to year 1999). This step implies a large loss of countries as only 18 of the 28 OECD countries have estimates for their returns to schooling. The assumption is that a person with a certain level of schooling in a country looks at the wages of people with similar schooling in other countries when deciding whether and where to migrate. Therefore a country that pays high wages to less educated workers should attract more workers in that group. This procedure is more accurate than simply proxying the earnings of all skill groups with the average GDP per capita in the countries of origin and destination. Such a procedure would completely miss the effects of the wage distribution on the skill distribution of immigrants.

Table 8.4 shows the estimated coefficients for regression (2), pooling all groups in column I, and separating them by group in specifications II to IV. The effects of the geographic variables are similar to what was estimated in Table 8.3, only the effects are smaller for distance and larger for sharing a common language than previously. The sizes of the groups of origin and destination, *ln(pop)*, are very significant in determining the number of emigrants, although their coefficients are smaller than one. This implies that larger groups or countries tend to receive a larger number of emigrants, but in numbers less than proportional to their original populations, so that the share of emigrants and immigrants tend to be smaller for larger countries. Consistent with previous results (e.g. Mayda, 2005) wages in the country of destination are a very important determinant of migration, with a positive elasticity close to 3 (which suggests that a wage increase of 1 per cent in the country of destination increases the stock of immigrants by 3 per cent) while the wage in the country of origin has a smaller and insignificant effect. Often the theory predicts an ambiguous

Table 8.4 Geographic and economic determinants of bilateral migration

Dependent variable: Ln (stock migrants)	I: All groups	II: Tertiary education only (16 yrs +)	III: Secondary education only (12–16 yrs)	IV: Primary education only (0–11 yrs)
Ln (distance)	−0.77** (0.10)	−0.78** (0.19)	−0.74** (0.18)	−0.89** (0.19)
Common border	0.63** (0.29)	0.20 (0.45)	0.41** (0.50)	1.08** (0.50)
Common language	1.83** (0.21)	2.20** (0.35)	1.79** (0.39)	1.12** (0.34)
Trade agreement	1.03* (0.24)	0.93* (0.40)	1.22** (0.40)	0.95** (0.44)
Within EU	−1.20** (0.27)	−0.89 (0.47)	−1.17** (0.49)	−1.94** (0.50)
Ln (individual wage) destination	2.92** (0.20)	1.81** (0.27)	3.11** (0.41)	5.84** (0.46)
Ln (individual wage) origin	0.40 (0.24)	−0.34 (0.40)	0.54 (0.40)	0.93 (0.50)
Ln (population) destination	0.66** (0.06)	0.61** (0.11)	0.62** (0.12)	1.46** (0.13)
Ln (population) origin	0.77** (0.06)	0.83** (0.11)	0.77** (0.11)	1.09** (0.13)
Tertiary education dummy	1.32** (0.28)	n.a.	n.a.	n.a.
Secondary education dummy	1.32** (0.36)	n.a.	n.a.	n.a.
Observations	918	306	306	306
R^2	0.35	0.34	0.32	0.31

Notes

Dependent variable: natural logarithm of the total stock of emigrants in each schooling group in year 2000. The zero values (only 2% of the total) have been substituted with ones.

The explanatory variables Ln (individual wage) are imputed for each education group as described in the main text.

Number of countries is 18. Each one has 17 observations on gross emigrants. Education groups are 3.

Specification I: People 15 years of age and older, all schooling groups pooled.

Specification II: Only people 15 years and older with some tertiary education.

Specification III: Only people 15 years and older with some secondary education.

Specification IV: Only people 15 years and older with some tertiary education.

Standard Errors are clustered by country couple

* = significant at 5%, ** = significant at 10%.

effect of this wage on emigration. On the one hand, people with very low wages (those in poverty) often do not have the means to emigrate, so that an increase in wages may lift these people out of poverty and hence raise the emigration rate; on the other hand, as the wage continues to rise and economic opportunities improve, the incentives to emigrate diminish. As a result of these two offsetting influences people often find a small or zero effect (or sometimes a non-linear effect) of wage changes in the country of origin on emigration flows. We also confirm the higher mobility of intermediate and highly educated workers. Moreover, this specification strengthens our previous finding that belonging to the EU actually has a negative effect on emigration flows. When we control only for differences in wages and population, living within the EU is associated with a much lower tendency to move between countries. Two hypothetical non-EU OECD countries would have more than twice the bilateral migration flows as two EU countries with identical wage, population and bilateral geographic characteristics! Part of the country-specific lack of mobility not due to wage differences, previously captured by country dummies in Table 8.3, is now absorbed by the EU effect.

Specifications II to IV in Table 8.4 confirm the stronger effects of common language on the migration of highly skilled individuals and, interestingly, the higher sensitivity to wages in the destination country for the less educated group. Confirming the non-monotonic effect of wages in the country of origin on labour flows, the emigration of highly educated individuals (who are certainly not poor even in poorer countries) responds negatively, though not significantly, to an increase in that wage. Less educated people, on the contrary, respond to higher wages in the country of origin with a higher, though not significant, emigration rate. The effect of the EU dummy in each regression confirms the lack of mobility particular to within-EU countries, but also shows a smaller negative effect on the group of highly educated relative to less educated.

In general the regressions show that highly educated workers are on average more mobile, less affected by distance and proximity and more affected by common language in their migratory choices than are the less educated. Moreover, migration flows for all skill groups respond very strongly to wages in the country of destination and less strongly to wages in the country of origin. Finally, the EU seems to have an unusually low level of cross-country mobility even relative to other OECD countries, once we control for the well-known geographic and economic determinants of emigration.

4 Ability to attract educated international migrants

In light of the above results we can begin to analyse the reasons for the relative inability of the EU to attract highly educated foreign-born workers. First of all there is a tendency of large economies to attract foreign-educated workers in smaller proportions than domestic workers. The percentage of foreign born from these groups is consequently lower in larger economies. However, the US, an economy of comparable size to the EU, has a 14 per cent share of highly educated residents who are foreign born relative to 5.9 per cent in the EU: clearly none of this difference is driven by the size of the economy. Second, the lower returns to education in many European countries compared to the US (though not to Canada and Australia, which have similar returns) and the sensitivity of migration of highly-skilled workers to the wages in the country of destination also explain some of the differences. In particular, looking at differences in the returns to schooling between Germany[12] (7.7 per cent per year of schooling) and the US (9.3 per cent per year of schooling) and differences in average incomes and years of schooling, one observes that the salaries for the highly educated are 30 per cent higher in the US than in Germany (in terms of purchasing power). Given our estimated sensitivity of emigration to wages (for highly educated workers), this translates into a 50 per cent larger inflow of highly educated to the US, all else equal. Yet this difference is still too small to explain the actual percentage differences in migration between the highly educated foreign born in the EU and the US. Using German high-skill wages as the representative skilled wage series for continental Europe, bringing these to the US levels would still only increase the share of foreign born to about 9 per cent (5.9 per cent +0.5*5.9 per cent). Five percentage points of difference, equivalent to nearly 100 per cent of the size of total immigration of highly-skilled workers in the EU, remain unexplained.

To be more precise in the quantification of the unexplained inability to attract educated foreign workers, we run specification (2) again, but add selected country of destination dummies. We add an 'EU' effect (equal to one when the destination is a EU country) and a 'US' effect (equal to one when the destination is the US). Then we add dummies for specifically selected immigration countries. Finally, we compare Germany and the UK as destination countries. The estimates of the coefficients on these dummies are reported in Table 8.5. Each column reports coefficients from one regression identical to specification II in Table 8.4 (hence restricted to highly educated workers) with the inclusion of these dummies.

The sign and magnitude of these estimates can be interpreted as the unexplained excess ability or inability of the destination country to attract skilled immigrants, once we control for the geographic and wage determinants of migration. Specification I includes only EU and US dummies as destination countries, while specification II adds a specific effect for Canada and Australia. Specification III includes 18 dummies to control for all observed and unobserved characteristics of the countries of origin. Finally, specification IV considers a specific effect for Germany and the UK as destination countries (these are the only two large EU countries included in the regression, as Italy lacks data on migration and France lacks data on the returns to schooling).

In each specification the EU effect is negative and significant relative to the average effect for OECD countries (standardized to zero). In contrast, the US effect is positive, significant and stands as the largest effect even when we include other immigration economies. Considering that the average share of

Table 8.5 Attraction of highly-educated international migrants: US and EU unexplained effects

Destination-country effects, highly educated migrants	I: Baseline	II: Including Canada and Australia	III: Controlling for country of origin effects	IV: Specific for Germany and UK
EU	−1.65** (0.36)	−0.58** (0.34)	−1.44** (0.26)	
Germany				0.04 (0.10)
UK				+2.79** (0.56)
US	+2.73** (0.59)	+4.77** (0.59)	+3.14** (0.48)	+6.13** (0.69)
Canada		+3.88** (0.44)		+4.58** (0.54)
Australia		+4.38** (0.53)		+4.89** (0.50)
Observations	306	306	306	306
R^2	0.42	0.54	0.46	0.57

Notes

The dependent variable is Ln (stock of migrants).

The values reported in each column are the estimated coefficients and standard errors for dummies specific to a country (or area) of origin of the emigrants, in a regression as specification II in Table 8.5.

The coefficient captures the excess capacity of attraction of highly educated migrants (if positive) or the disadvantage in attracting immigrants (if negative) of a country, after we control for the economic and geographic determinants of migration (such as wages population, distance and barriers).

* = significant at 5%, ** = significant at 10%.

highly educated foreign born in an OECD country is 2 per cent, the negative effect estimated in column 3 implies that the EU (even with wages and population identical to the US) would host a percentage of foreign born equal only to 0.84 per cent of its residents, while the US would receive 11.7 per cent of all its highly educated from abroad. This difference (likely to be due to a combination of policies, institutions, education opportunities, non-monetary incentives, and other factors) accounts for 80 per cent of the share of highly educated immigrants in the US, and over-accounts for the disadvantage of the EU. Somewhat unsatisfactorily, the largest part of the difference between the US and the EU in attracting skilled foreigners is captured by these unexplained dummies. Certainly more careful analysis of the immigration policies and institutional characteristics of the countries may reveal important determinants currently buried in the country fixed effect. Finally, specification IV shows that when we allow differences across EU countries, the UK emerges as the country that, for given wages and geographic characteristics, has the largest unexplained capacity to attract highly educated foreign born. While the specific effect of Germany as a destination country is equal to the OECD average (the coefficient on the dummy is not different from 0) the UK has a capacity almost four times as large as the average to attract educated immigrants (+280 per cent). This is still far from the US and other immigration countries, but remarkable for EU standards.

While Table 8.5 confines the analysis to the group of highly educated immigrants, similar regressions run for the groups of intermediate and less educated (not reported) produce similar results. We therefore wish to emphasize the low ability of the EU to attract workers in general at any level of human capital and skill. This tendency, already shown by the simple statistics on immigration of section 2, is dramatically confirmed by the econometric analysis. Particularly when compared to the US, the countries of the EU15 (with the possible exception of the UK) have a remarkably weak ability to attract workers.

5   Skill composition of native workers and skill composition of immigrants

Essential to any immigration policy is stipulation of not only the total number of immigrants allowed in the country, but also criteria for admitting them. For such decisions it is crucial to consider the skills, education and ability of immigrants, especially in assessing the effects of immigration on the wages and income of natives. Workers with different schooling levels are effectively different factors of production, since they perform different tasks and choose different occupations. Thus they are not perfectly substitutable. Hence by shifting the relative supply of different skills, the inflow of immigrants affects the relative scarcity (and wages) of different groups. Some groups of natives gain while others lose as a result of these inflows. Furthermore, if we believe that foreign-born workers are not perfect substitutes for natives even within the same education group (because of different abilities, occupational choice and working preferences –

see Ottaviano and Peri, 2005 for a fuller discussion) the gains for local workers from immigration would be differentiated even further. In particular, for a group of native workers with a certain educational attainment, most beneficial to them would be the inflow of workers with vastly different levels of education. These immigrants would complement their abilities and increase their productivity, while the inflow of workers with similar education and skills would compete for similar jobs, possibly pushing wages down and (at least temporarily) unemployment up.

Since all the immigration economies considered here are democratic, ultimately the selection of migrants is determined via immigration laws that are approved and supported by the citizens (natives). We should then expect that the combination of immigrants allowed in the country is one that benefits the majority of its citizens, particularly the median voters. In a political-economy equilibrium where the median voter chooses the immigration policy, the largest skill group in the country should limit the inflow of foreigners with the same level of education and encourage the inflows of those with different levels of education.[13] In particular, if one group has an absolute majority of people in the country, it should succeed in keeping the share of foreign born in that skill group among the smallest of all immigrant groups, in order to minimize competition from foreigners and maximize the benefits from complementarities. Table 8.6 shows the composition of the native population across education groups (upper panel, 8.6a) and the presence of foreign born in each skill group as the percentage of the total residents in that group (lower panel, 8.6b). The first four rows report figures relative to the immigration countries, the fifth row reports those for the EU15 and the last three rows show the figures for the three largest EU economies (France, Germany and the UK).

Each of the immigration countries (Australia, Canada, Switzerland and the US) follows the principle described above: the largest skill group in each country (in most cases an absolute majority, and marked in bold in the upper table) corresponds to the group with the lowest percentage of foreign born (marked in bold in the lower table). We report in Figure 8.2 the distribution of the native population across the three education groups (solid line) and the share of foreign born in each group (dotted line) for each of the immigration countries and for the EU. For each immigration country, represented in the top four panels (the US, Australia, Canada and Switzerland), it is easy to perceive the 'mirror image' behaviour of the two variables: the foreign born are relatively abundant in the groups where natives are less concentrated in absolute terms. For the EU on the other hand (bottom graph in the panel) the two variables 'move together': the foreign born are relatively abundant in those education groups (the less educated) already prominent within the native population.

This feature of these immigration countries is interesting because the educational compositions of their populations are different. Australia has a relative majority of less educated individuals and Canada has a rather balanced population (with a small majority of people with secondary schooling), while Switzerland and the US have relatively large intermediate groups, with an

Table 8.6 Education of natives and education of immigrants

a: Distribution of native born across education groups

	Low	*Medium*	*High*
Australia	**0.450**	0.163	0.388
Canada	0.309	**0.371**	0.320
Switzerland	0.256	**0.552**	0.192
USA	0.219	**0.511**	0.270
EU15	**0.535**	0.232	0.232
France	**0.548**	0.272	0.181
Germany	0.236	**0.570**	0.194
UK	**0.512**	0.287	0.201

b: Share of foreign born in each education group

	Low	*Medium*	*High*
Australia	**0.204**	0.268	0.268
Canada	0.192	**0.179**	0.238
Switzerland	0.321	**0.152**	0.277
USA	0.234	**0.101**	0.139
EU15	0.059	**0.040**	0.058
France	0.136	**0.087**	0.124
Germany	0.220	**0.099**	0.110
UK	**0.080**	0.086	0.160

Source: Author's calculations on OECD (2005) data relative to foreign born in year 2000 and Barro and Lee (2000) data relative to education of all residents in year 1999.

absolute majority of individuals with secondary school education. Correspondingly, the foreign born in Australia are over-represented in the group of medium and highly educated people (27 per cent of each group is foreign) and underrepresented in the group of less educated (20 per cent). Canada has a more balanced distribution of immigrant skills, with a small over-representation in the low and high schooling groups and under-representation in the medium schooling group. The US and Switzerland have a disproportionately large share of immigrants with high and low skills and a disproportionately small share in the intermediate group, thus complementing the distribution of natives. In general the presence of a large group of natives with a certain schooling level is associated with a relatively small share of foreign born in that group for all the large immigration economies.

This is, however, not true for the EU. While the absolute majority (53 per cent) and the median voters in the EU belong to the low-education group, this group is also the one with the largest share of foreigners. Possibly because European workers have other means of protecting their wages from market competition (unionization, insider's advantages) immigration policies have not been

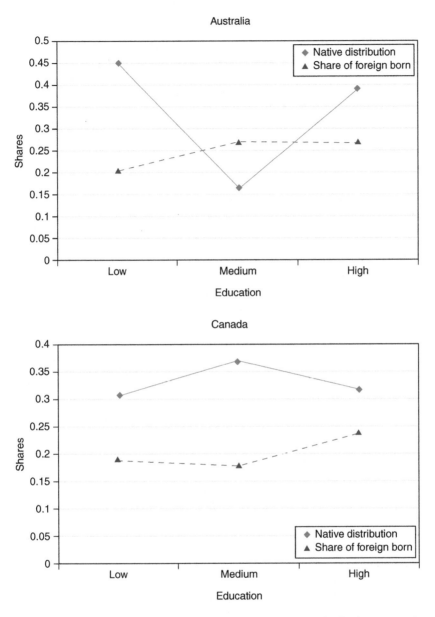

Figure 8.2 Education of natives and education of immigrants: distribution across three schooling groups.

continued

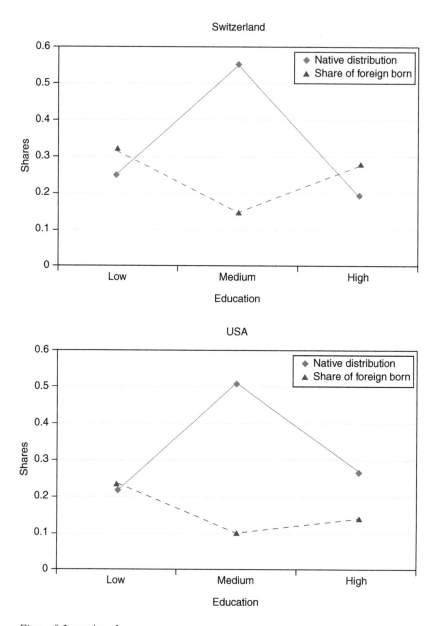

Figure 8.2 continued.

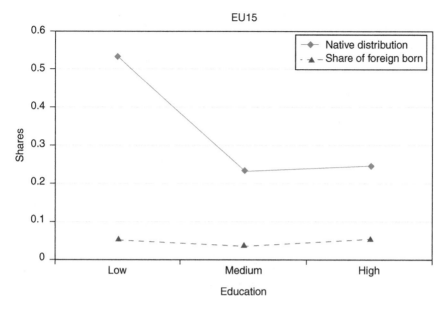

Figure 8.2 continued.

targeted to shelter these low education workers from competition, even though they constitute the majority of the labour force in the EU area. One explanation for this is that there is no common immigration policy in the EU; as such we should look at individual countries. At the country level, however, the discordance between immigrant skill levels in reality and those predicted by the political economy equilibrium remains in some countries. Interestingly, while the skill compositions of natives in France and the UK are similar to the EU average, with a majority of people with only primary education, the relatively uncompetitive French labour market attracts the largest share of foreigners among less skilled workers, while the more market-oriented UK attracts more highly educated workers. Germany has a native skill composition concentrated among the intermediate levels of education and, in line with the political economy equilibrium, attracts more from the two extreme groups of skills. Ultimately, labour market distortions that have artificially protected workers in the EU may have reduced their concerns over the skill composition of immigrants, leading to sub-optimal immigration policies, at least from the point of view of the majority. This is confirmed by the fact that countries where these distortions are stronger (such as France) exhibit an immigrant skill composition at odds with the one predicted by the political economy equilibrium, while those which are more market-oriented (such as the UK) show the largest presence of immigrants from education groups that benefit the country's majority, in line with the prediction of the political economy model. If immigration laws were established with an eye to the welfare of the native labour force, the EU would change the composition of its immigrant workforce, shifting it towards those with secondary and tertiary education who could most benefit the local economy. At the same time of course, better tertiary education and higher rewards to skills should complement any immigration policy if the EU is to compete for highly educated international migrants.

6 The impact of immigration on wages

If the skill composition of immigrants is complementary to that of natives, then immigration benefits the majority of natives. This idea is based on the intuitive principle that, for a given factor, increasing the supply of a complementary factor of production benefits the factor, while increasing the supply of a substitute harms it. Here, we present a simple model of production that, using reasonable estimates of the elasticity of substitution between education groups and between foreign born and natives (taken from the literature), allows us to quantify the effects of the stock of immigrants on the wages of each native group and the average wage for all groups. We calculate these effects for both the immigration economies and the EU in order to illustrate again the contrast between the potentially large gains derived from migrants in the immigration countries vis-à-vis the very small gains or losses to the majority of EU individuals. These differences are due to the varying appropriateness of immigrant skill distributions and to varying abilities to attract highly educated workers.

Production with imperfect substitutability of skills

In order to compute the effect of a change in the supply of skills (due to migration) on the wages of natives, we need to assume an aggregate production function. We follow the recent labour (Katz and Murphy, 1992; Borjas, 2003) and growth (Caselli and Coleman, 2005) literatures and specifically Ottaviano and Peri (2005). We assume that production of output, Y, in country i, takes place combining physical capital and the three types of labour inputs (classified by their schooling level) according to the following production function:

$$Y_i = A_i K_i^\alpha \tilde{L}_i^{1-\alpha} - \text{where } \tilde{L}_i = \left[\sum_{k=1}^{3} \left(\frac{L_{ki}}{\tau_{k,i}} \right)^{\frac{\delta-1}{\delta}} \right]^{\frac{\delta}{\delta-1}} \tag{3}$$

A_i is country i's total factor productivity, K_i is physical capital and $\tilde{L}$ is a CES labour composite of the three groups of workers with different education levels (Primary, Secondary and Tertiary). The terms $(1/\tau_{k,i})$ measure the efficiency of each group, while δ is the elasticity of substitution across these groups. Assuming the Cobb-Douglas combination of physical capital and the labour composite and considering the long-run accumulation of capital, any model with the above production function and optimal consumption converges to a balanced growth path with a constant real return to capital. Hence one can solve out K from (3) and calculate the wage (marginal productivity) of each type of worker as a function of total factor productivity, efficiencies $1/\tau_{k,i}$ and supplies $L_{k,i}$ of labour types.[14] Once we have these formulas we can evaluate the impact of changes in the supply of foreign-born workers on the wages of each group of native workers. It turns out that these elasticities depend only on the elasticity of substitution, δ, which we take from the literature to be 1.5,[15] and on the wage and employment shares of workers in each group. We measure the first as shares in the population of each education group and the second using the wages imputed to each group in each country according to the procedure described in section 3.2. Then we evaluate the wage elasticity of natives in each group to a change in the supply equal to the total foreign-born population. In this section we assume that the total supply of each skill group is the sum of natives and foreign born in that group: $L_{k,i} = H_{k,i} + F_{k,i}$, where $H_{k,i}$ is the total number of home-born residents in education group k, while $F_{k,i}$ is the total number of foreign-born residents in education group k. We evaluate the percentage change in wages for home-born workers when $F_{k,i}$ changes from 0 to the actual value for the year 2000 in each country.

Table 8.7a reports the results of this exercise for the four immigration countries and for the EU. Let us consider the effect of the stock of immigrants on Australian wages. Since Australia attracts mostly intermediate and highly educated workers, this influx increases the wage of less-educated workers by 3.7 per cent, while it reduces the wages of the other two groups by 2.4 and 3.2 percentage points. This group of less-educated individuals is the largest in Australia and nearly commands an absolute majority; hence the effect described above is beneficial to the largest skill group of the country. On the other hand Switzerland, which mostly attracts immigrants in the extreme education groups, experiences a wage increase for the intermediate (secondary) schooling group by 7 percentage points, while the other two groups experience wage losses of 11 and 5 percentage points. Similar to this pattern (but less pronounced) are the effects of migration into the US and Canada. Notice that the aggregate effect on native wages (last column) is close to 0 in all cases. This results from our assumption of aggregate constant return to scale in production and of perfect substitutability of home and foreign born in each education group.

Finally, consider the overall effects of immigration in the EU. The only group that benefits from immigration is the one with secondary education (+1 per cent in their wages). But this group accounts only for 23 per cent of the population, while the absolute majority of the population (with low levels of education) loses 0.4 per cent of its wage. Competition from foreign born at the low end of the education spectrum therefore harms Europe more than the US. One may argue that the solution is to promote educational policies rather than change immigration policies; many have stressed that the EU must increase its graduation rates in tertiary education, hence increasing the average education of native Europeans. It seems possible, however, that any benefits from educational restructuring might be undermined by current EU immigration policies.

Table 8.7 Calculated impact of the stock of immigrants (2000) on wages of different educational groups of natives

a: Assuming perfect substitutability between native and migrants in the same education group

	Low	Intermediate	High	Average
Australia	**+3.7%**	−2.4%	−3.2%	0.02%
Canada	+1.4%	**+2.0%**	−3.7%	0%
Switzerland	−11.2%	**+7.1%**	−5.1%	0.1%
USA	−8.4%	**+3.4%**	+0.4%	0.05%
EU15	−0.3%	+1%	−0.2%	−0.05%

b: Using the estimates of substitutability between natives and migrants in the same schooling group as in Ottaviano and Peri (2005)

	Low	Intermediate	High	Average
Australia	**+7.3%**	+0.9%	+5.6%	+5.5%
Canada	+4.6%	**+4.1%**	+3.7%	+4.0%
Switzerland	−4.8%	**+8.8%**	+3.8%	+4.3%
USA	−4.3%	**+4.5%**	+4.2%	+2.4%
EU15	+0.5%	+1.4%	+1.2%	+0.8%

Notes
The effects have been calculated by assuming a CES production function with elasticity of substitution between schooling groups of 1.5. The shares of native and foreign-born in each education group were taken from the census 2000, the share of total wage to each group has been calculated using the returns to schooling reported in Bils and Klenow (2000) and the procedure described in the text. The returns to schooling used are:
Australia: 6.4% per year of schooling
Canada: 4.2%
Switzerland: 7.2%
USA: 9.3%
EU15 (Germany): 7.7%.

Gains from complementarities

I have argued in previous articles (Ottaviano and Peri, 2005) that the above procedure, which assumes perfect substitutability between home and foreign-born workers within an education group, understates the gains from immigration accruing to natives. In that article we further showed, using both estimates and anecdotal evidence, that within the US, foreign-born workers choose different occupations, have different abilities, and bring different skills to production from those of natives (for a given level of schooling). Think, for instance, of a Chinese-born cook or of an Italian-born stylist living in the United States: they certainly have abilities and produce services that cannot be perfectly substituted by their US-born counterparts. We also showed that substitutability between home and foreign-born workers is particularly low within the group of highly educated workers, where talent, originality, and creativity are important attributes shaped by culture. In the US, most highly educated foreign-born residents work in the fields of science, technology and engineering, while natives are disproportionately employed in administration, law and education. As an extreme example, think how hard it would have been to substitute for natives that talented group of European-born physicists (Albert Einstein, Enrico Fermi *et al.*) who operated in the US during World War II, or the many Russian mathematicians who migrated to the US during the 1990s, or the Indian computer engineers that currently reside in Silicon Valley. They all brought talents complementary and very valuable to the US economy.

These considerations have two implications for our previous calculations. First, because these complementarities exist not only between particular groups but all groups, the host economy may increase the aggregate/average wage of its native workers from an influx of migrants (while single groups can still suffer from a wage decrease). Second, because these complementarities characterize creative, technological and scientific professions, attracting the highest-educated foreigners will have the most beneficial effects on domestic productivity (wages). An easy way to incorporate these assumptions in our model is to consider the supply of each type of labour ($L_{k,i}$ in equation 3) as a CES composite itself, made up of home and foreign-born workers, as follows:

$$L_{k,i} = \left[\left(\frac{H_{k,i}}{\tau_{Hk}} \right)^{\frac{\theta_k - 1}{\theta_k}} + \left(\frac{F_{k,i}}{\tau_{FK}} \right)^{\frac{\theta_k - 1}{\theta_k}} \right]^{\frac{\theta_k - 1}{\theta_k}} - \text{ for } k = \text{Low, Medium, High} \qquad (4)$$

$1/\tau_{j,k}$ are the efficiency factors of each group and the parameters θ_k is the elasticity of substitution between the home and foreign born in education group k. Based on the estimates in Ottaviano and Peri (2005) we choose that elasticity to equal 7 for the group with low schooling, 10 for the group with intermediate schooling and 4 for the group with high schooling. As argued above these estimates imply that highly educated workers benefit to a larger extent from the complementarities of its members. These values were estimated using US census data for the period 1970–2000. Table 8.7b reports the simulated effects of the stock of immigrants on the wages of natives under these assumptions. Looking first at the immigration countries, the group of natives of largest size is still the one that gains the most from immigration. Highly educated natives however now always gain, thanks to stronger complementarities with foreigners in the group. Finally, average wage gains are positive and large. The positive average effect is actually larger when the overall capacity of attracting immigrants, particularly the most educated ones, is larger. Australia enjoys an average increase of native wages by 5.5 per cent, Canada by 4 per cent and the US by 2.4 per cent. The group of highly-educated domestic workers in Australia gains 5.6 per cent in its wage and in the US the same group increases its wage by 4.3 per cent. Even in the EU15 (last row) the increase in immigrants now has a positive wage effect on each of the native education groups as well as on the average (+0.8 per cent). However these effects are much smaller than for the other economies and the largest group (less educated) still experiences the smallest benefit (+0.5 per cent).

7 Conclusions

The European Union is increasingly becoming an immigration economy. Therefore it is instructive to compare it to those economies that have attracted immigrants for a long time. Produced at a time when important policy discussions about reforming and unifying immigration laws across EU countries are being held, this paper provides facts that we believe should be carefully considered. First, the EU has not succeeded in increasing the internal mobility of its workers, not even the most educated ones. Rigid labour, housing and credit markets, along with insider privilege and entitlements for citizens to government transfers (hard to carry across countries) may be responsible for this immobility. If Western Europe is to become a society that aims at being inclusive and multicultural, it should first achieve greater internal integration. Second, the EU is still far from attracting talented and educated foreign born at the rate that the US does. In net terms the EU was still experiencing a drain of its highly educated individuals in the year 2000, which possibly has worsened in the last few years. Third, the composition of immigrants in the EU by schooling levels is more likely to penalize the earnings of the largest group of EU natives (still represented in the year 2000 by those with primary education only) while in most immigration economies the wages of the majority of workers grow from immigration. Some indications have emerged that the UK is probably the most successful large EU country in attracting foreign talent and selecting foreign born by education. If the large immigration economies (the US, Canada, Australia and Switzerland) are to be taken as a benchmark model, however, deep changes are needed to make immigration in the EU more similar to theirs in quality and quantity.

Notes

1 I thank Barry Eichengreen for inviting and stimulating this contribution. Peter Lindert provided very helpful and insightful comments and discussion. I also thank Anna Maria Mayda and participants to the Berkeley-Vienna Conference, 2005 for helpful comments. Ahmed Rahman provided outstanding assistance with the editing of the chapter. Errors are mine.
2 See, for instance, Stiglitz (2002).
3 See the debate between Samuelson (2004) and Bhagwati *et al.* (2004).
4 Here and in the rest of the chapter we refer to EU15 as 'European Union'. The Eastern and Central European countries (of recent accession to the EU) are excluded.
5 See for instance Hatton and Williamson (2002, 2004), Clark *et al.* (2002), Mayda (2005). For a more descriptive overview see Massey *et al.* (1993) and Zlotnik (1998).
6 There is a long tradition of analysing the impact of immigrants on US wages. Early influential papers are Altonji and Card (1991), Borjas (1987), Card (1990), Grossman (1982). More recent important articles are Borjas *et al.* (1997), Borjas (1999, 2003), and Card (2001). Baker and Benjamin (1994) analysed the impact of immigrants in Canada. For the impact of immigrants in Europe see Angrist and Kugler (2003).
7 See section 2.2 below for details.
8 EU15 includes the following countries: Austria, Belgium, Denmark, Spain, Finland, France, Germany, Greece, Italy, Ireland, Luxembourg, The Netherlands, Norway, Sweden, The United Kingdom. Italy is never included, however, in our statistics, due to lack of data.
9 See also the Report EEAG (2003) on the drain of talents from Europe.
10 See Feenstra (2003) for a survey of the gravity approach in the trade literature.
11 The native of each one of the 28 countries can migrate to any of the other 27. Hence the number of observations for the gross flows is $756 = 28 \times 27$.
12 Here and in the rest of the chapter we take German's returns to schooling as representative for the EU.
13 See Ortega (2004) for a formalization of this idea.
14 The details of the derivation and of the formulas are in Ottaviano and Peri (2005), pages 7 to 10.
15 See, for instance, Katz and Murphy (1992), Caselli and Coleman (2005), Ciccone and Peri (2005).

References

Altonji, J.J. and Card, D. (1991) 'The effects of Immigration on the Labor Market Outcomes of Less-Skilled Natives', in John M. Abowd and Richard Freeman (eds) *Immigration, Trade and the Labor Market*. Chicago: The University of Chicago Press.

Angrist, J. and Kugler, A. (2003) 'Protective or Counter-Productive? Labor Market Institutions and the Effect of Immigration on EU natives', *Economic Journal* 113: 302–331.

Baker, M. and Benjamin, D. (1994) 'The Performance of Immigrants in the Canadian Labor Market', *Journal of Labor Economics* 12: 455–471.

Barro, R.J. and Lee, J.W. (2000) 'International Data on Educational Attainment: Updates and Implications', manuscript, Harvard University, February 2000.

Bhagwati, J., Panagariya, A. and Srinivasan, T.N. (2004) 'The Muddles over Outsourcing', *Journal of Economic Perspectives* 18(4): 93–114.

Bils, M. and Klenow, P. (2000) 'Does Schooling Cause Growth?', *American Economic Review* 90(5): 1160–1183.

Borjas, G.J. (1987) 'Self-selection and the Earnings of Immigrants', *American Economic Review* 77(4): 531–553.

Borjas, G.J. (1991) 'Immigration and Self-Selection', in John Abowd and Richard Freeman (eds) *Immigration, Trade and the Labor Market.* Chicago: University of Chicago Press, pp. 29–76.

Borjas, G.J. (1999) *Heaven's Door*, Princeton and Oxford: Princeton University Press.

Borjas, G.J. (2003) 'The Labor Demand Curve is Downward Sloping: Reexamining the Impact of Immigration on the Labor Market', *Quarterly Journal of Economics*, Vol. CXVIII (4): 1335–1374.

Borjas, G.J., Freeman, R. and Katz, L. (1997) 'How Much do Immigration and Trade Affect Labor Market Outcomes?', *Brookings Papers on Economic Activity*, 1997 (1), 1–90.

Butcher, K. and Card, D. (1991) 'Immigration and Wages: Evidence from the 1980s', *American Economic Review*, Papers and Proceedings 81(2): 292–296.

Card, D. (1990) 'The Impact of the Mariel Boatlift on the Miami Labor Market', *Industrial and Labor Relation Review* XLIII: 245–257.

Card, D. (2001) 'Immigrant Inflows, Native Outflows, and the Local labor Market Impacts of Higher Immigration', *Journal of Labor Economics* XIX (2001): 22–64.

Caselli, F. and Coleman, W. (2005) 'The World Technology Frontier,' manuscript London School of Economics, April 2005.

Ciccone, A. and Peri, G. (2005) 'Long-Run Substitutability between More and Less Educated Workers: Evidence from US States 1950–1990', *Review of Economics and Statistic* 87(4) November 2005.

Clark, X., Hatton, T.J. and Williamson, J.G. (2002) 'Where do US Immigrants come from and why?', NBER Working Paper No. 8998.

EEAG (2003) 'Report on the European Economy 2003', European Economic Advisory Group (EEAG) at CESifo, Munich.

Feenstra, R. (2003) 'Advanced International Trade: Theory and Evidence'. Princeton, NJ: Princeton University Press.

Glick, R. and Rose, A. (2002) 'Does a currency union affect trade? The time-series evidence', *European Economic Review* 46(6): 1125–1151.

Grossman, J.B. (1982) 'The Substitutability of Natives and Immigrants in Production', *Review of Economics and Statistics* 64: 596–603.

Hall, R. and Jones, C. (1999) 'Why Do Some Countries Produce So Much More Output per Worker than Others?', *Quarterly Journal of Economics*, February 1999, 114(1): 83–116.

Hatton, T.J. and Williamson, J.G. (2002) 'What Fundamentals Drive World Migration?', NBER Working Paper No. 9159.

Hatton, T.J. and Williamson, J.G. (2004) 'International Migration in the Long Run: Positive Selection, Negative Selection and Policy', NBER Working Paper No. 10529.

Helliwell, J.F. (1998) 'How Much Do National Borders Matter?', Chapter 5, pp. 79–91. Brookings Institution Press.

Jones, C. (2002) 'Sources of US Economic Growth in a World of Ideas', *American Economic Review* 92: 220–239.

Karemera, D., Oguledo, V.I. and Davis, B. (2000) 'A gravity model analysis of international migration to North America', *Applied Economics* 32(13): 1745–1755.

Katz, L. and Murphy, K. (1992) 'Change in Relative Wages 1963–1987: Supply and Demand Factors', *Quarterly Journal of Economics* 107: 35–78.

Massey, D.S., Arango, J., Hugo, G., Kouaouachi, A., Pellegrino, A. and Taylor, J.E. (1993) 'Theories of International Migration: A Review and Appraisal', *Population and Development Review* 19(3): 431–466.

Mayda, A.M. (2005) 'International Migration: A Panel Data Analysis of Economic and non-Economic Determinants', manuscript, Georgetown University, May 2005.

OECD (2005) 'Public Data Files of the OECD Project on the stock of international Migrants', Organization for Economic Cooperation and Development, May 2005.

Ortega, F. (2004) 'Immigration Policies and Skill upgrading', mimeo Universitat Pompeu Fabra.

Ottaviano, G. and Peri, G. (2005) 'Rethinking the Gains from Immigration: Theory and Evidence from the US', NBER Working Paper #11672.

Samuelson, P. (2004) 'Why Ricardo and Mill Rebut and Confirm Arguments of Main-stream Economists Supporting Globalization', *Journal of Economic Perspectives* 18(3): 135–146.

Stiglitz, J. (2002) *Globalization and Its Discontents*, W.W. Norton & Company, June 2002.

Zlotnick, H. (1998) 'International Migrations 1965–96: an Overview', *Population and Development Review* 24(3): 429–468.

9 American fiscal policy in the postwar era

An interpretive history

Alan J. Auerbach[1]

1 Introduction

From a macroeconomist's perspective, the central issue surrounding fiscal policy has traditionally been its efficacy as a tool for stabilization. This focus on aggregate activity typically has led to a parallel concentration on fiscal aggregates: revenues, spending, and deficits. But a focus on aggregates masks significant changes that have occurred over the postwar years in US fiscal policy. Some of these changes, in turn, have consequences for the practice of stabilization and budget policy. Given the continuing evolution in the composition of revenues and spending, a look below the surface will provide some insight into the future challenges to the practice of fiscal policy.

This chapter begins, in the next section, with an overview of US fiscal policy during the postwar period. Section 3 considers the determinants of fiscal policy actions over this period, asking in particular how business cycle and budget conditions have affected tax and spending behavior. Section 4 provides a discussion of how the changing composition of spending, from discretionary spending to old-age entitlements, is likely to affect short-run spending behavior, and also how this shift affects budget sustainability and how we judge this sustainability.

2 A brief overview

Spending

Since 1962,[2] federal spending (excluding interest) has been relatively stable as a fraction of GDP. As seen in Figure 9.1, this share has ranged between just over 16 percent and just under 20 percent throughout the period. But the overall share's relative stability masks considerable changes in spending components. Defense spending has been trending steadily downward from a peak of nearly 10 percent at the height of the Vietnam War, with interruptions in this trend during the first half of the Reagan Administration and since September 11 2001. Non-defense discretionary spending rose during the mid-1960s and again in the mid-1970s and fell sharply at the beginning of the Reagan administration, but has maintained a roughly constant share of spending since 1986, between 3.3 and 3.8 percent of GDP.

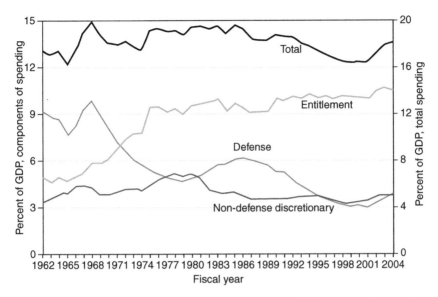

Figure 9.1 Federal non-interest spending as a share of GDP (source: Congressional Budget Office).

The main spending growth over the postwar period has occurred in entitlement programs, which grew sharply in the 1960s and 1970s and continued growing, albeit more slowly, for the remainder of the period. Entitlement spending has more than doubled as a share of GDP since the early 1960s, absorbing the 'peace dividends' provided by the conclusions of the Vietnam and Cold wars. Figure 9.2 shows spending on the three main entitlement programs, Social Security, Medicare and Medicaid, over the same period. While spending as a share of GDP on these fast-growing programs stabilized for a time in the 1990s, in part because of the economy's fast growth during this period, growth relative to GDP has resumed; and, as long-range projections make quite clear, these programs, as currently structured, will continue to grow quite rapidly relative to GDP for the foreseeable future. Within these three programs, the share going to medical care has been steadily increasing, to the point that combined federal spending on Medicare and Medicaid is now nearly as high as that on Social Security.

Over the last four decades, then, federal spending has been relatively stable as a share of GDP, with this stability produced by offsetting trends in defense spending (down) and entitlement spending (up), as other discretionary spending has remained relatively constant. Over shorter periods, the trends have varied. During most of the Reagan years, cuts in non-defense spending balanced a temporary defense build-up. Throughout the George H.W. Bush and Clinton administrations, sharply falling defense spending more than offset entitlement growth, and aggregate spending fell as a share of GDP. During the George W. Bush administration, spending in all three areas has grown as a share of GDP, for the

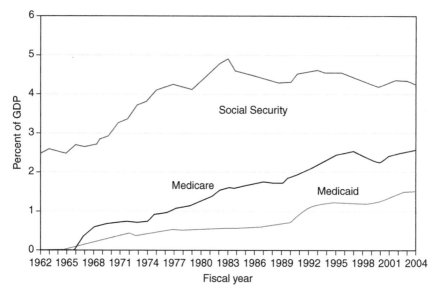

Figure 9.2 Trends in entitlement spending (source: Congressional Budget Office).

first time since the Johnson administration's simultaneous pursuit of the Great Society and the Vietnam War.

Revenues

As with spending, federal revenues have been more stable in the aggregate, as a share of GDP, than have the important revenue components. Prior to the late 1990s, as shown in Figure 9.3, revenues ranged between 17 and 20 percent of GDP, the stability provided by offsetting trends in payroll taxes, which rose with the growth of the Medicare and Social Security systems to which payroll taxes are dedicated, and corporate income and other taxes, which fell. There were several important structural changes in the individual income tax that reduced marginal tax rates, notably in 1964 and 1986. Nevertheless, the individual income tax shows little trend, although it has risen over short periods, as during the late 1970s, when bracket creep and high inflation drove average tax rates up, and even more throughout the mid-to-late 1990s, as income at the top of the taxable income distribution exploded with the economy and the stock market. Neither of these spurts in individual income tax revenues was sustained, the first being reversed by the massive cut in individual income tax rates included in the Economic Recovery Tax Act of 1981, the second by a series of tax cuts starting in 2001 and the stock market 'correction' that began in 2000.

Indeed, the years since 2000 have experienced a remarkably sharp drop in individual income taxes (as a share of GDP) – from 10.3 percent in fiscal year 2000 to 7.0 percent in fiscal year 2004. Further, this enormous drop in individual

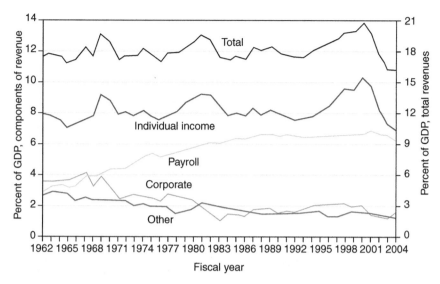

Figure 9.3 Trends in tax revenues (source: Congressional Budget Office).

income taxes since 2000 has been accompanied by sustained declines, as a share of GDP, in each of the other revenue categories. In all, revenues fell from 20.9 percent in fiscal year 2000 to 16.3 percent in 2004, the highest and lowest shares of GDP, respectively, during the entire period since 1962.

The downward trend in 'other' taxes reflects the declining use of indirect taxes as a source of revenue, a continuation of a trend of much longer duration. The modest level of corporate tax collections has received renewed attention of late, but the biggest decline, as a share of GDP, occurred between the late 1960s, when corporate taxes reached 4 percent of GDP, and the early 1980s.[3] Since 1983, corporate tax collections have ranged between 1.1 and 2.2 percent of GDP. During the last two decades, corporate taxes rose slightly after the Tax Reform Act of 1986, which shifted the tax burden from individuals to corporations, and again in the late 1990s, with the economy's strong growth. The recent weakness in corporate tax collections is clearly due in part to overall economic performance, and revenues from this source have started to recover. Innovations in tax avoidance techniques, including the use of off-shore transactions, have also been implicated, although there is no precise estimate of the importance.

Deficits

Figure 9.4 brings together the postwar trends in spending and revenues to show the evolution of the federal government's budget deficits, as a share of GDP. The strong growth in spending and the sharp decline in revenues over the past few years, just discussed, contribute to a remarkable drop in the federal budget

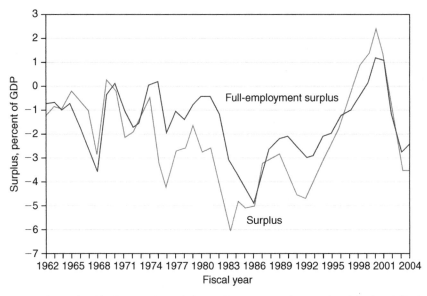

Figure 9.4 Federal budget surplus, relative to GDP (source: Congressional Budget Office).

surplus, from a high of 2.4 percent in fiscal year 2000 to a deficit of 3.6 percent just four years later, a swing of 6 percent of GDP. This deterioration follows an equally remarkable eight-year rise that began in 1992.

Also represented in the figure is the full-employment surplus (as estimated by CBO), which is less volatile. As a comparison of these two series indicates, the strong surpluses of the late 1990s were attributable, in part, to strong economic performance, although the full-employment surplus in fiscal year 2000, at 1.2 percent of GDP, is still the highest value achieved over the entire period. Only a small part of the deterioration since then is directly attributed to the business cycle by CBO. The current budget deficit as a share of GDP, even when adjusted, is still smaller than in the mid-1980s. That is, taken in historical context, the 2004 budget deficit does not stand out, even though most of it remains after cyclical factors are removed.

3 What has caused policy to change?

Over the longer term, the trends in various revenue sources and spending programs often have clear explanations, rooted in policy objectives and changing economic and demographic factors. For example, we have been turning away from indirect taxes as a revenue source for many decades, as our ability to collect direct taxes has improved; an aging population and steadily increasing per capita medical spending have contributed to prolonged and rapid growth in Medicare spending. Over the shorter term, though, other political and economic objectives may influence changes in policy, and it is interesting to consider the strength of these different influences. A fundamental challenge to doing so, however, is the difficulty of identifying the magnitude and timing of policy changes, both of which are important in considering the macroeconomic effects of policy.

Automatic stabilizers

Since the seminal paper by Brown (1956), it has been understood that measuring the magnitude of policy changes requires one control for changes that are not policy-driven. Increases in spending and, especially, declines in revenues that come about as a direct consequence of recession represent the automatic stabilizers implicit in policy. These automatic stabilizers, of course, may influence the magnitude of economic fluctuations, but they are not in any sense changes in the course of policy. Indeed, for those skeptical of the government's ability to time fiscal changes and effectively practice discretionary fiscal policy, automatic stabilizers provide at least some scope for countercyclical fiscal actions.

On the tax side, a key measure is the change in taxes with respect to a unit change in aggregate income. This may be roughly proxied by the tax share of GDP, but the two coincide only if the tax system is a proportional one, which ours is not. Changes in the structure of taxation and in the distribution of income can affect the strength of automatic stabilizers independently of the tax share of GDP. Given the changes that have occurred over the past several decades in the relative importance of different taxes, the progressivity of the individual income tax, and the income distribution, the relative stability of aggregate revenues as a share of GDP seen in Figure 9.4 does not necessarily imply a similar stability in the strength of tax-based automatic stabilizers.

Figure 9.5 presents estimates, for the period 1960–97, of the response of individual income and payroll taxes, the two most important revenue categories, to a unit change in income. (The figure updates one in Auerbach and Feenberg (2000) and is based on the methodology developed there.) There are several factors at work influencing this measure. Some, such as the widening dispersion of the income distribution, should have increased the sensitivity of taxes to income, given the progressive individual income tax rate structure. Other changes, such as the various rounds of marginal tax rate cuts that began in 1964 and continued in 1981 and 1986, should have decreased the sensitivity of taxes to income, as should the inflation indexing provision of the 1981 Act (which took effect in 1985), to the extent that one assumes (as this calculation does) that inflation is sensitive to cyclical income changes.

All in all, though, the measure in the late 1990s stands roughly where it did in the early 1960s. The tax cut of 1964 had a relatively small impact, given the very high incomes at which previous top marginal rates had applied. The 1981 and 1986 Acts had more noticeable impacts, but these simply undid the very large rise in sensitivity that had occurred during the 1970s as a result of bracket creep. The 1993 tax increase had a small effect and, if the figure was extended to the present, this increase would probably have been more than undone by the tax cuts of 2001 and 2003.[4]

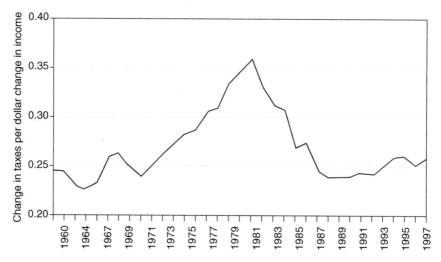

Figure 9.5 Automatic stabilizers: individual income and payroll taxes (source: NBER TAXSIM model).

Further adjustments

It is common to use changes in the full-employment deficit to measure changes in discretionary fiscal policy, given that these changes have been purged of the effects of automatic stabilizers. But there are considerable problems with this interpretation, as the following case study from the period leading up to September 11, 2001 illustrates.

As we now know, the economy had gone into recession several months prior to September 11, and the weakening economy contributed to the declining budget surplus. As Figure 9.6 shows, the full-employment surplus was relatively stable through the second quarter of 2001, while the unadjusted surplus was declining. However, the sharp drop in the surplus during the third quarter of 2001 is only slightly weakened by the full-employment adjustment, suggesting that a major expansionary policy change occurred during this quarter, either just before or just after September 11.

But what was this 'policy' change? There were few changes in spending programs during the period, but there were two factors, other than the economic slowdown, contributing to a decline in revenues. One was the phase-in of the Economic Growth and Tax Relief Reconciliation Act (EGTRRA), enacted in spring, 2001. The other was the sharp decline in revenues attributable neither to legislation nor to the economic slowdown, and hence categorized by CBO as 'technical' changes. Due to such causes as the decline in the stock market and the resulting drop in taxes on capital gains and compensation options, CBO (2002) revised downward its annual revenue forecasts by about $50 billion from those reported during the summer of 2001.

Thus, the large apparent change in discretionary policy that occurred during

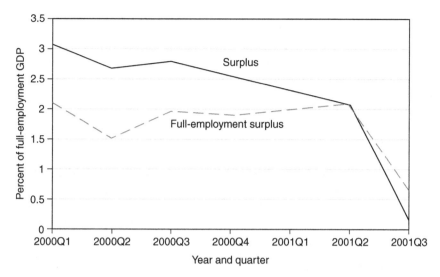

Figure 9.6 The budget surplus and September 11 (source: Congressional Budget Office).

the third quarter of 2001 derives largely from two sources; one was a policy change adopted earlier in the year, another was not a policy change at all. Clearly, the second source should not be counted as a change in policy; as to the first, some of the effects of policy might have been delayed until taxes actually were reduced, but this is not relevant if we are seeking to understand the determinants of policy decisions.

An alternative measure of policy changes

To avoid counting previously announced policy changes and changes in the budget that are not attributable to policy at all, I rely on a measure developed in Auerbach (2002, 2003), based on explicit policy changes. As described more fully in those papers, the changes in revenue and expenditure policy come from successive CBO forecasts that attribute changes from the previous forecasts of revenue and expenditures to legislative action, changes in macroeconomic projections, and changes in other economic factors not captured by macroeconomic projections. Thus, they measure changes in the government's explicit policy trajectory that occurred during the period.

The available information provides a continuous, roughly semiannual series (summer to winter and winter to summer) of policy changes in revenues and expenditures, beginning with changes between winter and summer, 1984. As each update includes policy changes for the current fiscal year and several subsequent years, I construct a summary measure equal to the discounted sum of the current fiscal year's change and that for the next four fiscal years, using a discount rate of 0.5.[5]

This measure of policy changes has its own problems, of course. Perhaps most notable is that even policies specified by legislation need not be credible. Indeed, in recent years, the credibility of legislative changes to the tax code has been intentionally undercut by the use of 'sunset' provisions. These provisions repeal tax cuts after a specified number of years, in many cases where those crafting the legislation have made quite explicit their intent that the provisions be permanent.[6]

Such a legislative maneuver may be understood as a response to the multi-year budget window used to evaluate and constrain tax legislation; changes that are intended to be permanent may be enacted at a lower measured revenue cost if they are scheduled to expire during the budget window.[7] But if the changes are intended to be permanent, and these intentions are credible, then it is not clear how the policy change in years beyond the sunset should be treated. Presumably, at least some weight should be given to an extension of the policy. Fortunately, the relatively short policy period (five years) considered, along with the heavy discounting of the policy changes for future fiscal years, makes this issue relatively unimportant here.

Empirical results

The first column of Table 9.1 presents a regression with this summary measure of policy changes in revenue as the dependent variable, with the previous quarter's GDP gap and the previous fiscal year's surplus as explanatory variables. (All variables are scaled by the contemporaneous CBO estimate of potential GDP.) The second column of the table presents the same regression, except that the dependent variable is policy changes to non-interest expenditures. In both equations, the coefficients indicate that policy has responded in a counter-cyclical manner, and has been responsive to budget conditions as well. The responsiveness in the two equations is of roughly the same order of magnitude. The coefficients suggest that about 14 percent of an increase in the budget surplus is immediately eroded by tax cuts and spending increases.

One of the advantages of this data source is that it provides projections of the budget surplus, under existing policy, which may be a more accurate measure of fiscal conditions than the lagged budget surplus. Using a weighted average of the lagged surplus and the projections of surpluses for the current and next three fiscal years,[8] I construct an alternative measure of fiscal conditions. The results for revenues and expenditures using this alternative measure are in the third and fourth columns of Table 9.1. The results for revenues are similar to those based on the lagged surplus, while the fit for expenditures is better, and the estimated coefficients larger.

Using these estimates, it is interesting to consider when policy has followed these simple feedback rules, and when it has deviated. Figure 9.7 presents residuals for the equations in the third and fourth columns of Table 9.1. On the spending side, there are notable negative shocks during the Gramm-Rudman period in the late 1980s. The fall, 1990 budget agreement between President

Table 9.1 Determinants of policy changes, 1984–2004

Independent variable	Sample period and dependent variable:							
	1984:2–2004:1				1984:2–1993:1, 2001:2–2004:1		1993:2–2001:1	
	Revenues	Expenditures	Revenues	Expenditures	Revenues	Expenditures	Revenues	Expenditures
Constant	-0.001	0.002	-0.001	0.002	-0.002	0.002	-0.0003	0.001
	(0.0003)	(0.0005)	(0.0004)	(0.004)	(0.001)	(0.001)	(0.0005)	(0.0003)
Budget surplus (−1)	-0.061	0.078	—	—	—	—	—	—
	(0.015)	(0.018)						
GDP gap (−1)	-0.052	0.076	-0.059	0.095	-0.046	0.096	-0.034	0.071
	(0.021)	(0.026)	(0.023)	(0.027)	(0.029)	(0.039)	(0.049)	(0.030)
Projected surplus	—	—	-0.066	0.094	-0.084	0.098	-0.042	0.085
			(0.016)	(0.019)	(0.021)	(0.028)	(0.036)	(0.022)
$\bar{R}^2$	0.285	0.291	0.278	0.366	0.386	0.331	0.070	0.656
Number of observations	40	40	40	40	24	24	16	16

Source: Congressional Budget Office.

Notes
Dependent variable: semiannual policy change in revenues or expenditures (excluding interest) relative to full-employment GDP.
Standard errors in parentheses.

Bush and Congress produced a positive revenue shock and a negative spending shock, both contributing to smaller subsequent deficits. The 1993 Clinton tax increase produced a positive revenue shock, but there were few other surprises during the Clinton period. Policy volatility returned during the current Bush administration, with the tax cuts of early 2001 and early 2003 producing large negative revenue shocks. The 2003 shock is larger than the 2001 shock, even though the 2001 tax cut was bigger, because of the different budget situations in the two years. When the 2001 tax cut occurred, there was a large budget surplus, and President Bush argued that it was the taxpayers' money and should be returned to them. When the 2003 tax cut occurred, the surplus was gone, replaced by a deficit, but tax cutting continued.

Also notable about the first part of 2003 is the large contemporaneous positive shock to spending. Note that this spending shock is due primarily to large increases in defense and non-defense discretionary spending. It does not include the introduction of the Medicare drug benefit in the fall of 2003, which does not register as a large change because its major budget impact will not be felt in the next few years.

Do recent fiscal actions indicate a change in behavior? With so short a sample of observation, it is difficult to tell. As the last four columns of Table 9.1 show, if one breaks the entire sample period down by Presidential party (i.e. Reagan, Bush, and Bush vs. Clinton), the estimated behavioral responses are relatively similar across parties. The estimates suggest stronger responsiveness by Republicans to both the GDP gap and the projected surplus, for both revenues and expenditures. These differences, though, are not significant. The differences in intercepts indicate that, for a zero budget surplus and a zero GDP gap, Republicans would

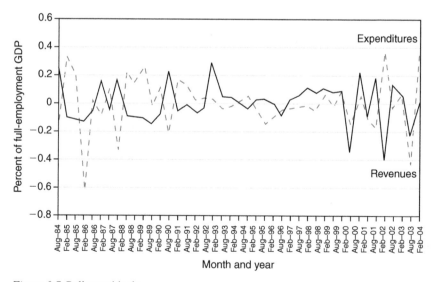

Figure 9.7 Policy residuals.

increase spending more than Democrats, and cut taxes more. It follows that, for conditions like those in the spring of 2001, when the budget was in surplus and there was a positive GDP gap, the predicted Republican response involves larger tax cuts and higher spending than the predicted Democratic response. Thus, some of the recent behavior may simply reflect a return to a Republican policy rule, but, again, it is hard to be very certain given the short period of observation. The real test will come during the next few years, as we observe how the government's tax and spending policies respond to the very large budget deficits that they have helped create, in a period of relative economic prosperity.

Determinants of structural policy changes

Although it is common to focus on aggregate changes in spending and revenues, structural policy changes are important as well. Some important tax reforms, such as the Tax Reform Act of 1986, was designed to be revenue-neutral, while attempting to change incentives to work, to allocate and finance capital, and engage in tax avoidance transactions. While one may apply a similar methodology to that used above to study changes in particular incentives,[9] the tax changes are generally difficult to summarize using concise measures suitable for econometric analysis. This leaves the case study as an alternative to understand the timing and shape of structural tax changes.

Much writing has been devoted to understanding the economic and political factors that precipitated the major tax changes of the 1980s, both occurring under President Reagan, the Economic Recovery Tax Act of 1981, and the Tax Reform Act of 1986.[10] Equally challenging to summarize and explain is the reform process since then, as marginal tax rates crept upward until 2001 and gaps in the taxation of different forms of income (notably the favorable treatment of capital gains) reappeared.

4 Implications of the evolving public sector

Figures 9.1 and 9.2 above showed that entitlement spending, particularly spending on Social Security, Medicare, and Medicaid, have been growing rapidly over the past few decades, accounting for a larger and larger share of total federal spending. There is little to suggest that this process will abate any time soon. Figure 9.8 provides the most recent intermediate projections by the Social Security and Medicare Trustees of benefits for their respective programs, as a share of GDP, through 2080. According to the projections, these two programs alone would, if not altered, account for more of GDP in 2080 than has all federal spending combined in any year shown in Figure 9.1. Recent long-term projections for Medicaid (CBO 2005c) paint a similar picture for growth of that program through 2050, as for Medicare.

In this chapter's context, there are at least three important issues raised by this strong and persistent trend in entitlement spending. First, what are the implications for the feasibility of fiscal policy? Second, how will short-run

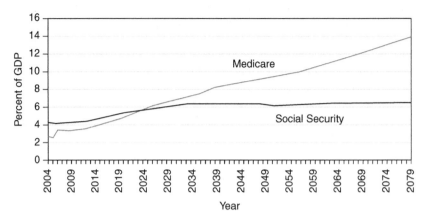

Figure 9.8 Social Security and Medicare projections (sources: Social Security – 2005 OASDI Trustees Report, Table VI.F4; Medicare – 2005 Medicare Trustees Report, Table III.A2 (interpolated after 2015)).

policy responses be influenced by the changing composition of spending? Third, how does this shift in spending affect the meaning of standard measures of fiscal balance and fiscal policy, such as the budget surplus?

Policy feasibility

The answer to the first of these questions is simple. Given the Trustees' projections for Social Security and Medicare and CBO's projections for Medicaid, current US fiscal policy clearly is unsustainable. Table 9.2 presents a variety of measures of how far policy is from being sustainable, following the same methodology as used in Auerbach *et al.* (2004) and updated to reflect the most recent CBO ten-year forecasts (CBO 2005b) and long-term forecasts (CBO 2005c).

The first two columns of Table 9.2 are based on the assumption that the current CBO baseline for taxes and spending as a share of GDP prevails through 2015, with taxes and all non-interest spending components other than Social Security, Medicare and Medicaid growing with GDP thereafter. The last two columns adjust this baseline to incorporate more realistic assumptions for the next decade about discretionary spending growth (for example, that discretionary spending grows with prices and population) and taxes (that sunset provisions do not take effect and that the Alternative Minimum Tax is not allowed to affect a growing share of taxpayers).

The first row of Table 9.2 presents estimates of the permanent increase in the primary surplus needed to make policy feasible, under these two baselines. Columns 1 and 3 measure this necessary increase over the period 2005–2080, where feasibility is associated with achieving the same debt:GDP ratio in 2080 as in 2005. Columns 2 and 4 measure the necessary increase over the infinite horizon, identifying the permanent increase in the primary surplus:GDP ratio

Table 9.2 Fiscal gaps

	Official baseline		Adjusted baseline	
	Through 2080	*Permanent*	*Through 2080*	*Permanent*
As a percent of GDP	4.98	8.38	7.59	11.11
In trillions of present-value dollars	24.7	67.8	40.0	96.1

Source: Author's calculations

needed for the present value of revenues to equal the present value of spending plus the initial stock of publicly-held national debt.

Under the official baseline assumptions, the fiscal gap through 2080 is 4.98 percent of GDP. This implies that an immediate increase in taxes or cut in spending of 4.98 percent of GDP – or over $600 billion per year in current terms – would be needed to maintain fiscal balance through 2080. The fiscal gap is larger under the adjusted baseline, because it assumes a lower level of revenue and a higher level of discretionary spending than the official baseline. Under the adjusted baseline, the fiscal gap through 2080 amounts to 7.59 percent of GDP. The fiscal gap is even larger if the time horizon is extended, since the budget is projected to be running substantial deficits in years approaching and after 2080. If the horizon is extended indefinitely, the fiscal gap rises to 8.38 percent of GDP under the official baseline and 11.11 percent of GDP under the adjusted baseline. The required adjustments represent substantial shares of current spending or revenue aggregates. A fiscal adjustment of 8.38 percent of GDP, for example, translates in 2005 into a reduction in non-interest spending of 45 percent or an increase in revenues of 48 percent.

One may also express these measures in absolute terms rather than as a share of GDP, by calculating the present value of the required increases in the primary surplus. This alternative method of presentation has recently been suggested by Gokhale and Smetters (2003), as a way of emphasizing how large the total imbalance is relative to the explicit national debt. These numbers are presented in the second row of Table 9.2, for the same assumptions as those in the first row of the respective columns.

Changing short-run fiscal behavior

A problem that must be faced in attempting to deal with this large fiscal gap is that entitlement programs are more difficult to change than other types of spending. Particularly when old-age programs such as Social Security and Medicare are concerned, long-range planning is involved on the part of beneficiaries, and this translates into the need for long-range planning for changes on the part of government. This suggests that short-run fiscal adjustments on the spending side should be smaller now than in the past, and should be smaller still in the future.

In illustration of this point, Table 9.3 presents regressions to explain annual changes in spending on discretionary items and on Social Security, Medicare, and Medicaid as a share of full-employment GDP. The independent variables, as before, are the lagged values of the budget surplus, as a share of GDP, and the full-employment gap.[11] As shown in the first three columns of Table 9.3, over the full available sample period, 1963–2004, total discretionary spending was responsive to both explanatory variables, although neither coefficient is significant. Excluding defense spending, which clearly has other important determinants as well, reduces standard errors substantially, making the budget surplus coefficient statistically significant. Note, though, that spending on the three major entitlement programs bears essentially no relationship to these same determinants; indeed, the coefficients, while insignificant, are actually negative.

Given that Medicare didn't even exist in 1963, and that budget rules governing discretionary spending have varied a lot over the full period, a look over a shorter, more recent period may be advisable. The last three columns of Table 9.3 present results since 1993. The coefficients for both discretionary spending aggregates are much larger and more significant over this period, indicating considerable responsiveness. But the major entitlements still show little responsiveness to the budget and the business cycle.

The meaning of traditional fiscal measures

In the fall of 2003, Congress enacted a major expansion of the Medicare program, the new Part D that will provide partial payment for prescription drugs for Medicare beneficiaries. Although there was considerable controversy over its cost over the official ten-year budget window, the short-run cost pales in comparison to the long-run cost, because (1) the program is not fully effective immediately, and (2) like the rest of Medicare, the annual cost is projected to grow more rapidly than GDP for the foreseeable future.

The jump in projected Medicare spending visible over the next few years in Figure 9.8 represents the phasing in of this new program, which is projected to account for roughly one-fourth of all Medicare spending, and 1 percent of GDP, by 2015.[12] In present value, the program has added an estimated $18.2 trillion dollars of implicit liability, net of premium payments by beneficiaries and projected contributions from states. This increment alone, which is projected to absorb 1.9 percent of GDP annually, is several times the current explicit national debt![13]

This episode highlights the problem of evaluating changes in the entitlement programs, like Medicare, that are occupying a growing share of federal spending. Like essentially all other components of spending, Medicare is accounted for on a cash basis, with trust fund accumulations duly recorded but increments to future liabilities ignored.

There is no ideal way to account for these liabilities. Treating them as equivalent to explicit debt suggests that they carry the same commitment, which they do not in a legal sense. But ignoring them suggests that they carry no

Table 9.3 Determinants of spending changes, 1963–2004

Independent variable	Sample period and dependent variable					
	1963–2004			1993–2004		
	All discretionary	Nondefense discretionary	Soc. Security/ Medicare/Medicaid	All discretionary	Nondefense discretionary	Soc. Security/ Medicare/Medicaid
Constant	−0.0001	0.001	0.001	0.001	0.0004	0.0003
	(0.001)	(0.001)	(0.0004)	(0.0004)	(0.0003)	(0.0004)
Budget surplus (−1)	0.057	0.047	−0.024	0.287	0.066	−0.011
	(0.047)	(0.022)	(0.015)	(0.039)	(0.029)	(0.034)
GDP gap (−1)	0.031	0.021	−0.019	0.344	0.077	0.029
	(0.037)	(0.017)	(0.011)	(0.052)	(0.039)	(0.045)
$\bar{R}^2$	−0.013	0.063	0.031	0.823	0.221	0.187
Number of observations	42	42	42	12	12	12

Source: Congressional Budget Office.

Note
Dependent variable: annual change in spending component relative to full-employment GDP (standard errors in parentheses).

Table 9.4 Implicit debt and deficits of the OASDI system (billions of dollars)

Year	Debt	Deficit	Portion of deficit due to change in	
			Base year	Projections
1997	7,724	426	523	−97
1998	8,151	173	581	−408
1999	8,324	765	604	161
2000	9,089	878	677	201
2001	9,967	704	731	−27
2002	10,671	403	731	−328
2003	11,074	797	747	50
2004	11,871			

Source: Author's calculations.

commitment at all, which historically has certainly not been the case. Also, finding that the present value of a stream of future spending is very large does not imply that the spending is unwise or unsustainable; after all, the stream of future tax revenues is large in present value, as well. But a change in policy that increases future spending commitments and provides no offset in the form of spending cuts or tax increases does worsen the government's fiscal position.

How one accounts for these large liabilities does not affect their magnitude, but it could affect policy decisions. Consider the illustrative calculations in Table 9.4, which update estimates in Auerbach (2002, 2003) and are explained in more detail there. For the debt of the OASDI system, the table presents annual estimates of the 'closed-group' liability, equal to the present value of benefits less contributions for those aged 15 and over in the year of the calculation.[14] This is one possible measure of the system's net liability, although there are others as well.

In the second column is the deficit, equal to the change in the debt from the beginning of the current year to the beginning of the next. The change in the closed-group liability from one year to the next equals the sum of two terms: increases in obligations to those remaining in the system plus the difference between liabilities to those entering the system and those leaving the system.

The next two columns provide a breakdown of the deficit into two exhaustive categories. The first of these categories, labeled 'Base year,' measures what the deficit would have been had no economic or demographic projections changed during that year; this measures the change in the debt holding projections fixed. The second, residual category measures the remaining portion of the deficit, due to changes in projections. This portion of the deficit is sometimes negative and sometimes positive, averaging −$64 billion over the seven-year period. But the component due to the changing base year is always positive, and averages $656 billion per year. This measure is positive and large, reflecting the fact that the retirement of the baby boom cohort is approaching. Deficit estimates like these for the Medicare system would be several times larger, given the relative magnitudes of the closed-group liabilities for the two systems, especially in 2003, when the new prescription drug benefit was introduced.

Would there have been a substantial tax cut in 2001 if a budget deficit of several percent of GDP had been reported, rather than a budget surplus? Would Congress have added a prescription drug benefit to Medicare in 2003, with no offsetting spending reductions or tax increases, had the full cost of the change been featured in the debate?

5 Conclusion

During the past several decades, fiscal policy has responded to changing circumstances. Spending on defense has risen and fallen with national security needs, and old-age entitlement programs have grown along with the aging and elderly populations. In the short run, spending and taxes have responded to cyclical and budget forces. But aging and increasing health care expenditures present unprecedented challenges to the fiscal system's ability to respond, for they generate a large sustainability gap that is not well-characterized by the traditional budget measures to which policy has responded in the past. The major fiscal changes required over the coming years may require changes in fiscal accounting as well.

Notes

1 This chapter was prepared for the second annual Berkeley-Vienna Conference on the US and European Economies in Comparative Perspective, September 2005. An earlier version was presented at the Federal Reserve Bank of Boston's conference on The Macroeconomics of Fiscal Policy, June 2004. I am grateful to participants at both conferences for comments.
2 The historical data in Figure 9.1, and the next three figures, are from CBO (2005a), which provides historical fiscal data since 1962.
3 For an analysis of the causes of this decline, see Auerbach and Poterba (1987).
4 Auerbach (2002) constructs an alternative time series for the strength of automatic stabilizers, based on CBO's full-employment deficit series. That series has different year-to-year patterns but has the same general shape over time, with the value in 2001 slightly below the value in 1960.
5 This high discount rate is chosen based on goodness-of-fit criteria. Because policy revisions between the winter and summer take effect starting midway through the current fiscal year, I reduce the weight on the current fiscal year by one-half and increase weights on subsequent years correspondingly, for winter-to-summer revisions.
6 See Gale and Orszag (2003).
7 See Auerbach (2006) for further discussion.
8 The weighting scheme is the same as that used for the dependent variables.
9 For example, Auerbach (2003) relates changes in the user cost of capital for US business fixed investment to lags in the output gap and the budget surplus, as well as to lagged investment. The results suggest that, as with aggregate revenues, investment incentives are responsive to cyclical and budget conditions.
10 See, for example, Steuerle (1992).
11 The use of actual spending data is necessary because there is not a consistent

breakdown by category in the CBO policy data used in Table 9.1. There is a potential problem that actual spending data will include changes that might be the automatic result of cyclical factors. This should not be a major concern, though, given that most automatic responses at the federal level are on the tax side or in entitlement programs other than those considered in Table 9.3.

12 See the 2005 Medicare Trustees Report (Boards of Trustees, Federal HI and Federal SMI 2005), Table III.A2.

13 Medicare Trustees Report, Table III.C21.

14 I am grateful to Kristy Piccinini for performing these calculations. The closed-group measures in Table 9.4 are somewhat lower for 2003 and 2004 than those provided by the corresponding Trustees Reports ($11.9 trillion and $12.7 trillion, respectively), presumably as the result of differences in assumed tax and benefit profiles. One cannot use the figures from the Trustees Reports to perform these calculations because they are not published for earlier years and do not offer a breakdown into the sources of change from one year to the next.

References

Auerbach, A.J. (2002) 'Is There a Role for Discretionary Fiscal Policy?' in *Rethinking Stabilization Policy: Proceedings of a Symposium Sponsored by the Federal Reserve Bank of Kansas City*, pp. 109–150.

Auerbach, A.J. (2003) 'Fiscal Policy, Past and Present,' *Brookings Papers on Economic Activity*, 1, pp. 75–122.

Auerbach, A.J. (2006) 'Budget Windows, Sunsets, and Fiscal Control,' *Journal of Public Economics*, 90, pp. 87–100.

Auerbach, A.J. and Feenberg, D. (2000) 'The Significance of Federal Taxes as Automatic Stabilizers,' *Journal of Economic Perspectives*, Summer, pp. 37–56.

Auerbach, A.J. and Poterba, J.M. (1987) 'Why Have Corporate Tax Revenues Declined?' in L. Summers (ed.) *Tax Policy and the Economy* 1, pp. 1–28.

Auerbach, A.J., Gale, W.G. and Orszag, P.R. (2004) 'Sources of the Long-Term Fiscal Gap,' *Tax Notes*, May 24, pp. 1049–1059.

Boards of Trustees, Federal Hospital Insurance and Federal Supplementary Insurance Trust Funds (2005) *2005 Annual Report*, March 23.

Board of Trustees, Federal Old-Age and Survivors Insurance and Disability Insurance Trust Funds (2005) *2005 Annual Report*, March 23.

Brown, E.C. (1956) 'Fiscal Policy in the 'Thirties: A Reappraisal,' *American Economic Review* 46, December, pp. 857–879.

Congressional Budget Office (2002) *The Budget and Economic Outlook: Fiscal Years 2003–2012*, January.

Congressional Budget Office (2005a) *The Budget and Economic Outlook: Fiscal Years 2006–2015*, January.

Congressional Budget Office (2005b) *The Budget and Economic Outlook: An Update*, August.

Congressional Budget Office (2005c) *The Long-Term Budget Outlook*, December.

Gale, W.G. and Orszag, P.R. (2003) 'Sunsets in the Tax Code,' *Tax Notes* 99, June 9, pp. 1553–1561.

Gokhale, J. and Smetters, K. (2003) *Fiscal and Generational Imbalances: New Budget Measures for New Budget Priorities*. Washington, DC: The AEI Press.

Steuerle, C.E. (1992) *The Tax Decade: How Taxes Came to Dominate the Public Agenda*. Washington, DC: Urban Institute Press.

10 Fiscal policy in Europe

The past and future of EMU rules from the perspective of Musgrave and Buchanan

Marco Buti and André Sapir[1]

1 Introduction

Views regarding the role of government and public spending have evolved over time, both influencing and reflecting the evolution of actual public intervention. For the last 40 years, the intellectual debate has been dominated by the views of Richard Musgrave and James Buchanan, who together published some years ago a fascinating account of their respective conceptions in *Public Finance and Public Choice: Two Contrasting Views of the State* (Buchanan and Musgrave, 1999). The 'public finance' view of the state is essentially that the state can and must correct the excesses of the market. By contrast the 'public choice' view holds that interventions by the state create problems of their own because the state acts not in the general public interest, as postulated in the public finance view, but in the interest of certain groups.

Nowhere has the role of government and public policy been more important than in Europe. This chapter begins with an overview of European fiscal policy since the Second World War. It distinguishes between two phases: a 'public finance' phase, associated with Europe's 'Golden Age', and a 'public choice' phase, during which Europe's public spending became unsustainable. Section 3 examines how the fiscal rules of Europe's Economic and Monetary Union (EMU), and in particular the Stability and Growth Pact (SGP), were meant to remedy the runaway growth in public spending and why they partly failed to deliver. Section 4 looks at the reform of the SGP enacted in 2005 and section 5 discusses whether the reform will be successful in delivering sustainable public finances. Section 6 concludes.

2 Sixty years of public finance in Europe: a bird's eye view

The 'Golden Age' (1945–73)

For 30 years, between the mid-1940s and the mid-1970s, Europe witnessed a 'Golden Age' of growth, stability and social cohesion. Post-war reconstruction created an economic and social environment which ensured that the three sides of this 'magic triangle' operated in a mutually reinforcing manner. The post-war 'welfare state' reflected a political consensus that was broadly shared across Western Europe. Business was guaranteed a stable economic, industrial and social environment for sustained growth that reflected an implicit social contract with the people that the creation of new wealth would be fairly distributed. This commitment was enshrined in the new features of the post-war consensus: a universal standard of social protection together with equal opportunity in education and employment regardless of birth.[2]

While economic stability and social cohesion were undoubtedly crucial conditions for European growth during those years, rapid economic growth was equally crucial to ensure the sustainability of economic stability and the social protection system.

Economic and social conditions in Western Europe during the years 1950–73 were remarkable. The region enjoyed average annual growth rates of well over 4 per cent for GDP and nearly 4 per cent for GDP per capita. As a result, Europe's standard of living caught up rapidly with the United States: compared to a benchmark of 100 for the US, GDP per capita (measured at purchasing power parity) in Western Europe rose from around 40 in 1950 to around 70 in 1973. Over the same period, inflation stood on average at 4 per cent and unemployment at 2 per cent.

Throughout this period, the size of the Welfare State increased considerably in Europe. By 1970 the share of total government expenditure in GDP reached between 35 and 40 per cent in most countries – yet still only slightly higher than in the United States, where it stood at 32 per cent of GDP.

The creation and expansion of the Welfare State was at that time viewed as a powerful tool in the hands of benevolent governments seeking to maximize social welfare. Most economists embraced the vision expounded by Richard Musgrave in his treatise *The Theory of Public Finance* published in 1959. Musgrave defined three major economic roles for government: the provision of public goods and other measures to correct for market failures and improve the *allocation* of resources; the *redistribution* of income to ensure that it was equitably distributed among households; and the *stabilization* of economic activity to attain high levels of employment with reasonable stability of prices.

Higher taxes and social expenditures were seen as means not only to improve the distribution of income, but also to improve the allocation of resources and growth (by correcting market failures in the labour market) and to promote the stabilization of output (via the automatic stabilizers provided by taxes and social expenditures). Moreover, high growth rates helped to keep public debt under control, thereby ensuring the sustainability of public finances. And indeed, during the 'Golden Age', the three sides of the Musgravian triangle seemed to reinforce one another. There appeared to be no trade-off between allocative efficiency, redistribution and stabilization.

This is well illustrated by the situation of France, Germany, Italy and the United Kingdom, the four largest European countries, where the share of total public expenditure (and revenue) in GDP reached 35–45 per cent in 1973 (see Figures 10.1 and 10.2), with about 15 per cent devoted to social expenditure (Figure 10.3).

Despite the rapid growth of public expenditure in these countries, their public debt basically remained under control during the period 1960–73 (Figure 10.4). In the United Kingdom, where the debt-to-GDP ratio was well over 100 per cent in 1960, it actually declined by nearly 60 percentage points. It also declined sharply in France, to less than 20 per cent in 1973. In Germany it remained constant around 20 per cent throughout the period. Only in Italy did the debt-to-GDP ratio grow, reaching around 50 per cent in 1973.

Table 10.1 shows, however, that underlying public finance decisions cannot take all the credit for the favourable development with respect to debt sustainability during the period 1961–73. In all four countries, it was a combination of high GDP growth rates and low real interest rates, producing 'negative snowball' effects, that led to substantial declines in public debts. In fact, apart from the United Kingdom, all countries ran primary budget deficits that tended to work in the opposite direction, and in Italy actually swamped the 'negative snowball' effect, resulting in an accumulation of debt.

Table 10.2 shows that public finance did however tend to play a stabilizing role during this period. Public debt decreased in 'good times' and increased in 'bad times' in Germany and Italy. And in France and the United Kingdom, two countries where the debt-to-GDP ratio decreased substantially during the period, the public debt actually decreased during both good and bad times.

Even in the 'public finance' heyday of the 1960s, however, not everyone shared Musgrave's activist and benign vision of the public sector in the economy. In *The*

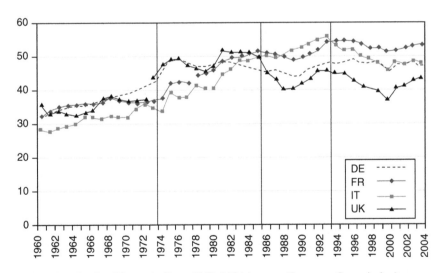

Figure 10.1 Total public expenditure 1960–2004 (source: European Commission).

Note
DE: new definition as of 1970 (from 1960 to 1990 data of West Germany) – FR: new definition as of 1978 – IT: new definition as of 1980 – UK: new definition as of 1973 – (former definition ESA79 – new definition ESA95)

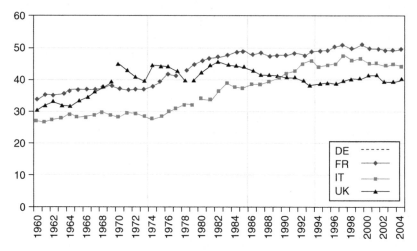

Figure 10.2 Total public revenue 1960–2004 (source: European Commission).

Note
DE: new definition as of 1970 (from 1960 to 1990 data of West Germany) – FR: new definition as of 1978 – IT: new definition as of 1980 – UK: new definition as of 1970 – (former definition ESA79 – new definition ESA95)

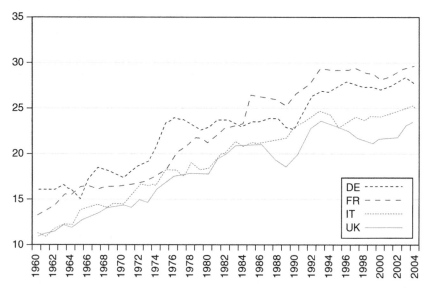

Figure 10.3 Public social expenditure 1960–2004 (source: OECD and European Commission).

Calculus of Consent, published in 1962, James Buchanan and Gordon Tullock presented a radically different view of the public sector. They argued that, in majoritarian political systems, special interest groups and coalitions tend to generate an over-expansion of the public sector, with increasing transfers in their favour and rising taxes, which lead to deleterious economic and social consequences.[3] To

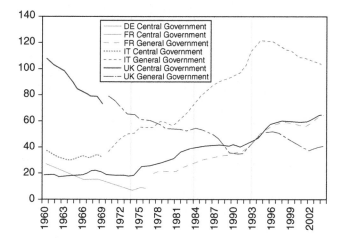

Figure 10.4 Gross Public Debt 1960–2004 (source: European Commission).

prevent such an outcome Buchanan and Tullock advised governments to adopt rules that would constrain the expansion of the public sector.

The next 30 years (1973–2005)

In the next 30 years, economic conditions in Europe were less rosy. Potential growth fell by nearly one full percentage point, and now stands at only 2 per cent a year, compared with almost 3.5 per cent in the United States, where growth has actually increased. And while it is true that GDP per capita increased at the same rate in Europe as in the United States throughout the period, this of course implies that the income gap between the United States and Europe has remained constant, and that the rapid catching-up process of the Golden Age actually stopped 30 years ago. Meanwhile, inflation first rose sharply during the 1970s and then fell steadily during the 1980s and 1990s, until around 2000 since when it has stayed around 2 per cent. By contrast, unemployment, which also rose rapidly during the 1970s and the early 1980s, never much declined thereafter, hovering instead between 8 and 10 per cent.

The 'magic triangle' started to unravel in the 1970s with the two oil shocks. Since then pressure has mounted as a result of three profound, interconnected changes in the socio-economic environment taking place across Europe and the world: changes in demographic patterns, technological breakthroughs and globalization.

Whereas rapid growth, macroeconomic stability and the Welfare State had been mutually supportive during the 'Golden Age', the mixture of slow growth, macroeconomic instability and a welfare system conceived in a different set of circumstances proved difficult to manage in the years after 1973. In fact three sub-periods must be distinguished.

Table 10.1 Breakdown of debt accumulation 1961–2004

In % of GDP	1961–2004			1961–73			1974–83			1984–92			1993–2004		
	Δ debt ratio	Snowball effect	Primary balance +SFA	Δ debt ratio	Snowball effect	Primary balance +SFA	Δ debt ratio	Snowball effect	Primary balance +SFA	Δ debt ratio	Snowball effect	Primary balance +SFA	Δ debt ratio	Snowball effect	Primary balance +SFA
Germany	47	21	26	0	−9	8	21	5	17	3	1	2	23	24	−1
France	26	−8	33	−20	−23	3	7	−11	18	13	8	5	25	18	7
Italy	63	−25	88	10	−31	41	18	−48	66	37	15	22	−1	38	−40
United Kingdom	−81	−62	−19	−58	−44	−14	−12	−31	18	−13	6	−20	2	6	−4

Source: Ecfin calculations on AMECO data and national sources. Calculations for 1961–70 for Italy and UK and for 1961–77 for France are based on central government debt figures from the Bordo-Jonung database.

Table 10.2 Debt accumulation in good and bad times 1961–2004

In % of GDP	1961–2004			1961–73			1974–83			1984–92			1993–2004		
	Δ debt ratio	Δ GT	Δ BT	Δ debt ratio	Δ GT	Δ BT	Δ debt ratio	Δ GT	Δ BT	Δ debt ratio	Δ GT	Δ BT	Δ debt ratio	Δ GT	Δ BT
Germany	47	3	44	0	–4	4	21	5	16	3	–1	4	23	3	20
France	26	5	21	–20	–13	–7	7	4	3	13	3	10	25	11	15
Italy	63	15	48	10	–2	12	18	–4	22	37	25	12	–1	–4	2
United Kingdom	–81	–35	–46	–58	–20	–37	–12	–8	–4	–13	–10	–3	2	4	–2

Source: Ecfin calculations on AMECO data and national sources. Calculations for 1961–70 for Italy and UK and for 1961–77 for France are based on central government debt figures from the Bordo-Jonung database.

From the mid-1970s to the mid-1980s

During the period 1974–85, the combination of slow growth and high unemployment resulted in increased demands for social protection, which had severe consequences for public finances. The share of total government expenditure in GDP grew rapidly after 1973, reaching 45–50 per cent in many European countries by 1985 – an increase of more than 10 percentage points compared to 1970. This spectacular increase mainly involved two items: government consumption and social transfers. It was financed partly by additional public revenue and partly by public borrowing (see Figure 10.5).

By the mid-1980s, Europe was stuck in a negative spiral: lower GDP growth and employment rates meant increasing public expenditure, which required increasing public revenue, which in turn implied higher social contributions and higher direct taxes, thereby reducing the incentive to work and to invest, and hence further reducing the prospects for output and employment growth.

There were two reasons why it was so difficult for Europe to break out of this spiral. First, shocks to the system were long-lasting. The slowdown of growth was not initially perceived as permanent, which led policy-makers to bet on stabilization rather than adjustment. But after the two oil shocks of 1973 and 1979, Europe was confronted with an ageing population, the information technology revolution and globalization, all of which substantially increased the demand for social protection. Second, the system seemed politically unable to reform itself and to establish a new social contract aimed at increasing growth while still preserving social welfare. It was caught in a dilemma: preserving the costly European social model required

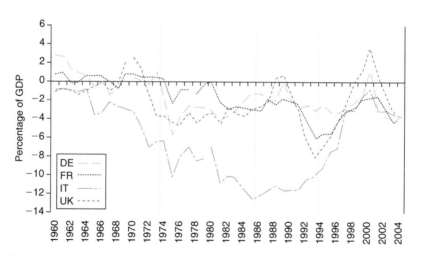

Figure 10.5 Budget balance 1960–2004 (source: European Commission).

Note

DE: new definition as of 1970 (from 1960 to 1990 data of West Germany) – FR: new definition as of 1978 – IT: new definition as of 1980 – UK: new definition as of 1970 – (former definition ESA79 – new definition ESA95)

higher GDP growth, but that higher growth could not be achieved without adapting the social model to the new socio-economic environment.

The over-expansion of social expenditures (see Figure 10.3) led to debt accumulation not only in Italy, but now also in France and in Germany (see Figure 10.4). As shown in Table 10.1, all four large European countries (even the United Kingdom by this stage) were running large primary budget deficits, which added substantially to their debt. This was, however, partially compensated for by the persistence of 'negative snowball' effects (except in Germany) during this period as the slowdown in GDP growth was accompanied by a reduction in real interest rates due to increased inflation.

Table 10.2 shows that public finance ceased to play a stabilizing role during the period 1974–83. Public debt now increased during both good and bad times in France, Germany and Italy, while in the United Kingdom it continued to decrease during both good and bad times.

In other words, compared to the 'Golden Age', when the three sides of the Musgravian triangle seemed to reinforce one another, the decade following 1973 witnessed the emergence of trade-offs between allocative efficiency and redistribution in the manner envisaged by Buchanan and Tullock.

From the mid-1980s to the mid-1990s

During the period 1984–92, persistent slow growth and high unemployment resulted in a sustained deterioration of public finances.

The over-expansion of social expenditures continued unabated (see Figure 10.3). By 1992, public social expenditure had reached 29 per cent of GDP in France (compared to 16 per cent in 1970), 27 per cent in Germany (against 17 per cent in 1970), 24 per cent in Italy (15 per cent in 1970) and 23 per cent in the United Kingdom (against 14 per cent in 1970). This led to further debt accumulation in France, Germany and Italy (see Figure 10.4). As shown in Table 10.1, all three countries still ran primary budget deficits during this period, although much less than during the previous decade. But now the 'snowball' effect had finally turned positive in all the four large European countries as real interest rates (which had increased due to disinflationary policy) became larger than GDP growth rates, thereby adding to debt accumulation.

Table 10.2 indicates that public finance failed to regain its stabilizing role during the period 1984–92. Public debt continued to increase during both good and bad times in France and Italy (but less so in Germany), while in the United Kingdom, it continued to decrease during both good and bad times. By 1992, the level of public debt had reached around 40 per cent in France (20 points higher than in 1974), Germany (24 points higher) and the United Kingdom (25 points lower), and more than 100 per cent in Italy (57 points higher).

Therefore the trade-offs between allocative efficiency and redistribution that had emerged during the previous decade continued to operate.

From the mid-1990s to the mid-2000s

In 1993, total government expenditure in the EU reached its highest-ever peak at 51 per cent of GDP, with 56 per cent in Italy (an increase of 25 percentage points since 1970), 55 per cent in France (up 18 points), 49 per cent in Germany (up 10 points) and 46 per cent in the United Kingdom (up 2 points only) – while it also reached a record high in the United States, but at a level of only 37 per cent. With public revenue in the EU meanwhile at only 45 per cent of GDP, this meant that 1993 was also the year when Europe's public borrowing reached its highest-ever peak at 6 per cent of GDP on average and 10 per cent in Italy, 7 per cent in the United Kingdom, 6 per cent in France and 3 per cent in Germany.

The Maastricht fiscal consolidation process, launched in 1993, was designed to put an end to the deterioration of public finances in most EU countries that had started 20 years earlier. And indeed by 1999, when the euro was introduced, public borrowing was down to less than 1 per cent. The turnaround was achieved by a combination of reduced government expenditure and increased government revenue. In 1999, total government expenditure in the EU had come down to 47 per cent of GDP (53 per cent in France, 48 per cent in Germany and Italy, and 39 per cent in the United Kingdom) – four points below the peak of 1993, but still about 10 points above the 1970 level. At the same time, total government revenue had reached 46 per cent of GDP (56 per cent in Italy, 55 per cent in France, 49 per cent in Germany and 46 per cent in the United Kingdom), its highest-ever level and again about 10 points above the 1970 level.

Thus, by the year 2000, it seemed that fiscal consolidation in the EU had been achieved. For the first time since 1970, the consolidated budget of the EU countries posted a positive balance.[4] Government expenditure also seemed to be under control. In reality, however, the spiral of low growth and high public expenditure was still more or less intact. 2000 was an exceptional year, with a growth rate of GDP in the EU at 3.5 per cent, one full point above the trend for the period 1986–2000. When the downturn hit in 2001, public expenditure and public borrowing started to rise again. Since 2003, total government expenditure has been above 47 per cent of GDP on average in the EU and public borrowing more than 2 per cent of GDP, and well above the 3 per cent mark in France, Germany and Italy (and also, although to a lesser extent, in the United Kingdom).

Thus, despite efforts at consolidation during this period, the debt-to-GDP ratio actually increased substantially in France and Germany (see Figure 10.4). As shown in Table 10.1, the main culprit was the 'snowball' effect due to the large positive gap between real interest rates and GDP growth rates. This effect was even larger in Italy, but there it was more than compensated by fiscal retrenchment that led to a small decrease in the debt ratio.

Table 10.2 indicates that during this period public finance regained its stabilizing role in Italy but, surprisingly, lost it in the United Kingdom, where public debt actually increased in good times and decreased in bad times. In France and Germany public debt continued to increase during both good and bad times, and by 2004 their level of public debt had reached well over 60 per cent (more than

40 points higher than in 1974). By contrast it remained around 40 per cent in the United Kingdom (25 points lower than in 1974) and around 100 per cent in Italy (about 60 points higher than in 1974).

During the two decades spanning the period from the mid-1970s to the mid-1990s, therefore, government expenditure increased sharply in all the large European countries except the United Kingdom. It fell slightly thereafter, although it remained at a very high level compared to the early 1970s. Moreover, the composition of public expenditure has changed dramatically over the last 30 years, with social expenditure accounting since the 1990s for about 60 per cent of total expenditure compared to barely 40 per cent in 1970.

The combination of high levels of public expenditure and a high share of it devoted to social spending is the main feature of European public finance for the past 30 years. It contrasts sharply with the situation that prevailed during the 30 years after the Second World War, when public expenditure was much lower and the share of it devoted to social spending was also lower. The shift meant that the benign use of public finance associated with Musgrave's view gave way to a deleterious approach more akin to that identified in Buchanan and Tullock's critique.

3 Enter Europe: the run-up to and early years of EMU

Maastricht and the Stability Pact: what was expected ...

After the rise in public spending of the previous years, several EU countries entered the 1990s with their public finances out of control. The period of strong growth in the second half of the 1980s was not used to reduce deficits and debt: the structural primary balance was merely stabilized at around balance and public debt continued to grow, albeit more slowly than before.

As Buchanan and Tullock (1962) and the ensuing 'political economy of public finance' literature argue, the only way to counter the deficit bias of governments is to adopt fiscal rules. But whilst several European countries already had public finance rules and guidelines in the early 1990s, they were often ineffective. Hence, the choice was made to set up rules at the EU level. The Maastricht criteria codified in the Treaty the imperative of consolidation as a condition for joining the euro area, and the Stability and Growth Pact (SGP) complemented these rules by aiming to make budgetary discipline a permanent feature of EMU. It is therefore commonly interpreted as a major building block of EMU's architecture: the SGP 'must rank as one of the most remarkable pieces of policy coordination in world history. Its construction makes it in some respects comparable to the founding of the Bretton Woods system' (Artis, 2002: 155).

The SGP is a two-pronged instrument. It consists of a dissuasive arm which aims to accelerate and clarify the excessive deficit procedure (EDP) of the Treaty, and a preventive arm which aims to strengthen the surveillance of budgetary positions and the surveillance and coordination of economic policies.

On the dissuasive side, the 3 per cent of GDP reference value for triggering the excessive deficit procedure should be treated as much as possible as a 'hard ceiling', the breaking of which would put in motion 'a quasi-automatic mechanism' (Stark, 2001) for imposing sanctions, with escape clauses defined as narrowly as possible and legally binding deadlines imposed for taking decisions for the countries to implement corrective measures. This feature strengthened the role of the 3 per cent deficit threshold which had been introduced relatively late in the negotiations for the Maastricht Treaty and then hedged with discretionary qualifications.

On the preventive side, Member States are required to commit themselves to a 'medium-term budgetary objective of close-to-balance or in surplus', creating a safety margin of the order of 3 percentage points of GDP against breaching the 3 per cent deficit ceiling, enough to ensure that movements in the budgetary balance in response to cyclical fluctuations would leave the deficit under 3 per cent of GDP in all cases bar a few rare recession episodes. In this way the so-called 'preventive arm' of the SGP fleshes out the provisions of the Treaty on the surveillance of economic policies, and it does so concretely by institutionalizing the annual submission by Member States, and examination by the Council, of stability programmes setting out their medium-term budgetary strategy to achieve and maintain the close-to-balance or in surplus objective, including the accompanying economic assumptions, and putting in place an early-warning mechanism whereby the Council addresses a recommendation to a Member State in the event of any 'significant divergence of the budgetary position from the medium-term objective, or the adjustment path towards it'.

Given that the political priority was to get the deficit under control, improving allocation efficiency and cyclical stabilization were seen as secondary objectives. However, restoring the basic conditions of fiscal discipline was considered a precondition for the pursuit of these other objectives, and ones which could only be pursued once the basic conditions of fiscal discipline were restored. It was considered a precondition, first, because the cut in public spending brought about by the budgetary consolidation was seen as efficiency-enhancing, in that it reduced the role of the state in the economy and opened up the way to lower average and marginal tax rates. Second, restoring fiscal prudence in normal times was also considered a precondition for using fiscal policy for stabilization purposes, as close-to-balance positions would allow automatic stabilizers to play fully without endangering the 3 per cent ceiling.

... *and what actually happened*

The imposition of the Maastricht budgetary targets at the beginning of the 1990s undeniably set in motion a genuine consolidation process. In most countries budget deficits declined substantially after 1993, the year which marked the entry into force of the Maastricht Treaty and in which the euro area registered the historically high deficit ratio of 5.5 per cent of GDP. Aided also by lower interest rates thanks to reduced risk premia, the cyclically-adjusted balance improved by 4.5 percentage points in the euro area between 1993 and 1999 (Figure 10.6), and by 1997 was brought back below the 3 per cent of GDP threshold in all Member States, except in Greece.

Amongst the large euro-area countries, Italy managed to reduce its budget deficit by 7 percentage points of GDP between 1993 and 2000, although the reduction in the interest burden explains a sizeable share of the retrenchment. In contrast, Germany and France, traditional bastions of fiscal prudence, struggled to reduce budget deficits and keep control of a public debt fuelled in the first part of the period by the costs of unification in the case of Germany and subdued economic performance in the case of France. In these countries public debt actually increased, though starting from a level below the 60 per cent of GDP reference value.

The composition of the fiscal consolidation is shown in Figure 10.7 which breaks down the discretionary fiscal policy changes into changes in total revenue and changes in primary expenditure. The diagonal from top right to bottom left indicates the direction of the budgetary adjustment: the area above it marks an improvement in the cyclically-adjusted primary balance, while the area below it indicates a structural deterioration. The diagonal from top left to bottom right marks the composition of the adjustment between expenditure changes and revenue changes.

In the run-up to EMU, the four large countries and the euro area as a whole lie above the top right–bottom left diagonal, meaning that their cyclically-adjusted primary balance improved during the period. Moreover, primary spending was reduced in all countries, though to a varying degree.

While the retrenchment in the run-up to EMU is commonly considered a success, the SGP, which was supposed to consolidate Maastricht's achievements, has fallen short of its framers' expectations. At close to 3 per cent of GDP the cyclically-adjusted deficit of the euro area remains no nearer the close-to-balance position than it was at the launch of EMU.

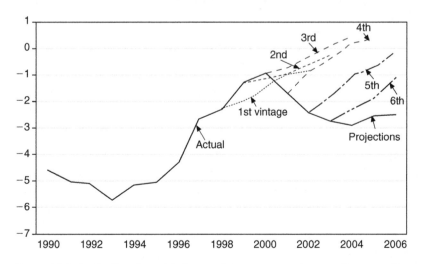

Figure 10.6 Cyclically adjusted balance of the euro area (source: European Commission).

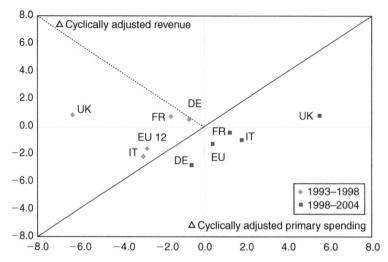

Figure 10.7 Composition of the adjustment: 1993–1998 vs. 1998–2004.

As shown in Figure 10.6 above, the cyclically-adjusted balance for the euro area as a whole has progressively deteriorated in the years since 2000, falling well short of the commitments enshrined in the early updates of national stability programmes. The turnaround in both direction and composition of discretionary fiscal policy is confirmed by Figure 10.7 which shows that the structural primary balances have deteriorated since the end of the 1990s: as the tax revenue was reduced, primary expenditure started to climb again.

This analysis shows that the de facto suspension of the excessive deficit procedure in the cases of Germany and France after November 2003 (see below), potentially signalling the amputation of the dissuasive arm of the Pact, had been preceded by a progressive loss of credibility of the preventive arm too, as evidenced by persistent negative gaps between fiscal projections and the outcomes of successive rounds of stability programmes. However, it is the three largest countries in the euro area (France, Germany and Italy) that appear to be most to blame for the credibility gap affecting stability programmes, as their fiscal projections suffered a significant bias towards the under-prediction of actual deficits.[5]

In sum, although the Maastricht process halted the unprecedented non-war debt increase of the previous two decades, the SGP 'mark I' has apparently failed to eradicate the underlying – and ultimately unsustainable – deficit bias of fiscal policies. In particular, this bias manifests itself through the continuation of the tendency to run expansionary policies or to fail to consolidate in good times, as shown by the deterioration of cyclically-adjusted balances in the last upswing. More importantly, EMU's fiscal rules do not seem to have brought about a shift towards more growth-friendly policies, including in the public finance area.

4 More intelligent, but more complex: the new Pact

The reform of the SGP

The failure of the SGP 'mark I' is epitomized by the repeated breaches of the 3 per cent of GDP deficit ceiling by individual Member States. Since 2002 six out of the 12 euro-area members have been subject to the excessive deficit procedure; the early-warning mechanism was invoked in four cases. Even more damaging to the credibility of the Pact was the perceived disavowal of the original framework, and specifically its enforcement mechanism, by key Member States. Already detectable in the apparent unwillingness of the Council to let the early-warning mechanism run its normal course in the cases of Germany and Portugal in February 2002, the crisis became explicit the following year. In November 2003 the excessive deficit procedures against France and Germany were de facto suspended following the Council's failure to endorse Commission recommendations that the procedures be stepped up.

While the debate in academic circles showed the depth of the division among economists, a certain consensus gradually emerged in the course of 2004 among the main policy players as to what changes were needed to the EMU fiscal framework. It was recognized that EMU needed numerical fiscal rules (since financial market discipline and national procedures were not deemed sufficient to ensure budgetary discipline) and that any radical changes to the rules introduced in 1992 (Maastricht Treaty) and 1997 (SGP) would be highly problematic. 'Internal adjustment' – as Buti *et al.* (2003) described it – of the existing framework rather than a radical overhaul of the rules came to be regarded as the only feasible way ahead. It was also acknowledged that complementary measures at the national level (such as better budgetary procedures and independent fiscal councils) would be highly desirable. There was agreement that internal reforms should include action to improve fiscal policy in good times, more consideration of public debt and long-term sustainability in assessing Member States' budgetary positions, a greater focus on cyclical developments and more transparency in fiscal data. Other aspects were more controversial: these included changes to the excessive deficit procedure and a stronger role for the Commission as enforcing agency.

The risks involved in embarking on a reform process under the pressure of unfavourable fiscal developments were also highlighted in the debate: the credibility of the framework itself could be endangered and the reform process could prove long and uncertain. It was also noted that if the problem was primarily one of adherence to the rules, the priority should be to ensure rigorous implementation of the existing rules rather than to change them. At the same time, it was widely recognized that simply attempting to apply the existing rules after the watershed of November 2003 was not an option. Re-establishing a sense of ownership of the fiscal rules by all parties would be the precondition for their effective enforcement.

At the request of the European Council, in September 2004 the Commission issued a Communication suggesting a number of changes to the Pact which, while preserving its overall architecture, aimed to avoid pro-cyclical policies, especially in good times; better defined the medium-term objective by taking into account country-specific circumstances and reforms; gave greater prominence to the debt criterion; modified the implementation of the excessive deficit procedure, in particular by allowing countries more time to correct an excessive deficit under certain circumstances; and improved the governance and enforcement arrangements (European Commission, 2004).

After a difficult and at times heated debate, agreement was reached at the ECOFIN Council of March 2005. The broad lines of the reform were set out in a report which envisaged changes to both the preventive and corrective arms of the Pact (Council, 2005).

On the preventive side (i.e. the medium-term targets and the adjustment path towards them), medium-term budgetary objectives (MTO) were now to be somewhat differentiated from one country to another on the basis of debt ratios and potential growth rates. Targets were to be specified in structural terms, i.e. cyclically-adjusted and net of the effects of temporary measures, and should range between a deficit of 1 per cent of GDP and a small surplus. The latter would apply to high-debt, slow-growth countries. Implicit liabilities were also to be taken into account, once the Council agreed on criteria and methodological aspects. Major structural reforms with long-term fiscal benefits were also to be taken into consideration both when defining the adjustment path towards the medium-term objective and when considering temporary deviations from the target.

On the corrective side (i.e. the application of the excessive deficit procedure), a modification was introduced in the definition of the 'exceptional cyclical circumstances' which may justify the reference value for the deficit being exceeded: a breach of the threshold would now be considered exceptional if it resulted from a negative growth rate or an accumulated loss of output during a protracted period of very low growth relative to potential. When evaluating deficits exceeding the 3 per cent limit, the Commission would now take into account a number of factors ranging from cyclical conditions to the implementation of the Lisbon agenda and policies to foster R&D and innovation, from debt sustainability to the overall quality of public finances, and from financial contributions to international solidarity to fiscal burdens related to European unification. However, any excess over the 3 per cent deficit threshold was to remain limited and temporary. Implementation of pension reforms establishing a compulsory funded pillar was also to be taken into consideration, especially when assessing whether an excessive deficit had been corrected.

While confirming that, as a rule, the deadline for the correction of an excessive deficit would remain the year after it is identified, the Council decided that the initial deadline could be set one year later if there were special circumstances, and could be revised at a later stage if unexpected adverse economic events with major unfavourable budgetary effects occurred.

The Council called for greater weight to be given to public debt, but was not able to agree on the Commission's suggestion of the quantification of the minimum debt reduction for countries with very high debt ratios.

The Council also outlined a number of steps to improve the governance of EU rules. It suggested closer cooperation between Member States, the Commission and the Council in the implementation of the Pact. It indicated the need to develop national budgetary rules and ensure that national parliaments are closely involved in the process. Finally, it called for reliable macroeconomic forecasts and budgetary statistics.

A first evaluation of the reform

These changes met with a sceptical reception. Some commentators argued that, given the host of exceptions to the 3 per cent rule and the greater discretion left to the Council, the Pact was de facto dead (Calmfors, 2005; Buiter, 2005). Even those who were traditionally critical of the old SGP, while appreciating the better balance between fiscal discipline and flexibility, viewed the reformed Pact as excessively prone to opportunistic interpretation and felt that it failed to tackle the root causes of fiscal imbalances (Coeuré and Pisani-Ferry, 2005).

In reviewing the debate on the SGP, Buti *et al.* (2005) highlighted four critical issues that any effective reform of the Pact needed to tackle: (1) overcoming excessive uniformity, (2) improving transparency, (3) correcting pro-cyclicality, and (4) strengthening enforcement.

Overcoming excessive uniformity

The new SGP introduces some elements of country-specificity in both the preventive and the corrective arms of the Pact. The close-to-balance rule of the original SGP, interpreted as 'broadly balanced budgets in cyclically-adjusted terms', treated equally countries with different levels of public debt, implicit and contingent liabilities, and public investment needs.

In the early years of EMU, the only dimension along which countries were differentiated was the variability of the cyclical component of the budget balance. In the new Pact, the way the MTO is set has been extended to encompass other dimensions, such as the financial fragility of the country embodied in stock of public debt and – in the future – the threat to long-term sustainability created by the implicit liabilities of pension systems, as well as the capacity of countries to 'grow out of their debt', assessed in terms of their potential growth (and therefore structural reforms aimed at boosting it).

The Council has taken a cautious approach by stipulating that, in order to safeguard the 3 per cent deficit ceiling, the medium-term target should never exceed a deficit of 1 per cent of GDP. If structural reforms entailing frontloaded costs are envisaged, deviations from the MTO are allowed, but only under strictly defined conditions. The new SGP also introduces elements of country specificity in the corrective arm of the Pact.

Whilst such changes may reduce the excessive uniformity of the rules, they may in some instances increase their complexity, with negative implications for transparency and enforcement.

Improving transparency

The original EU fiscal framework was widely criticized for its lack of transparency. First, the deficit indicator as defined by ESA-95 does not provide a full picture of countries' public finance imbalances. Second, the debt indicator (gross financial debt at face value) allows targets to be achieved via operations which do not improve fiscal sustainability, and tends to underestimate overall outstanding liabilities. Third, under the current system of national accounts, monitoring is hampered by delays in data provision and allows some manipulation of statistics with the result that the whistle is often blown far too late or only when the true data eventually surface. Finally, the forecasts underlying stability programmes have frequently turned out to be optimistically biased.

The new SGP includes potentially important provisions leading to improved transparency but also elements that work in the opposite direction.

In recent years, countries have frequently adopted one-off, cash-raising measures to meet the short-term deficit targets instead of making the necessary structural adjustment. The decision that compliance with the medium-term target as well as with the minimum annual adjustment of 0.5 per cent of GDP is to be assessed in *structural* terms, by netting out the estimated effect of the cycle and one-off measures, should lead to improved transparency.

The availability of high quality statistics and timely fiscal indicators still remains an issue. The new Pact acknowledges the importance of quality, timeliness and reliability of fiscal statistics and pledges to ensure the independence, integrity and accountability of both national statistical offices and Eurostat. The availability of better statistics should be complemented by a more comprehensive surveillance of fiscal variables.

The overly optimistic forecasts that are common in some Member States can translate into higher than projected deficits, since government revenues quickly respond to changes in potential output whereas adjustments on the expenditure side normally require a lengthy process of political decision-making. The new Pact indicates that budgetary projections should be based on realistic, even cautious macroeconomic forecasts.

While these changes should improve the quality and availability of fiscal indicators, others are likely to have a negative impact on the second aspect of transparency mentioned above, that is, the possibility of easily assessing compliance with the rules.

One of these – and indeed the most notable amendment to the corrective part of the Pact – is the specification of so-called 'other relevant factors' in the assessment of whether a deficit in excess of 3 per cent of GDP can be considered 'excessive' in the sense of the Treaty. Such factors – including the implementation of the Lisbon agenda and policies to foster R&D and innovation, the overall quality of public finances, financial contributions to international solidarity, and fiscal burdens related to European unification – may give countries running deficits in excess of the reference value easy escape routes. While there is an important safeguard in the provision that any excess over the 3 per cent deficit threshold should remain limited and temporary, the need to take such a long list of factors into account risks blurring the assessment.

The preventive part of the SGP has also become more complex. The medium-term objectives are no longer defined *ex ante*. They are instead objectives that countries set themselves in their stability programmes on the basis of commonly agreed criteria which may evolve over time.

Correcting pro-cyclicality

It is widely recognized that the original SGP did not provide sufficient incentives for countries to run prudent fiscal policies in good times, with the result that their room for manoeuvre was curtailed in bad times. The new agreement explicitly aims to correct pro-cyclicality by emphasizing the importance of reliable macroeconomic forecasts, including the commitment to step up consolidation in good times, relaxing the 'exceptionality clause', making the timing for the correction of the excessive deficit a function of the prevailing cyclical conditions and providing for the guarded possibility to repeat steps of the procedure in the event of adverse shocks.

While these changes go in the right direction, the question remains whether they go far enough in terms of sticks and carrots.

More could be done to step up peer pressure by using the early-warning procedure of the SGP not only in bad times when the deficit approaches the 3 per cent ceiling, but also in good times when a significant divergence from structural targets is detected. The idea of an early-warning procedure independent of the immediate danger of an excessive deficit is considered in European Commission (2004). However, the new SGP, while foreseeing the possibility for the Commission to issue 'policy advice' in this regard, did not incorporate this proposal.

Buti *et al.* (2003) and Sapir *et al.* (2004) have argued that the introduction of rainy-day funds may strengthen incentives for prudent fiscal behaviour in good times. These funds, which would be used in times of recession and replenished in upturns, might increase the incentive for governments not to waste the surpluses in good times and increase the room for manoeuvre in bad times. However, their establishment would require the current ESA accounting rules for computing budgetary statistics to be revised so, although interesting, such a move is not unproblematic.

Strengthening enforcement

A strong criticism of the Treaty and the old SGP is that enforcement is partisan: national authorities are supposed to apply the rules to themselves, and therefore have strong incentives for collusion and horse-trading. As indicated in Table

10.1, the new Pact includes provisions on enforcement which, like those on transparency, will cut both ways – with some strengthening it and others likely to weaken it.

As pointed out in Buti *et al.* (2003), enforcement is particularly problematic in the case of supranational fiscal rules applying to sovereign countries. One way of countering this would be to enhance national ownership of the rules so that there is a better chance that they become self-enforcing. In parallel, the Commission's role in the enforcement of the SGP should be strengthened.

On the first count (national ownership), the new provisions concerning governance – notably the involvement of national parliaments – go in the right direction, but are modest overall. In particular, the suggestion of establishing independent monitoring bodies at national level, which had been strongly advocated by Sapir *et al.* (2004) and mentioned in the initial proposals by the Commission (European Commission, 2004), was not accepted. On the second count (stronger role of the Commission), the new Pact does not introduce any significant change in the voting or the procedural arrangements. Evidently, the Council was not prepared to strengthen the authority of the Commission in the implementation of EU fiscal rules. Rather, provisions such as the considerations of 'other relevant factors' risk working against an effective enforcement of the rules, by reducing transparency and increasing the possibility of collusion within the Council.

5 The reformed Stability Pact from a political economy perspective: renewed ownership or green light for collusion?

The SGP as a supranational rule

Maastricht *cum* the SGP was the EU's response to the unsustainable budgetary developments of the previous decade. The choice to rely on a supranational rule had important implications.[6] By focusing on the budget deficit, the rule clearly aimed at fostering macroeconomic stability in the currency union rather than at tackling head-on the negative effects of public finance developments on growth. The choice of the budget deficit as the variable constrained by the EU rule was not only due to its potential macroeconomic spillovers and the fact that it is relatively simple to monitor and measure, but also because it is relatively neutral in terms of the social preferences of EU countries. This is obviously essential for a supranational rule which must fit countries with widely different levels of development, size of the public sector, and preferences along the efficiency/equity frontier.

From a (revised) Musgravian perspective,[7] abiding by the SGP could help reign in the threat of unsustainability while regaining room for fiscal stabilization. But seen from Buchanan's standpoint, the SGP, together with the pressure of tax competition in a single market, could eventually lead to lower public spending and a less intrusive role for the public sector in the economy, thereby helping to tackle one of the root causes of Europe's growth problem. While preserving this logic, the reformed Pact also makes allowance for structural public finance reforms aimed at boosting growth.

Does the new SGP incorporate the right political incentives?

Whether or not the new SGP will actually produce these effects depends on whether the new rules embody the right incentives for compliance. Table 10.3 compares how well five conditions judged essential for the success of the Pact were fulfilled in the SGP 'mark I' and how far they are likely to be met in the 'mark II' version.[8] Two scenarios for the new version are considered: an opportunistic 'collusive' scenario and 'genuine' adherence to the new rules.

Public visibility

The objective of meeting the Maastricht convergence criteria was the centre-piece of public finance strategies in many EU countries during the 1990s. Public visibility was greatly facilitated by the simplicity of the 3 per cent of GDP deficit criterion which provided a clear signpost for economic policies regardless of the government's political colour, especially in countries which entered the 1990s with very high deficits and looming unsustainability threats. The simple and the (largely) unambiguous definition of the fiscal requirements – especially that concerning the budget deficit – allowed effective monitoring by the European Commission which played the role of external agent entrusted with the correct interpretation and implementation of the Treaty criteria. High visibility, together with easy monitoring, was one of the reasons for preferring numerical targets over national procedural rules. The close-to-balance-or-in-surplus rule of the SGP had lower visibility than a simple deficit ceiling. The fact that, in the reformed Pact, the MTOs are set by national authorities (albeit within the range agreed upon by the Council) gives a better chance of renewed visibility under a genuine implementation of the new rules. However, a collusive approach by

Table 10.3 The old and the new stability pact: two readings

	Old SGP	*New SGP: collusion*	*New SGP: genuine*
1 Public visibility	High but fading	On the way to oblivion	Medium
2 Clear incentives	Blurred	Easier to get away with	Better rationale
3 Political ownership	Small MS	High deficit MS: DE+FR+IT	Germany and virtuous MS
4 Constraining calendar	CTB a moving target	MTO de facto never	MTO by the end of stability programme
5 Collegial culture	Acrimony prevailed	Mutual back-scratching	New collegiality based on trust

national governments would relegate the Pact to the backburner and, eventually, it would fade into oblivion.

Clear incentives

The Maastricht public finance requirements very clearly laid out rewards and penalties. Meeting the convergence criteria enabled budgetary laggards to join the virtuous countries in the new policy regime, while failure to comply carried the penalty of exclusion from the euro area. Market incentives were also crucial. Countries with high deficit and debt levels that adopted a credible adjustment programme were able to enjoy a reduction in interest rates which helped lower their public finance imbalances. The structure of incentives changed with entry into the euro area: the convergence of interest rates meant that the market incentives were reduced, the carrot of the prospect of entry was eaten, and the stick of the risk of exclusion was replaced by the much weaker threat of uncertain and delayed sanctions under the SGP. The experience of the early years of EMU showed that the Council was not ready to use the 'nuclear option' of pecuniary sanctions, especially against large countries. The new Pact offers easier ways out, for instance by allowing repetition of the various steps of the EDP procedure. However, if genuinely applied, its stronger economic rationale may in fact increase peer pressure on fiscal delinquents.

Political ownership

The debate on the fiscal requirements of EMU reflected Germany's concern with fiscal discipline: both the Maastricht fiscal criteria and the SGP clearly bear Germany's fingerprints. Macroeconomic stability came to be regarded as an essential precondition for Germany to agree to merge its monetary sovereignty into a single currency. After 2000, due to Germany's economic difficulties, political ownership of the SGP shifted towards smaller countries with structural surpluses which, though numerous, have a relatively small weight in the euro area. This was sufficient to keep the Pact alive but weakened the enforceability of the rules, especially vis-à-vis large countries. Under the new Pact, Germany once again holds the key to rigorous implementation of the new rules. If Germany is to retake political ownership of the rules it must accept a stringent application of the rules to itself, for otherwise high deficit countries will simply disregard them. Resistance by virtuous small Member States would in that case eventually be swamped in a collusive deal.

Constraining calendar

The Treaty set very clear deadlines for moving to the final stage of EMU. Countries wanting to join the first wave had no choice but to make the required consolidation effort to meet the convergence requirements. The SGP set very clear, short deadlines between the various steps of the excessive deficit procedure, but the 2003 November crisis over France and Germany led to a stalemate. However, the real problem was that the close-to-balance requirement of the Pact had no specific timetable, and was therefore treated as a moving target. The same fate might also befall the MTO in the new Pact if the collusion scenario materializes. In contrast, if the new rules are applied in earnest countries are likely to meet their MTO.

Collegial culture

During the run-up to EMU, the convergence process facilitated the progressive emergence of a collegial stability culture among national and EU officials. This facilitated peer pressure between national authorities and enhanced the role and authority of the European institutions. Once the SGP was implemented, however, this climate of mutual trust was replaced by acrimony between the Council and the Commission, and between large and small countries. Under the reformed Pact, if collusion prevails, the more complex setting would favour mutual back-scratching by fiscal sinners ('I help you now, you help me later'). However, a genuine application of the new rules would favour the emergence of a new collegial atmosphere based on trust.

What is the probability that the new SGP will be applied rigorously? According to most academic and policy commentators, the new rules bear the imprint of collusion as a birthmark. Yet while a certain degree of scepticism is justified, the SGP 'mark II' should not be written off too quickly. At EU level, if the new SGP were to fail, the damage to the reputation of the ECOFIN Council, and especially the Eurogroup, let alone the Commission, would be enormous. At the national level, the key to genuine implementation of the rules is held by large countries, especially Germany, and it will soon be clear whether or not this has been achieved.

5 Conclusion: could Buchanan meet Musgrave again?

The chapter has examined the role of fiscal policy in Europe since the Second World War. It has shown that the period can be divided into two distinct phases. During the 'Golden Age' that lasted until the mid-1970s, Europe witnessed a 'public finance' phase, when the three sides of Musgrave's triangle seemed to reinforce one another, with no apparent trade-off between allocative efficiency, redistribution and stabilization. During the next 30 years, Europe suffered a 'public choice' phase, with increasing public deficits and trade-offs between allocative efficiency and redistribution in the manner foreseen by Buchanan, leading to declining growth performance.

By the end of the 1980s, several countries had adopted public finance rules and guidelines to attempt to control their deficits, but these were often ineffective. Hence, the choice was made to set up rules at the EU level where it would allegedly be easier to resist 'public choice temptations'. The Maastricht criteria codified in the Treaty the imperative of consolidation as a condition for joining the euro area. As a complement, the Stability and Growth Pact aimed to make budgetary discipline a permanent feature of EMU.

The hope was that EU fiscal rules would help national governments find a mid-point between the views of Musgrave and Buchanan. Abiding by the SGP would help solve the threat of unsustainability and regain room for fiscal stabilization à la Musgrave. At the same time, the SGP could eventually lead to lower public spending and a smaller role of the public sector in the economy, thereby helping to tackle one of the root causes of Europe's growth problem as identified by Buchanan.

Clearly, the Stability Pact 'mark I' had a number of drawbacks, particularly asymmetric incentives and its lack of a long-term view, which limited its ability to fulfil its role. The reformed Pact goes some way towards correcting such problems while retaining the original architecture.

However, the question remains as to whether EU rules can succeed where national rules have failed. Our view is that EU rules can be helpful provided they are backed by national institutions and are better enforced at the Community level.

Successful application of the Pact will require increasing political accountability at national level. This applies to provisions concerning governance, namely the use of reliable forecasts and a stronger role for national parliaments. Member states should set up independent national boards in charge of budgetary monitoring and assessment – including via the provision of unbiased forecasts (Jonung and Larch, 2006) – so as to complement and reinforce the role of the Community authorities in this area.

The major weakness of the old rules was poor enforcement mechanisms. Will the new rules be more effectively enforced? The fact that in the new Pact there is a greater margin for discretion but no independent enforcer may increase the incentives for the Council to collude in subverting the implementation of the rules. However, as the new Pact has a better economic rationale and may increase fiscal transparency and national ownership of the rules, there may be a better chance of it becoming self-enforcing.

While the reformed SGP has been greeted with scepticism in many academic and policy circles, it would be wrong to assume that it is bound to become irrelevant. First, the reasons why fiscal rules were adopted in a monetary union of many sovereign countries in the first place are still valid. The future enlargement of the euro area to Central and Eastern European countries actually strengthens the need for a common fiscal framework (Orbán and Szapàry, 2004). Second, no viable alternative to a credible supranational rule emerged from the debate on the reform of the Pact, since all the other potential solutions came up against serious criticism of one kind or another. Third, many countries need sound fiscal policies leading to a reduction in debt levels also for purely domestic reasons – particularly the demographic shock which lies around the corner – and in this case an external anchor will continue to be useful. Finally, it is likely that, as soon as serious imbalances emerge in some countries threatening the stability of the euro area, the other euro-area members will step up the pressure for rigorous implementation of the rules.

Enforcement of the reformed SGP will, in the end, depend on politics. A better rationale for EU rules, echoing Musgrave's public finance goals, will not suffice. The key players will have to take renewed ownership of the rules and integrate them in their national policy framework. From Buchanan's perspective, the new rules will only be rigorously applied to the extent that the perceived long-term negative spillovers of fiscal misbehaviour in EMU outweigh the short-term political costs of attempting to limit the partner countries' room for manoeuvre. This issue goes to the heart of supranational policy rules and coordination and, while the early experiences of implementation of the reformed SGP are encouraging, the jury is still out on which of these forces will prevail.

Notes

1 Paper prepared for the second annual Berkeley-Vienna Conference on the US and European Economies in Comparative Perspective (Berkeley, 12–13 September 2005). The views expressed herein are those of the authors and do not necessarily represent those of the organizations they are affiliated with. The authors would like to thank Martin Larch and conference participants for useful comments and Vittorio Gargaro and Sophie Bland for valuable research assistance and editorial support.
2 See Sapir *et al.* (2004).
3 See also Buchanan (1967). Since then a burgeoning literature of 'political economics' has explored the interplay between political and institutional systems and public finances. For a thorough overview, see Persson and Tabellini (2000).
4 This, however, included one-off revenue of some 1 per cent of GDP arising from the sale of UMTS mobile phone licences.
5 As shown in Buti and van den Noord (2004a), producing over-optimistic forecasts is particularly tempting in electoral periods as a way to increase the room for manoeuvre of discretionary fiscal policy.
6 For a more detailed analysis of the SGP as a supranational rule, see Buti *et al.* (2003).
7 In a modern perspective, the dimension of sustainability is added to the original 'Musgravian triangle'. Sustainability is closely linked to the goals of efficiency and stabilization. After the shocks of the 1970s, the goal of ensuring cyclical stabilization has been broadened to one of preserving overall macroeconomic stability.
8 See Buti and Giudice (2002) and Buti and van den Noord (2004b).

References

Artis, M.J. (2002) 'The Stability and Growth Pact: Fiscal Policy in the EMU', in F. Breuss, G. Fink and S. Griller (eds) *Institutional, Legal and Economic Aspects of the EMU*. Wien-New York: Springer.
Buchanan, J.M. (1967) *Public Finance in Democratic Process*. Chapel Hill: University of Carolina Press.
Buchanan, J.M. and Musgrave, R.A. (1999) *Public Finance and Public Choice: Two Contrasting Visions of the State*. Cambridge, Mass.: MIT Press.
Buchanan, J.M. and Tullock, G. (1962) *The Calculus of Consent: Logical Foundations of Constitutional Democracy*. Ann Arbor: The University of Michigan Press.

Buiter, W.H. (2005) 'The "Sense and Nonsense of Maastricht" Revisited: What Have We Learnt about Stabilization in EMU?', *CEPR Discussion Paper*, 5405.

Buti, M. and Giudice, G. (2002) 'Maastricht's Fiscal Rules at Ten: an Assessment', *Journal of Common Market Studies* 40(5): 823–847.

Buti, M. and van den Noord, P. (2004a) 'Fiscal Discretion and Elections in the Early Years of EMU', *Journal of Common Market Studies* 39(4): 737–756.

Buti, M. and van den Noord, P. (2004b) 'Fiscal Policy in EMU: Rules, Discretions and Political Incentives', *Moneda y Crédito* 218: 265–308.

Buti, M., Eijffinger, S. and Franco, D. (2003) 'Revisiting the Stability and Growth Pact: Grand Design or Internal Adjustment?', *CEPR Discussion Paper*, 3692.

Buti, M., Eijffinger, S. and Franco, D. (2005) 'The Stability Pact Pains: a Forward-Looking Assessment of the Reform Debate', *CEPR Discussion Paper*, 5216.

Calmfors, L. (2005) 'What Remains of the Stability Pact and What Next?', Sieps, Report No. 8.

Coeuré, B. and Pisani-Ferry, J. (2005) 'Fiscal Policy in EMU: Towards a Sustainability and Growth Pact?', *Oxford Review of Economic Policy* 21(4): 598–617.

Council of the European Union (2005) 'Improving the Implementation of the Stability and Growth Pact', 7423/05, March.

European Commission (2004) 'Strengthening Economic Governance and Clarifying the Implementation of the Stability and Growth Pact', COM (2004) 581, September.

Jonung, L. and Larch, M. (2006) 'Improving Fiscal Policy in the EU: the Case for Independent Forecasts', *Economic Policy* 47: 491–534.

Musgrave, R.A. (1959) *The Theory of Public Finance: A Study in Public Economy*. New York: McGraw-Hill.

Orbán, G. and Szapàry, G. (2004) 'The Stability and Growth Pact from the Perspective of the New Member States', Hungarian National Bank Working Paper, 4.

Persson, T. and Tabellini, G. (2000) *Political Economics: Explaining Economic Policy*. Cambridge, Mass.: MIT Press.

Sapir, A., Aghion, P. and Bertola, G. (2004) *An Agenda for a Growing Europe: The Sapir Report*. Oxford: Oxford University Press.

Stark, J. (2001) 'Genesis of a Pact', in A. Brunila, M. Buti and D. Franco (eds) *The Stability and Growth Pact: The Architecture of Fiscal Policy in EMU*. New York: Palgrave.

Part II

Governance and social policy

11 Economic institutions and policies in the US and the EU

Convergence or divergence?[1]

Élie Cohen and Jean Pisani-Ferry

1 Introduction

Once upon a time, there were national varieties of capitalism. There were a German (or Rhineland) model, a Gallic model, a Scandinavian model, a British model, etc., as well as, outside Europe, a Japanese model and a Korean model. Some of these models were more distant from the US model of a modern market economy and some were closer, but each was specific. As recently as a quarter of a century ago, the common belief in academic as well as business and policy communities was that these idiosyncrasies were here to stay.

This belief was based on the view that transatlantic differences were primarily rooted in dissimilarities in the functioning of capital markets, as regards, for example, corporate ownership and governance structures; financing patterns; the regulatory framework; and relationships between states and markets. Goods markets and labour markets were part of the picture, but less essential. This is why the emphasis was put on alternative models or varieties of *capitalism*. According to this school of thought, complementarity between key features of those patterns, as well as between them and social ones, made the model self-reinforcing and led to the belief that it would survive the transformations of the world economy.

This was a flawed hypothesis. Over the last 25 years a major change has taken place in Europe as a consequence of globalization and European integration. The latter has proceeded through (1) the extension of EU-wide economic legislation within the framework of the Single Market, (2) the delegation of major policy functions such as competition policy and monetary policy to EU institutions, and (3) softer forms of intra-EU convergence through harmonization and peer pressure in fields such as privatization and fiscal policy. References to a French or a German model of capitalism nowadays are generally made in a normative way to blame procrastination or rearguard manoeuvres in coping with change.

However, significant differences remain in the social models. In spite of rhetorical references to the 'European social model' and of an obvious distance between Europe and the US, several varieties of it continue to coexist within the EU. Furthermore, not much convergence can be observed between, say, the costly but efficient social institutions of the Nordic countries and the much less developed welfare state of the UK.

This persistence is sometimes taken as a basis for claiming that the varieties of capitalism have survived the transformations induced by globalization – that only the focus of differentiation has changed. In fact, authors starting from very different conceptual backgrounds such as Amable (2003), Hall and Soskice (2001) and Rajan and Zingales (2003) seem to converge to consider that national varieties of capitalism still exist. Hence, a first methodological issue: can different forms of capitalism of the kind we have outlined remain in an era of globalization? Can these differences be rooted in capital market institutions? Can, alternatively, the persistence of specific 'social models' form the basis of lasting differentiation? Is there a role for the broader macroeconomic policy framework?

The second issue we intend to investigate is an empirical as well as a political one: assuming that national models fade away, is European integration leading to the emergence of a genuinely European type of market economy or to convergence on the US model? Over the last quarter of a century, US economic policy has experienced significant changes in both the micro and the macro fields as a consequence of the deregulation of the 1980s, the emergence of the 'new economy', the gyrations of fiscal policy in the 1990s and the early 2000s and the emergence of a new monetary policy philosophy under the chairmanship of Alan Greenspan. The question is whether this double move is leading towards convergence or renewed divergence of the EU and US. From a distant point of view, there is obviously convergence since both sides of the Atlantic are now characterized by limited government intervention in the markets and (at least in theory) prudent macroeconomic management. But this is a superficial characterization. The real question is whether the two sides are converging towards the same model of market economy, where the differences that remain are rooted and whether they can be expected to recede.

This chapter is organized as follows: section 2 surveys the literature on alternative models of market economies; section 3 reviews what the transformations of France and Germany over the last two decades imply for this analysis; section 4 discusses the way European integration transformed microeconomic institutions and policies in the EU; section 5 deals with macroeconomic policy; section 6 addresses the social dimension; and section 7 concludes.

2 A retrospective on 'varieties of capitalism'

Andrew Shonfield's seminal 1965 study of the interaction between politics and economics in core capitalist countries after the Second World War initiated a series of debates on the convergent or divergent character of the dynamics at work in advanced market democracies. According to Kitshelt *et al.* (1999), the main issues were 'to what extent capitalist countries are maintaining their path-dependent trajectories? Are there pressures toward greater institutional and policy convergence? And even if there are, are there also continuing and new sources of diversity?'

Throughout the 1980s and the 1990s, a significant body of research has been devoted to characterizing the different versions of capitalist economies. To quote just a few authors, Aglietta (1976) and Boyer (1986) proposed the concept of *régulation* (which does not translate into regulation but rather designates a consistent and self-reinforcing set of rules, institutions and practices) to distinguish between different types of market economies across time or space. Zysman (1983) introduced the distinction between 'market-led', 'bank-led' and 'state-led' financial systems. Albert (1991) contrasted the US type of market-led capitalism and the German-based *Rhineland* model. Cohen (1992) studied French social Colbertism. Crouch and Streek (1996) discussed whether European capitalisms would eventually converge on the US type or would follow distinctive paths. More recently, Hall and Soskice (2001) proposed a framework for analysing of *varieties of capitalism*.

This line of research has given rise to both an academic and a policy debate. The academic discussion has been devoted to the reasons for and the characterization of the core features of national varieties of capitalism. The policy discussion has been centred on the assessment of European integration and on the possible emergence of a European model that would not simply replicate the US model of a market economy.

As Dani Rodrik (2003) puts it, there is now widespread agreement to consider that 'first-order economic principles [such as] protection of property rights, market-based competition, appropriate incentives, sound money, and so on, do not map into unique policy packages'. Even from an efficiency standpoint, this indeterminate mapping leaves room for alternative institutional arrangements, especially in the presence of institutional complementarity as emphasized by Amable (2003). Furthermore, growth economics suggests that the nature of the efficient arrangements may depend on the degree of development: institutions that are growth-enhancing in a catching-up phase may become dysfunctional as the economy approaches the technology frontier (Acemoglu *et al.*, 2002). The issue, thus, is not whether differences exist but where they are rooted and how they can withstand the effects of markets integration.

Proponents of the variety of capitalisms approach frequently address the functioning of markets for goods, capital and labour, macroeconomic policy behaviour, and redistributional issues, all of which are regarded as being interconnected. However, the main focus of this line of research has been on the institutions that determine the functioning of the market for capital.

This focus is very clear in early work such as John Zysman's *Government, Markets and Growth* (1983), which provides an analytic framework for investigating the role of governments in financial systems and the impact of institutions on growth patterns. Zysman starts from a simple question: how is the financing of the economy organized in industrialized countries and how does it impact industrial performance? Zysman's model includes the organization of financial markets, credit policies, business financing patterns and the exercise of property rights. This provides the basis for analysing national varieties of capitalism and for elaborating ideal types. The US and Britain exemplify the 'market-led' type, where financial markets are the central institution channelling capital to the most profitable investments. Companies finance themselves on the market and must therefore convince shareholders, analysts, institutional investors and rating agencies – which implies the release of information on an ongoing basis. France and Japan are examples of the second, 'state-led' type. Through credit controls, specialized credit channels and interest rate subsidies, the state essentially substitutes financial markets in the allocation of resources to the various sectors of the economy. In this type of capitalism, there is a market for goods and services (although it may be subject to state intervention), but hardly for factors of production, as if allocation were too important a function to be left to market forces. Finally, Zysman sees Germany's system as 'bank-led' because funds are channelled to companies and investment projects through the banking system. The intimate relationship between a company and its bank is thus key to development and to capital accumulation. This arrangement favours long-term strategy over short-term results.

This variety of arrangements raises the issue of their relative efficiency. To explain why such different institutional settings and economic regimes could lead to apparently similar performance, Zysman argued that differing institutional arrangements for coordinating economic activity all had their strengths and weaknesses and that the market-led model was not universal. Thus, there was no normative implication in his approach.

The approach of Hall and Soskice (2001) is in some respects similar. They intend to 'bring firms back into the centre of the analysis of comparative capitalism' and put the emphasis on the relationships that firms establish internally (with their own employees) or externally (with suppliers, clients, shareholders, etc.). Consistent with this emphasis, they distinguish between 'liberal market economies' in which 'firms coordinate their activities primarily via hierarchies and competitive market arrangements' and 'coordinated market economies' in which they 'depend more heavily on non-market relationship to coordinate their endeavours with other actors'.

This latter distinction comes close to that of Rajan and Zingales (2003), although the purpose of these authors is normative rather than positive. Rajan and Zingales distinguish between 'relationship capitalism', by which they designate the system of managed competition that emerged in the developed economies after the Second World War in which the role of markets in allocating resources was contained, and 'arms-length capitalism', in which financial markets drive investment choices. While Rajan and Zingales put the emphasis on financial systems, they underline the resemblance between relationship capitalism, Rhenish capitalism, and bank-based system.

Although authors come from different backgrounds, and although their normative preferences certainly differ, that body of research thus converges on the key features that distinguish varieties of capitalism. Those are:

1   the pattern of corporate ownership and control;
2   the financing of corporations;

3   the degree of competition in goods and services markets and the regulation
     of entry; and
4   the role of the state in allocating resources.

3 Europe's transformations and the (partial) demise of national models

The events of the last decades lead to question the permanence of national varieties of capitalism. France and Germany, which were not long ago considered
archetypal of different kinds of varieties, have both – though to an unequal
extent – undergone deep transformations as a consequence of globalization and
European integration. They therefore provide appropriate test cases.

France's exit from the state-led model

In the second half of the 1970s, reactions to the oil shocks and the growth slowdown seemed to confirm the view that each country would follow its own path.
In the early 1980s, the socialist government of François Mitterrand nationalized
the financial system, thereby giving control over the allocation of capital to the
state. However, the government soon realized that it was politically untenable to
assume full responsibility for the level of capital reallocation that the period
called for. Although it embarked on a hands-on approach to the restructuring of
ailing sectors and companies, it was also quick to reverse its initial course and to
move towards financial deregulation.

Starting in the mid-1980s, a series of reforms were introduced which
amounted to a complete overhaul of the financial system. (State-owned) banks
were despecialized, interest rate subsidies were reduced and eventually eliminated, credit controls were scrapped, administrative controls on direct inward
and outward investment were eliminated, portfolio capital flows were freed, and
government policy clearly encouraged disintermediation. Simultaneously, the
traditional instruments of industrial policy (direct state aids and sectoral plans)
were progressively eliminated. Finally, from 1986 onwards, previously nationalized banks and companies, including those which had been nationalized after the
Second World War, were returned to the private sector by the newly elected
government of Jacques Chirac.

As a consequence of these transformations, French capitalism no longer
resembles Zysman's model of it. Except in a few sectors such as utilities and
defence industry, virtually all of the channels that made effective state guidance
possible have been eliminated. But neither does it resemble what the privatizers
of the 1980s had imagined: the ownership structure created on the occasion of
privatization has not passed the test of time.

Due to the absence of pension funds and more generally to the weakness of
institutional investors, the French financial market lacked agents that could exercise control over the newly privatized companies. When the privatization
process was launched, the government tried to overcome this difficulty by

mimicking the German system and creating a network of cross-ownership between the major banks and insurance firms and the major non-financial companies. This was achieved in the privatization process by allocating blocks of shares (known as *noyaux durs* – hard cores) to selected corporate shareholders. The major companies were thereby given reciprocal control. However, this artificially created structure did not last for long as the companies' strategic interest did not coincide with the role they had been given by the architects of the privatization process. Gradually, most of them got rid of the control blocks they had been given.

The result of this move was a dramatic increase in the share of non-residents in the capital of French companies. According to the Banque de France, foreign shareholders accounted for 29 per cent of the capital of all French companies in 2002. This is still a smaller proportion than in the UK where it reaches 37 per cent, but a significantly higher one than in Japan (18 per cent), Germany (15 per cent) or the US (11 per cent).[2] As Table 11.1 illustrates, in spite of the size discrepancy between the two economies, at end-2003 equity investment by non-residents exceeded the level reached in Germany.

Furthermore, the share of non-residents is much higher in the capital of listed companies, for which it reaches 38 per cent.[3] Former national champions like Total, Saint-Gobain, or CapGemini are now truly global companies, whose foreign shareholders account for about 60 per cent of total capital.[4] Others such as Péchiney or AGF have been taken over by foreign companies.

Wide-ranging liberalization and large scale privatization against the background of weak institutional investors have thus brought French-style capitalism to an abrupt end. This does not mean that resistance to liberalization has disappeared, nor that the state does not intervene in the markets. In 1997–2002, the socialist government of Lionel Jospin launched several industrial policy initiatives in the aerospace, telecom and banking sectors. From 2002 on, right-wing Prime Minister Jean-Pierre Raffarin embarked on a series of rescue initiatives to avoid the disappearance of flagship companies such as France Télécom or Alstom and advocated the promotion of 'industrial champions' (including by lending support to the 2004 takeover of Aventis, a Franco-German pharma company, by Sanofi, a French one) and in 2005, his successor Dominique de Villepin promoted 'economic patriotism' and explicitly defined a series of sectors where foreign takeovers were officially unwelcome.

What the evolution that has taken place means, however, is that the state has effectively been deprived of the instruments it could rely on to bolster its industrial policy initiatives. Ministers can still intervene to support an ailing company and promote negotiations with its creditors. This is however virtually the only initiative they can take – under the surveillance of the European Commission which has the power to order companies to reimburse illegal state aids. In fact, even in very publicized cases like the Sanofi-Aventis battle, the only tool the French ministers used was political pressure because they had no other legal or financial instrument at their disposal. Rajan and Zingales may be right when they point out the resilience of relationship capitalism, however the resistance of

Table 11.1 Non-resident portfolio equity investment in major economies at end-2003 (millions of US dollars)

Investment in	Investment from				
	United States	United Kingdom	Major euro area countries	Other	Total value of investment
United States	–	174,064	415,786	346,451	1,274,037
United Kingdom	420,684	–	176,787	76,205	894,006
Luxembourg	6,026	17,995	354,938	94,329	622,798
Japan	255,496	71,342	84,988	27,864	493,777
France	130,761	44,941	118,891	35,135	410,089
Germany	103,239	29,223	102,214	38,821	326,663
Netherlands	115,792	31,916	101,878	27,330	320,700
Total value of investment	2,080,302	664,067	1,896,729	840,721	6,910,332

Source: IMF, Coordinated Portfolio Investment Survey.

incumbents could not prevent the foreign takeover of companies such as Péchiney and AGF.

Germany's partial exit from the bank-led model

Changes have been less pronounced in Germany, as illustrated by a series of events such as the obstruction to a European Commission-initiated takeover directive by German members of the European Parliament and by Chancellor Schröder's staunch defence of the special character of Volkswagen, or the opposition expressed by the *Länder* to the implementation of EU competition legislation in fields such as local services, transportation and banking. In 2005, SPD general secretary Franz Müntefering even compared foreign investors to locusts, illustrating once again the German reluctance to accept the dominance of financial markets in the ownership and the control of companies.

Research by Marco Becht and colleagues confirms that as recently as in the mid-1990s, Germany was still very far from having converged on the British or American type of ownership structure. According to Becht and Böhmer (2003), a single blockholder controlled more than 25 per cent of the voting rights in 82 per cent of the German corporations. In more than half of the companies, the largest shareholder controlled 52 per cent of the voting rights against 20 per cent in France, 10 per cent in the UK and less than 5 per cent in the US (Becht and Röell, 1999). It would thus seem that, unlike the French model, the Rhineland model is alive and well.

Nevertheless, the transformation of German capitalism is underway, as illustrated by a series of transformations such as the successful hostile takeover of Mannesmann by Vodaphone in 2000 (in spite of strong and vocal opposition by the unions and the Chancellor), the merger of Allianz and Dresdner Bank and the transformation of Deutsche Bank into a global investment bank. Even that last dyke, national bank ownership, has ceased to be a taboo, as illustrated by the 2005 merger of Hypovereinsbank and Unicredito. Less anecdotally, the 2000 change in the tax law (effective 2001) that scrapped the taxation of capital gains on the sale of shares by companies was widely regarded as signalling the end of the traditional long-term bank holdings of industrial shares, as banks and other financial intermediaries became free to unwind their long-established capital links with companies without paying a tax penalty.

Italy's eventual opening of the financial sector

In Italy, resistance to the transformation of the local variety of capitalism was epitomized by the stubborn but eventually unsuccessful attempt by Governor Fazio to oppose the takeover of Italian by foreign banks. In the name of 'italian-ity', the governor tried in 2004–05 to make use of his discretionary powers to prevent foreign takeovers and to promote instead local solutions. However, evidence that in the process he had departed from the neutrality that is expected of a central bank governor eventually forced him to resign. Only a few weeks later, the takeover of Banca Nazionale del Lavoro by French bank BNP-Paribas was announced. It is widely expected that the policy of the governor appointed in early 2006, Mario Draghi, will distinguish himself from the protective attitude of its predecessor.

France, Germany so far to a lesser extent, Italy, and more generally continental Europe are thus moving away from the collection of country-specific models they were.[5] In part, these transformations simply amount to the adoption of a market-based model of a modern economy, of which the US offers a powerful example.

4 The European regulatory framework: an airlock or a shelter?

The two major forces behind the decline of national varieties of capitalism have been globalization and European integration. However, the European microeconomic regulation frameworks that have been gradually replacing national frameworks could be regarded as a building block or a stumbling block in a process of convergence towards the US model. While European integration contributes to the dismantling of pre-existing national regulatory frameworks, it can either play the role of an 'airlock compartment' that allows gradual adjustment to the pressure of globalization or, alternatively, a 'shelter' under which a genuinely European variety of capitalism could develop and replace national ones while remaining different from that of the US.

In order to shed light on this issue, we start by recalling the policy process that led to the replacement of national policy frameworks by a European one. We then look at a series of quantitative indicators in order to grasp the extent of the transformation that has affected European economies. Finally, we examine specific policies.

Integration through liberalization rather than common policies: the logic of the last decades

In the early 1980s, Europe and the US were both discussing the virtues of competitiveness policies. This discussion was motivated by the erosion of the market share of European and US producers vis-à-vis those of Japan and emerging Asia (Dertouzos *et al.*, 1989). Against the background of discussions on 'US economic decline' and 'eurosclerosis' a debate developed between, on the one hand, the proponents of active intervention relying on industrial policy, strategic trade policy and a soft stance towards national champions in competition policy decisions, and, on the other hand, the advocates of free-market solutions such as liberalization, deregulation, and privatization.

In this context, American pundits such as Clyde Prestowitz, Robert Reich, Lester Thurow or Laura Tyson depicted Japan and European countries as examples of successful competitiveness policy strategies. Europeans, however, had the feeling that their traditional approaches had reached their limits and targeted industrial policies a zone of decreasing – if not negative – returns.

During the following two decades, the EU was in fact not able to renew its interventionist toolkit and essentially relied on liberalization while the US, which had already started the deregulation of several sectors in the 1970s, kept a more balanced approach between liberalization and proactive policies.

In the early 1980s, Europe was suffering from stagflation, exchange crises and industrial restructuring, EC integration was stalled, and the Community machinery was overwhelmed by difficulties. National governments were frequently tempted by purely national, if not isolationist, solutions. Most if not all political energy was devoted to restructuring ailing sectors, negotiating adjustments to the Common Agricultural Policy, managing the consequences of monetary disturbances or quarrelling about budgetary contributions. The EC was able to liquidate but unable to build for the future. Europeans responded to this challenge with what was meant to be a two-track strategy: the launching of the Single Market programme and a series of projects tailored to prop up technological development.

The Single Market itself was not a new project, as the Commission had prepared a programme of 300 directives that were deemed necessary to go beyond the abolition of internal tariffs and to complete the integration of markets for goods, services and capital, but it provided new impetus. Among the member states, Germany and France, the traditional pillars of European integration, were looking for a new momentum, and the UK under Mrs Thatcher was keen on dismantling regulations and barriers. Jacques Delors was the political entrepreneur who succeeded in blending a demand for economic efficiency, a demand for political impetus, and the EC's traditional supply of integrationist policies into a single mobilizing project, Europe 1992.[6] The resulting Single European Act was a balanced compromise between liberalization (with the removal of physical, technical and tax barriers to economic integration), integration (with the adoption of qualified majority voting for a series of decisions) and political assertion (with the launching of new common policies and the addition to the EC budget of a significant redistributive component).

The economic agenda for bolstering European competitiveness thus relied on a liberalization arm through the removal of trade and non-trade barriers and an industrial policy arm through the adoption of a series of programmes (such as Esprit, Eurêka, etc.) devoted to the promotion of new technologies. Instead of choosing between free-market and interventionist policies, European reformers were aiming at a combination.

In retrospect, Europe's successful implementation of its liberalization agenda strongly contrasts with the very limited success of its industrial policy initiatives. Two decades after the adoption of the Europe 1992 objective, the integrationist programme initiated in the mid-1980s through the liberalization arm has by and large been implemented. Change has certainly been slow in some areas, such as services and public utilities. Furthermore, enlargement raises new issues as the Single Market involves countries of very dissimilar development levels. In spring 2005, the row over the Bolkestein directive aiming at a liberalization of services markets illustrated of this new tension.[7] Nevertheless, liberalization has made inroads into previously highly regulated sectors, state aids in individual member states have been cut down and competition policy has gained strength.

In contrast, little remains of the industrial policy arm. Attempts to rejuvenate the European economy through the promotion of common, forward-looking projects have had at best limited success and have certainly not been sufficient to overcome a deteriorating competitive position.[8] Most of the projects initiated in the 1980s have subsequently been abandoned or redirected towards the promotion of research. The few successes there are, in sectors such as aerospace, rely on special or bilateral agreements and do not belong to the remit of the Union.

Europe's behaviour in the allocation of third generation mobile telephone licenses provides an interesting case. The starting point was the EU success with the second generation. Early adoption of a common European standard, the GSM, had been a success and had facilitated the development of equipment manufacturing and services. Although this had not been the product of an explicit industrial policy, Europe had de facto succeeded in taking the lead in the development of mobile telecommunications (Cohen and Mougeot, 2001; Didier and Lorenzi, 2002). The European Commission's attempt to reiterate this success led in 1998 to relying on a similar approach for 3G mobile telecommunications. However, an ambitious timetable for the development of new services was adopted in spite of a lack of technological visibility. Europeans were wary enough not to embark on an explicit industrial policy, but they could not resist the temptation to stimulate the emergence of a sector in which they could pretend being more advanced than the US and possibly Japan. The result was that the new project was launched without having demonstrated that industry would be able to deliver on the technology's potential. In the event, it was not – at least within the envisaged time frame.[9]

A clear imbalance thus now exists between the former two arms, liberalization and industrial policy. Those who find little merit in industrial policies may regard this contrast as just another illustration of their intrinsic inefficiency. There is some truth in this view, but it must be observed that integration within the Single Market has not brought visible supply-side effects either. Europe still lags behind the US in terms of innovation and productivity growth, and if anything, the gap has increased in the period in which the growth effects of the 1992 programme were supposed to materialize (Emerson *et al.*, 1988; Baldwin, 1989).[10] Unlike the US, the EU preference for liberalization policies can thus not be explained by the success they had.

The failure of European active intervention partially results from the permanent conflict between interventionist and free-market leaning states within the EC, but equally from the Union's idiosyncratic disregard of industrial policy. Three factors explain the continuing European commitment to the removal of internal barriers and its near-abandonment of industrial policy:

- The first is that liberalization has become identified with European integration. The removal of intra-European barriers is by nature a liberalization policy. But it can be pursued on the basis of its integrationist merits only. In effect, the alliance that Jacques Delors had built to promote the Single Market programme brought together Eurosceptic Margaret Thatcher (on liberalization grounds) and free-market sceptic François Mitterrand (on integrationist grounds). The same applies today as pro-Europeans support the creation of a Single Market for railways or energy even though they may have reservations on the accompanying liberalization agenda.

- The second reason can be found in the decision mechanisms. Since the 1950s, European integration has proceeded in two different modes: a deep, supranational mode and a shallow, intergovernmental mode. Under the supranational mode, European countries have created common institutions and a genuine Community law enforced by the Community's own courts. Under the intergovernmental mode, national governments have agreed to coordinate their national policies, but these policies are executed by national institutions under national law and remain determined to a large extent by national policy-makers. As a decision mechanism, the first mode is certainly more efficient than the second. The strength of liberalization is that it proceeded through the first mode, while a weakness of industrial policy is that it relies on the second.

- The third reason is that the implementation of the liberalization agenda relies on powerful lock-in mechanisms which, once in place, do not require additional political impetus. The strength of liberalization may thus progress through a series of quasi-judicial decisions that do not require explicit political decisions. Industrial policy instead constantly requires discretionary decisions for which the EU governance system is ill-equipped.

European integration in the micro field thus primarily provides a framework for regulation. An implication of the prominence of overall liberalization over concrete initiatives is that the specifically European character of the policy may be less pronounced. Before turning to the investigation of specific cases, we briefly look at what the quantitative indicators may tell us.

A quantitative assessment

The degree to which policy responsibility has been transferred to the European level is hard to measure. A comprehensive attempt at a quantitative assessment has been made by Alesina et al. (2002), but while their indicators give an overall picture of the development of EU legislative activity (Figure 11.1) they do not provide a reliable measure of the degree to which effective responsibility has been transferred to Brussels in various sectors.

Indicators developed by the IMF (2004) for the measurement of structural reform provide complementary indications. Their purpose is to provide a consistent measure of the degree of liberalization of goods, labour and capital markets.

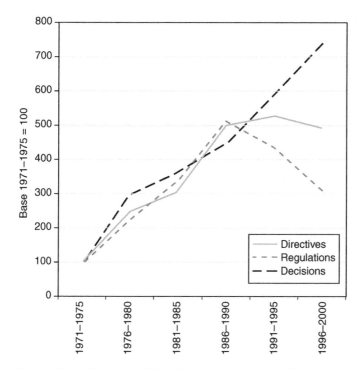

Figure 11.1 Indicators of EU legislative activity, 1971–2000 (source: Alesina *et al.* (2002)).

Although similar in intention to those of the OECD, they have the advantage of being available year by year, which helps in the assessment of the effect of European integration.[11]

Figure 11.2 plots for each of the three markets – goods, capital and labour – the mean and the standard deviation of the liberalization indicator for both the EU-15 and 20 OECD members (including all the EU-15). Three features stand out:

- First, markets differ in both the degree of liberalization and the dispersion of individual country performance. For capital markets, liberalization and convergence are complete. For goods, and even more for labour, liberalization is incomplete and convergence is partial.
- Second, the dispersion of country indicators is highest for goods markets. This suggests that the move towards liberalization takes place at different speeds in different countries, thereby initially increasing dispersion (before it eventually recedes as convergence takes place). This pattern was also observed for capital markets in the 1980s and the early 1990s, before convergence took place.
- Third, there is virtually no difference in the degree of liberalization or the dispersion of performance between the EU and the OECD. This means the

inclusion of the US, Japan and other non-EU countries does not alter the observed pattern. In other words, membership in the EU does not lead to an observable difference in behaviour.

Quantitative evidence thus suggests a limited EU effect on liberalization and convergence. It lends support to the 'airlock' rather than the 'shelter' view of European integration. But the indicators are admittedly crude and potentially misleading. Thus, we have to look at more direct evidence of the effects of integration.

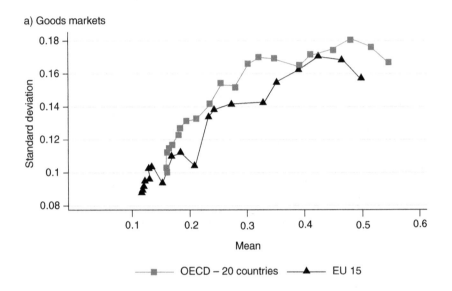

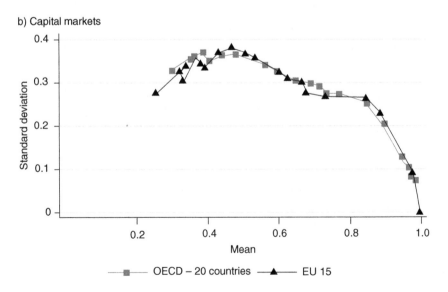

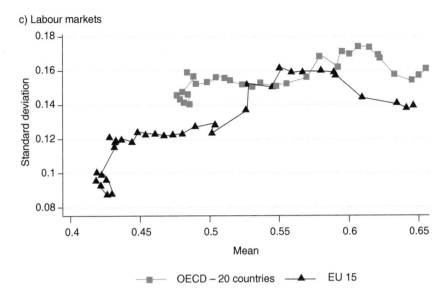

Figure 11.2 Indicators of market regulation and liberalization, 1975–1998 (source: OECD.

Note
For each country, the indicator takes values between 0 (no liberalization) and 1 (complete liberalization). The graph plots the mean of the indicator for the EU-15 or the OECD-20 (X-axis) against the standard deviation of the same indicator (Y-axis).

The Enron test

The corporate scandals of the early 2000s provided a test of the EU's willingness and ability to promote a specific variety of capitalism. Before the Enron affair broke out, convergence on the US model of corporate governance was slowly taking place as a consequence of three forces: first, European companies contemplating a listing on the NYSE were increasingly adopting US governance and disclosure rules; second, new accounting standards were being elaborated by the International Accounting Standards Board (IASB); third, national governments and private organizations were slowly adopting new regulatory frameworks.

The Enron affair and others which emerged simultaneously raised the question of the future of the convergence process. Detractors of the US corporate governance and control model were quick to take the occasion to express distrust in its market-based philosophy and to renew calls for a truly European approach to the issue. Furthermore, the US Congress reacted swiftly by passing the Sarbanes-Oxley legislation, which addressed perceived fault lines in the US system and took no account of European demands. This could have been a factor of divergence. As in the interwar period, when the stock market crash was accompanied by increasingly powerful distrust in the markets and the emergence of a much more regulated capitalism, the event could have been for the US and the EU the occasion of moving apart.

In the event, the US Congress took the lead in the definition and the design of appropriate measures and most Europeans decided to follow suit through the passing of similar legislation. Instead of pulling apart Europe and the US, the corporate scandals in effect accelerated European convergence on the US model.

The same can be said of the accounting standards. Although the process had been initiated before the US corporate scandals, the Enron/WorldCom affair drew attention to the issue and gave increased resonance to discussions that would otherwise have remained at a technical level. Here again the outcome of the process was not written in advance. The Europeans had chosen to delegate to the IASB the preparation of new accounting standards, hoping that the US would join and that truly international standards would in this way emerge. In fact, US accounting concepts frequently prevailed (especially as regards the fair value accounting) and the Europeans ended up adopting standards that certainly do not reflect a European idiosyncrasy.

Summing up

The question we started with was whether European integration could give rise to the emergence of a specific European variety of capitalism. A first conclusion from the observation is that this cannot be expected from proactive industrial policies. Due to a combination of factors, ranging from the internal weaknesses of the industrial policy approach to the identification between liberalization and integration and the implementation of liberalization through a series of powerful mechanisms, the EU has moved away from a discretionary approach and increasingly put emphasis on developing and enforcing rules of the game, thereby gradually adopting a more resolutely pro-market stance.

The question, thus, is whether the European legislative and regulatory framework is likely to shape a specific variety of firm behaviour. There are certainly many aspects of EU legislation that can hardly be found elsewhere. But the overall assessment is that the EU-wide regulatory framework is more of the 'airlock' type than of the 'shelter' type. More precisely, under present circumstances the strong forces that lead to harmonizing regulatory frameworks – free capital movements and the emergence of truly multinational companies – are not likely to be significantly countered by legislative initiatives. Thus, the micro regulation framework is unlikely to provide the shelter for developing a European model of capitalism.

How does this compare to the other side of the Atlantic? US policy retains a larger margin for discretion. Although it has also moved away from industrial policy, instruments are still in place: the defence and research budgets are far more considerable than those of the EU, and they are being used. Neither the executive nor Congress refrain from exercising political judgement when deemed appropriate. In 2005, rejection on purely political grounds of the takeover of an oil company, UNOCAL, by Chinese company CNOOC once again illustrated this feature of US attitude. The US government remains responsive to political pressures, while the EU increasingly defines itself by the rules it has committed to abide by. Because it regards itself a 'Community of law' and has developed a rules-based culture, the EU is likely to behave increasingly as the champion of rules in international economic relations.

As integration proceeds and competences are transferred to the EU level, more and more domains can be expected to be managed on the basis of a core set of principles. While the development of a more political and a more democratic Europe could be expected to counteract this tendency, the recent enlargement is going to reinforce it. The US, by contrast, is only slowly moving in the direction of a rules-based approach, because its domestic political setting implies that the administration remains responsive to the electorate's and the special interest groups' concerns.

5 Macroeconomic policy

Over the last quarter century, the approach to and instruments of macroeconomic policy have changed on both sides of the Atlantic. The change, however, has been less in the US than in Europe, where the role of monetary and fiscal policy has been transformed by financial market liberalization and the creation of Economic and Monetary Union (EMU).

Since the 1970s, the US has not experienced a discrete change in the way financial markets operate; it has not introduced any legal redefinition of the objectives of economic policy; its major economic policy institutions have remained virtually untouched; and the exchange rate regime has not been redefined. This high degree of continuity has certainly not precluded significant changes in the development of financial markets. Nor has it prevented an evolution in the approach to monetary and fiscal policy, as a consequence of both the succession of events and the economic policy controversies of the 1970s, the 1980s and the 1990s. But these strategic redefinitions have taken place against the background of a stable economic and institutional framework.

Europe, by contrast, has undergone a complete overhaul of its economic policy system(s). First, financial market regulations and restrictions on capital outflows which were widespread in the 1970s have been dismantled throughout the continent. Second, the objectives of economic policy and the corresponding assignment of instruments have been redefined. Third, all euro-area countries where the central bank was not fully independent from government have reformed their monetary institution and responsibility for monetary policy has been transferred to the European Central Bank. Fourth, exchange rate regimes have changed from fixed to floating, then to a floating-but-adjustable rates regime, and eventually either to floating (in non-euro countries) or to a full monetary union.

In some respects, the European countries are closer to the US now than they were a quarter of a century ago. When President Reagan and President Mitterrand both embarked on a fiscal reflation course in 1981, the US and the French economy responded in almost opposite ways, as could have been expected since one was a financially open economy with an independent, inflation-adverse central bank and the other was a financially closed economy whose central bank had to yield to government injunctions. Nowadays, both the financial environment and the monetary context of fiscal policy are broadly similar in Europe and the US. Unsurprisingly, a significant degree of convergence can be observed in the pattern of macroeconomic policy.

• Although the stated objective of monetary policy is not identical, price stability is a common goal. Differences in monetary policy reaction functions have been studied extensively in the literature. In their research on the post-1979 period, Clarida *et al.* (1998) have shown that in spite of rhetorical differences, the actual behaviour of the Fed and the Bundesbank had been in fact 'remarkably similar'. More recent studies (Artus and Wyplosz, 2002) suggest that the same can be said of the ECB.
• More surprisingly, there is also evidence of fiscal policy convergence. Figure 11.3 depicts the evolution of the general government balance in the US and the EU. By and large, the evolution has also been remarkably similar. While the short-term volatility in the deficit has been greater in the US, especially in recent years, the timing of the major reversals is similar.

There are, however, significant differences in the way macroeconomic policy is envisaged and implemented. First, quasi-constitutional constraints on economic policy are more prevalent in Europe, which implies that the discretionary component of both monetary and fiscal policy is less prominent than in the US. Second, there is more policy inertia in Europe, as Europeans have in a way 'locked in' the particular policy philosophy that characterized the late 1980s and early 1990s and are likely to stick to it while US policy is more likely to adapt to changing circumstances.

Rules vs. discretion

In the US, the Federal Reserve has been given by Congress a broad and somewhat loosely defined mandate and the FOMC has consistently maintained a significant margin of discretion. In the words of Governor Laurence Meyer (2002), 'while monetary policy can follow a rule-like behaviour, it can and should avoid the quarter-to-quarter commitment to a strict rule [...] No one policy rule can anticipate the appropriate response to all possible circumstances before they arise'. The implicit policy rule of the Federal Reserve under Alan Greenspan has been ironically described as 'study all the data carefully, and then set interest rates at the right level' (Mankiw, 2002), which is an accurate description of discretionary behaviour.

The ECB is characterized by both a narrower mandate and a greater inclination towards rules. It was given by the Maastricht Treaty the specific mandate of preserving price stability, for which its governing council initially adopted a

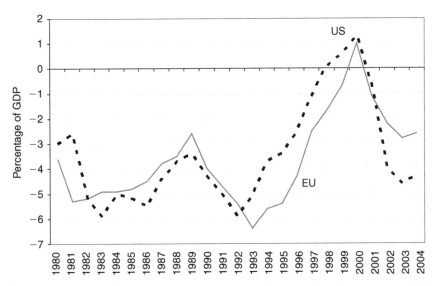

Figure 11.3 General government balance, US and EU15, 1980–2004 (source: IMF
WEO).

quantitative definition (inflation below 2 per cent over the medium term) and a
strategy partially relying on a quantitative objective for M3.[12]

Since the ECB has taken charge of monetary policy in the euro area, its actual
behaviour suggests that it has in fact retained a margin of discretion. In its first
years, it overlooked the evolution of M3 after having observed that this aggregate had almost always exceeded its growth target by a considerable margin. Furthermore, the ECB has kept its eye on the medium term and consistently allowed
inflation to exceed the 2 per cent threshold, provided that expectations remained
contained. In May 2003, the ECB governing council eventually adapted its monetary strategy: the objective was modified (inflation should now be below 2 per
cent but close to 2 per cent) and the monetary aggregate was downgraded from
being one of the two pillars of the strategy to an indicator status.

But its response to the slowdown of the early 2000s was much less aggressive
than that of the Federal Reserve, although growth in the euro area remained
deceptive long after the US economy had picked up. At a deeper level, the ECB
and the Fed have developed quite different philosophies on the role of a central
bank in a world of uncertainty. ECB officials lose no opportunity to emphasize
that, in the words of the bank's chief economist Otmar Issing (2002), 'central
banks must avoid becoming a source of additional uncertainty themselves when
there is only limited knowledge about the economy and the behaviour of economic agents'. By contrast, Alan Greenspan (2004) insists that in an environment of uncertainty 'the conduct of monetary policy in the United States has
come to involve, at its core, crucial elements of risk management' and that
'policy practitioners operating under a risk-management paradigm may, at

times, be led to undertake actions intended to provide insurance against especially adverse outcomes'. From the same premise – that the world is uncertain – the two central banks thus draw opposite conclusions as regards the role of monetary policy.

Differences in the approach to fiscal policy are also significant. In the US, there have been discussions of a balanced-budget rule but, so far, Congress remains free to vote whatever budget is deemed appropriate. And this freedom is being used: according to the OECD, the US cyclically-adjusted deficit as a percentage of GDP moved from a 1.1 per cent surplus in 2000 to a 4.3 per cent deficit in 2004.

In Europe, responsibility for fiscal policy remains in the hands of national governments but subject to the constraints of the 'no-excessive deficit' procedure of the treaty and of the Stability Pact. Constraints on national fiscal policy have continuously hardened from the early 1990s, when the treaty was negotiated, to the early 2000s, where the Stability Pact began to be enforced. While the member states' initial obligation was only to 'avoid excessive deficits' (Art. 104 of the EU treaty), by which it was understood that, in the absence of 'exceptional circumstances', they had to keep the general government deficit below a 3 per cent of GDP threshold, subsequent legislation has tightened the limitations on fiscal discretion. The Stability and Growth Pact of 1997 states that 'member states commit themselves to respect the medium term budgetary objective of positions close to balance or in surplus'.[13]

A look at the data suggests that since the launch of the euro, constraints have effectively been imposed. In the 1998–2004 period (the same as for the US), the aggregate cyclically-adjusted deficit of the euro area fluctuated between 1.3 per cent and 2.6 per cent of GDP. The amplitude of fiscal gyrations has therefore been four times smaller than in the US.

However, the jury is out as regards the implications of the 2005 reform of the Stability Pact. While emphasizing the rules, this reform has introduced significantly more recourse to economic judgement in the assessment of the fiscal situation of the member states. In a way, the EU has taken a step away from a mechanical rules system and towards a constrained discretion regime – in effect narrowing the gap that had opened up vis-à-vis the United States.

Inertia vs. responsiveness

Another, related characteristic of EU economic policy is inertia. Behavioural inertia results from the fact that most policy decisions for the euro area as a whole need to be taken collegially, which implies that they often require consensus-building and/or negotiations. This applies to the monetary policy decisions of the ECB, which are taken by a council consisting of six board members and (at the time of writing) 12 national central banks governors. Although information on the deliberations of that body is scarce (it does not publish minutes and generally does not vote), most ECB-watchers have pointed out that internal procedures make the European Central Bank a 'slow institution'

(Gros *et al.*, 2000, 2001; Alesina *et al.*, 2001). The same can be said of the Eurogroup in which the euro area's finance ministers gather to assess the economic situation and discuss policy coordination. Legal constraints notwithstanding, any discretionary decision to alter the policy stance is bound to require long negotiations between ministers even before it goes to the various parliaments. Quite apart from the member states' commitment to fiscal discipline, this is a significant constraint on the implementation of a coordinated fiscal policy.

Institutional inertia results from the fact that Europe's institutions (such as the ECB) or rules (such as the price stability objective and the no-excessive deficit procedure) are enshrined in a treaty that can only be modified by unanimity. Amendments to secondary legislation require almost as much consensus and political capital as a constitutional reform in a unitary state. Thus, it is likely that the set of rules and institutions that constitutes the EU economic policy system will exhibit a degree of stability. Moreover, those rules and institutions were all defined within a short time span, between the late 1980s and the late 1990s. As a consequence, they embody the policy thinking of a period in which industrialized countries were just emerging from high inflation and struggling with high public deficits and rising public debt ratios. This explains the very high priority given to credibility and discipline. In a way, the EU has 'locked in' the policy philosophy of that decade and has made it a permanent inspiration of its policy system.

This contrasts with the US, whose policy rules and institutions result from a sedimentation of influences, from the early Federal Reserve Act of 1913 and the post-depression Banking Act of 1935 to the Keynesian inspiration of the Employment Act of 1946 and the Humphrey-Hawkins Act of 1978 as well as neo-Ricardian, monetarist and supply-side influences.

The outlook

A major issue is whether the policy system of the euro area has reached an equilibrium or whether it can be expected to undergo further significant transformations. One view holds that the major choices have been made and that all the essential tenets of the system are in place. Another one emphasizes that the EU is still on a learning curve and that it is too early to say whether some form of collective governance can be expected to emerge.

If the first view is correct, the euro area can be expected to follow a medium-term-oriented, non-activist monetary policy and a fiscal policy that limits itself to letting the automatic stabilizers move freely, with very little aim at discretionary action, at least for the euro area as a whole.[14] In such a system, there would be built-in stabilizers, but neither monetary nor fiscal policy would take responsibility for the overall management of the economic cycle. The policy mix would be the *ex post* result of decisions taken by individual actors in accordance with predefined rules.

Assessing such systems per se is not the purpose of this chapter. Here, our focus is on a comparison with the US and on implications for EU–US relations. While some US policy-makers find merit in the idea of predefined rules, little in the country's political institutions or traditions suggests that it could go very far in this direction. As to the relationship between the EU and the US, one may speculate that US governments would generally be happy with a Europe that follows a rules-based approach to macroeconomic policy and leaves to the US the task of being the world's Stackelberg leader. However, circumstances could also arise in which the US would expect Europe to undertake discretionary action, either in connection with the exchange rate of the euro vis-à-vis the dollar, or in response to common shocks affecting both the US and Europe.

According to the second view, an alternative scenario would be for the participants in the euro area to develop institutions that would equip the area with an ability to make policy choices, including through discretionary decisions. When the Eurogroup was created in 1998 its (frequently but not exclusively French) promoters wanted it to be able to undertake policy coordination and for that purpose expected it to become a kind of collective executive body (Jacquet and Pisani-Ferry, 2000; von Hagen and Mundschenk, 2001). Further proposals have been made to assign to the Eurogroup or a euro-area council the responsibility of making decisions that apply only to the euro-area countries or to entrust the group with a capacity to vote by qualified majority on economic policy guidelines for the whole area (Lamy and Pisani-Ferry, 2002; Coeuré and Pisani-Ferry, 2004). The logic of these proposals is that the Eurogroup should, in some circumstances, be able to make decisions for the area as a whole even though implementation would be left to the national governments. If this approach prevails, the functioning of the euro area will move somewhat closer to the US model.

The jury is still out. A majority of member states certainly favours the status quo, but two recently introduced changes indicate that the euro-area policy system has not yet reached its equilibrium. First, the rotating Eurogroup presidency has been replaced by a fixed presidency. Although decision procedures remain unchanged, the adoption of a fixed presidency is a victory for the advocates of a more visible and more active Eurogroup. Second, the reform of the Stability Pact has introduced a dose of economic judgement in what was initially regarded as a purely rules-based system. Before deciding sanctions, ministers now have to exercise judgement as regards the origins of a deficit, the economic situation, or the nature of the expenditures.

For the longer run, Europe continues to hesitate between two views of monetary integration, which Maastricht tried to reconcile. On the one hand, there are those who, in a spirit reminiscent of the nineteenth-century gold standard, seek to depoliticize macroeconomic management and to ensure that economic policy abides by a set of fixed rules. On the other hand, there are those who, in the tradition of the twentieth century, regard fiscal and monetary policy as key instruments that have to be used for minimizing the adjustments imposed on society by external shocks. These two views are both compatible with the goal of price stability and a scrupulous respect of the central bank's independence. But they correspond to two different policy philosophies.

Summing up

For the macro field, the upshot of our analysis is that if anything, Europe has become more distant from the US. This assertion needs to be qualified, as differentiation takes place against the background of convergence on some basic macroeconomic and institutional principles – stable prices, an independent central bank, fiscal sustainability, etc. It may also be less long-lasting than suggested by the present policy setting. Nevertheless, the reasons to believe that even if it evolves, Europe will remain more inclined than the US towards a rules-based, non-activist, and rather inertial policy philosophy have roots in the Union's constitutional set-up, especially in the lesser role of the political process and the need to achieve consensus to amend the treaties.

6 The social dimension

The 'varieties of capitalism' approach regarded corporate ownership, control, financing and competition as well as competition and relationship with the state as the main factors behind international differentiation. For the reasons we have explained, we doubt this can still be the case in an area of globalization – although we recognize that convergence is far from complete and is bound to take time.

Our discussion on macroeconomic policy leads us to single out some factors of differentiation that may prove durable. But we recognize that even significantly different macroeconomic policy philosophies are unlikely to give rise to sharp differentiations. Assuming that US macroeconomic policy-makers will remain more willing than their EU counterparts to take on the role of insurers vis-à-vis the private sector, and that this may in turn reinforce the European private sector's relative risk-aversion in comparison to that of its US counterpart, this is unlikely to create a deep divide between the two sides of the Atlantic.

There is however a domain where very little convergence can be observed either across the Atlantic or even within Europe. It is the social sphere. Contrary to early expectations, global integration has not led to convergence in the level of social insurance spending or in the delineation of the relative responsibilities of states and markets in the provision of social services such as old-age insurance and health care. Neither have the principles underlying unemployment insurance and welfare assistance converged. Finally, labour market institutions remain worlds apart. Gøsta Esping-Andersen's (1990) notion of several worlds of welfare capitalism remains accurate. Furthermore, research into the motives for the differences between the US and Europe have emphasized permanent factors such as the nature of political institutions and the ethnic composition of the population (Alesina and Glaeser, 2004).

In a similar vein, convergence within Europe is hardly noticeable in spite of talks of a European social model. Labour market institutions remain extremely diverse and do not exhibit more pronounced convergence than within the OECD as a whole, as illustrated by Figure 11.4 taken from Pisani-Ferry (2005). While Blanchard and Giavazzi (2003) have pointed out that deregulation in the goods markets should over time translate into reform of the labour markets, the evidence so far is that the process is at best a slow one. The so-called 'European employment strategy' and the 'Lisbon strategy' adopted in 2000 to coordinate economic and especially labour market reforms have not delivered the expected results, and they have been looked at with increasing scepticism.

There is even less convergence in the fields of pensions, health care and welfare, which are very much in the realm of national states. In fact, except for very basic provisions regarding working conditions or gender equality at work, European harmonization has not extended to social policies, which remain the responsibility of national governments or social partners within countries. Boeri (2002) and Sapir (2005) can thus underline the persistence of no less than four social models within the EU-15 involving different degrees of efficiency and different trade-offs between efficiency and equity: a continental one (Germany, France), a Nordic one (Scandinavia, Netherlands), an Anglo-Saxon one (UK, Ireland) and a Mediterranean one (Italy, Spain).

A fundamental reason for this persistence is that labour mobility within the EU remains extremely low. In spite of the treaty provisions according to which the movements of persons is (together with those of goods, services and capital) one of the 'four freedoms' that form the basis of the Single Market, the untold consensus in the EU has for long been that mobility should remain as low as possible. Table 11.2 shows that in most of the EU-15 member states, and all large ones, residents from other EU countries represent a small fraction of the

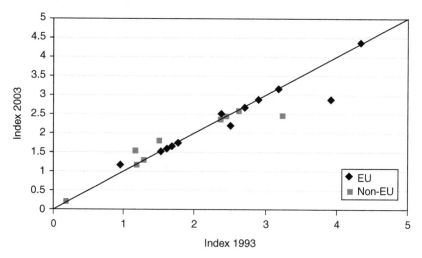

Figure 11.4 Employment protection for permanent workers, 1993 and 2003.

population. Furthermore, only in three countries (Britain, Ireland and Sweden) has the accession of the new member states from Central and Eastern Europe been accompanied by the liberalization of migrations. The 12 other members of the former EU-15 have made use of the possibility of keeping temporary restrictions for up to seven years.

In addition, the 2004 proposal by the Commission to introduce a 'home country principle' according to which providers of cross-border services would be subject to the legislation of their home country instead of that of the country where the service is being provided met fierce opposition in several member states, especially France where this proposal played a role in the rejection of the referendum on the European constitution. Although the issue involved many technical arguments, the main reason for popular rejection was, again, the fear that it would undermine the (French) social model. Similar reactions have been

Table 11.2 EU10 and EU15 nationals as percentage of destination country's working age population aged 15–64

Country of destination	Nationality	
	EU10[1]	EU15[1]
Belgium	0.2	2.7
Czech Republic	1.0	0.1
Denmark	0.1	0.2
Germany	0.2/0.9[2]	1.0
Estonia	0.0	0.1
Greece	0.1	:
Spain	0.0	0.1
France	0.0	0.0
Ireland	1.9	:
Italy	0.1	:
Latvia	0.0	0.0
Lithuania	0.0	0.0
Hungary	0.0	0.0
Malta	0.1	0.8
Netherlands	0.2	:
Austria	0.7/1.2[2]	:
Poland	0.0	0.0
Portugal	0.0	0.0
Slovenia	0.0	0.0
Slovakia	0.0	0.0
Finland	0.0	0.0
Sweden	0.1	0.0
United Kingdom	0.4	:

Source: European Commission Report on the Functioning of Transitional Arrangements on the Accession Treaty, 2006. Data sources differ from country to country.

Notes
1 EU10=New member states.
   EU15=Old member states.
2 First figure refers to foreign workers stock and second to work permits.

observed in other member states such as Belgium or Germany, as well as in Scandinavian countries.

More precisely, a distinction should be drawn between labour market regulation where some pressure towards convergence does exist and the redistribution and social insurance sphere where national models do not exhibit any convergence. The revised Lisbon strategy presented by the European Commission in 2005 puts emphasis on employment rate convergence and is underpinned by an ongoing benchmarking of national labour market policies. While wage negotiation patterns, unemployment insurance systems and employment protection regimes still differ from country to country, it can be argued that there is a trend towards convergence. Health care, pensions, and welfare systems, however, remain disconnected, as well as tax and redistribution systems.

It can even be speculated that against the background of different national preferences, one-dimensional convergence in the governance and the financing of the corporate sector contributes to maintaining and even to increasing divergence in the social models. For example, differences in collective risk aversion could in the past result in companies insuring their employees to a different degree against economic risks, yet in the context of global capitalism those differences are more likely to surface in public social insurance institutions.

Differences in some of the basic tenets of the social contract are thus likely to persist across the Atlantic and may even widen as US and European collective preferences regarding, for example, the degree of redistribution through taxes and transfers, or the degree of protection against economic risks that is provided by the social safety net seem to be more distant than they were in the 1970s. Within Europe, convergence is at best a very slow process driven by policy learning rather than mandated harmonization, explicit coordination or market pressure. As pointed out by Sapir (2005), it may lead the least efficient systems to reform themselves, therefore implying convergence in the efficiency dimension, but there is no reason to believe that convergence will extend to the equity dimension.

It is therefore in national preferences and their influences on the social institutions, rather than the nature of capitalism, that the most profound differences between developed economies are today located. This has led Amable (2003) to claim that diversity of capitalism is alive and well.

We do not agree. A situation where the rules and institutions governing capital, goods and services market regulation are to a very large extent common (either within Europe or between Europe and the US) while rules and institutions governing redistribution, social insurance and even labour markets remain diverse would bear little relationship with the one that gave rise to the varieties of capitalism school of thought. While it was an appropriate characterization until the 1980s, today we regard 'diversity of capitalism' as a misnomer which can only conceal the depth of the changes that have taken place. We prefer, instead, to speak of the coexistence and relationship between a global capitalism and diverse social institutions.

This is not a semantic issue. From an analytical standpoint, whether different varieties of capitalism coexist and how global capitalism adapts to societies characterized by differing social contracts are two different issues. To confuse them does not help tackling the research challenges.

7 Conclusions

In this chapter, we have examined how differences between the European and American economic systems and policies have evolved over the last quarter century. Our main conclusions are as follows:

1 There has been considerable convergence of Europe towards the US model of a market economy. Temporary exceptions apart, little remains of the traditional models of capitalism that were not so long ago considered permanent characteristics of the major European countries.
2 European integration has been a major driving force of this convergence. In both the macro- and the microeconomic fields, it has led to a near-complete transformation of the European regulatory framework. The US has not undergone similar transformations.
3 European integration could be regarded as providing a kind of 'airlock' for the adaptation of European economic regimes to globalization or as offering a 'shelter' for the emergence of a genuinely European variety of capitalism. In spite of (failed) attempts at developing European industrial policies, the evidence suggests that in the micro field, Europe has played the former rather than the latter role.
4 In the macro field, convergence is less pronounced. Although the end goals of US and EU macro policies are similar, differences are apparent in the definition of the role of macroeconomic policy, the degree of activism and the degree of inertia of principles, rules and institutions. Those differences are likely to be durable.
5 Europe's convergence towards a model characterized by a stability-oriented monetary policy, non-activist, sustainability-oriented fiscal policies, free competition in products and capital markets, and a very limited role for targeted government intervention is both a product of trends affecting the world economy and of idiosyncratic developments. European integration has increased the weight of common rules and reduced the scope for discretionary economic policy decisions. This can be observed both in the micro and in the macro fields. A difference is thus emerging between a rules-based Europe and the US, where discretion remains a major characteristic of economic policy.
6 European rules are generally enshrined in treaty or treaty-like legal texts whose revision requires unanimity or supermajority. There is thus an element of inertia in Europe which is absent in the US. Furthermore, European rules and principles have generally been defined within a short period of time and for that reason they tend to lock in a policy philosophy

characteristic of the 1980s and the 1990s. Forces of inertia do exist in the US, but they are probably less powerful.

7   Cooperation between a Europe that abides by rules and a US in which policy choices retain a distinctive discretionary character could result in the US taking the role of a Stackelberg leader while Europe would essentially follow its rules. However it could also lead to divergence and conflict. The EU is likely to behave increasingly as the champion of rules in international economic relations, and this may lead to enduring divergence with the US.

8   Labour markets and to an even higher degree redistribution and social insurance, pensions, and the provision of public services in education and health care are key areas in which virtually no convergence can be observed, and which have not (not yet, at least) been affected by European integration. The EU has thus produced bounded convergence, and here lies the true specificity of the European model.

9   This, however, should not justify continuing to speak of a persistence of diversity in the models of capitalism. We prefer, instead, to speak of the coexistence and relationship between global capitalism and diverse social institutions.

Notes

1 This chapter was prepared for the Second Annual Berkeley-Vienna Conference on The US and European Economies in Comparative Perspective, Berkeley, 12–13 September 2005. An earlier version of this chapter was presented on 11–12 April 2002 in the Harvard-wiiw Conference on EU–US relations. We thank the participants in both conferences as well as Barry Eichengreen and Jonah Levy for their remarks and criticisms on earlier drafts.

2 Data for other countries are for the year 2000. The French figure for that year was 27 per cent, slightly lower than in 2002.

3 The figure is even more impressive if we narrow the scope to the CAC40 companies, for which foreign shareholders account for 50 per cent of total shareholders (*Les Échos*, Audit de la France, 2002).

4 Although we do not have precise figures, only estimates (except for Total).

5 Another illustration of the change is the fact that Governor Fazio's manoeuvres to avoid the takeover of Italian banks by foreign banks have ended up in creating embarrassment for the Italian authorities.

6 It is significant that Jacques Delors, by his own confession, only set in motion the process of liberalization having found that no other direction for relaunching European integration would have gained the support of the Member States.

7 In spring 2005, a Commission proposal to introduce a framework law for the liberalization of the service sector was fiercely attacked by French politicians as it would have provided a more effective instrument to foster intra-EU competition in previously sheltered sectors. In the campaign before the referendum on the draft constitution, the 'Polish plumber' came to epitomize the fear of 'social dumping' in the services market. At the insistence of President Chirac and other heads of state, the directive project was temporarily withdrawn.

8 When the first *Esprit* Programme was launched in 1984, the dominant view was that Europe had to catch up with the US in the information technology sphere through producing computers and electronic components. Eight years after the launching of

the programme, in 1992, the results were mediocre: the EC was still buying three times as much as it sold to the US.

9 Furthermore, member states proceeded in an uncoordinated way as the Council had decided that the allocation of licences could be left to the member states. Some member states such as Finland and Sweden chose to give away the licenses for free, while others such as the UK and Germany opted for an auction procedure explicitly aiming at maximizing public revenue and others again to sell the licences in a beauty contest. As a result, the price of licences varied between 630 euro per user to 43 euros per user (Cohen and Mougeot, 2001).

10 Recent surveys such as Gros *et al.* (2001) do not provide evidence of an increase in European productivity growth that would even partially match what has been observed in the US.

11 We are grateful to Xavier Debrun from the IMF for having provided us with the data and to Karine Serfaty for research assistance.

12 ECB Council decision of 13 October 1998.

13 Resolution of the European Council on the Stability and Growth Pact of 17 June 1997.

14 This could be different for individual member states that could rely on discretionary fiscal policy to counteract asymmetric developments.

References

Acemoglu, D., Aghion, P. and Zilibotti, F. (2002) 'Distance to frontier, selection, and economic growth', NBER Working Paper, no. 9066.

Aglietta, M. (1976) *Régulation et crises du capitalisme*. Paris: Calmann-Lévy, reprint Paris: Odile Jacob, 1997.

Albert, M. (1991) *Capitalisme contre capitalisme*. Paris: Le Seuil.

Alesina, A. and Glaeser, E. (2004) *Fighting Poverty in the US and Europe: A World of Difference*. Oxford University Press.

Alesina, A., Angeloni, I. and Schuknecht, L. (2002) 'What does the European Union Do?', *unpublished manuscript*, June.

Alesina, A., Blanchard, O., Gali, J., Giavazzi, F. and Uhlig, H. (2001) *Defining a Macroeconomic Framework for the Euro Area*, Centre for Economic Policy Research, Monitoring the ECB series, no. 3.

Amable, B. (2003) *The Diversity of Modern Capitalism*. Oxford University Press.

Artus, P. and Wyplosz, C. (2002) 'Politique monétaire de la banque centrale européenne', *Rapport du Conseil d'analyse économique*, Paris.

Baldwin, R. (1989) 'The Growth Effects of 1992', *Economic Policy*, October.

Banque de France (2001) *Rapport annuel 2000 du Conseil national du crédit et du titre*.

Becht, M. and Böhmer, E. (2003) 'Voting Control in German Corporations', *International Review of Law and Economics* 23: 1–29.

Becht, M. and Röell, A. (1999) 'Blockholdings in Europe: An International Comparison', *European Economic Review* (43)4–6: 1049–1056.

Blanchard, O. and Giavazzi, F. (2003) 'Macroeconomic Effects of Regulation and Deregulation in Goods and Labor Markets', *Quarterly Journal of Economics*, August, pp. 879–907.

Boeri, T. (2002) 'Let Social Policy Models Compete and Europe Will Win', paper presented at a Conference hosted by the Kennedy School of Government, Harvard University, 11–12 April.

Boyer, R. (1986) *La théorie de la regulation: une analyse critique*. Paris: La Découverte.

Clarida, R., Gali, J. and Gertler, M. (1998) 'Monetary Rules in Practice: Some International Evidence', *European Economic Review*, vol. 42, no. 6, June.

Coeuré, B. and Pisani-Ferry, J. (2004) 'Autour de l'euro et au-delà', in *Perspectives de la coopération renforcée dans l'Union européenne*. Paris: Commissariat général du Plan.

Cohen, É. (1992) *Le colbertisme high-tech*. Paris: Hachette.

Cohen, É. (1996) 'Europe between market and power: industrial policies', in Yves Mény, Pierre Muller and Jean Louis Queremonne (eds), *Adjusting to Europe*. London: Routledge.

Cohen, É. and Lorenzi, J.-H. (2000) *Politiques industrielles en Europe*, Rapport du Conseil d'analyse économique no. 26, La Documentation française, Paris, available at www.cae.gouv.fr.

Cohen, É. and Mougeot, M. (2001) *Enchères et action publique*, Rapport du Conseil d'analyse économique no. 34, La Documentation française, Paris, available at www.cae.gouv.fr.

Crouch, C. and Streeck, W. (1996) *Les capitalismes en Europe*. Paris: La Découverte.

Dertouzos, M., Lester, R. and Solow, R. (1989) *Made in America*. Cambridge: MIT Press.

Didier, M. and Lorenzi, J.-H. (2002) *Enjeux économiques de l'UMTS*, Rapport du Conseil d'analyse économique no. 36, La Documentation française, Paris, available at www.cae.gouv.fr.

Emerson, M. *et al.* (1988) 'The Economics of 1992', *European Economy*, No. 35.

Esping-Andersen, G. (1990) *The Three Worlds of Welfare Capitalism*. Cambridge: Polity.

European Central Bank (2000) 'The Two Pillars of the ECB's Monetary Policy Strategy', *ECB Monthly Bulletin*, November.

Gali, J. (2001) 'Monetary Policy in the Early Years of EMU', paper prepared for the European Commission, available on www.econ.upf.es/%7Egali/html_files/research.htm.

Greenspan, A. (2004) 'Risk and Uncertainty in Monetary Policy', remarks at the meetings of the American Economic Association, San Diego, California, www.federalreserve.gov/boarddocs/speeches/2004/20040103/default.htm.

Gros, D., Davanne, O., Emerson, M., Mayer, T., Tabellini, G. and Thygesen, N. (2000) 'The Cost of Muddling Through', *Second Report of the CEPS Macroeconomic Policy Group*, Centre for European Policy Studies, Brussels.

Gros, D., Jimeno, J.F., Monticelli, C., Tabellini, G. and Thygesen, N. (2001) 'Testing the Speed Limits for Europe', *Third Report of the CEPS Macroeconomic Policy Group*, Centre for European Policy Studies, Brussels.

Hall, P. and Soskice, D. (eds) (2001) *Varieties of Capitalism*. Oxford: Oxford University Press.

IMF (2004) *World Economic Outlook*, Washington, DC: IMF.

Issing, O. (2002) 'The Role of Monetary Policy in Managing Economic Risks', address to the National Association of Business Economist, Washington, 26 March, available on www.ecb.int.

Jacquet, P. and Pisani-Ferry, J. (2000) *Economic Policy Coordination in the Euro zone: What Has Been Achieved? What Can Be Done?*, Centre for European Reform, London.

Kitshelt, H., Lange, P., Marks, G. and Stephens, J. (1999) 'Continuity and Change in Contemprary Capitalism', Cambridge University Press.

Lamy, P. and Pisani-Ferry, J. (2002) *The Europe We Want*, Policy Network, London.

Mankiw, N.G. (2002) 'US Monetary Policy in the 1990s', in Jeffrey Frankel and Peter Orszag (eds), *American Economic Policy in the 1990s*, Cambridge: MIT Press.

Meyer, L.B. (2002) 'Rules and discretion', Remarks at the Owen Graduate School of

Management, Vanderbilt University, 16 January, available on www.federalreserve. gov/boarddodcs/speeches/.

OECD (2004) *Economic Outlook*, June, Paris: OECD.

Pisani-Ferry, J. (2002) 'Fiscal Discipline and Policy Coordination in the Eurozone: Assessment and Proposals', paper prepared for the European Commission's Group of Economic Advisers, April.

Pisani-Ferry, J. (2005) 'What's Wrong with Lisbon?', CESifo Forum, Summer.

Rajan, R. and Zingales, L. (2003) *Saving Capitalism from Capitalists*. New York: Crown Business.

Rodrik, D. (2003) *Growth Strategies*, mimeo prepared for the *Handbook of Economic Growth*.

Sapir, A. (2005) Globalisation and the Reform of European Social Models, mimeo.

Shonfield, A. (1965) *Modern Capitalism*. New York: Oxford University Press.

Tyson, L. (1992) *Who's Bashing Whom: Trade Conflict in High Technology Industries*. Washington, DC: Institute for International Economics.

von Hagen, J. and Mundschenk, S. (2001) 'The Political Economy of Policy Coordination in EMU', paper prepared for the European Commission workshop on the functioning of EMU, mimeo.

Zysman, J. (1983) *Governments, Markets and Growth: Financial Systems and the Politics of Industrial Change*. Ithaca, NY: Cornell University Press.

12 Between neo-liberalism and no liberalism

Progressive approaches to economic liberalization in Western Europe

Jonah D. Levy

1 Introduction

In the literature of comparative politics, political economy, and globalization, progressive policy is typically portrayed as an *alternative* to economic liberalization: social democracy as an alternative to neo-liberalism (Garrett, 1998); a social investment strategy as an alternative to neo-liberal austerity (Boix, 1998); a coordinated market economy as an alternative to a liberal market economy (Hall and Soskice, 2001). Progressive approaches enable governments to *avoid* economic liberalization. It is by avoiding liberalization that progressive governments are able to project sovereignty and give expression to their political values.[1]

I believe that this dichotomous vision rests on a limited conception of economic liberalization. My central claim is that there is more than one way to liberalize. *How* a country liberalizes is as important as *whether* it liberalizes. Economic liberalization need not be synonymous with the harsh, neo-liberal methods of Ronald Reagan, Margaret Thatcher, or George W. Bush. It is possible to reconcile liberalization with concerns about equity and the disadvantaged, depending on how liberalizing reforms are constructed. Moreover, such progressive liberalizing reforms are not simply abstract possibilities, but rather the very real practice of a number of European governments.

I call this approach to economic and social reform 'progressive liberalism.' Progressive liberalism accepts many of the liberal arguments about the virtues of reduced government spending, lower taxes, and more flexible labour markets. Where it parts company is in the distributional arena. Progressive liberalism adopts a Rawlsian approach to economic liberalization, constructing liberalizing reforms so as to preserve or even enhance the well being of low-income and disadvantaged citizens. Simply stated, those at the bottom of the income scale should benefit more (or, in the worst case, suffer less) from economic liberalization than those at the top – and the favourable impact should be immediate, rather than a long-term, trickle-down effect of a stronger economy.

This chapter provides an overview of progressive liberal practices in Western Europe. It is organized into five sections. Section 2 analyses the linkages between left politics and progressive liberalism. Sections 3 to 5 describe three sets of progressive liberal reforms: deficit reduction in Italy and Sweden (Section 3); tax relief in France, Holland, and Britain (Section 4); and efforts to boost labour market participation in Holland and Sweden (Section 5). In each case, I show how European governments have sought to implement liberalizing reforms, while avoiding the increases in inequality and poverty associated with neo-liberalism. Finally, the conclusion (Section 6) briefly discusses the political and theoretical implications of progressive liberalism.

2 Left politics and progressive liberalism

The progressive approach to economic and social reform has long rested on a mixture of Marx and Keynes. Marx provided an endpoint, a sense of history or direction to reform. The goal of progressive policy was to move society towards socialism through structural reforms like nationalizations or codetermination that rolled back the frontiers of capitalism. Keynes offered more immediate and tangible relief (Przeworski and Wallerstein, 1984). Redistributive measures on behalf of the disadvantaged could be justified not only in social terms, but also in economic terms. The Keynesian strategy of sustaining aggregate demand centred on boosting the purchasing power of those who were most likely to spend. Given that the poor spend more of their income and save less than the rich, economic logic favoured channelling resources to the poor.

Since the late 1970s, both Marxism and Keynesianism have largely fallen into disrepute. Socialism failed to deliver either freedom or prosperity. It has ceased to offer a model for the future. The record of Keynesianism is more mixed. It can be argued that Keynesian policies helped smooth business cycles in the post-war boom period, although there were certainly many examples of mistimed and counterproductive stimulus packages (Boltho, 1982). Even if we allow that Keynesianism is desirable, however, it has become increasingly impractical. With the dramatic increase in trade flows, demand stimulus tends to 'leak,' sucking in imports (and swelling trade deficits), as opposed to reviving domestic production. Moreover, central bank leaders, who have grown in power and independence, generally frown on budget deficits, responding to Keynesian measures by tightening monetary policy and dampening growth. It also bears mentioning that Keynesianism is of little or no use when economic problems are located on the supply side, rather than the demand side (poor workplace organization, backwards technology, insufficient capacity, etc.), as has often been the case in recent times.

The eclipse of Marxism and especially Keynesianism has deprived left-leaning governments of their primary means for reconciling the promotion of economic efficiency with distributional commitments to low-income and disadvantaged groups. The neo-liberal paradigm, which has come to dominate economic policy-making, more or less denies this possibility. As British Prime Minister, Margaret Thatcher famously argued, 'There Is No Alternative' (TINA). In the 1980s and 1990s, Thatcher revived the British economy and restored full employment through a combination of tax cuts, deregulation, privatization, and curbs on social spending. These reforms were anything but painless. Poverty and inequality grew dramatically, while Britain's deindustrialized cities began to experience American-style social pathologies, including teenage pregnancy, drug abuse, and violent crime. Still, Thatcher contended, there was no alternative: the choice was between neo-liberal reform and no reform.

The recent experiences of leftist governments in major European countries would seem to confirm Mrs Thatcher's understanding. On the one hand, the leftist coalition of Lionel Jospin that governed France from 1997 to 2002 approximated the strategy of no liberalism, of resisting liberalism. On the other hand, the Social Democratic–Green coalition of Gerhard Schroeder that governed Germany from 1998 to 2005 followed a course of cautious neo-liberalism. Both strategies presented serious drawbacks.

The French left has generally defined progressive principles in terms of resistance to economic liberalism. The role of a progressive is to combat the extension of market forces, not to cultivate the market. A strategy of resistance to liberalization, while appealing to the leftist faithful, suffers two important problems. The first is that the left is placed on the defensive, championing what is in many cases an unpopular status quo. For example, in the name of progressive principles, Prime Minister Jospin refused to introduce any job search requirements into France's unemployment insurance system and guaranteed minimum income (RMI). Yet a strong majority of French voters supported some kind of reasonable job search obligation. Jospin's resistance to labour market reform lent credibility to conservative critiques that he was avoiding hard choices, that he was placating interest groups rather than modernizing the country – a charge that damaged Jospin badly in his unsuccessful campaign for the presidency in 2002.

The second problem of resisting liberalization is that such resistance cedes control of reform to actors other than a government of the left. To continue with the previous example, the Jospin government did not prevent the reform of the unemployment system. Rather, the reforms were initiated by the French employer association and extended by a government of the right that succeeded Jospin in 2002. Not surprisingly, these reforms, reflecting the preferences of employers and political conservatives, tended to be long on obligations for the unemployed and short on countervailing compensations. The same trajectory occurred in the case of pension and health care reform: Jospin resisted change, only to have his conservative successors enact reforms that slashed benefits and increased payments in a fairly regressive manner.

If the traditional leftist strategy has been to resist economic liberalization at every turn, self-styled 'modernizers,' such as Gerhard Schroeder in Germany, have frequently gone to the opposite extreme, pursuing an essentially neo-liberal agenda under the guise of 'modernization' and activism. The phrase 'Nixon goes to China' is invoked to describe this strategy (Pierson, 2001; Green-Pedersen, 2002). Just as only a fierce anti-Communist like Richard Nixon could recognize Communist China, only a Social Democratic leader like Schroeder could slash social spending, loosen labour market regulations, and lower taxes. Schroeder sought to appeal to German voters on two counts: first, as an economic modernizer, introducing needed market reforms into Germany's stagnant economy (the so-called 'Agenda 2010'); second, as a social modernizer, making Germany a more tolerant and cosmopolitan country through a number of 'post-materialist,' lifestyle reforms (liberalization of citizenship rules, gay rights, restrictions on nuclear power, etc.).

The principal drawback of Schroeder's Nixon-goes-to-China approach is that it hurt low-income and vulnerable groups. Both Schroeder's pension and tax reforms had regressive consequences and, in a reversal of roles, it was the centre-right Christian Democrats who were calling for a fairer sharing of costs and benefits. Schroeder's most controversial initiative was the 'Hartz IV' labour market reforms introduced at the beginning of 2005 that dramatically scaled back unemployment benefits. The presumption behind Hartz IV was that the unemployed were not taking jobs because benefits are too generous. Yet with the German economy in recession and unemployment having surged from four million to over five million during Schroeder's tenure in office, there was clearly a problem of job creation.

The Nixon-goes-to-China approach confronts electoral as well as social problems. It disorients and discourages the leftist faithful, who are inclined to either stay at home or punish the government at the polls. Shortly after assuming office, Schroeder's government was defeated in a series of regional *Länder* elections, losing control of the second chamber of parliament (the *Bundesrat*) in 2000. The Hartz IV reforms triggered a series of protests in German cities throughout 2004, notably in the East, led by union members and leftist politicians. Dissatisfied leftists within the SPD then broke away to create a new party, the WASG, which merged with the revamped former East German Communist party (PDS). The product of that merger, the *Linkspartei*, received over 8 per cent of the vote in the 2005 elections, draining support from the SPD and arguably costing Schroeder his position as chancellor. More generally, Schroeder's liberalizing reforms were so unpopular that he went down to defeat against a colourless and inexperienced conservative adversary, Angela Merkel, who – by all accounts – ran a very poor campaign.

Taken together, the Jospin and Schroeder experiences appear to validate the TINA perspective. Jospin preserved social protection at the expense of reform, while Schroeder pursued reform at the expense of social protection. Jospin and Schroeder do not represent the sum total of all options available to leftist reformers, however. In between the no reforms of leftist traditionalists and the neo-liberal reforms of the self-styled 'modernizers,' there is a third possibility – progressive liberal reforms.

The notion that economic liberalism can take more than one form has historical precedent in the plasticity and diversity of earlier, overarching economic and social arrangements. The post-war 'golden age' was marked by the so-called 'Keynesian compromise' or 'compromise of the Keynesian welfare state' (Offe, 1984; Przeworski and Wallerstein, 1984). The general framework of this compromise was that left parties and unions accepted the private ownership of the means of production and widespread managerial discretion in the organization of the workplace, while employers accepted Keynesian demand management and a sizable welfare state to cushion the working class from the vicissitudes of capitalism. Yet within this general framework, both Keynesianism and the welfare state admitted tremendous cross-national variation.

We may have all been Keynesians, in the words of Richard Nixon, but Keynesianism looked very different from one country to the next (Boltho, 1982; Hall, 1989). Many countries increased social spending and government deficits in a recession, in the classic Keynesian manner. Indeed, the operation of large welfare states tended to produce this effect automatically. Yet there was more than one way to engineer a budget deficit. The US tended to implement Keynesian ideas through tax cuts and military spending, rather than social spending. French authorities ran deficits primarily as a result of subsidies to business. Sweden privileged public investments in a recession. Under the general rubric of 'Keynesianism,' countries pursued very different economic strategies with very different distributional consequences.

The same observation could be made with respect to the welfare state. If welfare states expanded dramatically in the post-war period, social protection took very different forms from one country to the next (Titmuss, 1987; Esping-Andersen, 1990; Huber and Stephens, 2001). Gøsta Esping-Andersen identifies three varieties or 'worlds' of welfare capitalism: a liberal world, aiming to limit hardship among the 'deserving poor' and relying heavily on tax-subsidized private provision; a Christian Democratic world, seeking to preserve social order and hierarchy through income-based benefits; and a Social Democratic world, striving to expand citizenship and alleviate worker dependence on employment – what Esping-Andersen terms 'decommodification' (Esping-Andersen, 1985, 1990).

Another important insight provided by Esping-Andersen is that partisanship figured prominently in the construction of these various welfare regimes, and not just for parties of the left. Although the welfare state might appear to be at odds with everything that conservative parties stand for, Esping-Andersen and others have shown that centre-right Christian Democrats erected welfare regimes that were essentially as expensive as those established by the Social Democratic left (Esping-Andersen, 1990; Huber et al., 1993; Kersbergen, 1995). The reason is that Christian Democrats were able to forge welfare states that corresponded to their values and the interests of their constituents: providing the largest benefits to those who earned the most; dividing and demobilizing the working class; focusing on transfer payments, rather than social services, so as to keep the state bureaucracy small; and reinforcing traditional family structures, the so-called 'male breadwinner' model. In an analogous manner, this chapter suggests that left-leaning parties, operating on the apparently inhospitable terrain of economic liberalization, can construct liberalizing reforms in ways that are compatible with their political principles and the interests of their supporters.

I call this effort to reconcile market reform and distributional equity 'progressive liberalism.' Progressive liberalism fuses a liberal concern for efficiency with a Rawlsian commitment to low-income groups. Under progressive liberalism, the character of the liberalized economy – of the smaller government, lower taxes, and more flexible labour markets – is itself defined by progressive social principles and concerns for the disadvantaged. Liberalizing reforms are designed to benefit those at the bottom of the income scale more than those at the top and to do so immediately, rather than as the result of some uncertain, future, trickle-down effect.

Figure 12.1 situates progressive liberalism relative to the main alternative economic strategies. It draws two distinctions. The first relates to the *principal institution or agent of economic coordination*: the state in the top half of the figure; the market in the bottom. The second distinction relates to the *beneficiaries of state policies*: workers and low-income groups on the left side of the figure; employers and affluent groups on the right.

The top half of the figure is composed of two ideal-types of state guidance of the economy. *Social Democracy* (quadrant 1) represents the pro-labour variant of statism. Characteristic policies include: redistributive Keynesianism, Social Democratic welfare states, and various forms of *Marxisant* reforms, such as codetermination and nationalizations. The *developmental state* (quadrant 2) represents the pro-business variant of statism. Characteristic initiatives include: industrial policy, protectionism, and cheap credit. The corrupt or degenerated

Agent of economic coordination	Beneficiaries of state policies	
	Low-income groups	High-income groups
State	*Social democracy* – Socialism: nationalizations, codetermination – Redistributive Keynesianism – Social Democratic welfare state 1	*Developmental state* – Industrial policy, protectionism, cheap credit – Crony capitalism – Christian Democratic welfare state 2
Market	3 *Progressive liberalism* – Cuts in dysfunctional government programmes and programmes for affluent groups – Tax cuts for wage earners – Reduced protections for the non-employed, along with increased benefits for the employed	4 *Neo–liberalism* – Across-the-board spending cuts or cuts for programmes benefiting low-income groups – Tax cuts for the affluent – Reduced protections of workers and benefits for the non-employed

Figure 12.1 Progressive liberalism in comparative perspective.

version of this strategy is crony capitalism. When conservatives have expanded spending on social policy as well as industrial policy, this spending has tended to take the form of a Christian Democratic welfare state (also located in quadrant 2).

Over the past 25 years, there has been a general movement from the top of Figure 12.1 to the bottom, from state to market direction of the economy. (The movement has been somewhat less pronounced in social policy than in economic development policy.) Again, though, we can identify two variants, which are distinguished primarily by their distributional or class orientation. Both neo-liberalism (quadrant 4) and progressive liberalism (quadrant 3) seek to roll back dysfunctional regulations, increase labour market flexibility, and reduce state spending and taxation. But neo-liberalism tends to pursue these liberalizing objectives by redistributing resources upward, while progressive liberalism seeks to redistribute resources downward (or, at least, to limit the upward redistribution of resources). The result, as this chapter will show, is very different policies of economic liberalization. Whereas neo-liberalism cuts social spending across-the-board or targets low-income groups, progressive liberalism focuses cuts on dysfunctional programmes or those that benefit the affluent disproportionately. Whereas neo-liberalism reduces taxes on the highest earners, who pay the most taxes, progressive liberalism reduces taxes on wage earners, who have the greatest need and often confront the highest effective marginal tax rates. And whereas neo-liberalism promotes labour market flexibility by scaling back protections and benefits, progressive liberalism may curtail protections, but also takes measures to increase the returns to paid employment (to 'make work pay').

Progressive liberalism represents an ideal-type, not a widely diffused policy model. No government has openly proclaimed its allegiance to the progressive liberalism and implemented this agenda in a comprehensive, across-the-board manner. Still, the effort to reconcile liberalization and social justice has shaped the actions of a number of governments, however experimental and uncertain their strategies. By and large, the cases that come closest to the progressive liberal ideal-type are Sweden under the Social Democrats from 1994 to 2006, a Labour–Liberal coalition that governed Holland from 1994 to 2002, and Tony Blair's New Labour government in Britain. But even in countries like Italy, France, and Germany, one can find isolated instances of progressive liberal reform.

Progressive liberalism has generally been the product of *a constrained or corrective European left*. For parties of the right – even if the continental European right is different from the Anglo-American right – policies that expand the play of market forces fit well with their basic policy orientation, and the upward redistribution of wealth that accompanies such reforms benefits their electoral base. Thus, conservative parties are reasonably comfortable with a conventional neo-liberal agenda. For parties of the left, by contrast, economic liberalization challenges fundamental beliefs, while an upward redistribution of wealth harms their supporters. Consequently, the European left has tended to embark on liberalization with great reluctance, usually as a result of some kind of constraint. Progressive liberalization has emerged when this reluctant liberalization has been structured so as to assuage the distributional concerns of leftist advocates and voters.

All of the leftist governments examined in this chapter have operated in a constrained or corrective capacity. Often, the constraints have been economic or fiscal, such as Maastricht budget deficit targets. Both the centre-left in Italy and the Social Democrats in Sweden sought to reduce massive budget deficits in the 1990s. When the left gained power in these countries, the deficit exceeded 12 per cent of GDP, roughly double the peak US figure during the Reagan years and four times the Maastricht target. Qualifying for EMU was an explicit goal of the Italian government, meaning that the deficit had to be reduced quickly and dramatically.

Other constraints have been political, such as the need to govern in coalition with centre-right parties. In Holland, initial austerity reforms were conducted under a centre-right coalition from 1982 to 1989. The Labour party then entered the government as a junior partner in 1989, before leading a so-called 'Purple Coalition' with the Liberals from 1994 to 2002 (red of Labour + blue of the Liberals = purple). Thus, for Labour to have any influence, it needed to reach an agreement and make important concessions to centre-right allies.

Finally, in some cases, progressive reforms have emerged as a corrective to prior neo-liberal reforms by centre-right governments. This corrective undertaking has been most apparent in the case of Tony Blair's New Labour government in Britain, which assumed office after 18 years of Thatcherite reform. New Labour has accepted a considerable degree of economic liberalization, but has sought to harmonize the more liberal economic context with left values and constituent interests, in particular, by reducing poverty.

Progressive liberalism represents a possibility, not an inevitability. As we have seen, leftist governments in France and Germany have gravitated toward alternative approaches. If economic and political constraints have often laid the foundation for progressive reforms, other options remain available. Consequently, progressive liberalism is, to some extent, the product of strategic choice and political leadership.

The rest of this chapter describes progressive liberal policies of various European centre-left governments. My analysis focuses on three sets of liberalizing reforms: deficit reduction, tax relief, and labour market activation. For each case, I will proceed in four steps. First, I will define the traditional leftist position that opposes any change. Second, I will present the neo-liberal position, which favours change with regressive distributional implications. Third, I will show that the liberalizing reform in question does indeed harbour progressive potential. Fourth, I will describe how the reforms have been implemented in practice by European governments, so as to capture many of the benefits of neo-liberalism, while safeguarding or enhancing commitments to low-income and disadvantaged groups. I begin with the case of deficit reduction in Italy and Holland.

3 Reducing budget deficits and equity deficits

The commitment to increased government spending on social programmes has long been a defining feature of Social Democracy. Indeed, for Social Democratic scholars, the traditional measure of left power, of labour's 'power resources,' is social spending as a share of GDP. From this vantage, cuts in social programmes constitute a clear step backward.

The neo-liberal perspective on government spending is more critical. Social spending diverts resources from productive uses, crowds out private investment, and reduces work incentives. By and large, government spending is suspect, and reductions in social spending are desirable. The risk from a progressive standpoint, of course, is that such cuts – even if they generate some economic benefits – will increase the vulnerability and hardship of the poor.

Yet deficit reduction need not yield such regressive outcomes. The starting point for a progressive approach to deficit reduction is a more cold-hearted, calculating take on social spending. When systems of social protection absorb 30 to 40 per cent of GDP, as they do in most West European countries, 'not only the poor' are benefiting (Goodin and Le Grand, 1987). Much of the spending goes to middle-class or even affluent groups, and some of this money is used in ineffective or even counterproductive ways. In other words, a lot of social spending is at odds with progressive values and interests. By implication, then, it is possible to reduce social spending without undermining social justice.

The key to realizing this possibility is what I have termed turning 'vice into virtue' (Levy, 1999). The vice-into-virtue strategy targets inequities within the welfare system that are simultaneously a source of either economic inefficiency or substantial public spending. Savings are extracted, not from virtuous programmes that help the poor and disadvantaged, but rather from the attenuation of 'vices,' that is, cuts in programmes that concentrate benefits on the affluent, that are marked by patronage or fraud, that are patently dysfunctional, or that are at odds with stated programme objectives. An example of such an inefficient inequity might be generous disability pensions paid to hundreds of thousands of people who are neither sick nor disabled. By attenuating these historic 'vices' or inequities, progressive reformers may be able to extract resources with which to pursue a variety of 'virtuous' objectives, such as reducing budget deficits without slashing benefits to the truly needy. In more general terms, inherited welfare 'vices' can be manipulated so as to soften or even obviate the supposedly ineluctable trade-off between efficiency and equity.

The experience of Italy in the 1990s illustrates the possibilities for a vice-into-virtue approach to deficit reduction (Baccaro and Locke, 1996; Ferrera 1997; Mira d'Ercole and Terribile, 1998; Levy, 1999). Between 1992 and 1998, successive governments reduced the overall deficit from over 10 per cent of GDP to less than 3 per cent, enabling Italy to qualify for EMU. The reforms were conducted by a combination of technocratic governments, supported by parties of the left, and explicitly leftist governments, who were in office for the first time since the immediate post-war years. Tax and pension reform accounted for much of the deficit reduction. Obviously, some of these measures were painful. Still, the bulk of the savings came from the attenuation of unfair privileges that had been distributed to political supporters by the corrupt Christian Democratic establishment that had governed Italy throughout the post-war period. Three sets of 'vices' of the old Christian Democratic regime figured most prominently in the centre-left's austerity policies.

The first was the elimination of some of the most egregious forms of early retirement, notably so-called 'baby pensions' that allowed some civil servants to retire after a mere 20 years on the job. The left established a minimum retirement age of 57, while also requiring 35 years of contributions to qualify for a full pension. The second change was to harmonize the pension rules for all retirees. The main effect of the change was to scale back substantial government subsidies to many public-sector workers and to the self-employed, who are a relatively affluent group. The third change was to impose a minimum level of taxation on the self-employed. No longer could wealthy lawyers, doctors, and accountants pay little or no taxes by underreporting their earnings.

The Italian retirement age of 57 is still too low; further pension and budgetary reforms are likely to be necessary; and there was some fiscal backsliding under the right-wing Berlusconi government that governed from 2001 to 2006. For all these limitations, however, the changes of the 1990s bolstered Italy's fiscal position, while improving fairness and equity. Indeed, some Italian observers have gone so far as to describe the reforms as a 'success story' that 'makes transparent the conditions for financial sustainability and significantly reduces the large inequalities characterizing the old system' (Mira d'Ercole and Terribile, 1998).

It might be objected that the Italian experience is of little relevance to progressive reformers elsewhere because that country's system was so uniquely riddled with 'vices.' Scholars generally agree that among the three 'worlds of welfare capitalism' identified by Esping-Andersen, the Christian Democratic system (found in Germany, France, Austria, Belgium, and Holland) is the most problematic and unfair (Esping-Andersen, 1996b; Levy, 1999). It overtaxes labour, spends too much on 'passive' labour market programmes that pay people not to work (early retirement, disability pensions, unemployment benefits, etc.), favours 'insiders' at the expense of 'outsiders,' and excludes women and minorities from employment opportunities and welfare benefits. In the case of Italy, the genetic defects of the Christian Democratic welfare model have been magnified by endemic corruption (Ferrera, 1996). Still, if Italy represents an extreme case, it does not represent an isolated one.

The Italian experience of pension reform is echoed across a number of contexts. According to Myles and Quadagno, the main direction of pension reform has been to reduce deficits while heightening progressivity (Myles and Quadagno, 1997). In so-called 'Bismarckian' pension systems, like that of Italy, where benefits are proportional to earnings and financed by payroll taxes, reformers have tightened the links between contributions and benefits. The effect in most cases, as in Italy, has been to squeeze subsidies to the self-employed and other affluent groups that were paid for by payroll taxes levied on blue-collar workers. In so-called 'Beveridgean' pension systems, where benefits are flat rate and financed by general taxation, reformers have deployed 'claw-backs' or 'means-testing from the top.' Put simply, the principal source of savings has derived from eliminating or reducing the pensions of high-income groups. In an almost perfect illustration of the vice-into-virtue logic, Myles and Pierson note that Canada used part of the savings from reduced pensions for the affluent to pay for increased pensions for the needy (Myles and Pierson, 1997). The result was to bring elderly poverty rates down to near Scandinavian levels, despite the decrease in overall spending.

Moving beyond pension reform to the more general challenge of deficit reduction, the experience of Sweden in the 1990s suggests that vice-into-virtue strategies need not be confined to corrupt, Christian Democratic systems (Anderson, 1998; Palme and Wennemo, 1998; Levy, 2000; Lindbom, 2000; Palme, 2000).[2] Sweden is, in many ways, the hardest case for a vice-into-virtue argument. The Swedish welfare state was constructed by parties of the left, not the right, so contrary to Italian progressives, Swedish leftists did not inherit an array of conservative programmes that they could scale back. Moreover, Sweden is generally portrayed as something like social best practice – social pro-grammes are managed properly and efficiently; they are geared toward maximiz-ing labour force participation; and they are relatively free of archaic or sexist values (Esping-Andersen, 1990, 1996a, 1999; Huber and Stephens, 2001). Yet even in 'virtuous' Sweden, Social Democratic reformers found a number of 'vices' to correct.

I do not wish to suggest Swedish authorities completely avoided painful or regressive measures. Confronting a massive budget deficit of 13 per cent of GDP in 1994, the Social Democrats were forced to make difficult choices. In particular, they reduced the general replacement rates for unemployment, pension, and parental leave programmes from 90 per cent to 75 per cent of pre-vious wages (later raised to 80 per cent). That said, much of the savings came from attenuating vices, correcting programmes that had degenerated over the years and moved away from their stated objectives.

The case of sick pay provides an illustration (Anderson, 1998). Although the government had set sick pay at 90 per cent of wages, collective bargaining agreements often topped up these payments to a full 100 per cent. What is more, the reference wage for calculating sick pay included bonuses and vacation pay. As a result, employees could actually 'earn' more by staying at home than by going to work. Adding to the temptation, no medical exam was required if the employee were absent for less than one week, and even if employees were absent longer, the insurance board accepted any doctor's certificate more or less automatically. Not surprisingly, Swedish absenteeism was sky high. In the late 1980s, the average Swedish worker was out sick for five weeks every year, and Sweden was devoting 3 per cent of GDP to sick pay, roughly double the figure of any other European country.

When the Social Democrats returned to office in 1994, they attacked the 'vice' of sick pay paid to people who were not really sick through a series of changes. As noted above, the reimbursement rate was reduced to 75 per cent of wages (later raised to 80 per cent), and fringe benefits and vacation pay were excluded from the calculation of the reference wage. The government also prohibited collective bargaining agreements from topping up sick pay. Those out sick were required to submit medical documentation on a regular basis; the doctor had to explain how the injury or sickness prevented the patient from working; and the insurance office, rather than the physician, was given the final say over whether the patient was able to work. Finally, to induce employers to control absenteeism, companies were made financially responsible for the first four weeks of sick pay (while receiving tax breaks in compensation).

The effect of these reforms was to reduce Swedish absenteeism and sick pay spending by almost 60 per cent. Although some on the left denounced the changes as an erosion of social protection, the government replied that the purpose of sick pay is to protect sick people, not to provide unpaid vacations. And even with the reforms, Swedish employees were still taking an average of 12 days per year for sick leave – not exactly the American system.

The Swedish Social Democrats repaired other social programmes that had evolved in unintended or undesirable directions. The disability scheme had become a de facto early retirement programme, removing labourers from the workforce at the age of 58 (Wadensjö, 1991, 1999; Ebbinghaus, 2000). The Social Democrats tightened the definition of disability, protected the jobs of older workers, and reduced reimbursement rates for disability insurance to the same level as other social programmes, while expanding means-tested programmes to protect low-income disability pensioners (Hort, 2001; Swedish Government, 2001). The government not only saved money, but Swedish labour force participation rates for workers aged 55 to 65 are among the highest in the OECD (OECD, 2001a; Swedish Government, 2001). The government also closed loopholes in the advance maintenance allowance, a child support guarantee for custodial parents. Many Swedish couples had been making child support payments under the table, so that the custodial parent would qualify for the state advance maintenance allowance. The reformed system imposed a minimum payment of roughly $250 per month on the non-custodial parent, undercutting the possibilities for evasion.

The Social Democratic austerity package was balanced roughly evenly between spending cuts and tax increases. Employees were hit with higher payroll taxes, although the blow was softened by a reduction in value-added taxes on food, and payroll taxes were cut subsequently, as the Swedish economy recovered in the late 1990s. Businesses and high-income groups were also required to contribute to fiscal recovery. The government boosted taxes on capital and production and raised the top marginal income tax rate from 50 per cent to 55 per cent. Combining the effects of programme cuts and tax hikes, the Swedish government estimates that the wealthiest fifth of households paid 43 per cent of the costs of the fiscal consolidation programme, while the bottom fifth paid 11 per cent (Swedish Ministry of Finance, 2001: Annex 5). Again, my claim is not that poor people were spared entirely from the effects of austerity, but rather that even in virtuous Sweden, it was possible to extract much of the savings from affluent groups and from programmes like sick pay and disability that had evolved in unintended and undesirable directions ('vices').

No dimension of the liberal economic agenda is more wrenching and painful for progressives than cutting government spending. In hard economic times, governments often have no choice but to impose some of the burdens on citizens who can afford them the least. Still, progressive liberal austerity, of the kind implemented in Italy and Sweden in the 1990s, is very different from the regressive assaults on programmes for low-income groups associated with neo-liberalism. The existence of vices in the mammoth welfare states of Western Europe, of programmes that are tilted toward the affluent or that operate in perverse and unjust ways, offers opportunities for improving efficiency and equity at the same time. If the low-hanging fruit is most visible in the dysfunctional Christian Democratic regime, all the more so in a historically patronage-ridden system like Italy, such fruit has also grown, perhaps less luxuriantly, in the austere, northern climate of Scandinavia. Thus, all austerity packages are not created equal. In the next section, we will see that tax relief likewise offers opportunities for progressive distributional strategies.

4 Lower taxes, fairer taxes

Tax relief encompasses two kinds of changes. The first is tax *reallocation*: reforms that adjust the composition of taxation, while leaving the overall level of taxation as before. The second kind of relief is tax *reduction*, reforms that lower the overall burden of taxation and may also alter the composition of the tax burden.

Traditionally, tax relief has not been central to the vision of European progressives. The way to deliver benefits to constituents was through increased social spending. From this perspective, taxation was a necessary evil more than a component of progressive strategy. Indeed, the tax systems of large welfare states like Sweden were often less redistributive than those of the residual liberal systems, like the US or UK (Steinmo, 1993; Kato, 2003). Part of the reason was that higher expenditures required substantial taxes on all groups, not just the affluent. No less important, taxation was rarely seen as the arena where Social Democracy found expression; rather, taxation was a support for the progressive policies that were enacted on the spending side.

The neo-liberal approach to tax reform encompasses both an aggregate and a distributive dimension. In aggregate terms, neo-liberals see government spending and taxation as too high. Society's resources are being diverted from their most productive use by excessive government spending. Moreover, much of this spending erodes work incentives by providing citizens with an alternative to paid employment. Thus, neo-liberals favour tax cuts as a way of lowering the burden on saving and investment, not to mention constraining future government spending.

The second dimension of the neo-liberal approach is distributional. Tax relief should be focused on affluent groups, rather than low-income groups. The case can be made on equity grounds, in that the affluent tend to pay the most taxes, hence they should receive the most relief. From an electoral perspective, to the extent that it is parties of the right that are conducting tax reform, an upward redistribution of wealth favours their voters. Finally, there is an economic argument. The affluent have a higher propensity to save and invest, hence to generate growth and employment opportunities for the rest of the population.

The central risk of the neo-liberal tax-cutting agenda, from a progressive standpoint, is that it will redistribute substantial resources from low-income to affluent groups. This concern is certainly not ill founded. In Britain, the Thatcher and Major governments did not reduce overall taxation during their 18 years in office from 1979 to 1997, but they did make the composition significantly more regressive (Giles and Johnson, 1995; Adam and Frayne, 2000; Clark and Leicester, 2002; Kato, 2003). The top marginal income tax rate was reduced from 83 per cent to 40 per cent; the corporate tax rate fell from 52 per cent to 35 per cent; and the top inheritance tax rate was slashed from 75 per cent to 40 per cent. To pay for all these tax cuts, which strongly favoured high-income groups, the Thatcher and Major governments increased a series of regressive taxes that are paid disproportionately by average and low-income groups. The national sales or value-added tax (VAT) more than doubled, from 8 per cent to 17.5 per cent, and employee payroll taxes jumped from 6.5 per cent to 10 per cent. Taken together, this combination of tax cuts for the affluent counter-balanced by tax hikes for average and low-income workers accounted for roughly one-third of the massive 40 per cent increase in inequality under the Tories.

The 2001 and 2003 tax cuts enacted by the Bush administration in the United States tell a similar tale (Krugman, 2003; Steurle, 2004; Hacker and Pierson, 2005). The tax cuts were incredibly regressive: the richest 1 per cent of Americans are slated to receive 36 per cent of the benefits, a share roughly equal to that of the bottom 80 per cent of Americans (Hacker and Pierson, 2005). This regressive outcome is the product not only of generous income tax cuts for high earners, but also of the phasing out of the highly progressive Estate Tax, which applied only to inherited estates valued at more than $675,000, that is, to the top 2 per cent of all estates.

If the Thatcher/Major and Bush experiences point to the perils of tax relief, they do not represent the sum total of tax relief strategies. Tax relief can be progressive if constructed properly. Two features of contemporary tax systems, in particular, open the possibility for progressive reform. The first is that tax systems impose significant burdens on average and low-income groups, not just the well to do. When the public sector absorbs 40 to 60 per cent of GDP, as is the case throughout Western Europe, it is not just the rich who are paying taxes. The fiscal contribution of middle- and low-income groups is especially significant if the definition of 'taxes' is extended beyond the income tax to include social security charges (or payroll taxes). Although low-wage workers generally pay little or no income tax, they pay hefty social security taxes. Even in the United States, Social Security and Medicare taxes total 15.3 per cent of earnings (up to a ceiling of around $90,000 per year). The burden is especially heavy, reaching 40 to 50 per cent of wages, in the Christian Democratic or Bismarckian welfare states – such as Germany, France, Italy, and Holland – which finance their systems of social protection primarily through social security contributions. Thus, there is a lot of room for cutting the taxes of average and low-wage groups. Instead of cutting inheritance taxes or the income taxes of the very rich, as under the Bush reforms, governments may choose to reduce the burden of less privileged groups.

The second feature of the tax system that creates possibilities for progressive tax reform is that every tax system contains inequities and irrationalities ('vices'). The heavy taxation of labour income, described above, is not just inequitable; it also generates perverse incentives. In many countries, the combination of income taxes, social security charges, and means-tested benefits that are reduced or withdrawn as income rises imposes very heavy marginal tax rates on people moving from unemployment or other social benefits to paid employment. These tax rates can easily exceed 70 per cent – far higher than the rates confronted by those at the top end of the income scale. Consequently, reforms that reduce the tax burden on low-wage workers are good for social justice, but also increase work incentives, improving the functioning of the labour market.

A further opportunity for welfare-enhancing tax reform arises from sizable positive or negative 'externalities,' that is, gaps between social costs and the costs borne by the agent. Environmental policy is a classic example: households and businesses do not bear the full costs of their energy consumption and pollution, consequently they have an incentive to over-consume scarce natural resources and to over-pollute. An 'eco-tax' that raised the costs of polluting and consuming natural resources would reduce harmful behaviour, while generating fiscal resources that could be put to other uses.

A final feature of the tax code that merits mention is its malleability. Paul Pierson has demonstrated that efforts to retrench or redirect social spending programmes tend to be fraught with difficulty, as current recipients mobilize to protect their benefits (Pierson, 1994). Social policy has, therefore, seen relatively little change over the past 25 years. Tax codes, by contrast, have been reformed on a regular basis. The less visible and understandable character of taxation creates opportunities for progressive authorities to redirect benefits in a way that would be much more difficult on the spending side.

Progressive tax relief has operated through both reallocation and reduction. The reforms of the French left since the early 1990s offer an example of progressive reallocation (Levy, 1999, 2004b).[3] One of the hallmarks of the Christian Democratic or Bismarckian welfare state found in France is an over-reliance on wage-based contributions. Occupational programmes were constructed originally along actuarial lines: wage-based contributions by employers and workers would fund the old-age, accident, family, and unemployment insurance programmes from which employees would eventually benefit. Over the years, however, political authorities grafted social policy missions onto these insurance schemes. In most countries, for example, health coverage and minimum pensions have become available to all citizens regardless of prior contributions. Yet many of these programmes continue to be funded under the occupational insurance system. In other words, even when Bismarckian, employment-based programmes evolved into universal (or Beveridgean) schemes, their mode of financing has tended to remain Bismarckian. Social insurance has been called upon to finance social assistance, Bismarck to pay for Beveridge.

The conflation of Bismarck and Beveridge is both unfair to low-wage workers, who pay for benefits enjoyed by all citizens, and detrimental to employment, since it raises the post-tax cost of labour. Consequently, in 1991, the French left began shifting the financing of universal programmes away from Bismarckian payroll taxes to a flat tax, the *contribution sociale généralisée* (CSG), which is levied on all earnings, including those from capital and real estate. In 1998, the Jospin government raised the CSG to 7.5 per cent of wages, while all but eliminating employee health insurance contributions. The reform was revenue-neutral, but it boosted worker purchasing power by over 1 per cent. Today, in the wake of these fiscal reforms, the CSG brings in more money than the French income tax.

Holland, like France, has a Bismarckian welfare state that over-taxes labour. As in France, excessive payroll taxes erode wage-earner purchasing power and discourage hiring. Dutch authorities have responded to this problem through a combination of tax reallocation and tax reduction (Levy, 2004b).[4] The main revenue-neutral strategy for reducing taxes on labour has been to 'green' the tax system, that is to replace taxes on labour with taxes on energy consumption and pollution (First Dutch Green Tax Commission, 1998; Second Dutch Green Tax Commission, 2000; Abrate, 2004). Greening the tax system holds out the possibility of a so-called 'double dividend' (Koskela *et al.*, 1999; OECD, 2001b). The first dividend is that a tax on energy or pollution internalizes the costs to the agent, thereby reducing socially damaging behaviour. The second dividend is that with the revenues generated by new environmental taxes, governments can lower taxes elsewhere.[5]

Dutch authorities have been at the forefront of European efforts to green the tax system. In the 1990s, the share of green taxes in total government revenues rose from 8.6 per cent to 14.1 per cent (Second Dutch Green Tax Commission, 2000: 7). Like most European countries, the Netherlands imposes heavy taxes on energy and transportation (i.e. gasoline). Where Holland broke new ground was with the introduction of a so-called 'Ecotax' in 1996, which extends to pollution and the use of natural resources (extraction of fresh ground water, tap water, and the disposal of garbage) (Abrate, 2004). Today, environmental taxes in the Netherlands total between 3.5 and 4.0 per cent of GDP, among the heaviest – by some measures, the heaviest – in Europe (Abrate, 2004: 246). The growth in green taxes has generally been accompanied by reductions in payroll taxes, boosting employee take-home pay and lowering labour costs to employers.

Dutch authorities have used tax reduction as well as tax reallocation to reduce the fiscal burden on wage earners. Indeed, tax policy has played a central part in the Dutch strategy of job growth through negotiated wage restraint. In 1982, confronting a stagnant economy, double-digit unemployment, and most important, a newly-elected centre-right government that was threatening to emulate the industrial relations practices of Mrs Thatcher, Dutch trade unions reluctantly agreed to dampen their wage demands. The resulting 'Wassenaar agreement' made the revival of corporate profitability the centrepiece for relaunching investment and employment. By the late-1990s, Dutch unemployment had fallen below the US rate, while inequality and poverty had increased little, if at all. This ability to reconcile full employment and social cohesion led a number of observers, including the OECD, to speak of a 'Dutch miracle' or 'Dutch model' (Visser and Hemerijck, 1997; OECD, 1998).

One of the keys to this felicitous outcome was tax policy. In the 1990s, as the Dutch economy recovered, budget deficits turned to surpluses, and a Christian Democratic government gave way to a Labour–Liberal 'purple' coalition, Dutch authorities targeted tax relief at ordinary wage earners (OECD, 1994a; Dutch Government, 1998, 1999; OECD, 2000; Dutch Ministry of Finance, 2001; Dutch Government, 2002; Dutch Ministry of Finance, 2004). By boosting take-home pay, tax relief helped sustain wage moderation in the face of tighter labour markets. According to an IMF report, 'The impact of cuts in taxes and social security contributions was quite substantial; whereas the real wage of the average production worker increased by only 0.9 per cent over the 1983–98 period, the corresponding net real wage went up by 14.8 per cent' (Bakker and Halikas, 1999: 25). In other words, tax policy has essentially spelled the difference between wage stagnation – a difficult sell to union members – and appreciable gains in take-home pay. It has underwritten a win-win game between Dutch employers and workers that has increased employment and equity in tandem.

Like Dutch authorities, Britain's New Labour government has deployed tax reductions on behalf of progressive, redistributive objectives (Levy, 2004b).[6] When Tony Blair became the British prime minister in 1997, he inherited a double legacy from his Conservative predecessors. On the positive side, the British economy was no longer the sick man of Europe, as it had been in the 1970s. In the late 1990s, economic growth exceeded the European average, public finances were in excellent shape, and the country neared full employment. On the downside, the impressive economic turnaround under Margaret Thatcher and John Major had been purchased at a very high social price. Income inequality had increased by 40 per cent and childhood poverty had tripled (Goodman, 2001; Brewer *et al.*, 2002; Clark and Leicester, 2002; Piachaud and Sutherland, 2002).

The Blair government's response to this dual legacy has been to use some of the fruits of the former legacy (a stronger economy) to alleviate the latter (child poverty). In 1999, Prime Minister Blair announced the goal of eliminating all child poverty within a generation. Subsequently, the British Treasury translated this goal into quantitative targets: a 25 per cent reduction of childhood poverty (measured as 60 per cent of median income) by 2004; 50 per cent by 2010; and 100 per cent by 2020 (Brewer and Gregg, 2001). Thus, New Labour is acting as a *corrective* left, seeking to undo some of the shocking increases in poverty and inequality introduced by the Conservatives.

New Labour is also a *constrained* left. A combination of political and economic constraints has led the government to make tax reform the primary vehicle for pursuing its redistributive objectives. Politically, Tony Blair was able to end Labour's 18-year exile from office by reassuring financial markets, the business community, and moderate voters that his brand of politics would be different from the ruinous tax-and-spend policies of the 1970s. The renaming of the party as 'New Labour' was part of this effort to break with the past, as were reforms designed to curb the power of the trade unions within the party. In the run-up to the 1997 election, Blair added a further reassurance by pledging to adhere to the rigorous spending targets of the Conservative government – targets that, ironically, few expected even the Conservatives to respect. So the new government found itself with relatively little room to increase social spending. Cutting taxes, by contrast, resonated with the values of business and finance. The complexity of tax reform also provided a less visible way of channelling resources than a straightforward spending programme. Indeed, Treasury officials referred to the government strategy as 'redistribution by stealth.'

The government has sought to distance itself from the traditional Labour party by insisting that the best way to fight poverty, including childhood poverty, is through paid employment, as opposed to social benefits. It has launched a series of so-called 'New Deals' designed to move benefit claimants into the labour force (Lødemel and Trickey, 2000; Judge, 2001; British Government, 2002). The first New Deal centred on youths under the age of 25. Subsequently, New Deals have been established for workers over 25, older workers, lone parents, partners of the unemployed, and the disabled.

The New Deals were inspired by US welfare-to-work programmes. They include increased surveillance, mandatory meetings with caseworkers to design a programme for securing a job, and, in some cases, benefit loss as punishment for non-cooperation. Labour's goal is not simply to move people into the workforce, however, but also to move them out of poverty. The government is especially concerned about childhood poverty, given its highly publicized targets for reduction. Consequently, work must pay and pay well, especially for families with children. Toward this end, the government reestablished the national minimum wage in 1999 at a level of £3.60 per hour ($5.40). The minimum was raised to £4.20 ($6.30) in October 2002 and to £4.85 ($7.27) in October 2004. The minimum wage is currently £5.35 per hour. It will rise to £5.52 per hour in October 2007. Still, there are clear limits to this strategy, given the risk of pricing British workers out of jobs. Consequently, the government's efforts to make work pay for low-wage employees (especially workers without children) have centred on tax policy. British authorities have mobilized five sets of tax reductions or credits to alleviate poverty (British Treasury, 2002; Brewer, 2003; British Government, 2003b; British Treasury, 2003; Levy, 2004a, 2004b).

The first is income taxes. In contrast to recent US practice, the Blair government focused income tax cuts on *low* earners, rather than high earners, slashing the bottom tax rate from 20 per cent to 10 per cent, while keeping the top rate unchanged at 40 per cent. Second, the government has scaled back the taper rate dramatically (the rate at which public benefits are withdrawn as income rises), from 70 per cent to 37 per cent. Third, acknowledging that childcare costs reduce the returns to employment, New Labour established a means-tested Childcare Tax Credit (CTC). The CTC can cover as much as 70 per cent of childcare expenses up to £135 per week ($203) for one child and £200 per week ($300) for more than one (Chote *et al.*, 2003). Fourth, the administration increased income support and tax credits for low-income workers (the equivalent of the Earned Income Tax Credit in the United States) to as much as £90 per week ($135). Fifth, the government created and expanded a collection of tax credits for low-income families. These were gathered into a single programme, the Integrated Child Credit (ICC) in 2003, providing between £33 ($50) and £110 ($165) per week, depending on earnings. Taken together, the combination of a higher minimum wage and tax credits raised the minimum weekly income guarantee for a family with one child and one full-time worker by almost one-third in four years, from £182 ($273) in 1999 to £241 ($362) in 2003 (British Government, 2003a: 90).

The tax policies of the Labour government have brought genuine improvements in the plight of low-income households. Between 1997 and 2003, tax policies boosted the income of the poorest tenth of the population by 15 per cent, as compared to 3 per cent for the richest decile (Chote *et al.*, 2003: 6). Government policies have been especially generous to lone parents on low incomes. According to the OECD, for a lone parent with two children, earning two-thirds of the average production wage, the British tax system is the most generous of all the affluent democracies, with an effective tax rate of *negative* 10.8 per cent (OECD, 2002: 36). Perhaps most important, the Labour government met its initial childhood poverty target – a 25 per cent reduction between 1998/99 and 2004/05 (Brewer *et al.*, 2004). While there is clearly more work to be done and while this work may prove expensive, for the first time in over a quarter-century, British social indicators are heading in the right direction.

This section has shown that it is entirely possible to reallocate or reduce taxes in ways that are compatible with progressive principles and concerns for the disadvantaged. Progressive reform has generally grown out of two features of the tax code. The first is what I have termed 'vices,' that is, the inevitable inequities, irrationalities, and perverse incentives that have infiltrated the tax system over the years. Fixing these 'vices' can generate resources for more virtuous fiscal objectives. The second feature is significant taxation of wage earners. A critical starting point is to frame 'tax reform' as including social security charges or payroll taxes, rather than just being confined to income taxes. Once the artificial exclusion of social security charges is effected, then the opportunities and rationale for cutting taxes on low-income groups are increased immeasurably.

This section has also shown that channelling tax relief to low-income groups, rather than high-income groups, is not simply a matter of choosing equity over efficiency. Rather, there are plenty of compelling economic reasons for focusing tax relief on the bottom of the income scale. Because of the withdrawal of means-tested benefits, the lowest earners often confront the highest effective marginal tax rates. To the extent that efficiency is equated with countering marginal effects, economic logic would dictate focusing relief on low-wage workers. Moreover, as the Dutch case illustrates, in countries suffering from high unemployment, concentrating tax relief on average and low-wage earners has the added advantage of facilitating wage moderation, since post-tax wages rise even if nominal wages are stagnant. Wage moderation then accelerates the pace of job creation and the return to full employment. Thus, an efficiency-enhancing tax reform can just as easily favour those at the bottom of the income scale as those at the top. In the next section, we will see that efforts to move the unemployed or non-employed into the workforce, what the Europeans describe as 'labour market activation,' can likewise be structured so as to yield progressive distributional outcomes.

5 More jobs, better jobs

The term 'labour market activation' derives from the distinction between so-called 'passive' labour market expenditures that pay people not to work (unemployment insurance, early retirement, etc.) and so-called 'active' labour market expenditures that help people find jobs. Labour market activation conveys two main ideas. The first is that people should derive their income primarily from paid employment, as opposed to government transfers. The second notion is that the goal of policy is not simply to minimize unemployment, but also to maximize total employment. In other words, in addition to reducing *formal* unemployment, the goal of activation is to move people *outside* the labour force – stay-at-home mothers, disabled workers, early retirees, discouraged workers – into the labour force. Part of this activation strategy may also entail loosening regulations that limit part-time and temporary employment, so as to expand the supply of jobs available to those not working.

Progressives have voiced a number of concerns about labour market activation policies. For those pushed into the labour market, 'activation' entails the transformation of an unconditional right of citizenship into a privilege that is dependent on the goodwill of the caseworker (King, 1999; Handler, 2003). Activated workers are at risk of being coerced, humiliated, and deprived of personal dignity and rights (Cloward and Piven, 1971). They can be forced to take substandard jobs at substandard wages, on pain of losing their benefits. The risk is all the greater if pressures to seek employment are combined with an easing of restrictions on less desirable part-time and temporary jobs. In addition to hurting the activated workers, such substandard jobs undercut the wages and employment conditions of others in the labour market. In short, activation transforms Marshallian citizens into a reserve army of the unemployed, mobilized on behalf of capital and against the rest of the workforce.

The progressive criticisms point to real risks associated with activation, but one can also identify possible benefits. Moving people into paid employment has the potential to improve their economic well-being and sense of self-worth if conducted properly. The judgement about the merits of activation strategies depends to considerable extent on how such measures are conceived and implemented. Are recipients abused, forced into lousy jobs? Do they benefit financially from working? Do they receive support and services that they need? The answers to these questions – hence the character of activation – vary widely.

The progressive liberal approach to labour market activation is distinguished from a neo-liberal strategy in two main ways. The first is a concern for the *quality* of employment, for improving the situation of activated workers, not just for the *quantity* of employment. Whereas the neo-liberal approach favours more jobs, the progressive liberal approach favours more *and better* jobs, jobs that provide better living circumstances and life chances.

The second feature of the progressive liberal approach to labour market activation is a much more extensive, positive role for public policy. The neo-liberal strategy consists primarily of withdrawing state protections, so as to increase work incentives and employment opportunities. It is largely a negative approach, rolling back state interventions that are seen to be at the heart of labour market dysfunctions. The neo-liberal strategy is also a 'thin strategy.' It rests on a relatively limited or 'thin' set of policy instruments. The progressive liberal strategy may include some 'thin' measures, but it goes much further. It entails positive as well as negative reforms; it re-regulates as well as deregulating labour markets; and it demands much more of the state as well as of the individual – a plethora of public policies to support workers as they reenter the labour force. As a result, 'thick,' progressive labour market policies are often as expensive, or even more expensive, than the passive labour market programmes that they replace.

This section describes two sets of progressive liberal, labour market reforms. The first is the expansion of part-time employment in the Netherlands. The second is a reform of the unemployment system in Sweden. Both changes have increased pressures on the unemployed and those outside the labour force to take jobs, but they have also increased pressures on the state. 'Thick' accompanying regulations and supports have sought to protect activated workers against exploitative employment practices and to boost their living standards.

Traditionally, most European countries have placed heavy restrictions on part-time and temporary employment (Levy, 2004a). Unions and the left, in particular, have been wary of part-time and temporary employment for three reasons. The first is that, even under the best of circumstances, such jobs are unlikely to be sufficient to sustain a family. Given that most European societies were long organized according to the so-called 'male breadwinner model,' male workers needed to be able to earn enough to support a non-employed wife and children. A second reason why progressives have been wary about part-time and temporary employment is that companies have often sought to use these jobs to pay substandard wages and benefits. Left unchecked, the spread of 'atypical employment' risks fostering a vulnerable, exploited 'reserve army,' forced to toil without the protections afforded full-time, core, unionized workers. The third and related concern of progressives is that atypical employment will place downward pressure on the wages, benefits, and rights of core workers. Full-time workers will be forced to either make hefty concessions to employers or see their jobs migrate to the atypical sector.

Neo-liberal reformers have generally sought to remove restrictions on part-time and temporary jobs. They argue that temporary and part-time jobs are better than no jobs and may even enable the employees to secure full-time jobs at some point in the future (Lindbeck and Snower, 1988; Friedman, 1990: ch. 8; OECD, 1994b). Neo-liberals are not too concerned that employers might use part-time and temporary workers to undercut the wages and working conditions of core, full-time workers. Indeed, from a neo-liberal perspective, if part-time and temporary employment threatens the status of full-time workers, this is a good thing. Full-time workers are privileged 'insiders'; their high wages and job protections come at the expense of 'outsiders,' who are unable to obtain jobs on these terms (Olson, 1982; Lindbeck and Snower, 1988). Weakening the privileges of insiders attenuates the 'insider-outsider problem,' making labour markets more flexible, better able to create jobs for all.

Despite these risks, promoting part-time and temporary employment may have a legitimate place in a progressive agenda. In an era of mass unemployment, it can be argued that part-time or temporary jobs are better than no jobs, and many jobs can only exist on a part-time or temporary basis. A significant segment of the economy is seasonal in nature, for example. In sectors like agriculture, construction, and retail trade, there is a lot of demand for workers at certain times of the year, but that demand would dry up if the workers had to be retained permanently.

Changes in the economy have spawned a number of legitimate business needs for part-time or temporary employment. Intensified international competition and shorter product cycles make it harder for employers to forecast their labour needs. To compete in fast-changing markets, companies often seek to employ a portion of their workforce on fixed-term contracts, so that they can reduce costs when demand drops. Another economic change, the shift from manufacturing to services, has expanded the need for part-time employment. The consumption of many services is concentrated at a few times in the day (noon, after work), so companies need to be able to hire part-time workers to meet these moments of peak demand.

Business is not the only potential beneficiary of part-time and temporary employment. With the mass entry of women into the labour market, many employees have substantial caring responsibilities. Mothers with young children, single mothers, and daughters caring for elderly parents often cannot work a full-time job.[7] For them, the choice is a part-time job or no job.

Part-time employment can also be an important vehicle for combating poverty. Dual-income households constitute a form of risk spreading. Even if the male breadwinner loses his job, his wife is still bringing home a paycheck (and may be able to increase her hours to limit the family income loss). Dual-income households are at lower risk of poverty, therefore, than single-earner households, even if the second income is from a part-time job. Moreover, as wages at the bottom of the pay spectrum have stagnated or declined in the post-OPEC period, a second (part-time) income has often prevented families from sinking into poverty. Finally, part-time jobs can help preserve the skills and job contacts of mothers with young children. As a result, mothers are less at risk of being unable to find a job when their children are older and they wish to return to paid employment. Perhaps even more important, they possess an independent earning capacity in the event that separation, divorce, or death deprives them of a partner's income.

Temporary and part-time employment offers a number of potential benefits, then: more jobs, jobs that are often better suited to the needs of working mothers, protections against household poverty. From a progressive standpoint, the problem is not part-time or temporary employment per se, but rather the way in which such employment is generally promoted.

The thin, neo-liberal approach is not the only way to promote part-time and temporary employment. The Netherlands has become the world champion of atypical employment, in particular part-time employment, but has done so in a very different manner from the neo-liberal approach (Visser and Hemerijck, 1997; OECD, 1998; Levy, 1999). Holland has greatly increased part-time employment over the past 20 years. From 1979 to 1996, part-time employment increased from 16.6 per cent to 37.4 per cent of total employment, far and away the highest figure of any OECD nation.

Part-time employment has not been synonymous with worker exploitation, however. While relaxing prohibitions on part-time employment, Dutch authorities and social partners have simultaneously upgraded the (hourly) wages and benefits of part-time and temporary workers to the levels enjoyed by their full-time counterparts. In this way, Dutch employers are now able to hire part-time and temporary workers in response to genuine needs for flexibility, but not as a means of evading wage rates and benefits paid to full-time workers.

The equalization of working conditions has occurred through a combination of collective bargaining and legislation. Over 80 per cent of collective bargaining agreements mandate pro rata wages and fringe benefits for part-time work, and the gap between part-time and full-time (hourly) wages has narrowed to only 5 per cent. In 1993, the government put an end to the provision exempting jobs of less than one-third the normal working week from the application of the legal minimum wage and related social security benefits. The 1995–96 'flexibility and security' agreements guaranteed pension and social security benefits to all part-time and temporary employees. Most recently, the Working Hours Adjustment Act of 2000 gave part-time workers an explicit right to equal treatment in all areas negotiated by the social partners, including wages, basic social security, education and training, childcare, holiday pay, and supplementary pensions (Hemerijck and Vail, 2006). With few exceptions, these changes have improved the conditions surrounding part-time and temporary employment, as opposed to undercutting the position of full-time employees. In other words, harmonization has occurred as much through a race to the top as to the bottom.

Part-time employment in the Netherlands has been largely female employment (although the rate of male part-time employment in Holland is also the highest in the world, more than double the OECD average). Roughly three-quarters of part-time jobs are held by women, as a generation of Dutch house-wives has entered the labour force on a part-time basis. Whether this situation is transitional, with younger Dutch women gravitating toward full-time jobs, or whether the Dutch one-and-one-half earner model constitutes a stable alternative to the Swedish dual-earner model, is an open question. What is not in question is that the expansion of part-time employment in the Netherlands has been con-ducted in such a way as to protect the interests of both established, full-time workers and new part-time workers.[8]

So-called 'welfare-to-work' or 'work-first' programmes have likewise lent themselves to progressive construction. As noted above, state initiatives to move claimants of unemployment or welfare benefits into paid employment run the risk of bullying vulnerable citizens into taking substandard jobs. That said, such strategies also hold potential benefits to both society and the activated individual (Ellwood, 1988; Field, 1995; Deacon, 1996; Field, 1997; Deacon, 2002). From a societal perspective, paying people not to work is incredibly wasteful, especially when the recipients of passive benefits are capable of holding jobs. Moreover, the legitimacy of welfare state can be jeopardized when programmes are per-ceived as rife with abuses or encouraging behaviour at odds with social norms. When one-seventh of the adult population in Holland is receiving a disability pension, for example, it is only a small step to conclude, in the words of a centre-right prime minister, that 'the Dutch welfare state is sick' (Visser and Hemerijck, 1997). Finally, social expectations about work have changed over the years, and it could be argued that the welfare state should evolve with the times. If in the 1950s, a 'good mother' was someone who stayed at home full-time with her children, rather than pursuing 'selfish' career interests, today, the vast majority of mothers are employed, and it seems unfair for mothers on welfare not to have to go to work like everyone else (Orloff, 2001).

It is not just society that stands to benefit from welfare-to-work initiatives, but also the activated themselves. A job often brings an increased sense of self-worth and pride. Reliance on earnings, as opposed to social transfers, reduces personal dependence of the activated individual on the whims of policy-makers and caseworkers (although it substitutes a dependence on employers). From a political perspective, people who are employed are a much more sympathetic constituency, making it easier to upgrade benefits subsequently. Activation neu-tralizes a wedge issue, transforming 'them' (the non-working poor) into 'us' (hard-working people, who are struggling to get by) (Ellwood, 1988; Weir, 1998). When people who are not working are poor, opponents of government intervention can always argue that the solution to their problem is to get a job; when people who *are* working are poor (or lack health insurance), the case for government support becomes much stronger. Once again, then, the assessment of activation depends very much on how such measures are constructed.

The thin, neo-liberal strategy attributes unemployment to personal failings or excessively generous benefits, rather than broader social and economic factors.

It, therefore, emphasizes cutting benefits and training opportunities. This approach is guided by the English Poor Law principle of 'less eligibility': welfare benefits should be (considerably) less attractive than the worst paid employment. Typically, benefit levels are lowered, as under the Thatcher government, so that claimants will have more incentive to accept a job. In addition, neo-liberals advocate scaling back alternatives to employment, such as training programmes and higher education, which are seen as undermining job search and parking the unemployed temporarily in useless programmes.

Coercion and control also figure prominently in the neo-liberal approach. Eligibility rules are tightened in an effort to move people off the public rolls. Claimants are forced to meet with caseworkers more regularly (meetings that can be quite unpleasant) and can lose their benefits as punishment for missing meetings or declining job offerings.

The neo-liberal approach emphasizes moving people into jobs, with little regard for the quality of those jobs. The main metric of 'success,' under this approach, is the reduction in welfare caseloads, as opposed to improvements in the living standards of welfare leavers. A second measure of success is the reduction in government spending, made possible by shrunken welfare rolls. Relatedly, the work-family tensions arising from paid employment, such as childcare and elderly care, are seen largely as a 'private' matter to be handled by the individual, rather than the government.

The thin, neo-liberal approach is most closely approximated by the 1996 welfare reform in the United States (Weaver, 1998; Weir, 1998; Weaver, 2000). The title of the US legislation, The Personal Responsibility and Work Reconciliation Act of 1996 (PWORA), reflects the emphasis on personal failings as the root cause of poverty and unemployment. The central objective of the 1996 reform was to move people off welfare. Again, the language was revealing: Aid to Families with Dependent Children (AFDC), the welfare programme dating to the 1930s, was replaced by *Temporary* Aid to Needy Families (TANF). The 50 states administering welfare were required to cut their caseloads by 50 per cent by the year 2002 or else face steep penalties. By contrast, no targets were set for the earnings and living standards of welfare leavers. Indeed, states were not even required to collect data on the plight of former beneficiaries.

The 1996 welfare reform was also supposed to save money – an estimated $52 billion over a five-year period, primarily by denying benefits to legal immigrants, reducing spending on food stamps, and tightening eligibility for Supplemental Security Income (Weaver, 1998). The legislation capped the federal government's financial commitment to welfare. PWORA replaced AFDC's open-ended federal commitment to match state spending on welfare recipients with a block grant: if welfare rolls surged, it would be the states, rather than the federal government, that would foot the bill. Moreover, since the federal grant is not indexed to inflation, it has declined in real terms by around 20 per cent since 1996.

While greatly increasing the obligations on welfare mothers, the 1996 legislation provided little in the way of support services. In moving from welfare to work, claimants often fall between two health insurance stools, earning too much to qualify for Medicaid, but holding low-end jobs that do not provide health insurance. Since single mothers, by definition, have children, they also confront increased outlays for childcare. Transportation to and from work represents a further need. Yet the 1996 legislation offered scant help with these challenges. As two scholars wryly note, 'Expanded access to assistance for working families was in no way mandated by TANF' (Gais and Weaver, 2002: 39).

The 1996 welfare reform in the US incarnated the thin, neo-liberal approach. Benefits and government spending were cut; states were required to reduce caseloads, but not to improve the well-being of welfare leavers (or even to track their status); and while tightening work requirements, US authorities provided little in the way of accompanying services or benefits, such as childcare. Yet welfare-to-work programmes need not be conducted in the harsh US manner. In several European countries, such reforms have been conducted with more generous intentions and supportive public policies. As described in the previous section, Britain's 'New Deal' intensified job search requirements, but was accompanied by a number of measures to make work pay for those who entered the labour market: a higher minimum wage, childcare subsidies, assorted tax breaks and credits.

Recent reforms in Sweden extend the 'thick' approach to activation further still (Levy, 2004a). The Swedish strategy has revolved around three sets of policies. The first has been the commitment to traditional 'active labour market policy,' as pioneered by Sweden in the 1950s: heavy investments in job training, job matching, and geographical relocation for displaced workers (Hort, 2001). This approach was bolstered during the 1990s, by the 'Adult Education Initiative,' which allowed the unemployed to pursue higher education full time while still receiving their unemployment benefits. The university population doubled in the 1990s (Björklund, 2000), and many young Swedes were able to reenter the labour market with a stronger knowledge and skill base.

The second strand of Swedish activation was a reform of the unemployment insurance system in 1999 (OECD, 2001a; Swedish Government, 2002). The reform established a so-called 'activity guarantee.' This initiative corresponded more closely to the thin neo-liberal approach, tightening supervision and increasing the demands on claimants. Even so, the activity guarantee was not entirely coercive. The reform simultaneously increased unemployment benefits by up to 30 per cent and was supported by the LO trade union.

The 'activity guarantee' was designed to remedy the problem of the quaintly-named 'benefits carousel.' Formally, unemployment benefits in Sweden expire after two years. In practice, however, whenever benefits were about to end, recipients would be placed in a training programme. They would remain in the programme for six months, thereby requalifying for another two years of unemployment benefits. Thanks to this 'carousel,' there was no effective time limit on the receipt of unemployment benefits. Another problem with the 'benefits carousel' was that the unemployed received the attention of public authorities only at the end of their two-year benefit period. The rest of the time, they were left to their own devices. This benign neglect by public authorities created opportunities for fraudulent unemployment claims. It also left many unemployed workers isolated, discouraged, and depressed.

The 'activity guarantee' broke with the logic of the 'benefits carousel' and lax public supervision. After 100 days of unemployment, claimants are no longer allowed to remain at home. They must be 'active' for eight hours per day, with 'activity' defined as a job, a training programme, a public internship, or some other kind of structured routine outside the home. The 'activity guarantee' has helped some unemployed people by providing contact with caseworkers and placement opportunities. It has also made it more difficult to cheat the system. Claimants can no longer receive unemployment benefits while holding a job under the table, since they must account for their actions eight hours per day. Not coincidentally, recent Swedish statistics reveal a sharp drop-off in the unemployment rolls at the 100-day mark.

The third dimension of the Swedish activation strategy has centred on carrots, instead of sticks. The goal has been to reduce the financial penalties on employment – to lessen the 'poverty trap,' as it is commonly called. The thin neo-liberal strategy for 'making work pay' is to slash unemployment benefits (the principle of 'less eligibility'), while perhaps tendering some kind of tax credit to low-income earners. As we have seen, Sweden increased unemployment benefits, rather than cutting them. Consequently, in order to 'make work pay,' Swedish authorities needed to also boost the financial pay-off from holding a job.

One way of 'making work pay' has been to reduce taxes on labour income. A 7 per cent employee payroll tax, which had been imposed as part of the austerity measures of the 1990s, was phased out over a four-year period, from 1999 to 2003 (Swedish Government, 2002). This change put money in the pockets of Social Democratic constituents, while also increasing the pay-off for moving from welfare to work.

Swedish authorities have done more than cut taxes. They have also lowered 'taper rates,' that is, the rate at which transfer payments are withdrawn when a claimant earns money from work. Swedish policy has always been based on the assumption that the best way to combat poverty is to allow people to combine government transfer payments with earnings from work. This orientation is especially important for single mothers, who can often only work part time because of their child-rearing responsibilities. Poverty rates among single-parent households have been kept at very low levels by allowing lone parents to combine earnings from a (typically part-time) job with social benefits (Gustafsson, 1995).

The third way in which Swedish authorities have increased the returns to employment has been by phasing out means-tested benefits. Swedish Social Democrats despise means-tested programmes, not only because they see such programmes as stigmatizing, but also because the means test functions as an additional income tax, one that is concentrated on the poor. Typically, as a person moves from welfare to work, means-tested benefits are reduced, sometimes drastically. Most Swedish social programmes are, therefore, organized on a universal basis. In contrast to the United States, the unemployed in Sweden do not have to worry that they will lose health care or childcare benefits should they take a job, since these benefits are available to all citizens at little or no cost. Nonetheless, means-tested programmes have always existed around the edges of the Swedish welfare state, and they were expanded in the 1990s, as fiscal austerity made it more difficult to provide universal benefits at an adequate level. With the return to more flush fiscal times in the past few years, the Social Democrats made it a priority to curtail means testing.

In 2002, a sliding scale for childcare fees was replaced by the 'maximum fee,' which limits the maximum parental contribution to about £100 per month, cutting costs for the average family by 40 to 50 per cent (OECD, 2001a; Swedish Government, 2002). Children of the unemployed also became eligible for public childcare, so that their parents would be able to search for work. The Social Democrats attempted to reform another means-tested programme, the housing allowance. Arguing that housing costs are primarily a problem for households with one income, they proposed to turn the means-tested housing allowance into a non-means-tested benefit for single mothers. Even in 'woman-friendly' Sweden, however, this proposal proved politically unfeasible. As a fallback, the Social Democrats have frozen the housing allowance, allowing it to wither on the vine, while channelling the savings into a universal child allowance that is not means-tested. The result, again, is to phase out means testing.

The thick, Swedish approach to activation has activated public authorities as well as the non-employed. Under the 'activity guarantee,' the non-employed are held accountable for their actions during the workday. But the government is also held accountable. The unemployment benefits of people who genuinely cannot find jobs have been increased by up to 30 per cent. Swedish public authorities also forged expensive new instruments, such as the Adult Education Initiative, to boost the human capital and employment prospects of job seekers. Most important, the Social Democrats retooled public policies across a range of areas to improve the financial returns from employment: lowering taxes on labour; allowing people to combine substantial earnings from work with social transfers; providing high-quality, universal services virtually free of charge; and phasing out means-tested programmes. In short, the thick, Swedish policy has been geared not only to move people from welfare to work, but also to improve their welfare in the process.

The punitive, US approach to labour market activation is understandably unappealing to progressives, but it is not the only option. A more humane and supportive approach is also possible. The thick activation strategy deployed in Holland, Sweden, and Britain under New Labour moves beyond the thin, neo-liberal agenda of coercion, 'less eligibility,' and scaled-back state protections. It regulates as well as deregulates labour markets; it promotes good jobs as well as more jobs; it increases the income and opportunity of the activated as well as their obligations; and it forces state authorities to rethink and expand their interventions across a range of policy areas, including areas outside formal labour market policy (taxation, social services, and means-tested benefits, to name just a few). In short, thick, progressive liberal activation represents a very different set of policies, with very different economic and social consequences, as compared to thin, neo-liberal activation. It offers a valuable set of policy instruments for improving the lot of the disadvantaged.

6 Conclusion

This chapter has identified the elements of a progressive approach to economic liberalization. The hallmark of progressive liberalism is the effort to reconcile the pursuit of economic efficiency through liberal, market-supporting reforms with traditional leftist distributional commitments to low-income and disadvantaged groups. Progressive liberalism has generally been the product of constrained or corrective left governments that are compelled for political or economic reasons to move in a liberal direction, but determined to allocate the costs and benefits of such reform in an equitable manner.

The progressive liberal reforms of constrained or corrective European governments have differed in fundamental ways from the harsh neo-liberal strategies of Margaret Thatcher, Ronald Reagan, and George W. Bush. The austerity budgets of Italy and Sweden extracted the largest savings from what I call 'vices,' that is, programmes that either privileged affluent groups or had evolved in unintended and undesirable directions. The tax relief of France, Holland, and Britain concentrated reductions on low-income wage earners, yielding both a social benefit in the form of lower poverty and increased take-home pay for those at the bottom of the income scale, and an economic benefit in the form of improved work incentives and wage moderation that facilitated further hiring. Finally, the labour market activation programmes of Holland, Sweden, and Britain increased employment levels, but also the living standards and workplace rights of those who took jobs. In short, under progressive liberal reforms, efficiency and equity have advanced together.

The findings of this chapter point toward three theoretical conclusions. The first is that there are varieties of economic liberalism. Neo-liberalism is a subset of liberalism, not a synonym. There is more than one way to reduce government spending, alleviate the tax burden, and encourage labour market participation. Progressive liberalism achieves these goals, while safeguarding or even enhancing Rawlsian distributional priorities. It represents a different kind of liberalism, not a diminished liberalism.

The second conclusion relates to the strategies of left parties. It is often argued that in the contemporary context of globalization, European integration, and intensified competition, left parties must shift their programmatic strategies from economic or 'material' issues to 'post-materialist,' lifestyle issues (Kitschelt, 1994). The optimal strategy is to more or less accept the neo-liberal economic agenda of the right, while seeking to carve out a distinct identity in the post-materialist arena. To be progressive today is to combine neo-liberal material policy with liberal, pluralistic post-materialist policy (i.e. support for environmental protection, feminism, gay rights, and outreach to minorities and immigrants). Certainly, there are plenty of good reasons for supporting a post-materialist agenda, but as the experience of Gerhard Schroeder in Germany suggests, such an agenda may not be enough to secure re-election (and some post-materialist issues, like outreach toward immigrants, are probably electoral losers, even if justified for other reasons). More importantly, this chapter has demonstrated that the left can still appeal to the electorate on material issues, even in a context of globalization and economic liberalization. Accepting economic liberalism need not mean accepting the distributional priorities of the right. Contrary to Mrs Thatcher's assertions, 'There Is a Progressive Materialist Alternative' to neo-liberalism (TIAPMA, not TINA) – and that alternative is progressive liberalism. Consequently, whatever the virtues of post-materialist reforms, such reforms should be seen as a complement to a progressive material agenda, rather than an alternative.

The third conclusion concerns the relationship between politics and economic liberalization. By and large, this relationship is portrayed in binary terms: political leaders can either accept and accommodate economic liberalization or they can resist it (Keohane and Milner, 1996; Friedman, 1999). This chapter suggests a third possibility: political choices can define the character of economic liberalization, its contours and distributional implications. Given that there is more than one way to liberalize, it is politics that selects among these alternatives. It is politics that determines the extent to which liberalizing strategies approximate progressive liberalism as opposed to neo-liberalism. Simply put, the decision to pursue economic liberalization is not where politics ends; it's where politics begin. Thus, it is politics, not some overarching logic of globalization or competitiveness, that has and will continue to structure the kind of society in which we live.

Notes

1 Throughout this chapter, it should be clear that I am using the word 'liberalism' in the European sense – a belief in limited government, maximum individual liberty, and free markets – as opposed to the contemporary US usage, conveying faith in government activism and social programmes. I mean the liberalism of John Locke, Adam Smith, or *The Economist* magazine, not of Lyndon Johnson and Edward Kennedy. The closest American approximation of the concept would probably be 'libertarianism.'

2 In addition to written sources, this account is based on interviews with Swedish officials in the finance ministry, prime minister's office, and parliament, as well as business and labour leaders, in June 2000 and March 2002.

3 In addition to written sources, this account is based on interviews with French officials in the finance ministry, the prime minister's office, and the Socialist party in June 2000, June 2002, and June–July 2004.

4 In addition to written sources, this account is based on interviews with Dutch officials in the finance ministry and Labour party in March 2002.

5 Less discussed in the economic literature is a potential 'national dividend': to the extent that countries import energy resources, environmental taxes will reduce transfers to (foreign) suppliers of energy, bolstering the balance of payments.

6 In addition to written sources, this account is based on interviews with British officials in the treasury, prime minister's office, and Labour party in June 2000 and June 2002.

7 Without denying that men are sometimes the primary care-givers, for purposes of linguistic simplicity, I am equating care-givers/part-time workers with women, and bread-
winners/full-time workers with men.
8 Perhaps for this reason, Dutch women voice considerable satisfaction with part-time
work. According to a recent survey, only 7 per cent of part-time female employees
wish to work full-time; conversely, 35 per cent of those working full-time would like
to work part-time (Survey cited in OECD 1998: 36). In other words, if the Dutch
labour market perfectly mirrored the expressed preferences of the female population,
the result would be *more* women working part-time, not fewer. This satisfaction with
part-time work may be a product of false gender consciousness among Dutch women
or the absence of quality childcare facilities that would make full-time work more
attractive. Still, one cannot ignore the fact that part-time employment is unusually
attractive in the Netherlands, owing to the alignment of (hourly) wages and benefits on
the rates paid to full-time workers. Indeed, part-time employment is not just attractive
to women. One-sixth of all Dutch men work part-time, the highest figure in the OECD
by far and more than double the OECD average.

References

Abrate, G. (2004) 'The Netherlands', in *Tax Systems and Tax Reform in Europe*, in L.
Bernardi and P. Profeta (eds). London, Routlege: 241–269.
Adam, S. and Frayne, C. (2000) *A Survey of the UK Tax System*. London, Institute for
Fiscal Studies, Briefing Note No. 9.
Anderson, K. (1998) *The Welfare State in the Global Economy: The Politics of Social
Insurance Retrenchment in Sweden, 1990–1998*, Ph.D. Thesis, Department of Political
Science, University of Washington.
Baccaro, L. and Locke, R. (1996) 'Learning From Past Mistakes? Recent Reforms in
Italian Industrial Relations'. *Indsutrial Relations Journal* 27(4): 289–303.
Bakker, B.B. and Halikas, I. (1999) 'Policy Reforms and Employment Creation', in *The
Netherlands: Transforming a Market Economy*, C.M. Watson, B.B. Bakker, J.K.
Martijn and I. Halikas (eds). Washington, DC, IMF, Occasional Paper No. 181: 16–41.
Björklund, A. (2000) 'Denmark and Sweden – Going Different Ways', in *Why Deregu-
late Labor Markets?* G. Esping-Andersen and M. Regini. Oxford, Oxford University
Press: 148–180.
Boix, C. (1998) *Political Parties, Growth, and Equality: Conservative and Social Demo-
cratic Economic Strategies in the World Economy*. Cambridge, Cambridge University
Press.
Boltho, A. (ed.) (1982) *The European Economy: Growth and Crisis*. New York, Oxford
University Press.
Brewer, M. (2003) *The New Tax Credits*. London, Institute for Fiscal Studies, Briefing
Note No. 35.
Brewer, M. and Gregg, P. (2001) *Eradicating Child Poverty in Britain: Welfare Reform
and Children Since 1997*. Institute of Fiscal Studies Paper, 3 May.
Brewer, M., Clark, T. and Goodman, A. (2002) *The Government's Child Poverty Target:
How Much Progress Has Been Made?* London, Institute for Fiscal Studies, Comment-
ary No. 88.
Brewer, M., Goodman, A., Myck, M., Shaw, J. and Shephard, A. (2004) *Poverty and
Inequality in Britain: 2004*. London, Institute for Fiscal Studies.
British Government (2002) *National Action Plan for Employment*. London, Department
for Work and Pensions.

British Government (2003a) *2003 Budget*. London, HM Treasury.

British Government (2003b) *Employment Action Plan*. London, Department for Work and Pensions.

British Treasury (2002) *The Child and Working Tax Credits*, Report Number Ten in Series on the Modernisation of Britain's Tax and Benefit System, April 2002. London, HM Treasury.

British Treasury (2003) *Budget 2003 Press Notices*. 9 April 2003. London, HM Treasury.

Chote, R., Emmerson, C. and Simpson, H. (2003) *The IFS Green Budget*. Institute of Fiscal Studies Commentary 92, January 2003.

Clark, T. and Leicester, A. (2002) *How Have Reforms to the Tax and Benefit System Affected Inequality?* London, Institute for Fiscal Studies.

Cloward, R. and Piven, F.F. (1971) *Regulating the Poor: The Functions of Public Welfare*. New York, Vintage Books.

Deacon, A. (1996) *Stakeholder Welfare*. London, Institute of Economic Affairs.

Deacon, A. (2002) *Perspectives on Welfare: Ideas, Ideologies, and Policy Debates*. Buckingham, Open University Press.

Dutch Government (1998) *National Action Plan for Employment*. The Hague, Ministry of Finance.

Dutch Government (1999) *National Action Plan for Employment*. The Hague, Ministry of Finance.

Dutch Government (2002) *National Action Plan for Employment*. The Hague, Ministry of Finance.

Dutch Ministry of Finance (2001) *Revision of Taxation 2001*, Updated Version.

Dutch Ministry of Finance (2004) *Taxation in the Netherlands 2004: Information for Companies Operating Internationally*. The Hague, Ministry of Finance.

Ebbinghaus, B. (2000) 'Any Way Out of "Exit from Work"? Reversing the Entrenched Pathways of Early Retirement', in *From Vulnerability to Competitiveness: Welfare and Work in the Open Economy*. F. Scharpf and V. Schmidt (eds). Oxford, Oxford University Press: 511–553.

Ellwood, D. (1988) *Poor Support: Poverty in the American Family*. New York, Basic Books.

Esping-Andersen, G. (1985) *Politics against Markets: The Social Democratic Road to Power*. Princeton, Princeton University Press.

Esping-Andersen, G. (1990) *The Three Worlds of Welfare Capitalism*. Princeton, NJ, Princeton University Press.

Esping-Andersen, G. (1996a) 'After the Golden Age? Welfare State Dilemmas in a Global Economy', in *Welfare States in Transition: National Adaptations in a Global Economy*, G. Esping-Andersen (ed.). Thousand Oaks, CA, Sage: 1–31.

Esping-Andersen, G. (1996b) 'Welfare States without Work: The Impasse of Labor Shedding and Familialism in Continental European Social Policy', in *Welfare States in Transition: National Adaptations in a Global Economy*, G. Esping-Andersen (ed.). Thousand Oaks, CA, Sage Publications: 66–87.

Esping-Andersen, G. (1999) *Social Foundations of Postindustrial Economies*. Oxford, Oxford University Press.

Ferrera, M. (1996) 'The "Southern Model" of Welfare in Social Europe'. *Journal of European Social Policy* 6(1): 17–37.

Ferrera, M. (1997) 'The Uncertain Future of the Italian Welfare State'. *West European Politics* 20(1): 231–249.

Field, F. (1995) *Making Welfare Work*. London, Institute of Community Studies.

Field, F. (1997) *Reforming Welfare*. London, Social Market Foundation.

First Dutch Green Tax Commission (1998) *The Dutch Green Tax Commission: A Summary of its Three Reports, 1995–1997.*

Friedman, M. (1990) *Free to Choose: A Personal Statement*. Chicago, University of Chicago.

Friedman, T. (1999) *The Lexus and the Olive Tree*. New York, Farrar, Straus, Giroux.

Gais, T. and Weaver, R.K. (2002) 'State Policy Choices Under Welfare Reform', in *Welfare Reform and Beyond: The Future of the Safety Net*, I. Sawhill, R.K. Weaver, R. Haskins and A. Kane (eds). Washington, DC, Brookings: 33–40.

Garrett, G. (1998) *Partisan Politics in the Global Economy*. New York, Cambridge University Press.

Giles, C. and Johnson, P. (1995) 'Tax Reform in the UK and Changes in the Progressivity of the Tax System, 1985–1995'. *Fiscal Studies* 15(3): 64–86.

Goodin, R.E. and Le Grand, J. (eds) (1987) *Not only the Poor: Middle Classes and the Welfare State*. London, Allen and Unwin.

Goodman, A. (2001) *Inequality and Living Standards in Great Britain: Some Facts*. London, Institute for Fiscal Studies, Briefing Note No. 19.

Green-Pedersen, C. (2002) *The Politics of Justification: Party Competition and Welfare-State Retrenchment in Denmark and the Netherlands*. Amsterdam, Amsterdam University Press.

Gustafsson, S. (1995) 'Single Mothers in Sweden: Why Is Poverty, Less Severe?', in *Poverty, Inequality, and the Future of Social Policy*, K. McFate, R. Lawson and W.J. Wilson (eds). New York, Russell Sage Foundation: 291–325.

Hacker, J. and Pierson, P. (2005) 'Abandoning the Middle: The Bush Tax Cuts and the Limits of Democratic Control'. *Perspectives on Politics* 3(1): 33–53.

Hall, P. (ed.) (1989) *The Political Power of Economic Ideas: Keynesianism across Nations*. Princeton, NJ, Princeton University Press.

Hall, P. and Soskice, D. (eds) (2001) *Varieties of Capitalism: The Institutional Foundations of Comparative Advantage*. Oxford, Oxford University Press.

Handler, J. (2003) 'Social Citizenship and Workfare in the US and Western Europe: From Status to Contract'. *Journal of European Social Policy* 13(3): 229–243.

Hemerijck, A. and Vail, M. (2006) 'The Forgotten Center: State Activism and Corporatist Adjustment in Holland and Germany', in *The State after Statism: New State Activities in the Age of Liberalization*, J. Levy (ed.). Cambridge, MA, Harvard University Press.

Hort, S. (2001) 'Sweden – Still a Civilized Version of Workfare?' in *Activating the Unemployed: A Comparative Appraisal of Work-Oriented Policies*, N. Gilbert and R.V. Voorhis (eds). New Brunswick, NJ, Transaction: 243–266.

Huber, E. and Stephens, J. (2001) *Development and Crisis of the Welfare State: Parties and Policies in Global Markets*. Chicago, University of Chicago Press.

Huber, E., Ragin, C. and Stephens, J.D. (1993) 'Social Democracy, Christian Democracy, Constitutional Structure, and the Welfare State'. *American Journal of Sociology* 99(3): 711–749.

Judge, K. (2001) 'Evaluating Welfare to Work in the United Kingdom', in *Activating the Unemployed: A Comparative Appraisal of Work-Oriented Policies*, N. Gilbert and R.V. Voorhis (eds). New Brunswick, NJ, Transaction: 1–28.

Kato, J. (2003) *Regressive Taxation and the Welfare State: Path Dependence and Policy Diffusion*. Cambridge, Cambridge University Press.

Keohane, R. and Milner, H. (eds) (1996) *Internationalization and Domestic Politics*. Cambridge, Cambridge University Press.

Kersbergen, K. v. (1995) *Social Capitalism: A Study of Christian Democracy and the Welfare State*. New York, Routledge.

King, D. (1999) *In the Name of Liberalism: Illiberal Social Policy in the United States and Britain*. Oxford, Oxford University Press.

Kitschelt, H. (1994) *The Transformation of European Social Democracy*. Cambridge, Cambridge University Press.

Koskela, E., Schob, R. and Sinn, H.W. (1999) *Green Tax Reform and Competitiveness*, NBER Working Paper No. 6922.

Krugman, P. (2003) *The Great Unraveling: Losing Our Way in the New Century.* New York, W.W. Norton.

Levy, J. (1999) 'Vice into Virtue? Progressive Politics and Welfare Reform in Continental Europe'. *Politics & Society* 27(2): 239–273.

Levy, J. (2000) *Can the Left Reform the Welfare State without Becoming the Right? The Case of Sweden*. Paper presented to the annual meeting of the American Political Science Association. Washington, DC. 1 September 2000.

Levy, J. (2004a) 'Activation through Thick and Thin: Progressive Approaches to Labour Market Activation', in *Social Policy Review 16*, N. Ellison, L. Bauld and M. Powell (eds). London, Palgrave: 187–208.

Levy, J. (2004b) *Progressive Tax Relief in Western Europe*. Paper presented to the annual meeting of the American Political Science Association. Chicago, IL. 1–5 September 2004.

Lindbeck, A. and Snower, D. (1988) *The Insider–Outsider Theory of Unemployment*. Cambridge, MA, MIT Press.

Lindbom, A. (2000) 'Dismantling the Social Democratic Welfare Model? Has the Swedish Welfare State Lost its Defining Characteristics?' unpublished essay, Department of Political Science, Uppsala University, Sweden.

Lødemel, I. and Trickey, H. (eds) (2000) *'An Offer You Can't Refuse': Workfare in International Perspective*. Bristol, Policy Press.

Mira d'Ercole, M. and Terribile, F. (1998) 'Pension Spending: Developments in 1996 and 1997', in *Italian Politics: Mapping the Future*, L. Bardi and M. Rhodes (eds). Boulder, CO, Westview: 187–208.

Myles, J. and Pierson, P. (1997) 'Friedman's Revenge: The Reform of "Liberal" Welfare States in Canada and the United States'. *Politics and Society* 25(4): 443–472.

Myles, J. and Quadagno, J. (1997) 'Recent Trends in Public Pension Reform: A Comparative View', in *Reform of Retirement Income Policy: International and Canadian Perspectives*, K. Banting and R. Boadway (eds). Kingston, University School of Policy Studies: 247–271.

OECD (1994a) *Economic Survey: Netherlands, 1993–1994*. Paris, OECD.

OECD (1994b) *The OECD Jobs Study: Facts, Analysis, Strategies*. Paris, OECD.

OECD (1998) *Economic Survey: Netherlands, 1997–1998*. Paris, OECD.

OECD (2000) *Economic Survey: Netherlands, 1999–2000*. Paris, OECD.

OECD (2001a) *Economic Survey: Sweden, 2000–2001*. Paris, OECD.

OECD (2001b) *Environmentally Related Taxes in OECD Countries: Issues and Strategies*. Paris, OECD.

OECD (2002) *Taxing Wages, 2001–2002*. Paris, OECD.

Offe, C. (1984) *Contradictions of the Welfare State*. London, Hutchison.

Olson, M. (1982) *The Rise and Decline of Nations*. New Haven, CT, Yale University Press.

Orloff, A.S. (2001) 'Ending the Entitlements of Poor Single Mothers: Changing Social

Policies, Women's Employment, and Caregiving', in *Women and Welfare: Theory and Practice in the United States and Europe*, N. Hirschmann and U. Liebert (eds). New Brunswick, NJ, Rutgers University Press.

Palme, J. and Wennemo, I. (1998) *Swedish Social Security in the 1990s: Reform and Retrenchment*. Stockholm, Print Works of the Cabinet Office and Ministries.

Palme, J.C. (2000) *Summary: Interim Balance Sheet for Welfare in the 1990s*. Report to the Minister for Health and Social Affairs, Government of Sweden.

Piachaud, D. and Sutherland, H. (2002) *Child Poverty*, unpublished manuscript.

Pierson, P. (1994) *Dismantling the Welfare State? Reagan, Thatcher, and the Politics of Retrenchment*. New York, Cambridge University Press.

Pierson, P. (2001) 'Coping with Permanent Austerity: Welfare State Restructuring in Affluent Democracies', in *The New Politics of the Welfare State*, P. Pierson (ed.). New York, Oxford: 410–456.

Przeworski, A. and Wallerstein, M. (1984) 'Democratic Capitalism at the Crossroads', in *The Political Economy: Readings in the Politics and Economics of American Public Policy*, T. Ferguson and J. Rogers (eds). Armonk, NY, M.E. Sharpe: 335–348.

Second Dutch Green Tax Commission (2000) *'Greening' the Tax System: An Exploration of Ways to Alleviate Environmental Pressure by Fiscal Means*.

Steinmo, S. (1993) *Taxation and Democracy: Swedish, British, and American Approaches to Financing the Modern State*. New Haven, CT, Yale University Press.

Steurle, C.E. (2004) *Contemporary US Tax Policy*. Washington, DC, Urban Institute Press.

Swedish Government (2001) *Action Plan for Employment*. Stockholm, Swedish Government Offices.

Swedish Government (2002) *Action Plan for Employment*. Stockholm, Swedish Government Offices.

Swedish Ministry of Finance (2001) *Spring Budget Bill*. Stockholm, Swedish Government Offices.

Titmuss, R. (1987) 'Welfare State and Welfare Society', in *The Philosophy of Welfare: Selected Writings of Richard Titmuss*, B. Abel-Smith and K. Titmuss (eds). London, Allen & Unwin: 141–156.

Visser, J. and Hemerijck, A. (1997) *'A Dutch Miracle': Job Growth, Welfare Reform, and Corporatism in the Netherlands*. Amsterdam, Amsterdam University Press.

Wadensjö, E. (1991) 'Sweden: Partial Exit', in *Time for Retirement: Comparative Studies of Early Exit from the Labor Force*, M. Kohli, M. Rein, A.-M. Buillemard and H. v. Gunsteren (eds). Cambridge, Cambridge University Press: 284–323.

Wadensjö, E. (1999) 'Sweden: Revisions of the Public Pension Programmes'. *Industry and Trade* (Reprint No. 535, Swedish Institute for Social Research): 101–115.

Weaver, R.K. (1998) 'Ending Welfare As We Know It', in *The Social Divide: Political Parties and the Future of Active Government*, M. Weir (ed.). Washington, DC, Brookings: 361–416.

Weaver, R.K. (2000) *Ending Welfare As We Know It*. Washington, DC, Brookings Institution.

Weir, M. (ed.) (1998) *The Social Divide: Political Parties and the Future of Active Government*. Washington, DC, Brookings.

13 Is there a European welfare model distinct from the US model?

Agnes Streissler

1 Theoretical considerations

What is being compared?

This chapter compares types of welfare states, in order to determine whether such a thing exists as a 'European welfare state model' distinct from the US model.

Comparisons are made from a geographical and a time perspective. First, to find out whether differences between Europe and the US are larger or more significant than differences between European states (or between US states). Second, to find answers to the question of whether over time, different models converge or behave independently.

Which national/geographical entities are compared?

In many respects there are no data available for a EU15-average, and as for European aggregates, there are no time series going back beyond the early 1990s. For purposes of long run comparisons we have only national data. And these differ in major respects. This in turn has serious consequences once one starts comparing them with data for the US. The claim, for example, that the income distribution in the US is more unequal than in Europe is, as Galbraith has pointed out, correct only as long as the US is compared with individual European states, but when the two economic areas are compared.

> It is true that the United States is substantially more unequal than the countries of Northern Europe, and somewhat more unequal, by most measures, than the countries of Southern Europe. But these pairwise comparisons ignore the component of inequality contributed by differences in average pay across European countries – differences which remain far more substantial than comparable differences across American states.
>
> (Galbraith, 2002: 107)

This objection hints at a fundamental problem in comparing Europe and the US: What *territorial unit* do we mean? On one side we have the federation of the US with 52 federal states, on the other the – much looser – union of European states with (in 2003) 15 members. Should one compare the federal level of the US with the supranational European Union (in which case the US would certainly turn out the more extensive welfare state)? Or is one to compare individual states of the US with individual member states of the EU (in which case the European states would definitely come out first)? Actually, either one of these approaches would be more appropriate than the comparison attempted here (and so far in all official international statistics), i.e. a comparison on the national level: EU member states are being compared with the federal level of the United States.

Similarly, we run into difficulties when we try to make up groups of states. In this chapter states are often put together in groups: the Scandinavian countries, the Benelux states, the Central European states, the Mediterranean countries, etc.

But even within such groups major differences may exist. Think of Sweden and Norway: Norway has oil, it can afford a generous welfare state, while Sweden was forced, though rather late, to reform its system in a restrictive manner. Germany is a special case: reunification brought grave problems. Spain and Italy, though both Mediterranean countries and both, relative to other parts of Europe, late starters in their economic development, show little similarity in their welfare 'models' (for this problem see also Maître *et al.*, 2005: 168f).

I tried to solve this problem by looking at both aggregate and the individual data. I group countries according to systemic and geographic characteristics. For these groups, I calculate unweighted averages. For Europe as a whole I calculate both an unweighted and a population-weighted average. The population weight is intended to show the relative importance of the country groups while the unweighted average shows the impact different models have: population or economic weight is not always the relevant indicator of the importance of a country – one can witness this in today's Europe of 25. Very small countries like Slovakia or Estonia have a massive impact on the discussion of optimal taxation systems. Conservatives always cite their success story when arguing in favour of cutting taxes. On the contrary, liberals (or in European terminology, leftists) look towards the Nordic countries for *best practice* – again, these countries are not very large (economically or by population), nevertheless they are important players in the welfare discussion.

Convergence or path dependency?

One of the first questions to be answered when comparing types of welfare states is the question of whether they tend to converge over time. Especially with respect to the US, this question has become more urgent lately: is Europe about to copy the US model? There are those who would welcome this; for them the US represent the ultimate form of capitalism, while the EU is over-regulated. Others shudder at the idea of Europe taking over the US model, for they see the United States as deficient in welfare policies and as dominated by multinationals, on the one hand, and poverty and inequality, on the other.

> [...T]he American Model has become a stylized battleground for Europeans, a terrain for struggle between those who would destroy European social democracy, those who would defend it, and those who would adapt it as best they can.
>
> (Galbraith, 2002: 101)

There are two competing hypotheses: one of them states that the development of national societies shows an irreversible trend towards *institutional convergence*. This hypothesis relies on strong assumptions, namely, that there is one 'proper' route to development which, sooner or later, all societies will follow; in addition, it is assumed that institutions are sufficiently prone to influences of market competition so that mutual adaptation will occur over time.

> In other words: the convergence hypothesis is a particular variant/special brand of the functionalist argument, viz. that functional requirements transnationally lead to convergence of national institutions.
>
> (Traxler, 2002: 471)

The opposing hypothesis is *path dependency*: societies will change only along and within the limits of their particular 'development corridors', which are determined by the particularities of their respective institutions. Mutual adaptation may occur, but institutional variety and international differences will persist.

> - There exist functionally equivalent solutions systematically covariant with alternative institutional arrangements. Dysfunctional arrangements may become obsolete in the course of economic internationalization. Nevertheless, the institutional pluralism will continue as more than one arrangement will prove to be compatible with the dictates of the market.
> - The institutional arrangements are so insensitive to any dictates of adaptation that it is the benefit programmes that have to adapt to the institutional situation rather than the other way around. This is a consequence of imperfect markets in conjunction with high costs of institutional change.
>
> (Traxler, 2002: 473)

In subsequent sections we shall discuss diverse welfare models. The Welfare State is frequently regarded as an important element in the *structural convergence* of present-day societies; at the same time, however, it may trigger *divergences* – due to differing institutional structures (Flora and Heidenheimer, 1981: 8).

> [C]ultural change seems to be path dependent. Economic development tends to bring pervasive cultural changes, but the fact that a society was historically shaped by Protestantism or Confucianism or Islam leaves a cultural heritage with enduring effects. [...] Finally, modernization is probabilistic, not deterministic. Economic development tends to trans-form a given society in a predictable direction, but the process and path are not inevitable. Many factors are involved, so any prediction must be contingent on the historical and cultural context of the society in question.
>
> (Inglehart and Baker, 2000: 49)

These institutional structures are not stable over time. They cannot be clearly and exactly distinguished once and for all, for they are continually changing. All welfare states face similar challenges (see the next section), and it is true for nearly all societies that different groups have different rights and different ways of access to their systems. One cannot speak of convergence; all we can say is that it becomes more difficult to distinguish exactly between actual systems (Cochrane *et al.*, 2001: 20).

Hence I take the position that one can see parallel developments rather than convergence. There is plausible evidence for path-dependency, but external shocks may divert societies from their given path. Especially the last years in Europe show clearly that systems that were sustainable for some decades may not be sustainable anymore. Nevertheless one cannot speak of clear conver-gence, as cultural factors also matter. This becomes very clear when one regards social reforms in the last decade in Europe: when politics tries to reform within the system, they will get much less resistance than with reforms against the system (e.g. Scandinavia vs. Germany). This view is shared to some extent by Wilensky, although in his analysis he reaches the conclusion of 'convergence' of welfare states:

> The welfare state is at once one of the great structural uniformities of modern society and, paradoxically, one of its most striking diversities. In the past century the world's 22 richest countries [...], although they vary greatly in civil liberties and civil rights, have varied little in their general strategy for constructing a floor below which no one sinks. The richer these countries became, the more likely they were to broaden the coverage of both population and risks. At the level of economic development they achieved in the past 30 years, however, we find sharp contrasts in spending, taxing, and the organization of the welfare state and, of course, in the poli-tics of the welfare state.
>
> (Wilensky, 2002: 211)

The structural correlates of industrialization push all rich democracies toward convergence at a high level of social spending; differences in the power of mass-based political parties as they interact with national bargaining patterns (especially the structure, functions, behaviour, and interplay of labour, the professions, management and the government) explain the substantial differences in patterns of taxing and spending that remain among the countries equally rich. There is no uniform 'crisis' of the welfare state, although there is much hysterical talk about it. Instead there is a slowdown in the rate of expansion and some reductions in benefits per person, with variation in the targets and the fairness of cuts.

(Wilensky, 2002: 247)

The development of systems of welfare states

Many Western capitalist welfare states face similar challenges:

- Aging populations produce demographic pressure.
- Traditional family models are no longer dominant; therefore one can no longer rely on long-established familial self-help models.
- De-industrialization destabilizes labour markets, so job-focused social benefits decrease noticeably.
- Advanced societies also have in common an expanded 'middle-class', increased class mobility and meritocracy, more minority-group cleavages and reduced rates of economic growth.

(Wilensky, 2002: 243)

Different welfare states react differently to these problems. This is due to their different histories. According to Durkheim, it was a process of *structural-functional differentiation* that brought traditional forms of social organization to an end. The regulating structures – markets, associations, bureaucracies – developed differently in different countries. Countries with a dominant *protestant state church* developed responsibility for social welfare quite early, while catholic countries tended to maintain the traditions of private charity and clung to the principle of subsidiarity (according to which social responsibilities are entrusted to the lowest possible level of the communal hierarchy).

Thus, differences in the existing associative structures and their historical development may explain some of the differences in the development of the welfare state.

(Flora and Alber, 1981: 43)

Apart from the church, it is the strength and cohesion of *labour parties* and *labour unions* that determine a welfare model. This may have undesired consequences: in countries such as in France and Germany, socialists and communists rivalled and even fought one another, hampering the development of solidarity and respective benefit systems (see Flora and Alber, 1981).

From 1900 to the Second World War, Western capitalist societies saw the take-off of modern welfare states. The most significant structural change in the development of public expenditure was the redistribution of incomes via social transfer payments.

The classical phase, initiated in Germany, was completed by the beginning of the First World War. By then, nearly all Western countries had some sort of accident insurance for employees; many countries also had incipient systems of health insurance. Of the various types of insurance, *accident insurance* conflicted least with liberal concepts of individual responsibility: accidents on the job are inevitable to a certain extent and it would have been inefficient to deal with each case individually. Therefore, a sort of automatic compensation was introduced early on, with the employers eventually moving from individual liability to a system of risk-pooling.

Health and old age insurance are somewhat farther removed from liberal principles so they came only later. Farthest removed from them, however, is *unemployment insurance*: even today how far this encourages the 'unworthy poor' is still being discussed.

Nonetheless, the time between the two wars was a phase of expansion in which more risks (as those just mentioned) and other groups of persons were included and some more countries set up insurance systems. A number of states adopted the idea of guaranteed minimum wages. After the Second World War the systems were rounded out. Thus, some countries extended their social security to the self-employed; in fact, systems of comprehensive ('universal') social security were established.

Those systems developed parallel to one another; there is no reason, according to Flora and Alber, to speak of a process of diffusion. It was a historical coincidence – namely, Bismarck's hatred of the socialists – that Germany became the first country to establish a social security system. Those countries that introduced social security systems later did so on a noticeably higher level. Their systems were more refined and more inclusive.

Today, within the European Union, a variety of welfare state models exist, with the common feature that comprehensive social protection is a fundamental right. These different welfare states have shown to be able to reform and adapt their welfare states to demographic and social changes to vastly different degrees.

The US developed along different lines from the beginning, as feudalism in its European form never existed there, nor had a powerful labour movement emerged before democratic structures were established. In the twentieth century the US welfare state saw two major extension phases: the New Deal (in the 1930s) and the Great Society (in the 1960s), which in some aspects indicated a turn towards European welfare state models. After the Vietnam trauma and increased orientation towards domestic affairs in the early 1970s, the New Right became stronger in the United States, and the American welfare model began to develop away from its European counterpart. In the last few decades, social policy responsibilities have increasingly been transferred from federal to state levels; this did not change in the 1990s during the administration of President Clinton. All in all, the development of US social policy has resulted in what Wilensky calls an 'elaborate welfare mess' – it is expensive, non-transparent and unable to cope adequately with social problems:

> Although the United States is not alone in cultivating the welfare mess, it is exceptional in the vigour of its means testing, the inadequacy and inefficiency of its programmes, and the harassment of its welfare poor.
>
> (Wilensky, 2002: 717)

To my mind, Wilensky is too negative about the United States and too positive about the good performance of (mainly European) corporatist welfare regimes.

The world of Esping-Andersen

One book has become indispensable to writers on social policy, especially to those interested in international comparisons, namely, Esping-Andersen's *The Three Worlds of Welfare Capitalism* (1990).

Esping-Andersen distinguishes three types of social welfare states, according to the following criteria:

- the degree of *decommodification*: this indicates how far an individual is economically independent from the market and/or from selling his labour on the market. Indirectly it also indicates whether and how far social benefits are dependent on (former) gainful employment;
- the degree of *social stratification*: this indicates how far welfare regulations influence social position – are they effective only *ex post*, indirectly, or do they actively determine the social position of the persons benefited?

Thus, the author distinguishes:

'Liberal' welfare states: these stress individual liberty and unhampered market mechanisms. Their benefit systems rely on income-dependent payments, whose stigmatizing effects are expressly taken into account. Benefits paid by the government are intended primarily for the lowest income brackets. Social security payments are scanty, while government encourages private provision for risks. Policies in the interest of a particular class are more or less unknown. Examples of such states are Australia, Canada and the United States, while Great Britain and Japan fit in here only with qualifications.

'Conservative' welfare states rely on social security benefits that tend to maintain traditional distinctions of class and status. The redistribution of income is not high among their priorities. Examples of this type are Italy, France and Germany. Such states often have catholic–absolutist traditions. In order to avoid misunderstandings about the word 'conservative', often the term 'corporatist' is

resorted to instead. This may be correct for Austria and Germany, but not for France with its statist traditions. Also, the use of the word overlooks that 'socialist/ social-democratic' states have tended to introduce or re-introduce corporatist elements into their systems. The success, for example, of the employment policies of Denmark and the Netherlands is to a considerable extent due to the consensus reached by 'social partnerships' of employers and employees.

'Socialist' welfare states have the most comprehensive and highly redistributive systems. They too show some class stratification, but aim at minimizing class differences. As for employment policies, they rely on active labour-market measures. While their labouring classes strongly influence politics, socialist/-social-democratic parties in such states tend to form coalitions also with other social groups, for example farmers. Examples are the Netherlands, Denmark, Sweden, and Norway.

Table 13.1 lists those countries that are most typical – as rated by Esping-Andersen's cluster method – of the respective regime. The only exception is Great Britain, a 'liberal' regime but with reservations in view of certain socialist features. When one looks at Esping-Andersen's list, it becomes clear that there is hardly a country that neatly fits the characterization of one regime, as the systems tend to overlap.

It may be objected that Esping-Andersen's clustering was not properly done: cardinally comparable data were first reduced to ordinal rankings; the resulting ranks were accorded points arbitrarily and those points were used in the cluster analysis (Prettenthaler and Sturn, 2003: 391). Still, the results achieved may be used for further analyses, even though with some critical reservations (to be explained in the following section).

Mixed economies of welfare

Feminist economists have been critical of the fact that, in Esping-Andersen's world, the role of women and/or the family is neglected. It makes a difference whether a system shows a high degree of decommodification because the government offers social security benefits that so far have been offered by the market, or whether we have a system in which social security has never been offered via the market because it has always been provided privately, i.e. within the family. Decommodification may denote either that social benefits had

Table 13.1 Clusters of welfare states according to regimes

'Conservative'	'Liberal'	'Socialist'
Austria	Switzerland	Denmark
Belgium	USA	Finland
France	(Great Britain)	Netherlands
Germany		Norway
Italy		Sweden

Source: Esping-Andersen 1990, 74.

formerly been commodified, or that they had never been commodified at all and therefore remained invisible.

Esping-Andersen took this criticism to heart and in a subsequent work (*Social Foundations of Postindustrial Economies*, 1999) introduced the concept of *de-familialization*: the degree to which families are divested of social responsibilities, be it by the market or by government.

The role of families as an agent of social welfare is also taken into account in the concept of mixed economies of welfare. This focuses on the fact that there exists a variety of agencies/agents offering social security benefits and that the relation among them must be analysed. Different authors use different classifications, but most of them distinguish between the factors State, Market, a Third Sector and the Family.

Kuhnle and Alestalo (2000: 8) classify European mixed economies accordingly: Great Britain provides welfare services via Market and Family (probably the same could be said of the US); in continental Europe, State, Family and Third Sector are responsible for welfare; in Scandinavia it is almost exclusively the State; in Southern Europe, Family and Third Sector.

Johnson (1999) points out that this classification has ideological undertones, for focusing on 'mixed welfare economies' implies a turning-away from state-centred discussions of welfare policies:

> The maintenance of a split between provision, on the one hand, and finance and regulation, on the other, is a common theme in analyses of mixed economies of welfare. The general aim is to reduce the state's role as a direct provider of services, but to retain its role in finance and regulation. In this way, state agencies become enablers rather than providers.
>
> (Johnson, 1999: 25)

Therefore, the concept of mixed welfare economies is advocated by feminists, on the one hand, who expect an increased visibility of informal (women's) services therefrom, and on the other hand by critics of bureaucracies, who expect that a division among more providers will increase the efficiency of social services.

The analysis of *mixed economies* requires some caution, but it enables us to realize what has been invisible so far: the services of families, especially women. Some authors have recently even inquired into the importance of ethnic minorities. This is an important problem, not only in the US, but also in Europe. Ethnic minorities are not only systematically disadvantaged in Western capitalist societies; they are also the ones who perform the meanest and worst paid jobs. They are underpaid and quite often have fewer social rights. Welfare states may also be classified according to the manner in which they treat such minorities: Sweden and also the US may be regarded as assimilating, multicultural countries, while France, Great Britain, and the Netherlands have quasi-assimilating regimes with strong post-colonial tendencies; Austria and Germany, on the other hand, simply have exclusive guest-worker regimes (Castles; Miller 1999, quoted in Cochrane *et al.*, 2001b, 17).

2 Empirical analysis

I now want to compare the social policy systems of Europe and the United States in two respects: first I look at equal opportunities – what can social policy systems do to level out different situations and to further equal opportunities? Second I want to examine the organization of the different welfare states. In these two factors (equal opportunities and organization) lie the core differences between the two models on both sides of the Atlantic.

Distribution of opportunities

Are opportunities equally distributed, regardless of sex, of ethnic origin, of health, etc.? Internationally comparable data is scarce and has its flaws. I mainly use OECD data which has a strong focus on the labour market.

Underlying the analysis is the hypothesis that in a comprehensive view opportunities are more equally distributed in countries which also have more equally distributed incomes. Therefore I look at income distribution and social expenditures first (we know from social policy analysis that there is a very high correlation between gross social expenditures and income distribution, for example, see Prettenthaler and Sturn, 2003).

Social expenditures and income distribution

With regard to *gross expenditure*, in particular public expenditure, there are significant differences between Europe and the United States. For example, in 2001, European welfare states, on average, spent 27 per cent of GDP for social policy measures, compared to only 16 per cent of GDP in the case of the US. However, in the 1990s, the growth of social expenditures began to slow. Table 13.2 shows that total social expenditures do not differ very much at all – net total expenditures in the United States in 2001 were just as high as in Europe. That is an indication that insurance against social risks is important to both Europeans and Americans, but the extent to which it is publicly provided differs.

Statistical information indicates that in the first half of the twentieth century the unequal distribution of *market incomes* was slowly but steadily decreasing, and already at that time it was the Scandinavian countries where incomes tended to be most equally distributed. Income relations were stable in the 1950s and 1960s, and the only noticeable shifts occurred between the richest and the poorest income segments. Especially in the United States this was a period when large income shares were accounted for in particular by the middle class, while in the following decades the richest groups gradually increased their income shares. Changes in income distribution were found in all countries in the 1970s and 1980s. Since the late 1980s income distribution has become considerably

Table 13.2 Public and total social expenditure (in percentage of GNP), 2001

	Public social expenditure (%)		All social expenditure (%)	
	Gross	Net	Gross	Net
Norway	27.00	22.40	29.40	23.80
Sweden	34.10	27.10	38.20	29.70
Denmark	34.20	26.10	35.80	26.90
Scandinavia	**31.77**	**25.20**	**34.47**	**26.80**
Belgium	30.90	26.50	30.90	26.50
Netherlands	24.60	20.60	31.70	25.50
Benelux	**27.75**	**23.55**	**31.30**	**26.00**
Germany	30.60	28.10	33.30	30.10
Austria	29.60	23.60	31.40	24.90
Central Europe	**30.10**	**25.85**	**32.35**	**27.50**
Italy	n.a.	n.a.	n.a.	n.a.
Spain	21.70	18.80	22.10	18.90
Mediterranean	**21.70**	**18.80**	**22.10**	**18.90**
France	n.a.	n.a.	n.a.	n.a.
United Kingdom	25.40	23.30	30.60	27.50
United States	15.70	17.10	26.70	25.60
Anglo-Saxon	**20.55**	**20.20**	**28.65**	**26.55**
Europe	**27.34**	**23.34**	**30.16**	**25.34**
Europe weighted	**27.34**	**23.69**	**30.20**	**25.81**
United States	**15.70**	**17.10**	**26.70**	**25.60**

Source: OECD 2005a. Data chart EQ 7.2. Own calculations.

more unequal in the US than in Europe (possibly with the exception of the United Kingdom).

Regarding *disposable incomes* (i.e. taking into account taxes and transfers; see Table 13.3) distribution is most equal in the Scandinavian countries. The United States and the United Kingdom saw the strongest increases in inequality until the mid-1980s, and the other countries followed this trend in the next decade. This development is primarily due to changes in the labour market: as a result of rising numbers of insecure jobs and growing unemployment rates, in almost all countries the lowest income groups did not participate in general economic growth. Contrary to the United States, however, in Europe attempts were made to prevent structural changes from showing their full effects on wages. This resulted in higher social stability but at the expense of employment and eventually led to *increased unemployment rates*. An analysis of poverty trends (Table 13.4) shows in which ways lower income segments actually benefited from the different approaches in the individual countries:

Table 13.3 Distribution of disposable income – development over time

	Relation of richest decile to poorest decile			
	Middle of 1970s	*Middle of 1980s*	*Middle of 1990s*	*End of 1990s*
Norway	n.a.	2.90	3.00	2.80
Sweden	2.80	2.60	2.70	3.00
Denmark	n.a.	2.90	2.70	2.80
Scandinavia	**2.80**	**2.80**	**2.80**	**2.87**
Belgium	n.a.	3.20	3.20	n.a.
Netherlands	2.70	2.80	3.20	3.10
Benelux	**2.70**	**3.00**	**3.20**	**3.10**
Germany	n.a.	3.30	3.70	3.50
Austria	n.a.	2.90	3.00	3.30
Central Europe	n.a.	**3.10**	**3.35**	**3.40**
Italy	n.a.	3.80	4.60	4.60
Spain	n.a.	n.a.	n.a.	4.10
Mediterranean	n.a.	**3.80**	**4.60**	**4.35**
France	n.a.	**3.30**	**3.40**	**3.40**
United Kingdom	3.10	3.60	4.10	4.20
United States	4.90	5.70	5.50	5.40
Anglo-Saxon	**4.00**	**4.65**	**4.80**	**4.80**
Europe	**2.87**	**3.27**	**3.58**	**3.55**
Europe weighted	**2.19**	**3.34**	**3.69**	**3.67**
United States	**4.90**	**5.70**	**5.50**	**5.40**

Source: Förster; Mira d'Ercole 2005. Annex Table A-3. Own calculations.

In the US, poverty rates were higher than in Europe both in the 1980s and in the 1990s (at the end of the 1990s, approximately 9 per cent of the European population were regarded as poor, compared to 17 per cent in the United States). Periods of poverty were also considerably longer. While the reforms undertaken by the United States in the 1970s and 1980s may have reduced the number of people who were granted 'unjustified' social benefits compared to the period of the Great Society, collateral damage in the form of general increases in (child) poverty is considerable.

Equal opportunities for women

The situation of women in various welfare systems is summarized in Table 13.5. Here massive differences are evident within Europe, but a number of differences between Europe and the United States can also be identified.

For instance, part-time work is a proven way for European women to reconcile job and family responsibilities, while part-time work is less common in the United States, which leads to the conclusion that wage levels and social insurance protection are insufficient for part-time options. This corresponds with the fact that the differences in employment rates between males and females have recently been lower in the United States than in Europe.

Although the US is generally regarded as economically liberal, equality of opportunity remains a distant goal. Wage differences between men and women are greater in the United States than in Europe (Table 13.6), while, seats in Parliament/Congress are significantly less often occupied by a woman (Table 13.7).

It is worth noting that although rates of active political participation are low in the United States, the share of women in administrative and managerial jobs is much larger than in any European country (Table 13.7). Internationally comparable data are very scarce on this subject, as there are different definitions of managerial work. In an ILO study we find some qualitative evidence suggesting that in Europe it is again the Scandinavian countries where women have the best chance of 'breaking through the glass ceiling'. But even there, the labour market is so segregated that women's participation rates in private-sector management jobs are low.

Table 13.4 Poverty – development over time

	Middle of 1980s	*Middle of 1990s*	*End of 1990s*
Norway	6.90	10.00	6.30
Sweden	5.30	6.40	5.30
Denmark	7.00	5.00	4.30
Scandinavia	**6.40**	**7.13**	**5.30**
Belgium	10.50	7.80	7.80
Netherlands	3.40	6.30	6.00
Benelux	**6.95**	**7.05**	**6.90**
Germany	6.40	9.40	9.30
Austria	6.10	7.40	8.90
Central Europe	**6.25**	**8.40**	**9.10**
Italy	10.30	14.20	12.90
Spain	n.a.	n.a.	11.50
Mediterranean	**10.30**	**14.20**	**12.20**
France	**8.00**	**7.50**	**7.00**
United Kingdom	6.90	10.90	11.40
United States	18.30	17.00	17.10
Anglo-Saxon	**12.60**	**13.95**	**14.25**
Europe	**7.47**	**9.20**	**8.65**
Europe weighted	**7.84**	**10.11**	**9.63**
United States	**18.30**	**17.00**	**17.10**

Source: Förster; Mira d'Ercole 2005. Annex Table A-3. Own calculations. Poverty thresholds at 50% of median income for the entire population.

Equal opportunities for immigrants and ethnic minorities

Immigrants and ethnic minorities are other groups that are often neglected in comparisons of welfare states, but whose social situation tends to be more precarious than that of the population as a whole. Unfortunately, international data hardly exist in this field. Still, the following facts may be extracted. Within Europe, immigration and integration policies depend on the nature of the welfare system. While West Central European countries tend to regard immigrants from the perspective of labour migration and thus are reluctant to grant them all rights related to welfare and social policy, the Scandinavian states and the Netherlands understand themselves to be multi-cultural societies (the latter with a strong post-colonial tradition; in the last years right-wing populist parties have undermined this consensus). However, integration achievements in these countries are also due to lower immigration rates. In recent years the European Commission has focused on this topic attempting to draw up at European level guidelines for third-country nationals.

The only comparable international data is from OECD employment statistics (Tables 13.8–13.10). One of the problems here is that foreign workers and

Table 13.5 Gender employment gap and part-time employment

	Difference in employment rates (%)		Part-time work (2003) (%)	
	1980	2003	Women	Men
Norway	22.50	7.00	33.40	9.90
Sweden	13.00	3.90	20.60	7.90
Denmark	12.00	9.20	21.90	10.50
Scandinavia	**15.83**	**6.70**	**25.30**	**9.43**
Belgium	34.00	16.80	33.40	5.90
Netherlands	40.00	15.80	59.60	14.80
Benelux	**37.00**	**16.30**	**46.50**	**10.35**
Germany	31.00	13.50	36.30	5.90
Austria	32.53	15.50	26.10	3.20
Central Europe	**31.77**	**14.50**	**31.20**	**4.55**
Italy	41.00	26.50	23.60	4.90
Spain	48.00	25.40	16.50	2.50
Mediterranean	**44.50**	**25.95**	**20.05**	**3.70**
France	**28.00**	**11.30**	**22.80**	**4.70**
United Kingdom	23.00	14.70	40.10	9.60
United States	24.50	12.50	18.80	8.00
Anglo-Saxon	**23.75**	**13.60**	**29.45**	**8.80**
Europe	**30.02**	**14.91**	**30.99**	**7.06**
Europe weighted	**32.71**	**16.88**	**29.05**	**5.89**
United States	**24.50**	**12.50**	**18.80**	**8.00**

Source: OECD Employment Outlook 2002 and 2004.

Table 13.6 Women's wages in comparison to men's wages, 1999

	Only full time employment (%)			Total (%)		
	Median	Lowest 20%	Highest 20%	Median	Lowest 20%	Highest 20%
Norway	n.a.	n.a.	n.a.	n.a.	n.a.	n.a.
Sweden	90.00	92.00	84.00	88.00	91.00	81.00
Denmark	93.00	96.00	87.00	92.00	95.00	88.00
Scandinavia	**91.50**	**94.00**	**85.50**	**90.00**	**93.00**	**84.50**
Belgium	94.00	91.00	91.00	93.00	91.00	92.00
Netherlands	86.00	85.00	80.00	87.00	86.00	81.00
Benelux	**90.00**	**88.00**	**85.50**	**90.00**	**88.50**	**86.50**
Germany	83.00	80.00	80.00	83.00	78.00	80.00
Austria	80.00	76.00	80.00	79.00	76.00	80.00
Central Europe	**81.50**	**78.00**	**80.00**	**81.00**	**77.00**	**80.00**
Italy	91.00	90.00	87.00	93.00	91.00	93.00
Spain	93.00	86.00	95.00	88.00	84.00	91.00
Mediterranean	**92.00**	**88.00**	**91.00**	**90.50**	**87.50**	**92.00**
France	**93.00**	**89.00**	**89.00**	**93.00**	**90.00**	**91.00**
United Kingdom	85.00	85.00	80.00	79.00	79.00	76.00
United States	79.00	83.00	78.00	76.00	82.00	78.00
Anglo-Saxon	**82.00**	**84.00**	**79.00**	**77.50**	**80.50**	**77.00**
Europe	**88.83**	**87.00**	**85.17**	**87.25**	**85.83**	**85.00**
Europe weighted	**88.06**	**85.29**	**85.26**	**86.41**	**84.03**	**85.22**
United States	**79.00**	**83.00**	**78.00**	**76.00**	**82.00**	**78.00**

Source: OECD 2002, 97. Own calculations.

Table 13.7 Women's political and business 'power'

	Seats in Parliament (%)		Women's share of administrative and managerial workers (%)
	1987	2004	2002/03
Norway	34.0	36.0	30.0
Sweden	32.0	45.0	30.0
Denmark	29.0	38.0	26.0
Scandinavia	**31.7**	**39.7**	**28.7**
Belgium	8.0	35.0	31.0
Netherlands	20.0	37.0	26.0
Benelux	**14.0**	**36.0**	**28.5**
Germany	n.a.	32.0	36.0
Austria	11.0	34.0	27.0
Central Europe	**11.0**	**33.0**	**31.5**
Italy	13.0	12.0	21.0
Spain	9.0	36.0	30.0
Mediterranean	**11.0**	**24.0**	**25.5**
France	**7.0**	**12.0**	n.a.
United Kingdom	6.0	18.0	33.0
United States	5.0	14.0	46.0
Anglo-Saxon	**5.5**	**16.0**	**39.5**
Europe	**13.4**	**27.1**	**29.4**
Europe weighted	**10.74**	**25.0**	**29.36**
United States	**5.0**	**14.0**	**46.0**

Source: United Nations Statistics Division 2005. Own calculations.

foreign-born workers are mixed up. Another problem is that these statistics only illustrate the situation in the labour market – they do not tell us anything about cultural or political integration or about the quality of life in general of migrants.

Nevertheless this comparison reveals that in the United States, in spite of significantly higher immigration rates, integration is much more effective: the situation of immigrants is characterized by lower unemployment rates, higher qualification levels, and smaller differences between nationals and non-nationals in the labour market.

However, there is a problem group whose situation more closely resembles that of European immigrants: African-Americans. Accounting for 12 per cent of the overall population, they may be regarded as involuntary 'immigrants' and are strongly affected by the social policy backlash felt since the 1970s. Meanwhile, subtle racism (expressed in the prejudice that to be on welfare equals to be black) has also penetrated large segments of the Democrats. As a result of segregation, African-Americans often do not attain the same educational levels as other groups, and eventually, causing their opportunities for social participation and advancement to further deteriorate. Although there is no doubt that immigrants in Europe and black people in the United States are socially and materially disadvantaged, they are important service providers, as they are over-represented among workers in health and social assistance services.

Equal opportunities via education policies

For an analysis of social opportunities in the US it is indispensable to include the educational system. In Europe, one usually thinks about education policies more in terms of economic growth policy – education is one of the main aspects of the Lisbon strategy. It is equally important for social cohesion. The education system is also one of the most important levers for equal opportunity, as it can balance deficiencies in the individual background (be it lack of language in a migrant background or be it a low educational level of one's parents).

Table 13.8 Share of immigrants, 1998

	Immigrants in population		*Immigrants in labour force*	
	in 1,000	*as %*	*in 1,000*	*as %*
Norway	165	3.70	67	3.00
Sweden	500	5.60	219	5.10
Denmark	256	4.80	94	3.20
Scandinavia	**307**	**4.70**	**127**	**3.77**
Belgium	892	8.70	375	8.80
Netherlands	662	4.20	208	2.90
Benelux	**777**	**6.45**	**292**	**5.85**
Germany	7,320	8.90	2,522	9.10
Austria	737	9.10	327	9.90
Central Europe	**4,029**	**9.00**	**1,425**	**9.50**
Italy	1,250	2.10	332	1.70
Spain	720	1.80	191	1.20
Mediterranean	**985**	**1.95**	**262**	**1.45**
France	**3,263**	**5.60**	**1,587**	**6.10**
United Kingdom	2,207	3.80	1,039	3.90
United States	26,300	9.80	16,100	11.70
Anglo-Saxon	**14,254**	**6.80**	**8,570**	**7.80**
Europe	**1,928**	**5.25**	**788**	**5.09**
Europe weighted	**2,306**	**5.17**	**911**	**5.17**
United States	**26,300**	**9.80**	**16,100**	**11.70**

Source: OECD 2001, 170. Own calculations.

Table 13.9 Labour force participation and unemployment of immigrants, 1998

| | Participation in labour market (%) | | | | Unemployment rate (%) | | | |
| | Men | | Women | | Men | | Women | |
	Nationals	Non-nationals	Nationals	Non-nationals	Nationals	Non-nationals	Nationals	Non-nationals
Norway	87.00	85.50	78.10	64.80	3.40	5.90	4.00	6.00
Sweden	79.10	70.50	73.40	52.90	9.30	23.20	7.50	19.40
Denmark	84.10	69.40	76.00	51.60	3.80	7.30	6.10	16.00
Scandinavia	**83.40**	**75.13**	**75.83**	**56.43**	**5.50**	**12.13**	**5.87**	**13.80**
Belgium	72.90	69.00	55.10	40.70	6.50	18.90	10.90	24.10
Netherlands	83.20	66.50	63.50	40.80	3.10	11.60	5.60	14.10
Benelux	**78.05**	**67.75**	**59.30**	**40.75**	**4.80**	**15.25**	**8.25**	**19.10**
Germany	79.40	77.30	63.40	48.70	8.50	17.30	10.10	15.90
Austria	79.80	84.30	62.40	63.40	4.80	10.30	5.30	8.90
Central Europe	**79.60**	**80.80**	**62.90**	**56.05**	**6.65**	**13.80**	**7.70**	**12.40**
Italy	73.60	89.10	44.40	54.00	9.60	5.10	16.70	17.60
Spain	75.90	84.00	47.70	52.20	14.00	10.90	26.60	24.00
Mediterranean	**74.75**	**86.55**	**46.05**	**53.10**	**11.80**	**8.00**	**21.65**	**20.80**
France	**75.00**	**76.10**	**62.50**	**49.00**	**9.60**	**22.00**	**13.50**	**26.80**
United Kingdom	83.00	78.10	67.40	56.10	6.80	10.70	5.20	9.40
United States	74.20	79.70	60.80	52.70	4.30	4.90	4.50	6.00
Anglo-Saxon	**78.60**	**78.90**	**64.10**	**54.40**	**5.55**	**7.80**	**4.85**	**7.70**
Europe	**78.97**	**77.41**	**62.33**	**51.91**	**7.53**	**13.65**	**10.36**	**17.05**
Europe weighted	**78.15**	**79.87**	**59.36**	**52.94**	**8.40**	**13.06**	**12.05**	**17.21**
United States	**74.20**	**79.70**	**60.80**	**52.70**	**4.30**	**4.90**	**4.50**	**6.00**

Source: OECD 2001, 173. Own calculations.

Table 13.10 Educational level of nationals and non-nationals, 1998

	Lower secondary education (%)		Higher secondary education (%)		Tertiary education (%)	
	Non-nationals	Nationals	Non-nationals	Nationals	Non-nationals	Nationals
Sweden	30.80	20.40	41.50	50.30	27.70	29.30
Germany	48.50	13.20	37.00	62.20	14.40	24.60
Italy	47.10	56.30	38.30	34.30	14.60	9.30
France	63.30	33.40	22.90	45.40	13.80	21.10
United Kingdom	65.10	43.90	14.70	32.50	20.20	23.70
Europe	50.96	33.44	30.88	44.94	18.14	21.60
Europe weighted	51.43	31.64	32.94	48.27	15.59	20.04
USA	35.00	15.70	24.10	35.00	40.90	49.30

Source: OECD 2001, 181. Own calculations.

Therefore, I cmpare selected aspects of educational systems (Table 13.11). Education obviously plays an essential role in the United States: unlike social expenditure, in the US the public sums spent on education are similar to those in Europe, with both the primary and the tertiary sectors better funded than the European average.

Correspondingly, a larger share of the population graduates than in Europe (in Europe, one out of four people have completed at least tertiary education, compared to 38 per cent in the United States; Table 13.12). However, regarding the individual literacy fields, the PISA results for the US are not as favourable (Table 13.13). Except for reading, US scores are lower both compared to the OECD-average (namely, 500) and the EU-average. It is not clear what the reason is for this – one might suppose that it could reflect an 'elitist' approach (high support 'isles of excellence' but low support for mass institutions), but this is contradicted by the fact that variance of student performance is not significantly higher in the US than in Europe.

Table 13.13 highlights differences within Europe: the highest scores are reached in Finland (which is not shown in this table[1]) and in the Netherlands. The Central European and Mediterranean countries have lower scores.

State, market or mixed economy – how is the welfare system organized?

Since the 1980s, scepticism towards state intervention has shifted the focus (both in life and in social policy research) to other agents, namely the private and third sectors as well as informal networks.

States have changed their roles by cooperating with other agents. Here one must bear in mind that a 'state' is not a uniform structure, as it consists of various administrative levels with different responsibilities. Interactions between these levels are not always free of conflict.

Particularly in the United States, business has always played an important role in social policy. Private supplementary insurance accounts for one third of social policy expenditure, and enterprises provide occupational welfare services for employees, although to decreasing extents due to the difficult economic situation during the last few years (see Table 13.14). This should not be forgotten when shifts of responsibility from state to private structures are advocated also for social policy. Although, many social services may also be provided by private business, this always implies that certain persons or groups will be excluded.

Recent developments in the US have shown that occupational welfare benefits have become options only for highly qualified workers. If mixed systems are attempted in this field, the danger is that upper and middle classes may withdraw from agreements based on social solidarity, which have been widespread (often implicitly adhered to) in Europe. While wealthier groups turn to private insurance, public funds for disadvantaged people are getting increasingly smaller.

Table 13.11 Expenditure on educational institutions as % of GDP, 2001

	Sources of fund			Expenditure by level	
	Public	Private	Total	Primary and secondary	Tertiary
Norway	6.1	0.2	6.4	4.6	1.3
Sweden	6.3	0.2	6.5	4.3	1.7
Denmark	6.8	0.3	7.1	4.3	1.8
Scandinavia	**6.4**	**0.2**	**6.7**	**4.4**	**1.6**
Belgium	6.0	0.4	6.4	4.2	1.4
Netherlands	4.5	0.4	4.9	3.3	1.3
Benelux	**5.3**	**0.4**	**5.7**	**3.8**	**1.4**
Germany	4.3	1.0	5.3	3.6	1.0
Austria	5.6	0.2	5.8	3.9	1.2
Central Europe	**5.0**	**0.6**	**5.6**	**3.8**	**1.1**
Italy	4.9	0.4	5.3	3.7	0.9
Spain	4.3	0.4	4.9	3.2	1.2
Mediterranean	**4.6**	**0.4**	**5.1**	**3.5**	**1.1**
France	**5.6**	**0.4**	**6.0**	**4.2**	**1.1**
United Kingdom	4.7	0.8	5.5	3.9	1.1
United States	5.1	2.3	7.3	4.1	2.7
Anglo-Saxon	**4.9**	**1.6**	**6.4**	**4.0**	**1.9**
Europe	**5.3**	**0.5**	**5.7**	**3.9**	**1.2**
Europe weighted	**5.0**	**0.5**	**5.6**	**3.8**	**1.1**
United States	**5.1**	**2.3**	**7.3**	**4.1**	**2.7**

Source: OECD 2004, Table B2.1a and B2.1b. Own calculations.

This may pave the way to income inequalities and poverty rates as high as in the United States.

The third sector (also referred to as non-profit organizations or voluntary sector) is an alternative to private structures. Its actual form depends on national history, and especially religious and cultural traditions. In the last few years, however, marketization has also developed in this field.

Still, in Europe the third sector is subsidiary to the public sector and is often financially supported to a considerable degree, while in the US its market orientation is more pronounced (Tables 13.15 and 13.16). However, this also means that it is strongly particularistic, i.e. the interests of certain groups are better represented than others. Again, underprivileged, marginalized groups are often neglected.

Last there is the informal sector. Apart from communitarian approaches (based on the view that necessary social services in a community ought to be

Table 13.12 Educational attainment in %, 2002

	Secondary degree		Tertiary degree	
	Men	*Women*	*Men*	*Women*
Norway	66	64	29	33
Sweden	60	58	30	35
Denmark	72	69	25	30
Scandinavia	**66**	**64**	**28**	**33**
Belgium	54	50	27	29
Netherlands	58	60	27	22
Benelux	**56**	**55**	**27**	**26**
Germany	65	74	28	19
Austria	76	80	17	12
Central Europe	**71**	**77**	**23**	**16**
Italy	71	65	10	10
Spain	45	41	25	24
Mediterranean	**58**	**53**	**18**	**17**
France	**62**	**56**	**23**	**25**
United Kingdom	72	73	28	27
United States	57	57	38	38
Anglo-Saxon	**65**	**65**	**33**	**33**
Europe	**64**	**63**	**24**	**24**
Europe weighted	**65**	**64**	**23**	**21**
United States	**57**	**57**	**38**	**38**

Source: OECD 2004, Table A1.1a and A1.1b. Own calculations.

provided on the basis of volunteer work and a sense of solidarity) its primary agents are families. Summarizing, one may say that only in the Scandinavian countries (and partly in France) are families supported in such a way that family and job responsibilities can actually be reconciled. In the US, the problem of combining job and family duties is regarded as a private matter. At the same time, however, families are expected to meet high moral expectations in order to be eligible for social benefits.

How do people feel about their quality of life?

Comparing equal opportunity policies, one sees that in Europe and the United States this has a different connotation: whereas in Europe equality of opportunity is fostered via income and distribution policies and to a certain extent via strengthening the position of women, in the United States immigrants find a better climate of equal opportunity. Education policy is a traditional Anglo-

Table 13.13 PISA 2003 – mean scores in student performance in different fields

	Mathematics	*Reading*	*Science*
Norway	495	500	484
Sweden	509	514	506
Denmark	514	492	475
Scandinavia	**506**	**502**	**488**
Belgium	514	492	475
Netherlands	538	513	524
Benelux	**526**	**503**	**500**
Germany	503	491	502
Austria	506	491	491
Central Europe	**505**	**491**	**497**
Italy	466	476	486
Spain	485	481	487
Mediterranean	**476**	**479**	**487**
France	**511**	**496**	**511**
United Kingdom	n.a.	n.a.	n.a.
United States	483	495	491
Anglo-Saxon	**483**	**495**	**491**
Europe	**505**	**494**	**496**
Europe weighted	**498**	**490**	**496**
United States	**483**	**495**	**491**

Source: OECD 2005b. Tables 2.5c., 6.2, 6.6. Own calculations.

Table 13.14 Occupational welfare in the United States (% of population)

	1979		*1989*		*1996*	
	Pensions	*Health*	*Pensions*	*Health*	*Pensions*	*Health*
Workers/total	51.10	70.20	44.30	63.10	47.00	62.60
Gender						
Men	56.20	75.10	46.40	66.80	48.30	65.20
Women	42.80	62.20	41.20	57.90	45.30	59.10
Education						
No high school graduation	44.40	62.20	28.70	46.20	25.40	43.80
High school graduation	51.00	70.20	42.60	61.70	43.90	59.50
'Some' college education	51.40	71.80	45.80	64.30	47.90	63.40
College graduation	59.30	79.40	54.50	75.10	59.70	74.80
Postgraduate education	62.20	79.50	62.00	78.40	67.30	79.50

Source: Seeleib-Kaiser 2000, 121.

Saxon theme but finds entrance into the social policy arena more and more in Europe also.

Looking at the organization of the welfare system we have found that the market is more important in the US than in Europe. In Europe, state and family dominate, with a growing importance of the Third Sector.

So we see different systems – the question is whether one of these systems is preferable to another. And here the data clearly say 'no'. It can be shown that people in the United States are not unhappier than people in Europe (Table 13.17). On an average, the most contented people live in the Netherlands and in Denmark.[2]

The US also ranks high in the UN human development index (Table 13.18). Although its relative position has declined in recent years, the theory of path dependency has essentially been confirmed also in this regard: the majority of people are satisfied with the system they live in and its values. Why then should significant convergence processes take place?

Culture matters

This leads to the concluding insight that the fundamental differences between the United States and Europe are rooted in different traditions and mentalities.

Compared at an aggregated level (Tables 13.19 and 13.20), Americans are more often members of some group (interestingly enough also political groups, which include parties, local political initiatives and so on). This conforms with the results of the comparison of third-sector activities. In Europe we see high group activity in Scandinavia (which is probably due to the high union organization, resulting from the connection of unemployment insurance and union membership).

Compared to Europe, the US is more strongly oriented towards tradition, with a strong focus placed on religion and authority. Europeans are more emancipated as a rule and thus make heavier demands on the state as a political community. This is connected to differences in the development of democracy in the United States and Europe. In the US, the absence of feudalist periods and class struggle, paralleled by scepticism towards state functions based on the country's specific history, has prevented a welfare state of the European kind from being established.

3 Conclusion

In spite of variations within Europe, the system of the United States definitely differs from European welfare state models. The individual policy areas are organized along different lines; there is no universal family policy and no general unemployment insurance system. Poverty policies, whether in the form of cash benefits or housing and health support for the poor, are not federal but state responsibilities. The federal government has withdrawn from social policy to a growing extent and merely provides financial assistance in the form of block

Table 13.15 Third sector employment 1995

	Employment in the third sector (%)				Third sector employment in % of total non-agricultural employment	
	Education	Health	Social services	Other	Paid staff	Volunteers
Norway	11.20	6.00	14.00	68.80	2.70	4.40
Sweden	6.80	0.90	10.50	81.80	1.70	5.10
Denmark	n.a.	n.a.	n.a.	n.a.	n.a.	n.a.
Scandinavia	**9.00**	**3.45**	**12.25**	**75.30**	**2.20**	**4.75**
Belgium	30.50	23.90	22.90	22.70	8.60	2.30
Netherlands	23.10	29.50	20.30	27.10	9.20	5.10
Benelux	**26.80**	**26.70**	**21.60**	**24.90**	**8.90**	**3.70**
Germany	7.60	21.80	27.20	43.40	3.50	2.30
Austria	n.a.	n.a.	n.a.	n.a.	3.80	1.10
Central Europe	**7.60**	**21.80**	**27.20**	**43.40**	**3.65**	**1.70**
Italy	14.80	18.00	26.10	41.10	2.30	1.50
Spain	20.60	10.50	30.80	38.10	2.80	1.50
Mediterranean	**17.70**	**14.25**	**28.45**	**39.60**	**2.55**	**1.50**
France	**14.60**	**9.20**	**27.40**	**48.80**	**3.70**	**3.70**
United Kingdom	25.40	8.00	16.00	50.60	4.80	3.60
United States	18.50	34.20	22.10	25.20	6.30	3.50
Anglo-Saxon	**21.95**	**21.10**	**19.05**	**37.90**	**5.55**	**3.55**
Europe	**17.18**	**14.20**	**21.69**	**46.93**	**4.31**	**3.06**
Europe weighted	**16.42**	**14.64**	**24.59**	**44.35**	**3.86**	**2.62**
United States	**18.50**	**34.20**	**22.10**	**25.20**	**6.30**	**3.50**

Source: Comparative Nonprofit Sector Project, 2005. Tables 1 and 3. Own calculations.

Table 13.16 Sources of revenue in the third sector, 1995

	Government (%)	Philanthropy (%)	Private fees and payments (%)
Norway	35.00	6.90	58.10
Sweden	28.70	9.10	62.30
Denmark	n.a.	n.a.	n.a.
Scandinavia	**31.85**	**8.00**	**60.20**
Belgium	76.80	4.70	18.60
Netherlands	59.00	2.40	38.60
Benelux	**67.90**	**3.55**	**28.60**
Germany	64.30	3.40	32.30
Austria	50.40	6.10	43.50
Central Europe	**57.35**	**4.75**	**37.90**
Italy	36.60	2.80	60.60
Spain	32.10	18.80	49.00
Mediterranean	**34.35**	**10.80**	**54.80**
France	**57.80**	**7.50**	**34.60**
United Kingdom	46.70	8.80	44.60
United States	30.50	12.90	56.60
Anglo-Saxon	**38.60**	**10.85**	**50.60**
Europe	**48.74**	**7.05**	**44.22**
Europe weighted	**48.67**	**7.66**	**43.66**
United States	**30.50**	**12.90**	**56.60**

Source: Comparative Non Profit Sector Project 2003, Table 4. Own calculations.

grants. Medicare and Social Security are the only federal responsibilities still remaining, but they have increasingly been under pressure as well. While this has resulted in lower overall social expenditure than in Europe, the middle classes have been forced to take out insurance on a private basis. People with irregular income from employment as well as poor people depend on state welfare programmes, which, however, they are not entitled on the basis of civil or human rights however, as eligibility depends on discretion and generosity in each individual case.

While Europe and the United States converged towards each other after the First World War and in particular in the 1960s, when the Great Society was proclaimed in the US, in the 1970s and 1980s the two models tended to drift apart. In the 1990s, US positions were increasingly often taken over in Europe, and as a consequence of the Maastricht convergence requirements, cutbacks in welfare spending were inevitable. Nevertheless, from a present-day point of view there are no actual indications that Europe is getting closer to the United States.

The same is evident with regard to social policy outputs. In particular, income

Table 13.17 Life satisfaction – percentage of respondents with high life satisfaction

	1990–91	*1999–2002*
Norway	77.5	78.8
Sweden	84.1	79.6
Denmark	85.8	85.5
Scandinavia	**82.5**	**81.3**
Belgium	77.7	78.5
Netherlands	84.3	89.6
Benelux	**81.0**	**84.1**
Germany	71.6	78.6
Austria	63.7	82.7
Central Europe	**67.7**	**80.7**
Italy	70.7	69.6
Spain	67.2	65.3
Mediterranean	**69.0**	**67.5**
France	**58.8**	**65.8**
United Kingdom	75.0	73.2
United States	79.3	78.7
Anglo-Saxon	**77.2**	**76.0**
Europe	**72.3**	**75.4**
Europe weighted	**69.6**	**73.5**
United States	**79.3**	**78.7**

Source: OECD 2005a, Table CO1.1. Own calculations. Respondents were asked to define their life satisfaction on a scale of 1 to 10. This table shows the proportion of those giving the answers 7 to 10.

distribution is much more unequal in the United States than in Europe. According to Krugman (2002: 25) a pronounced erosion of the middle classes is taking place in the US, as in recent years the strongest increases in incomes have been registered for the richest 1 per cent or even the richest 0.1 per cent of society. Krugman describes the rise of a plutocracy: the rich are buying politicians, intellectuals and public opinion to an unparalleled extent. While social conventions had been determined by the New Deal and the Great Society for 30 years and consequently income equality was regarded as a positive value, now the situation has changed towards 'anything goes'. Rich groups shape the tax system to their advantage, while the situation is getting more and more precarious for the middle classes. In the past, employees in large enterprises could compensate for the lack of welfare institutions by means of occupational benefits, but today these jobs also have become insecure and as a consequence the majority of employees have no employment-related health insurance or pension plans.

This change in atmosphere has had strong effects on welfare states. It challenges the long-maintained theory that the lean welfare state of the United States

Table 13.18 Trends in the human development index (United Nations)

	1975	*1980*	*1985*	*1990*	*1995*	*2002*
Norway	0.856	0.875	0.887	0.899	0.924	0.956
Sweden	0.862	0.872	0.882	0.892	0.924	0.946
Denmark	0.866	0.874	0.881	0.889	0.905	0.932
Scandinavia	**0.861**	**0.874**	**0.883**	**0.893**	**0.918**	**0.945**
Belgium	0.845	0.861	0.874	0.895	0.925	0.942
Netherlands	0.860	0.872	0.886	0.900	0.921	0.942
Benelux	**0.853**	**0.867**	**0.880**	**0.898**	**0.923**	**0.942**
Germany	n.a.	n.a.	n.a.	n.a.	0.905	0.925
Austria	0.839	0.853	0.866	0.889	0.908	0.934
Central Europe	n.a.	n.a.	n.a.	n.a.	**0.907**	**0.930**
Italy	0.827	0.845	0.855	0.878	0.895	0.920
Spain	0.817	0.837	0.853	0.875	0.893	0.922
Mediterranean	**0.822**	**0.841**	**0.854**	**0.877**	**0.894**	**0.921**
France	**0.846**	**0.862**	**0.874**	**0.896**	**0.913**	**0.932**
United Kingdom	0.839	0.846	0.856	0.876	0.914	0.936
United States	0.861	0.882	0.896	0.912	0.923	0.939
Anglo-Saxon	**0.850**	**0.864**	**0.876**	**0.894**	**0.919**	**0.938**
Europe	**0.844**	**0.858**	**0.869**	**0.888**	**0.911**	**0.934**
Europe weighted	**0.838**	**0.852**	**0.864**	**0.885**	**0.907**	**0.930**
United States	**0.861**	**0.882**	**0.896**	**0.912**	**0.923**	**0.939**

Source: United Nations 2004.

is more conducive to limiting unemployment. The cost this entails is rising numbers of working poor and a perpetuation of poverty (Castles, 2000: 210).

One should not forget that the US's greatest achievements in social policy go back to a time when the majority of workers had traditional forms of employment – but residual social policy combined with well-structured occupational welfare services can provide security for large parts of society only if long-term employment is the rule rather than the exception (see also Seeleib-Kaiser, 2000: 102).

Are social policy outputs in Europe are better, or is the US rather a pioneer and model in the sense that Europe has yet to learn that the state and civil society should share social policy responsibilities to a larger extent?

Closer inspection leads to the conclusion that actually, it is neither. The United States and Europe have different systems with different histories. While in the United States comprehensive social policies trickled down from federal to state levels, in Europe various forms of national social welfare systems were established, and the discussion of what responsibilities should be transferred to European Union level has started only recently.

Table 13.19 The importance of traditional values in the 1990s

	Survival vs self-expression	Traditional vs secular	Percentage who go to church at least once a month	Percentage who say God is important
Norway	1.45	1.2	13.00	15.00
Sweden	2.20	1.4	10.00	8.00
Denmark	1.20	1.2	n.a.	n.a.
Scandinavia	**1.62**	**1.27**	**11.50**	**11.50**
Belgium	0.75	0.2	35.00	13.00
Netherlands	2.00	0.5	31.00	11.00
Benelux	**1.38**	**0.35**	**33.00**	**12.00**
Germany	1.25	1.3	33.00	14.00
Austria	0.70	0.1	n.a.	n.a.
Central Europe	**0.98**	**0.70**	**33.00**	**14.00**
Italy	0.55	−0.1	47.00	29.00
Spain	0.40	−0.6	40.00	18.00
Mediterranean	**0.48**	**−0.35**	**43.50**	**23.50**
France	**0.60**	**0.15**	**17.00**	**10.00**
United Kingdom	1.10	−0.15	25.00	16.00
United States	1.50	−1.20	59.00	48.00
Anglo-Saxon	**1.30**	**−0.68**	**42.00**	**32.00**
Europe	**1.02**	**0.33**	**27.17**	**14.50**
Europe weighted	**0.86**	**0.18**	**30.71**	**16.02**
United States	**1.50**	**−1.20**	**59.00**	**48.00**

Source: Inglehart; Baker 2000. Chart 1, Tables 6 and 7. Own calculations.

Table 13.20 Proportion of respondents who are active or inactive members by type of group

	Church–religion	Sport–cultural	Political–unions	Other groups
Norway	32.10	49.80	58.70	1.45
Sweden	71.40	52.30	73.00	2.20
Denmark	11.90	41.70	62.30	1.20
Scandinavia	**38.47**	**47.93**	**64.67**	**1.62**
Belgium	11.90	37.20	29.70	0.75
Netherlands	34.70	69.60	40.50	2.00
Benelux	**23.30**	**53.40**	**35.10**	**1.38**
Germany	13.50	32.10	13.90	1.25
Austria	25.40	31.50	30.00	0.70
Central Europe	**19.45**	**31.80**	**21.95**	**0.98**
Italy	10.30	18.50	16.70	0.55
Spain	6.60	12.80	8.10	0.40
Mediterranean	**8.45**	**15.65**	**12.40**	**0.48**
France	**4.40**	**21.50**	**9.50**	**0.60**
United Kingdom	5.00	12.00	13.20	1.10
United States	57.10	55.70	49.60	1.50
Anglo-Saxon	**31.05**	**33.85**	**31.40**	**1.30**
Europe	**16.51**	**30.38**	**26.14**	**1.02**
Europe weighted	**12.72**	**24.70**	**18.98**	**0.86**
United States	**57.10**	**55.70**	**49.60**	**1.50**

Source: OECD 2005b. Chart CO 3.2. Own calculations.

It is hardly conceivable that the United States will emulate European best practice. Politics are too strongly dominated by groups that dismiss values such as solidarity and are convinced that individual capabilities and achievement orientation are the best stepping stones for advancement.

On the other hand, Europe will not uncritically follow the US model. There are sufficient instances of best practice within Europe. The Scandinavian countries continue to rank best with regard to most wealth indicators. However, it is the conservatively oriented countries of continental Europe (Germany, Austria, and, as far as can be concluded from existing data, the Mediterranean countries) that have to catch up in order to meet the challenges of the twenty-first century. In these countries, social policies oriented towards the past are overly heavy burdens. While the Anglo-Saxon world prioritizes education (orientation towards the future), the Scandinavian countries have adopted a mix that combines solidarity with weaker social groups and responsibility for the future.

Thus, there is a distinction between the European and the US welfare model. Extensive welfare states based on social protection as a civil right are among the essential constituting elements of Europe, while US citizens are sceptical towards the state and state institutions. There is a European way of reforming the Welfare State which may differ only slightly in certain aspects from the US model (for example, concerning the importance of workfare) but which is based on a different definition of what welfare and social security are about.

Restructuring will be necessary, independent of budgetary economies. States in which families are responsible for a major part of social policy necessities will have less favourable prospects than those where the state assumes responsibility for education and actively promotes equality of men and women. This may be a lesson to learn for both Europe and the US – although as in the past they will probably find different answers.

The question of whether welfare models converge or diverge also depends on the time horizon. In a globalized world most external shocks are no longer country-specific (there are of course exceptions like German re-unification or the Vietnam War). But even when problems become the same (regarding family structure, social mobility, minority problems, etc.), nevertheless the answers are not.

What we see is not so much a convergence process (which would imply that there is a *first best solution* towards which models converge) but that it is a parallel development as solutions are different and sustainable to different degrees. There is no *first best solution* which works for all countries but rather country specific solutions which must be system compliant.

Notes

1 Finnish score in Mathematics: 544; in Reading 543; in Science 548.
2 It is not really explainable why life satisfaction should have risen so much in Austria in the past decade.

References

Castles, Francis G. (2000). Models for Europe? Lessons of Other Institutional Designs. In: Stein Kuhnle (ed.) *Survival of the European Welfare State*. London: Routledge. 202–216.

Cochrane, Allan, John Clarke and Sharon Gewirtz (2001) 'Comparing Welfare States'. In: Allan Cochrane *et al.* (eds), *Comparing Welfare States* (2nd ed). London: Sage. 2–27.

Comparative Nonprofit Sector Project CNP, 2005. Online. Available HTTP: www.jhu.edu/~cnp/compdata.html>.

Esping-Andersen, Gøsta (1990) *The Three Worlds of Welfare Capitalism*. Cambridge: Polity Press.

Esping-Andersen, Gøsta (1999) *Social Foundations of Postindustrial Economies*. Oxford: Oxford University Press.

Flora, Peter and Jens Alber (1981) 'Modernization, Democratization and the Development of Welfare States in Western Europe'. In: Peter Flora; Arnold Heidenheimer, *The Development of Welfare States in Europe and America*. New Brunswick: Transaction Publishers. 37–80.

Flora, Peter and Arnold Heidenheimer (1981) 'Introduction'. In: Peter Flora; Arnold Heidenheimer, *The Development of Welfare States in Europe and America.* New Brunswick: Transaction Publishers. 17–36.

Förster, Michael and Marco Mira d'Ercole (2005) 'Income Distribution and Poverty in OECD Countries in the Second Half of the 1990s'. *OECD Social, Employment and Migration Working Papers 22.* Paris: OECD.

Galbraith, James K. (2002) 'What is the American Model really about? Soft Budgets and the Keynesian Devolution'. *Der öffentliche Sektor – Forschungsmemoranden 3–4,* 101–109. Also online. Available HTTP: <www.puereview.ae.poznan.pl/2003v3n1/ 03-1-galbraith.pdf>.

Inglehart, Ronald and Wayne E. Baker (2000) Modernization, Cultural Change, and the Persistence of Traditional Values. *American Sociological Review 65.* 19–51.

Johnson, Norman (1999) *Mixed Economies of Welfare: A Comparative Perspective.* Hemel Hempstead: Prentice Hall.

Krugman, Paul (2002) 'Der Amerikanische Albtraum'. *De Zeit 7.* November. 25–29.

Kuhnle, Stein and Matti Alestalo (2000) 'The Declining Resistance of Welfare States to Change?' In: Stein Kuhnle (ed.) *Survival of the European Welfare State.* London: Routledge. 3–18.

Maître, Bertrand, B. Nolan and C.T. Whelan (2005) 'Welfare regimes and household income packaging in the European Union'. *Journal of European Social Policy 15/2.* 157–171.

OECD, 2002. *Employment Outlook.* Paris: OECD.

OECD, 2004. *Education at a Glance – Tables. Online.* Available HTTP: <www.oecd. org/document/7/0,2340,en_2649_34515_33712135_1_1_1_1,00.html> (downloaded June 2005).

OECD, 2005a. *Society at a Glance – Raw data. Online.* Available HTTP: <www.oecd.org/els/social/indicators> (downloaded June 2005).

OECD, 2005b. *PISA 2003. Online.* Available HTTP: <www.pisa.oecd.org> (downloaded June 2005).

Prettenthaler, Franz and Richard Sturn (2003) 'Führt der Wohlfahrtsstaat zu mehr Gleich-heit? Vergleichende Analyse von Umfang, Entwicklung und Wirkung von Sozialaus-gaben', in Österreich und anderen OECD-Ländern seit 1960. *Wirtschaft und Gesellschaft 3/29.* 389–413.

Seeleib-Kaiser, Martin (2000) 'Kulturelle und politisch-institutionelle Determinanten des US-amerikanischen Wohlfahrtsstaates'. In: Herbert Obinger; Uwe Wagschal. *Der gezügelte Wohlfahrtsstaat – Sozialpolitik in reichen Industrienationen.* Frankfurt: Campus, 95–129.

Streissler, Agnes (2003) *USA und Europa: Ein Vergleich der Sozialsysteme.* Arbeitspa-pier 46. Wien: Austrian Institute for International Affairs.

Traxler, Franz (2002) 'Die Institutionen der Lohnregulierung: Funktion und Wandel im internationalen Vergleich'. *Wirtschaft und Geselschaft 4/28.* 471–488.

United Nations Statistic Division (2005a) 'Statistics and indicators on women and men'. Online. Available HTTP: <unstats.un.org/unsd/demographic/products/indwm/indwm2. htm> (downloaded June 2005).

United Nations Statistic Division (2005b) *Human Development Report 2004.* Online. Available HTTP: <hdr.undp.org/statistics/data/indic/indic_8_1_1.html> (downloaded June 2005).

Wilensky, Harold L. (2002) *Rich Democracies – Political Economy, Public Policy, and Performance.* Berkeley: University of California Press.

14 The Welfare State and Euro-growth

Peter H. Lindert

1 Introduction

Governments all over the world now tax and transfer large shares of the national product. Even governments in low- and middle-income countries tax and transfer more than any government did before the twentieth century. Have today's social transfers raised or lowered the growth of national production? Have they raised or lowered economic inequality?

The mainstream view sees a trade-off between growth and equality. On this view, Europe's welfare states have equalized incomes at a cost in terms of national product, relative to the alternative of keeping taxes and transfers as low as in the United States or Japan. I read history differently. The experiences of the rich countries seem to show that Europe's welfare states have equalized incomes and improved life expectancy at zero cost in terms of national product.

The road to these conclusions needs to start by clarifying what I mean and what I do not mean by social transfers and the Welfare State. Social transfers consist of these kinds of tax-based government spending:

- basic assistance to poor families, alias 'poor relief' (before 1930), 'family assistance,' 'welfare' (in America), or 'supplemental income';
- public aid to unemployed workers (unemployment compensation and help in securing new jobs);
- public pensions, excluding those for government and military employees;[1]
- public health expenditures; and
- housing subsidies.[2]

Such tax-based transfers tend to redistribute income somewhat progressively, as Beveridge and other pioneers had hoped. Their progressivity is not uniform or easily measured, however. I define a welfare state as a country resembling those European countries the media often call welfare states. These countries devote 20 per cent of GDP or more to social transfers, and that 20 per cent threshold conveniently, though arbitrarily, defines a welfare state for present purposes.[3]

The Welfare State does *not* include any direct market controls by government, such as worker protection laws, high minimum wages, import barriers, hours restrictions, or government ownership of industry. This exclusion is important to my conclusions about growth, since related research confirms that there are negative growth effects from some kinds of direct market interventions. Among welfare state transfer *programmes*, only unemployment compensation has a negative effect on national product, and this limited effect is offset by the pro-growth effects of other kinds of social transfers (Lindert, 2004; Allard and Lindert, 2006). Clarifying these definitions sets us on the road to the following conclusions:

1   The Welfare State is not an endangered species among the industrialized OECD countries. Since 1980, social transfers have continued to take a slowly rising share of GDP in most OECD countries. There is no race to the bottom.

2   OECD experience since 1980 does not show any negative econometric effect of larger tax-financed transfers on national product.

3   There are good reasons for this. High-budget welfare states feature a tax mix that may be more pro-growth and pro-health than the tax mixes of low-budget America, Japan, and Switzerland. The high-budget states also have more efficient health care, better support for child care and women's careers, and other features that mitigate the negative incentives on transfer recipients.

4   Western Europe's flaws in economic institutions and policies are separate from the social transfers that have always defined the Welfare State. Europe has restricted competition in labour markets, in product markets, and in higher education, to the detriment of its economic growth. These mis-steps seem more serious in Southern Europe than in Northern Europe.

5   To judge the new pressures that population ageing will bring to government budgets in this century, we can use OECD pension experience from the 1980s and 1990s. The countries with the oldest populations had already begun to cut the relative generosity of their transfers to the elderly *per elderly person*. They did not, however, cut the average shares of public pensions or other transfers in GDP, nor did they lower the absolute real value of the average pension.

6   Transfers to the elderly will be under more severe pressure in some countries than in others. On the pension front, perhaps the biggest trouble is brewing for Italy and Japan. On the health care front, the United States is in the most trouble, with its combination of unregulated markets and socialized medicine aimed at the elderly alone.

2 What is not wrong with the Welfare State

Little retreat since 1980

As an economic species, the Welfare State has shown strong survival instincts in the countries where it emerged in the twentieth century. Within the expanding OECD, the number of welfare states is stable or expanding. Since 1980, these exits, entries and borderline cases have stood out:

- Ireland definitely left the ranks of welfare states on the 20 per cent yardstick.
- Switzerland took Ireland's place in the late 1990s, silently becoming a welfare state with major increases in pensions and public health.[4]
- Others are approaching the 20 per cent borderline from above and from below. The Netherlands dropped down to the border, with major cuts in its disability and other *programmes* after 1995. Japan is approaching welfare state status, now transferring over 17 per cent of national product.
- In Eastern Europe, at least the Czech Republic, Hungary, and Poland are preserving their welfare states, both through the depression of the 1990s and through the subsequent recovery.
- Six other OECD countries continue to hover near the 20 per cent borderline: Australia, Canada, New Zealand, Portugal, Spain, and Britain.

The 'free lunch puzzle'

The Welfare State's survival over the last quarter-century has puzzled many observers. Don't tax-based social transfers dampen the incentive to be productive, dragging down the growth of the economy? This fear rests on some familiar and plausible suspicions about taxes and transfers. We often suspect that tax and transfers cut the productivity of both the taxed and the subsidized, since both sides face higher marginal tax rates of exerting themselves productively. Many have also suspected that welfare states tend to run bigger government budget deficits.

Yet experience from the late nineteenth century to the early twenty-first fails to support these common suspicions. So say the numbers, both when you look at them in the raw and when you statistically measure the different forces that determine economic growth. There is no international correlation at all between the share of social spending in the economy and either the level or the growth of GDP. Of course, places differ in other ways than just in their views of taxes and welfare, so we need an econometric analysis that gives many forces their due. Several economists have performed such tests, and most have found no robust or significant negative effect of higher social transfers on GDP per person.[5] The effect could just as easily be positive, say the majority of tests, with a zero effect near the centre of the confidence interval.

Before we accept this null result, the past literature needs to be re-shaped to fit the issue of social transfers and the Welfare State. Three key refinements concern the choice of fiscal variable, simultaneity, and non-linearity. First, no past study showing a negative growth effect in a large sample has ever used social transfers as the fiscal variable. Rather, they used total government spending or total taxes, so that any kind of unproductive government consumption, unrelated to the Welfare State, could appear to drag down growth.[6] Second, very few of the studies addressed the simultaneous feedback from GDP itself to social spending. Finally, the literature has generally failed to test for the non-linearity of the costs of taxes and transfers. Since conventional theory clearly predicts that costs should rise non-linearly with the rate of taxation and transfers, the statistical tests must allow for this curvature. Elsewhere, I have presented test results honouring all these commitments. In all the new tests, as in most earlier studies, the Welfare State looks like a free lunch, for the nation as a whole.[7]

Facing facts like these, someone believing in a high cost of the Welfare State has a tough choice to make. One can be strong, standing by long-held beliefs and demanding alternative econometric tests until one of them forces the data to confess. Or one can be weaker, and retreat in the face of the apparent facts. The more promising road is to accept the statistical verdict, and then explore how that could be true. In fact, there are good reasons why the net cost is probably zero, when you look at how welfare states run in the real world.

One key: imagined blunders versus real-world policies

The usual tales about the high incentive costs of the Welfare State are based on a compelling economic logic. The logic might have been borne out in the real world if governments had blundered by simply taxing capital and entre-preneurship and effort heavily, while offering young adults the chance to avoid a lifetime of work with a near-wage benefit. Yet the overriding fact about such blunders is that *they never happened*. Only if we extend the econo-metric estimates out into a world that never happened, a blundering world that taxes 40 per cent of capital and top incomes and pays people who never work, would some of the estimated equations predict those high costs of foolish policy. Within the range of true historical experience, there is no clear net GDP cost of higher social transfers. The econometric evidence suggests – though it cannot yet quantify – major roles for the following institutional and historical facts.

The welfare-state tax mix looks better

A closer look reveals that the high-budget welfare states actually favour types of taxation that mainstream economists think are better for economic growth.[8] To see how their choice of taxes departs from some common beliefs about the sloppy and bloated welfare state, consider the kinds of taxes shown in Exam Question 1. Many think of the Welfare State as a place where big government soaks the rich, taxing corporations, capital, and top property incomes so heavily that many of them try to take their money out of the country. Not so. The correct answer in Exam Question 1 is answer (a), that the Welfare States do not tax cor-porations or capital or top property incomes more heavily than low-social-budget countries like the United States or Japan. One might have been misled on this point back in the 1970s or 1980s when reading news that the top income tax rates were very high in, say, Sweden. Yet even back then corporations and the richest seldom paid the top statutory rates, thanks to a host of deductions and loopholes. And since the early 1990s Sweden and other European countries have simplified their tax systems so as to levy lower top tax rates.

Exam Question 1

Which of the following tax rates is **not** higher in big-government welfare states than in a small-government country like the United States?

a   tax rate on corporations, capital, and top property incomes
b   tax rate of labour income
c   tax rate on general consumption (like sales tax)
d   sin taxes (on tobacco, alcohol, gasoline)

If the high-budget welfare states do not tax corporations, capital, and top property incomes any more heavily than does the United States, what other taxes do they levy to pay for those bigger social budgets? For one thing, they do levy higher taxes on the human earnings of everybody from janitors up through doctors and lawyers, labelled as 'labour income' in answer (b). This kind of tax could by itself have negative effects on economic growth. Yet North American economists, when polled on the subject of taxation, feel that taxing labour income is definitely better for economic growth, because labour supply is less sensitive to taxation than in capital supply. One should also note that the heavy taxes on labour bring the tax burden to rest on the same income groups that vote in favour of the Welfare State. To a large extent, workers themselves pay for the safety nets designed to protect the least fortunate among them.

Welfare-state governments also levy heavier taxes on general consumption, the kind of levy mentioned in answer (c). Such taxes, in the efficient form of a European 'value added tax' (VAT), are favourites among economic conservatives. They have the pro-growth virtue of not double-taxing savings. It is striking that this kind of taxation takes a bigger tax bite in the Welfare States of Europe than in the United States, where conservatives have traditionally called for it.[9]

Finally, it is the Welfare States, especially those in the Nordic countries, that have the heaviest 'sin taxes.' Again, they have chosen taxes that mainstream economists would defend. Such addictive products as alcohol, tobacco, and gasoline bring negative externalities to society, in the form of bad health and bad air. How does relying on these kinds of taxes harm economic growth and well-being? Yet these are the kinds of taxes that are kept lower in the United States.

Their work supply disincentives are not much worse

It is natural to fear that the Welfare State, in addition to taxing those who work, also discourages work by transfer recipients. Giving generous unemployment compensation seems like the most obvious example of a policy that cuts jobs and output by subsidizing non-work. It turns out that this fear is qualitatively correct, but the effects on GDP are small enough to be outweighed by the favourable effect of other welfare state transfers on GDP.

More generous unemployment compensation does indeed cut the share of adults who work. A rich econometric literature has made this point, and our latest tests agree.[10] But by how much does it cut GDP? The solid findings on the work losses from raising the level of unemployment benefits miss the mark here, for at least two reasons. For a start, they usually focus on the simple 'replacement ratio,' the ratio of a standard unemployment benefit to the average wage rate. Users of this key parameter of unemployment compensation miss these facts: only a fraction of the unemployed qualify for such standard benefits, only a further fraction of those who qualify actually claim the benefits, and these in turn draw benefits only for a fraction of a year. When we multiply the replacement ratio by the fractions covered and paid, the effective rate of unemployment compensation actually moves in a lower and narrow fractional range. Between 1975 and 1998 the well-known replacement ratio for core OECD countries averaged 34 per cent of an average wage, with a standard deviation of 15 per cent. Yet the more relevant measure of the effective rate of unemployment compensation averaged only 13 per cent of the wage, with a standard deviation of 8 per cent.[11] So instead of imagining the job effects of two-deviation jumps in the replacement ratio from, say, 30 per cent to 60 per cent of an average wage, we should be measuring the effects of a jump from 13 per cent to 29 per cent.

A second difficulty with the usual thought experiments is that they stop with estimating effects on jobs, with no extension to GDP effects. Yet we know that any labour-supply restriction cuts output less than it cuts employment, while raising labour productivity. That would happen even if labour were of uniform quality. Add to this the fact that unemployment compensation typically looks attractive only to persons with below-average earning potential, leading to a further rise in output per worker. All things considered, unemployment compensation only has a small effect on GDP.

While many observers over-estimate the percentage effects of classic unemployment compensation on GDP, they also overlook the way in which basic family assistance, alias welfare, is often designed to avoid discouraging work. The unemployed are given retraining and job search help, and are pressured to take it. To illustrate how a higher-budget welfare state has actually given some people *more* incentive to take a job, consider the case of jobless single mothers. The realities of recent history on this front are illustrated by Exam Questions 2.

Exam Question 2

In which case was a poor single mother given the **least** incentive to get a job?

a   USA under Reagan
b   USA under Clinton
c   Britain under Tony Blair today
d   Sweden's welfare state today

What has given poor single mothers the least incentive to work has been a policy environment that takes away their welfare and other public benefits as soon as they get a job. What would make a country actually do that, and face such women with a huge marginal tax rate? The desire to keep welfare expenditures very low, so that no one person above the poverty line gets any aid. Such penny-pinching, known as strict means testing, was practised by the conservative Thatcher-Reagan revival of the early 1980s. Hence (a) is the correct answer to Exam Question 2.[12]

Later on, bipartisan reforms in the Clinton years improved work incentives at the bottom of the US income spectrum. The first improvement came when the Earned Income Tax Credit (EITC) was made more generous in 1993. That, and accompanying adjustments of state-level benefits, gave jobless single mothers a stronger incentive to take that first low-paying job and get started on an employment history. Then the 1996 welfare reform added a tough-love dimension by setting term limits on welfare. The combination of the two has decreased welfare caseloads without raising poverty, even after the recession of 2001–02. Meanwhile, Britain under Tony Blair made a similar reform to the EITC, undoing the strict means testing of the Thatcher era. And a welfare state like Sweden never had such a heavy tax on getting a first job, because family benefits were retained when one got a job, and the tax rate on extra earnings remained moderate.

Investing in women's careers

The Welfare States also gain jobs and productivity through public policies that invest in career continuity and skills accumulation for mothers. This matters a lot, now that such a large share of women's adulthood is career-oriented. Welfare states provide paid parental leaves and public day care with qualified providers. While it is not easy to estimate the gains in productivity from micro-data, there is at least one aggregate sign of strong gains: women in such countries have market wage rates that are much closer to wage rates for men in the United States or Japan or Switzerland.[13]

Public health: Uncle Sam's Achilles heel

The strongest pro-growth dimension of social transfers occurs in public health, the social sector where reliance on ordinary market mechanisms breaks down most frequently. The best international OECD evidence on this front comes from the regrettable experience of a single outlier nation, the United States.

Americans die younger than people in countries that have a greater share of their health expenses paid for by taxes. The US ranks nineteenth out of 20 rich OECD countries in life expectancy, just ahead of Portugal. Not all of this is due to the health care system. Americans have worse health habits and slightly more pollution exposure. The health habits of the US are world famous – especially bacon double cheeseburgers, fries, Krispie Kremes, double lattes, soft drinks, and a high homicide rate. Yet when you weigh all the separate effects statistically, the health care system looks guilty of causing a significant part of early death.

The best attempt to quantify these sources is an OECD panel study summarized in Table 14.1. Using the new OECD standardized measures of premature mortality and a pooled cross-section approach, Zeynap Or finds that a greater public-expenditure share, for given total expenditures, significantly reduces mortality, especially among men, among OECD countries since 1980.[14] Table 14.1 reports some of the cross-sectional part of the results. In the mortality-change perspective, where minus signs are good, some familiar factors lower mortality down towards the world-best Japanese standard. Those factors include higher income, white-collar occupations, cleaner air, abstention from bad consumption habits, and greater total spending on health care. On balance, though, a more public approach to the same health care expenditures also helps significantly. It explains a small but significant part of America's greater mortality.

The more private American system also costs more. Part of the extra expense of American health care is a justifiable purchase of higher-quality care, a tendency that the rest of the world will soon emulate. Part of it, though, consists of higher bureaucratic costs. Contrary to the usual rhetoric assuming that bureaucracy means government bureaucracy, the private health insurance sector in the United States imposes greater administrative costs trying to keep people from being insured and compensated than other countries spend administratively on providing public care to all. The World Health Organization has ranked the United States thirty-seventh in the quality of health care delivery. Obviously, the US has the best cutting-edge medical care in the world, but few can afford it. Little wonder that in recent surveys of opinions about health care, Americans were more dissatisfied about their health care than were people in most other surveyed countries.

The locus of the American health care problem is not the public sector as such. Rather it centres on the country's peculiar combination of unregulated markets, strong supplier lobbies, and the lobbying power of the elderly. Two historical traps have hobbled American health care. The first trap came in the 1940s and 1950s, when health insurance was chained to employment. As Milton Friedman and others emphasized, one culprit was the regime of wage controls in the Second World War. Unable to compete by offering higher wage rates in tight labour markets, employers competed with new health insurance packages. By 1954, tax legislation and support decisions by the courts finished the welding of this link of health insurance to jobs.[15] The second trap was sprung by the passage of Medicare in 1965. Medicare used tax revenues taking an increasing share of GDP to bid for health services in a context of uncontrolled prices, so that greater effective demand on behalf of seniors made health care less and less affordable for those under 65.

Only time will tell whether the United States can escape the trap of its overworked health care system. Canadian history suggests that in a federal system,

Table 14.1 Health care systems and other determinants of life saving, selected countries versus Japan in 1992

Explaining premature years of life lost (PYLL) per 100,000 persons living in 1992 relative to Japan, both sexes (Negative = better life-saving relative to Japan).

	France	Netherlands	Sweden	UK	US	OECD average
Actual excess mortality (PYLL) relative to Japan	34.7	19.3	6.0	28.2	61.3	31.1
Amount of excess PYLL due to differences in:						
Income and occupations	-5.9	-8.6	-9.9	-4.5	-18.7	4.9
Pollution	6.3	8.8	10.4	9.9	14.5	8.5
Four bad consumption habits	25.9	14.9	6.7	15.0	12.7	13.5
Total health expend's per capita	0.3	4.1	5.2	5.7	0.9	5.3
Public share of all health expend's	-0.9	-1.3	-3.1	-2.8	8.5	-0.6
Not explained by any of these	8.9	1.4	-3.3	4.8	43.6	-0.5

Sources: All estimates are from Or (2000/1), which displays results for 21 countries, 1970–92.

Notes

PYLL = Premature years of life lost before age 70, per 100,000 of population. An infant death counts as a loss of 70 years, and a death at age 65 counts as 5 years lost. Thus the United States excess of 61.3 relative to Japan in 1992 is equivalent to 6.13 excess US deaths at age 60 per 100,000 of population where the corresponding Japanese would have survived to age 70. Alternatively, the 61.3 figure is equivalent to almost one (61.3/70) extra infant death per year per 100,000 of population.

Income and occupations = the sum of two products of (regression coefficients * the differentials or changes) in two independent variables. The two are real GDP per capita in 1990 international dollars and the share of white collar workers in the total labour force.

Pollution = the contribution to PYLL from NO emissions per capita, in kilograms per year.

Four bad consumption habits = the contributions to premature mortality made by (1) litres of alcoholic beverages per person over 15; (2) consumption expenditure on tobacco per person over 15, US$ at 1990 price levels and PPPs for tobacco consumption; (3) butter consumption per capita, in kg per year; and (4) sugar consumption per capita, in kg per year.

Total health expenditures per capita is measured in US$ at 1990 price levels and PPPs for medical consumption.

Public share of total expenditures = the share of public expenditure in total health expenditure.

Not explained by these = the sum of the residual, or prediction error, plus (for Panel (A.)), the fixed effect for that country.

the reforms would have to come from below. Over half a century ago, Saskatchewan and other provinces took the lead in universal health insurance, long before the federal government stepped in. Perhaps innovative states could lead the United States toward the healthy heresy of extending 'socialized medicine' to the under-65 population.

3 Western Europe's policy defects

While the American approach is at its worst in the health care sector, Western European growth and well-being have been dragged down by other policy failures. The common denominator in Europe's shortcomings is protectionist restrictions on competition.

European anti-competitiveness shows up in higher education, the social sector that is most removed from the poor, the sick, and the elderly. Higher education calls for a mixture of market competition and limited public subsidy. Here the United States and Canada have chosen a better institutional mix than Western Europe or Japan. North American government subsidies for higher education seem to approximate the (hard to measure) amount appropriate to the fact that higher education does bring some 'external' benefits, some favourable spillovers to the general population through the advancement of knowledge. Yet we have avoided making the government pay for all of higher education, or even half of it. We force public universities to compete with each other and with private universities for research grants, for faculty talent, and for student talent. Individual faculty members have to compete by teaching well, since America attaches more importance to student evaluations of faculty than does any other country. By contrast, top universities in Western Europe and Japan have not been allowed, or forced, to compete sufficiently with each other and with American universities.

The European anti-competitive bent has also slowed the retreat from nationalization and from restrictive product-market restrictions on competition. The restrictiveness of product-market regulations has been easing up in all OECD countries since 1980, but at unequal rates. As Figure 14.1 shows, continental Europe has been particularly slow to ease up on anti-competitive regulations in seven key sectors, as indexed by the OECD. This has perhaps compromised European GDP.[16]

Of Europe's anti-competitive institutions, perhaps the costliest in the long run are the many restrictions on labour-market flexibility. Here let us focus on employee anti-protection laws (EPLs), which greatly raise the cost of dismissing employees. The conventional fear that EPLs cost jobs has not been shared by all authors in the recent debates. Some have rightly pointed out that the hypothesized job losses from EPL strictness do not show up in all equations.[17] Yet the balance of statistical work still indicts EPLs.[18]

Even if they do not raise unemployment very much, they redistribute it in a way that seems to cut labour productivity in the long run. EPLs create insiders and outsiders. While the insiders whose jobs are protected might enjoy more

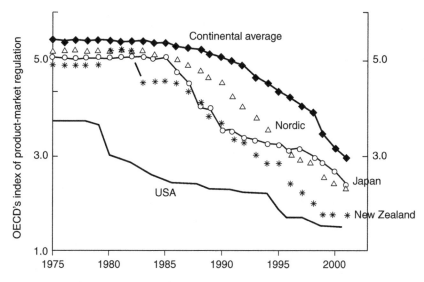

Figure 14.1 The restrictiveness of product-market regulations, 1975–2001.

productivity-enhancing training at work, human investments in the job-market outsiders is delayed for years. Table 14.2 underlines the effects on outsiders by showing the relative unemployment rates for two groups of outsiders, namely youth (15–24) and women. Where EPLs defend the insiders most strictly, a Southern European tendency here represented by Greece and Italy, unemployment runs relatively high among youths and women. Where it is low to the North, as shown here for Ireland and Denmark, youths and women are more fully employed.

In theory, the favourable effects for insiders and the unfavourable effects on outsiders might happen to balance out, at least in the first few years after EPLs are tightened. Yet over a generation or two the share of the workforce's adult

Table 14.2 Employee protection laws redistribute unemployment toward outsiders: four countries in 2002

	Ratios of unemployment rates		
	EPL strictness	Youth 15–24/men 25–64	Women 25–64/men 25–64
Greece	3.8	4.2	2.4
Italy	3.3	3.8	1.8
versus			
Ireland	1.3	1.7	0.8
Denmark	1.6	1.6	1.2

Source: OECD, standardized unemployment rates.

history that was lost to the career delays of outsiders goes on rising, at the expense of productivity.[19]

These protections of privilege are unrelated, however, to the safety nets and egalité of the Welfare States.

4 Longer life in the twenty-first century: a crisis for social budgets?

If the Welfare State seems innocent of dragging down growth in the twentieth century, might it nonetheless fail in the twenty-first? Daily media coverage emphasizes that a rapidly ageing population may find it harder and harder to keep budgets in balance and to sustain economic growth. Will the Welfare State be one of the casualties in this ageing world? For most countries, the budgetary tensions have centred on public pensions, and to a lesser extent on health care budgets.

Three familiar sources of pension trouble

Ageing too fast

The trend toward improved senior longevity and lower fertility is pressuring high-income countries to recalibrate their pension programmes. Actuarial changes are been forced not only on public pensions and health systems, but on private job-based plans as well. If ageing were the only problem, then we could rank different countries' dangers just by looking at the UN projections for population ageing out to, say, the middle of this century. As of 2050 the countries with the highest population shares over age 65 will probably be Italy and Japan. North America, Australia, and New Zealand face less difficulty here, thanks to their accepting immigrants and their generally higher fertility. Most developing countries also face less demographic threat over this half-century. The exceptions tend to be East Asian: China, Taiwan, and Singapore are all ageing so rapidly that by mid-century they will face pension problems as severe as those faced by most OECD countries today.

Asking for trouble with early retirement policy

A second source of pension trouble is avoidable, but widespread in Southern and Western Europe. Stuck with their own laws against firing workers, several European countries have tried to buy out seniors by subsidizing early retirement of workers in the 50–64 age range. The implicit tax on staying at work peaked at the start of the 1990s. Italy is in particularly deep trouble here, yet Italian politics has thus far produced only timid and partial roll-backs of the subsidies to early retirement.

Asking for trouble with overall government deficits

The budget pressures that can crush social programmes need not relate to ageing or to retirement policy alone. They can come from any source. Whatever raises the overall government deficit and national debt relative to annual GDP can force a country to cut back on any kind of spending, including pensions and other social transfers. Even if pensions were ostensibly protected in a special lock-box fund, a desperate government could always raid the lock box. The OECD country subject to the most pressure from its overall budget deficit is Japan, where the deficit has been about 6–8 per cent of GDP for over a decade. The United States has suddenly vaulted into second place in the deficit/GDP ranks since 2002, thanks to its mixture of spending jumps and tax cuts.

These pressure points will cause more pain in some countries than in others. Perhaps the top victims will be Italy and Japan on the pension front, and the United States on the health insurance front.

Basic perspectives on OECD pension solutions

PAYGO is sustainable

When the population gets older, something has to give. Annual pension benefits simply cannot continue to keep up with annual incomes of the employed. Wage-indexed pensions appear unsustainable, and need to be shifted to price indexation.

Most public pension systems are now on a pay-as-you-go (PAYGO) basis. In the aggregate, the current generation of workers pays for the retirement of the currently elderly, and not for its own retirement. Given that PAYGO is the prevailing current system, many have slipped into thinking that PAYGO is doomed and must be replaced with a funded or defined-contribution system.

This is incorrect, however. No pension whatsoever is immune to the need to adjust to longevity. Suppose that the only pillar of your retirement were your individual savings. If you work and save for Q years, and draw on savings for an estimated R years of retirement, you must set your annual savings and retirement benefits so that the accumulated value of your savings just covers your retirement needs. For any given rate of return you get on your savings, you cannot enjoy more retirement (raise the ratio R/Q) without cutting your retirement consumption relative to your earlier wage. The same holds if you add a second private pillar and convince your employer to share your retirement costs, presumably by accepting a lower rate of straight pay. You and your employer are still subject to the same actuarial logic as you would be by yourself. Nor is the third pillar any different: a public system, like a private pension plan, must adjust the relative retirement benefit to the ratio of years spent in the two phases of adult life.

But just as ageing is a problem in any pension system, so too there is some parametric adjustment in any system that can fix the problem. Making the pension system sustainable is no more difficult under a PAYGO public system than under any other. There are two ways to avoid raising the tax rate and still balance the pension budget, even though we live longer:

1   Slow down the rise of retired/working ratio, by raising retirement age (or fertility or immigration), and
2   Make benefits rise more slowly than the average income of the employed.

Yet real benefits need not be cut, as long as income grows. Suppose that over a half-century the elderly share doubles, as it threatens to do for Italy and Japan. If real incomes continue to double every half-century or faster, as in the past, the country could leave its real benefits *and* its retirement age *and* its tax rate the same forever. Real benefits per retiree could even go on rising as long as the ageing is less severe than in Italy or Japan, or the full-benefit retirement age is raised, or both.

The implied OECD solutions of the 1980s and 1990s

Keeping PAYGO in equilibrium is not purely hypothetical. In fact, several countries of Northern Europe did much of the necessary adjusting in the 1980s and 1990s. It is instructive to see which adjustments their political systems tended to make. By drawing on the underlying econometric estimates of what determines social budgets, we can forecast the likely non-linear effects of population ageing on taxes and transfers.[20] Figure 14.2 gives the revealed

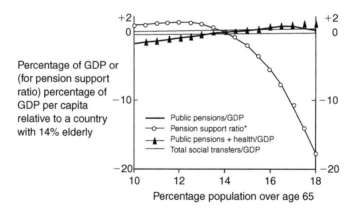

Figure 14.2 How population ageing affected taxpayers, pensioners, and other transfer recipients, 1978–55 (source: Regressions in Lindert (2004, vol. 2,
App. Table E3), without fixed-country effects).

Note
* Pension support ratio = (public pensions/elderly)/(GDP/capita).

policy response to ageing, holding other things equal. When the over-65 share of the population rose from 14 per cent to 18 per cent (a rise of 29 per cent), there was no change in the shares of pensions or other social transfers in GDP. The cost to taxpayers of all social transfers, including pensions, therefore rose hardly at all (a statistically insignificant 0.5 per cent of GDP). Essentially, the full burden of the adjustment fell on the elderly themselves, in relative terms. The crude pension support ratio, measured as the ratio of (pensions per elderly) to (GDP per capita), dropped 18 per cent, other things equal. It did not show up as a real drop on pension benefits because GDP per capita was growing. Some countries achieved this by encouraging later retirement, others by indexing pensions to something that grew more slowly than the growth of earnings. In principle, this kind of adjustment in tax-based pensions could continue forever. In the 1980s and 1990s it was part of a larger set of social transfers that did not bring any loss of GDP to those high-budget countries of Northern Europe.

How do funded and private systems really differ from PAYGO?

Even though the long-run equilibrium requirements for different private and public pension systems are analogous, there is still the widespread belief that switching from PAYGO to a funded (defined contribution) system or a more private system would bring benefits, and that these benefits somehow relate to the ageing problem. While the proposals are complex and varied, a core feature is that individual earners take their paycheck contributions out of the public PAYGO system. Despite the 'privatization' label, government compulsion is involved: even those whose set-asides are voluntary are compelled to keep their extra private savings locked away until retirement.

Compelling households to save more allegedly serves four goals: (1) bringing government deficits under control, (2) promoting national saving, (3) improving the rate of return on investments in retirement, and (4) building in a political pre-commitment to a fixed set of rules. Yet it is not clear that any of these four goals is well served by what are often called 'reforms' of the public pension system.

Government budget deficits will be raised, not lowered, for a generation or longer. Honouring the implicit pension promises to those currently in middle age or older means that pension budgets cannot be cut for at least a quarter century. The general taxpayers must offset each dollar that is withdrawn from the public pension system and shifted to personal private accounts. The extra burden on general taxpayers is as immediate as the exit of savings into personal private accounts. Chile's experience dramatized this new burden on the general taxpayers.

Eventually, if the system stays in place beyond the decades in which the government compensates the earlier cohorts, continued compulsory savings would indeed raise the national savings rate. But that is at least a quarter century off, and we still await clear evidence that the nations in question are under-saving. A simpler way to address the savings issue is to switch from the current income tax systems that double-tax saving.

In the American debate, at least, one hears that switching from social security contributions to private (forced) savings gives investors a better rate of return, by letting them choose something other than the government bonds that social security implicitly or explicitly buys. This is questionable. Private financial markets already equilibrate between bonds and other assets, so that differences in rates of return tend to reflect differences in perceptions of risk. Inducing some investors to shift out of bonds and into, say, stocks raises the rate of return on bonds and lowers the rate of return on stocks. If any rate-of-return gap had actually existed, the rate of return could not go up as much as that gap would imply. Even the existence of a gap in favour of holding stocks, as implied by the literature on 'the equity premium,' is in doubt, both for the past and especially for the future. That past equity premium was based on measurements that may not have adjusted correctly for risk or for survivor bias in the stock indices. Believing that there will be an equity premium in the future implies that investors will be persistently and systematically mistaken about stocks versus bonds – a strange support for the belief that they will make the right choices when investing their privatized retirement funds.

Furthermore, making it profitable or compulsory to shift from government bonds to other assets means a greater government debt service burden, simply because this portfolio shift and the greater government deficit will raise interest rates on those bonds.

There is no reason to believe that starting a defined-contribution plan has any more permanence than a PAYGO set of benefits. Most countries with PAYGO pensions today had defined-contribution plans earlier, but overthrew them. Consider three famous examples. The original Bismarck social security innovations of the 1880s started as defined-contribution plans, but began shifting within a few years to more PAYGO, and more burdens on general taxpayers. The US Social Security Act of 1935 set up a funded system, not PAYGO. The system was defined-contribution at the aggregate cohort level, though it gave low earners a better rate of return than high earners. Yet political forces gradually abandoned the funded system in favour of PAYGO, under pressure from the powerful elderly lobby (Miron and Weil, 1998). Finally, Margaret Thatcher's famous privatization of Britain's public pensions still exists, but with important modifications drifting back toward progressive redistribution and PAYGO. While the Blair government has retained much of the defined-contribution features of the Thatcher era, it has raised minimum income guarantees for pensioners significantly, at the expense of the general taxpayers.[21] The political tendency is clear: democracy finds it at least as easy to switch out of funded defined-contribution systems toward PAYGO as vice versa. All pension 'reforms' reflect temporary and reversible shifts in political mood.

In the process of switching to defined contribution and privatized plans two kinds of elderly poor fall behind – those whose lower lifetime earnings yield less pension support under the less progressive reform designs, and those whose retirement investments turned out worse. Furthermore, the financial service sector gets a windfall gain if government has compelled households to buy its services. Of all the effects of such compulsory private savings, this is perhaps the clearest.

5 Conclusion: what happened to the trans-Atlantic trade-off between equity and efficiency?

This chapter's claims that the Welfare State is not the problem, and will not be the problem even in an older society, may seem at odds with two common assertions about a trade-off between how Americans and Europeans have accepted, or must accept, a trade-off between equity and efficiency. One common assertion is correct: in practice, the American political balance has accepted more inequality, more poverty, and lower wages as a price to be paid for higher GDP.[22] That is how political tastes have differed across the Atlantic, and nothing in this chapter overturns such a conclusion.

Yet the evidence in this chapter helps us reject a second, more common, assertion. Many assert that policy-makers *must* trade away some equality to get more efficiency. As we have seen, however, there has been no net GDP cost of the Welfare State. Furthermore, both America and Western Europe have passed up opportunities to promote either GDP or equality without reducing the other. America is deficient in health care for the young and poor, in developing mothers' human capital, and in taxing addictive health hazards. Europe is deficient in letting outsiders compete in labour and product markets. In terms of economic jargon, all countries are somewhere within, and not on, the social possibility frontier sketched in Figure 14.3.

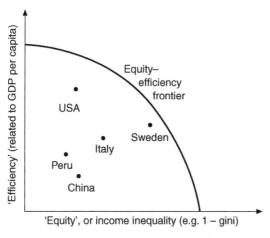

Figure 14.3 Nobody is on the equity–efficiency frontier.

Even without the evidence in this chapter, the second assertion should have flunked a simple political reality check. That is, what we know about the political process rejects the assertion that policy-makers *must* trade away some equality to get more efficiency. Ask yourself: what countries do you know that have exhausted all opportunities to promote both growth and equality? Even the European welfare states, which have pressed relatively hard to equalize incomes, still sacrifice both efficiency and equity by protecting agricultural landholders at the expense of food purchasers and general taxpayers. As argued here, they also protect senior high-paid workers at the expense of younger job entrants. Similarly, the United States protects agricultural landholders while raising the cost of food, and we have seen that it subsidizes civilian medical care only for those residents who have already survived to the age of 65, at the expense of public care for the young and the poor. There is no necessary trade-off, just homework that has not been finished on either side of the Atlantic.

Notes

1 It is desirable to exclude the contributory amounts paid by one's self or one's employer. They are not a controversial redistribution of resources, but rather just part of one's employment contract. It is not easy, however, to remove all employer and employee contributions from the expenditure data. As a smaller step toward isolating non-contributory payments, I have tried to exclude government–employee, and military, pensions from the OECD measures used here.

2 The underlying data sets do not permit us to add 'tax expenditures' (tax reductions) to the social transfers.

3 As of 1995, the Welfare States, ranked by the share of total social transfers in GDP, included Sweden, Finland, Denmark, Norway, Belgium, France, Netherlands, Germany, and Italy. Also included for 1995, but only slightly above the 20 per cent line, were the United Kingdom, Austria, and Spain (Lindert, 2004, vol. 1, 177).

4 It is not clear why OECD data show such a strong rise in Swiss pensions and health expenditures, as a per cent of GDP, since the early 1990s. The elderly share of the population has not risen much, and is low by OECD standards. One might have suspected a role for relatively sluggish growth of the GDP denominator, but Switzerland's growth has been relatively poor since 1975, well before the rise in the shares of pensions and health care in GDP.

5 The literature is rich, even when we focus just on studies explaining the determinants of GDP per capita, and set aside the determinants of employment. Much of the literature is surveyed in Slemrod, 1995, Atkinson, 1999, and Lindert, 2004, vol. 2, Chapters 18 and 19. Perhaps the most plausibly specified set of econometric tests finding a significant and sizeable cost of larger government is Fölster and Henrekson, 1999 (with a rebuttal by Agell *et al.*, 1999). Its relevance to the issue of social transfers is limited, however, by its focus on the effects of total taxes. These taxes go to finance all government consumption and investment, not just social transfers.

6 This fiscal mis-match also shows up in the literature on global growth econometrics, which shows negative GDP effects of wasteful non-social government consumption. For example, the Barro and Lee, 1993; Barro, 1997 measure of government consumption excludes the social transfers that are the expenditures of interest here. A further

mismatch between the global econometric studies and the issue of welfare-state programmes arises from their including kleptocratic governments in the global sample, a choice that supports no conclusions about the growth effects of a rich-country welfare state.

7   Lindert, 2004, Chapters 10, 18, and 19, and the sources cited there. The underlying data sets are available at www.econ.ucdavis.edu/faculty/fzlinder.

8   Wilensky, 2002, Kato, 2003, Lindert, 2004, Timmons, 2005.

9   Note that the case in favour of taxing consumption rather than income or earnings is not documented here with any empirical evidence. Rather it is attributed to economic orthodox thinking. Some studies do seem to find that taxing consumption is less distortionary, and better for growth (e.g. Kneller *et al.,* 1999). While this seems plausible, current econometric work by Gayle Allard and myself, which allows for predicted non-linearities not incorporated by the Kneller–Bleaney–Gemmell analysis, does not find this result to be robust.

10   For an overview of the rich earlier literature, see Meyer, 1995, Nickell, 1997, and Blanchard and Wolfers, 2000. For the new tests, see Allard, 2003; Lindert, 2004, Vol. 2, Ch. 19; and Allard and Lindert, in progress.

11   The effective rate of unemployment compensation here means Gayle Allard's 'net reservation wage' (Allard, 2003, with updates on her web site at ie.edu).

12   In fairness to Reagan, the correct answer should have been 'The US under Johnson and Reagan.' At times, Lyndon Johnson's Great Society programmes also had the defect of pulling back benefits sharply with the start of labour earnings. This feature was partly removed by reforms under Nixon, Ford, and Carter. Then the Reagan administration brought back the high marginal tax rates, by limiting the public tolerance to any welfare mother with significant earnings.

13   Lindert, 2004, Chs. 10, 11.

14   Or 2000.

15   Thomasson, 2002, 2003.

16   Like some earlier studies, Allard and Lindert (2006) find a negative effect of product market regulations on GDP per person of working age. The negative effect is not robust, however, in the face of reasonable alternative regression equations. The progress of product-market liberalization since 1980 has also been noted by Blanchard, 2004, who sees it as a hopeful sign for European productivity growth.

17   Baker *et al.*, 2005, Freeman, 2005.

18   OECD, 1994, Blanchard and Portugal, 2003; Lindert, 2004, Ch. 19 and Appendix E; Allard and Lindert, 2006.

19   Allard and Lindert, 2006.

20   Lindert, 2004, Chs. 7, 8 and appendices.

21   Blundell and Johnson, 1999; Disney *et al.*, 2004.

22   See, for example, Alesina and Glaeser, 2004.

References

Agell, J., Lindh, T. and Ohlsson, H. (1999) 'Growth and the Public Sector: A Reply', *European Journal of Political Economy* 15: 359–366.

Alesina, A. and Glaeser, E. (2004) *Fighting Poverty in the US and Europe: A World of Difference*. Oxford: Oxford University Press.

Allard, G. (2003) 'Jobs and Labor Market Institutions in the OECD'. Doctoral dissertation, University of California – Davis.

Allard, G.J. and Lindert, P.H. (2006) 'Euro-Productivity and Euro-Jobs since the 1960s: Which Institutions Really Mattered?' in T.J. Hatton, K.H. O'Rouke and A.M. Taylor (eds) *The New Comparative Economic History: Essays in Honor of Jeffrey G. Williamson*. Cambridge, MA: MIT Press, pp. 365–394.

Atkinson, A.B. (1999*) The Economic Consequences of Rolling Back the Welfare State*. Cambridge: MIT Press.

Baker, D., Glyn, A., Howell, D. and Schmitt, J. (2005) 'Labor Market Institutions and Unemployment: A Critical Assessment of the Cross-Country Evidence,' in D. Howell (ed.) *Fighting Unemployment*. Oxford: Oxford University Press, pp. 72–118.

Barro, R.J. (1997) *Determinants of Economic Growth: A Cross-Country Empirical Study*. Cambridge: MIT Press.

Barro, R.J. and Lee, J.-W. (1993) 'Winners and Losers in Economic Growth'. *Proceedings of the World Bank Annual Conference on Development Economics*. Washington: World Bank, pp. 267–314.

Blanchard, O. (2004) 'The Economic Future of Europe', *Journal of Economic Perspectives* 18(4) (Fall): 3–26.

Blanchard, O. and Portugal. P. (2001) 'What Lies Behind an Unemployment Rate: Comparing Portuguese and US Labor Markets', *American Economic Review* 91(1) (March): 187–207.

Blanchard, O. and Wolfers, J. (2000) 'The Role of Shocks and Institutions in the Rise of European Unemployment: The Aggregate Evidence', *Economic Journal* 110(462) (March): C1–C33.

Blundell, R. and Johnson, P. (1999) 'Pensions and Retirement in the United Kingdom,' in J. Gruber and D. Wise (eds) *Social Security Progammes and Retirement around the World*. Chicago: University of Chicago Press, pp. 403–436.

Disney, R., Emmerson, C. and Smith, S. (2004) 'Pension Reform and Economic Performance in Britain in the 1980s and 1990s,' in D. Card, R. Blundell and R.B. Freeman (eds) *Seeking a Premier Economy: The Economic Effects of British Economic Reforms, 1980–2000*, 233–273.

Fölster, S. and Henrekson, M. (1999) 'Growth and the Public Sector: A Critique of the Critics', *European Journal of Political Economy* 15 (June): 3337–3358.

Freeman, R.B. (2005) 'Labour Market Institutions without Blinders: The Debate over Flexibility and Labour Market Performance'. NBER Working Paper 11286 (April).

Kato, J. (2003) *Regressive Taxation and the Welfare State: Path Dependence and Policy Diffusion*. Cambridge: Cambridge University Press.

Kneller, R., Bleaney, M. and Gemmell, N. (1999) 'Fiscal Policy and Growth: Evidence from OECD Countries', *Journal of Public Economics* 74(2) (November): 171–190.

Lindert, P.H. (2004) *Growing Public: Social Spending and Economic Growth since the Eighteenth Century*. Two volumes. Cambridge: Cambridge University Press.

Meyer, B.D. (1995) 'Lessons from the US Unemployment Insurance Experiments', *Journal of Economic Literature* 33(1) (March): 91–131.

Miron, J.A. and Weil. D.N. (1998) 'The Genesis and Evolution of Social Security,' in M.D. Bordo, C. Goldin and E.N. White (eds) *The Defining Moment: The Great Depression in the American Economy in the Twentieth Century*. Chicago: University of Chicago Press for the NBER, pp. 297–322.

Nickell, S.J. (1997) 'Unemployment and Labor Market Rigidities: Europe versus North America', *Journal of Economic Perspectives* 11(3) (Summer): 55–74.

Or, Z. (2000) 'Determinants of Health Outcomes in Industrialised Countries: A Pooled, Cross-Country, Time-Series Analysis', *OECD Economic Studies* 30(1): 53–77.

Slemrod, J. (1995) 'What Do Cross-Country Studies Teach about Government Involvement, Prosperity, and Economic Growth?' *Brookings Papers in Economic Activity* 2, 373–431.

Thomasson, M. (2002) 'From Sickness to Health: The Twentieth Century Development of US Health Insurance', *Explorations in Economic History* 39(3) (July): 233–253.

Thomasson, M. (2003) 'The Importance of Group Coverage: How Tax Policy Shaped US Health Insurance', *American Economic Review* 93(4) (September): 1373–1384.

Timmons, J.F. (2005). 'Left, Right, and Center: Partisanship, Taxes, and the Welfare State'. ITAM, Mexico DF, February 16.

Wilensky, H. (2002) *Rich Democracies: Political Economy, Public Policy, and Performance*. Berkeley: University of California Press.

15 The policy of insolvency EU–US

Dieter Stiefel

1 Introduction

America is different. This has been the basic impression of Europeans from Alexis de Tocqueville until today (Lévy, 2006). One of these differences concerns bankruptcy policy. Famous cases of insolvency such as Enron show this clearly (Barreveld, 2002; Rapoport and Dharan, 2004; Dembinski *et al.*, 2006). Above all, Chapter 11 is both well-known and debated in Europe. In past years, airlines have been the main users of petitions of insolvency as a means to reduce staff costs or even to transfer pension liabilities onto public institutions (Delta, *New York Times*, 23 April 2006: 22; or Eastern Airlines in 1989). Bankruptcy policy is thus part of a country's economic and legal culture, and it varies between the US and the EU countries quite considerably.

Writing on bankruptcy policy is like aiming at a moving target. The way economic failure is dealt with varies not only from country to country but also over time. Bankruptcy regulations are either a reaction to economic and political changes (such as the crisis of dot.coms at the end of the 1990s) or to the repercussions of legal reform. This was especially evident with the Bankruptcy Reform Act of 1978 in the US. In 1984, there were approximately 62,000 business bankruptcy filings and 286,000 filings by individuals and married couples. Twenty years later, in 2004, the number of business bankruptcy filings had fallen by half to 34,000, while the number of filings by individuals and married couples had increased more than five-fold to 1,583,000. Concern about the rising number of individual bankruptcies led Congress to adopt reforms of the personal bankruptcy law in 2005 (White, 2001: 1).

Differences in bankruptcy policy are therefore historically explicable. This chapter deals first with the long-term development of bankruptcy policy in the US. It then proceeds to compare it with Germany, France and Great Britain. Subsequently, it will discuss the efforts of the European Union to achieve uniformity in this field. Finally, we shall deal with the question of how far away the European Union still is from a common policy in comparison with the US.

2 The development of American insolvency proceedings

Over the last 200 years, American bankruptcy law has been through three clearly distinct phases (Skeel, 2001: 3–5). In the eighteenth century, the US was still predominantly an agrarian country and it was a matter for debate whether a bankruptcy law was necessary or at all sensible. Although the constitution contained a clause according to which the Congress had the right 'to establish [...] uniform Laws on the subject of Bankruptcies' (US Constitution, Art. I, Sec. 8, clause 4), Washington did not exercise this right for a long time and legislation on insolvency was introduced only with the Federal States. Basically, the Federal States were responsible for property and contract law and the federation simply issued banknotes and was thus fundamentally responsible for bankruptcy law. However, the decentralised regulation made it possible for debtors to change Federal State in the case of bankruptcy, and this reduced and complicated creditors' options. For this reason, a uniform insolvency law was sensible for the whole of the US. All the debtor's assets could be assessed no matter where they were located. Federalists, on the other hand, feared that a federal bankruptcy law might endanger farmers' property and reduce the influence of the Federal States and benefit the Union. Republicans held the view that the future of America lay in trade and commerce, and that therefore a bankruptcy law was necessary in order to guarantee creditors a right of access to a debtor's assets. Farmers and plantation owners in the South feared that the 'money men' of the North could force them to pay under the terms of the bankruptcy law and the financial world of the North wanted uniform regulation of the debt collection. This conflict between industrial and agrarian interests went on throughout the nineteenth century and was essentially a conflict between the Northeast and the Southwest of the US.

In the years 1800, 1841 and 1867, bankruptcy laws were introduced as a consequence of financial crises; however they were soon repealed. Essentially, these were cases of ad hoc legislation meant to cope with the consequences of an economic crisis and they would appear superfluous at the first economic improvement. Until the law of 1841, the central element of bankruptcy law was still penalty, and imprisonment was common. The law of 1841 led to a change of thinking. This law foresaw for the first time a wilful petition of bankruptcy on the part of the debtor. It also foresaw for the first time acquittal at the end of bankruptcy proceedings, which ultimately led once again to the repealing of this law. The equally short-lived law of 1867 distinguished for the first time between individuals and enterprises. It was only in 1898 that the Congress issued a lasting federal bankruptcy law which was essentially a triumph for lobbying organisations (board of trades, chambers of commerce) which had been created in the meantime. The continuity of the Republican majority gave the law of 1898 the necessary time to establish the bankruptcy proceedings. With the law, which remained in force for 80 years, the principle of bankruptcy had changed from a crime against the community and an individually punishable act, to an economic condition in which liabilities exceed assets. This law showed, as

Charles Warren, the historian of US bankruptcy observed, an awareness that the continual operation of a firm in trouble is more important for the nation than the closing and selling of a firm for the benefit of the creditors (Warren, 1934: 144). However, the 1898 law foresaw only the liquidation of the enterprise.

The failure to establish an insolvency law which would be valid for the entire United States, therefore, goes back to the ideological confrontation between the interests of creditors and debtors on the one hand, and the scepticism towards governmental bankruptcy proceedings on the other. The Democrats defended the interests of the debtors and were for the regulation on the part of individual states, whereas the Republicans were in favour of the interests of the creditors and of a federal regulation which would be valid for all the states. The Democrats wanted voluntary petition of bankruptcy on the part of the debtor as protection against creditors, whereas the Republicans fought for the rights of the creditors and wanted to give the right of petition of bankruptcy only to them. Individual Federal States, including Florida and Texas, had already issued laws for the protection of indebted farmers, to whom they conceded either temporary or permanent remission of debts. The political representatives of these states were thus vehemently against federal regulation. Only at the end of the century, when the Republicans controlled both Houses, could a lasting insolvency law be established.

There was also a second development, which proved to be invaluable for American bankruptcy proceedings: the crisis of the railways. The companies for the construction of railways were the first large share-based companies in the nineteenth century. As a result of overexpansion and fluctuation of economic activity, many societies encountered financial difficulties. There was a period in which up to 20 per cent of the railway system was run by insolvent companies. The companies and their creditors, however, did not resort to the state, as happened in Europe, but to the courts. The political structure and the distribution of expertise between the States and Washington prevented a governmental solution for the railways which stretched over many Federal States. By the end of the nineteenth century, the courts, therefore, had to develop a reorganisation technique which was called 'equity receivership'. The courts changed the bankruptcy proceeding – originally meant as a liquidation – to a rehabilitation proceeding. To a larger extent than the Bankruptcy Act of 1898, this legal proceeding was the foundation of the American way in the rehabilitation of firms. This did not emerge on the basis of a master plan, but from the lack of a legal basis with which to deal with enterprise insolvencies which spread over numerous Federal States. Thus, legal and economic practice created the foundation of insolvency law.

However, this form of rehabilitation of firms turned out to be unsatisfactory. It was both time consuming and unjust. The courts had little control over the reorganisation plan and the committee, which represented the interests of the shareholders and was mainly composed of insiders in connection with creditors. There was no independent control of the reorganisation plan and, as the legal confirmation required the majority of the credit claims, recalcitrant creditors were paid in cash for their support. This led to injustice and delays (Altman, 1971: 5). Criticism was also levelled against the generous fees of banks and lawyers and against the length of the proceedings.

In the twentieth century, new problems emerged. Above all, the world economic crisis, which in the US lasted throughout the 1930s, brought about the collapse of many firms. In connection with the New Deal, the State also developed the intention to intervene more strongly in the economy. This led to the Chandler Act of 1938, in which the role of banks and lawyers was reduced and – similarly to the English model – bankruptcy proceedings were conducted in a more administrative manner. According to the Chandler Act, insolvency of companies was dealt with entirely under Chapter X and Chapter XI, and was actually only meant for small private firms. According to Chapter XI, the court can leave to the current management the development of a rehabilitation plan without any supervision on the part of the Securities and Exchange Commission. The firm could take on new loans, which had to be secured in a preferential way. Thanks to the relatively short duration of these proceedings, this method was regarded as successful. There was, however, no clear formal definition for the application of Chapter XI and so it was not surprising that companies began to test this grey area. With time, larger and larger firms filed for bankruptcy under Chapter XI, which thus became the usual form of the rehabilitation of a firm.

In the 1960s, renewed discussion on bankruptcy law emerged, concerning, above all, consumer loans. The reform of bankruptcy law had its starting point in the report of the Brookings Institution, *Bankruptcy: Problem, Process, Reform* (Stanley and Grith, 1971). This was one of the most ambitious analyses of the bankruptcy problem ever to have been undertaken in the US. The influence of this study is undisputed; it led, according to the adopted point of view, to criticism or praise. The tenor of the study was its emphasis on the social importance of the problem. At its beginning (Stanley and Grith, 1971: 1) it observed that every fifth American was either directly affected by a case of bankruptcy, as a debtor or a creditor, or he knew someone who had gone bankrupt. Every year, thousands of Americans filed a bankruptcy petition and courts cancelled debts amounting to a total of around $2 billion. On the other hand, the economic significance of insolvencies was relativised: the $2 billion debts, which were cancelled every year via bankruptcy proceedings, made up only 0.2 per cent of outstanding private debts – and could be considered as the expenses of the existing loan system. Bankruptcy was therefore not so much an economic problem as a human one (Stanley and Grith, 1971: 40). The focus of this major reform was the increasing number of private bankruptcy cases. In its shadow, however, the conditions for company insolvencies also changed.

The study mentioned above led, after long discussions and some amendments, to the 1978 Bankruptcy Code. This Code brought about a completely new form of bankruptcy law in the US. Since then, the best law firms have dealt with insolvencies and declarations of bankruptcy by individuals and companies have reached an unexpected number. In the new law, the old chapters X, XI and XII were subsumed under a new Chapter 11. As a consequence there were now only two chapters for companies, namely Chapter 11 for their reorganisation and Chapter 7 for their liquidation. As is customary in the American legal system, the law sets guidelines only. Its legal and economic application, however, was left to the judicial system in the form of precedence.

3 US insolvency proceedings today

In the US, there is a distinction between personal bankruptcy and commercial bankruptcy. The essential element of personal bankruptcy is the 'discharge' from financial liabilities. Creditors can thus no longer prosecute the debtor; he is free from previous financial liabilities. US law, however, foresees exceptions for the possibility of discharge, in the case of fraud or crime this cannot be granted, but also in the case of specific debts such as alimony, tax arrears, student loans, and financial obligations which resulted from driving while intoxicated. Discharge is thus granted to the respectable debtor or for respectable debts (Gross, 1997: 27). An essential advantage of American law for the debtor is that he continues to exercise control over the proceedings. A person who files for bankruptcy can decide whether to hand over his assets to the court and thus to be immediately free from his obligations, or to keep his assets and make payments within the framework of a 3–5 year rehabilitation plan.

In practice, three quarters of personal bankruptcies are no-asset cases. In a no-asset case, the debtor receives from the court an 'immediate discharge' and is freed from his debts without payment. This development is mainly due to the success of credit card companies in the US. While in 1978 only around 40 per cent of all families had at least one credit card, by 2000 this share was over 80 per cent. In 1978, 172,000 Americans filed an application for personal bankruptcy, by 1996 the number had risen above one million, with a tendency to increase further (Skeel, 2001: 188). When a personal bankruptcy petition is filed, the loss essentially concerns the consumer loans on credit card, as the latter are unsecured. Credit card companies factor the loss into their business plans. The receivables which are cancelled in a case of private bankruptcy are passed on to other credit card customers, especially onto the rate of interest, which in the case of an overdraft is substantially higher than bank interest rates.

The second possibility is the presentation of a Rehabilitation Plan according to Chapter 13. Here the debtor maintains control over his assets and commits to pay back a certain part of his debts over a period of three to five years. This form is meant for persons with regular income and dates back to the 1930s. This procedure is therefore an option in view of the possible future income of the debtor, but the creditors must be able to expect at least the same financial result as with liquidation of the current assets. Chapter 13 is advantageous if the debtor wants to keep the value of his assets, and it also enables him to preserve his social image. Even in Chapter 13 the creditors' claims cannot be fully satisfied, because the purpose of the proceedings is the economic continuation and not the financial ruin of the debtor. However, this chapter can be applied only within certain limits of debts: in the case of secured debts, the sum must be lower than

$750,000 and in the case of unsecured ones, lower than $250,000. These limits appear arbitrary (Warren, 1996: 29–30). Most debtors, however, do not complete the proceeding described in Chapter 13, which requires a lot of rigour. An unexpected expense is enough to ruin everything, and the debtor finds himself using Chapter 7.

Such essentials as house furniture, cars, and tools for one's profession up to a certain sum cannot be used to satisfy the creditors. US federal law regulates the extent of discharge, but allows the individual states to issue their own provisions. This has indeed been done by 35 states. What is inaccessible to the creditors varies greatly in the US. The assessment of what is necessary for personal survival and well-being in the present and future depends on various estimates. The bankruptcy system protects automobiles, televisions and hi-fi equipment, but not works of art. It protects domestic property: more than half of the people in private bankruptcy are, and in fact remain, house owners (Sullivan *et al.*, 1989: 328), but in New York only up to a value of $10,000, whereas in Florida (the debtor's haven), Texas and five more states this amount is unlimited. Thus, a debtor can escape bankruptcy even with assets in the region of millions, as long as this is in domestic property.

In a certain sense, bankruptcy law in the US is a substitute for a weakly-constructed social system. The health care system and unemployment support are limited, so the only replacement available for families whose survival is threatened is the bankruptcy system. Unemployment represents two thirds of the grounds for bankruptcy, while health costs in case of illness make up 20 per cent. In the US the bankruptcy system is a protective measure against the pressure of the market economy. The state has here drawn a socio-political line to guard against the dangers of credit companies. The Bankruptcy Court is therefore comparable to a hospital for patients in financial troubles (Sullivan *et al.*, 1989: 328). There are, however, also voices which assert that one should not regard the bankruptcy system as a panacea for all social problems (Gross, 1997: 131).

The number of personal (non-business) bankruptcy filings increased from 241,000 in 1980 to more than 1.6 million in 2003 – more than six-fold. During the six-year period from 1980 to 1985, a total of 1.8 million personal bankruptcy filings occurred; while during the six-year period from 1998 to 2003, there were 8.6 million filings. Since the same individual cannot file for bankruptcy under Chapter 7 more often than once every six years, this means that the proportion of households that filed for bankruptcy rose from 2.2 per cent in 1980–85 to 8.2 per cent in 1998–2003. An important issue in personal bankruptcy is to explain the increase in the number of filings. Because it is so favourable to debtors, 70 per cent of personal bankruptcy filings occurred under Chapter 7. Ninety-five per cent of debtors who file under Chapter 7 have no non-exempt assets and repay nothing to creditors. Thus, a new bankruptcy law was adopted in 2005 (Bankruptcy Abuse Prevention and Consumer Protection Act), of which the main changes are in the area of personal bankruptcy. Individual debtors must take financial counselling before filing for bankruptcy. Also, they must pass a series of means tests in order to file for bankruptcy under Chapter 7. If household income is greater than the median and disposable income over a five year period exceeds either $10,000 or 25 per cent of the unsecured debt, then debtors must file for bankruptcy under Chapter 13 rather than Chapter 7. In addition, the homestead exemption is limited to $125,000 unless debtors have owned their homes for 3.3 years at the time they file for bankruptcy. These changes are expected to reduce the number of personal bankruptcy filings by debtors who have relatively high earnings and they will also prevent millionaire debtors (O.J. Simpson is a recent example) from moving to high exemption states such as Texas and Florida to shelter their millions from creditors. But the reform seems unlikely to substantially reduce the overall number of bankruptcy filings, since most debtors who file for personal bankruptcy are in the lower half of the household income distribution in their states (White, 2005: 45–46).

Firms are also free to decide whether to file a petition for bankruptcy either for liquidation or for reorganisation. As in the case of personal bankruptcy, Chapter 7 foresees that the firm will hand over all of its assets to a Trustee who is appointed by the authority unless at least 20 per cent of the creditors' unsecured claims request that the trustee be appointed by the creditors. The function of the trustee is the liquidation of the firm and the realisation of all assets. The proceeds are then distributed according to the order of precedence of the creditors. Chapter 7 is rarely the first choice; in most cases, it is the second option after Chapter 11; however, around 80 per cent fail and are consigned to Chapter 7 (Warren, 1993: 31).

The alternative to this procedure is Chapter 11. Numerous big firms made use of Chapter 11 in order to reorganise themselves financially and to exercise pressure on their creditors, suppliers and employees. Chapter 11 foresees reorganisation of the firm on the recommendation of the management. Management remains – at least temporarily – in place and continues to run the firm. Management thus not only preserves its influence on the administration of the firm, but also on the company reports which would have been carried out independently had a trustee been appointed. Management gets some breathing time – an 'exclusivity period' of at least four months (120 days). In the case of large firms, however, the Court prolongs this period for as long as is necessary. The continuation of the firm's activity by management makes the option of bankruptcy more attractive than it would otherwise be. 'No other bankruptcy system in the world gives the managers of a troubled firm so much influence' (Skeel, 2001: 9). Management does not have to liquidate the firm, even if this would be more advantageous to the creditors than the continuation of the firm. Of course, it is criticised in the US, too, since the people who remain in the leading positions are those who led the firm to its ruin. The counterargument is that only the current management really know the firm and new management would need precious time to become acquainted with it. However, in real insolvency cases, that is, those which are not entered into for other business goals, at least part of the management is replaced, in order to make a better impression on the creditors. Despite this, studies show that only in smaller firms does management remain in position, whereas in bigger ones insolvency proceedings, even when they come under Chapter 11, are accompanied by some fluctuation. Elisabeth Warren mentions that in the biggest 'Chapter 11 cases' in the 1980s, in the 18 months prior to and after the declaration of insolvency, 91 per cent of CEOs were replaced. Other investigations show a 71 per cent to 91 per cent turnover rate of the top management within two years after the declaration of bankruptcy (Warren, 1993: 66).

Reorganisation now takes place through the negotiations with the creditors. The reorganisation divides the creditors into classes with similar claims and presents a plan to every class of creditor. Shareholders and creditors vote on this plan. If the plan is rejected, management and/or the creditors can present a new plan. When every class of creditors has accepted the plan, the latter is confirmed by the Court and the firm begins to operate again. A typical reorganisation plan foresees a quota of 25 per cent to 50 per cent for unsecured loans (White, 1996: 475). Losses are eligible for tax reduction.

This is the normal case for big firms, although the procedure can usually last for two years or more (Franks and Torous, 1996). Therefore, Chapter 11 is, as a rule, considerably more costly than Chapter 13, not only because it lasts longer but also because one must utilise costly services, above all those of lawyers, trustees, accountants and investment bankers. Firms in trouble generally file for bankruptcy under Chapter 11. This must often, however, move later to Chapter 13. One study discovered that only one quarter to one third of firms are actually reorganised according to Chapter 13. The percentage of big firms is around 60 per cent (White, 1996: 478).

If the plan is rejected by one or more classes of creditors and agreement cannot be reached, the plan can nonetheless be confirmed by the Court. This is referrred to as 'cram down'. The liquidation value of the firm is assessed and the reluctant class receives its part according to the priority rule, i.e. preferential creditors must be entirely satisfied before the next class of creditors can be considered. It has been observed, however, that the priority rule is often broken. This is because the creditors with high guarantees always agree to a reduction of their receivables in favour of less secure receivables and even of the shareholders in order to obtain their approval of the reorganisation plan. Thus, even share holders can obtain a part, albeit usually small, of the bankruptcy proceeds (Bhandari and Weiss, 1996: 109). A study has recorded such infringement in about two-thirds of the cases analysed; the disadvantaged creditors, however, were usually granted a higher interest rate for their receivables (White, 1996: 260).

An advantage of this proceeding is the 'automatic stay', that is, an automatic moratorium, as a consequence of which the firm does not have to pay back its previous debts during the proceedings. Chapter 11 temporarily frees the firm from its creditors and affords the necessary breathing time to restructure its finances and to reach a solution. Preferential payments are also excluded. All payments to unsecured creditors are invalid from 90 days before a bankruptcy petition; if the creditor is an insider, then this period is extended to one year. The regulation of the debt problem thus takes place in an orderly manner.

In American law, management and owners/shareholders are not personally liable for the debts of a firm which according to corporate law has limited liability (shares etc). Management runs the firm without exposing itself to risks and in the case of bankruptcy can continue its activity in another firm without being burdened by the mistakes of the past. The different treatment of personal bankruptcy and commercial bankruptcy is seen as peculiar. Whereas an individual person is liable for his financial blunders, bankruptcy affects the firm but the people who caused its financial ruin leave all their obligations behind (Gross, 1997: 29). The purpose of this generosity towards the management is to permit the timely commencement of the bankruptcy proceedings and to prevent the management from continuing running the insolvent firm at high costs in the attempt to avoid bankruptcy by all means (White, 1996: 207).

The stigma of bankruptcy has weakened in the US in the last decades and the costs of a bankruptcy petition for the firm have clearly abated. With Chapter 11, the emphasis has shifted towards the debtor. It is difficult for the creditor to replace management in a proceeding, the deadline for the reorganisation is often postponed, and the peculiar situation emerges in which creditors who lend sums of money to the firm which has already filed for insolvency are put first in the list of preferences. Some firms, therefore, file for bankruptcy under Chapter 11 in order to obtain further loans. The declaration of bankruptcy no longer necessarily means that a firm is finished; rather than a last resort for the weak and for failures, it can be an instrument of the rich and powerful. Because of the costs and length of the proceeding, Chapter 11 is for large firms or, in the words of a New York lawyer: 'Bankruptcy is not for bankrupts'. Chapter 11 is an insider business; one needs a large amount of financial means, knowledge and experience in order to be able to play this game well and take advantage of it in an innovative way. It has been observed that Chapter 11 saves the jobs of the management and not the assets (Mizsei, 1993: 32). If the reorganisation fails, it is the creditors and the firm that bear all the costs and its management are no worse off than with an immediate liquidation.

An innovation of the law of 1978 was that the concept of receivables is interpreted in a broad sense. It included not only the legal obligations of the past but also those that the firm may be burdened with in the future, even if these cannot be appraised yet. This has led to completely new use of the insolvency proceedings: thus, for example, an asbestos firm reacted to the threat of class-action lawsuits with a declaration of bankruptcy and thus reached a favourable agreement; smaller firms filed for bankruptcy in order to avoid the costs of the environment pollution they had caused; a petroleum corporation reduced penalty payments to a business rival because of the unfair take-over of a company thanks to insolvency proceedings; airlines forced their unions to accept dismissals and salary reductions and thus reduced their expenses; steel firms in an insolvency proceeding were able to delegate pension liabilities to the public authorities and avert a take-over attempt by a business rival.

Bankruptcy has therefore become a strategy for avoiding financial burdens and risks. Firms – mostly together with their banks – can instigate insolvency for many reasons. These strategic bankruptcies have three essential elements: first, they pursue a short-term goal that they cannot reach without a bankruptcy proceeding; second, liabilities which had not been considered before or had been valued differently become concrete; and, finally, these cases always contain an innovative legal strategy which is meant to underpin the representation of a firm's insolvency (Delaney, 1997: 161). These strategic insolvencies are spectacular, but in the final analysis they are an exception. In these cases, too, there is a problem that may but does not necessarily have to lead to a firm's demise but endangers the continual success of the company's activity. The example of the airlines, for which the reduction of staff costs is a question of survival, shows that this company policy, unlike in some European countries, is reached not through negotiations with the unions but rather in the last resort through the threat of bankruptcy. Here bankruptcy law is a substitute for the social policy approach of other countries.

A market-conforming variant of the insolvency proceeding is the 'workout'. As an insolvency proceeding casts doubt on the ability of a firm to fulfil its obligations, contracting parties are encouraged to break the arrangements they have concluded with the firm. Customers will pay their bills only reluctantly, and suppliers will supply only against payments in cash. An informal insolvency proceeding in the form of negotiations between all parties concerned reduces these disadvantages and saves them the direct proceeding expenses and the changes of the legal situation which result from court involvement. Such a proceeding, however, is possible only if it is initiated relatively on time and the firm concerned is still in a relatively good state. Also, the management must be in a good position to secure concessions from its creditors. The most important instrument here is the threat of bankruptcy and willingness to cut costs, above all with regard to the staff, in order to convince the creditors. Thus, this type of market-conforming insolvency is considered only in cases in which the whole sector is in a structural crisis, as in the case of the airlines. If the management is seen as responsible for the firm's difficulties, then a workout becomes unthinkable. Also, workouts are not necessarily encouraged by the legislator, because losses are not eligible for tax depreciation. A variant of this market-oriented bankruptcy model is the 'pre-packaged bankruptcy petition'. Nearly all firms attempt, before resorting to Chapter 11, to reach a workout agreement with the creditors out of court. This, however, requires that all creditors must accept the solution and that the receivable reliefs are not eligible for tax reduction. The solution is pre-packaged bankruptcy, in which an already prepared reorganisation plan accepted by most creditors is presented to the court for approval.

4 Development in the European countries

Great Britain

Until 1986, the focus of British bankruptcy law was protection of the creditor's receivables. The most important aspect of this was that management was in all cases removed from a firm's leading positions. Since 1986–87 there have been three possibilities:

- liquidation
- receivership
- voluntary reconstruction.

The Insolvency Act of 1986 foresees that management will file a bankruptcy petition as soon as there is no prospect of a continuation of the firm's activity. If this does not happen, exclusion can be imposed on every management role for up to 15 years, and managers are personally liable for any additional damage. In the first five years, this regulation was applied to over 1,000 board members. In all cases, the firm is handed over to a trustee who is supposed to represent the interests of the creditors. Both the firm itself and the creditors can apply for liquidation. This step must be approved by the court, but it can be appealed. The liquidator disposes of the firm, settles business transactions, and distributes the proceeds among the creditors. The British insolvency proceeding foresees the appointment of an administrator chosen by the court or by the creditors. This administrator is also paid by the creditors. If the assets available are too few, the state bears the bankruptcy expenses, and there is thus no dismissal of the bankruptcy petition on the grounds of unavailable funds. However, the bankruptcy administrator is as a rule self-financed. The proceeds of the liquidation first have to cover the expenses for the proceeding, and then they are distributed to the creditors with special guarantees and next to preferential creditors, such as certain taxes and the claims of the employees. The claims of the employees are guaranteed within limits by the state, which then represents them as creditor. Only after all this is it the turn of other creditors.

The bankruptcy administration is a complicated proceeding. A creditor with a fixed charge can appoint a bankruptcy administrator, called the receiver, specifically for mortgaged assets. The receiver is only responsible for this one creditor and his fixed charge. This receiver realises the specific assets for which he is appointed, satisfies this creditor, and hands over the remaining value to the liquidator. A creditor with a floating charge, that is with a security which extends to the whole firm, can appoint an administrative receiver who assumes the control of all assets (with the exception of the fixed charges) and is liable to creditors according to the priority of their receivables. Normally, this is the procedure of large banks or a group of banks, as British firms mostly possess a credit agreement with only one bank. As long as the receiver is in office, assets which are indispensable for the running of the firm cannot be extracted from it. Although the appointment of a receiver cannot be appealed, other creditors can request the appointment of a liquidator, which would make the receiver superfluous. The lack of a court and the possibilities of the secured creditor lead to a quick resolution of the financial liabilities. If there are no secured creditors, no receiver can be appointed. The only alternative until 1986 was the liquidator.

Bankruptcy administrators are also known as licensed insolvency practitioners. They are usually professional accountants whose reputation is of paramount importance as only a small group of banks deal with a large part of the appointments of receivers. The receiver decides whether a firm will continue to operate. If cash flow is positive, then this is easily the case. If it is negative, new financial means must be taken up. The receiver is personally liable for all liabilities incurred after his appointment and will be careful in taking up new loans. His main aim will be to reach the highest possible satisfaction of the creditor by whom he was appointed. Whatever else he can obtain is distributed among the remaining creditors according to the order of preference of their receivables. There are some regulations which should protect the remaining creditors; however, the receivership is in general regarded as a proceeding in which the remaining creditors are damaged while all benefits are destined to the floating charge holders, and the continual operating of the firm is sacrificed to the interests of this creditor. Receivership therefore encourages liquidation, all the more so because this can be requested at any time by the other creditors.

The decision as to whether the firm should continue operating is mostly taken under time pressure and with limited information; therefore liquidation is a frequent solution. Management are not involved in the proceedings and is under pressure to avoid insolvency whenever possible. The debtor therefore no longer controls the firm. If a firm can be sold in its entirety, it often happens that current management takes the lead, since its knowledge of the firm allows it to submit the best offer and take decisions more quickly than anyone else.

The Insolvency Act of 1986 foresees a third possibility, that of an administrative receivership, through which the proceeding can be more debtor-friendly and premature liquidations are avoided. An administrative receiver is appointed at the request of the firm or creditors via the court. Appointment of an administrator by the court is the fundamental difference from the US law (Chapter 11), in which the operations of the firm are conducted by current management. Management in Great Britain, however, lose control over the firm in all cases. The accompanying role of lawyers and management consultants is also lacking, whereas it is essential in the US. The British bankruptcy administrator is a licensed profession. He represents the claims of all creditors. Thus, an area of conflict which existed with the receiver now disappears. The administrator has a much stronger position than the receiver: he can suspend existing loans, interest rates or leasing payments, take up new loans and cannot be replaced by a liquidator. Also, he is not personally liable for financial commitments which are made after his appointment. The appointment of the administrator brings about an automatic three-month stay during which a rehabilitation plan is developed, which must be accepted by more than 50 per cent of creditors (as measured by the value of receivables). The court, too, can impose a rehabilitation plan on the creditors. The administrator is regarded as a way of finding a more debtor-friendly and reorganisation-friendly solution (Franks and Torous, 1996: 456). The difference, however, is that the rehabilitation plan is prepared by the administrator and not by management, which during this phase has only a limited role. In addition, creditors with a fixed or floating charge can block appointment of the administrator by appointing their own receiver or liquidator. Therefore, the option of an administrator is possible only when the majority of creditors agree from the outset. In addition, such proceedings are costly and only larger firms can afford them. During the first ten years after the appointment of an administrator, of 202,000 firm insolvencies 78 per cent resulted in liquidation, 20 per cent in bankruptcy trusteeship, and less then 1 per cent in the appointment of administrators (Hoshi, 1998: 26–27). The proceedings work, therefore, only for very large firms, in which the preservation of assets is of utmost importance.

British law gives the firm the opportunity to solve its problems with its most important creditors through a legal workout. The court confirms the voluntary arrangement with a 'scheme of agreement'; this is conditional on 75 per cent of each class of creditors giving their consent. This procedure is mainly chosen for complex reorganisations, because a voluntary arrangement with the mediation of the court becomes binding for all creditors. In the ten years after the introduction of this regulation, this procedure, too, represented around one per cent of insolvencies.

Considerably more successful are informal workouts in which the firm itself – or more often its bank – appoints a consultant and accountant before opting for a formal workout. In two-thirds of cases, this method allows a solution to be found for the continuation of the firm's activity (Hill, 1994: 37). As a consequence of the strictness of British insolvency law, only real insolvency cases are considered for formal proceedings; otherwise there is a tendency towards an extrajudicial resolution.

British insolvency law is rapid and relatively inexpensive. Creditors obtain control of the firm and thus higher reliability of the original credit agreement. However, this can lead to premature insolvency petitions and underinvestment, as the management's personal liability advises extreme caution (Franks and Torous, 1996: 464). In principle and in spite of all reforms, however, British law still assumes that it is the creditors' money that is at stake and that it is therefore their concern to control the proceeding. Most rehabilitations and liquidations occur without involving the courts or with only minor involvement to secure legal certainty. The market must regulate its own errors, because 'companies are not rescued in courtrooms, but in the market-place' (Hill, 1994: 47). In Britain there is no 'rescue culture': rehabilitation is not regarded as a first possibility but as a last resort. What becomes obvious here is the conviction that a firm's failure should be punished. Insolvency proceedings should not be an opportunity to redress aberrant developments. Continental European practice, like in Britain, foresees the appointment of a bankruptcy administrator or trustee in order to continue the activity of the firm. Here, however, the courts are more strongly involved in the proceedings. There is no equivalent of administrative receivership and of secured creditor's influence. Bankruptcy legislation is more debtor-friendly and reorganisation generally lasts longer. Regulations for private bankruptcy are very far from the strictness characterising company insolvencies. Although in this case, too, a debtor's assets and income are realised to mere subsistence level for the benefit of the creditors, this phase lasts only two years in the case of debts of up to £20,000, and three years for larger debts. After this relatively short time, the person concerned is free from its previous obligations.

France

French insolvency law belongs to the tradition of Roman law and was first laid down in the Napoleonic Code in 1807. All later laws were based on these principles. The Code provided for the equal treatment of all creditors, the appointment of a bankruptcy administrator by the courts and the creation of a committee of creditors. Regulations focused on creditors' interests and regarded insolvency as an offence on the part of the debtor and thus entailing penal consequences (Lafont, 1994: 15). The twentieth century brought about a series of legislative amendments, the most important of which were in 1984, 1985 and 1994. In the economic crisis of the 1980s, with increasing unemployment and bankruptcies, the structure of insolvency proceedings changed profoundly. In France, its essential aim is to save the firm and maintain the working place. The law of 1985 eliminated the need to create a creditors' committee, in order to accelerate the proceeding and to reach the following aims:

- reintegration of the firm into the economy
- strengthening of employment
- satisfaction of the creditors' receivables.

The aims of this legislative amendment were therefore primarily of a social and politico-economic nature; creditors' interests, which until then had been of primary importance, became secondary. The law was therefore thought of as a socio-economic instrument that now bore little resemblance to the regulations of the Napoleonic Code.

A bankruptcy petition can be made by the firm, the creditors, the state attorney or the courts. Management is obliged to file a petition for insolvency within 15 days. However, these sanctions are not strict, which is why the firm itself rarely completes the petition (Hoshi, 1998: 30). Petitions for insolvency are therefore more often filed by a creditor who needs only to prove that the firm has not honoured its payments.

Courts examine the insolvency application and issue a decree of reconstruction. An automatic stay ensues, which means that debts can no longer be demanded or paid individually. This decree envisages the appointment of an administrator, who supervises the management, and a period of observation that is initially of six months but can be extended twice. The bankruptcy administrator represents the state and not creditors. He is chosen from a list of administrators authorised by the court and is responsible, personally and without limitation, for this activity and must be therefore appropriately insured. His authority is set down by the court. During the period of observation, he must examine the company's economic and social condition and assess the prospects for rehabilitation. If his examination gives positive results, he develops a reorganisation plan. This plan refers not only to the financial aspect of creditors' claims but also to the firm's organisation, cuts in the number of employees, and replacement of management. How high the restructuring rate must be is not explicitly stated; in most cases, instalments are paid over a period of seven or eight years.

If the administrator's examination gives negative results, a liquidation plan is developed whose aim is to sell the firm either in its entirety or in parts. The firm is then liquidated and the new owner is released from previous liabilities. Either plan – reorganisation and liquidation – is subject to court approval. The French model is clearly even more interventionist than Chapter 10 of the Chandler Act (Bolton, 2002: 19). It leaves hardly any space for negotiations between creditors and debtors. Decisions on reorganisation or liquidation as well as their development are taken exclusively by the administrator and the court. Of course, an administrator will consult all persons concerned and therefore also creditors, but it is a court that has the last word. A 1994 amendment strengthened the position of creditors further by eliminating the automatic period of observation and leaving this to the court's discretion. This is meant to permit more rapid treatment of hopeless cases. For firms with temporary liquidation difficulties, the law of 1984 introduced another proceeding in which the court appoints a 'conciliator' whose task is to develop a financial plan and submit it to the creditors. This method, however, has been rarely applied, as it requires the voluntary approval of creditors. Only in Paris was it reactivated for the rehabilitation of real estate firms at the beginning of the 1990s. Another rather flexible proceeding allows a company to designate a 'guardian', normally a trustee firm, which is authorised by the court for insolvency proceedings and acts as a sort of consultant to supervise the company's reconstruction before it becomes truly insolvent. This proceeding has permitted some spectacular cases of rehabilitation.

Germany

In Germany, too, bankruptcy proceedings follow an administrative model, in spite of the fact that there was no uniform law until 1999. The legal fundamentals were the bankruptcy law, the 1935 restructuring law, and the law of 1990 that regulated insolvency proceedings in East Germany after reunification. In addition to these, there were several civil and criminal regulations that also referred to bankruptcy proceedings. German bankruptcy proceedings are predominantly applied to the liquidation of a debtor's assets, in order to satisfy creditors' claims. Restructuring, that is to say a voluntary agreement with a creditor, played a minor role. Both debtors and creditors can file a bankruptcy petition. Creditors must prove their business partner's inability to pay, while debtors must submit a record of their assets and liabilities as well as a list of their creditors. Debtors must file a bankruptcy petition no later than three weeks after their inability to pay or over-indebtedness has become apparent. Management is personally liable for any damage that may result from a belated insolvency petition (Fialski, 1994: 26). German insolvency law, therefore, stresses creditors' interests. However, the importance of a company's survival for employment has become increasingly clear in Germany, too.

If assets are sufficient to cover court expenses, the insolvency judge will institute the proceeding and appoint an expert to examine the reasons for insolvency. At the same time, a debtor's assets are confiscated in order to prevent their disposal. If the proceeding is confirmed, a bankruptcy administrator is appointed from a list of authorised lawyers and trustees and the date for the creditors' meeting is decided. Normally, the administrator later becomes the trustee of the insolvent firm. Previous management is replaced. The bankruptcy administrator liquidates the debtor's assets and continues operating the firm only if this can secure receivables. Courts can also elect a committee of creditors for support and control of the bankruptcy administrator. During the first creditors' meeting, the provisional trustee submits a report on the causes of insolvency and the assembly normally confirms the trustee for the ensuing procedure. In the second creditors' meeting, which often takes place immediately after the first, creditors' receivables are examined and approved. In a third and last meeting, creditors vote on the final report of the trustee.

Creditors with solid guarantees do not take part in insolvency proceedings, as they can enforce their receivables independently thanks to their right of preferential treatment. Most of the loans given to firms are provided with preferential, securitised guarantees. In practice this means that after the satisfaction of creditors' claims with specific guarantees, there no longer are assets for the bankruptcy proceeding. In three-quarters of cases, the proceeding is therefore rejected on the grounds of unavailable funds. The debtor's assets are distributed first to those obligations incurred by the bankruptcy administrator in order to continue operating the firm, then to court expenses, employees' claims up to six months earlier, taxes and public dues, and finally to the unsecured creditors.

In German law, a debtor is not freed from his obligations. An individual remains liable for his remaining debts for 30 years, that is to say for the rest of his life. Management can also be liable for its personal assets, if creditors can accuse them of negligence. If a penal proceeding ends with a conviction, it is always a minor one (around 14 days probatory), but it lays the basis for a civil prosecution for material compensation. Managers who receive a criminal conviction as a result of an insolvency proceeding are barred from holding high office in the firm for five years.

German insolvency law also provides for enforced restructuring. A debtor offers his creditors a specific quota and presents a plan of how he intends to render these services. The creditors' assembly holds a vote and if 50 per cent of the creditors present with a share of 75 per cent of the total amount outstanding agrees the restructuring is accepted. This is binding on both creditors who were absent and those who voted no and relieves the debtor from any other liability. Nonetheless, this insolvency proceeding with a reorganisation aim is only of minor importance, because during the proceeding there is no debt moratorium for secured receivables and because a quota of 35 per cent is required (40 per cent if instalments exceed one year). Cases of insolvency that can be solved with restructuring are comparatively rare: they make up only 1 per cent of the total, as low as that of Great Britain. Hence, it is common – in an estimated 20 per cent of cases – to reach a workout outside the court proceeding.

In Germany, a 1999 decree introduced a new codification of insolvency law that put an end to the traditional dichotomy between bankruptcy and restructuring. The new insolvency law combines all regulations on insolvency and, with its stronger emphasis on company rehabilitation, has brought German regulations closer to Chapter 11, thus following the international trend. The new law revokes secured creditors' privileges to make use of their guarantees even during the insolvency proceeding. It introduces an automatic three-month stay, creates classes of creditors and allows creditors to present their own reorganisation plan. The main aim of this law, however, remains the best possible satisfaction of creditors. In addition to liquidation, the new law foresees an insolvency plan that replaces restructuring and enforced restructuring. The legal context for this is flexible. It is usually the bankruptcy administrator who presents the plan to the creditors. He can also continue operating the firm in order to satisfy creditors with future proceeds. The plan, however, can also recommend the selling of the firm or its liquidation. The new law allows current management to continue operating the firm, albeit under a trustee's supervision, and endeavours to promote reorganisation by means of a debt moratorium and agreements below 35 per cent.

Methods of dealing with bankruptcy and insolvency have raised discussions both in the US and in Europe and have led to amendments to the law. Criticism has been levelled against excessive privileging of creditors' interests in Great Britain and Germany, and against infringements of creditors' rights in order to reach rehabilitation in the US and in France. The regulatory changes of 1986 in Great Britain and 1999 in Germany attempted to redress this imbalance as the amendments of 1994 had done in France and in the US. Whilst insolvency policy seems to be growing more uniform, at least with regard to individual regulations, different political principles remain. The question as to which direction is economically more efficient depends on the success of the reorganisation, its costs and above all the individual who bears the expenses, since any macroeconomic advantage is hard to demonstrate.

A popular argument maintains that managers who have nothing or little to lose in a case of insolvency are more ready to take risks than those for whom doing so can be life-threatening. Numerous studies confirm this (Hoshi, 1998: 33). Few figures are available for the triumphs of rehabilitation in insolvency proceedings. Most statistics do not follow the development of a firm after an insolvency proceeding has been completed; only for individual cases do we know how successful rehabilitation was – that is, how long the firm continued to exist and whether a new structure was found that put the company firmly on its feet again.

It has also been argued that an overly lax insolvency legislation subverts the behaviour of the firm. However, one of the crucial innovations of the nineteenth century was the introduction of a limited responsibility for companies in the form of the joint-stock form and limited liability. This permitted outside capital to flow into firms that represented the driving force of the emerging credit services sector. Firms constantly operate with limited liability for their financial obligations; insolvency legislation is simply part of liability limitation.

European Union

On 31 May 2002, the European Insolvency Regulation (EIR) came into force. The long history of the EIR is typical of the European integration process and is mainly due to extremely different economic and legal cultures in member states. But the US, too, had to wait over 100 years for the emergence of a uniform insolvency law in all Federal States.

Whilst the Brussels agreement of 1968 regulated the jurisdiction and the recognition and enforcement of judgments, the field of insolvency remained – with the exception of few bilateral conventions – unregulated. In a note of 1959, the EEC points out disturbances and difficulties in the economies of member states when courts are unable to assess or support legal claims in the European economic area. 'Legal protection of rights and legal security on the European market depend essentially on a satisfactory regulation of recognition and enforcement of judgements between member states' (Morscher, 2002). In 1960, a commission of experts attempted to reach a uniform agreement regulating these matters. The year 1970 saw preliminary drafts of an agreement on bankruptcy, restructuring and related proceedings. The bill, however, did not develop. In 1980 the Commission worked on a new bill, which was only marginally revised in 1984. All of these bills were ultimately rejected. Criticism was levelled against their impractical nature, their overly complex regulations and marked French influence. In addition to the efforts of the Commission and of the EU Council, the Council of Europe had worked on the international protection of creditors' rights since 1979. This led to the European Convention on Certain International Aspects of Bankruptcy, also known as the Istanbul Bankruptcy Agreement, in 1990. The bill limited itself to the mutual recognition of bankruptcy proceedings and asserted the administrator's cross-national competencies, but it left other questions open. Although the Istanbul agreement was not ratified by all member states and therefore never came into force, it was an essential preparation. During a meeting of the EU ministers of justice in 1989, it was once again observed that the absence of an insolvency agreement for the Community must be regarded as a grave flaw in the common market. It was considered unacceptable that the activity of companies was increasingly regulated by Community law, whereas in the case of insolvencies only national law was applied. The Council created a working group for 'bankruptcy agreement' which operated from 1991 to 1995. By 1992 a bill was presented which the Council passed without major changes as a European agreement on insolvency proceedings in 1995. However, this agreement never came into force either, because Great Britain refused to ratify it. In 1999 the Committee on Legal Affairs and Citizens' Rights observed that the Community was at the same point as 20 years earlier. A resolution of the European Parliament invited the

Commission to develop a regulation on the basis of the 1995 bill. On the initiative of Germany and Finland, the transformation of the insolvency agreement of 1995 into a regulation of the Council was finally proposed, which ultimately prevailed as the European Insolvency Regulation (EIR) of May 2000 (Morscher, 2002).

The EIR is meant to regulate reorganisation and liquidation where they concern more than one EU member state. In principle, EU law is valid for all member states, but Denmark, Great Britain and Ireland are allowed to reject it under the terms of their accession treaties. Of the three, only Denmark has so far rejected this convention. The convention is valid between EU countries but not for insolvencies that concern other states. The EU avoided a uniform definition of the notion of 'insolvency'; instead it listed the various national insolvency laws. The convention governs a whole series of law cases. The regulation does not concern pre-insolvency proceedings or insolvencies of banks, insurance companies and financial institutions. The EU convention invalidated other agreements between states, such as the Nordic Convention and nine bilateral treaties between EU member states.

The EU feared that insolvent debtors might have an incentive to shop for a favourable jurisdiction. As national legislation could not prevent this, the EU opted for a compromise between the universal and territorial approaches. Special consideration was given to the different property rights and to the rights of the persons involved. This led to the conclusion that a uniform EU insolvency law could not be reached. In order to encourage efficient collaboration, the EU convention focuses on the following fields:

1   In what country and under which law must an insolvency petition be filed and a proceeding be initiated. The EU convention allows two proceedings, a primary and a secondary one. The primary proceeding must be initiated in an EU country that represents the debtor's 'centre of interests'. Every conflict that concerns this centre of interests is dealt with by the court where the insolvency petition was filed. The bankruptcy legislation of the country hosting the centre of interests is valid for the whole proceeding, and this also applies to other EU countries. However, creditors' rights for preferential and secured receivables depend on the country in which the business was concluded, because the law of that country was the basis on which the business was done and business partners must be able to rely on it. In addition to a primary proceeding, the trustee or, according to national laws, a party concerned, institute a secondary proceeding that is valid only for this specific country. A debtor must have an establishment in this country as a basis for regular business transactions; a loose connection such as banknotes is not enough. A secondary proceeding concerns only assets and receivables declared in this country, and follows the insolvency law of the country in which it takes place and not that of the primary proceeding. The primary proceeding is universal, whereas the secondary one is limited to the state in which it was instituted. If a primary insolvency proceeding is instituted in an EU country, there is a strict priority policy. Every subsequent proceeding

in another member state can only be a secondary proceeding. Secondary proceedings are only valid for branches of companies and the like, whereas legally independent subsidiaries do not fall under these regulations and are dealt with in separate proceedings. The EIR, however, does not exclude all conflicts of jurisdiction if for example, a primary proceeding had been instituted but a court in another country noticed flaws in the proceeding and instituted a new primary proceeding itself. Generally speaking, creditors will have to consider more than one legal system in the future. A German limited company (GmbH), for instance, may be partly subject to German insolvency law, but its assets can also be realised according to the principles of any other insolvency law within the European Union (Bert and Schlegel, 2003).

2   The recognition of this country's legal system. The petition of insolvency in an EU country is automatically recognised by all other member states. If the automatic stay is valid in this country, then it must be recognised as a legally regulated debt cancellation in other EU countries. There is the possibility of objection if this procedure is in conflict with constitutional laws or fundamental rights in this country. The liquidator or trustee can carry out his functions in all EU countries but he must also take into consideration local insolvency legislation.

Trustees taking part in proceedings are expected to collaborate and submit reports and have the right to take part at every proceeding, even those in other countries. Although the overall aim of a primary proceeding is a fair distribution, secured creditors in particular can be treated differently as a result of a different legal situation in various EU countries. The European proceeding is not European insolvency law; it only creates a relatively comfortable possibility to approach the ideal of the best possible creditor satisfaction on the basis of different national insolvency systems. At EU level, much remains to be done.

5   Conclusions

Generally speaking, there is worldwide convergence towards a more debtor-friendly insolvency policy. Differences between the US and the EU are in the degree of involvement of courts, administrators or trustees in the management of an insolvent company. In this respect, the US and Great Britain are diametrically opposed cases. Whilst in the US rehabilitation proceedings take place with a minimal participation of courts, elsewhere the courts are present in both proceedings and supervision. A further difference is in the restructuring of interests between creditors and debtor. On the other hand, creditors' interests are nowhere as strongly represented as in Great Britain. Germany abandoned the strong emphasis on creditors' interests with the 1999 law. There are also differences in the consideration given to other stakeholders such as employees. Especially in France, large firms protect employees' interests. Finally, there are differences in the personal responsibility of the debtor or of management and in the extent of debt moratorium.

In the US, it is usually debtors who file insolvency petitions, whereas in Europe it is mostly their creditors. It is assumed that the stricter is insolvency law towards management, the bigger is the danger of a belated insolvency petition. The early filing of a petition is meant to help minimise losses and increase the chance of saving the company. Europeans do this with strict, personal sanctions on management, whereas the US system assumes that milder treatment of previous management can lead to earlier filing on insolvency petitions. American managers are encouraged to file by the 'carrot' represented by Chapter 11, whereas European ones by the 'stick' of their legal sanctions (White, 1996: 478).

The most important difference, however, is that in the US there are largely uniform insolvency proceedings, from which the EU, in spite of all its efforts, is still far away. This chapter has described only three EU countries; if it had considered all 25, the picture would have been more complicated still. Not only is the legal tradition different, but so is legal certainty (La Porta and Lopez-de-Silanes, 2001; Claessens and Klapper, 2002).

Bibliography

Altman, E.I. (1971) *Corporate Bankruptcy in America*. Lexington, MA: Heath Lexington Books.

Altman, E.I. (ed.) (2002) *Bankruptcy, Credit Risk and High Yield Junk Bonds*, Malden, US: Blackwell.

Baird, D.G. (1996) 'A world without bankruptcy', in Jagdeep S. Bhandari and Lawrence A. Weiss (eds) *Corporate Bankruptcy. Economic and Legal Perspectives*. Cambridge: Cambridge University Press.

Barreveld, D.J. (2002) *The Enron Collapse. Creative Accounting, Wrong Economics or Criminal Acts?* Writers Club, San Jose.

Berle, A.A. and Means, G.C. (1933) *The Modern Corporation and Private Property*, New York: Transaction Publishers.

Bert, P. and Schlegel, U. (2003) 'Das EU-Insolvenzrecht offenbart Tücken im Detail', *Frankfurter Allgemeine Zeitung*, 20 August.

Bhandari, J.S. and Weiss, L.A. (1996) *Corporate Bankruptcy. Economic and Legal Perspectives*. Cambridge: Cambridge University Press.

Bolton, P. (2002) *Towards a Statutory Approach to Sovereign Debt Restructuring: Lessons from Corporate Bankruptcy Practice around the World*, unpublished manuscript, Princeton University.

Bufford, S.L., Adler, L.D., Brooks, S.B. and Krieger, M.S. (2001) *International Insolvency*, Washington, DC: Federal Judicial Center.

Carruthers, B.G. and Halliday, T.C. (1998) *Rescuing Business: The Making of Corporate Bankruptcy Law in England and the United States*. New York: Oxford University Press.

Claessens, S. and Klapper, L.F. (2002) 'Bankruptcy around the World: Explanation of its Relative Use', World Bank Publicy Research Working Paper 2865, July.

Claessens, S., Djankov, S. and Mody, A. (2001) *Resolution of Financial Distress. An*

International Perspective on the Design of Bankruptcy Laws, WBI Development Studies, Washington.

Cofer, C. and Appley, M. (1964) *Motivation: Theory and Research*. New York: John Wiley and Sons, Inc.

Colman, P.J. (1974) *Debtors and Creditors in America: Insolvency, Imprisonment for Debt, and Bankruptcy 1607–1900*. Madison: Wisconsin Historical Society Press.

Cybinski, P.J. (2003) *Doomed Firms. An Econometric Analysis of the Path to Failure*. Aldershot: Ashgate Publishing.

Delaney, K.J. (1997) *Strategic Bankruptcy*, Berkeley: University of California Press.

Dembinski, P.H., Lager, C., Cornford, A. and Bovin, J.M. (eds) (2006*) Enron and World Finance. A Case Study in Ethics*. New York: Palgrave Macmillan.

Dewing, A.S. (1953) *Financial Policy of Corporations*. New York: Ronald Press Co.

Fialski, H. (1994) 'Insolvency Law in the Federal Republic of Germany', in Stilpon Nestor, *Corporate Bankruptcy and Reorganisation Procedures in OECD and Central and Eastern European Countries*. Paris: OECD.

Franks, J.R. and Torous, W.N. (1996) 'Lessons from a comparison of US and UK insolvency codes', in Jagdeep S. Bhandari and Lawrence A. Weiss (eds) *Corporate Bankruptcy. Economic and Legal Perspectives*. Cambridge: Cambridge University Press, pp. 450–466.

Geus, A. de (1997) *The living Company. Growth, Learning and Longevity in Business*. Boston, MA: Harvard Business School Press.

Gratzer, K. (1998) 'Reasons for filling a bankruptcy', CeFin Seminar Paper, Huddinge.

Gratzer, K. (2000) *Business Failure in an International Perspective*, unpublished manuscript, Stockholm.

Gross, K. (1997) *Failure and Forgiveness*. New Haven, CT: Yale University Press.

Hart, O. (2000) 'Different Approaches to Bankruptcy', Working Paper 7921, National Bureau of Economic Research, Cambridge, September.

Hausch, D.B. and Ramachandran, S. (2001) 'Corporate Debt Restructuring: Auctions Speak Louder than Words', in Stijn Claessens, Simeon Djankov and Ahoka Mody (eds) *Resolution of Financial Distress. An International Perspective on the Design of Bankruptcy Laws*, WBI Development Studies, Washington, pp. 91–106.

Hill, S. (1994) 'Corporate Workouts – Options under UK Legislation', in Stilpon Nestor, *Corporate Bankruptcy and Reorganisation Procedures in OECD and Central and Eastern European Countries*, Paris: OECD.

Hirschman, A. (1970) *Exit, Voice, and Loyality*. Cambridge, MA: Harvard University Press.

Hoshi, I. (1998) 'Bankruptcy, Reorganisation, and Liquidation in Mature market Economies: Lessons for Economies in Transition', in Leszek Balcerowicz, Cheryl W. Gray and Iraj Hoshi (eds) *Enterprise Exit Processes in Transition Economies. Downsizing, Workouts, and Liquidation*. Budapest: Central European University Press.

International Monetary Fund (1999) *Orderly and Effective Insolvency Procedures. Key Issues*, IMF Legal Department, Washington, DC.

Jackson, T.H. (1986) *The Logic and Limits of Bankruptcy*. Cambridge, MA: Harvard University Press.

Klikovits, A. (2002) 'EU und Insolvenzrecht: Ende Mai manches neu!', *forum.ksv*, Vienna, April.

Kosstal, J. (2000) '5 Jahre Privatkonkurs (Schuldenregulierungsverfahren)', *forum.ksv*, Vienna, April.

Lafont, H. (1994) 'The French Bankruptcy System', in OECD, *Corporate Bankruptcy* and Reorganisation Procedures in OECD and Central and Eastern European Countries. Paris: OECD.

La Porta, R. and Lopez-de-Silanes, F. (2001) 'Creditor Protection and Bankruptcy Law Reform', in Stijn Claessens, Simeon Djankov and Ashoka Mody (eds) Resolution of Financial Distress. An International Perspective on the Design of Bankruptcy Laws, WBI Development Studies, Washington, DC, pp. 65–90.

Lévy, H.-B. (2006) American Vertigo. Traveling America in the Footsteps of Tocqueville. New York: Random House.

Mason, J.R. (2001) 'Reconstruction Finance Corporation Assistance to financial Intermediaries and Commercial and Industrial Enterprises in the United States, 1932–1937', in Stijn Claessens, Simeon Djankov and Ashoka Mody (eds) Resolution of Financial Distress. An International Perspective on the Design of Bankruptcy Laws, WBI Development Studies, Washington, DC.

Matis, H. and Stiefel, D. (1994) Die Weltwirtschaft. Struktur und Entwicklung im 20. Jahrhundert, Ueberreuter, Vienna.

McQueen, J. (1992) Bankruptcy: the Reality and the Law. Lancaster: Bankruptcy Association of Great Britain and Ireland.

Mischon, C. (1984) Materialien zur Insolvenzentwicklung in der Bundesrepublik Deutschland von 1976 bis 1983, No. 74, IFM: Bonn.

Mitchell J. (1993) 'Creditor Passivity and Bankruptcy: Implications for Economic Reform', in C. Mayer and X. Vives (eds) Capital Markets and Financial Intermediation. Cambridge: Cambridge University Press.

Mizsei, K. (1993) Bankruptcy and the Post-Communist Economies of East Central Europe, Toronto: HarperCollins.

Morscher, M. (2002) Die Europäische Insolvenzverordnung (EuInsVO), Schriftenreihe Euro-Jus, Band 6, Krems, Austria.

Nelson, P.B. (1981) Corporations in Crisis. Behavioral Observations for Bankruptcy Policy. New York: Praeger Publishers.

Presoly, C. (2002) Chapter 11 – Unternehmensreorganisation in den USA im Rechtsvergleich zum österreichischen Recht, Linzer Schriften zum Unternehmensrecht. Vienna.

Rapoport, N.B. and Dharan, B.G. (eds) (2004) Enron: Corporate Fiascos and their Implications. New York: Foundation Press.

Rowat, M. and Astigarraga, J. (1999) 'Latin American Insolvency Systems: a Comporative Assessment', IMF Working Paper, No. 433.

Sennett, R. (1998) Der flexible Mensch. Die Kultur des neuen Kapitalismus. Berlin.

Skeel, D.A. Jr. (2001) Debt's Dominion, A History of Bankrupty Law in America. Princeton: Princeton University Press.

Stanley, D.T. and Grith, M. (1971) Bankruptcy: Problem, Process, Reform. Washington, DC: Brookings Institution.

Stiglitz, J.E. (2001) 'Bankruptcy Laws: Basic Economic Principles', in Stijn Claessens, Simeon Djankov and Ashoka Mody (eds) Resolution of Financial Distress. An International Perspective on the Design of Bankruptcy Laws, WBI Development Studies, Washington, DC.

Sullivan, T., Warren, E. and Westbrook, J.L. (1989) As we Forgive our Debtors: Bankruptcy and Consumer Credit in America. Oxford: Oxford University Press.

Sullivan, T., Warren, E. and Westbrook, J.L. (2000) The Fragile Middle Class: Americans in Debt. New Haven, CT: Yale University Press.

Swaim, C.H. (1994) 'United States Bankruptcy – Reorganisation Laws', in OECD,

Corporate Bankruptcy and Reorganisation Procedures in OECD and Central and Eastern European Countries. Paris: OECD.

Warren, C. (1934) *Bankruptcy in United States History*. Buffalo, NY: William S. Hein & Co.

Warren, E. (1993) *Business Bankruptcy*, Washington, DC: Federal Judicial Center.

Warren, E. (1996) 'Bankruptcy policy', in Jagdeep S. Bhandari and Lawrence A. Weiss (eds) *Corporate Bankruptcy. Economic and Legal Perspectives*. Cambridge: Cambridge University Press.

White, M.J. (1996) 'The corporate bankruptcy decision', in Jagdeep S. Bhandari and Lawrence A. Weiss (eds) *Corporate Bankruptcy. Economic and Legal Perspectives*. Cambridge: Cambridge University Press, pp. 207–231.

White, M.J. (1996) 'The costs of corporate bankruptcy: A US–European comparison', in Jagdeep S. Bhandari and Lawrence A. Weiss (eds) *Corporate Bankruptcy. Economic and Legal Perspectives*. Cambridge: Cambridge University Press, pp. 467–500.

White, M.J. (2001) 'Bankruptcy Procedures in Countries undergoing Financial Crisis', in Richard Posner, Stijn Claessens, Simeon Djankov and Ashoka Mody (eds) *Resolution of Financial Distress. An International Perspective on the Design of Bankruptcy Laws*, WBI Development Studies, Washington, DC, pp. 25–26.

White, M.J. (2005) 'Economic Analysis of Corporate and Personal Bankruptcy Law', Working Paper 11536, National Bureau of Economic Research, August.

Williamson, O. (1970) *Corporate Control and Business Behavior*. Englewood Cliffs: Prentice Hall.

Yemin, E. and Bronstein, A.S. (1991) 'The Protection of Workers' Claims in the Event of the Employer's Insolvency', *Labour Management Relations Series No. 76*, Geneva: International Labour Office.

16 Phases of competition policy in Europe

Andreas Resch

1 Introduction

Representatives of the European Union have raised the prospect of a convergence of American antitrust law and European competition law. One must keep in mind, though, that capital markets, corporate governance and competition policy have developed in a different manner in the two economic areas. In the US, modern antitrust legislation began in 1890 with the Sherman Act. From the 1980s on, in accordance with the Chicago school, efficiency considerations gained weight.[1] In Europe, in contrast, competition policy developed in a different manner.

The aim of this chapter is to demonstrate how specific aspects of European history give capital markets, corporate governance and competition policies their special flavour. The focus is on four phases of European competition policy: developments prior to the First World War, the inter-war period, the era of competition policy under American influence after the Second World War, and recent developments.

2 The emergence of modern industry, cartelisation, and the state of the competition legislation in Europe before 1914

In Europe, hand in hand with industrial growth and the integration of local markets, collusive behaviour among firms emerged in the second half of the nineteenth century. From the 1880s on, a revival of protective duties and barriers to trade was conducive to monopolistic tendencies at the national level.

While in the United States the Sherman Act provided for a special antitrust law, no specific legislation was passed in Europe before the First World War. As a rule, constraints of trade in Great Britain were inhibited by Common Law which caused uncertainty for cartels. In France, Article 419 of the Code pénal threatened profiteering but was hardly ever applied (Isay, 1955: 25). In practice it was allowed to organise cartels, although their provisions could not be enforced in courts. In Austria-Hungary a similar legal situation prevailed. In Germany it was generally assumed that cartels were an instrument for controlling the instability created by cut-throat competition and price warfare. In addition, freedom of contracting constituted one of the governing principles of competition laws. This implied that price agreements were not only permitted but also enforceable in courts. Anti-cartel action was taken only in extreme cases, for instance when a cartel could lead to monopoly or to extreme exploitation of consumers (Scherer, 1994: 24; Fezer, 1985: 51–68).

British policies of free trade were an obstacle to the development of stable industrial cartels. In France one of the earliest collusive agreements was the Marseille cartel in soda, concluded in 1838. Beginning in the 1840s, cartels in the iron and coal industry appeared. Later on also the chemical industry, glass and porcelain, sugar, salt, soap, petroleum, paper, textiles and other sectors were cartelised (Liefmann, 1930: 48).

Around 1900 Germany was the centre of the cartel movement. By 1905 there were 385 cartels involving 12,000 firms. Until 1910 the number of cartels increased to 700 (Schröter, 1996: 132).

In the Austro-Hungarian Empire the cartel movement spread in a similar way. Experts estimated the number of Austrian cartels before the First World War to have reached approximately 200. The most powerful organisation regulated the iron and steel industry (Resch, 2002: 107–132).

International cartelisation developed in line with agreements at the national level. In 1879 the federation of Luxembourg-Lorraine crude iron works came into existence. The year 1884 saw the creation of the first International Rail Manufacturers' Association (Wurm, 1994: 258). In 1897 there existed 40 international cartels with German participation. Great Britain was involved in 22, Austria in 13, Belgium in ten and France in nine (Liefmann, 1930: 182).

In contemporary opinion, this development was indicative of the emergence of 'monopolistic capitalism' or 'organised capitalism'.[2] Interlocking directorates and supervisory boards, collusive agreements among firms, interlocking structures of politics and business were seen as crucial aspects of organised capitalism. The strong position of banks was a feature of this institutional environment. Banks acted as shareholders, financial intermediaries, and voters by proxy. Yet, their controlling power seems to have been widely overestimated by contemporaries (Wellhöner, 1989; Ziegler, 1997: 131ff.; Wixforth, 1995: 29ff.). Recent research has shown that banks participated in business networks but usually failed to dominate them. Also, in spite of the great number of cartels, their capacity to effectively restrain market competition was limited. National cartels in general faced foreign competition because of limited restrictions on foreign trade. Furthermore, in most cases they were not able to build reliable barriers against actual and potential competition in their own countries.[3] But in spite of the limited power of cartels, a specific continental or German blend of corporate governance emerged, thanks to the joint effect of their collusive practices, the strong position of banks as shareholders and financiers, and the prevailing structures of interlocking directorates.

In a system with open capital markets and labour markets for managers, as it has emerged in the US, the market forces are important factors in corporate governance. In the German or continental European system however, closed market structures prevailed. Consequently, market forces were unable to provide for effective corporate governance. This role was taken over by block shareholders, either the founding families of stock corporations or the banks. This system survived the economic and political upheavals of the twentieth century. In a historical and comparative perspective it appears that the formation of bank–industry networks was particularly marked in countries with strong cartelisation, like Germany, France, or the late Habsburg Empire.[4]

3 Cartels during the inter-war era

The inter-war period was the most cartel-intensive era in modern history. In the first phase after 1918 Europe had to cope with the consequences of the war. It achieved a fragile economic reconstruction until 1929. The new European order provided the institutional framework for the political and economic relations on the continent. During the 1920s many attempts were aimed at mending the broken world. At the Conference of Genoa a new international currency system was established, and from the mid-1920s a network of trade agreements provided for liberalised international economic relations. The Great Depression ended this first phase. The international currency system broke down and the national economies erected new trade barriers. During the slump most international cartels dissolved. They re-emerged in the 1930s, within the framework of a disintegrated world economy.

In Europe, competition legislation made little progress in the 1920s. Most countries failed to create specific laws dealing with cartels and restraint of trade. In certain cases, notably Great Britain, France, or Austria, cartels were threatened by new laws against forcing up prices. In Germany influential leaders such as Walther Rathenau prepared plans for 'Gemeinwirtschaft' (social economy) after the experience of the war (Nörr, 1994: 33). Among the relevant results of this era were the Kali syndicate[5] and the coal syndicate. In 1923 Germany suffered from political turmoil (Hitler's coup in Bavaria, crisis in Saxony and the occupied Ruhr area) and hyperinflation. The legislature conceded an Enabling Act conferring on the government far reaching power. Based on this power a cartel act was passed, which can be seen as the beginning of modern cartel legislation in Europe. The new law declared cartels as legal and at the same time aimed at controlling the abuse of market power (Neumann, 1998: 44; Liefmann, 1930: 207; Isay, 1955: 40).

On the international level, in the difficult economic circumstances after the First World War, plans were laid to overcome economic disintegration by means of private agreements. French politicians like Etienne Clémentel, Louis Loucheur and the young Jean Monnet, cognizant of their country's strong political position following the First World War, favoured Franco-German economic integration.[6] Monnet joined the secretariat of the League of Nations. In his new function he promoted international economic entente (Gillingham, 1991: 5).

In 1925, the Assembly of the League of Nations, following a proposal by the French, initiated a World Economic Conference to be held in Geneva in 1927.[7]

One of the main points of the Conference was to be economic reintegration by means of international cartels and agreements. However, leading experts submitted studies on cartels to the Preparatory Committee for the Conference. The discussions in the Committee and the studies soon disclosed the antagonistic positions of the participants.

At the beginning of the preparatory talks, Louis Loucheur expressed in cautious words what he hoped to achieve: 'I would not like that somebody imagines that the conference had to reach real international conventions.... The conference has to achieve statements to a certain number of principles.'[8]

The French Professor of Economics, William Oualid, suggested in his study submitted to the Preparatory Committee an international approach. He recommended conveying a Draft Convention to the member states of the League of Nations that aimed at safeguarding a 'normal equilibrium between production and consumption, stable prices and supplies, and regular employment' by international industrial agreements (Oualid, 1926: 32). To ensure control over the organisations, he intended '... to entrust to a special administration, technical or juridical institutions, the duty of supervising or tracking down injurious combinations and compelling them to supply all necessary information on their working, and to empower these institutions to order or instigate their regularisation, prosecution, repression, or prohibition. The widest publicity is given to their decisions with a view to the deterrent, disciplinary, and moral effect on the economic education of the public' (Oualid, 1926: 34). This institutional framework should be created by 'a programme of making national laws on industrial and commercial agreements uniform by means of a Convention ...; of publicity for agreements by way of declaration to the League of Nations and presumption that those not declared are unlawful; of attaching these institutions to an international institution; of establishing national and international procedures and sanctions' (Oualid, 1926: 35).

German experts shared a positive attitude towards cartelisation, but they did not recommend steps to establish control on an international level. The former German Minister of the Reich, Professor Julius Hirsch, stated somewhat vaguely in his paper submitted to the Preparatory Committee: 'In so far as agreements in the nature of cartels are effected between the nations, their greatest use lies in the fact that they bring together economic groups that are still divided into hostile camps under the influence of the world war.... In so far as international monopolies and kindred agreements represent a rationalisation in world trade and industry as well, the favourable effects of this function should be intensified as much as possible.... The League of Nations might establish a general observation post from which the formation of monopolies ... can be observed' (Hirsch, 1926: 22–24).

The British member of the Preparatory Committee, Sir Arthur Balfour, noticed that in his country the setting-up of each kind of cartel would face great difficulties. British experts held the opinion that only a return to the liberal international economic system of the pre-war era could provide for normalisation and stabilisation of the economy. The Swedish economist Gustav Cassel warned that weak development of the international economy would not be overcome by monopolies: 'However the responsibility for this unfortunate development may be divided, a situation in which Europe, by aid of unemployment doles, is storing up industrial labour which is not allowed to perform useful work in the service of the world's economy, while at the same time agriculture and colonial production suffer from an insufficient and too highly priced supply of industrial products, must be looked upon as the most emphatic expression of the fundamental fallacy of monopolism' (Cassel, 1927: 45).

At the end of their discussions the experts could only agree on the vague statement: 'The Conference has examined with the keenest interest the question of industrial agreements, which have recently considerably developed and have attracted close attention from those sections of the community whose interests are affected by them and from the public opinion of the various countries. The discussion has revealed a certain conflict of views and has occasioned reservations on the part of the representatives of different interests and countries. In these circumstances, the Conference has recognised that the phenomenon of such agreements, arising from economic necessities, does not constitute a matter upon which any conclusion of principle need be reached.'[9]

While the Economic Conference and other similar attempts at international diplomacy did not achieve concrete results, the practical development of cartels advanced in the 1920s. From the middle of the 1920s on, the international institutional environment provided a framework conducive to strategic behaviour and business diplomacy of various interest groups.

The International Steel Cartel can be seen as the most important historic example of an international industrial agreement in this period. The pre-war structures of the European steel industry were massively affected by the treaty of Versailles. The return of Alsace-Lorraine to France doubled the country's theoretical capacity of steel production and increased its dependence on Ruhr coke and coal.[10] The French were interested in access to the German market and achieving general regulation of the steel output. On the other hand, German industry needed access to the French market for machinery and settlement of the question of the Saar ores. During the first years after the war Ruhr industrialists were reluctant to conclude an agreement. The inflation which lasted until 1923 facilitated their export sales.[11] They had embarked on a construction programme to be completed in 1924. In 1923 France occupied the Ruhr. German room for manoeuvre in international negotiations was limited by the clauses of the Versailles peace treaty (tariffs, coal deliveries, etc.), and domestic cartels had dissolved after the war. Following the death of Hugo Stinnes in 1923 the steel properties of his conglomerate were taken over by the newly founded Vereinigte Stahlwerke.[12] The formation of this new German steel giant lasted until 1926 (Reckendrees, 2000). The period ended in 1924 with the formation of the new crude steel syndicate (Rohstahlgemeinschaft). The organisation served as a parent cartel for a host of product syndicates and embraced 90 per cent of the industry's production (Feldman, 1977: 162). It could confront French companies as a monopoly agency of great power (Maier, 1975: 526). After Germany had regained her tariff sovereignty in 1925, trade negotiations with France commenced on the official diplomatic level. At the same time industrialists embarked on private negotiations to settle the questions concerning the steel industry. Both levels were firmly interwoven in a complex set of strategic behaviour. French domestic industrial organisations were relatively underdeveloped. The Comptoir Sidérurgique had been suspended in 1921, while the Comité des Forges served as an informal directorate for the industry in general (Gillingham, 1991: 25).

German and French needs were complementary enough to allow for an understanding to be reached in 1926. Germany was to absorb French steel, France was to absorb German finished goods and the Saar question was to be settled (Maier, 1975: 531). The steel industries of France and Germany, together with the works of Belgium and Luxembourg, formed an international steel cartel. The agreement covered the entire steel production of all members, for domestic consumption as well as export. Production was controlled by a quota system. Quotas, together with a system of penalty payments for excess production, should result in higher prices (Wurm, 1994: 257). The steel producers of Czechoslovakia, Austria, and Hungary joined the syndicate in 1927 (Teichova, 1974: 141; Hexner, 1946b: 73; Resch, 2003: 58).

In a like manner, various cartels for finished or semi-finished goods made of iron or steel were agreed upon. In 1926 the old rail cartel was revived. The earlier abbreviation of 'IRMA' (International Rail Manufacturers' Association) was changed to 'ERMA' (European Rail Manufacturers' Association) because as a consequence of the US-antitrust legislation the US steel industry hesitated to participate officially in the agreement. But American participation was secured by an unofficial reduction of the British quota. Other international cartels of the iron industry were aimed at regulating the business for crude iron, rolled wire, ferromanganese, and rolled materials.

Further cartels of international importance emerged to organise the markets for magnesite, carbide, glue, explosives, Chile saltpetre, aluminium, copper, bottles, plate-glass, electric bulbs, paper and some textiles.[13] Many continental European countries participated in these international cartels. The British industrialists did not yet enter into an agreement with the international raw steel cartel but took part in several other international combinations.

Ultimately, the international steel cartel disappointed the hopes of the politicians and businessmen who had contributed to its emergence. The quota system was too rigid for the development of the respective industries. The Germans renegotiated some clauses of the quota and payment agreement soon after they signed the steel agreement. The organisation disintegrated in 1930–31.

All in all, the system of trade agreements of the late 1920s stimulated the emergence of national and international cartels. Some of these international organisations, like the steel cartel, developed in line with international trade negotiations.

But the market power and stability of these collusive organisations was limited by many factors. In many countries cartel treaties could not be enforced in courts. In Germany first attempts to control abuses of market power were made, and in some countries cartel members were threatened by laws against profiteering. Under the circumstances of a fairly free international market economy most economic players could with credibility leave their respective cartel and to become outsiders in the domestic and foreign markets. Cartels could not shield themselves from actual or potential competition. So the agreements tended to be unstable. Only industries showing particular structural features could effectively be cartelised. Some had concluded technology sharing agreements, like the industries for electric bulbs and chemistry. Elsewhere, there existed entry barriers because of substantial set up costs and sunk costs, as in the heavy industries. The absence of specific competition legislation did not only mean a lack of abuse control. It also meant that national governments did not lend power to the market organisations. Early attempts by France to achieve international agreements for the regulation of markets remained without practical result.

Under such circumstances most national and international cartels dissolved during the great slump. The obvious failure to stabilise the European economic order by means of international cartels did not prevent industrialists and politicians from further attempts made under the new conditions of the 1930s.

During the Great Depression the international currency system collapsed, and extensive new barriers to trade were imposed. International financial and goods markets broke down, and the international economy dramatically disintegrated. These developments were causes as well as consequences of increasing interventionism and economic nationalism. As a result, in the 1930s various forms of corporatism and state interventionism gained influence in Europe.

French politicians and economists continued to propagate industrial agreements as a 'remède infaillible'[14] to revive international trade and production (Nocken, 1989: 80). On the one hand, many national governments began to support cartels to strengthen them as members of international agreements (Wurm, 1989: 18–29). In their view, cartels were to be a weapon of competitive nationalism. On the other hand, strength in international organisations could protect industrialists against domestic political influence. Even in Great Britain a general reconsideration of free trade and cartelisation occurred. In 1932 the Import Duties Act and the Ottawa Conference ended the era of free trade. The government developed attempts to reorganise coal mining and cotton industry, and central organisations of the industry gained more influence. In France as well, the administration worked out special projects for certain industries.

Another consequence of this prevailing trend was that European countries for the first time implemented special cartel legislation.[15] States aimed at controlling the cartels, but in the first instance they wanted to strengthen domestic industrial groups to compete for the narrow remaining international markets. Thus, they sought to use domestic cartels as institutions of economic nationalism in the framework of international agreements. For example, the Nazi regime in Germany, after initially being hostile, encouraged the formation of cartels (Gillingham, 1985: 23).

In many countries, cartel acts were passed which required compulsory registration of all valid agreements. Stronger government control over cartels was the aim. At the same time registration and affirmation improved the legal certainty of the registered organisations which stabilised the agreements. In Hungary, for example, after 1931 cartels had to submit their formative treaties to the ministry of economics. In 1933 registration became compulsory in Czechoslovakia, Poland, and Romania.

In many countries, common attempts of governments and private organisations to regulate certain industries resulted in laws providing for enforced cartelisation. In fascist Italy cartels became a part of the corporatist economic structures. In 1932 a law for compulsory cartelisation was passed. Germany followed suit in 1933, allowing for the formation of state enforced cartels (Feldenkirchen, 1985: 129–144; Nocken, 1985: 167–175; Wessel, 1985: 188–201). Given that those laws were hardly ever applied, the possible threat to use them sufficed to create additional pressure on the outsiders of the existing collusive organisations. In Italy, only the steel and silk industries were directly affected by enforced organisation (Schröter, 1996: 136).

Other countries embarked on the enforced organisation of single industries. For example in the United Kingdom in 1930 the Coal Mines Act was passed. The French government attempted the organisation of the coal mining and silk industry.

In many cases the state administration protected existing cartels from new entrants. In Italy a special law impeded the market entry of new firms. Governments used existing laws, e.g. building regulations, to frustrate entry. In some cases special laws were passed to obstruct new competitors. For example, in Austria in 1933–34 the Hungarian firm Manfred Weiss AG built a new factory for tubes in Vienna. A few weeks before it was opened some industrialists succeeded in lobbying for a law forbidding the erection of new tubes factories. Only after lengthy negotiations with the Austrian tubes cartel and the state authorities, Weiss obtained a license to open the works in 1936 (Resch, 2003: 77–78).

On an international level, quota agreements among national cartels were frequently reinforced by preferential duties for quantities within the negotiated quotas or by barter agreements. After winding up in 1930–31, the international steel cartel was re-established in a modified form in 1933, under the name International Steel Export Cartel (ISEC) (Barbezat, 1993: 157–175; Wurm, 1994: 257). The old members, Belgium, France, Germany and Luxembourg, now established an agreement that was to relate exclusively to steel exports. The quota system was extended to particular steel commodities, and the prices were to be regulated directly through export syndicates. Furthermore the cartel was to promote cartels of merchants in importing countries. The 1933 arrangement consisted of a general agreement and a set of sectional comptoir agreements for specific goods as heavy rails, merchant bars, etc. (Hexner, 1946b: 82–84).

Following intense negotiations, the British steel industry entered the agreement in 1935. Bargaining positions had changed as a consequence of the devaluation of the pound sterling in 1931/2 and the implementation of protective tariffs. In the United Kingdom the Import Duties Advisory Committee, a governmental agency, and the British Iron and Steel Federation cooperated to exert economic pressure on the continental producers. Simultaneously, they organised the domestic production. Cartel members on the continent were confronted with a tariff wall threatening them with loss of their British markets. They had no choice but to agree that imports to the United Kingdom would be restricted to 670,000 tons for the first year and later to 525,000 tons. After Parliament had ratified the agreement, the British Iron and Steel Federation inaugurated a licensing system under which imports within agreed quotas were admitted upon payment of preferential duties (Stocking and Watkins, 1947: 194ff.).

The ISEC was extended into a world cartel when the US steel industry entered in 1938. The Steel Export Association of America agreed to recognise the domestic markets of the European members as their exclusive marketing territory. In return, the cartel recognised certain areas as American spheres of influence.

The ISEC survived political tensions in Europe in the 1930s. When the Nazi party seized power in Germany in 1933, this did not change the behaviour of the German industrialists in the ISEC. In 1935, when the Saar returned to the German customs area, the Ruhr absorbed the output previously sold in France. After the 'Anschluss' of Austria in 1938 German quota shares were increased by the Austrian share as part of the central European group. After the invasion of Czechoslovakia in March 1939 the German group did not require the dissolution of the Czechoslovakian group. The ISEC did not cease to exist until the beginning of the war in September 1939 (Hexner, 1946b: 90–91).

As in the 1920s, the international steel agreement was embedded in a network of further cartels covering rails, tubes, cold rolled brands and strips, wire products, etc. (Lovasy, 1947, table 2). A web of agreements in coal and coke complemented those in steel. In November 1936 an international coke cartel was concluded. During the last years before the Second World War, the steel and coke cartels functioned as one of the main channels of influence for British and French economic appeasement policy. Until the early months of 1939, both the British and French hoped that economic deals with Nazi Germany would prevent war – a strategy that ended in failure (Gillingham, 1989: 96–101).

Not only in the iron and coal industries but also in other sectors of industry, cartels shaken during the years of the economic downswing began to re-emerge. The international tin cartel for example re-emerged in 1931. The aluminium cartel was renewed in 1931. The European nitrogen cartel was re-established in 1932, and Chile and Japan joined during the next years. The dyestuff cartel, founded in 1927, was deepened by means of new treaties with the British industry (Imperial Chemical Industries) and Japanese and Far Eastern producers in 1934. The network of cartel agreements in the chemical industry was extended (Teichova, 1974: 277ff.). After the decay of the old railway rolling stock cartel during the early 1930s, a new international organisation emerged in 1935. It included producers from Germany, the United Kingdom, the US, and other countries. In the same year a new organisation of the industry for enamel goods appeared. The list could easily be extended.[16]

Cartels in general achieved maximum strength during the 1930s. Monopolistic pricing was made possible to a certain extent on the domestic and international level. About 40 to 50 per cent of world trade was affected by international industrial agreements. British, French and American industries participated. It seems that German firms played the greatest part. The strong position of German industry in the international organisations may have provided for a certain dispersion of German practices of 'organised capitalism', which featured producer regulation and a close relationship between state and industry. But this development was in line with the French tradition of state intervention and with the British turnaround in economic policy.

Due to the petrifaction of existing organisations and the obstruction of new entrants, the market process was blocked in the 1930s. Without such a market process, there was no continuous search for best solutions (as stipulated by the Austrian School of Economics) and no continuous process of 'creative destruction' (in the sense of J.A. Schumpeter). Capital markets and job markets for managers were more regulated than ever, and goods markets were effectively controlled. This must have massively increased the deficiencies of the system of corporate governance prevailing in continental Europe.

4 European traditions and 'Americanization' of competition policy after the Second World War

After the Second World War, the United States sought to transplant US antitrust notions to its sphere of influence. The Potsdam Agreement of July 1945 proposed to dismantle powerful vested business interests and cartels in Germany. The Americans regarded German cartels as weapons of economic warfare. Their plans aimed at reconstructing democratic and efficient economic structures in Germany. But during the early stages of the Cold War the main focus shifted from dismantling German industry to rebuilding the German economy as that of a prospective ally.

However, American politics continued to be somewhat contradictory (Asbeek Brusse, 1997: 164–169; Milward, 1984: 362–420). German cartels were declared illegal by the Allied Military Government. In 1947 general laws aiming at decartelisation were passed first for the American zone, and later for the joint British–American 'bizone'. Specific regulations to dismantle I.G. Farben, large coal and steel syndicates, major banks and the film industry followed (Wank, 1985: 205).

The European powers were not enthusiastic about American style antitrust. In Europe, a sceptical attitude towards the uncontrolled powers of a free market system prevailed. Various forms of collective economic regulation appeared quite compatible with the prevailing trends of corporatist state interventionism: French planification, British nationalisation of heavy industry, and the German social market economy. Consequently, the Americans were not successful in embedding their attitudes of antitrust within a multilateral framework. Various options were tried in vain, including the International Trade Organisation, the Council of Europe and the General Agreement on Tariffs and Trade (Asbeek Brusse and Griffiths, 1997: 165).

Only the European Community for Steel and Coal (ECSC) provided for explicit antitrust clauses. The formative treaty prohibited in Article 65 agreements and concerted practices that aimed to 'prevent, restrict, or distort the normal operation of competition' within the Community. Article 66 forbade 'unauthorized concentrations' and permitted the Community's High Authority to combat abuses committed by enterprises possessing a dominant market position. Thus for the first time a transnational competition policy was adopted in conjunction with trade liberalisation within the ECSC (Scherer, 1994: 33).

The strong antitrust clauses of the treaty were the result of specific historical circumstances. In some respect the Plan Schuman, which led to the emergence of the ECSC, can be seen in the tradition of French plans for French–German economic integration developed in the inter-war era. Around 1950, France needed an understanding with Germany to safeguard the domestic plans for modernisation created by Jean Monnet. Western Germany gradually regained its sovereignty from 1949 on, and allied control over the heavy industries was to be loosened. The French iron industry depended on free access to German coal production. Furthermore, as German re-industrialisation went ahead, the German iron and steel industry gained significant cost advantages over that of France, mainly because of cheaper coal (Milward, 1984: 377).

German, French, Dutch and Belgian industrialists would have clearly preferred to return to the old international steel exporters' cartel. But this was impossible because of the strong American anti-cartel commitment. Consequently, French planners were willing to subject their own industry as well as the industry of the other participants to a supra-national regime as provided by the ESCS.

American authorities were suspicious that the old cartel should be restored. So Schuman had to provide for antitrust policies and for the free integration of the national coal and steel markets. After complicated diplomatic negotiations, the formative treaty was signed in April 1951. It created a common market for coal and steel encompassing Belgium, the Federal Republic of Germany, France, Italy, and the Netherlands. The former direct authority of the allied forces to control the Ruhr gave way to the High Authority as defined in the treaty. In the years to come, the High Authority was anxious to keep the goodwill of the industrialists, who had opposed the anti-cartel alignment. Ignoring Monnet's wishes, the High Authority declined to embark on severe anti-cartel measures. In July 1953 cartel registration was required. Of the 80 syndicates registered by 1958, the ECSC had dissolved only three, none of them important. Even the German coal syndicate Deutscher Kohleverkauf, successor of the old Ruhr syndicate, was only reluctantly dismantled in 1953. A new export cartel, the Entente de Bruxelles, was formed in March 1953, shortly before the opening of the common market for steel (Gillingham, 1991: 336). Thus, the Schuman Plan was an important step for the integration of Europe but the ECSC was, in spite of its rigid antitrust clauses, very ineffective in fighting cartels.

In another strategy that did not prove very successful, the Americans tried to influence European national competition legislation via the European Recovery

Programme. Marshall Plan administrators attempted to use their power over counterpart funds as leverage for this objective (DeLong and Eichengreen, 1993: 217). Around 1950, anti-cartel laws began to appear in several countries participating in the Marshall Plan. In many cases these laws were passed to satisfy the Americans but were not really taken very seriously. For example, the Austrian Government in the commentary to the cartel law, passed in 1951, expressed the conviction that cartels were not necessarily harmful but on the contrary could be useful because of their stabilising economic effects (Tüchler, 2003: 131). Cartel legislation was also passed in the Netherlands in 1951 and France in 1953, but failed to have far reaching consequences (Asbeek Brusse and Griffiths, 1998: 15ff.; Mohand, 1998: 205ff.).

In Germany a draft cartel law was passed in 1951 under the control of the Allied Forces. It was replaced in 1957 by German legislation. The new law was influenced by American antitrust and by the German Ordo-liberal school. It established a per se rule against cartels and vertical agreements. Exemptions provided for an approach according to rule of reason.[17] So in fact the German tradition of distinguishing between 'good' and 'bad' cartels could be continued.

In 1957 in Rome the member states of the ECSC reached an agreement to found the European Economic Community (EEC) and Euratom. The Treaty of Rome resulted from two different approaches to extended economic co-operation. French officials wished to integrate further economic sectors, whereas the Dutch preferred overall economic integration (Asbeek Brusse, 1997: 59). The negotiations proceeded under less American influence than the process leading to the ECSC. As a result, the founding treaty of the EEC was less equivocal in its adoption of pro-competitive measures.

Article 85 of the Treaty of Rome prohibited all cartels and restrictive practices distorting competition. It sounded like a per se prohibition, but it contained far reaching exemptions for agreements that contributed 'towards improving the production or distribution of goods or promoting technical or economic progress while reserving to users a fair share in the (resulting) profit', provided that the agreements did not go beyond what was essential to attain those objectives, and provided also that competition was not eliminated on 'a substantial portion of the products in question'. Thus a complex balancing process was instituted, following a 'rule of reason' approach (Scherer, 1994: 35).

Article 86 prohibited the abuse of a dominant position. Furthermore, Article 90 aimed to control state monopolies. Article 92 prohibited state aid that threatened to distort competition (Laudati, 1998: 385–386). Regulation 17/1962 provided for a strong role of the European Commission in enforcing EEC competition law. Commission powers included investigation, fining, consulting with governments, and even conducting 'dawn raids'. Yet until the late 1980s those powerful instruments were hardly used (Gillingham, 2003: 249).

The European Commission usually took a hard line towards anticompetitive violations. In general, decisions were guided by the principle of preventing agreements that hampered the integration of EEC markets. Offences such as price fixing, quotas, and market sharing agreements were prosecuted, if they affected the Common Market. In addition, the commission stood against vertical agreements between producers or importers and distributors. Exemptions or block exemptions were not granted for agreements between groups of producers and distributors. Furthermore, exemptions were denied if parallel imports were impeded (George and Jacquemin, 1990: 214ff.).

The common competition policy at the EEC level successively required some harmonisation of national legislation. Following the entry into force of the Treaty of Rome in 1957, each of the member states enacted some form of competition law or modified already existing laws. The second wave of laws was enacted in the 1970s and early 1980s. The third wave of national legislation compliant with EC law followed in the 1990s (Laudati, 1998: 381–410).

5 Recent developments

During the last decades of the twentieth century the competitive environment has changed. Globalisation, the fall of the Iron Curtain and new technologies as well as the development of the Internal market of the EU, the European Monetary Union and EU enlargement have all imposed new demands on EU competition policy.

The first half of the 1980s was characterised by massive crises of 'old industries', such as steel production, the chemical industry and textiles. Painful restructuring became inevitable. Politics at the national and EC levels responded with massive state subsidies and a temporary encouragement of collusive agreements.

From the second half of the 1980s on, subsidies were reduced and directed towards the promotion of research and development. State subsidies in general declined (Gillingham, 2003: 253–254). The successive privatisation of state-owned industries and the liberalisation of international financial markets gradually changed the structure of European capital markets, and the number and scope of mergers increased (Neal and Barbezat, 1998: 80–84).

The reform process of the EU competition policy had to cope with those new developments. In 1989, after long negotiations, a Merger Regulation (4064/1989) was passed, enabling the Commission to tackle cases surpassing certain thresholds of market share or turnover (George and Jacquemin, 1990: 233–234). The merger rule aimed at a market structure conducive to viable competition. Interestingly, this responds to an approach the Americans had tried to implement in Europe during the 1940s and 1950s, but with little success. Evidently, their seed germinated with a time lag of 40 years. In the meantime, from the late 1970s on, US antitrust politics developed towards a more differentiated approach. In accordance with the findings of the Chicago school, concerns for the market structure were complemented by efficiency-oriented aspects.

In Europe as well, questions of efficiency gained more weight in decision-making process. But it seems that Europe's common competition policy was more eager to inhibit collusive behaviour, vertical restraints and mergers than the American authorities (George and Jacquemin, 1990: 223–234).

According to the changed economic environment the number of cases the Commission had to deal with increased greatly (Pons and Sautter, 2004: 29–62). In 2000 the Commission took 345 final decisions for Article 81 and 82 cases.[18] The number of mergers and so-called phase 2 investigations reached a record high in 1999 and 2000. More than 2,000 mergers have been reviewed since 1990. 95 per cent of the mergers notified were directly authorised by the Commission, 5 per cent required further investigation, and only 1 per cent were blocked.

As a side-effect of globalisation, the international aspects of competition policy gained in importance. Though many cases of international relevance were handled uniformly by the antitrust authorities in Europe and the US, the much discussed decisions on Boeing/McDonnell and GE-Honeywell highlighted the relevance of this development. Commissioner Mario Monti raised the prospect of a convergence of American antitrust law and European competition law (Gifford and Kudrle, 2003: 727–780).

In October 2001 an International Competition Network (ICN) was launched by 16 national competition authorities as a forum to address practical competition enforcement and international policy issues (Weinrauch, 2004: 160). Negotiations of a WTO competition law agreement have not produced sizable results so far.

US antitrust agencies favour an approach that emphasises the extraterritorial application of the Sherman Act combined with bilateral cooperation in investigation and enforcement. This goes well with the development of antitrust law under a common law case-by-case model. In 1982, the US Congress adopted the Foreign Trade Antitrust Improvements Act (FTAIA) to simplify the extraterritorial reach of US antitrust laws. Recently, a case regarding to the international vitamin cartel provided for some clarification of the extraterritorial reach of the Sherman Act. The foreign vitamin distributor Empagran who had purchased cartelised goods in Australia, Ecuador, Panama, and Ukraine presented the jurisdictional question of whether foreign plaintiffs, who had suffered overcharges in transactions occurring outside the US could maintain claims in US courts under US antitrust law. In *amicus curiae* briefs filed in the Supreme Court, several European governments argued that permitting such claims would interfere with global antitrust enforcement and fail to respect the sovereign authority of other nations.[19] The case presented the Supreme Court with a question at the intersection of antitrust policy and international jurisdictional law. The court adopted a narrow interpretation of the FTAIA, holding that the plaintiffs own claim must arise from the effects of conduct on US commerce. The court unanimously ruled that the FTAIA should not be read as a general prohibition against price fixing in all parts of the world but as an exception for foreign commerce that affected domestic commerce.[20] The opinion signals a serious interest on the part of the Supreme Court in using principles of comity instead of extraterritorial jurisdiction.[21]

In Europe, antitrust legislation has been an important vehicle of the market integration. According to this tradition, the EC in general has been more willing to promote international antitrust policy. The Commission has been active in discussions within the WTO, the OECD, the ICN and the United Nations Conference on Trade and Development (UNCTAD) (Dabbah, 2003: 130–132; Weinrauch, 2004: 157–160).

The most important reform of competition law within the EC started with the White Paper issued by the Commission in April 1995. The Commission's proposal to amend regulation 17, dating from the year 1962 was adopted by the Council on 16 December 2002 (Pons and Sautter, 2004: 50–62).

The changes were of a kind to allow the Commission to concentrate on big international cases. Antitrust federalism helped to reach this goal. Smaller cases are dealt with on a national level. The proponents of the reform are convinced that it will help EU antitrust regulators to gain 'Muscle for Big Cases'.[22] Critics are afraid that the consistency of application of the law in different countries may be a critical issue and that in some cases a nationalistic approach may re-emerge.[23]

The aim expressed by Mario Monti, at convergence towards American antitrust law, will not easily be achieved (Gifford and Kudrle, 2003). Simple imitation of American regulations might even have unexpected and detrimental effects because of the different history of the business environment. As a result of the historical development of the European economy, the structures of business still differ in comparison to North America. In Germany more than 90 per cent of all listed stock corporations are part of a Konzern (Prigge, 1998: 970). Crossholdings provide for tendencies of collusive practices and restrict the development of open capital and job markets. They limit the threat of takeover, which is an important element of corporate governance in open market structures (Wenger and Kaserer, 1998: 504).

Consequently, in the European system of corporate governance, the control exercised by blockholders and competitive product markets remains one of the most important powers for coping with agency problems. Blockholders can be private persons and families or banks. Bank influence derives from chairmanship of supervisory boards, proxy votes and blockholdings (Franks and Mayer, 1998: 657). Bank managers, like industry managers, are part of interwoven Konzern structures and crossholdings. They are not as free as private shareholders to execute their control functions. Studies are inconclusive as to whether interlockings via bank shareholdings act as an efficient mechanism for solving corporate governance problems.[24] According to recent studies the system of mutual stockholdings provokes the danger of collusion among managers tied together. This may also be why stock option programmes do not work as well in continental Europe as in the USA (Wenger and Kaserer, 1998: 531).

The openness of competitive goods markets has been ensured by the strict competition policy of the European Commission. As mentioned above, the aim was to advance the integration of the European markets. More or less as a side-effect, strengthened product market competition became a vital part of European corporate culture. It is one of the forces that make poor management performance apparent to outsiders (McDonnell and Farber, 2003: 818). Because of this, effects on corporate governance as well as effects concerning efficiency have to be considered in connection with European competition policy.

At present, European capital markets are experiencing a phase of gradual change. Banks are scaling down their holdings, and lending to corporate customers has become less important (Mülbert, 1998: 485). Capital markets as opposed to bank intermediation has gained importance. Crossholdings have been considerably reduced (Wenger and Kaserer, 1998: 510). All this bodes yet further changes in the structure of corporate governance in Europe.

6 Conclusion

Our overview has revealed that until the 1960s a positive attitude towards cartels prevailed in Europe. Structures of bank influence, closed job markets for managers, and corporate control by banks and blockholders had developed. From the 1960s on, anti-monopolistic policy gained weight as a means of market integration at the EC level, while American antitrust policy was somewhat relaxed from the 1980s on. In Europe, market competition became an important disciplining force for managers, given the growing structures of capital markets and corporate governance.

Capital markets and corporate governance in Europe have developed towards American patterns during recent years. One could argue that under such conditions European competition policy should adopt American style antitrust. That would give less weight to the promotion of competition per se as a goal of competition policy and as a mean for economic integration, and adopt a more pronounced efficiency orientation. But, since the historical peculiarities of European business structures seem to persevere in a number of ways, Europeans should be cautious about a rash convergence.

Notes

1 For a concise overview see Posner, 2001: 33–48; Rubinfeld, 2001; Motta, 2004: 1–9.
2 As a famous contemporary study see Hilferding, 1910.
3 As a case study for Austria before 1914 see Resch, 2002.
4 Hopt, 1998: 235.
5 The first potassium convention in Germany was formed in 1876 under massive state intervention. Schröter, 1993: 76.
6 Bussière, 1994: 274; Bussière, 1992: 257–263.
7 League of Nations (LON), C. 356. M. 129, Report and Proceedings of the World Economic Conference held at Geneva, May 4 to 23, 1927.
8 Quoted after Hara, 1994: 269.
9 LON C. 356. M. 129. 1927.II. League of Nations. Report and Proceedings of the World Economic Conference, Vol. I, pp. 49–50.
10 Teichova, 1988: 18–20.
11 Holtfrerich, 1980; Feldman, 1997: 631–697.
12 Feldman, 1998: 841ff.
13 As a concise contemporary overview see LON Archives Geneva, Economic Committee, Doc. E 465 (a–e) (1929).
14 Ballande, 1936: 323.

15 For a comparative overview see Friedländer, 1938; Lovasy, 1947: 10–11.
16 See for example Lovasy, 1947, table 1–3; Hexner, 1946a; Stocking and Watkins, 1947.
17 Neumann, 1998: 41–53; Kamacke, 1998: 143–159; Katzenbach, 1990: 189–205.
18 The articles were renumbered in 1992/93 as a consequence of the Maastricht treaty. Former Article 85 became 81, 86 since then is 82.
19 See, for example, Briefs of the Governments of the Federal Republic of Germany and Belgium and of the United Kingdom of Great Britain and Northern Ireland and the Kingdom of the Netherlands, 2003 US Briefs 724.
20 *F. Hoffmann-LaRoche Ltd.* v. *Empagran S.A.*, 124 S.Ct. 2359, 159 L.Ed.2d 226 (2004); www.oyez.org/oyez/resource/case/1746/ (01.17.2005). Joseph E. Stiglitz and Peter R. Orszag argue in their brief in support of the respondents that failing to provide an effective deterrent against global cartels undermines protection against antitrust abuses within the US itself. Because of that reason they plead for allowing foreigners harmed by global cartels to file suits in the United States. US Briefs 724, No. 3, March 15, 2004.
21 For a more differentiated comment see Buxbaum, 2004.
22 The Wall Street Journal Europe, 29 April 2004.
23 Fortune, 3 May 2004.
24 Gorton and Schmid, 1996; Mülbert, 1998: 485; Wenger and Kaserer, 1998: 499 ff.

References

Asbeek Brusse, Wendy (1997) 'Regional Plans for European Trade, 1945–1957', in *The Economic Development of the EEC*, edited by Richard T. Griffith, Cheltenham, Lyme: Elgar, pp. 45–63.

Asbeek Brusse, Wendy and Richard T. Griffiths (1997) 'The Management of Markets: Business, Governments and Cartels in Post-War Europe', in *Business and European Integration since 1800*, edited by Ulf Olsson, Göteborg: (Meddelanden från Ekonomisk-Historiska Institutionen vid Göteborgs Universitet; 71) pp. 162–188.

Asbeek Brusse, Wendy and Richard Griffiths (1998) 'Paradise Lost or Paradise Regained? Cartel Policy and Cartel Legislation in the Netherlands', in *Competition Policies in Europe*, edited by Stephen Martin, Amsterdam: Elsevier, 15–39.

Ballande, Laurence (1936) *Essai d'étude monographique et statistique sur les ententes économiques internationales*, Paris.

Barbezat, Daniel (1993) 'A Price for Every Product, Every Place: The International Steel export Cartel, 1933–1939', in *Coalitions and Collaboration in International Business*, edited by Geoffrey Jones, Aldershot: Elgar, pp. 157–175.

Brief of the Governments of the Federal Republic of Germany and Belgium (2003) *F. Hoffman-LaRoche Inc.* v. *Empagran S.A.*, US Briefs 724.

Brief of the United Kingdom of Great Britain and Northern Ireland and the Kingdom of the Netherlands (2003) *F. Hoffman-LaRoche Inc.* v. *Empagran S.A.*, US Briefs 724.

Bussière, Èric (1992) *La France, la Belgique et l'organisation économique de l'Europe*, Paris: Min. de l'Économie des Finances et du Budget, Comité pour l'Histoire Économique et Financière de la France (Histoire économique et financière de la France: Études générales).

Bussière, Èric (1994) 'La SDN, les cartels et l'organisation économique de l'Europe durant l'entre-deux-guerre', in *International Cartels Revisited (1880–1980)*, edited by Dominique Barjot, Caen: Éditions-Diffuson du Lys, pp. 273–283.

Buxbaum, Hannah L. (2004) 'National Courts, Global Cartels: *F. Hoffman-LaRoche Ltd.* v. *Empagran, S.A.* (US Supreme Court 2004)', in *German Law Journal* No. 9 (1 September 2004).

Cassel, Gustav (1927) *Recent Monopolistic Tendencies in Industry and Trade*, Geneva: League of Nations C.E.C.P. 98.

Dabbah, Maher M. (2003) *The Internationalisation of Antitrust Policy*, Cambridge: Cambridge University Press.

De Long, J. Bradford and Barry Eichengreen (1993) 'The Marshall Plan: History's Most Successful Structural Adjustment Program', in *Postwar Economic Reconstruction and Lessons for the East Today*, edited by Rudiger Dornbush, Wilhelm Nölling and Richard Layard, Cambridge, Mass.: MIT Press, pp. 189–230.

Feldenkirchen, Wilfried (1985) 'Das Zwangskartellgesetz von 1933. Seine wirtschaftliche Bedeutung und seine praktischen Folgen', in *Kartelle und Kartellgesetzgebung in Praxis und Rechtsprechung vom 19. Jahrhundert bis zur Gegenwart*, edited by Hans Pohl, Stuttgart: Steiner, pp. 145–165.

Feldman, Gerald (1977) *Iron and Steel*, Princeton, NJ: Princeton University Press.

Feldman, Gerald (1997) *The Great Disorder*, New York, Oxford: Oxford University Press.

Feldman, Gerald (1998) *Hugo Stinnes*, Munich: Beck.

Fezer, Karl-Heinz (1985) 'Die Haltung der Rechtswissenschaften zu den Kartellen bis 1914', in *Kartelle und Kartellgesetzgebung in Praxis und Rechtsprechung vom 19. Jahrhundert bis zur Gegenwart*, edited by Hans Pohl, Stuttgart: Steiner, pp. 51–68.

Franks, Julian and Colin Mayer (1998) 'Bank Control, Takeovers, and Corporate Governance in Germany', in *Comparative Corporate Governance*, edited by Klaus J. Hopt a.o., Oxford a.o.: Oxford University Press, pp. 638–662.

Friedländer, Heinrich (1938) *Die Rechtspraxis der Kartelle und Konzerne in Europa*, Zürich: Polygraphischer Verlag.

George, Ken and Alexis Jacquemin (1990) 'Competition Policy in the European Community', in *Competition Policy in Europe and North America: Economic Issues and Institutions*, edited by W.S. Comanor a.o., Chur a.o.: Harwood, pp. 206–245.

Gifford, Daniel J. and Robert T. Kudrle (2003) 'European Union competition law and policy: how much latitude for convergence with the United States?', in *The Antitrust Bulletin*, 48, 3, Fall 2003, pp. 727–780.

Gillingham, John R. (1985) *Industry and Politics in the Third Reich: Ruhr Coal, Hitler and Europe*, Stuttgart: Steiner.

Gillingham, John (1989) 'Coal and Steel Diplomacy in Interwar Europe', in *Internationale Kartelle und Aussenpolitik. International Cartels and Foreign Policy*, edited by Clemens A. Wurm, Stuttgart: Steiner, pp. 96–101.

Gillingham John (1991) *Coal, Steel and the Rebirth of Europe, 1945–1955*, Cambridge a.o.: Cambridge University Press.

Gillingham, John (2003) *European Integration, 1950–2003*, Cambridge: Cambridge University Press.

Gorton, Gary and Frank A. Schmid (1996) *Universal Banking and the Performance of German Firms*, NBER WP 5453, February.

Guyon, Janet (2004) 'Europe Braces for the Mini-Marios', *Fortune*, 194, 9, 3 May 2004, p. 46.

Hara Terushi (1994) 'La Conference Économique Internationale de 1927 et ses effets sur la formation des cartels internationaux', in: *International Cartels Revisited (1880–1980)*, edited by Dominique Barjot, Caen: Éditions-Diffuson du Lys, pp. 265–272.

Hexner, Ervin (1946a) *International Cartels*, Chapel Hill, NC: University of North Carolina Press.

Hexner, Ervin (1946b) *The International Steel Cartel*, Chapel Hill, NC: University of North Carolina Press.

Hilferding, Rudolf (1910) *Das Finanzkapital*, Vienna: Wiener Volksbuchhandlung.

Hirsch, Julius (1926) *National and International Monopolies from the Point of View of Labour, the Consuming Public, and Rationalisation*, League of Nations – International Labour Office, C.E.C.P. 99, Geneva 1926.

Holtfrerich, Carl-Ludwig (1980) *Die deutsche Inflation 1914–1923*, Berlin, New York: de Gruyter.

Hopt, Klaus J. (1998) 'The German Two-Tier Board: Experience, Theories, Reforms', in *Comparative Corporate Governance*, ed. by Klaus Hopt, Oxford, New York: Oxford University Press, pp. 228–283.

Isay, Rudolf (1955) *Die Geschichte der Kartellgesetzgebungen*, Berlin: de Gruyter.

Kamacke, Ulrich (1998) 'Vertical Restraints in German Antitrust Law', in *Competition Policy in Europe*, edited by Stephen Martin, Amsterdam: Elsevier, pp. 143–159.

Kantzenbach, Erhard (1990) 'Competition Policy in West Germany: A Comparison with the Antitrust Policy of the United States', in *Competition Policy in Europe and North America: Economic Issues and Institutions*, edited by W.S. Comanor a.o., Chur a.o.: Harwood, pp. 189–205.

Laudati, Laraine L. (1998) 'Impact of Community Competition Law on Member State Competition Law', in *Competition Policies in Europe*, ed. by Stephen Martin, Amsterdam: Elsevier, pp. 381–410.

League of Nations (LON) Archives Geneva (1929) Economic Committee, *Doc. E 465 (a–e)* (1929).

League of Nations (LON) (1927) C. 356. M. 129, *Report and Proceedings of the World Economic Conference held at Geneva, May 4th to 23rd, 1927*, Vol. 1.

Liefmann, Robert (1930) *Kartelle, Konzerne und Trusts*, Stuttgart: Moritz.

Lovasy, Gertrud (1947) *International Cartels. A League of Nations Memorandum*, Lake Success, New York.

Maier, Charles S. (1975) *Recasting Bourgeois Europe*, Princeton, NJ: Princeton University Press.

McDonnell, Brett H. and Daniel A. Farber (2003) 'Are efficient antitrust rules always optimal?', in *The Antitrust Bulletin*, Fall 2003, pp. 807–835.

Milward, Alan S. (1984) *The Reconstruction of Western Europe 1945–51*, London: Methuen & Co.

Mitchener, Brandon (2004) 'EU Antitrust Regulators Gain Muscle for Big Cases', in *The Wall Street Journal Europe*, XXII, 4 April 2004, pp. A1 and A8.

Mohand, Souam Said (1998) 'French Competition Policy', in *Competition Policies in Europe*, edited by Stephen Martin, Amsterdam: Elsevier, pp. 205–227.

Motta, Massimo (2004) *Competition Policy*, Cambridge: Cambridge University Press.

Mülbert, Peter O. (1998) 'Bank Equity Holdings in Non-Financial Firms and Corporate Governance: The Case of German Universal Banks', in *Comparative Corporate Governance*, edited by Klaus J. Hopt, Oxford: Oxford University Press, pp. 473–505.

Neal, Larry and Daniel Barbezat (1998) *The Economics of the European Union and the Economics of Europe*, New York, Oxford: Oxford University Press.

Neumann, Manfred (1998) 'The Evolution of Cartel Policy in Germany', in *Competition Policies in Europe*, edited by Stephen Martin, Amsterdam: Elsevier, pp. 41–53.

Nocken, Ulrich (1985) 'Die Nationalökonomie und das Zwangskartellgesetz von 1933', in *Kartelle und Kartellgesetzgebung in Praxis und Rechtsprechung vom 19. Jahrhundert bis zur Gegenwart*, edited by Hans Pohl, Stuttgart: Steiner-Verl., pp. 167–175.

Nocken, Ulrich (1989) 'International Cartels and Foreign Policy: The Formation of the International Steel Cartel 1924–1926', in *Internationale Kartelle und Aussenpolitik. International Cartels and Foreign Policy*, edited by Clemens A. Wurm, Stuttgart: Steiner, pp. 33–82.

Nörr, Knut Wolfgang (1994) *Die Leiden des Privatrechts. Kartelle in Deutschland von der Holzstoffkartellentscheidung zum Gesetz gegen Wettbewerbsbeschränkung*, Tübingen: J.C.B. Mohr.

Oualid, William (1926) *The Social Effects of International Industrial Agreements*, League of Nations, C.E.C.P. 94, Geneva.

Pons, Jean-Francois and Timothée Sautter (2004) 'Ensuring a Sound Competition Environment: Rules, Practice, Reforms and Challenges of European Competition Policy', in *Competition Policy in Europe*, edited by Johann Eekhoff, Berlin, Heidelberg, New York: Springer, pp. 29–62.

Posner, Richard A. (2001) *Antitrust Law*, Second Edition, Chicago, London: The University of Chicago Press.

Prigge, Stefan (1998) 'A Survey of German Corporate Governance', in *Comparative Corporate Governance*, ed. by Klaus J. Hopt, Oxford: Oxford University Press, pp. 894–989.

Reckendrees, Alfred (2000) *Das 'Stahltrust'-Projekt*, Munich: Beck.

Resch, Andreas (2002) *Industriekartelle in Österreich vor dem Ersten Weltkrieg*, Berlin: Duncker & Humblot.

Resch, Andreas (2003) 'Große Marktmacht in einer kleinen Volkswirtschaft: die österreichischen Kartelle in der Zwischenkriegszeit', in: *Kartelle in Österreich*, edited by Andreas Resch, Vienna: Manz, pp. 45–94.

Rubinfeld, Daniel L. (2001) 'Antitrust Policy', in *International Encyclopedia of the Social and Behavioral Sciences*, Vol. 1, Amsterdam: Elsevier, pp. 553–560.

Scherer, F.M. (1994) *Competition Policies for an Integrated World Economy*, Washington, DC: The Brookings Institution.

Schröter, Harm (1993) 'The International Potash Syndicate', in *International Cartels Revisited*, edited by Dominique Barjot, Caen: Èditions-Diffusion du Lys, pp. 75–92.

Schröter, Harm (1996) 'Cartelization and Decartelization in Europe, 1870–1995: Rise and Decline of an Economic Institution', *Journal of European Economic History*, 25, 1996, pp. 129–153.

Stocking, George W. and Myron W. Watkins (1947) *Cartels in Action*, New York: The Twentieth Century Fund.

Teichova, Alice (1974) *An Economic Background to Munich*, Cambridge: Cambridge University Press 1974.

Teichova, Alice (1988) *Internationale Grossunternehmen*, Stuttgart: Steiner.

Tüchler, Michael (2003) 'Die Entwicklung des österreichischen Kartellrechts', in *Kartelle in Österreich*, edited by Andreas Resch, Vienna: Manz, pp. 121–148.

US Supreme Court (2004) F. Hoffman-LaRoche Ltd. v Empagran S.A., 124 S.Ct.

Wank, Rolf (1985) 'Die alliierten Entflechtungsmaßnahmen – Politische und juristische Aspekte', in *Kartelle und Kartellgesetzgebung in Praxis und Rechtsprechung vom 19. Jahrhundert bis zur Gegenwart*, edited by Hans Pohl, Stuttgart: Steiner, pp. 202–208.

Weinrauch Roland (2004) *Competition Law in the WTO*, Graz: NWV.

Wellhöner, Volker (1989) *Großbanken und Großindustrie im Kaiserreich*, Göttingen: Vandenhoeck & Ruprecht.

Wenger, Ekkehart and Christoph Kaserer (1998) 'German Banks and Corporate Governance: A Critical View', in *Comparative Corporate Governance*, edited by Klaus J. Hopt, – Oxford: Oxford University Press, pp. 502–536.

Wessel, Horst A. (1985) 'Die Haltung der Unternehmer zur Zwangskartellierung', in *Kartelle und Kartellgesetzgebung in Praxis und Rechtsprechung vom 19. Jahrhundert bis zur Gegenwart*, edited by Hans Pohl, Stuttgart: Steiner, pp. 188–201.

Wixforth, Harald (1995) *Banken und Schwerindustrie in der Weimarer Republik*, Cologne, Weimar, Vienna: Böhlau.

Wurm, Clemens A. (1989) 'Politik und Wirtschaft in den internationalen Beziehungen', in *Internationale Kartelle und Aussenpolitik. International Cartels and Foreign Policy*, edited by Clemens A. Wurm, Stuttgart: Steiner, pp. 1–31.

Wurm, Clemens (1994) 'The politics of international cartels: Great Britain, steel and cotton textiles in the interwar period', in *International Cartels Revisited (1880–1980)*, edited by Dominique Barjot, Caen: Éditions-Diffusion du Lys, pp. 255–264.

Ziegler, Dieter (1997) 'The Influence of Banking on the Rise and Expansion of Industrial Capitalism in Germany', in *Banking, Trade and Industry*, edited by A. Techova, Cambridge: Cambridge University Press, pp. 131–156.

17 European Union expansion

A constitutional perspective

Dennis C. Mueller[1]

1 Introduction

The original intent of Jean Monnet and the other founders of the European Union was to join economically Germany, France and enough other European countries sufficiently closely to make certain that they would never go to war against one another again. Thus, the motivation behind the founding of the European Union was to provide a form of public good for all of Europe. In describing the European Union's raison d'être today, we would expand the list of collective goods that can be provided more efficiently at the European level, and would explicitly include the gains to all Europeans from free trade. The European Union's raison d'être is to help Europeans achieve the possible gains from a more efficient *allocation* of goods and services.

To achieve the collective benefits from providing public goods to all Europeans, one must determine the types and amounts of public goods Europeans want and then supply them. There are essentially two types of institutional structures for accomplishing these tasks: a federalist or a confederalist structure. Which of these two structures is best suited to these tasks depends upon the characteristics of the distribution of citizen preferences across Europe for public goods, and thus also on the characteristics of the public goods themselves. The European Union's institutional structure has both federalist and confederalist attributes. This mixture creates certain problems in achieving the goal of optimally providing public goods within the EU, and in deciding whether or not to admit new members and upon what terms. These issues are the subject of this chapter.

We begin by reviewing the criteria for establishing a federalist state or a confederation (Sections 2 and 3). In so doing we shall employ the metaphor of viewing the state as a club and thus make reference to the theory of clubs. Section 4 discusses the optimal design of federations and confederations, while Section 5 takes up the benefits and costs of admitting new members. Given the important role heterogeneity plays in the analysis, Sections 6 and 7 are devoted to a description of the kinds of heterogeneity of preferences that are relevant, and the costs of these heterogeneities. Section 8 extends the analysis to the EU, while the final section returns to the issue of EU expansion, and the possible forms future expansion might take.

2 States as clubs: federalism

The need for clubs

Imagine people distributed in varying densities across a given land mass living in an anarchist regime. They produce that which they need to survive, supplemented by that which they can obtain through exchange. There exist certain goods – roads, fire protection – that no single person or family can supply optimally. Thus, incentives exist for groups of individuals to agree to provide these goods collectively. In the tradition of contractarianism and the new constitutional political economy we can imagine various groups of individuals reaching separate agreements to provide different public goods. Let us call each union of a group of people to provide one or more public goods a *club*.

The characteristics of a public good – joint supply and nonexclusion from benefits – often give a *geographic* dimension to any club formed to provide a particular good or service. A fire station benefits only those within a certain radius that covers the distance that its trucks can reach in a reasonable amount of time, a dam protects only those who live lower down along the river. This property of public goods leads us to expect that many clubs that are formed to provide public goods have a geographic dimension to them.[2] The natural self-interest of individuals should thus lead them to create and join many clubs of different geographic dimensions to provide the many possible public goods that could make them better off.[3]

The essence of a *club* is that it is a *voluntary* association of individuals to achieve some mutually beneficial goal. As such, the formation of clubs to provide public goods is much in the spirit of Wicksell's (1896) *voluntary exchange* approach to government, and of the FOCJs of Frey and Eichenberger (1996).[4] Consistent with these approaches, one might simply define a state as a club formed to provide one or more public goods. Given the many sorts of public goods that individuals might wish to consume and the different geographic dimensions of their benefits, one might well expect that a given individual would be a citizen of several clubs/states, some of which would provide public services to individuals in a small geographic area, others to larger numbers of individuals spread across much larger areas. Although there is nothing that we have said so far that would imply that a series of voluntarily joined clubs would take on the hierarchical structure of a federalist state, these clubs would resemble the optimal federalist state, as described in the economics literature of federalism, in that governmental *functions* would be associated with different levels of government in accordance with the geographic spillovers from the various public goods, and the relationship between the benefits from membership in a club and the size of the club.

Optimal club size

The public good benefits from club membership may be of two, fundamentally different types: (1) benefits that grow without bound as club size expands, or (2) benefits that eventually decline as club size expands, and may even turn negative on the margin beyond some size. Under the first heading we can place the benefits from free trade to members of a customs union, or the net benefits to a club member from providing a public good when there is no crowding. In the latter case, if the benefits to a member do not fall as the club size increases, his *net* benefits from membership will increase as the club size grows and the fixed costs of providing the public good are spread over more and more dues/tax payers.[5]

For many sorts of public goods, like transportation, environmental and recreation systems, adding consumers leads to congestion costs beyond some certain club size. When such crowding occurs, an optimal club size exists at which the benefits to existing members from spreading the costs of providing the public good over one more member just equal the additional congestion costs that this new member brings with her.[6]

The costs of heterogeneity under federalism

Although all citizens can in principle benefit from the provision of a pure public good, all do not necessarily have the same preferences for the public good. Institutions must be established to aggregate the diverse preferences of the citizens in a given polity to determine the optimal quantities and characteristics of the public goods offered by that polity. In all European countries except for the United Kingdom these institutions take the form of a proportional representation electoral system to elect members of parliament, and the use of the simple majority rule within the parliament to aggregate the preferences represented there. This method of aggregating preferences imposes certain costs on some or even all citizens, when citizen preferences differ from one another.

To see what is involved, assume that a polity provides a single public good, say roads, and its citizens must decide the amount, x, to be spent on roads. The population can be divided into five groups, each of which favours a different expenditure on roads. Let x_1 be the expenditure favoured by group 1, x_2 the expenditure favoured by group 2, and so on. Assume that $x_1 < x_2 < x_3 < x_4 < x_5$. An election is held and the parties representing groups 2 and 3 win together enough seats to form the government and decide the amount of x for the community. It is reasonable to assume that the expenditure on roads that this coalition chooses, x^*, falls between x_2 and x_3, i.e. $x_2 \leq x^* \leq x_3$. Under this assumption, x^* must differ from the most preferred quantity of x of one of the groups, and most likely differs from the quantities most preferred by both groups. Thus, the need to form a coalition to be able to decide the quantity of the public good imposes costs on each group in comparison to what it would experience, if it could decide the quantity of the public good alone.[7]

Similar losses also exist for members of the other three groups obviously, and these losses are likely to be even greater than those experienced by the groups whose representatives were able to form the government. Thus, the necessity of all members of a community having to consume the same quantity of any public good it provides imposes some loss of utility on virtually all members, as opposed to what would occur if all members had the same tastes. Two consequences follow: first, we can now identify a second possible cost to the existing members of a community from expanding its membership. Even when no crowding takes place, the existing members may be made worse off from the admittance of new members, if the new members have different preferences from old members, and the increased heterogeneity of the community shifts the chosen quantity of the public goods supplied away from those favoured by the old members. Second, there may exist gains for all individuals from free migration across communities, if this migration can result in communities with more homogeneous preferences for public goods.[8] A possible advantage of having a federalist governmental structure with numerous communities within the federation providing different bundles of public goods is that it would allow citizens the opportunity to improve the levels of utility that they obtain from publicly provided goods and services by resorting themselves into communities of more homogeneous preferences.

3 Confederations as clubs

My *American Heritage Dictionary* defines a *confederation* as a group of states united for a common purpose. One might well also define a *club* as a group of individuals united for a common purpose. A confederation is thus a kind of club of nations,[9] and we expect it to share the following two properties of clubs: (1) membership is voluntary. (2) Members voluntarily join because they expect to be made better off. The 'common purpose' that brings them together involves their obtaining mutual benefits. The benefits from membership in the club or confederation are a form of a public good to club members.

When the members of a club are autonomous states, the issue arises of whether it is the interests of the citizens of these states that are being advanced by the confederation, or the interests of the members of the governments that represent these citizens. The simplest case to consider, and the one which is most compatible with the confederate form of government being the optimal way to advance the interests of the *individual citizens* within it, is to assume that every person within a given state has identical preferences for the public goods that the confederation provides, and that the representatives of the governments of each member state faithfully represent the preferences of their citizens.

Under these assumptions, a club of states has all of the properties of a club of individuals. Namely, optimal club size is infinite in the absence of crowding or preference heterogeneity across club members, optimal club size is likely to be finite when either of these two phenomena are present.

When every person within a given state has identical preferences for the public goods that the confederation provides, an obvious and simple way to represent these preferences is to have each of the constituent state governments send representatives to an assembly, and for these state delegations to have seats or voting rights in this assembly proportionate to their populations. Such a system of representation would produce an assembly of representatives for the confederation that would resemble that which one would expect to arise under a system of proportional representation in which the citizens of the confederation elected representatives to the assembly directly.

The situation can be quite different, however, if the preferences of the citizens within each state are heterogeneous. Assume, for example, that the population of each state can be divided into five groups as in the previous section, with the five groups in each of the states having the same five most preferred quantities of the public good x, $x_1 < x_2 < x_3 < x_4 < x_5$. Assume further that there are ten states in the confederation. In five of these, parties representing the groups favouring x_1 and x_2 form governments with narrow majorities, in the other five states parties favouring x_3 and x_4 form governments with substantial majorities. If the populations of the five states favouring x_1 and x_2 give them a slight majority in the confederation's assembly, and this assembly uses the simply majority rule, then the quantity of the public good chosen using the confederate form of representation will lie between x_1 and x_2, where a quantity between x_3 and x_4 would have been chosen using the simply majority rule under a system of proportional representation in which citizens across the confederation elect their representatives directly.

With heterogeneous preferences within states, the outcomes from a confederate form of representation can differ from those under proportional representation when citizens elect representatives directly, *even if the unanimity rule* is used in the confederate assembly. In the above example, individuals who favour the quantity x_5 are not represented in any of the ten governments, and thus their preferences would presumably receive no weight in any compromise over x that representatives of the ten governments were able to reach under the unanimity rule. These considerations imply that a confederate form of government is the optimal way to represent citizen preferences *only* when these preferences are homogeneous within each member state and heterogeneous across them.

4 The optimal design of the State

Much of the public choice literature that deals with constitutions, and essentially all of the recent constitutional political economy literature, assumes that constitutions are written by the citizens of a country and are *unanimously* agreed to by these citizens.[10] Although these assumptions are highly unrealistic as *descriptions* of the way actual constitutions of nation states are written, they do accurately describe how confederations come into being. Since the potential members of a new confederation are themselves nation states, it is possible for each of them to remain in the existing 'state of anarchy' should they not find the conditions for joining the confederation to their advantage. Unanimity is not merely a hypothetical ideal when it comes to the formation of a confederation, it is a practical necessity. Although all countries that meet to discuss forming a confederation may not choose to join it, the agreement among those which do join must be unanimous. The contract all joiners sign must be seen as a Pareto move *by all signers*.[11] Both the contractarian perspective on the initial constitution and the assumption of unanimous agreement among all signers is fully justified, when a new polity is created through the joining of previously autonomous states.

Although when states form a new polity the process of state formation is that of a confederation, the new state need not take on that form. The existing states might form a federal superstate with the former autonomous states being sub-states in the superstate. Our previous discussion suggests that this federalist structure is optimal, when citizen preferences for the public goods provided by the superstate are heterogeneous *within* the separate countries which form it. The formation of the United States of America might be viewed as an example of such a process. Alternatively, if citizen preferences for the public goods provided by the superstate are homogeneous within each member country and heterogeneous across them, then a confederation will be optimal. Since the European Union was founded as a confederation of states, and has effectively functioned as a confederation throughout its history, one must assume that citizen preferences for the public goods provided by the EU are homogeneous within each member country, *if the EU is organized optimally for revealing its citizens' preferences and providing them with public goods.*

Once the superstate has been created, it must decide on a voting rule to be used to make the various collective decisions, which will advance the interests of its citizens. If a federal structure has been chosen, these collective decisions will presumably be made by a parliament in which citizen preferences are represented through parties, which have competed for votes across the super-state. If a confederation has been chosen, the collective decisions will be made in an assembly filled with representatives from the elected governments in each member country. In either case, the assembly making collective decisions must operate with some voting rule. Following Buchanan and Tullock (1962: 63–91) the selection of the optimal voting rule has been analysed in the public choice literature as depending on decision-making costs and the external costs of collective decisions.[12] These costs are depicted in Figure 17.1. The majority required to make a decision, m, runs from zero to one along the horizontal axis, with $m=1.0$ being the unanimity rule, $m=0.5$, the simple majority rule, and so on. The time taken to reach the required majority increases with the size of this majority, with the usual assumption being that these decision-making costs, D, increase at an increasing rate as m rises. Under the unanimity rule, each member of the committee can effectively veto any proposal that would make her worse off, and there are no external costs from collective decisions. As the majority required to pass an issue falls, the likelihood of a member being made worse off increases, and thus so too do the external costs of collective decisions, E. Here also the usual assumption has been that E increases at an increasing rate as m declines. The optimal majority, m^*, is found at the point where the sum of these two curves is at a minimum.

It is reasonable to assume that m^* will differ for different types of collective decisions and for different communities. In particular, the more heterogeneous

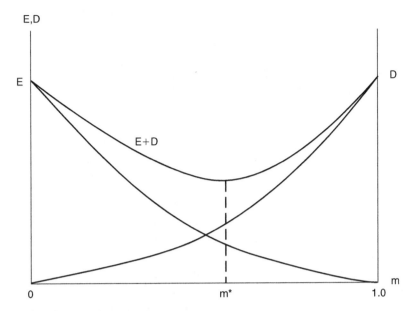

Figure 17.1 Choosing the optimal majority.

the members of the assembly are, the longer it is likely to take them to reach a collective decision. Thus, the *D*-curve is likely to pivot to the left as heterogeneity increases. This change alone would imply lower optimal majorities for more heterogeneous committees. It is also likely, however, that *E* pivots to the right as heterogeneity increases, as the danger of a collective decision being made that lies far from a member's most preferred outcome increases. Thus, the net effect on the choice of a voting rule from an increase in heterogeneity cannot be predicted without knowing by how much each curve shifts. What can be said unequivocally, however, is that the combined costs associated with collective decision-making are greater, the greater the heterogeneity of the community.[13]

5 The benefits and costs of EU expansion

Benefits

If *x* is a pure public good, then additional citizens can enjoy the benefits of consuming *x* without imposing any costs on the rest of the community. If these additional citizens bear some of the costs of supplying *x*, then existing members of the community benefit from allowing new members in. An example of such an *x* might be a satellite, whose signals can be selectively beamed to particular people. The costs per person of launching and maintaining such a satellite fall as the size of the community paying for the satellite increases.

When one thinks of the EU, there are very few public goods that it provides that have these characteristics. Indeed, most of the EU's budget goes into agricultural subsidies and other redistribution programmes, which certainly do not resemble pure public goods. Many might regard the euro as a kind of EU public good, but it is not 'supplied' to all members, and there is no technical reason why one would have to join the European Union to join the European Monetary Union (EMU). If Canada wanted to adopt the euro and existing members of the EMU agreed, it would be entirely feasible to replace the Canadian dollar with the euro without having to admit Canada into the EU. Similar arguments apply with respect to the benefits from participation in the Shengen agreement.

As noted at the start of this chapter, a primary objective in forming the EU was to prevent future wars in Europe – and the achievement of this goal has been its most successful accomplishment. To the extent that new members into the EU refrain from starting or joining in wars with other member countries, *because* of their EU membership, all existing and new members benefit. Spreading and preserving peace and democracy are arguably the greatest benefits from EU expansion.

Another set of benefits from EU membership come through the harmonization of various rules and regulations that make doing business in different European countries easier. Here again, however, one might argue that many of these benefits might be obtained without having to become a full member.

Costs

Congestion

Austria has more trucks transiting it than any country in the EU, and this truck traffic increased with the addition of the ten new member countries to its north and east on 1 May 2004 (*Die Presse*, 2004). Congestion in the skies and on the beaches of Europe may also be expected to increase with expansion. Many have also been concerned with congestion in the job market. Too many workers from the poorer new member countries seeking jobs in the rich countries. Images of a hypothetical Polish plumber taking business away from French plumbers coloured the debate in France over the draft EU constitution prior to the French referendum on it. Although this possibility cannot be dismissed out of hand, in the long run the migration of workers to the richer countries should increase both the supply of workers and the demand for them, *if the richer EU countries liberalize their legal environments to make the creation of firms and jobs easier.*

The draft constitution of the EU creates a new animal called the 'European Union citizen'. Although the full implications of this article are unclear, one possible consequence might be that EU citizens will not only have the right to migrate to richer countries in search of employment, but – as EU citizens – would have the right to claim access to a rich country's generous welfare system soon after taking up residency. Should the courts interpret EU citizenship in this way, it could be the death of the Welfare State in Europe as it exists today (Sinn, 2004).

Heterogeneity

If x was a public good supplied to the 15 member countries of 30 April 2004, and the range of their preferences over x was from x_1 to x_5, then a reasonable outcome of collective decision-making in the EU would have been a choice of x of, say, x_3. If the preferred quantities of x of the new member countries are, say, x_6, x_7, and x_8, then the addition of the ten new countries would likely shift the chosen quantity of x in the EU away from that favoured by the original member countries imposing costs upon them.[14]

Effects on the basket of public goods provided

As discussed at the beginning of this chapter, most public goods have a geographic dimension to them, unlike the satellite example given above. As the boundaries of the EU expand, the number of public goods that can be optimally supplied to all member countries is likely to decline. Ironically, expansion of the EU should probably carry with it a *contraction* of the work of Brussels, at least in so far as it is involved in providing public goods. There has been much discussion in recent years of an 'inner' and an 'outer core' of member countries, of EU countries moving at two speeds, and so on, with the connotations surrounding these terms usually interpreted negatively at least among the slow-moving, outer core countries. The geographic dimensions of public goods suggests, however, that a subdivision of their provision in the EU might well be optimal. Instead of the EU being thought of as only a single club of 25 or more countries, it might well be optimal to divide the EU into several smaller clubs – a British Isles–Scandinavian club, a Mediterranean club, a central European club, and so on – for the provision of some public goods with spillovers across individual country borders.

The optimal voting rule

The ten new members to the EU range from tiny islands in the Mediterranean with tourism as their main industries, to tiny countries in the Baltic sea with diverse economies, to giant Poland with its huge agricultural sector. The new entrants differ from the 15 previous members most conspicuously in their relative incomes. The average new member income per capita is less than half of that of the existing members.

This increase in heterogeneity in the EU can be expected to shift upward both the E and D curves in Figure 17.1 raising the total costs of collective decision-making in the EU. As noted above, the effects of the shifts in these two curves on the size of the optimal majority for passing an issue is ambiguous. This ambiguity stands in sharp contrast to the seeming consensus among the drafters of the new constitution that the expansion necessitated a reduction in the size of the effective majority to pass issues in the Council. The reason for this contrast can be seen in the fact that the rise in decision-making costs falls entirely on members of the Council, for it is they who will have to spend more time search-ing for proposals that will achieve the required majority. This increase in decision-making costs need not concern EU citizens, for they are not directly engaged in reaching collective decisions. On the other hand, the rise in the exter-nal costs of collective decision-making falls largely on EU citizens. In particu-lar, citizens in the 15 pre-May 2004 member countries can expect to bear the costs of future collective decisions in the EU falling further from their most pre-ferred outcomes. This difference in who bears the costs of expansion helps to explain why citizens in the 15 pre-May 2004 member countries seem to be less enthusiastic about the expansion than their representatives in the Council and Commission in Brussels.

6 The nature of heterogeneous preferences

Preference heterogeneity plays a very important role in our analysis of the optimal structure for the EU, federation or confederation, of the optimal voting rule, and of the costs and benefits from expansion. Given its importance, it is appropriate that we pause here to consider the nature of the kinds of preference heterogeneity that can raise the costs of membership in a community. The list of heterogeneities that follows is not meant to be exhaustive, and no importance should be given to the order of presentation.

Tastes

In the example involving the choice of x, individuals are assumed to have differ-ent preferences with respect to the optimal quantity of a pure public good. An example of such a good might be a maximum speed limit on limited-access highways imposed across all EU members. Some people are highly risk averse and favour low speed limits, others are more concerned with the costs of travel-ling at low speeds. If these preferences are relatively homogeneous within coun-tries and heterogeneous across them, then setting a common speed limit across all countries will impose costs on some of the member countries.

Income

Poor people buy smaller quantities of some private goods, like meals in restaur-ants and holidays on the beach, and lower qualities of other private goods. The addition of poorer countries to the EU can be expected to shift the provision of EU-wide public goods towards the provision of lower quantities and qualities of public goods.

Ideology

A communist wishes to see the state own all means of production and little or no scope for the market. An economic liberal favours strong property rights and market institutions. Ideological differences over economic institutions have been prominent in Europe over the last century and have imposed huge costs on its citizens. The most conspicuous of these are certainly the costs on those trapped in communist countries after the Second World War. The 'stop-go' economic policies followed by successive Conservative and Labour governments in Britain during the 1960s imposed costs of a lesser sort on its citizens. The Red Brigades and other left-wing terrorist groups caused much fear and suffering and a not insignificant number of deaths during the 1970s. In 2005, the leadership of Britain and France were at loggerheads over whether the future of Europe will be better if it liberalizes its labour and product markets, or strives to preserve and extend to the Union's new members the state interventions in the market that have underpinned the 'social market economy'. This debate in the EU is likely to continue for some time.

Race

It might not be possible to tell whether a man is an economic liberal by simply looking at him, but it is easy to tell whether his skin colour is black or white. Race is the most conspicuous of all heterogeneities that divide people, and continues to be a common cause of friction in racially-mixed societies. For complex sociological or perhaps genetic reasons, many white people do not wish to work or live alongside black people, and discriminate against them in their social and economic interactions. This discrimination tends to drive the races apart both physically and economically with blacks and whites clustering together in largely segregated communities, and black people occupying the lower ranks of the income distribution. Although the United States is the most prominent country that has been troubled by racial problems, it is not alone. I can think of no country in the world with a non-negligible black minority in which black people have achieved economic equality with white people in the sense of having equal per capita incomes, and equal probabilities of occupying the top managerial and other positions of status in the country.[15]

Religion

If one lists the 'trouble spots' of the world over the last decade – Israel, Iraq, Afghanistan, Kosovo, India, Bosnia, Northern Ireland – one immediately recognizes that religious differences have been a factor in all of these countries, and in most have been the primary if not the sole cause of conflict. One also immediately recognizes that the religious clashes have also not always been between Islam and Christianity, or even have involved Islam. In India, Muslims and Hindus have engaged in violent confrontations, and in Northern Ireland it is Catholics and Protestants that persist in killing one another. In Iraq, Sunni Muslims kill Shiite Muslims, because they regard them as apostates. The power of religious beliefs to lead to kill one another should not be underestimated. All of the major religions of the world seem capable of fuelling sufficient hatred against other religions to generate physical violence when members of different religions live near one another.[16]

Culture

The typical European family today often chooses to have no children, or at most one or two. It places great store in educating its children, ideally up through the university. The typical Romani family has six, eight or more children who usually receive little formal education. Although there are some racial differences between Romani and other Europeans, the most conspicuous gulf between them is in their living styles, or what we might call cultures. The Romani are ostracized and discriminated against by other Europeans, because of the dramatic differences in their cultures. The fact that these differences are reinforced and enhanced by this ostracism and discrimination does not make them any less important as a source of conflict. The violence that has characterized relationships between the Basques and other Spaniards might also be attributed to cultural differences.

Language

When seen on the street it would be difficult to tell the difference between a Flemish Belgian and a Walloon, only when they begin to speak in their mother tongues does the difference between them stand out. This difference has been a continuous cause of friction within the country over the past decades. Although these frictions have not escalated to the kinds of violence seen in Spain between Basques and other Spaniards, or in Northern Ireland, it has imposed costs on the community. Language differences contribute to the gap separating Basques from other Spaniards, Catalans from other Spaniards, and Corsicans from other French. Language differences are a frequent cause of conflict between groups, which otherwise seem quite homogeneous.

Sexual orientation

Differences in sexual orientation across people have become a more important source of friction in recent years, as homosexuals have become less inhibited in showing signs of affection for one another in public. Here we have an example of one form of heterogeneity that can lead to conflicts because of another form of heterogeneity. The animosity that some people feel and show toward homosexuals arises in part at least, because they believe that God has forbidden homosexual relationships. When race, religion and culture all combine to reinforce the differences between groups, the costs of heterogeneity can become quite large.

Commentary

It is common among social scientists to attribute the costs of heterogeneity to prejudices that some people have against members of other groups, and to argue that these prejudices arose out of the cultural and educational environment in which these people were raised. The problems caused by heterogeneity can then be 'solved' by better education, by inculcating the proper values into citizens, and so on. Recent work in evolutionary psychology calls these assumptions into question. Aggressive behaviour against members of *other* groups is to some extent genetically determined. During the Pleistocene period, when humans lived in tribes of hunters and gatherers, loyalty to one's group and animosity to other groups would increase survival chances. Such loyalty and animosity became part of our genetic make-up, which may be triggered by signals that identify who is a member of *our* group and who is not. Race, language, religion and the other heterogeneities discussed here can be such triggering signals.[17]

To say that group loyalty and animosity are partly genetically driven does not imply, of course, that we are condemned to racial, linguistic and religious conflict. For large parts of the last millennium Catholics and Protestants in Europe went about killing one another. Now they live peacefully side be side in *most* of Europe, but not all. Education can counteract genetic tendencies toward group animosities, but, at a minimum, European history suggests that the learning process can take some time. It is just as big a mistake to *over*estimate the power of education as to underestimate it. Rapidly increasing the racial, linguistic and religious heterogeneity of Europe may bring with it increasing group conflict with its associated costs.

7 The nature of the costs of heterogeneity

If individuals have single-peaked, concave utility functions defined over a single-dimensional issue, x, then the utility loss to an individual from the choice of an x, which differs from her ideal point increases more than proportionally with the distance between the chosen x and her ideal point. Thus, if the continual expansion of the EU leads to continually greater degrees of heterogeneity across the EU in citizen preferences (tastes) for EU-wide public goods, expansion is likely to erode citizens' perceived benefits from the EU in member countries, *unless these costs are offset by other benefits from expansion.*

Some of the other forms of heterogeneity listed in the previous section can also impose real costs on citizens. Signs in a community with two language groups might have to be printed in two languages. Parliamentary debates, court proceedings and other public events might require translators. Television stations might have to broadcast in two languages, or one might need more stations than would otherwise be the case. Religious differences might also impose real costs on members of the community. If the minority religion succeeds in getting its religious holidays declared as national holidays along with the religious holidays of the majority religion, the number of public holidays in the country may exceed the number which all citizens deem optimal. In the extreme case, of course, racial, linguistic and religious differences can lead to violent clashes between the different groups with their attendant costs.

Many of the costs of heterogeneity are not *real* costs as in the above examples, but *psychological* costs. A white person does not resent living next to a black person, because the black person favours a different speed limit than the white person, but merely resents seeing and knowing that a black person is her neighbour. The presence of the black person gives rise to a *psychological externality*.[18] The sight of two men holding hands or kissing in public gives rise to a negative, psychological externality for the person who believes homosexual relationships to be a sin. Indeed, the mere *thought* that two people are having a homosexual relationship in private may give rise to a psychological externality.

The common way to eliminate a negative externality is to prohibit the action that causes it. If secondary smoke from cigarettes causes an externality, smoking is banned in public places. Bans against homosexuals committing certain sexual acts in public – or even in private – have been common, and still exist in many places today; black people have been banned from certain places frequented by white people; and most recently in France Muslim women have been banned from wearing head scarves in public buildings. Such bans impose obvious costs on the minority whose activity has been circumscribed. Should the ban not be imposed, the costs fall on the majority experiencing a psychological externality. When such externalities exist for two groups living together in a community, one group must suffer losses for the benefit of the other group, *whatever* the community decides with respect to the action. The only way that the imposition of costs on one group can be avoided is by separating the two groups by a great enough distance so that the externality disappears.

8 The costs of heterogeneity in the European Union

Article 21 of the Charter of Rights, which is (was?) to be included in the new EU constitution begins with the sentence, 'Any discrimination based on any ground such as ... [17 criteria] ... shall be prohibited.' Among the 17 criteria for discrimination, which are prohibited, are all of the usual suspects – race, sex, religion – and then some others. Article 21 thus annunciates the liberal ideal of racial, sexual, religious, etc. equality shared by liberals in Europe and around the globe. If an article in a constitution could eliminate racial prejudice, then racial inequality in the United States would have vanished long ago. If people perceive psychological externalities from some of the differences among people enumerated in Article 21, then there will be costs from having and increasing heterogeneity within the European Union.

Fifty years ago, France was a relatively homogeneous French-speaking country with a largely white, Catholic population. Today France has the largest Muslim population in Europe, and its major cities are surrounded by black ghettos with high unemployment rates, particularly among young males, and high crime rates, a situation resembling what once existed, and to some extent still exists in the United States today, except that there the ghettos tend to span the city centres.

The bombings of 11 March 2004 in Spain are a vivid reminder of the potential costs of heterogeneity. They were not set off by deranged Spanish citizens, or even by those alienated from the government like the Basques. They were set off by people from a culture and of a religion quite different from that of most Spaniards. The underground bombings in London in the summer of 2005 indicate that even citizens educated and raised in a country can differ from their neighbours to a degree that makes them kill their neighbours. The costs of heterogeneity can be quite high.

Over the last 30 or 40 years support for 'the government', for those in government, and for the political parties that represent citizens in government has declined dramatically in virtually every developed, democratic country in the world (Pharr and Putnam, 2000; Dalton, 2004). One important explanation for this decline is that the preferences of citizens for what they want from government have become more heterogeneous and citizens have become more demanding of government to satisfy these heterogeneous preferences (Dalton, 2004, Ch. 7). Greens demand severe restrictions on the use of automobiles and nuclear power, non-greens object; homosexuals demand the right to marry, religious conservatives object; some demand the right to have abortions, religious conservatives again object. It is impossible for governments to satisfy all of these demands simultaneously, and compromises leave all sides disaffected. Support for the government wanes, because it is not seen as meeting the demands of the citizens.

This alienation is clearly visible in Europe at the nation state level and could easily manifest itself at the European Union level, if the draft constitution with its accompanying Charter of rights were to come into effect. To give but one example, the question of same-sex marriages has become a hot topic in the United States recently. Imagine that the draft constitution comes into effect, and a homosexual group in one member country sues to have same-sex marriages allowed citing Article 21 of the Charter. If the court agrees with the homosexual group, then same-sex marriages should be allowed in *all* member countries, since the Charter guarantees every EU citizen the same set of rights. While this decision might be welcomed in some member countries, it would be strongly opposed in some others. Within the latter, alienation against the EU would be fostered. When preferences on issues such as this are strong and heterogeneous, enforcing a single outcome across all of Europe will have considerable costs.

9 European Union expansion: with or without immigration?

As already noted, the primary benefits from the European Union have come through the elimination of wars between its members. The preservation of peace and democracy in the existing member countries, and their spread to new members are the most likely benefits from expansion, along with the economic benefits of an ever expanding common market. All of these gains can be realized *without* requiring that the citizens of one member country be free to migrate to and take up residence in another member country.

Free migration and rights to employment in all member countries have been a feature of the European Union from early on. To date, migration among the member countries has been rather modest, and this feature of the EU has not been a cause of much concern. The differences in income between the new members and the pre-existing 15 are sufficiently great, however, that the right to free migration may prove to be unpopular in some of the richer countries, if it is exercised by too many people. With this in mind some existing member countries, like Austria and Germany, chose to restrict the immigration rights of the new members for an initial period. Such restrictions have been only partially successful, however, and the migration of workers from some of the new member countries has already become a cause of some concern in some of the old member countries.

Income aside, the ten new member countries do not differ greatly from the existing 15. All have white, European populations. All have Christian heritages. One can be fairly optimistic that the integration of these ten countries will not impose great heterogeneity costs on the previous members, even if migration from the new members proves to be greater than has been the case following past expansions.

As one looks further east, however, the potential dangers from further expansion and liberal migration appear to loom larger. In particular, many Europeans on both the right and the left of the political spectrum have great reservations about allowing Turkey into the EU. Although political correctness often forces politicians to be circumspect about the origin of their fears if Turkey were to join, its large and rapidly growing Muslim population must be an important component of the explanation.

The benefits to the European Union from admitting Turkey could be great, however. Indeed, the whole world would benefit if peace and democracy could be spread to the Middle East, and no country in this region is a better candidate for helping to achieve this goal than Turkey. If Turkey were allowed into the EU *without* its having the rights to free migration that have characterized EU membership until 1 May 2004, the existing EU members would receive all of the benefits from Turkey's entry without many, if any, of the potential costs. Turkey too could expect to be a large net beneficiary.

With these considerations in mind, I see essentially three possible scenarios for the EU's future development.

1   Roll up the red carpet. Call a halt to EU expansion, perhaps after admitting Croatia and the Western Balkans. Except for transition periods, rights to migration continue to exist and are extended to rights to citizenship in other member countries after relatively short periods of residency. Europe becomes an island of peace and prosperity surrounded by some occasionally quarrelsome and unpleasant neighbours.

2   Extend the red carpet, continue to allow free migration, and hope that all European Union citizens become as enlightened and tolerant as the people

who drafted the Charter and the constitution. Should this hope prove in vain, this scenario risks the eventual undoing of the EU experiment as some countries begin to perceive the costs of membership, as enumerated above, to exceed the benefits.

3 Continual expansion to include countries which meet the criteria of being liberal democracies with well-functioning market economies, but allow each member country – new and old – to define its own criteria for residency, employment and citizenship. The EU continues to expand as a confederation with each member country able to control the inward flow of people from both within and outside of the EU. Here it should be noted that freedom to *travel* within the EU could be assured to all EU citizens without granting them rights of residency or eventual citizenship. Considerable migration could still be expected, but each country would control both the amount and the identities of the migrants to ensure that the benefits from migration exceed the costs.

Option 3 would allow the EU to gradually expand across all of Europe and into the Middle East, eventually absorbing not only Turkey, but perhaps Israel, Russia and many of its former satellites like Ukraine, if they could eventually meet the criteria for entry. Admittedly, this is a big if, and one would expect that some countries would have to be bypassed because they failed to meet the entry criteria, while countries to their east were admitted. The pressure to reform on a non-democratic country surrounded by a sea of democratic ones would, presumably, be very great, however, and one might hope that eastward expansion would eventually result in the inclusion of all countries along the way.

Option 3 resembles the dream of Woodrow Wilson and others for the League of Nations, and of others who have dreamed of a 'world government'.[19] To some it may appear Utopian, but I would argue that it is less Utopian than thinking that option 2 could be followed without great risks. The rejection of the draft constitution by France and the Netherlands and the postponement of the ratification process in other countries, presents an opportunity to rethink what the European Union is and what it should become. A tightly integrated federalism with citizens free to migrate at will across the Union and sharing a common set of rights wherever they resided might have been feasible with an EU of six member countries, perhaps even of 15, it seems far less feasible with 27, and would become increasingly difficult if expansion were to continue. Option 3 promises far greater benefits to both existing and new member countries than either of the other two options, with potentially lower costs than the second option. It is worthy of careful consideration.

Notes

1 This chapter builds on an earlier paper of mine (Mueller, 2002).
2 Exceptions exist, of course. One category would be that of 'cultural clubs', like religions. It may be possible to join a religious club and receive the benefits from membership regardless of where one lives. See, Mueller (1996a, Ch. 20).

3 Schmidt-Tenz and Schmidtchen (2002) emphasize the likelihood of different sized protective states being optimal for different laws.

4 FOCJs stands for *functional, overlapping and competing jurisdictions.* Frey and Eichenberger advocate allowing individuals to create their own political communities to provide local public goods.

5 If B is the benefit to each member of a customs union from free trade, and n is the number of members of the union, then it is reasonable to assume that B initially grows rapidly as membership expands, but eventually its growth, although still positive, tapers off as the bulk of the gains from free trade have been realized. This relationship can be captured by positing an exponential relationship between B and n.

$$\beta = \alpha + \beta \ln n \tag{1}$$

A similar relationship between B and n arises for a pure public good, when there is no crowding. If α is the utility a club member experiences from consuming the pure public good, and β is the public good's total costs, then the benefits an individual obtains from club membership, net of his share of the public goods costs are

$$B = \alpha - \beta/n \tag{2}$$

Both equations (1) and (2) imply an optimal club size of infinity.

6 Congestion costs can be introduced into equation (2) by adding a term as given in equation (3).

$$B = \alpha - \beta/n - \gamma n^2 \tag{3}$$

Equation (3) implies an optimal size for club membership, $n^* = (\beta/2\alpha)^{1/3}$.

7 Let the members of group i have identical preferences for spending on roads, $U_i = K_i - b_i(x_i - x^*)^2$, where x_i is the amount each member of this group wishes to see spent on roads, and b_i is an intensity weight specific to group i. If $x_i = x^*$, a member of the group experiences a utility level K_i. The *loss* L to a member from having to consume x^* rather than x_i, increases linearly with its intensity weight, and exponentially with the distance between $x_i - x^*$, $L = -b_i(x_i - x^*)^2$.

8 See Tiebout (1956); Inman and Rubinfeld (1997a); and Mueller (2003, Ch. 9). The latter two references also discuss the kinds of externalities from migration that negate the potential benefits from 'voting with the feet'.

9 Indeed the European Community was often referred to in its early years as the Club of Rome.

10 This is of course the approach pioneered by Buchanan and Tullock (1962).

11 It is, of course, possible that countries that choose not, or are not allowed to join are adversely affected by the formation of a confederation. Thus, the emphasis in the text.

12 See also Mueller (2003: 74–78).

13 See also the discussion in Kafoglis and Cebula (1981).

14 Alesina and Spolaore (2003) present a general analysis of the trade-off between the benefits of size and the costs of heterogeneity in determining the optimal size of a state and in Chapter 12 relate their analysis to the question of EU expansion.

15 In the past when I have made this observation, some people have occasionally pointed to Brazil as a counterexample of successful racial integration. A fairly recent article in the *Economist* (2003) indicates that this is not so, however. Black people in Brazil are demanding the same sort of quotas in hiring and university admissions to achieve racial equality that black people in the US have long demanded.

16 Buddhism has not figured in the violence experienced by the seven countries listed in the text, but recent violent clashes between a Muslim minority in the south of Thailand and the Buddhist majority in this country suggest that it too can be a source of religious conflict.

17 See Pinker (1997: 509–517), and for a general discussion of the challenge raised by

evolutionary psychology to traditional thinking in sociology and psychology, Tooby and Cosmides (1992).

18 I first introduced the concept of a psychological externality in Mueller (1996b).

19 It resembles most closely the scenario described by Peter Bernholz (1985), who also saw the European Community of that time as the building block for a much larger peaceful union of states.

References

Alesina, Alberto and Enrico Spolaore (2003) *The Size of Nations*, Cambridge MA: MIT Press.

Bernholz, Peter (1985) *The International Game of Power*, Berlin: Mouton.

Buchanan, James M. and Gordon Tullock (1962) *The Calculus of Consent*, Ann Arbor: University of Michigan Press.

Dalton, Russell J. (2004) *Democratic Challenges, Democratic Choices*, Oxford: Oxford University Press.

Frey, Bruno S. and Reiner Eichenberger (1996) 'FOCJ: Competitive Governments for Europe,' *International Review of Law and Economics*, 16 (3), September, pp. 315–327.

von Furstenberg, George M. and Dennis C. Mueller (1971) 'The Pareto Optimal Approach to Income Redistribution: A Fiscal Application,' *American Economic Review*, 61, September, pp. 628–637.

Goodman, S.F. (1996) *The European Union*, 3rd edn, London: Macmillan.

Inman, Robert P. and Daniel L. Rubinfeld (1997) 'The Political Economy of Federalism,' in Dennis C. Mueller, ed., *Perspectives on Public Choice*, Cambridge: Cambridge University Press, pp. 73–105.

Kafoglis, Milton Z. and Richard J. Cebula (1981) 'The Buchanan-Tullock Model: Some Extensions,' *Public Choice*, 36, pp. 179–186.

Koester, Ulrich and Stefan Tangermann (1990) 'The European Community,' in Fred H. Sanderson, ed., *Agricultural Protectionism in the Industrial World*, Washington, DC: Resources for the Future, pp. 64–111.

Mueller, Dennis C. (1996a) *Constitutional Democracy*, New York and Oxford: Oxford University Press.

Mueller, Dennis C. (1996b) 'Constitutional and Liberal Rights,' *Analyse & Kritik*, September, 18, pp. 96–117.

Mueller, Dennis C., ed. (1997a) *Perspectives on Public Choice*, Cambridge: Cambridge University Press.

Mueller, Dennis C. (1997b) 'Federalism and the European Union: A Constitutional Perspective,' *Public Choice*, 90, pp. 255–280.

Mueller, Dennis C. (2002) 'Constitutional Issues Regarding European Union Expansion,' in Bernard Steunenberg, ed., *Widening the European Union*, London: Routledge, pp. 41–57.

Mueller, Dennis C. (2003) *Public Choice III*, Cambridge: Cambridge University Press.

Pharr, Susan and Robert Putnam, eds (2000) *Disaffected Democracies: What's Troubling the Trilateral Democracies*, Princeton: Princeton University Press.

Pinker, Steven (1997) *How the Mind Works*, London: Penguin Books.

Schmidt-Tenz, Hans Jörg and Dieter Schmidtchen (2002) 'Adapting the Acquis Communitaire: Towards an Economic Theory of Optimal Legal Areas,' in Bernard Steunenberg, ed., *Widening the European Union*, London: Routledge, pp. 58–79.

Sinn, Hans-Werner (2004) 'The New Systems of Competition,' *Perspektiven der Wirtschaftspolitik*, 4, pp. 23–38.

Tiebout, Charles M. (1956) 'A Pure Theory of Local Expenditures,' *Journal of Political Economy*, 64, pp. 416–424.

Tooby, John and Leda Cosmides (1992) 'The Psychological Foundations of Culture,' in J.H. Barlow, L. Cosmides, and J. Tooby, eds, *The Adaptive Mind*, Oxford: Oxford University Press, pp. 19–136.

Wicksell, K. (1967) 'Ein neues Prinzip der gerechten Besteuerung,' *Finanztheoretische Untersuchungen*, Jena, 1896; translated as 'A New Principle of Just Taxation,' 1958; reprinted in Richard A. Musgrave, and Alan T. Peacock (eds), *Classics in the Theory of Public Finance*, London: Macmillan, pp. 72–118.

'Out of Eden' (2003) *The Economist*, 5 July, pp. 35–36.

'Experten geben sektoralem Fahrverbot wenig Chancen' (2004) *Die Presse*, 19 May, p. 5.

18 Europe's constitutional imbroglio

Gérard Roland[1]

1 Introduction

The rejection of Europe's Constitution by a comfortable majority of voters in France on 29 May 2005 (54.7 percent) and a few days later on 1 June in the Netherlands (61.6 percent) delivered a painful end to a constitutional process that had started under very good auspices.

With hindsight, the simple existence of a text for a European Constitution should have been seen as a very unlikely event. A few years ago, the prospect of the enlargement of the European Union to 25 had raised fears that the EU would simply become a large free-trade area and that the post-Second World War European project of peace on the continent via a closer political integration may never materialize. Europe had lost its historical opportunity in the aftermath of 1989, claimed the pessimists. The Nice Treaty had made decisions on voting weights in the European Council and on the number of seats in the European Parliament after enlargement. It seemed inevitable that decision-making would become much more difficult in the enlarged EU (Baldwin *et al.*, 2001). However, a seemingly unimportant event, the institution of a Convention to establish the Charter of Fundamental Rights, was to have deep-reaching consequences. The Belgian presidency prepared a declaration, the Laeken declaration, destined to renew the impetus for reform and to move farther ahead than the bland Nice outcome. The most revolutionary act would prove to be the abandoning of the traditional instrument of the intergovernmental conference (IGC) and the decision to mandate instead a Convention to prepare these reforms. Intergovernmental conferences are always composed of country representatives who have in mind only the interests of their country. This leads often to quite inefficient bargaining. The convention was to be composed not only of representatives of national governments but also of members of the European Parliament and of national parliaments. Even more interestingly, it included representatives from the accession countries which, at the time, had not yet officially entered the EU. Members of the Convention were to act not as country representatives but as conventioneers trying jointly to prepare a draft Constitution. Despite a very strict deadline and a sometimes idiosyncratic presidency by the aging former French president Giscard d'Estaing, the Convention fulfilled its task. The IGC that took place in the fall of 2003 could not make any progress over the work of the convention. The rejection of the referenda by a large majority in France on 29 May by 54.7 percent of the votes and on 1 June in Holland by 62.8 percent came all the more as a bitter blow to most observers of the European Constitutional process.

The rejection of the Constitution by voters had not been predicted by the French and Dutch executive. President Chirac wanted to use the referendum instrument to consolidate his role as leader of the right in France and to buy himself an option on the next presidential mandate against his rival Sarkozy. Holland is one of the six founding countries of the EU and has always been very pro-European. Here also, a rejection appeared very unlikely.

What happened? Why this massive rejection? Why the seemingly increasing distance between parliaments where overwhelming majorities were ready to support the Constitution and the dissatisfied populations? It is important to understand the reasons for the rejection in order to figure out how to go forward. What does this rejection spell for the future of the European integration process? What are the possible options on the table for the policy-makers in the coming months and years?

I will suggest answers to these questions in this chapter. I will argue that, while fraught with numerous difficulties, the best option available is a sufficiently substantial revision of the Constitution. The price to pay is a delay of several years before a new text for the Constitution can be proposed to European voters. However, the Constitution should not be seen as the major priority for EU institutions right now. A major reason for the negative referendum outcome is the stagnant economy in major European countries like France and Germany. In Spain where the economic situation is better and where the EU is perceived to have improved the economy, a large majority voted in favor of the Constitution. Without substantial progress in reforms to bring Europe back to a path of stronger growth, less rigid labor markets and a sustainable public pension system, there are great chances that a revised Constitution would meet the same fate as this one. The compromise reached in the Council in June 2007 is probably the best one can hope for at this stage.

2 The reasons for the No

There has been much speculation in the media about the reasons for the French and Dutch rejection of the Constitution. Among those cited were the prospect of Turkish entry, the Polish plumber, the lack of social Europe, etc.... What are we to make out of this? Fortunately, quite detailed Eurobarometer surveys were conducted in the two countries two days following the referendum. They give us a more accurate picture than the impressionistic comments in the media.

First of all, it would be wrong to blame the outcome on voters' lack of interest. The turnout was quite large in both countries. In France, the turnout rate was 69.3 percent, a figure that is very close to the Maastricht turnout which was of 69.7 percent. In the Netherlands where a referendum was held for the first time, the turnout rate was of 62.8 percent. The debates were very passionate in France and reached deep layers of society. One may question the extent to which these debates addressed the real issues of the Constitution but it is uncontroversial to state that very large debates took place on visions for the future of Europe. Following the referendum, *Libération*, one of the major French newspapers, reported stories on the divorces taking place among left-wing couples due to disagreements on how to vote.

Despite a high turnout in both countries, it is fair to state that the French No was more solid than the Dutch one. French voters do not blame a too-late campaign or lack of information. Only 37 percent complained that the campaign started too late compared to 67 percent in the Netherlands. French voters were in general quite confident in the information they had in order to decide: 70 percent said that they had sufficient information to vote. Voters who considered themselves ill-informed tended to abstain. In Holland, lack of information is paradoxically the most cited reason for voting No: 32 percent of those who voted No cited lack of information as a reason for why they voted No. French voters made their decision rather early in the campaign (60 percent). The picture that emerges thus is that a strong and resolute opposition had built up in France while in Holland voters were more confused and dissatisfied with the organization of the campaign and the information they had. The outcome of the French referendum certainly had a momentum effect on Dutch voters. However, if this momentum effect was important, it must have started playing a role as soon as the French polls predicted a victory of the No. Indeed, a majority of No in the Netherlands was already predicted more than a week before the day of the French referendum.

The reasons for the No were also characteristically quite different in the two countries. In France, the main motivation was dissatisfaction with the economy. Overall, 57 percent of those who voted No cited fear of more unemployment and outsourcing and dissatisfaction with the French economic situation and its high unemployment rate.[2] There is also a strong leftist economic reasoning behind the rejection: 35 percent of those who voted No consider that the Constitution is too 'liberal', i.e. pro-free-market and does not give its due to 'social Europe'.[3] Opposition to Chirac was an important motive and was cited by 18 percent as a reason for voting No.

Despite the strong resolve of voters, the text of the Constitution was not a key determinant of the vote: only 18 percent of respondents mentioned it as a key determinant of their vote. This should be compared with 32 percent who mentioned the French economic situation as the key determinant and 32 percent who mentioned their overall opinion of Europe. Moreover, 47 percent of those who voted No mentioned the French situation as the main determinant of their vote.

The reasons for the Dutch No were more scattered and diffuse but also very different from the reasons put forward in France. The main reason for the No vote is the lack of information mentioned above. The second main reason is the fear of loss of national sovereignty cited by 19 percent of those who voted No. Opposition to the government was cited by 14 percent and 13 percent thought that 'Europe is too expensive' which can be interpreted as dissatisfaction with the cost-benefit ratio of the European budget.

Apart from that, some of the motives emphasized by the press seem to have played a very small role in the French and Dutch vote. Thus, for example, opposition to Turkish membership in the EU was cited only by 6 percent of those who voted No in France and 3 percent in the Netherlands. The complexity of the Constitution was also cited by the media as a major cause for its rejection. However, it is only cited by 12 percent of those who voted No in France as a motive and by 5 percent in the Netherlands. The theme of the complexity of the Constitution is partly a red herring. In France, it was mocked by the No campaign who called it a telephone book, a great exaggeration for those who have seen the version distributed in France. Of the 325 pages, part I, which is the most important one and contains the rules of functioning of the EU, has only 48 pages and is rather concise. The Charter of Fundamental Rights of EU citizens, which was put together before the Convention, contains 23 pages. Titles III–V of part III which contains the enumeration of the competences of the EU and is mainly a rehash of the existing Treaties, and was hardly discussed at the Convention, contains 166 pages. In a way, it is a bit naïve to complain about the length of the Constitution. Apart from skills at concision, the shorter a Constitution, the more of an incomplete contract it represents. The longer it is, the less incomplete the contract. In the case of the EU which still comprises sovereign nations, it is hardly surprising that pressures for precision and detail should take place. This is seen as a guarantee of the sovereignty of European nations. This does not mean that it is impossible to write a shorter Constitution. One can easily reduce it to 150 pages by mentioning that the competences of the Union are those developed in the previous Treaties. It is doubtful whether this would represent an improvement.

The age and social composition of the No voters in France and Holland is also interesting. In both countries, the rejection was very strong among manual workers (76 percent in France and 74 percent in Holland). In France, rural areas voted No (61 percent) whereas urban areas supported the Constitution (53 percent of Yes and 55 percent in Paris). There was also a clear age divide in France. Those above 54 supported the constitution (54 percent) whereas age groups below rejected it, in particular those between 18 and 24 (59 percent rejection) and those between 40 and 54 (63 percent rejection).

Some other aspects of the survey were less surprising. Most French and Dutch voters are in favor of European integration. As stated in the media, the No did not challenge the last 50 years of European history. Those who voted Yes voted mainly out of support for European integration. Nevertheless, the enthusiasm for the Constitution was not great. Only 10 percent of those who voted Yes in France and 12 percent in the Netherlands said the latter would help smoothen the functioning of European institutions.

All in all, the rejection of the Constitution reflects less a dissatisfaction with the Constitution than with the economic situation (the contrast between the outcome of the Spanish referendum in a growing economy with the outcome of the French and Dutch referendum in stagnant economies is striking) in general as well as economic fears for the future. Commentators have sometimes drawn the conclusion that since it was mostly a protest vote rather than a rejection of the Constitution, one should therefore ask voters to vote again but this time on the Constitution. This reasoning is flawed. If given the same opportunity to vote in the near future on the same Constitution, it is likely that voters will use the vote to express the same protests. Politicians cannot, and of course should not, control the behavior of voters. The right answer is rather to first address the issues behind the protests before coming back to them with a Constitution project. The protest votes expressed by French and Dutch voters are an indication of the necessity to do something about the lingering European economy.

3 What is at stake?

Given the reasons for the referendum outcomes in France and Germany and the confusion around the Constitution issues, it is worthwhile considering what was at stake in the rejection of the Constitution. This allows us to understand if there is an urgency to move forward fast.

It is worthwhile noting that the Constitution did not contain any major step forward in European integration like the Single European Act or the European Monetary Union. It fulfilled the task of simplifying the multiple Treaties but did not propose any real drastic changes in the catalogue of competences of the Union. A careful status quo has been maintained. There is no question of eliminating the Common Agricultural Policy or of any drastic step forward on defense. This was a disappointment to many for different reasons but there simply was not, and is not at the current stage, a consensus to make any changes to the status quo. This does not mean that such a consensus cannot evolve. The Constitution however gave instruments to the EU institutions to be able to change both the catalogue of competences (Article I-17) and to shift from unanimity rule to a qualified majority rule in certain areas (Article IV-7a). Defense is, however, ruled out from the latter. In other words, the Constitution stated that both competences and voting rules could be changed by unanimity in the Council. I have claimed elsewhere (Roland, 2005) that these flexibility clauses are the most important advantage of the Constitution since it considerably reduces the transaction costs associated with any further move in European integration while at the same time respecting national sovereignty. Another important flexibility provided by the Constitution is that it made enhanced cooperation easier to initiate, something that is also important as a tool to further European integration as it allows a subset of countries to move forward in an area of integration without requiring all countries of the EU to participate.

The Constitution draft indeed aimed mostly at making the decision process more flexible compared to the Nice Treaty and making the EU more democratic by addressing Europe's democratic deficit. Other notable changes were a considerable reduction of the qualified majority rule in the Council (55 percent of Member States and 65 percent of the European population) compared to the Nice Treaty, a generalization of the co-decision rule giving more powers to the European Parliament and the election of the president of the Commission by the latter.[4]

Let us review some other significant changes apart from those 'cleaning up' the Treaties and simplifying the number of legal instruments. A first change was the replacement of the current six month rotating presidency of the Council by an elected president within the Council (by qualified majority) for a mandate of two-and-a-half years, renewable once. Another change was the institution of a European 'Foreign Minister' present both in the Council and in the Commission as one of its vice-presidents. This merges in a single job that of the Commissioner for External Affairs and of the High Representative for Common Foreign and Security Policy. The latter is a clearly desirable objective.

To conclude, the Constitution did not affect the existing catalog of competences of the EU relative to the Member States. It contained significant advances in simplifying the existing rules of functioning of the institutions and to make decision-making easier in a Europe of 25. However welcome these changes would have been, they do not represent drastic changes in the functioning of the EU. They affect the work of the Commission, the Parliament, the Council and EU institutions in general but much of that is perceived by the public as 'internal kitchen' of little concern to citizens. The rejection of the Constitution does not create an immediate challenge to the survival of the EU. The outcome of the referenda had no effect on the stock markets. One can claim that there was some minor temporary effect on the euro but it is debatable. In other words, financial markets do not expect that the rejection of the Constitution will have any major effect in Europe.

In a nutshell, while there clearly has been a missed opportunity to adopt a European Constitution, the failure of this attempt does not create a sense of urgency. This does not mean nothing should be done about it.

4 What are the options for the future?

What are the options on the table with respect to the future of the Constitutional process? Three basic options are available: (1) do nothing and forget about a European Constitution; (2) go back to the French and Dutch voters with the same Constitution and ask them to vote again; (3) go back to the drawing board and make non-cosmetic changes to the existing draft before going back to the voters. Let us examine in turn the advantages and disadvantages of each of these options.

(1) The 'British' Constitutional option: no constitution

This is a real option. The UK has never had a Constitution and has evolved over the centuries from one of the first regimes of separation of powers praised by Montesquieu and others to become one of the world's leading parliamentary democracies. The question is not whether it is better or not to have a Constitution for Europe, the question is rather whether Europe can do without and still evolve in a desirable direction.

A first argument to support this view is that many of the positive changes brought about by the Constitution could be implemented without the adoption of the current Constitution. A good example is that of the EU Foreign Minister. All it takes is the political will in the Council to implement this change. Of course, without a Constitution, this is not guaranteed. However, the Council should play a critical role both in the choice of the High Representative for Common Foreign and Security Policy and the EU Commissioner for External Affairs. It could thus nominate the same person for both jobs. Many other changes, apart from the voting rules in the Council and most legal changes, can be implemented without the Constitution. One of the first reactions of major EU politicians such as Giuliano Amato after the referendum debacle, was precisely to try to pick out which of the innovations of the Constitution could be adopted without its ratification.

Second, one can argue that maintaining the status quo is not as bad as many have stated, one can even argue that it is not bad at all. The most important difference implied by the rejection of the Constitution is that one maintains the Nice rules for qualified majority. It is generally agreed that these rules make it very difficult to adopt new legislation (see, for example, Baldwin *et al.*, 2001). However, it is not necessarily clear why this should be considered a bad thing. Most of the legislation related to economic and monetary integration has been passed (liberalization of services being a big exception) and one is less stuck in the middle of an unfinished process of European integration compared to a few years back. Even though further steps in European integration are desirable, such as progress in defense and security, there is not a consensus right now around these issues and any significant further step in European integration would anyway require unanimity of the Member States. So it is not clear why maintaining the Nice rules rather than the more flexible majority rule of the Constitution would make a big difference. One can even argue that the strong hurdles created by the Nice rules are a protection against possible overcentralization zeal by the Commission.

Third, one has not yet given time to let the Nice rules evolve. One example that has not received sufficient media attention relates to the process of selection of the Commission president and the Commission. An important change brought about by the Nice Treaty is that the Council's proposal for the Commission president must not be approved by unanimity any more but by qualified majority. This reduces the power of individual countries to block a candidate for Commission president. On the other hand, the Members of the European Parliament have never hidden their intention to increase the power of the European Parliament in the selection of the Commission president. The objective is to make the choice of the Commission president analogous to that in other parliamentary democracies. The European Parliament has indeed – since the Maastricht Treaty – the power to veto the Commission. An attempt was made after the 2004 elections. The winning party, the European People's Party proposed Chris Patten as the president of the Commission. This was rejected by the Council that eventually opted for Jose Manuel Barroso. The European Parliament thus scored a defeat here. Nevertheless, a very important event was the EP's threat to veto the Commission to protest against the choice of Rocco Buttiglione as Commissoner for Justice and Home Affairs. This rejection will have wide-ranging consequences in the future. Indeed, for the first time, the EP has been able to overrule the tradition that individual countries impose the name of their Commissioner. After the Buttiglione event, countries still keep the power to nominate their Commissioner but they now know that the EP can veto it. Discussions have already taken place among prominent MEPs as to how the Patten episode could be avoided in the future. One idea that is circulating is that the main party groups could announce, before the EP elections, who their candidate is for the presidency of the Commission. In effect, this is the German rule whereby the top parties announce before the election their candidate chancellor. If this were to happen for the 2009 elections, even though the Council still has the agenda-setting power over the Commission presidency, the Council might feel forced to pick the candidate of the winning party. Indeed, provided the European parties had campaigned all over Europe and given visibility to their candidate for the Commission presidency, the European Council would have to make a very good case for why it would not want to pick the candidate of the winning party. If that is the case, despite its current formal power, the Council's power to choose the Commission president would become comparable to that of the German or Italian president or of the remaining European monarchs. All in all, there is a lot of room for evolution within the changes provided by the Maastricht, Amsterdam and Nice Treaties.

There are of course obvious dangers in abandoning the project of a European Constitution. The first and immediate danger is that of negative momentum that could hurt the still fragile European institutions. One saw this very clearly in the budget debacle following the French and Dutch referendum. It is difficult to tell what would have happened in the event of a successful referendum in France and Holland, but the situation would clearly have been less tense. President Chirac thought he could deflect his own failure on the referendum by calling for a renegotiation of the British rebate, leading the British to retaliate by calling for a renegotiation of the CAP. These points were thrown in at the last minute without serious preparation and made it virtually impossible to reach an agreement in the middle of such improvised moves. Immediately, one heard voices including that of a member of the Italian government to unravel EMU. This did not go very far but is an indication of the negative momentum generated by the referendum outcomes.

A second danger is associated with the holdup power that individual countries or small groups of countries have with the Nice rules. Indeed, efficiency-enhancing and even Pareto-improving pieces of legislation might be vetoed by individual countries unless some other piece of legislation that they favor is also included. This exercise of holdup power has been characteristic of the functioning of the EU under unanimity rule in the past. It imposes costs on the EU as a whole and is a source of inefficiency both in terms of delays in decision-making but also in terms of rents given to the countries exercising their holdup power.

Third, and this is probably the most important disadvantage of not adopting the Constitution, it will be in the future much more difficult to agree on deepening European integration in matters such as defense and security (Berglöf *et al.*, 2003). The London bombings in July 2005 are a clear reminder that the EU needs to think ahead and meet the challenges of the twenty-first century. The London bombings and the threat of radical Islamic terrorism concern all European countries and require the need for an efficient, flexible and accountable European executive that can meet the challenge and rapidly adjust to new situations. Sooner or later, the European public will recognize more and more the need to integrate strong defense and security pillars in the EU. This will again require Treaty changes that must be ratified by 25 countries. Such treaty changes are extremely laborious and the costs of ratifying new Treaties increase dramatically as the number of Member States increases. The Constitution created flexibility for such changes. This will be seen in the future as a lost opportunity.

Fourth, having a Constitution has a power of commitment that one should not neglect. A Constitution is to a nation akin to what marriage vows are to a couple. The common will of having a joint Constitution is a signal of a political willingness and commitment to live together under the same set of European rules. True, a Constitution does not have the magical powers sometimes ascribed to it. Without a sufficient consensus underlying the Constitution, it is nothing more than a piece of paper. However, one can argue that a Constitution has marginal effects that may have important impacts in the long run. The marginal effect of a Constitution is its effect in those situations where the usual consensus breaks down or threatens to break down. In that case, the Constitution acts as an important buffer to solve conflicts in an orderly way based on the written law. This marginal effect does not operate all the time, it hardly ever operates but it does operate in critical moments where the absence of a Constitution might lead to unnecessary conflicts.

Option 2: retake the vote

This option has been expressed implicitly or explicitly by many European leaders and heads of state. It is also consistent with our analysis of the reasons for the No in France and the Netherlands.

The main advantage of this option is that it allows the saving of time and avoidance of a renegotiation of the Constitution that might be more likely to lead to a worse outcome than the current draft. This is coupled with the fact that such an option might very well have a chance at succeeding. Such a scenario is not implausible. The Irish were asked to vote again on the Nice Treaty. So, one can argue that adequate timing might allow the current Constitution to be ratified after all, leaving aside the uncertainty about the outcome of a British referendum, a problem that has been there all along.

There are, however, a number of disadvantages with this scenario. The first and very important one is the risk that the democratic credibility of the EU becomes irreversibly tarnished. The EU suffers from the perception (and the reality) of a democratic deficit which is related to the fact that there are too many layers between the European electorate and the European institutions. European voters simply do not have the possibility to oust the European Commission as is the case in other normal democracies where a majority of voters can change the identity of the executive. European voters face a much more difficult collective action problem than do voters in normal democracies. It is not clear where the EU would be rated on the Freedom House or Polity index! Asking voters to vote again because the outcome of the elections does not please those in power is not worthy of a healthy democracy. It is a shame that it happened in Ireland with the ratification of the Nice Treaty. This was a dangerous precedent that ought not to be repeated. Arguing that the behavior of voters was unrelated to what they were asked to vote on cannot be a good argument to repeat an election. Only electoral fraud or total mismanagement of a campaign could be good arguments for redoing an election. Neither case was present in France (the Dutch referendum fits more the mismanagement story but not necessarily convincingly so). The loss of credibility that would be associated with the move to retake the vote might be permanent and irreversibly damage the reputation of the EU. It would also dangerously damage the reputation of the current political elites in Europe and might foster political instability in many countries.

A second argument is that it is not clear that the current consensus on the Constitution cannot and will not evolve. While it is difficult to argue that the current Constitution draft could have easily been improved upon given the various political constraints faced, there is no good reason not to think that the consensus cannot evolve, albeit slowly. There are obviously areas where the Constitution could be improved but where a consensus fails to exist right now. The right time might be when a consensus can be found to significantly push forward integration on security and defense issues. Also, the Constitution's double majority system of weights (number of countries and number of citizens), while logical and reasonable, might be a true headache in the perspective of Turkey's accession to the EU. With the agreement on the mini-Treaty reached in the Council in June 2007, this option is fortunately excluded provided the intergovernmental conference decided at the Council meeting does not meet an unexpected hurdle.

Option 3: a 'non cosmetic' revision

The third and only remaining option is in a way a painful one because it involves going back to the drawing board and renegotiating the Constitution. This implies a new Convention, a new Intergovernmental Conference and a new ratification process.

There are clear disadvantages to such an option. First of all, it is not clear from the referendum results in which direction to go. French and Dutch voters have not exactly given a mandate to a new Convention on which issues they want revisited. Indeed, dissatisfaction with the economic situation suggests that the latter be dealt with first before presenting voters with a new Constitution project. If the constitutional process is put on its wheels again, it is quite likely that all the arguments that have been put forward by all participants in the debates of the past few years will only be repeated by all sides and it is clear that one would reach a better compromise than the current one.

A second disadvantage is that a revision of the current draft that would be more than cosmetic revision might take a very long time. There is a real danger that the momentum that emerged after the Laeken declaration might be lost. The timing was in a way very good. Participants from the New Member States came generally with enthusiasm and the desire to genuinely contribute to a Constitution that is as good as possible rather than go and defend their country interests. It is not clear whether this positive, deliberative spirit of the Convention can be recreated that easily. If the discussions get bogged down and no progress is made, this is likely to add even more to the negative momentum. Europe would be discouraged.

There are, however, also obvious advantages to such a scenario, the first one being that there are many possibilities for non-cosmetic change. Let us simply list a few: (1) revision of the majority rule in the Council to somewhat mute the population rule (a return to logarithmic style weights – see Widgren and Kirman, 1995 – would be a solution), (2) a shortening of the parts on competences, (3) a bolder move to integrate defense and security, (4) measures to have a truly European party system in European elections rather than have national parties present their lists. Many other items could be added to the list.

A second advantage is that a renewed constitutional process may allow not simply repetition of the steps of the past but the consideration of how to have larger debates within the European populations and to organize large public forums to allow opinions to express themselves. Such a measure seems absolutely necessary not only to reduce the democratic deficit but also to inform more European voters on Europe, to make European institutions more accessible and more readable to them. There is indeed a striking difference between the overwhelming majorities found in parliaments of European nations to approve the Constitution and the referendum results where the population is more divided, even in countries where the Yes prevailed such as in Spain and Luxembourg. A renewed constitutional process should be an opportunity for such large debates.

A third and important advantage is that this is the only way to go forward in the Constitutional process without irreversibly tarnishing Europe's democratic credentials, as discussed above.

All in all, if one weighs the pros and cons of the three options outlined, it would seem that the last argument strongly favors the road of a non-cosmetic revision. Also, the commitment power of a constitution argues against abandoning the idea of a Constitution altogether.

However, this is not sufficient. Many conditions need to be fulfilled to reignite Europe's Constitutional process.

The first one is the necessity of the organization of large debates within civil society, as argued above, before the gathering of new convention. Given the split between Europe's political elites and voters, it is desirable to organize cross-country forums to foster dialog beyond the current narrow European elite and to better involve the European population in debates on the Europe that they want. There should be particular value in having forums involving population groups from more than one country so that Europeans from one country can have dialog with Europeans from other countries and learn to know their way of thinking and their views on European integration.

A second condition is that referenda should be simultaneous and pan-European and they should preferably be linked to European Parliament elections. One of the important weaknesses of Europe today is that Europe-wide issues are decided in national elections. The elections to the European Parliament are organized simultaneously but voters are asked to vote for national party lists rather than for European party lists. There are good reasons for organizing the referenda this way. A first advantage would be that the debates would be synchronized all across Europe. Voters in France would be made to notice arguments made in Germany and vice versa. Voters would better understand that they are voting for Europe-wide issues rather than national issues. Linking the referenda to the European Parliament elections, possibly of 2014, would add to the mobilization and create positive externalities between the two campaigns.

Third, a mechanism must be explicitly provided to allow countries that reject the Constitution to keep benefits from the existing EU while not participating in the decision-making process of the 'New EU'. This is a tricky issue in international law that experts should look into. However, it is quite likely that the referendum will fail in a few countries who may consider rejoining the EU later. However, the existing Treaties should be made to work for them in the event of a rejection.

An important remark is warranted at this stage as to what should be the priorities in the next few years for European institutions. One of the first lessons from the referendum is that voters seem more worried about the state of the European economy rather than about the European Constitution. Going back to the voters with a new Constitution might generate the same rejection if one does not do something about the European economy and give it a strong medicine for growth (see the Sapir Report, 2004). The Lisbon process that was addressing the economic woes of Europe was more or less stalled to give priority to the Constitutional process. It is time to change the priorities and to put economic reform back on the agenda in Europe. The responsibility for doing this falls on national governments. The European Commission has neither the legitimacy nor the mandate to reform Europe's pension systems and labor market systems. However, the EU can be an appropriate forum where countries commit jointly to reform targets and to timetables using the 'Open Method of Coordination'. The EU can thus help the governments who want to move ahead in their reform process. Solving Europe's structural problems and boosting its growth rate should be the priority right now.

5 Conclusion

In conclusion, the referenda in France and the Netherlands have shown the gulf that exists between European voters and EU institutions. That gulf can only be overcome by non-cosmetic revision of the Constitution which is likely to take time. The main advantage of the compromise reached under German presidency is not that closure is reached on the Constitution, but that the issue of the Constitution is put aside for the moment while Europe grapples with other more urgent issues for the welfare of European citizens.

The referendum outcomes have mostly shown the dissatisfaction of European voters with the status quo and the absence of economic reforms that would do something about sluggish growth and high unemployment in Europe. These economic problems must start to be dealt with seriously before one can hope to ratify a new European Constitution.

Notes

1 I thank Jeff Frieden, Dennis Mueller and Jean Pisani-Ferry for their stimulating comments.
2 People were allowed to cite more than one motive so that the numbers add up to more than 100 percent.
3 If we interpret this consistently, it means that they feared that the Polish plumber would take away jobs from French workers but they seem quite keen at the same time on using EU funds to finance the unemployment benefits of Polish plumbers in Poland.
4 The latter change is more ambiguous and can be interpreted as a continuation of the status quo where the president of the Commission is de facto chosen by the Council and the EP ratifies.

References

Baldwin, Richard, Erik Berglof, Francesco Giavazzi and Mika Widgrén (2001) 'Nice Try: Should the Treaty of Nice be Ratified?', *Monitoring European Integration* 11, London: CEPR.

Berglöf, E., B. Eichengreen, G. Roland, G. Tabellini and Ch. Wyplosz (2003) *Built to Last: A Political Architecture for Europe*, CEPR series, Monitoring European Integration, No. 12, London, 2003.

Roland, G. (2005) 'In praise of the European Constitution', in *Designing the New EUropean Union* edited by H. Berger and T. Moutos, Cambridge, MA: MIT Press.

Sapir, A, Ph. Aghion, G. Bertola, M. Hellwig, J. Pisani-Ferry, D. Rosati, J. Vinals, H. Wallace, M. Buti, M. Nava, P. Smith (2004) *An Agenda for a Growing Europe. The Sapir Report*, Oxford: Oxford University Press.

Widgren, M. and A. Kirman (1995) 'European Economic Decision Making: Progress or Paralysis?', *Economic Policy* 21: 423–460.

19 From accidental disagreement to structural antagonism

The US and Europe: old and new conflicts of interest, identities, and values, 1945–2005

Michael Gehler[1]

1 Introduction

Europe is older than the United States of America, but the history of the US pre-dates that of the European Union. Both histories are hardly conceivable without their specific developments and mutual influences. The history of American unification is of course older than that of European unification. Nevertheless, informative comparisons may be made, even if different circumstances must correspondingly be taken into account.

Our topic is therefore extremely multifaceted. The historic change in relations between the EU and the US from cooperation during the Cold War to estrangement and confrontation after the end of the Cold War will be depicted here on the levels of alliance, security, trade, and economic policy. The discussion will thus cover political cultures and mentalities that in many ways lay submerged or were consciously covered up during the Cold War but came to light after its end. This analysis is complicated by the fact that in contrast to the US, the EU cannot be viewed either as an independent participant or as one that puts up a united front with a single opinion, and the various European states (for example, France and the United Kingdom) have had and continue to have diverging political interests in relation to the goals of the US.

2 Parallels and differences in the constitutional histories of the US and EU

The Gulf Crisis of 2001–02 and the invasion of Iraq in 2003 have also obscured the commonalities, similarities, and parallels in the histories of the founding of the US and the EU.[2] The US, which came into being in the eighteenth century with four million citizens, and the enlarged EU, which in 2004 had 455 million inhabitants but lacks a single common language, hardly seem comparable.[3] And the EU, because of its unique institutional structure, cannot mutate into some kind of 'United States of Europe', a term that is often attributed to Richard

Coudenhove-Kalergi or Winston Churchill. The circumstances of the 'EU convention' of 2002/03 were nevertheless comparable with the convening of the Constitutional Convention in Philadelphia on 21 February 1787. The EU faced the same dilemma as the Americans, namely connecting the model of confederation with that of a federal structure. The founders of the United States did not see themselves as 'Americans'. For the 'union citizens' of Europe, a feeling of European attachment and loyalty was and is underdeveloped. The US Constitution left open the question of the borders of the individual states and examined the possibility of new states joining on a case-by-case basis, similar to the EU, which is also not territorially fixed but has requested the guarantee of and adherence to the 'Copenhagen Criteria' (1993) from the candidates for accession.[4]

Neither the old US confederation (1777–81) nor the US under the federal constitution that replaced it can be equated with the central state of the European type (France, Great Britain, Italy, or Spain) which lacks the openness to federalism that existed in both US models. The gravest shortcoming of the EU consists of the absence of a second chamber of parliament. Without the additional chamber of the Senate, there would have been no United States. The demographically smaller states felt themselves backed up against the wall by the larger states, just as Luxembourg, Austria, Finland, and Sweden today. The United States' response was the equal representation of all members through two legislators in the Senate.[5]

In contrast to the Bill of Rights (1791) and the Thirteenth Amendment to the Constitution on the abolition of slavery (1865), the European Charter of Fundamental Rights (2000) was already established and was ceremonially declared before the proclamation of a European constitution.[6] The role of the European Court of Justice in the development of community law as the basis for a future European constitution comes quite close to that of the US Supreme Court in interpreting the US Constitution.[7] A comparison of the US Federal Reserve Bank System and the European Central Bank (ECB) reveals a substantial difference, however. While the United States only succeeded in having a central monetary authority 126 years after the adoption of the Constitution, the European monetary union was already realized in advance. The structure with governors of the Federal Reserve Bank and the ECB are, nevertheless, quite similar. Although the political decision-making processes may be comparably lengthy, the United States is still ahead of the EU with regard to the speed of implementation. Whether or not the convention process of the EU will lead to a comparably efficient chief executive is questionable.[8]

3 Old shared interests in the Cold War era

Integration by US intervention and the rescue of the European nation state

The formation of blocs in the West (the Organization for European Economic Co-operation, or OEEC, in 1948 and the North Atlantic Treaty Organization,

NATO, in 1949) was followed by the formation of blocs in the East (COMECON in 1949 and the Warsaw Pact in 1955). These combinations were to rule on the continent for decades, until 1989–90.[9]

As Werner Abelshauser noted, the integration of Western Europe is inconceivable without US support of self-help for West Germany and for Europe in general. This was the state of affairs for long stretches of time after the inauguration of the Marshall Plan in 1947–48.[10]

The twentieth century has been described as 'the American century', and the rise of the US has been closely associated with Europe's decline.[11] But Western Europe's re-ascent could only have been possible with American assistance. Militarily through its troop presence and economically with the European Recovery Programme (ERP)[12], the US had become a dominating factor on the western portion of the continent, even to the point of being a European power or, as Tilman Mayer puts it, for a long time a 'European guarantee force that keeps the balance in the process of European integration as a whole'.[13] Viewed in this way, European integration served within a larger containment concept as a substitute peace treaty for Germany. Hanns Jürgen Küsters called this an 'integration peace'.[14] The European associations and pressure groups advocating a (Western) European federation during 1946–48 acted to a large degree in the interests of the US and were at times also financed by the CIA.[15]

The character of Western European economic integration as an attempt to restore the European nation-states[16] – that is, only establishing supranational structures on a restricted basis – was completely in keeping with American national security interests.[17] A unified, politically independent, and strong Europe did not correspond to the interests of either the United States or the USSR. The 'Reconstruction of Western Europe 1945–51'[18] was closely connected with the implementation of the European Recovery Programme (ERP) but not linked with a US concept for a unified federalized and politically strong whole Europe. As a purely intergovernmental organization, the OEEC that was formed on 16 April 1948 guaranteed the distribution of reconstruction funds. But an orientation of Europe to a single constitution was not one of its objectives. The Council of Europe, founded on 5 May 1949, also could not fulfil the hopes and wishes of the European federalists and constitutionalists.[19]

NATO (1949), as an expression of transatlantic military integration,[20] was of far greater significance to the US than either the European Coal and Steel Community (ECSC – 1952)[21] or the European Economic Community (EEC – 1958).[22] In any case, Article 5 of the North Atlantic Treaty did not provide for any automatic (that is, unconditional and compelling) mutual assistance clause as did Article 5 of the Western European Union (WEU).[23] The US apparently did not want to enter into commitments and obligations that were too far-reaching with regard to Europe, as was the case with the WEU in 1954–55.

Different interests: FRG, France and UK

The 'Adenauer Republic', which was completely Western in orientation and ultimately integrated into NATO, was 'America's Germany', as Thomas A. Schwartz called John McCloy's relationship to the Federal Republic of Germany,[24] and an 'occupied ally', as Hermann-Josef Rupieper once called it.[25] It was the most important ally that the US could ever wish for in the Western Europe of the first Cold War (1949–55).

The United Kingdom, with its 'special relationship' to the US,[26] also played an important role. Foreign Minister Ernest Bevin made very clear what Great Britain wanted to be: 'A World Power as opposed to a purely European Power.'[27] But the years from 1951 to 1955 proved to be Winston Churchill's 'last campaign' and his 'last defeat' in the Cold War (John W. Young)[28]: There was no equal partnership with the US. The UK now wanted to instrumentalize the Europeans and the EEC for its own interests, that is, to also prevent or at least counteract the deepening of core-Europe.[29]

For the American Secretary of State Dean Acheson, it was clear that 'The key to progress towards integration is in French hands, even with the closest possible relationship of the US and the UK to the continent, France and France alone can take the decisive leadership in integrating Western Germany into Western Europe.' This would be 'the last chance for France to take the lead' in the event that 'Russian or German, or perhaps Russian–German, domination was to be avoided'.[30]

From the point of view of American power, France would serve as a promoter and leader of European integration while the UK could serve as a protagonist in order to apply the brakes to the speed of Europe's integration. Great Britain first ruled out membership in the European Coal and Steel Community and thus initiated its abdication as Europe's leading power, which it then, as a further consequence, had to cede to France.[31] After the failure of the project, it was left only with a reduced free trade zone, the European Free Trade Association (EFTA – 1959–60), which sealed the trade policy split of Western Europe.[32] With its conflicting and varying posture of 'using Europe and abusing the Europeans' (Wolfram Kaiser),[33] Britain's policy towards Europe, with a clear priority towards enlargement, was of no little use for America's policy towards Europe.[34]

The Eisenhower and Kennedy administrations had a relatively unambiguous position with respect to the EEC which was supposed to serve their geostrategic interests and act as a bulwark against communism. An association with the neutrals was therefore opposed, as it was feared that it might water down and weaken the EEC.[35]

De Gaulle was aware of his leading role in Europe when he twice refused Britain's acceptance into the EEC by exercising the veto (1963 and 1967). The British were not ready to give up their 'special relationship' with the US with regard to the policy on nuclear weapons and to integrate the French into a trilateral atomic force, which caused de Gaulle to ally himself more closely with

Germany. De Gaulle's first veto of 14 January 1963 was spectacular as he denied the British their chance in Europe.[36] German–French-rapprochement intensified and Cold War cooperation in arms procurement followed.[37]

Commonalities

What conflicts of interest really existed between Europeans and Americans? It is helpful to first mention the commonalities: there were agreements between Americans and Europeans in the defeat of Nazi rule *and* in the suppression of a Germany that was overly powerful, as well as in the economic reconstruction and the democratization of the political life of Europe, especially in the countries of the former Axis powers and their allies. There was agreement on the importance of defence against, the containment of, and the repelling of Communist–Soviet threats, on the liberalization of trade within the Western European and Western-global spheres (OEEC and the General Agreement on Tariffs and Trade, or GATT, respectively), on the intra-European balance of payments with the European Payments Union (EPU), on the closing of the dollar gap and the convertibility of European currencies (EMS), on cooperation within the Organization for Economic Co-operation and Development (OECD),[38] on the normalization of international relations and in the process of reducing tensions (the Conference on Security and Co-operation in Europe, or CSCE), but also on the implementation of the NATO two-track decision ('double resolution') as well as in the ending of the Cold War in Europe.

It was clear from the very beginning of NATO's existence that there would not be only a single containment. The intention was to practise a triple containment, as was noted internally by the former NATO Secretary General Lord Hastings Lionel Ismay, 'To keep the Russians out, the Germans down, and the Americans in'.[39]

When viewed in this way, one may speak of a broad-reaching convergence of the political objectives of the states of Western Europe with those of the US. These consisted of a definitive solution to the problem of Germany through control and integration – for the West the subject was the obstruction of the neutralization of a unified Germany, which had repeatedly been suggested by the Soviet Union – and in the continuation of the economic integration of Western Europe as a bulwark against Communism. It was clear that the neutralization of Germany would be the end of NATO in Europe.

Would a unified and politically strong whole Europe – as has been formed today after the EU enlargement to include the central and eastern parts of the continent – have been in the interests of the US? Beate Neuss has thrown up the question of whether during the years from 1947 to 1957 the United States could be seen as 'Europe's midwife'. According to Neuss, it was and acted accordingly. The US practised a European policy of 'integration by intervention'.[40]

From a National Security Council perspective, an independent Europe as a sort of 'third force' was not an acceptable US goal. Rather, Western Europe was seen as part of the US empire which, as described by Geir Lundestad, served as an 'empire by invitation' as well as an 'empire by integration'.[41]

In spite of the different military capacities, there was, in view of the common enemy in the East, a basis for communication and coordination: at the end of the 1960s, NATO came to an agreement on a comprehensive strategy based upon the Harmel Report, named after Belgian Foreign Minister Pierre Harmel, which unified both offensive and defensive elements. The alliance carried out a policy of military deterrence that was nevertheless closely connected with elements of détente.[42] In so doing, both American and European security policy objectives were served. After the USSR's intervention in Afghanistan in 1979, an additional important consensus could be found in the subsequent NATO double resolution (1982), even though this was already very controversial in Europe.

The aforementioned results completed the agreements with regard to the Western European–American policies of interest up until the envisaged central goals had been reached: in the wake of the arms race with which it could not keep up, the Soviet empire first splintered (1989–90) and then collapsed (1991), Germany reunited peacefully (1990), and the Warsaw Pact and COMECON dissolved (1991). Germany remained politically and economically integrated into Western Europe.

Apart from the significance of security policy, the increased relevance of the transatlantic society of communication, especially the importance of trade and commerce between EU Europe and the US, must be emphasized. In 2003, half a million air passengers crossed the Atlantic every day, while 1.4 billion e-mails were sent across the Atlantic Ocean. Around one million telephone calls were made. Foreign investment was and is the centrepiece of transatlantic economies, which are enormously dependent upon one another. Every day in 2004, more than $2 billion changed hands between Europe and the US. Forty per cent of this took place within multinational corporations that are located on both sides of the Atlantic. Although the EU and the US together make up no more than 12 per cent of the world's population, they produce nearly 40 per cent of the global gross domestic product.[43]

With a population of 293 million, the US is behind that of the EU which, after the enlargement of 1 May 2004, was now home to 454 million people. In terms of area, the US with its 9,583,000 km^2 (3,700,000 square miles) is more than twice the size of the EU with its 3,885,000 km^2 (1.5 million square miles). At 5.2 per cent, the unemployment rate in the US was significantly lower than that in the EU (8.9 per cent in 2005). And Europe is older than the United States: the proportion of the population over 65 is 12.4 per cent in the US, compared with 16.3 per cent in the EU. Life expectancy is the same, and the gross domestic product is about equal: $11 trillion in both the US and the EU.[44]

Differences of opinion and selective conflicts in Western European–American relations were not inconsequential. Just how far these extended into the fundamental structural long-term basis still needs to be determined. What appears certain, though, is that conflicts surfaced publicly only for a relatively short period and, with a view towards the more important goals of the Cold War, were soon swept aside once again. Western Europe and the US were in the same camp in a way that they no longer are today.

4 Old clashes of interest in the Cold War era

The old clashes of interest also partially exist in the new Europe, but they are mixed with a new potential for conflict with differences that are more difficult to resolve. Considered from an historical perspective, they consist of questions of the structure of European integration. One example of this was the intensely debated European Defence Community (EDC) that failed in August 1954 due to resistance from France, which no longer wanted to give in to pressure from the US. Efforts by the Western Europeans that had until then been made to create their own security framework were regarded in Washington with a mixture of willingness for cooperation and assistance along with, however, a generous dose of mistrust and suspicion.[45]

There was also the manner, pacing, and implementation of decolonization that, in the same year, was vehemently pushed by the US in the Indochina War of 1954, while the European powers continued to maintain their colonial stance as, for example, during the Suez Crisis in 1956. Later on, the dispute was about the participation of the Western Europeans, above all else the West Germans, in the Vietnam War (1957–75), with serious points of difference between Richard Nixon and Ludwig Erhard as well as the cooperation and involvement in nuclear policy with the Multilateral Nuclear Force (MLF). The latter culminated in the nuclear partnership being brought into question by Charles de Gaulle and by French command structures that were detached from NATO.[46]

Divergences and conflicts also came into existence through disarmament talks which led to the controversy surrounding the creation of a nuclear free zone in Europe; this played a considerable role, especially outside of the EC core of Europe. The 1957 'Rapacki Plan', with its various later versions in the 1960s, promoted by Polish Minister for Foreign Affairs Adam Rapacki, is worth mentioning here. A complex of problems later arose around embargo policies and technology transfers towards the East in the final period of the Cold War. This hard-line stance also influenced non-EC countries like Austria[47] and Sweden which did not always act as secret allies of the West when Washington wanted them to participate in a boycott of strategic goods against the USSR.

The initiative by Valéry Giscard d'Estaing and Helmut Schmidt for the creation of a European Monetary System (EMS) in 1978–79 was an attempt to bring European monetary rates closer to each other, to create a common basket of currencies as the core for a future single currency, and in so doing to throw off the yoke of the dominance of the US dollar. On the monetary level, this was a noteworthy attempt by Europe to emancipate itself.[48]

These differences of opinion between Western Europeans and Americans were articulated over the course of the various phases of the Cold War in the form of differences in political mentality, political culture, and values. These were swept under the rug again for reasons of loyalty, compliance, and solidarity within the transatlantic alliance. They then disappeared from public discussion and thus also, to a large extent, from public opinion.

5 New clashes of interest after the end of the Cold War

The decade after the officially proclaimed end to the Cold War (1990–2000) – which really only ended in Europe with the 'Charter of Paris' – brought dissent between the US and Europe back to the forefront. In the meantime, signs of a structural antagonism had developed, as had the beginnings of institutional drifting apart or dichotomies between the EC or EU states and the US. The change from the old EEC and the younger EC to the new EU was referred to as 'cautious revolution.'[49] That was associated with three different areas: developments after 1989 during the period of 'liberty revolutions' in Europe,[50] developments in the US during the conservative revolution, and developments in the world associated with the new globalization and Islamic revolution.

Foreign and security policy: growing divergences

In matters of foreign policy and security policy, the US has continued to reject a genuine European security policy. Deputy Secretary of State Lawrence Eagleburger argued that no matter how strong the EC became, the role of the US in Western European affairs should not be reduced. 'The president will remain the pre-eminent spokesman for the free world in the decade ahead,' he said in 1989. In November 1991, George Bush made it known that, with regard to Europe's defence, the EU would never make the US obsolete. 'If our premise is wrong – if, my friends, your ultimate aim is to provide independently for your own defence, the time to tell us is today.'[51]

At the end of the 1980s, the US tried to link the question of troop withdrawal from the continent with disputes over trade issues. But in the 1990s, Europeans could not be put under pressure with such a policy. The European allies realized very quickly that they had won more manoeuvring room. German Foreign Minister Klaus Kinkel pointed out in 1996 that 'the end of the cold war' is also 'the end of taking things for granted in the transatlantic alliance'. According to Wolfram F. Hanrieder, American hegemony in Western Europe then declined.[52]

The Europe (of the EU) after 2000 was different from the Europe (of the EC) in 1989 in which the fear of a new and restrengthened Germany dominated. This fear dissipated as a result of the further integration of Germany through the Treaty of Maastricht (1993),[53] in the face of technological and economic stagnation at the end of the Helmut Kohl era, so that the question poses itself today: what is to become of Germany and of EU Europe? How is the 'Eastern enlargement' to be financed given prevailing economic and financial relationships? After the fall of the Iron Curtain, a second Marshall Plan was not seriously considered by the US for the countries of Central and Eastern Europe, but the Eastern enlargement of NATO that was successfully implemented in the medium and long-term very much was. Security and military integration (meaning influencing Europe via NATO) was even more important for the US than the economic and political integration (emancipation) of Europe.

This was first of all provided within the framework of the Western European

Union (WEU) which, with the Treaty of Maastricht, was to have its status enhanced. As in the cases of the Common Foreign and Security Policy (CFSP) or the Common European Security and Defence Policy (CESDP), the bid to become independent alongside NATO was assessed negatively by the US.[54]

We have arrived at a remarkable, indeed even paradoxical contradiction: Washington repeatedly complained about Europe's lack of military capacity and the inadequacy of burden sharing, yet at the same time asserted its opposition when thoughts turned towards setting up independent European security structures.

(Fair instead of free) Trade and money

The EU home market that was developed to a certain degree in 1993 already made US economic circles sit up and take notice. With the European Economic Area (EEA) that entered into force in 1994, Western Europe was the strongest and – in terms of production – largest economic area in the world. *Fair trade* was now demanded from the Americans instead of the principle of *free trade* that had been championed up until that point[55] – precisely as a result of the strong economic relations, trade policy interconnections, and transnational corporate cooperation between the New and Old Worlds.

Europe was perceived differently by the US in the World Trade Organization (WTO) than had been the case in GATT. In the European Recovery Programme and GATT,[56] the US had been represented more as a European power *in Europe*; in the WTO, it appears today to be a former European power (with greatly reduced troop presence on the continent) that stands *outside of* or *next to* Europe. Within the framework of the WTO, a vehement and bitter trade war has raged for years.[57]

The implementation of Economic and Monetary Union (EMU) was at the time (1999) a major alarm bell for financial circles in the US. The supremacy of the dollar – which, in spite of currency turbulences in the 1970s, managed to strengthen its position as the leading global currency – seemed to be threatened by the introduction of the euro (2002). With this step, the EU became a challenge for the US.[58] With it, the predominance of the dollar has been loosened, if not broken. The ascent of Europe to being a world power as described by Walter Laqueur[59] was, however, a development that had already begun previously. It is no wonder, then, that in the area of military and security policy, views diverged further.

If an even more far-reaching consensus was reached between the US and Europe after Saddam Hussein's attack on Kuwait, and then in the Kosovo conflict and the beginning of the war against the Serbian part of Yugoslavia in 1999, there were already major irritants not only among the European alliance partners but also between the transatlantic alliance partners, irritants that would only escalate during the Iraq crisis of 2001–02 and in the Iraq War of 2003. NATO's continued existence was seriously called into question for the first time. The unconcealed aspirations of the George W. Bush administration for American hegemony increased the alienation with 'old Europe', a term used by US Secretary of Defense Rumsfeld in January 2003.

6 September 11 as a catalyst of the estrangement

The attacks on the World Trade Center and the Pentagon on 11 September 2001 initially produced sympathy with the victims and brought about 'unrestricted solidarity'. But with regard to background and causes, they then led to different evaluations in Europe and the US. The danger of terrorism was assessed differently. The debate surrounding the question of how to proceed acted to accentuate divergences.[60]

Foreign and security policy: different evaluations

Exporting democracy, rule of law, security, and stability to endangered regions in order to prevent insecurity and instability at home, was the strategy of the European Communities, especially with enlargement towards the south in 1981–86, but also with the enlargement encompassing Central and Eastern Europe in 2004.[61] This strategy presupposes the will to eliminate inequality, to level out differences in affluence, and thus to eliminate the causes of dictatorial systems and political extremism. With such a strategy, the US too would be able to attack the root of terrorism. But while on one side, Washington has stepped up its military budget and accumulation of weapons of mass destruction, the EU states rely more upon soft power strategies (diplomacy, foreign aid, trade and economic sanctions, cultural dialogue, etc.). It is not by chance that the EU, as far as foreign aid is concerned, is a global *payer*, in contrast to the US, which is a global *player* in the area of nuclear missiles and high-tech armaments. In the year of the Iraq War, the 'defence' budget of the United States was larger than the total defence spending of the next twenty-five industrialized countries combined. In 2003, American military outlay amounted to 395 billion euros annually, as compared with 160 billion euros for the 15 EU states.[62]

The issue of burden sharing between NATO and the EU states became more pressing in view of the potential for international conflict. After 11 September 2001, the urgency of the question of burden sharing increased. This was particularly the case after the war against the Taliban regime in 2001, which was already politically difficult to push through in Europe, and the subsequent operation in Afghanistan. From the European perspective, not only has military action in non-European regions been called increasingly into doubt, there have also been questions about the political objectives.

September 11 had only a short-lived effect upon European solidarity with the victims of the attacks and with the US. The broader consequences brought to the fore the structural differences between the larger EU states and the United States.

As much as NATO, through its enlargement to the east and southeast of the continent, could be seen on the one hand as a possible shoring up of Europe and, on the other hand, as a trust-building measure between the EU and the United States, the Anglo-American military intervention in Iraq in 2003 revived the structural antagonism between the US and the majority of the continental

European states. In the conflict between, on the one hand, a European multilateralism of civil societies and, on the other hand, American unilateralism oriented towards armaments building, as has been manifested in the Third Gulf War, it would appear that in the long term, a possible compromise may lie within the framework of the United Nations. But the Bush II administration has not favoured the UN.

September 11 and the Iraq War once again made it clear that the EU, in spite of the painful experience of passivity and incompetence during the Balkan wars (1991–95 and 1999), had not found a common foreign and security policy, nor could its strategic interests be defined in the intervening period. That was not America's fault; nevertheless, the accusation of 'unilateralism' provided a scapegoat. In military terms, the United States is a superpower, and the EU states once more seemed nearly powerless. It is therefore not surprising that the discussion was about Hobbesian America and Kantian Europe.[63]

During the Balkan crisis in the 1990s, Europe's military incompetence and paralysis of security policy became clear. The EU states were not able to formulate a common position, nor were they capable of acting effectively on the military level. During this time, the majority of the population in the West supported an American intervention. Against this background, the US saw itself compelled to intervene twice (in Bosnia and Herzegovina in 1995 and in Kosovo in 1999). In the Middle East, greater engagement by the US was repeatedly called for by the European side. This also took place against the background of a further military technology lag in relation to the US. As a result of the poor economic situation in Europe and problems with the fulfilment of the convergence criteria concerning the European Monetary Union (EMU), an increase in the defence expenditures of the EU states at the end of the 1990s and the first years of the new millennium was not to be expected. More and more, the EU states seemed to be fare dodgers on the US military policy bus. Therefore, since 1989–90, the highly unequal distribution of the burden in defence and security policy provided increasing potential for conflict in transatlantic relations. But it also came to light through the Iraq War that Europe was not as weak and powerless as it seemed, nor could the US act as powerfully and independently as it wanted. It was and is not in the position to put the world in order alone, let alone to govern alone, and consequently it is dependent upon allies.[64]

'*Either you're with us or you're against us': the new American* '*democracy*'

The US position on the Iraq crisis was 'either you're with us or you're against us'. The violation of international law led to irritations and ill feelings in Europe. In 2002–03, the failure to sign the environmental protection agreements at Kyoto, the imposition of import duties on steel from Europe, the rejection of the International Criminal Court in The Hague,[65] the incarceration of more than 600 alleged terrorists at Guantánamo Bay in Cuba in violation of human rights and international law, the announced intention of acting against Iraq even without a UN mandate, and differences of opinion on the Middle East conflict increased the alienation between the individual states of EU Europe and the US.

The PATRIOT ('Providing Appropriate Tools Required to Intercept and Obstruct Terrorism') Act of 26 October 2001, associated with a massive limitation of civil rights and liberties, was a first warning signal of the curbing of generally accepted forms of freedom and liberty. Attorney General John Ashcroft demanded that the Patriot Act be made into law within three days. When that period of time expired, he made the members of Congress responsible for any terrorist attacks that could take place while the law was under discussion.

The Guantánamo detention camp that was set up in 2002 – with its prisoners held far from their homeland, without legal counsel, due process, a trial, a sentence, and any prospect of an end to their incarceration – became a symbol of the 'undemocratic policies' of the Bush administration and the US widely lost credibility as a leading force of democracy.[66]

7 The Iraq War as the low point of a severe crisis in relations at all levels

Different conjectures have been made about the background of the Iraq War. It was often assumed that the US had sought this clash because of its need for oil. But it was more about the need for control of access to this raw material which gave the US a means of exerting pressure upon Asia and Europe. The age in which only the US, Europe, and Japan were economic powers has been relegated to history. The industrial dynamics and economic ascent of China increased the competition for resources, which has driven up prices for raw materials, above all for oil and copper. With the continuation of the liberal policy of economic reform by India, a shift in the world economy towards Asia has been predicted.[67]

Split within the EU and loss of importance of NATO

Making access to Iraqi petroleum for others more difficult or preventing it altogether was one of America's intentions. If, against the background of September 11, the military attack against the Taliban in Afghanistan seemed justified and legitimate, then a military intervention against Saddam Hussein seemed far less so. While the Kosovo crisis of 1998–99 was able to delay a drifting apart of the Atlantic alliance, the Iraq crisis of 2002–03 prevented a common European security policy and caused a split within the EU states and a marginalization of NATO.[68] Denmark, the United Kingdom, Italy, Spain, Portugal, Poland, the Czech Republic, and Hungary sided with the US and supported its attack against Iraq, while France, Germany, Belgium, and Luxembourg reacted negatively. The neutral states were also more or less on the side of the latter. Viewed this way, there was, in the words of Ludger Kühnhardt, in addition to the 'hot war in Iraq' also a 'cold war within the West'. America's war in Iraq had been justified by weapons of mass destruction: 'This policy of the USA was fed not with hate, but rather with fear. That was underestimated in Europe. Moreover, it still is not understood that at its core, the new challenge for the world order is not just an intellectual creation of the neoconservative ideologues around President Bush. It is rooted in the sense of living of the vast majority of Americans, no matter what their political orientation. These components, too, were and are underestimated in Europe.'[69]

The initiative for the development of independent military structures for the EU that was pursued by Germany and France against the background of the Iraq War led to suspicion on the part of US leadership. America's ambassador to NATO, Nicholas Burns, viewed this as 'the most serious threat to the future of NATO'. Part of the background of the conflict was the diplomatic pressure by the US on Great Britain to block German and French plans for more military cooperation, which London repeatedly portrayed as exaggerated. France's Michel Barnier, European Commissioner for Institutional Reform and Regional Policy, emphasized that European defence would also be in America's interest. The conflict needed to be 'dedramatized'.[70]

In March 2003, American–French relations had hit rock bottom. Washington and London waged war against Iraq without the approval of the United Nations. Chirac had attempted to prevent this war on three levels. *First*, he rebuked the Eastern European states that had shown solidarity with Bush with the words, '*Ils auraient mieux fait de se taire*' ('They missed a good opportunity to keep quiet') and not without reason, particularly since they contravened the principle of a common European foreign and security policy. *Second*, France blocked an application in NATO for military aid to Turkey that was desired by the US. *Third*, France led the faction against the war in the UN Security Council along with Russia and China. National Security Advisor Condoleezza Rice could not hide the disappointment of the State Department. Her reaction was, 'Punish France, ignore Germany, forgive Russia.' Relations between the two countries remained cool until June 2004, when on the occasion of the festivities for the 60th anniversary of the Normandy invasion ('D-Day'), a more conciliatory tone was adopted.

French–British rivalry and the Turkish refusal

French–British relations from 1950 to 1990, which were anything but conflict-free, represent a revealing field of research. Until 1972, France achieved the exclusion of Great Britain from the European Communities and thus enjoyed its hegemony on the continent, while the United Kingdom attempted to maintain a sort of hegemonic position outside of Europe – in vain, since the US had long since grabbed this position. If the periods of the Schuman Plan and the ECSC (1950–65) as well as the period when de Gaulle was in office (1958–69) are relatively well researched, this cannot yet be said of the following decade. With frustrations among the Europeans, above all on the part of France under Jacques

Chirac, the conflict surrounding Iraq in 2002–03 might possibly also have had to do with the French no longer being able to carry out a hegemonic policy à la Bush.[71] While Great Britain under Tony Blair was 'blessed' with this hegemonic policy in which it actively took part during the war, Paris rejected involvement, in a manner reminiscent of the severity of the irritations during the Suez crisis of 1956.

If France therefore formed the spearhead of the resistance against participation in the war against Iraq, then the refusal by Turkey to be the deployment zone and staging ground was the real surprise from a NATO partner that had always been dependable, if not submissive. Ankara forbade Washington to use its territory and thus prevented the opening of a northern front against Iraq. Even the attempt to bribe the Turks was not successful. Ankara insisted upon \$32 billion in the form of a US aid package,[72] which was then even too much for Washington. In the end, the Turkish parliament did not give the green light for the staging of US troops. The loss of this aspiring EU member in the alliance supporting US military intervention and the costly transfer of the US 4th Infantry Division from the north to the Gulf region was a serious defeat for the US and a real expression of the 'coalition of the unwilling'.

The power of states and empires has as a rule corresponded to their level of economic strength. At the end of President Ronald Reagan's term in office, the US had an enormous budget deficit. Paul Kennedy compares this combination with the situation of Great Britain before 1914. The peak had already been reached without it yet being completely recognized. Kennedy views the US policy in Iraq as 'appalling mistakes': 'The president's advisors made both military and political mistakes, and now we are paying a high price for them.'[73]

Seldom has the contradiction between, on the one hand, the demand for a policy of democracy and human rights by the US and, on the other hand, the realities of the politics of power and resources so come to light as during the Iraq War, which approached an American *Götterdämmerung*. The Europeans saw themselves proven correct in their mistrust and scepticism of America's war policy. When Bush declared war on terrorism, he also used this as an excuse to wage war against Iraq. When statements by his administration – according to which a link existed between Saddam's regime and Al Qaida, and weapons of mass destruction being stored in Iraq – turned out to be problematic and false, the President curtly declared that the US had invaded Iraq in order to establish democracy there. This set the rest of the world against the US. The fact that for some time after the first Gulf War there had been Swiss, French, and German contacts and deliveries of nuclear know-how for Saddam's nuclear armament industry may indeed create a guilty conscience on the part of European states, but it does not change anything in the misrepresentations and suspicions contained within US policy in relation to Saddam.

New EU foreign and security doctrine and disputes about steel trade

Within the framework of the Italian presidency of the Council of the European Union in the second half of 2003, the issue was not only the establishment of the competencies of EU institutions on the one hand and between the union and the member states on the other. It was also the attitude of EU Europe towards the deployment of military force against the background of the war in Iraq which forced the EU to reconsider patterns of behaviour for crises of that sort. The reform process resulted in a draft which saw the European Parliament emerge as the clear winner vis-à-vis the Commission. In addition to the tangible forms of democratization, intergovernmentalism was asserted with respect to the supranational body of law. The application of military force in international relations was among the most important subjects for discussion in the new EU security doctrine. In the end, it placed the priority on diplomacy and consequently upon peaceful settlement prior to the use of arms, thus asserting the German and French positions. The original version had left more room for military 'preventive strikes', while in the end, the discussion was more about 'preventive engagement', that is, conflict avoidance through a combination of diplomatic, economic, trade, and security means that provided for military force only as a final resort. Germany insisted that every reference to preventive strikes be deleted from the text. The use of force in international relations remained unresolved. In the course of the debates, the 'potential' danger that came from weapons of mass destruction was downgraded. But an 'effective multilateralism' was the aim. 'We do not want any security doctrine that copies the view of the US. We are not going through this exercise in order to satisfy the Americans.... We have drawn up this document because it comprises the European worldview,' remarked a seasoned German diplomat. On 12 December 2003, the EU heads of state or government meeting in Brussels adopted the security doctrine formulated by the High Representative of the Common Foreign and Security Policy, Javier Solana. Critics referred to the modest means of exerting pressure short of military force. EU diplomats explained this as resulting from the absence of an EU foreign minister and the lack of authority, as well as from the institutional weakness of the EU with its presidency changing every six months.[74]

In security policy, the main point of discussion was the firm establishment of an EU obligation for mutual military assistance. Although this was originally suggested by the Italian presidency of the Council, it did not come about owing to the reservations and misgivings of the neutral and alliance-free states (Ireland, Sweden, Finland, and Austria). A clause emerged which was non-automatic, that is, the requirements for solidarity in the security and military area could be made dependent upon national considerations and, in so doing, watered down. Thus, in the case of war or defence, the alliance-free states could, even with reference to another EU member, fall back upon reservations with regard to the common European foreign and security policy.[75]

In the case of the battle against terrorism, dubious regimes, and the proliferation of weapons of mass destruction, the EU states, in their resolutions of 12 December 2003, committed to common operations. It was decided to build up the EU military committee and to create an independent EU planning office. In the meantime, the EU had already taken over the international police mission in

Bosnia and Herzegovina and the NATO peace mission in Macedonia, as well as outside of Europe within the framework of Operation Artemis in the Bunia region in the Democratic Republic of the Congo. More recently, in its dealings with the Iranian nuclear weapons programme, a European security policy has become apparent. Not only Germany and France, but also Great Britain worked in combination here. Prime Minister Blair followed the core European line and, unlike Bush, did not count Iran among the 'axis of evil'. With this, London's new rapprochement with Paris and Berlin became apparent.[76]

Given intense irritations in the context of America's war against Iraq, the dispute over steel trade in 2002–03 aroused the attention of the media. In March 2002, the US had raised tariffs by up to 30 per cent on steel imports in order to provide the US steel sector with a three year breather. The EU threatened punitive tariffs and complained to the WTO which, in March 2003, declared the tariffs to be illegal, a decision against which the US lodged an appeal. In November of that year, the WTO rejected this appeal and authorized punitive tariffs, whereupon President Bush abolished the tariffs in December 2003. Washington explained the cancellation as resulting from the recovery of the industry. The background was, however, more complex: it included protests by the US steel processing industry (including automobile manufacturers) and the American government's fear of sanctions. The EU, Japan, China, and other countries had already threatened sanctions and successfully complained about the tariffs before the WTO, which had granted the EU the right to raise $2.2 billion per year in retaliatory tariffs beginning in the middle of December. The EU nations already wanted to apply the leverage to the so-called 'swing states' upon which the 2004 American presidential election would depend, for example, on citrus fruit from Florida, where the 2000 election was decided.[77]

Emancipation from NATO or strengthening of the former alliance?

At the NATO summit in Istanbul on 28 and 29 June 2004, Jacques Chirac let Bush know that there would no longer be a blank cheque for US military strikes. 'We want to be partners, not servants,' he declared, articulating a position for the future of NATO. With regard to the insistence of the US for the EU to accept Turkey as a full EU member as quickly as possible, the French president replied that meddling 'in internal [European] affairs' was not welcome.[78] Was the US outside of Europe? Was the time of the US as a European guarantee power over? The alliance remained split. There continued to be no common NATO action in Iraq. The NATO mission in Afghanistan was threatened with failure. Since the Iraq controversy, a continued policy of military intervention was subject to more intense discussion.

A few days before the official transfer of power in Iraq, the US and the EU agreed the support of the interim government in Baghdad. At the EU summit in Ireland, Washington and Brussels agreed to help with the elections planned for the beginning of 2005. According to a declaration, both wanted to help with the debt reduction of Iraq. George W. Bush let it be known that 'the bitter differences over the war are over'. However, thousands of people peacefully demonstrated against the US President with the slogan 'Stop Bush'.

Western Europe is not Central and Eastern Europe. That became especially clear with regard to security policy and transatlantic relations. The expansion of the EU by ten new states to a total of 25 members on 1 May 2004 intensified differences within the union. NATO's 'Eastern enlargement' formed the security flank of the subsequent economic and political integration of the candidate countries. Above all else, it enlarged the American zone of influence in Central, Eastern, and Southern Europe. At the same time, with regard to the future European security policy, this led to a division into pro-American and US-critical EU states. The enlargement of the EU in 2004 strengthened the 'transatlanticists' in the union, particularly since the new EU members (Poland, the Czech Republic, Hungary, Slovakia, and the Baltic nations) had strong leanings towards the US for historical and anti-Russian (that is, security) reasons. Through this, the pro-NATO states (Great Britain, Italy, the Netherlands, and Spain) appeared to receive more support than the 'autonomists' (Belgium, France, Luxembourg, and Germany under the Red–Green coalition). The realization of a common EU defence policy as well as a foreign and security policy will almost certainly be delayed by this lasting split.

8 Bush visit to Europe and failure of the EU Constitutional Treaty ratification 2005

After the 2004 election victory by Bush against the Democrat John Kerry, who had far more sympathy in Europe, a continuation of the 'conservative revolution' was to be expected in the field of American domestic and foreign policy. The dangers that were feared in Europe as a result of this election consisted of continued US interventionism and isolationism. The lesson from the Iraq War – a 'mistake'[79] in the view of the historian Gordon A. Craig – was, however, clear and unambiguous: the US would hardly again be in the position to act as unilaterally as it had done in 2001–03. The war against Iraq, but above all else its occupation, extracted such a high price in blood and money that Bush could not continue his policy of preventive strikes.

Against this background, it came as no surprise that the re-elected president showed a change in attitude towards the EU states. On the occasion of Bush's visit to Europe in February 2005, talk was of the beginning of a 'new era' in transatlantic relations. But assessments and expectations were in any case so exaggerated as to be out of touch with reality. There continued to be fundamental differences of opinion between the various EU states and the US in the area of the decision on war and peace; on the question of the restructuring of the future world order; and with regard to international trade.

Decision-making on war and peace

In the area of ensuring peace and in the matter of the eventuality of possible military conflicts, four potential areas of conflict emerged.

First: in the dealings with *Iran*, Germany, France, and the United Kingdom pursued a soft power strategy with incentives and negotiations in order to prevent the Iranian leadership from putting its nuclear enrichment plans into operation, while the US favoured tougher action all the way to a preventive strike.

Second: with regard to *Iraq*, Great Britain, Italy, Poland, and others stood by the side of the US, while Germany and France opted against a military presence. A European concept for reconstruction was lacking for the time being. The impression that the EU was apathetic or passive towards the problems in Iraq was, however, erroneous. In 2003 and 2004, it contributed €320 million toward reconstruction. For 2005, the Commission suggested paying €200 million for the establishment of public services, jobs, the fight against poverty, and the reconstruction of civil society. In 2003, the EU states had promised additional financial means to the extent of more than €1 billion. Furthermore, EU money was to be provided with the restoration of law and order as well as for the elections.

Third: irreconcilable differences developed on the question of lifting the European arms embargo against *China* which had been imposed after the suppression of the student protests in Tiananmen Square. The US saw Europe as encouraging the People's Republic in its hostile actions against Taiwan. Europe was interpreted in Washington as counteracting America's policy of stabilization in Asia.[80] In March 2004 Javier Solana, EU's top foreign policy official, spoke of the evolving 'comprehensive strategic partnership' between China and Europe. European leaders made no secret of the fact that China is their most effective counterweight to US hegemony. France held its first joint naval manoeuvres with China.[81]

Fourth: different priorities resulted in the Middle East policy. As a result of the conflict between Ariel Sharon and Yasser Arafat, the positions of the US and the EU also hardened. Not least as a result of the strong Zionist lobby in the US, America stood firmly behind Israel, while the EU states backed the demands the Palestinians. For a long time, the US had avoided both compelling Israel to adhere to the UN resolutions that provided for withdrawal from occupied territories and the speedy realization of a Palestinian state. After the death of Arafat, a new opportunity opened up for the peace process. The United States, with its Israel policy in tow, must prove its credibility.

Future world order, trade, Southeast Asia, drop in dollar value and the Airbus-Boeing race

With respect to the *United Nations*, the US showed little willingness to pay its membership dues for the world organization (millions are due) and to take it seriously, especially politically. At the 60th anniversary of its founding in San Francisco on 26 June 2005, the absence of the Americans was conspicuous. The Europeans wanted to extend and strengthen the UN. The call by Germany for a seat on the UN Security Council, which Bush neither rejected nor supported, seems unrealistic, just as a reform of the UN without the US also appears impossible.

In the area of *climate protection*, the US, as the world's largest energy user and polluter (especially with CO_2 emissions) continues to refuse to sign the Kyoto Protocol. The US uses approximately one third more energy than the Europeans, even though the EU has 165 million more inhabitants. Now that the protocol has come into force, this also means a competitive disadvantage for the EU signatories. Because of this, further conflicts can be expected.[82]

Clashes on trade policy are nearly routine. The Bush administration protects the US economy through *subsidies* and *punitive tariffs*, which is why a series of complaints have been filed with the WTO. In reference to export subsidies, the US yielded in 2004 with a new proposed statute, but the EU did not want to halt the sanctions until it had entered into force. With regard to meat with hormones, the EU maintained its import ban. It had fulfilled WTO conditions, but the US nevertheless levied punitive tariffs to the amount of $165 million per year, about which the EU complained to the WTO. In the area of *genetic engineering*, the EU import ban was dropped because harm to health could not be proven. The US attacked the labelling requirement which the EU introduced in place of the ban.

Although these sorts of trade squabbles gave rise to coverage in the media, they accounted for no more than one per cent of bilateral trade. 'Ninety-nine per cent goes smoothly,' reported EU Trade Commissioner Pascal Lamy, former cabinet head for EU Commission President Jacques Delors (from 1985–94). He was, however, concerned about the exploding budget deficit of the US, which made vigilance necessary with regard to possible protectionist measures.[83]

Trade with Southeast Asia (Brunei, Burma, Cambodia, East Timor, Indonesia, Laos, Malaysia, the Philippines, Singapore, Thailand, and Vietnam) has provided the EU and the US with a fascinating race for more than a decade. Between 1990 and 2002, trade volume between the EU and the ASEAN nations grew from €37 billion to €101 billion (an increase of 200 per cent), while the trade volume between the US and the ASEAN nations increased from $45 billion to $117 billion (an increase of 160 per cent). Both the EU and the US have trade deficits with the ASEAN countries (imports of 6.3 per cent of GDP and exports of 3.9 per cent for the EU, and imports of 6.0 per cent and exports of 4.2 per cent for the US respectively). While the US is striving for bilateral free trade agreements, the EU is looking for multilateral arrangements. From the military and security standpoint, the EU has no chance to pit itself against the US position in Southeast Asia. In any case, a European-Southeast Asian dialogue exists which can be viewed as a constructive contribution to the fight against terrorism.[84] In addition, the European Court of Justice is perceived very positively as a possible exporter of law.

The rapid drop in the value of the dollar in the wake of Bush's war policy led to reactions by central banks which wanted to reduce the portion of the US currency in their reserves. So far there is not much evidence of this. The issuing banks of Asia are no longer willing to finance America's debts and are turning more to the euro. China, Japan, and South Korea, the reigning powers of the Asian currency markets, agreed on the sidelines of the ASEAN summit in Laos in December 2004 to cooperate more closely on currency issues. Joint action ought to strengthen their position with respect to the US. In February 2005, the South Koreans announced that in the future, a larger portion of their currency reserves would be invested in Europe, whereupon the value of the dollar dropped. At the same time, the exchange rate of the Russian ruble was linked to a basket of currencies consisting of the euro and the dollar. It still consisted of 90 per cent dollars, but this is scheduled to fall to 50 per cent in favour of the euro.

Technical development also contains areas of competition and conflict. For example, in the dispute over support for Boeing and Airbus, a compromise appears to be possible: if the US is the leader in the area of high technology of warplanes, then the Europeans hold that position in civil aeronautics. It is not without reason that a dispute has erupted between the EU and the US over assistance for aircraft manufacturers. Washington maintained that the Airbus subsidies amounting to €15 billion. Support is higher than a treaty from 1992 allows, according to which no more than one third of the development costs may be subsidized. In 2004, both sides filed complaints against each other with the WTO, but in the beginning of 2005, they then attempted to reach an agreement through negotiations. But in the end, the dispute flared up again. EU Trade Commissioner Peter Mandelson suggested successive reductions in the subsidies for both Airbus and Boeing in order to defuse the dispute.[85]

US request for help

In the wake of Bush's visit to Europe, the media was already talking about a 'transatlantic thaw', even though a change in relations was not recognizable. The friendliness of Bush concealed a 'request for help'.[86]

The request may have resulted from multiple threats to the US after September 11: *first*, from the overextension of its own sphere of power and the increases in intervention costs associated with it; *second*, from the need for energy and resources, which continued to grow; *third*, from the loss of or lack of support from allies (Germany, France, Turkey, etc.); *fourth*, from an increasing lack of success in cultural integration with respect to the Asian area and Islamic-dominated regions; and *fifth*, from the spread of nuclear weapons, including to rogue states such as North Korea or even to terrorist factions. On top of that, it became clear that the US could no longer simultaneously control several flash-points nor carry on several preventive wars.

Zbigniew Brzezinski, former US national security advisor, reckoned that a genuine improvement in relations could 'only come about gradually'. Before Bush's visit to Europe, he warned of a deepening rift between Americans and

Europeans. Brzezinski referred to the US position of emphasizing common burdens but making decisions alone, while the Europeans demanded common decisions but left the burdens up to the US. He characterized a split between the EU and the US as a 'form of madness'. 'The result would be more global unrest and difficulties. In the short term, probably more for America than for Europe, but in the long term, presumably more for Europe than for America.'[87]

In spite of a great deal of demonstrative paying of respects and exchanges of pleasantries, Bush's European trip in February 2005 did not contribute to any decisive overcoming of the differing views on fundamental issues. The working meeting with Chirac and the heads of state and heads of government of the EU and NATO showed that a great deal of mistrust was still concealed behind the unity put on display. The two sides were 'just different,' commented France's former foreign minister Hubert Védrine on American–French relations: Europeans and Americans had not drifted apart since the end of the Cold War. Rather, the period of the Cold War had just concealed fundamentally different interests.[88]

All the same, Bush and Chirac issued a joint declaration in which Syria was called upon to withdraw from Lebanon. In matters concerning actions in the nuclear conflict with Iran, the planned lifting of the arms embargo against China, and climate policy, the two statesmen agreed to disagree.[89]

Worsening of US–German relations and French double strategy

With the end of the Cold War in Europe (1990) and the withdrawal of Russian troops from East Germany and Berlin (1994–95), Germany and Europe have gone 'out of business' for American geostrategic and security policy. Although there were still around a quarter of a million American soldiers in Germany in 1989, by August 2004 only approximately 73,000 remained (57,000 land forces and 16,000 in the air force). In the summer of 2004, it was also emphasized that the largest American troop transfer since the end of the Cold War of soldiers who had been stationed in Germany was not a punitive action because of Germany's 'No' to the Iraq War (as the conservatives in the United States Congress had demanded) but rather took place against the background of a worldwide restructuring of US units in accordance with the goal of more mobile, more flexible, and smaller troop segments and special units in view of the 'danger of terrorism'. The Pentagon justified realignment that had already been planned before the Iraq War not only from Europe but also from Japan and South Korea in the direction of Eastern and Southeastern Europe by referring to their proximity to possible Asian trouble spots. What was targeted was above all the resource-rich Black Sea and Caucasus region. The eastern enlargements of NATO (1999 and 2004) were the crowning conclusion of the Cold War in Europe that had been won through the policy of the alliance.[90]

German–American relations have been tense since 2002. The Red–Green coalition rejected the Iraq War. During the election campaign, Schröder had declared that Germany would not participate 'in any adventures'. When Minister

Justice Herta Däubler-Gmelin (of the Social Democratic Party) compared Bush's Iraq policy with the methods of Adolf Hitler, Condoleezza Rice characterized relations with Germany as 'poisoned'. Däubler-Gmelin had to resign, but the bell could hardly be unrung. After the end of the Iraq War, both sides made efforts at normalization. Although the German government refused any military engagement in Iraq, it did agree to the training of Iraqi policemen and soldiers in the United Arab Emirates. In Afghanistan, Germany with its 2,200 soldiers represented the largest troop contingent after the US. In contrast to Bush, who characterized NATO as a 'vital institution', Gerhard Schröder had judged NATO to no longer be 'the primary location at which the transatlantic partners consult about and coordinate their strategic ideas' and thus was a source of irritation both for the Pentagon and the State Department.[91]

The French pursued a double strategy. The return to an integrated NATO Supreme Command, which Paris had carried on since the middle of the 1990s, showed that it was with self-assurance that France desired a new alignment of transatlantic cooperation. It placed its generals at the head of the NATO operations in Kosovo and Afghanistan. At the same time, France pushed for greater recognition of the 'European pillar'. It thus made a clear distinction between NATO and EU values. A high-ranking French diplomat stated that the alliance must not become a miniature UN Security Council.[92]

Double standard in nuclear politics

The narrow degree to which the US knows how to bring a moderating and controlling influence to bear upon, and intervene in, the proliferation of nuclear weapons materials, as well as being at the same time caught in a multipolar relationship of dependency with regard to nuclear weapons, became noticeable in the Review Conference of the Non-Proliferation Treaty (NPT) that took place in New York when, on 27 May 2005, no agreement was reached on a Final Document. The US supported the viewpoint of Israel but was not successful with its position towards Iran.

Another future area of competition can be recognized in the conquest of outer space. The EU has an ambitious plan with its Project Galileo. Beginning in 2008, 30 satellites are to make possible a precise overview of events in the world. In that context, it will be necessary for Europe to overcome its dependency upon the US global positioning satellite system. In this connection, the involvement of the Russian Federation and China with test satellites and financial support for Galileo are worthy of note.

The failure of an EU Constitutional Treaty

The European Union still has much more to accomplish at home. With the subject of union citizenship, which has not really come to life since the Maastricht Treaty, it finds itself in a growing crisis of legitimacy.[93] The EU Constitutional Treaty, which was concluded by the 25 heads of state or government in

June 2004 under the Irish presidency of the Council of the European Union, was rejected in referenda by the French population on 29 May 2005 and the Dutch population on 1 June 2005. As a result, ratification was called into question. Luxembourg's presidency of the Council in the first half of 2005 reacted with a decree for a pause to reflect. In any case, crises in the history of European integration are nothing new. They have led to rethinking, have prompted compromises, and have stimulated new approaches.[94] Therefore no strong reasons exist for raising the question of 'apocalypse now' and talking about the 'end of Europe'.[95]

American reactions varied. Those who did not wish for a politically powerful Europe expressed derision and malice, while those who had hoped for a strong EU as a partner alongside the US reacted with dismay and anxiety. At a meeting with EU representatives in June 2005, President Bush gave an indication that he considered the second option to be the desirable one. But up until now, a militarily autonomous EU that acted with political unity did not lie in the interests of the US. In that respect, it was suggested that the rejection or delay of the ratification of the EU Constitutional Treaty strengthened the emphasis of American policy on NATO as the instrument of European security. Associated with the negative votes in France and the Netherlands is the consequence of a further division of Europe, such that greater cooperation in the security sector of the Common European Security and Defence Policy in core Europe is improbable for the time being. Europe will not be a great military power a lofty sense of foreign policy mission in the near future; nor will there be a US without double standards, messianism, and hypermilitary power.

9   Ways out of a crisis in relations? Summary and additional identity analysis of the different political cultures

Since the Bush II administration took office, the relationship of the European public to the US has been characterized by a complete inversion of attitudes, feelings, and judgments. During the Cold War, it was the Americans who were able to break Stalin's blockade of Berlin in 1949 with the airlift. John F. Kennedy was still being celebrated for it years later. His use of the phrase '*Ich bin ein Berliner*' as standing for a 'free Europe' is legendary. At the same place in 1988, the widely cheered Ronald Reagan challenged, 'Mr. Gorbachev, tear down that wall!' In contrast to this is the (Western) Europe-wide potential for demonstrations and protests against the US that has existed since 2002. The personal security of George W. Bush on his trips to Europe in 2002 and 2005 could only be guaranteed by a colossal contingent of police and a gigantic apparatus of his own security agents travelling along with him.

During his visits to Europe, Bush declared that he harboured no bitterness against Chirac, who had been the most prominent opponent of the Iraq invasion. But he also called into question Chirac's idea of a world in which a united Europe could represent a counterweight to the US. 'Why,' he stressed, 'if we share the same values and goals?'[96] But is that really the case?

Different identities, political cultures and historical experiences

A study of the *Realpolitik* alone would not be able to explain the ferocity of transatlantic irritations and conflicts at the beginning of the twenty-first century. Attention would also have to be given to the history of ideas, identity, and culture in order to better understand the disagreement. Both approaches would have to be integrated with each other in order to increase the possibilities for insight. At first glance, the American terms of 'democracy', 'freedom', 'free market', and 'human rights' appear to be identical and not in conflict with those of Europe. But in practice, there are massive differences.

The differences between France and the US are worthy of note. In contrast to Great Britain, Spain, and Germany, France has never waged war against the US. The especially severe condemnations between Paris and Washington in 2002–03 were thus all the more astonishing. One reason why Paris and Washington argued so vehemently was the fact that both nations have developed an ideological and moral sense of mission and make demands for political structuring that range far beyond their borders. Both take special credit for the spread of modern democracy and place great value upon the recognition of this moral and political 'higher quality'. A competitive situation has arisen in the struggle between them to define moral superiority.

More recent differences of opinion on Iraq policy between France and the US probably have more to do with the different formations of national identity since the eighteenth century than with the diverging political interests. Both states derive their legitimacy and the identities that grow from it from their founding documents (1777–81 and 1787 for the US and 1789–91 for France) in which the separation of state and religion takes on a primary significance. There was an important difference in the US, namely, the protection by the state of the exercise of religion. The fact that France does not have such a protection and is uninterested in granting one also affects its treatment of religious minorities. Tensions that result from this, especially with regard to the large Muslim minority, also explain France's attitude with regard to the war on terrorism that was proclaimed by the US and the occupation of Iraq in which French units have not been involved. Old differences in the attitude towards the role of religion in politics may likewise explain opposing political positions, such as the acceptance of membership of Turkey in the EU.[97]

The historical overview has shown that between 1945 and 1990 as well as later on, a multitude of European–American disagreements were present when France did not agree with the US. In these cases, the rest of (continental) Europe often did not share the opinion of the US while the United Kingdom repeatedly took the side of the United States. Italy and Spain also followed the British in the Iraq War.

The conflict surrounding the Iraq War was not about different political interests that are superficial, change rapidly, and can disappear by themselves. Rather it was primarily based upon structural conditions that remain relatively unchanged (dispositions of mentality, systems of government, and experiences in history). The issue in this regard is (1) really about the different identities and attitudes of Europeans and Americans, (2) about different political systems and political cultures of North American and European democracies, and (3) about different historical experiences.

With regard to point (1): because there is no one central government in Europe, the tendency when reacting to a problem is to intensely analyse and consider it before implementing a solution. On the other hand, in the US, by virtue of its concentration of power and wealth of resources, there is the inclination to focus complete concentration upon the task to bring about a rapid solution.[98]

With regard to point (2): neither the US government's decisiveness and speed of reaction nor the European nation-states' complicated, cumbersome decision-making processes are conducive to implementing an effective foreign service or a common security policy.

With regard to point (3): while the 'American dream' emphasizes the success of the individual, the European counterpart gives preference to the public good, which is based upon the different demographics, histories of development, and spaces of the two continents. The immigrants to America came from Europe in the eighteenth and nineteenth centuries during the final stages of Protestantism and in the early days of the Enlightenment, which emphasized the central position of the individual. Both ideologies took their 'founding fathers' from Europe and maintained them in the puritanical form. As engaged Christians and Protestants of the industrial world and passionate champions of capitalism and the nation-state in one, they had to fend for themselves from the very beginning and were forced to organize their survival without societal support. In far more densely populated Europe, Protestantism and the Enlightenment remained in a relationship of tension with the older feudal aristocracy as well as with Catholicism and paternalism, which were oriented towards the mutual commitment and responsibility of a far more hierarchical society. The European Middle Ages, with lineages and families, papacies and empires, monasteries and Lateran Councils, professions and guilds, etc. had a far more intense effect upon the EU Europe of the twentieth century than has been assumed, as Michael Mitterauer has shown.[99]

The year 1968 with its student unrest had far more broad-based societal repercussions and mental effects in Europe than in the US. It was not only about the calling into question of authoritarian patterns of thought and elites, but rather also about a peaceable way of life that mobilized neutralist-pacifist currents at the beginning of the 1980s against the implementation of the NATO Double Resolution.

Through long stretches of the twentieth century, Europe, as a result of dictatorships, totalitarianism, expulsions, mass murder, and repression, was partly (in the words of Mark Mazower) a 'dark continent'.[100] The collective memory of the aerial warfare which was borne primarily by the civilian population – and not only in Germany! – is very much alive. The military generation was traumatized in many ways by the experience of the Second World

War. These consequences of a culture of memory that spans more than 50 years, 'a mixture of Christian image of man, the philosophy of the Enlightenment, anti-totalitarianism, democracy, and human rights led to a free market economy and social responsibility' and consequently also to different assessments of reality on the two sides of the Atlantic.[101]

Against this background, the European democracies are rather tendentially oriented towards negotiation, mediation, and reconciliation, with an emphasis on diplomacy, dialogue, and multilateralism. An internal balance of interests is also reflected in an external reaching of consensus which may lead to indecision or inflexibility, and is interpreted as weakness and inability from the American point of view.

Better understanding, but different US–EU political doctrines remain

Responsibility for heightening the structural antagonism between the EU states and the US must rest more on the American side. The end of the Cold War, the disappearance of the ideological antipode of the USSR, and the behaviour of the sole remaining economic and military superpower, which mutated from a hegemonic power to an imperial one, generated new conflicts of interest. What was decisive was not differing interests but rather a lack of communication and the absence of mutual understanding of the other side's political culture.

The political consequences have been dramatic. It was not the rapid disintegration of the alliance against terrorism that formed in the wake of 11 September 2001 – which would not have held together for long without that event – but rather the intensified decline of the Atlantic alliance that was one of the most spectacular consequences of American foreign policy under George W. Bush. The low point was reached with the American war against Iraq. During the time of the Cold War, there had been transatlantic clashes and tensions. The Suez Crisis of 1956 and the withdrawal of France from the integrated NATO command in 1966 have already been mentioned. The debates surrounding the deployment of medium-range missiles at the beginning of the 1980s and the Balkan wars – in particular, the problems in the conflict in Kosovo (whose status remains unsettled to the present day) – are further examples. The transatlantic differences surrounding the Iraq War are, however, without precedent with respect to their extent, intensity, and, for the time being, their pettiness. The Bush government was reproached for having missed an historic opportunity to lead NATO into a new era. It was only after the fact that it corrected its mistake by transferring the command of the International Security Assistance Force (ISAF) that was deployed in Afghanistan to the alliance. However, the reconstruction there is still to come, a chain of events that will make a rethinking of US trade and development policy necessary for the entire region. In Iraq, there was and is no (united) NATO presence to take care of internal security.[102]

Ronald D. Asmus, Europe expert in the State Department under President Clinton, developed a strategy for overcoming the transatlantic rift, based on the idea of America giving way and Europe connecting. The US would have to treat

Europe as a first class partner and advocate a strong, united, and pro-Atlantic Europe. The impression would have to be done away with of carrying out a policy of division with respect to the 'old' continent. On the other hand, the insistence of the EU to go its own way and to behave as a counterweight to the US is dangerous both for transatlantic relations and for European integration. 'Any attempt to consolidate Europe as an anti-American base is doomed to split the continent.... A European policy of the counterweight is the right recipe for bringing about a split of Europe from the US. No American politician, no matter which school of thought to which he may belong, would agree to restrict a partnership with Europe for the sake of American freedom of action'.[103]

Think tanks on both sides of the Atlantic are running at full capacity in attempting to develop suggestions for a new relationship between the US and the EU. The Centre for European Reform (CER) in London and the Brookings Institution in Washington have enumerated what would be necessary in order to patch up the rift: in a 'strategic dialogue' in which the US would listen to the objections of the EU on the Iraq issue. In return, the EU would train 5,000 Iraqi officials and 29,000 policemen annually. The US would support the talks which the British, Germans, and French have been carrying out with Iran. The EU would declare itself willing to punish Iran if uranium enrichment is found there. The 'Pact between the USA and Europe' was signed by the former British foreign secretary, Sir Douglas Hurd, and the historian and political scientist, Timothy Garton Ash.[104]

The consequences of the Iraq War made clear the complex interdependence of the economic relations between the US and Europe as well as their mutual dependency and vulnerability. It was recognized with Bush's visit to Brussels in February 2005 that the Americans were more dependent upon the Europeans than the other way around.[105]

The consequences of US policy have already begun to have effects: during Bush's term of office, Russia has at minimum doubled its military spending, tested new missiles, and built better nuclear weapons. The Russians once again carried out large-scale manoeuvres, as did China. The air force of the nuclear power Israel is technologically further developed than that of any other NATO member with the exception of the US.

During the Cold War, it seemed that common views and values were shared by the US and EEC/EC-Western Europe in the areas of democracy and human rights. But the appearance was deceptive. After 11 September 2001, a rift opened up in these fundamental matters. With the EU coming together more strongly, commitments among EU members with regard to the common corpus of legislation of the union also grew. Along with this, a greater conflict in solidarity with the US also came into existence.

Hypothetically, the US would not be able to join the European Union because it would not meet the common EU corpus of legislation. The gap in political culture between EU-Europe and the US is large.[106] Undivided relationships of rule and exercise of power of the indirectly representative presidential democracy and unrestrained financial transactions dominate the political culture of the

US far more than that of the EU states. Through these 'values', Europe has in the end experienced more of an 'Americanization' than the US has an 'EUropeanization'. The majority of EU states have directly democratic systems of government with stronger civil society components and share a common EU corpus of legislation ('acquis communautaire') as well as the Copenhagen Criteria of 1993 which, for example, make the accession by Turkey more difficult, if not impossible, even though it has been able to be a member of NATO since 1952 without any problem, in spite of violations of human rights and minority rights as well as military coups.

The European development of international law, with the sort of critical inquiry of Hugo Grotius of the true authority that determines what a 'just war' is, does not have any comparable tradition in the US. Grotius's fundamental work *De iure belli ac pacis* (1625) found its way into the Treaty of Westphalia in 1648. His ideas, which were detached from the influence of organized religion, ended the controversy surrounding the 'just war' and based the regulation of international relations on state sovereignty, whereby international law was established as one of the principles of the equality of states, while a legal system that was characterized by reciprocity was established as an institution. The trailblazing codification took place at the end of the nineteenth and beginning of the twentieth centuries with the Hague Conferences in Europe, not in the US. The US under the leadership of George W. Bush broke with this foundation of European legal history in 2003 with the Iraq War, after both the Europeans and the Americans had jointly violated these principles in the course of the Kosovo crisis and the air war against Yugoslavia in 1999.

Different understandings of sovereignty likewise played a role during the Iraq crisis. The US has a far more flexible idea of the state and of changing its borders than either the EU or its individual countries. There is a degree of sovereignty which the individual EU countries are not prepared to give up or even allow to be infringed upon. The issue with the American intervention against Iraq also had to do with the sovereignty of an independent state which, in contrast to the US, a number of EU states wanted to see respected. This was also expressed on the issue of specifying the tasks of the UN weapons inspectors on Iraqi territory which had always been settled and agreed upon with the Iraqi national leadership under Saddam Hussein. For some Europeans, the war against Iraq was a problem above all because it was an attack on the sacrosanct principle of state sovereignty, the retention and safeguarding of which seemed to take precedence over the rights of the Iraqi people.[107]

The strong mixing of state, nation, and religion that has grown over centuries in the US has also led to an increased estrangement with Europe and even to a tendency not to show solidarity on the part of a number of EU states. The Iraqi crisis made the limits of solidarity clear,[108] particularly since in the matter of religiosity, a clear drifting apart has set in. Forty-eight per cent of people in Western Europe almost never go to church. It is not only the practical exercise of religion that has diminished but also the belief in God itself. While in recent decades, above all after the end of the Cold War, there has been a de-Christianization in Europe, a re-Christianization has set in within the US. In comparison to Europe, twice as many people in North America participate weekly in religious ceremonies. Hardly an American can be characterized as an atheist, compared with 15 per cent of Europeans. Like Max Weber in his essay on Protestant ethics and the capitalist economic system, US economists Robert Barro and Rachel McCleary reached the conclusion that religion influences economic outcomes through convictions concerning work ethic, honesty, thriftiness, and openness towards strangers. Longer workdays and weeks and less vacation time are the decisive causes for the greater labour input in the US. Another difference is recognizable with violence against individuals and criminality: the number of murders is four times higher in the US. One quarter of all prison inmates in the world are in US detention centres.[109]

The Bush doctrine amounts to an 'America first doctrine' of an unlimited exercise of power which contains nationalistic and jingoistic elements. EU doctrine, on the other hand, if there even is such a thing at all, is a self-restricted and delimited concept of the division of rule and the granting of power. The separation of powers in international relations has top priority. In the meantime, the EU has also turned into a community of common values, but up until now, it has not understood how to 'sell' this to the European public.

The collapse of communism in Europe and the Soviet Union in 1989–91 overshadowed the growing alienation and differences between European and American political cultures. After the end of the Cold War, a lack of interest and feeling of apathy by the US towards Europe set in. This went hand in hand with a growing tendency by Europeans to 'emancipate' themselves from the US. US foreign policy in the Iraq War revealed itself to be security policy and a policy of securing resources. The fact that massive profiteering was in play was likewise obvious.

Within the 'transatlantic alliance', the Iraq conflict indeed appeared to be more the expression of a structural antagonism than of an accidental dissent. This structural antagonism was expressed in a foreign policy chasm correlated with a growing consciousness of a difference in values (respect for human rights, the environment, willingness for international solidarity, prevention of conflict through non-interventionist military strikes, submission to supranational decision-making structures, etc.). Therefore Harald Müller is fully correct when he speaks of a '*transatlantisches Schisma*'.[110]

This structural antagonism is expressed in a growing asymmetry of power between the EU and the US that is accompanied by an increasing strategic divergence. Through the arbitrary decision-making of George W. Bush and his circle of power (Dick Cheney, Donald Rumsfeld, Paul Wolfowitz, and others), this antagonism has intensified.

The question is whether the EU as a 'preventive world power' (as Werner Weidenfeld calls it)[111] can prevent a 'second Vietnam'. The economic and political problems within the EU's own space are already large (the requirements for stability in the Balkans and their ultimate entry in the EU, the pacification of the united continent, the westernization of Russia, its own constitutionalization, etc.). But added to these are how long the alienation between the Old and New

Worlds will remain and what consequences can result from it. Predictions about this are hardly possible. And that also cannot be the task of a historian.

Historical judgement

If Western Europe's relations with the US during the Cold War lay between partnership and conflict, then the relationship between a number of EU states and the US after the end of the Cold War (1990–2005) clearly lies more on the side of conflict than of partnership. It is clear in retrospect that transatlantic relations have been far more important for the US than European integration has. Washington has also never really been ready for a supranational *transatlantic* integration; rather, its center of focus has been its own national security interests.

The suffering, tragedies, and catastrophes of the nineteenth and twentieth centuries in Europe (emigration as a result of famine, impoverishment, and mass misery against the background of Manchester capitalism in the nineteenth century; recession, economic crisis, and unemployment in the 1930s; and persecution, expulsion, and destruction against the background of fascism and Nazism and as a consequence of both world wars which, once again, began as European wars) have led in Europe to the desire for balance, mediation, and peace.

The European yearning for peace is very old[112] and was betrayed during the Iraq crisis. Since at least the nineteenth century, the United States had become the land of the future for millions of Europeans. During the Cold War, when differences in values had not been so clearly brought to light, something akin to a common Atlantic destiny came into existence. This defined the perspective of Western Europe to the US while the political division of the continent deepened. (Soviet) Russia turned into an adversary, while the prospects of the Far East were summarized by the motto 'North Atlantic instead of Asia'. In place of the fixation upon the US, it may well be that in the twenty-first century, the 'return to Asia' is the 'need of the moment' for Europe.[113] In the struggles of world powers, the issue in the end is not Europe's independence from the US, which, against the background of the globalization of communications technologies and economies, is no longer possible, because both sides need each other and, in the event of a split, would also lose more than they would win. The issue is Europe's *political* self-assertion.[114]

Notes

1 The author would like to thank Professor Ron Hassner of the University of California, Berkeley for a provocative and stimulating comment which was very helpful in finalizing this chapter.
2 See the interesting reflections by Henningsen (1997).
3 Hitchcock (2004); Gehler (2005).
4 Burghardt (2002), p. 8.
5 Ibid., pp. 3–8.

6   Gruber (2005).
7   Höreth (2005).
8   Burghardt (2002), pp. 3–8.
9   Calleo (2001), pp. 87–110.
10 Abelshauser (1981, 1984, 1989); Maier and Bischof (1992).
11 Bischof (2001).
12 Hogan (1987).
13 Argued conclusively and convincingly by Mayer (2002), pp. 143–144; for this and the preceding period see Harper (1996), for the later development see Duignan and Gann (1994); Varsori (1995); Heller and Gillingham (1996).
14 Küsters (2000).
15 Aldrich (1995).
16 Milward (1992a), pp. 21–45.
17 Michael Calingaert (1996).
18 Milward (1992b), pp. 90–125, 299–306, 462–502.
19 Gasteyger (1966), p. 39; Coudenhove-Kalergi (1966), pp. 79–80; Posselt (1987), pp. 322–371; Piepenschneider (2001), pp. 69–77.
20 Heller and Gillingham (1992).
21 Schwabe (1988), pp. 211–239; Schwabe (1987), pp. 166–182.
22 Haas (1958), pp. 240–280, 283–313.
23 Paganon (1997), pp. 93–102.
24 Schwartz (1991).
25 Rupieper (1991); for a broader perspective, see Hanrieder (1995), pp. 29–37, 39–65; for the beginnings see also Wurm (1995).
26 Louis and Bull (1986).
27 Steininger (2005), p. 168.
28 Young (1996), pp. 327–341.
29 Dell (1995), pp. 29–67, 68–103; see chapters 2 and 3 in Kaiser (1996a).
30 Steininger (2005), p. 168.
31 Young (1994).
32 Beloff (1963).
33 Kaiser (1996b), pp. 204–227; see also Young (1993), pp. 165–183.
34 Concerning European and American Rejection of Britain's Alternatives to the Common Market 1956–1960 see Giauque (2002), pp. 47–76; Hathaway (1990).
35 Rathkolb (1996); Gehler and Steininger (2000); see also Winand (1993) and Giauque (2002).
36 Kaiser (1995), Steininger (1996), Paxton and Wahl (1994).
37 Concerning Adenauer, De Gaulle and the Franco-German Treaty of 1963, see Giauque (2002); for a general overview see Kocs (1995), pp. 245–259.
38 Thiemeyer (2004).
39 Yost (1998), p. 52; for another Ismay-quotation see Hanrieder (1995), p. 39: 'NATO was created to keep the Soviets out, the Americans in, and the Germans down'; see also the collection edited by Steininger et al. (1993).
40 Concerning the 'Interventionistische Integrationspolitik' of the US see Neuss (2000), pp. 345–357; see also Jordan (1991); Killick (1997); Giauque (2002); Knipping (2004).
41 Lundestad (1998), pp. 13–28; Cromwell (1992).
42 Asmus (2003); see also Asmus and Pollack (2003).
43 'Handelskommissar Pascal Lamy über die wirtschaftlichen Beziehungen USA/Europa: das wachsende US-Defizit als größte Sorge,' *Format*, vol. 46 no. 1 (2004), p. 21; Kühnhardt (2003), p. 2; for a rediscovery of EUropean–US–American commonalities see Ash (2004).
44 'Die USA und die EU im Vergleich', *Der Standard*, 22 February 2005.
45 Steininger (1990); Dockrill (1994).

46 Concerning de Gaulle's Challenge to the Atlantic Framework 1960–69 see Lundestad (1998), pp. 203–264; Paxton and Wahl (1994); Conze (1995).

47 Bischof (1999).

48 Hanrieder (1995), pp. 333–360; Lundestad (1998), pp. 83–98. In that regard, see also the volume by Knipping and Schönwald (2004).

49 Hackett (1995); see also Neuss (2000), pp. 358–361; Calleo (2001), pp. 176–181; a very useful and critical overview is presented by Bischof (2005).

50 Kühnhardt (1994), pp. 212, 262, 300.

51 Steininger (2005), pp. 179–180.

52 Concerning Europe's new political order and the decline of US-hegemony see Hanrieder (1995), pp. 361–388; Kupchan (2003), pp. 69–88; Krell (2003).

53 Calleo (2001), pp. 185–206.

54 In that regard, see also Fröhlich (1998).

55 Neurauter (1998), pp. 88–97; see also Duignan and Gann (1994), pp. 227–272.

56 Brusse (1996).

57 See, for example, 'Grobes Geschütz für die EU gegen die USA. WTO bewilligt 4 Milliarden Dollar an Strafzöllen', *Neue Zürcher Zeitung*, 31 August/1 September 2002, p. 19.

58 The new lines of conflict were described by Kupchan (2003), pp. 65–69.

59 See chapters II and IV and the epilogue in Laqueur (1992).

60 Bierling (2004), p. 444.

61 For a systematic approach to the historical expansions see Preston (1997).

62 Camp (2003), p. 13; Kühnhardt (2003), p. 3.

63 Kagan (2003), pp. 7–8, 10, 45, 87–88; 'Europa als loyale Kritkerin der USA' (2002).

64 Larres (2004); Nye (2002); Mann (2003).

65 Kreß (2002).

66 'Morde, Schändung und Folterungen. Zahlreiche Dokumente belegen weitere Misshandlungsfälle durch das US-Militär', *Münchner Merkur*, 9 December 2004; Rauscher (2005); Dworkin (2005).

67 Frey (2005).

68 See, for example, Meiers (2001); Kissinger (2002); Rühl (2003). According to Andrew S. Moravcsik NATO is relevant, but the real transatlantic work started to be done over at the European Union. In European eyes, NATO seems 'an anachronistic organization': see Moravcsik (2004); for this topic see also Sloan (2003).

69 Kühnhardt (2003), p. 1; Barber (2003).

70 'Europäer und USA streiten über Militär', *Handelsblatt*, 17–18 October 2003.

71 The author would like to thank Professor Ron Hassner of the University of California, Berkeley for this suggestion.

72 Camp (2003), p. 13.

73 Eckert (2005); see also Kennedy (1987); conerning the European Communities, their potential and problems see Kennedy (2003), pp. 695–721, and the US, the problem of the number one and her relative decline, ibid., pp. 758–787; concerning the relatively unsuccessful unspoken empire see Ferguson (2004), pp. 200–285.

74 Dembinski and Wagner (2003), pp. 31–38; Böhm (2003); Wojahn (2003); Dempsey (2003): 'Words of war: Europe's first security doctrine backs away from a commitment to US-style pre-emption. The EU's stance reflects antipathy for the US invasion in Iraq. But the moderate tone will help secure agreement among member states'. See also 'Europa ringt um sein Verhältnis zur Gewalt. Neue EU-Sicherheitsdoktrin setzt auf Diplomatie statt Waffeneinsatz – Deutlicher Einfluss deutscher Positionen', *Financial Times Deutschland*, 5 December 2003.

75 Communication to the author on 1 September 2004 from Dr Gunther Hauser, Austrian Ministry of Defence; see also Hauser (2005).

76 Since June 2003 trilateralism had become something of an obsession for Chirac; see Stephens (2003).
77 'US scraps steel tariffs and avoids sanctions. Bush eases European relations but angers American steelworkers by lifting protectionists measures': see Buck and Sanchanta (2003). See also Koch (2003).
78 Gehler (2005), p. 331.
79 Conversation with Gordon A. Craig by Michael Gehler along with Ludger Kühnhardt in Palo Alto during a stay at Stanford University, 5 June 2004.
80 Bertram (2005).
81 Glain (2004).
82 'Die Streitpunkte zwischen Europa und den USA ...', *Format*, vol. 46 no. 1 (2004), p. 21.
83 'Die Streitpunkte zwischen Europa und den USA ...', *Format*, vol. 46 no. 1 (2004), pp. 20–21; Scherpenberg (2000).
84 Dosch (2004), p. 9.
85 Föderl-Schmid (2005).
86 Winder (2005).
87 'Das Ergebnis wären mehr globale Unruhen und Schwierigkeiten. Kurzfristig wahrscheinlich mehr für Amerika als für Europa, aber langfristig vermutlich mehr für Europa als für Amerika.' See 'Trennung Europa-Amerika wäre eine Form von Wahnsinn', *Der Standard*, 21 February 2005.
88 Brändle (2005).
89 Leibl (2005).
90 Busse (2004); 'USA machen mit Truppenabzug ernst. Die Verlagerung von Einheiten soll keine Strafaktion wegen Deutschlands "Nein" zum Irak-Krieg sein', *Coburger Tageblatt*, 17 August 2004.
91 *Der Standard*, 21 February 2005, p. 27.
92 Schlenker (1997); Smonig (2005).
93 Kirt (2003), pp. 95–106.
94 Kohler (1969); Loth (2001); Kirt (2001).
95 See, for example, Kirt (2005b); a hopeful future for the US is seen by Duignan and Gann (1994), pp. 276–313.
96 'Warum, wenn wir doch Werte und Ziele teilen?', see Schneider (2005).
97 The author would like to thank Prof. Ron Hassner of the University of California, Berkeley for this suggestion.
98 Kühnhardt (2003), p. 2.
99 Mitterauer (1999). For a modern history of Europe covering the history of ideas, spirits, and institutions, see Schmale (2000 and Gehler (2005)).
100 Mazower (2000), pp. 117–156, 207–265.
101 Kühnhardt (2003), p. 2.
102 Asmus (2003).
103 'Jeder Versuch, Europa als eine antiamerikanische Basis auszubauen, ist dazu verdammt, den Kontinent zu spalten [...]. Eine europäische Politik des Gegengewichtes ist das geeignete Rezept, um eine Scheidung Europas von den USA zu bewirken. Kein amerikanischer Politiker, welcher Richtung er auch angehört, wäre damit einverstanden, einer Partnerschaft mit Europa zuliebe die amerikanische Handlungsfreiheit einzuschränken.' – see Asmus (2003). See on the other hand also Haseler (2004).
104 Herrmann (2005); two years earlier Pöttering and Kühnhardt (2003) presented ideas for a common Atlantic treaty.
105 See also Drekonja-Kornat (2003).
106 Camp (2003), *The End of the Cold War and US-EU-Relations*, p. 25.

107 The author would like to thank Professor Ron Hassner of the University of California, Berkeley for this suggestion.
108 Haller (2004).
109 Rifkin (2004a).
110 Müller (2003a, 2003b, 2004).
111 Weidenfeld (2004), p. 36; 'Interview mit Werner Weidenfeld', *Süddeutsche Zeitung*, 20 March 2003.
112 Plessen (2003); concerning transatlantic differences see Haller (2004), pp. 35–104.
113 Schoettli (2004).
114 de Montbrial (1998); Schmidt (2000).

References

Abelshauser, Werner (1981), 'Wiederaufbau vor dem Marshallplan. Westeuropas Wachstumschancen und die Wirtschaftsordnung in der zweiten Hälfte der vierziger Jahre', *Vierteljahrshefte für Zeitgeschichte (VfZ)* 29 (1981), pp. 545–578.

Abelshauser, Werner (1984), 'Der Kleine Marshallplan. Handelsintegration durch innereuropäische Wirtschaftshilfe 1948–1950', in Helmut Berding (ed.), *Wirtschaftliche und politische Integration in Europa im 19. und 20. Jahrhundert*, Göttingen: Vandenhoeck & Ruprecht, pp. 212–224.

Abelshauser, Werner (1989), 'Hilfe und Selbsthilfe. Zur Funktion des Marshallplans beim westdeutschen Wiederaufbau', *Vierteljahrshefte für Zeitgeschichte (VfZ)* 37 (1989), pp. 85–113.

Aldrich, Richard J. (1995), 'European Integration: An American Intelligence Connection,' in Anne Deighton (ed.), *Building Postwar Europe: National Decision-Makers and European Institutions, 1948–63*, London: St. Martin's Press, pp. 159–179.

Ash, Timothy Garton (2004), *Freie Welt. Europa, Amerika und die Chance der Krise*, Munich (Hanser) Lizenzausgabe für die Bundeszentrale für politiche Bildung, Bonn.

Asmus, Ronald D. (2003), 'Rumsfelds falscher Ehrgeiz,' *Rheinischer Merkur*, vol. 42, p. 6.

Asmus, Ronald D. and Kenneth M. Pollack (2003), 'Werte statt Waffen. Bush und seine Neokonservativen sind im Irak gescheitert', *Die Zeit*, 4 September, p. 10.

Barber, Benjam R. (2003), *Imperium der Angst. Die USA und die Neuordnung der Welt*, Munich: Beck.

Baumann, Birgit (2005), '"Besuch bei einem Freund." Bush und Schröder wollen einen Neuanfang ihrer Beziehungen', *Der Standard*, 19–20 February.

Beloff, Max (1963), *The United States and the Unity of Europe*, Washington, DC: Brookings Institution.

Bernath, Markus (2005), 'Der langsame Aufstieg vom Nullpunkt. Bush und Chirac nennen sich nun Freunde', *Der Standard*, 22 February.

Bertram, Christoph (2005), 'Neue transatlantische Herzlichkeit?', *Der Standard*, 19–20 February.

Beschloss, Michael (2002), *The Conquerors. Roosevelt, Truman and the Destruction of Hitler's Germany, 1941–1945*, New York: Simon & Schuster, pp. 283–292.

Bierling, Stephan (2004), 'Die Europäische Union und die USA', in Werner Weidenfeld (ed.), *Europa-Handbuch, Bd. 1: Die Europäische Union – Politisches System und Politikbereiche,* Gütersloh: Verlag Bertelsmann-Stiftung, pp. 443–467.

Bischof, Günter (1999), *Austria in the First Cold War, 1945–55. The Leverage of the Weak*, Basingstoke: Macmillan Press.

Bischof, Günter (2001), 'Das amerikanische Jahrhundert: Europas Niedergang – Amerikas Aufstieg', *Zeitgeschichte*, No. 28 (March/April), vol. 2, pp. 75–95.

Bischof, Günter (2005), 'American Empire and its Discontents: The United States and Europe Today', in Michael Gehler, Günter Bischof, Ludger Kühnhardt, and Rolf Steininger (eds), *Towards a European Constitution. A Historical and Political Comparison with the United States (Europapolitische Reihe des Herbert-Batliner-Europainstitutes 3)*, Vienna: Böhlau, pp. 185–207.

Böhm, Wolfgang (2003), 'EU setzt auf Versöhnung mit den USA', *Die Presse*, 18 June.

Brändle, Stefan (2005), 'Ein intimes Arbeitsessen mit Jacques. Präsident Chirac will Scherben kitten', *Der Standard*, 19–20 February.

Brinkbäumer, Klaus (2005), 'Willkommen in Bushland', *Der Spiegel*, No. 9, 28 February, pp. 120–124.

Brusse, Wendy Asbeek (1996), 'The Americans, GATT, and European Integration, 1947–1957: A Decade of Dilemma', in Francis H. Heller and John R. Gillingham (eds), *The United States and the Integration of Europe: Legacies of the Postwar Era*, New York: St. Martin's Press, pp. 221–249.

Buck, Tobias and Mariko Sanchanta (2003), 'Brussels trade commissioner greets US lifting of steel tariffs as success for Europe', *Financial Times/Europe*, 5 December.

Burghardt, Günter (2002), 'Die europäische Verfassungsentwicklung aus dem Blickwinkel der USA', Lecture at Humboldt University Berlin, 6 June 2002 (Walter Hallstein-Institut für Europäisches Verfassungsrecht Forum Constitutionis Europae FCE 4/02), pp. 2–14.

Busse, Nikolas (2004), 'Der Job in Europa ist erledigt. Für die Amerikaner verliert der alte Kontinent an strategischer Bedeutung', *Frankfurter Allgemeine Zeitung*, 11 July, p. 8.

Calingaert, Michael (1996), *European Integration Revisited: Progress, Prospects and U.S. Interests*, Boulder CO: Westview Press.

Calleo, David P. (2001), *Rethinking Europe's Future (A Century Foundation Book)*, Princeton: Princeton University Press.

Camp, Glen D. (2003), *The End of the Cold War and US-EU-Relations (ZEI Discussion Paper C 122)*, Bonn: ZEI.

Conze, Eckart (1995), 'Hegemonie durch Integration? Die amerikanische Europapolitik und de Gaulle', *Vierteljahrshefte für Zeitgeschichte*, vol. 43, pp. 297–340.

Coudenhove-Kalergi, Richard N. (1966), *Paneuropa 1922 bis 1962*, Vienna: Herold.

Cromwell, William C. (1992), *The United States and the European Pillar: The Strained Alliance*, London: Macmillan.

Dell, Edmund (1995), *The Schuman Plan and the British Abdication of Leadership in Europe*, Oxford: Oxford University Press.

Dembinski, Matthias and Wolfgang Wagner (2003), 'Europäische Kollateralschäden. Zur Zukunft der europäischen Außen-, Sicherheits- und Verteidigungspolitik nach dem Irak-Krieg', *Aus Politik und Zeitgeschichte*, 28 July 2003 (B 31–32/2003), pp. 31–38.

de Montbrial, Thierry (1998), *Dialog am Ende des Jahrhunderts. Der europäische Gedanke als Selbstbehauptung eines Kontinents*, Munich: Europaverlag.

Dempsey, Judy (2003), 'Words of war', *Financial Times*, 5 December 2003.

Der Standard, 'Trennung Europa-Amerika wäre eine Form von Wahnsinn', interview with Zbigniew Brzezinski, 21 February, p. 27.

'Die Streitpunkte zwischen Europa und den USA und Handelskommissar Pascal Lamy über die wirtschaftlichen Beziehungen USA/Europa: das wachsende US-Defizit als größte Sorge', *Format*, vol. 46, no. 1, pp. 20–21.

'Die USA und die EU im Vergleich', *Der Standard*, 22 February 2005.

Dockrill, Saki (1994), 'Cooperation and Suspicion: The United States' Alliance Diplomacy for the Security of Western Europe, 1953–54', *Diplomacy & Statecraft*, vol. 5, March, pp. 138–182.

Dosch, Jörn (2004), 'Das Verhältnis der EU und der USA zur Region Südostasien', *Aus Politik und Zeitgeschichte*, 17 May (B 21–22/2204), pp. 7–14.

Drekonja-Kornat, Gerhad (2003), 'Besser kuschen?', *Die Presse*, 21 June.

Duignan, Peter and L.H. Gann (1994), *The USA and the New Europe 1945–1993*, Oxford: Blackwell.

Dworkin, Ronald (2005), 'Amerika zerstört seine Selbstachtung. Die Lager in Guantánamo haben die Vereinigten Staaten weltweit in Verruf gebracht. Zu Recht', *Die Zeit*, 7 July, p. 35.

Eckert, Andreas (2005), 'Prognose inclusive. Zum sechzigsten Geburtstag des Historikers Paul Kennedy', *Frankfurter Allgemeine Zeitung*, 17 June.

'Europäer und USA streiten über Militär', *Handelsblatt*, 17–18 October.

'Europa ringt um sein Verhältnis zur Gewalt. Neue EU-Sicherheitsdoktrin setzt auf Diplomatie statt Waffeneinsatz – Deutlicher Einfluss deutscher Positionen,' *Financial Times Deutschland*, 5 December.

'Europa als loyale Kritikerin der USA. Überlegungen zum Disput Amerika–Europa', *Neue Zürcher Zeitung*, 3/4 August, p. 7.

Ferguson, Niall (2004), *Colossus. The Price of America's Empire*, New York: Penguin Press.

'Flüchten Sie vor Bush, Herr Chomsky?', *Welt am Sonntag*, 16 January, p. 8.

Föderl-Schmid, Alexandra (2005), 'EU kommt USA im Streit um Airbus entgegen', *Der Standard*, 31 May.

Frey, Eric (2005), 'Bereit für das asiatische Zeitalter. Chinas und Indiens wirtschaftlicher Aufstieg setzt Europa unter Druck – zum Glück', *Der Standard*, 22 February.

Fröhlich, Stefan (1998), *Der Ausbau der europäischen Verteidigungsidentität zwischen WEU und NATO (ZEI discussion paper C19)*, Bonn: ZEI.

Gasteyger, Curt (1966), *Einigung und Spaltung Europas*, Frankfurt am Main: Fischer Bücherei.

Gehler, Michael and Rolf Steininger (eds) (2000), *Die Neutralen und die europäische Integration 1945–1995. The Neutrals and the European Integration 1945–1995* (Institut für Zeitgeschichte an der Universität Innsbruck, Arbeitskreis Europäische Integration, Historische Forschungen, Veröffentlichungen 3), Vienna: Böhlau.

Gehler, Michael (2005), *Europa. Ideen – Institutionen – Vereinigung*, Munich: Olzog.

Gehler, Michael, Günter Bischof, Ludger Kühnhardt and Rolf Steininger (eds), *Towards a European Constitution. A Historical and Political Comparison with the United States (Europapolitische Reihe des Herbert-Batliner-Europainstitutes 3)*, Vienna: Böhlau.

Giauque, Jeffrey Glen (2002), *Grand Designs and Visions of Unity. The Atlantic Powers and the Reorganization of Western Europe, 1955–1963*, Chapel Hill: University of North Carolina Press.

Glain, Stephen (2004), 'Bullets for Beijing. The big EU powers are moving to lift the ban on arms sales to China in a frontal challenge to US policy and power in Asia', *Newsweek*, 9 August, pp. 34–35.

'Grobes Geschütz für die EU gegen die USA. WTO bewilligt 4 Milliarden Dollar an Strafzöllen', *Neue Zürcher Zeitung*, 31 August/1 September, p. 19.

Gruber, Simon (2005), 'Die Grundrechtscharta und der Grundrechtskonvent (1999–2000). Analyse und vergleichender Rückblick auf die Verfassungsentwicklung in den USA (1787–1791)', in Michael Gehler, Günter Bischof, Ludger Kühnhardt and Rolf Steininger (eds), *Towards a European Constitution. A Historical and Political Comparison with the United States (Europapolitische Reihe des Herbert-Batliner-Europainstitutes 3)*, Vienna: Böhlau, pp. 271–302.

Haas, Ernst B. (1958), *The Uniting of Europe. Political, Social and Economic Forces 1950–1957*, Stanford: Stanford University Press.

Hackett, Clifford (1995), *Cautious Revolution: The European Union Arrives*, Westport CT: Greenwood Press.

Haller, Gret (2004), *Die Grenzen der Solidarität. Europa und die USA im Umgang mit Staat, Nation und Religion*, Berlin: Aufbau Taschenbuch-Verlag.

'Handelskommissar Pascal Lamy über die wirtschaftlichen Beziehungen USA/Europa: das wachsende US-Defizit als größte Sorge', *Format*, vol. 46, no. 1, 2004, p. 21.

Hanrieder, Wolfram F. (1995), *Deutschland, Europa, Amerika. Die Außenpolitik der Bundesrepublik Deutschland 1949–1994*, Paderborn: Schöningh.

Harper, John Lamberton (1996), *American Visions of Europe. Franklin D. Roosevelt, George F. Kennan, and Dean G. Acheson*, Cambridge: Cambridge University Press.

Haseler, Stephen (2004), 'Europa, nukleare Supermacht. Unter deutsch-französischer Führung entwickelt sich ein Gegengewicht zu den Vereinigten Staaten,' *Die Zeit*, 28 October, p. 13.

Hathaway, Robert M. (1990), *Great Britain and the United States. Special Relations since World War II (Twayne's International History Series 4)*, Boston: Twayne Press.

Hauser, Gunther (2005), 'Towards a Comprehensive Security System', in Michael Gehler, Günter Bischof, Ludger Kühnhardt and Rolf Steininger (eds), *Towards a European Constitution. A Historical and Political Comparison with the United States (Europapolitische Reihe des Herbert-Batliner-Europainstitutes 3)*, Vienna: Böhlau, pp. 365–411.

Heller, Francis and John R. Gillingham (eds) (1992), *NATO: The Founding of the Atlantic Alliance and the Integration of Europe*, London: St. Martin's Press.

Heller, Francis H. and John R. Gillingham (eds) (1996), *The United States and the Integration of Europe: Legacies of the Postwar Era*, New York: St. Martin's Press.

Henningsen, Manfred (1997), 'Zögerliche Blicke über den großen Teich. Die Gründungsgeschichte der USA und der EU zeigt viele Parallelen,' *Das Parlament*, no. 30–31 (25 July).

Herrmann, Frank (2005), 'Blair macht gern einen Umweg nach Brüssel', *Der Standard*, 19–20 February.

Hippler, Jochen (2003), 'Unilateralismus der USA als Problem der internationalen Politik', *Aus Politik und Zeitgeschichte*, 28 July (B 31–32/2003), pp. 15–22.

Hitchcock, William I. (2004), *The Struggle for Europe. The Turbulent History of a Divided Continent, 1945 to the Present*, New York: Anchor Books.

Hogan, Michael (1987), *The Marshall Plan: America, Britain, and the Reconstruction of Western Europe, 1947–1952*, Cambridge: Cambridge University Press.

Höreth, Marcus (2005), 'The European Court of Justice and the U.S. Supreme Court: Comparable Institutions?' in Michael Gehler, Günter Bischof, Ludger Kühnhardt and Rolf Steininger (eds), *Towards a European Constitution. A Historical and Political Comparison with the United States (Europapolitische Reihe des Herbert-Batliner-Europainstitutes 3)*, Vienna: Böhlau, pp. 143–162.

'Interview mit Werner Weidenfeld', *Süddeutsche Zeitung*, 20 March.

Jordan, Robert S. (1991), 'The Political Involvement of the United States in Europe', in

Robert S. Jordan (ed.), *Europe and the Superpowers. Essays on European International Politics*, London: Pinter, pp. 27–46.

Kagan, Robert (2003), *Macht und Ohnmacht. Amerika gegen Europa in der neuen Weltordnung*, Berlin: Siedler.

Kaiser, Wolfram (1995), 'The Bomb and Europe: Britain, France, and the EEC Entry Negotiations 1961–1963', *Journal of European Integration History*, vol. 1, no. 1, pp. 65–85.

Kaiser, Wolfram (1996a), *Großbritannien und die Europäische Wirtschaftsgemeinschaft 1955–1961. Von Messina nach Canossa*, Berlin: Akademie-Verlag.

Kaiser, Wolfram (1996b), *Using Europe, Abusing the Europeans. Britain and the European Integration, 1945–1963*, London: Macmillan Press.

Kennedy, Paul M. (1987), *The Rise and Fall of Great Powers. Economic Change and Military Conflict from 1500 to 2000*, New York: Random House.

Kennedy, Paul M. (2003), *Aufstieg und Fall der großen Mächte. Ökonomischer Wandel und militärischer Konflikt von 1500–2000*, Frankfurt/Main: Fischer Taschenbuch-Verlag.

Killick, John (1997), *The United States and European Reconstruction, 1945–1960*, Edinburgh: Keele University Press.

Kirt, Romain (ed.) (2001), *Die Europäische Union und ihre Krisen (Schriften des Zentrums für Europäische Integrationsforschung/Center for European Integration Studies 30)*, Baden-Baden: Nomos.

Kirt, Romain (2003), *Wege aus der Legitimationskrise. Die Europäische Union auf der Suche nach einem neuen Selbstverständnis*, Esch-sur-Alzette, Luxembourg: Editions Le Phare.

Kirt, Romain (2005a), *Die Europäische Union und ihre Nicht-Verfassung. Über einen Staatenverbund und sein weltweit einzigartiges Grundgesetz*, Alzette sur Esch: Editions Le Phare.

Kirt, Romain (2005b), *Apocalypse now? Der Aufstieg Amerikas und das Ende Europas*, Alzette sur Esch: Editions Le Phare.

Kissinger, Henry (2002), 'Die Risse werden größer. Der Anfang vom Ende? Die Zukunft der NATO ist ungewiss. Schuld daran: Eine aus dem Tritt geratene Allianz', *Welt am Sonntag*, 1 December, p. 15.

Knipping, Franz (2004), *Rom, 25. März 1957. Die Einigung Europas (20 Tage im 20. Jahrhundert)*, Munich: Deutscher Taschenbuch-Verlag.

Knipping, Franz and Matthias Schönwald (eds) (2004), *Aufbruch zum Europa der zweiten Generation. Die europäische Einigung 1969–1984 (Europäische und Internationale Studien, Wuppertaler Beiträge zur Geisteswissenschaft 3)*, Trier: WVT, Wissenschaftlicher Verlag Trier.

Koch, Rainer (2003), 'USA drängen Partner zu Nato-Einsatz in Irak. Colin Powell präsentiert bei Herbsttagung Szenario für Mission', *Financial Times Deutschland*, 5 December.

Kocs, Stephen A. (1995), *Autonomy or Power? The Franco-German Relationship and Europe's Strategic Choices, 1955–1995*, Westport CT: Praeger.

Kohler, Beate (ed.) (1969), *Erfolge und Krisen der Integration (Europäische Schriften des Bildungswerks Europäische Politik 20)*, Cologne: Europa-Union Verlag.

Krell, Gert (2003), 'Arroganz der Macht, Arroganz der Ohnmacht. Die Weltordnungspolitik der USA und die transatlantischen Beziehungen', *Aus Politik und Zeitgeschichte*, 28 July (B 31–32/2003), pp. 23–30.

Kreß, Claus (2002), 'Ein großes Vermächtnis. Amerikas Kampf gegen den Internationalen Strafgerichtshof', *Frankfurter Allgemeine Zeitung*, 12 July, p. 6.

Kühnhardt, Ludger (1994), *Revolutionszeiten. Das Umbruchjahr 1989 im geschichtlichen Zusammenhang*, Munich: Olzog.

Kühnhardt, Ludger (2003), 'Wieder Freundschaft nach dem Krieg? Reflexionen über das deutsch-amerikanische Verhältnis', *Forum. Vortragsreihe des Instituts der deutschen Wirtschaft Köln*, vol. 53, no. 37, 9 September, pp. 1–4.

Kupchan, Charles (2003), *Die europäische Herausforderung. Vom Ende der Vorherrschaft Amerikas, Reinbek*, Hamburg: Rowohlt.

Küsters, Hanns-Jürgen (2000), *Der Integrationsfriede. Viermächte-Verhandlungen über die Friedensregelung mit Deutschland 1945–1990 (Dokumente zur Deutschlandpolitik Studien Bd. 9)*, Munich: Oldenbourg Wissenschaftsverlag.

Laqueur, Walter (1992), *Europa auf dem Weg zur Weltmacht 1945–1992*, Munich: Kindler.

Laqueur, Walter (2006), *Die letzten Tage von Europa. Ein Kontinent veraüdert sein Gesicht*, Berlin: Ullstein.

Larres, Klaus (2004), ' "Bloody as Hell". Bush, Clinton and the Abdication of American Leadership in the Former Yugoslavia, 1990–1995', *Journal of European Integration History*, vol. 10, no. 1, pp. 179–202.

Leibl, Friederike (2005), 'Ein Geben und Nehmen unter Freunden,' *Die Presse*, 23 February.

Loth, Wilfried (ed.) (2001), *Crises and Compromises: The European Project 1963–69 (Veröffentlichungen der Historiker-Verbindungsgruppe bei der Kommission der Europäischen Gemeinschaften/Publications du Groupe de liaison des professeurs d'histoire contemporaine auprès de la Commission européenne 8)*, Baden-Baden: Nomos.

Louis, Roger and Hedley Bull (1986), *The 'Special Relationship.' Anglo-American Relations Since 1945*, Oxford: Clarendon Press.

Lundestad, Geir (1998), *'Empire' by Integration. The United States and European Integration, 1945–1997*, Oxford: Oxford University Press.

Maier, Charles S. and Günter Bischof (eds) (1992), *Deutschland und der Marshall-Plan*, Baden-Baden: Nomos.

Mann, Michael (2003), *Die ohnmächtige Supermacht. Warum die USA die Welt nicht regieren können*, Frankfurt am Main: Campus.

Mayer, Tilman (2002), 'Leitende Ideen in der transatlantischen Integration. Zu Fragen von Integration, Zusammenarbeit und dem Gleichgewicht der Kräfte in Europa und innerhalb der transatlantischen Beziehungen', in Reinhard C. Meier-Walser and Susanne Luther (eds), *Europa und die USA. Transatlantische Beziehungen im Spannungsfeld von Regionalisierung und Globalisierung*, Munich: Olzog, pp. 137–147.

Mazower, Mark (2000), *Der dunkle Kontinent. Europa im 20. Jahrhundert*, Berlin: Alexander Fest-Verlag.

Meiers, Franz-Josef (2001), 'Die Gemeinsame Europäische Sicherheits- und Verteidigungspolitik als Zankapfel zwischen den USA und Europa', in Erich Reiter (ed.), *Jahrbuch für internationale Sicherheitspolitik*, Hamburg: Mittler, pp. 433–452.

Milborn, Corinna (2004), 'Eiskalte Beziehungen? Mit der Wiederwahl von George Bush ist klar: Das Verhältnis zwischen den USA und Europa bleibt getrübt. Für Europa an sich eine Chance auf eine eigene Stellung in der Weltpolitik – die aber nicht genützt wird', *Format*, vol. 46, no. 1, pp. 18–20.

Milward, Alan S. (with the assistance of George Brennan and Federico Romero) (1992a), *The European Rescue of the Nation State*, London: Routledge.

Milward, Alan S. (1992b), *The Reconstruction of Western Europe 1945–51*, reprint edn, London: Routledge.

Mitterauer, Michael (1999), *Die Entwicklung Europas – ein Sonderweg? Legitimationsideologien und die Diskussion der Wissenschaft*, Vienna: Picus-Verlag.

Moravcsik, Andrew (2004), 'Europe Takes Charge', *Newsweek*, 5 July, pp. 26–27.

'Morde, Schändung und Folterungen. Zahlreiche Dokumente belegen weitere Misshandlungsfälle durch das US-Militär', *Münchner Merkur*, 9 December.

Müller, Harald (2003a), *Amerika schlägt zurück. Die Weltordnung nach dem 11. September*, Frankfurt/Main: Fischer Taschenbuch-Verlag.

Müller, Harald (2003b), 'Ein transatlantisches Schisma. Der Konflikt über den Irak-Krieg hat es an den Tag gebracht: Europa und die USA legen die gemeinsamen Werte höchst unterschiedlich aus', *Frankfurter Rundschau*, 4 December, p. 10.

Müller, Harald (2004), 'Das transatlantische Risiko – Deutungen des amerikanisch-europäischen Weltordnungskonflikts', *Aus Politik und Zeitgeschichte*, 19 January (B 3–4/2004), pp. 7–17.

Murphy, John (2004), *The United States and the Rule of Law in International Affairs*, New York: Cambridge University Press.

'Nato urgiert mehr Einsatz', *Der Standard*, 11 February.

Neurauter, Tamara (1998), *Die USA und die europäische Integration im Spiegel des Wall Street Journal und der Washington Post, 1983/84 und 1991–1993*, Diplomarbeit, University of Innsbruck, Austria.

Neuss, Beate (2000), *Geburtshelfer Europas? Die Rolle der Vereinigten Staaten im europäischen Integrationsprozess 1945–1958*, Baden-Baden: Nomos.

Nye, Joseph S. Jr. (2002), *The Paradox of American Power. Why the World's only Superpower Can't Go It Alone*, Oxford: Oxford University Press.

Paganon, Jean-Félix (1997), 'Western European Union's Pivotal Position between the Atlantic Alliance and the European Union', in Anne Deighton (ed.) (1997), *Western European Union 1954–1997: Defence, Security, Integration*, Oxford: St Antony's College, pp. 93–102.

Parsi, Vittorio Emanuele (2006), *L'alleanza inevitabile. Europa Stati Uniti oltre l'Iraq*, Milan.

Paxton, Robert O. and Nicholas Wahl (eds) (1994), *De Gaulle and the United States: A Centennial Reappraisal*, Oxford: Berg.

Piepenschneider, Melanie (2001), 'Ein gescheiterter Integrationsversuch als Geburtshelfer – Der Europarat und die Anfänge der europäischen Einigung', in Romain Kirt (ed.), *Die Europäische Union und ihre Krisen (Schriften des Zentrums für Europäische Integrationsforschung/Center for European Integration Studies 30)*, Baden-Baden: Nomos, pp. 69–77.

Plessen, Marie-Louisen (ed.) (2003), *Idee Europa. Entwürfe zum 'Ewigen Frieden'. Ordnungen und Utopien für die Gestaltung Europas von der pax romana zur Europäischen Union. Eine Ausstellung als historische Topographie.* Catalogue of the exhibit of the same name at the Deutsches Historisches Museum, Berlin for the inauguration of the exhibition hall designed by I. M. Pei, 25 May to 23 August, Berlin: Henschel.

Posselt, Martin (1987), *Richard Coudenhove-Kalergi und die Europäische Parlamentarier-Union. Die parlamentarische Bewegung für eine 'Europäische Konstituante' (1946-1952)*, Ph.D. dissertation, University of Graz, Austria.

Pöttering, Hans-Gert and Ludger Kühnhardt (2003), 'EU-USA. Plädoyer für einen Atlantischen Vertrag', *Integration*, vol. 26, no. 3, July, pp. 244–250.

Prantner, Christoph (2005), 'Hilfsdienstleister für die USA. Die Nato such trotz neuer Doktrin und globaler Einsätze ihre Rolle', *Der Standard*, 23 February.

Preston, Christopher (1997), *Enlargement and Integration in the European Union*, London: Routledge.

Rathkolb, Oliver (1996), 'The Austrian Case: From "Neutral Association" to a "Special Arrangement" with the EEC 1961–1963', in Richard T. Griffiths and Stuart Ward (eds), *Courting the Common Market: The First Attempt to enlarge the European Community 1961–1963*, London: Lothian Foundation Press, pp. 285–302.

Rauscher, Hans (2005), 'Guantánamisierung der US-Demokratie,' *Der Standard*, 28–29 May.

Rifkin, Jeremy (2004a), 'Glückliches Europa ...', *Die Zeit*, 14 October, p. 10.

Rifkin, Jeremy (2004b), *The European Dream. How Europe's Vision of the Future is quietly Eclipsing the American Dream*, New York: Penguin.

Rühl, Lothar (2003), 'Strategische Folgen der Irak-Krise für die Nato. Allianzpolitik mit doppeltem Boden beidseits des Atlantiks', *Neue Zürcher Zeitung*, 12 February, p. 7.

Rupieper, Hermann-Josef (1991), *Der besetzte Verbündete. Die amerikanische Deutschlandpolitik 1949–1955 (Studien zur Sozialwissenschaft 95)*, Opladen: Westdeutscher Verlag.

Scherpenberg, Jens (2000), 'Konkurrenten und Partner: Die Außenwirtschaftsbeziehungen zwischen den USA und EU', in Peter Rudolf and Jürgen Wilzewski (eds), *Weltmacht ohne Gegner. Amerikanische Außenpolitik zu Beginn des 21. Jahrhunderts*, Baden-Baden: Nomos.

Schlenker, Hans-Heinz (1997), 'Europäer kämpfen gegen US-Dominanz', *Salzburger Nachrichten*, 1 September.

Schmale, Wolfgang (2000), *Geschichte Europas*, Vienna: Böhlau.

Schmidt, Gustav (2004), *Geschichte der USA*, Darmstadt.

Schmidt, Helmut (2000), *Die Selbstbehauptung Europas. Perspektiven für das 21. Jahrhundert*, Stuttgart: Deutsche Verlags-Anstalt.

Schneider, Susi (2005), 'Bush: Lob für "Säulen der Freiheit"', *Der Standard*, 21 February.

Schoettli, Urs (2004), 'Die Neugeburt des Morgenlandes', *Neue Zürcher Zeitung*, 30 August.

Schwabe, Klaus (1987), 'Die Vereinigten Staaten und die Einigung Europas 1945–1952', in Otmar Franz (ed.), *Europas Mitte*, Göttingen: Muster-Schmidt, pp. 166–182.

Schwabe, Klaus (1988), '"Ein Akt konstruktiver Staatskunst" – die USA und die Anfänge des Schuman-Plans', in Klaus Schwabe (ed.), *Die Anfänge des Schuman-Plans 1950/51/The Beginnings of the Schuman Plan*, Baden-Baden: Nomos, pp. 211–239.

Schwabe, Klaus (2006), *Weltmacht und Weltordnung. Amerikanische Außenpolitik von 1898 bis zur Gegenwart. Eine Jahrhundertgeschichte*, Paderborn: Schöningh.

Schwartz, Thomas Alan (1991), *America's Germany: John J. McCloy and the Federal Republic of Germany*, Cambridge, MA: Harvard University Press.

Sloan, Stanley R. (2003), *NATO, the European Union, and the Atlantic Community. The Transatlantic Bargain Reconsidered*, Lanham MD. Rowman & Littlefield.

Smonig, Reinhold (2005), 'Paris drängt in die Kommandozentrale', *Die Presse*, 21 February.

Steininger, Rolf (1990), 'John Foster Dulles, the European Defense Community, and the German Question', in Richard H. Immerman (ed.), *John Foster Dulles and the Diplomacy of the Cold War*, Princeton: Princeton University Press, pp. 79–108.

Steininger, Rolf (1996), 'Great Britain's First EEC-Failure in January 1963', *Diplomacy & Statecraft*, vol. 7, pp. 404–435.
Steininger, Rolf (1997), '1961: Europe "at Sixes and Sevens". The European Free Trade Association, the Neutrals, and Great Britain's Decision to Join the E.E.C.', *The Journal of European Economic History*, vol. 26, pp. 535–568.
Steininger, Rolf (2005), 'Die USA und die Integration Europas. Vom Zweiten Weltkrieg bis zur Gegenwart', in Michael Gehler, Günter Bischof, Ludger Kühnhardt and Rolf Steininger (eds), *Towards a European Constitution. A Historical and Political Comparison with the United States (Europapolitische Reihe des Herbert-Batliner-Europainstitutes 3)*, Vienna: Böhlau, pp. 163–184.
Steininger, Rolf, Jürgen Weber, Günter Bischof, Thomas Albrich and Klaus Eisterer (eds) (1993), *Die doppelte Eindämmung. Europäische Sicherheit und deutsche Frage in den Fünfzigern*, Munich: v. Hase & Köhler.
Stephens, Philip (2003), 'Why Chirac and Blair have decided to pull together', *Financial Times*, 5 December, p. 13.
Thiemeyer, Guido (2004), 'From Convertibility to the Werner-Plan. European Monetary Integration 1958–1969. Changing World Economic Structures as Incentives for European Monetary Integration', in Régine Perron (ed.), *The Stability of Europe. The Common Market: Towards European Integration of Industrial and Financial Markets? (1958–1968)*, Paris: Presses de l'Université de Paris-Sorbonne, pp. 161–178.
'USA machen mit Truppenabzug ernst. Die Verlagerung von Einheiten soll keine Strafaktion wegen Deutschlands "Nein" zum Irak-Krieg sein', *Coburger Tageblatt*, 17 August.
Varsori, Antonio (ed.) (1995), *Europe 1945–1990s. The End of an Era?* London: Macmillan Press.
Weidenfeld, Werner (2004), 'Europa – aber wo liegt es?' in Werner Weidenfeld (ed.), *Europa-Handbuch, Bd. 1: Die Europäische Union – Politisches System und Politikbereiche*, Gütersloh: Verlag Bertelsmann-Stiftung, pp. 15–40.
Winand, Pascaline (1993), *Eisenhower, Kennedy, and the United States of Europe*, New York: St. Martin's Press.
Winder, Christoph (2005), 'Transatlantisches Tauwetter', *Der Standard*, 19–20 February.
Wojahn, Jörg (2003), 'Schwerpunkt Konfliktverhütung. Solana legt EU-Sicherheitsdoktrin vor – Gegenakzente zum US-Kurs', *Der Standard*, 20 June.
Wurm, Clemens (ed.) (1995), *Western Europe and Germany. The Beginnings of European Integration 1945–1960*, Oxford: Berg.
Yost, David S. (1998), *NATO Transformed: The Alliance's New Roles in International Security*, Washington, DC: US Institute of Peace Press.
Young, John W. (1993), *Britain and European Unity, 1945–1992*, Houndmills, Basingstoke: Macmillan Press.
Young, John W. (1994, 1998), *Britain, France and the Unity of Europe 1945–1951*, Leicester: Leicester University Press.
Young, John W. (1996), *Winston Churchill's Last Campaign. Britain and the Cold War 1951–1955*, Oxford: Clarendon Press.

Index

Page numbers in *Italics* represent Tables and page numbers in **Bold** represent Figures

For Product Safety Concerns and Information please contact our EU
representative GPSR@taylorandfrancis.com Taylor & Francis Verlag GmbH,
Kaufingerstraße 24, 80331 München, Germany

Batch number: 08153795

Printed by Printforce, the Netherlands